FUNDAMENTALS
OF MODERN BUSINESS

FUNDAMENTALS
OF MODERN BUSINESS

ROBERT W. HAMILTON

Minerva House Drysdale Regents
Chair in Law
University of Texas

LITTLE, BROWN AND COMPANY
Boston   Toronto

Library of Congress Catalog Card No. 88-80099

ISBN 0-316-34116-9

Fifth Printing

EB

**Published simultaneously in Canada
by Little, Brown & Company (Canada) Limited**

Printed in the United States of America

SUMMARY OF CONTENTS

IV

◇

FEDERAL TAXATION   257

V

◇

THE PRINCIPLES OF BUSINESS ORGANIZATIONS   299

VI

◇

SECURITIES AND INVESTMENTS   415

VII

◇

A SURVEY OF CORPORATE PRACTICE   495

III

◇

ACCOUNTING, INSOLVENCY, AND VALUATION 147

CHAPTER 7

FUNDAMENTALS OF DOUBLE ENTRY BOOKKEEPING   149

CHAPTER 8

FUNDAMENTAL ACCOUNTING PRINCIPLES   163

Contents

CHAPTER 5

COMMERCIAL ANNUITIES AND RETIREMENT PLANS   103

CHAPTER 6

LIFE INSURANCE   129

CONTENTS

Contents

CHAPTER 9

HOW TO READ AND USE FINANCIAL STATEMENTS   193

Contents

IV

◇

FEDERAL TAXATION   257

V
◇

THE PRINCIPLES OF BUSINESS ORGANIZATION 299

CHAPTER 13

SELECTING THE FORM OF A BUSINESS ORGANIZATION   301

Contents

CHAPTER 17

MERGERS AND TAKEOVERS   381

VI

◇

SECURITIES AND INVESTMENTS   415

CHAPTER 18

AN OVERVIEW OF THE PUBLIC MARKETS FOR STOCKS AND BONDS   417

Contents

CHAPTER 19

INVESTMENT STRATEGIES FOR THE SMALL
INVESTOR   459

VII

◇

A SURVEY OF CORPORATE PRACTICE   495

CHAPTER 22

◆

INSIDE COUNSEL: LAWYERS WHO WORK FOR A CORPORATION 507

CHAPTER 23

◆

THE FINE ART OF GIVING LEGAL ADVICE AND OPINIONS 517

◆ ACKNOWLEDGMENTS

I would like to thank my secretary, Gretchen Woellner, who patiently worked on numerous drafts and kept everything together during the year I was living in London. For their assistance, I also thank the editorial staff at Little, Brown and Company, particularly Virginia Vitzthum and Betsy Kenny.

A number of colleagues, family members, friends, and others read drafts of chapters and made useful comments and criticisms. Among those whose comments were particularly helpful are Sander Shapiro, Scott Killingsworth, Elliott Goldstein, Morey W. McDaniel, Russell Weintraub, Meredith Hamilton, Ernest E. Smith, John J. Sampson, Calvin Johnson, and Jay Westbrook. Of course, the mistakes that remain are my own.

I gratefully acknowledge the permissions granted to reproduce excerpts from the following materials.

M. Granof, *Financial Accounting Principles and Issues*. Copyright © 1985 by Prentice Hall.

The Wall Street Journal. Reprinted by permission of *The Wall Street Journal* © Dow Jones & Company, Inc. 1988. All rights reserved.

R. Hamilton, *Cases and Materials on Corporations Including Partnerships and Limited Partnerships* (3d ed. 1986). Copyright © 1986 by West Publishing Co.

FUNDAMENTALS
OF MODERN BUSINESS

◆ INTRODUCTION

This book is written primarily for the benefit of law students who have no prior business background and who feel insecure in law school classes dealing with corporations, securities, taxation, and similar matters. It discusses the fundamentals of business activity and of business law. It also discusses the practice of corporation law and the concepts and tools with which every successful corporate practitioner must be familiar. These concepts are partly financial in nature and partly legal, and they partly address the relationship between lawyers and sophisticated clients.

Students do not begin law school with a common background in business, economics, or finance. Some law students have a head start on others: They may have gained experience running their own business or through employment before going to law school or while in school. They may have taken courses in accounting, finance, or business in undergraduate or graduate school. A few may have been fortunate enough to have inherited money that they have invested and as a result learned something in the process. A few law students may be quite sophisticated and knowledgeable. These tend to be older students who have had substantial careers before going to law school: Certified public accountants with years of experience or former employees of stock brokerage firms, for example, but these students are rare. All law students — those with some, a lot, or no background in business — probably have about equal prospects of becoming successful corporate lawyers. Those that will become successful corporate lawyers will probably learn most of the tools of their trade the hard way, through experience, just as today's corporate lawyers did.

When students with varying backgrounds are brought together in a large law school class on corporations or income taxation or other subjects dealing with business and financial concepts, students without a business background tend to feel overwhelmed and fail to participate in class. At the same time, the more experienced students will dominate the class discussion, causing the instructor to believe that the level of sophistication of the class is higher than it really is. As a result, the insecurity of the less sophisticated student is increased rather than decreased by the classroom experience.

This book is designed to relieve this insecurity. It provides an introduction to business and business-related concepts for law students with little or no prior experience or knowledge. It concentrates on practical fundamentals that underlie the modern business world and draws shamelessly from several different courses that regularly appear in the law school curriculum. The book is designed to be a morale builder as well as an educational tool. Throughout there is an emphasis on vocabulary. Words such as *amortize, accounts receivable,* and *balloon notes* may strike fear in the heart of the uninitiated: Such terms are defined and discussed in this book and the underlying concepts are not difficult.

Many students may find some of the discussion in this book to be elementary: On the other hand, it is unlikely that anyone will find all of this book elementary. Basically, it attempts to carry the discussion to the point that a person, understanding what is in this book, can speak the same language as a person sophisticated in business transactions. While it will not make a corporation lawyer out of the reader, this book does discuss many things that a corporation lawyer must understand, and it should enable the reader to talk with such a lawyer with some confidence that he or she is at least on the same wavelength.

A formidable theoretical literature exists on business-related topics: management techniques and management goals, financial analysis, portfolio theory, decision analysis under conditions of uncertainty, the theory of the firm, multiple regression analysis, beta values, internal rates of return, efficient capital markets, and the like. Most of this theoretical literature is not law-related but is the product of economists, business school professors, and management specialists. Without in any way deprecating the importance and usefulness of these concepts in other contexts, relatively little attention is given them here because the corporate lawyer rarely encounters them in day-to-day practice. On the other hand, every corporate lawyer must have a working understanding of accounting concepts, the time value of money, federal income taxation, and insolvency, all discussed at some length in subsequent chapters.

Regrettably, the law applicable to business and corporate transactions is often complex, uncertain, and, to people in the business world at least, confusing. Indeed, for someone faced with difficult business choices in the face of massive uncertainty, the complexity and uncertainty of legal rules surrounding transactions is often frustrating. Fortunately for the lawyer, business as it relates to law is easier to understand than law as it relates to business. A lawyer should always be able to understand what goal a client is pursuing and the means he or she is using to get there.

This book is not a substitute for standard treatises in subjects, such as corporations or securities regulation, that are part of the traditional law school curriculum. Again, however, it does contain background information and discussion of fundamental principles in those specific areas, which should help students who are concerned that they lack the business background to understand these subjects. Also to some extent, this book may give a brief sketch of some of the issues discussed in those courses.

While this book is written primarily for law students and beginning lawyers, it will also be useful to business students, college students generally, and persons not in school at all, who feel a need for a better grasp of the subjects here discussed.

I

BASIC FINANCIAL CONCEPTS

CHAPTER 1

DEBT AND INTEREST

§1.1 Introduction

Debt is what makes the modern American economy go around. For individual consumers, the purchase of houses, of cars, of washing machines, and of other so-called big ticket items would be very difficult if not impossible without the widespread availability of easy credit. The same thing is true of both small and large businesses. Virtually every business today relies on debt to finance its operations. The notion that the best business is a debt-free business is now obsolete (if it ever was really true). From a business standpoint, there are substantial tax incentives and economic forces (including sheer necessity for more capital than owners can sometimes provide) that encourage every business in the modern economy to utilize borrowed money on a large scale. It is often more profitable for businesses with the power to raise large amounts of permanent capital to utilize debt in their operations rather than to raise additional permanent capital. (It is also viewed as safer in terms of the vulnerability of the entity to an unwanted takeover bid from outside interests.)

Entrepreneurs owning their own businesses often find that the use of borrowed capital permits greater growth and greater returns. Debt, in short, is not only a practical necessity for most businesses; it also fuels economic growth in the modern economy and helps to maximize earnings. On the other hand, debt is dangerous. A business that incurs debt also assumes fixed commitments that may run many years into the future. Economic conditions may change and debt incurred in an earlier era may become a crushing burden. In short, debt increases risk.

A preliminary examination of debt and interest is appropriate for another reason. Many business transactions not involving loans in the traditional sense come down to an immediate exchange of money for rights to receive (hopefully) larger sums of money in the future. The purchase of an existing business, for example, involves an immediate payment today for the right to receive the profits earned by that business in the future. The process of determining whether a contemplated purchase is desirable involves comparing the value of future payments with the payments required to be made today; this calculation turns out to be integrally related to the concept of debt and interest. Valuation is the subject of Chapters 2, 3, and 11.

§1.2 Debts, IOUs, and Promissory Notes

When one person (the creditor) lends money to another (the debtor), the first question that arises is what evidence of that debt the creditor should demand. Small noncommercial loans are frequently evidenced simply by a cancelled check, or acknowledged by a handshake, or a simple "thank you." Of course, a debt exists any time there is a loan, even if it is not evidenced by any writing or formality, and the creditor may enforce the repayment obligation upon proving that a loan was in fact made and not repaid.

A slightly greater level of formality occurs when the debtor executes an *IOU* — a written acknowledgment by the debtor that a debt exists. The initials "I.O.U." simply stand for "I owe you." An IOU may simplify the evidentiary requirements otherwise imposed on a creditor seeking to enforce a debt but it is not, by itself, a promise to repay the debt.

In the modern world, debts may be freely sold, assigned, or traded without the prior consent of the debtor. A person purchasing or otherwise acquiring a debt is known as an *assignee* and may enforce the creditor's claim against the debtor (subject to whatever defenses arising out of the same transaction that the original debtor may have against the original creditor). The debtor may also agree in the original transaction to waive defenses he may have in a suit brought by an assignee, and such a waiver will be given effect in some circumstances.

A higher level of formality and potentially greater legal consequences occur when the debtor is required to sign a promissory note. A promissory note states that the debtor "promises to pay to the order of" the creditor the amount of the debt, together with interest. Unlike an IOU, a promissory note itself embodies a promise to make a payment at some future time. One advantage of a promissory note is that the holder can sell or assign the underlying obligation simply by transferring the promissory note to a third person.

A promissory note may be made payable to the order of a specific person or to "bearer." A bearer note is payable to whoever has physical possession of the piece of paper; the debt is transferred simply by physical transfer of the paper. A promissory note payable to the order of a person is usually transferred by *indorsement*. The payee of the note writes on the back of the note "Pay to the order of Y," signs his or her name, and delivers the note to Y. Y can then enforce the note as though he or she were the payee, or may indorse the note to Z by following the same process.

A promissory note is said to be in *negotiable form* if it meets minimal statutory requirements: It must 1) be signed by the maker; 2) contain only an unconditional promise to pay a certain sum in money; 3) be payable on demand or at a definite time; and 4) be payable to order or bearer. Most notes used in commercial transactions are in negotiable form. The advantage of a note in this form is that, if the person acquiring the note is a *holder in due course* (that is, is a person who acquires the note for value and without knowledge of possible defenses), he or she is able to enforce the promise of payment set forth in the note free of certain defenses that the debtor might have had if suit had been brought directly by the creditor on the underlying transaction. The negotiation of a promissory note to a holder in due course results in a debt becoming an article of commerce largely freed from the underlying transaction that gave rise to it: The debt ceases to be a personal obligation between the creditor and debtor.

To illustrate: Assume that a seller of certain computer equipment originally received cash for a portion of the purchase price and lent the buyer the balance, taking a negotiable promissory note executed by the buyer. The buyer, however, has stopped making payments on the ground that the equipment did not perform as warranted. Obviously, if the seller directly seeks to enforce the buyer's promise to pay the balance of the purchase price, the defense of breach of warranty will be raised. It may not be completely ethical, but if the seller can negotiate the promissory note to a holder in due course, for example, a bank, the buyer will not be able to assert the defense of breach of warranty against the holder in due course. In other words, in the hands of a holder in due course, the promissory note is enforceable in and of itself without regard to the underlying commercial transaction that gave rise to it. If the buyer is forced to pay the holder in due course in full, he or she may then turn around and sue the seller for breach of warranty, so that at least theoretically, the wrongdoer — the seller whose product did not conform with his or her warranties — ends up ultimately being held responsible. In the process, however, the innocent purchaser of the promissory note is permitted to enforce it in accordance with its terms, and the defense of the maker can only be asserted against the other party to the original transaction in a separate law suit.

It is, of course, possible in the preceding hypothetical that the holder in due course will be unable to get satisfaction from the buyer even though he or she obtains a judgment. The seller, who indorsed the note to the holder in due course, is then liable to take back the note from the holder in due course and return any consideration paid since an indorser warrants that the instrument will be honored when it is presented. Other persons in the chain of transfer may also be liable if they transferred the instrument with knowledge of the maker's insolvency. In other words, if the buyer refuses to pay and the holder in due course is compelled to go back against the seller/indorser or earlier transferees on their warranties, the same result is reached — the wrongdoer ends up holding the bag.

The cutting-off of defenses described in the previous paragraphs does not apply to certain "real" defenses, such as forgery or duress. Also, if the person acquiring the note is not a holder in due course or if the transaction is cast as an "assignment" of a note rather than as a "negotiation," no defenses are shut off (unless the maker agrees to waive them) and the holder of the note stands in precisely the same shoes as the original lender. The difference between assignment, ("I hereby assign the attached note to Z") and negotiation ("pay to the order of Z") may seem to be mere semantics; however, different legal consequences often flow from different words. The detailed rules about the negotiation of promissory notes and other types of commercial paper, who qualifies as a holder in due course, and the rights of such a holder, all appear in Articles Three and Four of the Uniform Commercial Code, and are covered in detail in advanced law school courses in commercial law.

Almost all commercial loan-type transactions are evidenced by promissory notes. Most of them are in negotiable form. Forms for negotiable promissory notes appear in all form books, and printed promissory notes in negotiable form with blanks to be filled in can be obtained from a legal stationer.

Bonds and *debentures* are gussied-up promissory notes used by corporations to borrow long-term funds. Such instruments are often publicly held and widely traded. See §15.9.

§1.3 Secured and Unsecured Loans

Creditors often are not satisfied with the protections and rights available to a simple creditor, or even to a holder in due course of negotiable commercial paper. Such a creditor is *unsecured*: His or her right to collect on the claim (or the right of a holder in due course to enforce the note in accordance with its terms) depends on the debtor being good for the amount due when a judgment is obtained. The time when collection is sought is more critical than the time the transaction occurred: An unsecured debtor may have numerous assets when the debt is created but business reverses or unwise transactions may make the debt uncollectible when enforcement is sought. A holder in due course is no better off than the original creditor in this regard since even if the holder gets a judgment on the promissory note, he or she still has to collect on the judgment. Not even a holder in due course can squeeze blood from a turnip.

Creditors increase the likelihood of repayment by requiring, at the time of the transaction, that the debtor grant an interest in some or all of his or her property to secure the repayment of the loan. If the transaction involves the sale of goods on credit, the seller will normally take a *security interest* in the goods sold; in other types of transactions, the security interest may involve various kinds of tangible or intangible property or rights. Typically the property or assets remain in the control of the debtor until a default on the loan occurs, when the creditor may take judicial steps or self-help to seize the property or rights in which he or she has an interest in order to satisfy the debt. Historically, these creditor-owned interests in debtors' property were called *liens* or *chattel mortgages*; under the Uniform Commercial Code, they are called *security interests* or *purchase money security interests*, though references to liens still regularly appear in cases involving personal property. Basically, a lien or security interest is an intangible property interest that allows the creditor, if the loan is not repaid, to seize the property subject to the lien to satisfy the unpaid loan; usually the property is sold and the proceeds applied against the unpaid loan.

Notice of a security interest in the debtor's property is publicly made by filing with a public office to *perfect* the security interest against claims of subsequent creditors. (There are some important exceptions to the filing requirement for perfection; where an exception is applicable the security interest is perfected either by other means, such as taking possession of the collateral, or automatically.) A failure to perfect means that subsequent creditors may obtain competing security interests senior to the unfiled interest and that a bankruptcy trustee may be able to avoid the unfiled security interest, reducing the creditor to unsecured status.

The process by which a secured creditor realizes upon the security is usually described as *foreclosure*, though in the case of consumer goods it may involve *repossession*. Typically, the seized property is sold and the proceeds applied to the payment of the debt. If the proceeds of the sale of seized property are not sufficient to discharge the loan (as is usually the case), the creditor continues to have an unsecured claim against the debtor for the balance, usually called a *deficiency* or *deficiency judgment*. If the proceeds exceed the loan balance, unpaid interest, and allowable fees or charges (often including attorney's fees), the debtor is entitled to the balance.

Everyone has heard of automobiles or washing machines of luckless debtors being repossessed by hard-hearted creditors, or the equipment and land of farmers being put up for sale at auction at the direction of one or more creditors. While such events do obviously happen with some regularity when debtors are individuals, most enforcement efforts involve something less than foreclosure. For one thing, creditors often take security in property of dubious value but of personal value to the debtor as a device to encourage payment. Second-hand furniture probably will not bring very much upon resale, but the threat of foreclosure could mean the potential loss of a family's cherished items and only furniture, and payment of the secured loan may be made to ensure that the furniture is not lost. Many secured creditors threaten and cajole: They may make numerous threatening telephone calls or even post property for foreclosure. Foreclosure, however, is not free of cost and in most industries, at least, is a last resort. Automobile repossession in many areas is an exception because of the relative mobility and ease of marketability of the collateral.

Even though substantial businesses that raise capital by borrowing are also often required to pledge machinery and other business assets as security for the loans, foreclosure is even less common in the case of businesses than in the case of individuals. A business is typically worth more as a going enterprise than it is broken up and sold in parts. Thus, when a substantial business runs into financial difficulty and secured creditors begin making threatening noises to seize the railroad's freight cars or the manufacturer's machinery and equipment, the debtor usually seeks protection from foreclosure in the federal bankruptcy courts by filing a petition for reorganization so its operating assets can be preserved as a single unit. See Chapter 10. While secured creditors holding liens on operating assets are in a better position than unsecured creditors in a reorganization proceeding, there is no assurance that in bankruptcy a secured creditor will be able to realize directly upon his or her security.

Much of the law relating to obtaining and perfecting security interests appears in Article Nine of the Uniform Commercial Code and is covered in detail in advanced commercial law courses in law school. However, legal problems relating to security interests also involve bankruptcy, collection practices, and the like. These problems are sufficiently complicated that there is often at least one additional advanced course in law school curricula to deal with them.

§1.4 Simple Interest and Compound Interest

At the first level, everyone understands the concept of interest on a debt: Interest is the amount paid by a borrower for the use of the lender's money. Interest is the cost of a loan to a borrower; it is the return from owning capital to the lender. The amount of interest owed by a borrower is apparently a function of three variables: (1) the number of dollars borrowed, (2) the period for which they are borrowed, and (3) the rate of interest being charged.

Rather surprisingly, interest is a concept of some complexity. In order to determine how much interest actually is to be earned on a specific loan, one must know not only the stated interest rate, the period the loan is to be outstanding, and the amount borrowed, but also the periods when interest is to be computed, and, if the loan is to continue for more than one interest period, whether the interest is to be calculated as simple interest or compound interest.

The virtually universal practice is to quote interest rates on an annual basis. There is no uniformity, however, as to the manner in which the actual computation is to be made. Interest quoted at the rate of 6 percent per year may actually mean interest calculated at 0.5 percent per month due at the end of each month or it may mean interest at the rate of 1.5 percent per quarter due at the end of every three-month period, or 3 percent semi-annually, due at the end of six months, or 6 percent due at the end of a year. Usually, these different calculations lead to different results. The times when payments are to be made on a loan may or may not coincide with the times when interest is calculated.

The computation of interest over several periods also involves an assumption as to whether the earned interest is in effect withdrawn every period so that each period's interest is computed on a stable principal, or whether the earned interest from the previous period is left with the borrower and treated as principal thereafter, itself to earn interest in the future period. The former is called *simple interest* and the latter *compound interest*.

A good example of compound interest involves the deposit of money with your friendly Savings and Loan Association. In this transaction, you are, of course, the lender and the Association is the borrower who pays you interest at a specified rate. Let us assume that you have $10,000 that you deposit with an Association that advertises that it pays 8 percent per year, compounded quarterly. The word *quarterly* means, first of all, that while the Association quotes its interest rate as 8 percent per year, it actually calculates interest at the rate of 2 percent for each accounting period of three months and adds that amount of interest to your account at the end of that period. Thus, if you left your $10,000 with the Association for three months, you would be credited with $200.00 (2 percent of $10,000), which you could withdraw without reducing your account below $10,000.

Let us assume that you do not do this; rather you do not do anything except let the Association use your money for another three months. If the Association computed its obligation on a simple interest basis, you would simply earn another $200.00 during the second three months. If the Association computed its obligation on a compound interest basis (as most savings and loans institutions do and as your Association expressly promised to do when it advertised that its 8 percent rate was *"compounded quarterly"*), it would consider that you had $10,200 on loan to the Association throughout the second quarter, and interest would be calculated on this amount at the end of six months, so that you would earn $204.00 during this period rather than simply $200.00. This is compound interest. The additional $4.00 reflects interest on the last period's interest. Over several accounting periods, the difference between compound and simple interest becomes increasingly significant. If you left your compound interest investment with the Association for a full year, you would have an account worth $10,824.32; at the end of two years, it would be worth $11,716.59. If only simple interest were paid, the investment would be worth $10,800 after one year and $11,600 after two years. At the end of ten years your investment will be $22,080.40 at compound interest; if only simple interest were paid, the account would be worth $18,000. The compounding of interest thus significantly increases the growth rate of capital. If the interest rate is 6 percent (compounded quarterly), the investment doubles in 11.75 years; at 8 percent, in about 9 years; at 10 percent, in about 7 years.

If the Association had calculated the interest it owed you on a simple interest basis, in effect it would be ignoring the interest earned in previous periods in calculating the current period's interest; or to put it another way, it would assume that you had withdrawn the interest earned at the end of each accounting period even though you had not in fact done so. Presented in this way, it seems clear that compound interest more accurately reflects the reality of loan transactions over several accounting periods than does simple interest. The continued existence of simple interest computations here and there in the economy probably reflects a lack of sophistication by some lenders, the somewhat greater complexity of compound interest calculations as compared to simple interest calculations, and possibly an illogical remnant of the historical antipathy to the payment of interest at all. One can imagine, for example, a creditor making a two-year, 6 percent loan, and concluding that he should receive the original principal of the loan plus an aggregate of 12 percent in interest at the end of two years. The creditor may not realize that he is in fact charging less than 6 percent per year; or in other words that he is worse off setting up the transaction this way than if he made a one-year loan at 6 percent for that year and then "rolled over" that entire loan — principal and interest — at the end of that year into a second one-year loan at 6 percent for the second year.

The apparent complexity of compound interest transactions may have been a serious problem when all calculations were made with paper and pencil, and some lenders may have concluded that the additional interest was just not worth the apparent number of repetitive calculations or the use of a mathematical formula. This calculation problem, however, has been entirely eliminated by the development of compound interest tables, and recently, with the development of inexpensive and convenient electronic calculating devices and computers described briefly in §1.8.

One of the peculiarities of compound interest calculations is that whenever interest is compounded more frequently than the quoted annual rate, the actual interest rate earned for the year is more favorable to the lender than the quoted rate. In the above example, the quoted rate is 8 percent, but the actual rate of return for the first year is 8.243 percent. The quoted rate is sometimes also called the *nominal* rate, while the actual rate earned is usually called the *effective* rate of interest or the *yield*. Some advertisements set forth both rates in seeking to attract potential depositors. If compound interest is calculated on an annual period, of course, the effective rate at the end of one year is identical to the quoted nominal rate.

§1.5 Daily Compounding of Interest

As described above, interest paid by lending institutions is usually compounded for periods of less than one year, though rates are usually quoted on an annual basis. A few financial institutions advertise that their interest is "compounded daily" or "compounded continuously." All that means is that interest is computed each day (or each hour) and is added to principal to compute the following day's (or hour's) interest. Because compound interest rate calculations rapidly approach a limit as the interest rate and the time period is divided into smaller and smaller segments, the daily compounding of interest increases only slightly the productivity of money over quarterly compounding. For example, if you invest $10,000 with an institutional borrower offering to pay 8 percent interest per year compounded daily, your investment after three years will be worth $12,712.14. If the interest had been compounded quarterly, as most traditional institutional borrowers do, your investment would be worth $12,682.42. If it were compounded only annually, it would have been worth $12,597.12. If it were compounded hourly, every day and night for the three years, it would be worth $12,712.36, almost exactly the same as it would on the basis of daily compounding! In short, do not be misled by advertisements that promise a great deal because interest is compounded daily, hourly, or constantly.

§1.6 Exact or Ordinary Interest

Bankers also distinguish between *ordinary interest* and *exact interest*. These terms arose in connection with the computation of interest for periods of less than one year. When calculations were made by paper and pencil, and many loans were for days, weeks, months, or fractions of years, it greatly simplified matters to consider a year to consist of 360 days based on 12 months of 30 days each. Interest computed on the basis of these simplifying assumptions is ordinary interest and is still used by many banks, and in the computation of interest on corporate, agency and municipal bonds. Exact interest treats the year as consisting of 365 or 366 days, as the case may be, and ignores months. With the development of modern calculating devices, the computation of exact interest, like the calculation of compound interest, has been greatly simplified, though it is obviously more complicated to count the specific number of days in each month than it is to assume that each month has 30 days. While the difference involved is usually relatively small, one suspects that many banks and financial institutions continue to use ordinary interest because it imparts a small upward bias in the amount of interest charged borrowers.

When calculating interest, it is customary to exclude the day the loan is made and include the day in which it is repaid.

§1.7 Formulas to Calculate Compound Interest

The examples so far make one important point about compound interest problems: The calculations appear to be complex since they involve more than simple arithmetic or multiplication. Indeed, if one were to compute the interest at the end of each period, add it to the previous balance and then compute the interest for the next period, the calculation in many instances would be laborious if not interminable. There is, however, a formula for computing compound interest that has frightened generations of nonmathematicians. That formula is:

$$FV = P \times (i + 1)^t$$

where i is the interest rate, t the number of time periods, P the principal and FV the future value after t periods.

Obviously there must be a way to make the calculations even quicker than by using this formula. For many years financial institution employees used a booklet that gave compound interest computations (and other calculations described below) for one dollar by interest rates and by periods. These tables were called, not surprisingly, *compound interest tables*.

Table 1-1 is an example of a compound interest table. It shows the future value of $1 at various interest rates for 50 time periods. Assume you deposit $1,000 in a bank that pays 8 percent per year compounded quarterly. If you leave the money there for ten years, how much will be in the account after ten years? Since the interest is compounded quarterly, the question involves a calculation over 40 periods at 2 percent per period. Looking in the "40" row and "2%" column, we see that $1 will grow to 2.2080 after 40 periods. Hence, $1,000 will have grown to $2,208. Another question: Assume you will need $10,000 in five years for law school tuition. If a bank will guarantee a 6 percent rate compounded semiannually, how much must you deposit today to have $10,000 in five years? This requires a calculation over 10 periods at 3 percent. Using the "10" row and "3%" column, we find that $1 deposited today will have grown to $1.3439 in five years. Hence you must deposit

$$\frac{\$10,000}{1.3439} = \$7,441.03$$

It should be cautioned that these hypotheticals are not entirely realistic. First, no account is taken of the income tax that would be due on the periodic interest earned. Second, most banks today will not guarantee a fixed interest rate over time (though other financial devices exist that may permit "locking in" a fixed rate.)

Table 1-1
Future Value After n Periods of $1 Invested Today

No. of periods	2%	3%	4%	5%	6%	7%	8%
1	1.0200	1.0300	1.0400	1.0500	1.0600	1.0700	1.0800
2	1.0404	1.0609	1.0816	1.1025	1.1236	1.1449	1.1664
3	1.0612	1.0927	1.1249	1.1576	1.1910	1.2250	1.2597
4	1.0824	1.1255	1.1699	1.2155	1.2625	1.3108	1.3605
5	1.1041	1.1593	1.2167	1.2763	1.3382	1.4026	1.4693
6	1.1262	1.1941	1.2653	1.3401	1.4185	1.5007	1.5869
7	1.1487	1.2299	1.3159	1.4071	1.5036	1.6058	1.7138
8	1.1717	1.2668	1.3686	1.4775	1.5938	1.7182	1.8509
9	1.1951	1.3048	1.4233	1.5513	1.6895	1.8365	1.9990
10	1.2190	1.3439	1.4802	1.6289	1.7908	1.9672	2.1589
11	1.2434	1.3842	1.5395	1.7103	1.8983	2.1049	2.3316
12	1.2682	1.4258	1.6010	1.7959	2.0122	2.2522	2.5182
13	1.2936	1.4685	1.6651	1.8856	2.1329	2.4098	2.7196
14	1.3195	1.5126	1.7317	1.9799	2.2609	2.5785	2.9372
15	1.3459	1.5580	1.8009	2.0789	2.3966	2.7590	3.1722
16	1.3728	1.6047	1.8730	2.1829	2.5404	2.9522	3.4259
17	1.4002	1.6528	1.9479	2.2920	2.6928	3.1588	3.7000
18	1.4282	1.7024	2.0258	2.4066	2.8543	3.3799	3.9960
19	1.4568	1.7535	2.1068	2.5270	3.0256	3.6165	4.3157
20	1.4859	1.8061	2.1911	2.6533	3.2071	3.8697	4.6610
21	1.5157	1.8603	2.2788	2.7860	3.3996	4.1406	5.0338
22	1.5460	1.9161	2.3699	2.9253	3.6035	4.4304	5.4365
23	1.5769	1.9736	2.4647	3.0715	3.8197	4.7405	5.8715
24	1.6084	2.0328	2.5633	3.2251	4.0489	5.0724	6.3412
25	1.6406	2.0938	2.6658	3.3864	4.2919	5.4274	6.8485

Table 1-1 (*cont.*)
Future Value After n Periods of $1 Invested Today

No. of periods	2%	3%	4%	5%	6%	7%	8%
26	1.6734	2.1566	2.7725	3.5557	4.4594	5.8074	7.3964
27	1.7069	2.2213	2.8834	3.7335	4.8223	6.2139	7.9881
28	1.7410	2.2879	2.9987	3.9201	5.1117	6.6488	8.6271
29	1.7758	2.3566	3.1187	4.1161	5.4184	7.1143	9.3173
30	1.8114	2.4273	3.2434	4.3219	5.7435	7.6123	10.0627
31	1.8476	2.5001	3.3731	4.5380	6.0881	8.1451	10.8677
32	1.8845	2.5751	3.5081	4.7649	6.4534	8.7153	11.7371
33	1.9222	2.6523	3.6484	5.0032	6.8406	9.3253	12.6760
34	1.9607	2.7319	3.7943	5.2533	7.2510	9.9781	13.6901
35	1.9999	2.8139	3.9461	5.5160	7.6861	10.6766	14.7853
36	2.0399	2.8983	4.1039	5.7918	8.1473	11.4239	15.9682
37	2.0807	2.9852	4.2681	6.0814	8.6361	12.2236	17.2456
38	2.1223	3.0748	4.4388	6.3855	9.1543	13.0793	18.6253
39	2.1647	3.1670	4.6164	6.7048	9.7035	13.9948	20.1153
40	2.2080	3.2620	4.8010	7.0400	10.2857	14.9745	21.7245
41	2.2522	3.3599	4.9931	7.3920	10.9029	16.0227	23.4625
42	2.2972	3.4607	5.1928	7.7616	11.5570	17.1443	25.3395
43	2.3432	3.5645	5.4005	8.1497	12.2505	18.3444	27.3666
44	2.3901	3.6715	5.6165	8.5572	12.9855	19.6285	29.5560
45	2.4379	3.7816	5.8412	8.9850	13.7646	21.0025	31.9204
46	2.4866	3.8950	6.0748	9.4343	14.5905	22.4726	34.4741
47	2.5363	4.0119	6.3178	9.9060	15.4659	24.0457	37.2320
48	2.5871	4.1323	6.5705	10.4013	16.3939	25.7289	40.2106
49	2.6388	4.2562	6.8333	10.9213	17.3775	27.5299	43.4274
50	2.6916	4.3839	7.1067	11.4674	18.4202	29.4570	46.9016

Table 1-1 (*cont.*)
Future Value After n Periods of $1 Invested Today

No. of periods	9%	10%	11%	12%	13%	14%	15%
1	1.0900	1.1000	1.1100	1.1200	1.1300	1.1400	1.1500
2	1.1881	1.2100	1.2321	1.2544	1.2769	1.2996	1.3225
3	1.2950	1.3310	1.3676	1.4049	1.4429	1.4815	1.5209
4	1.4116	1.4641	1.5181	1.5735	1.6305	1.6890	1.7490
5	1.5386	1.6105	1.6851	1.7623	1.8424	1.9254	2.0114
6	1.6771	1.7716	1.8704	1.9738	2.0820	2.1950	2.3131
7	1.8280	1.9487	2.0762	2.2107	2.3526	2.5023	2.6600
8	1.9926	2.1436	2.3045	2.4760	2.6584	2.8526	3.0590
9	2.1719	2.3579	2.5580	2.7731	3.0040	3.2519	3.5179
10	2.3674	2.5937	2.8394	3.1058	3.3946	3.7072	4.0456
11	2.5804	2.8531	3.1518	3.4785	3.8359	4.2262	4.6524
12	2.8127	3.1384	3.4985	3.8960	4.3345	4.8179	5.3503
13	3.0658	3.4523	3.8833	4.3635	4.8980	5.4924	6.1528
14	3.3417	3.7975	4.3104	4.8871	5.5348	6.2613	7.0757
15	3.6425	4.1772	4.7846	5.4736	6.2543	7.1379	8.1371
16	3.9703	4.5950	5.3109	6.1304	7.0673	8.1372	9.3576
17	4.3276	5.0545	5.8951	6.8660	7.9861	9.2765	10.7613
18	4.7171	5.5599	6.5436	7.6900	9.0243	10.5752	12.3755
19	5.1417	6.1159	7.2633	8.6128	10.1974	12.0557	14.2318
20	5.6044	6.7275	8.0623	9.6466	11.5231	13.7435	16.3665
21	6.1088	7.4002	8.9492	10.8038	13.0211	15.6676	18.8215
22	6.6586	8.1403	9.9336	12.1003	14.7138	17.8610	21.6447
23	7.2579	8.9543	11.0263	13.5523	16.6266	20.3616	24.8915
24	7.9111	9.8497	12.2392	15.1786	18.7881	23.2122	28.6252
25	8.6231	10.8347	13.5855	17.0001	21.2305	26.4619	32.9190

Table 1-1 (*cont.*)
Future Value After n Periods of $1 Invested Today

No. of periods	9%	10%	11%	12%	13%	14%	15%
26	9.3992	11.9182	15.0799	19.0401	23.9905	30.1666	37.8568
27	10.2451	13.1100	16.7386	21.3249	27.1093	34.3899	43.5358
28	11.1671	14.4210	18.5799	23.8839	30.6335	39.2045	50.0656
29	12.1722	15.8631	20.6237	26.7499	34.6158	44.6931	57.5755
30	13.2677	17.4494	22.8923	29.9599	39.1159	50.9502	66.2118
31	14.4618	19.1943	25.4104	33.5551	44.2010	58.0832	76.1435
32	15.7633	21.1138	28.2056	37.5817	49.9471	66.2148	87.5651
33	17.1820	23.2252	31.3082	42.0915	56.4402	75.4849	100.6998
34	18.7284	25.5477	34.7521	47.1425	63.7774	86.0528	115.8048
35	20.4140	28.1024	38.5749	52.7996	72.0685	98.1002	133.1755
36	22.2512	30.9127	42.8181	59.1356	81.4374	111.8342	153.1519
37	24.2538	34.0039	47.5281	66.2318	92.0243	127.4910	176.1246
38	26.4367	37.4043	52.7562	74.1797	103.9874	145.3397	202.5433
39	28.8160	41.1448	58.5593	83.0812	117.5058	165.6873	232.9248
40	31.4094	45.2593	65.0009	93.0510	132.7816	188.8835	267.8635
41	34.2363	49.7852	72.1510	104.2171	150.0432	215.3272	308.0431
42	37.3175	54.7637	80.0876	116.7231	169.5488	245.4730	354.2495
43	40.6761	60.2401	88.8972	130.7299	191.5901	279.8392	407.3870
44	44.3370	66.2641	98.6759	146.4175	216.4968	319.0167	468.4950
45	48.3272	72.8905	109.5302	163.9876	244.6414	363.6791	538.7693
46	52.6767	80.1795	121.5786	183.6661	276.4448	414.5941	619.5847
47	57.4176	88.1975	134.9522	205.7061	312.3826	472.6373	712.5224
48	62.5852	97.0172	149.7970	230.3908	352.9923	538.8065	819.4007
49	68.2179	106.7190	166.2746	258.0377	398.8818	614.2395	942.3108
50	74.3575	117.3909	184.5648	289.0022	450.7359	700.2330	1083.6574

Within the last few years handheld calculators have become available with compound interest and other calculations built into their memories. One has only to enter any three of the four possible variables: the interest rate per period, the number of periods, the original principal amount and the future value. The calculator supplies the missing variable in a matter of seconds. The calculations in the preceding section, and the other calculations in this chapter were all made with the use of such a calculator, which originally cost about $30.00.

§1.8 On Careful Reading and "Flim Flam"

Members of the general public are encouraged every day by ingenious advertisements to deposit excess funds with banks, savings and loan associations, and other financial institutions. For many years, the maximum rates that such institutions could pay for funds in various classes of deposits were sharply regulated by the federal government. By 1986, however, these restrictions had disappeared, partly due to the wave of deregulation that swept through the federal government and partly because of the development of unregulated competition from *money market funds* created by the mutual fund industry (itself a fascinating story described in §19.5). With the disappearance of regulation came a bewildering proliferation of depository rules governing specific accounts that create a significant opportunity for deception.

Essentially, depository institutions are now free to pay interest on checking accounts, or to create new types of savings accounts that may or may not include the privilege of writing checks. The institution may pay whatever interest rate it chooses, calculate the interest in any manner it chooses, and may impose whatever restrictions it desires on the amount in the account, the period during which funds must remain in order to earn interest at the advertised levels, the number of checks written, and so forth. In fact, most public advertising of these new accounts is limited to the applicable interest rates and does not describe the restrictions, service charges, or penalties that might be applicable. As a result, careful reading is essential and some practices that have surfaced today can better be described as "flim flam" of the consumer. For example:

1. A bank offers a 5.25 percent annual interest rate, compounded monthly, for deposits of $1,000 or more. It does not disclose that it also imposes a "service charge" of $6.00 per month on deposits of less than $2,500. The result is that a customer who deposits exactly $1,000 earns in the first year, not approximately $54 but minus $18.

2. A bank advertises "we pay interest on the highest balance on deposit in the full quarter." Let us assume that you decide to invest your excess funds in this institution; you deposit $8,000 but decide to withdraw $1,000 to buy a new washing machine and dryer two months later. Shortly before the quarter ends, you have saved $1,500 and you deposit that amount, increasing the balance to $8,500. When you receive your statement at the end of the quarter, however, you discover that interest was calculated on $7,000, not $8,500. How come? The bank officer explains that the bank construes its advertisement to

mean the calculation should be made on the highest balance kept in the account *every day* for the entire quarter. Your "highest balance" maintained every day throughout the quarter was $7,000 and interest was calculated on that amount. In other words, interest is in fact being calculated on the lowest balance in the account during the quarter and the bank's advertisement seems misleading, if not a rip-off.

3. A bank publishes an advertisement that states "interest compounded daily." The bank construes this to mean not that the interest is compounded daily but that it is compounded quarterly based on the average of the depositor's daily balance in the account. Again this advertisement seems clearly misleading, given the well-understood meaning of compounding.

4. Fees may be based in part on the activity in the account and in part on the amount deposited: Smaller accounts pay larger fees than larger accounts.

An examination of the practices followed by several Washington, D.C. banks conducted by the staff of a congressman also revealed widely varying practices with respect to the manner of calculation of interest. It found, for example, that banks were using as a year a period varying from 336 days to 372 days in calculating interest.

In this new and unregulated world careful reading of fine print is required. One may have to ask questions of the financial institution before opening the account, and one must always be on the alert against flim flam.

§1.9 The Consumer as Borrower

The last sections dealt with the pleasant situation where you were the lender. Unfortunately that will not always be the case. You may borrow money as a consumer and you may represent clients who are involved in consumer loans. This section briefly discusses loan practices in these types of high-risk loans.

Everyone has seen advertisements for "easy" loans, "household" loans, and "small" loans. Companies involved in this loan business are usually regulated by state law, but the essence of their business is lending money at very high rates of interest. These rates may be advertised on a monthly basis; a rate of 3 percent per month is 36 percent per year. Small loan companies operate under special exceptions to usury statutes (discussed in a separate section below); rates of 50 percent per year or more are not uncommon. Pawn shops may charge even higher rates of interest. The cost of these loans is so great that they should be utilized only as a last resort.

§1.10 Credit Cards

Everyone is also familiar with bank credit cards that charge interest at the rate of 1½ percent per month or a lower rate for larger transactions. One can use these cards to buy things now and pay later; one can also use them to buy travelers checks, to borrow money, to get "cash advances" from automated machines, or to cover overdrafts in a checking account. All of these transactions essentially constitute loans on which the annual interest rate usually exceeds 18 percent per year. Actually, the effective interest rate involved in the use of credit cards depends on specific transactions. If we assume that the issuer of the card charges a 1½ percent per month fee on the closing balance on a specified day (the usual system), a purchase or extension of credit late in the monthly accounting period has the same cost as an identical transaction earlier in the period. Thus the effective interest rate depends on the day during the month that the charge is made. For persons who can obtain such cards (and that may not always be easy for young individuals "just starting out"), the convenience of using them as a credit device may exceed the relatively high interest cost.

Some consumer credit card plans provide for no interest charge if there is prompt payment of the entire balance within the following billing period. To the extent this privilege is exercised, these cards provide what are in effect short-term interest-free loans. Plans with this feature are still profitable because banks often charge annual membership fees and retailers and other merchants are charged a fee based on volume of use.

Another type of card that is superficially similar is the so-called *bank debit card*. These cards do not involve the extension of credit at all. Rather, your bank account is immediately and automatically charged with the amount of each purchase as soon as the merchant reports it.

Even though interest rates generally declined in the mid-1980s, effective interest rates on credit card transactions initially remained at relatively high rates, but gradually came under increasing competitive pressure. Some banks in smaller communities offer bank credit cards on a national basis, seeking to acquire users by charging lower interest rates than banks in larger cities.

A *PIN* (*personal identification number*) is a security device designed to prevent the possessor of a stolen or found credit card from using it to withdraw cash or cash equivalents from automated teller machines. The PIN must be entered manually by the user to effectuate the transaction.

§1.11 Other Consumer Loans

Another type of consumer loan involves loans made in connection with the purchase of automobiles or big ticket appliances. Many loans of this type appear to involve favorable interest rates and other terms. Of course, this may be in part because the loans are secured by the goods being sold. Because used goods often depreciate very markedly when they leave the showroom floor, however, this is often not the most likely explanation. Since the loans are usually arranged through the seller, there is also the possibility that the price is somewhat higher than it would be for a straight cash purchase, with the excess being compensation for the favorable credit terms. This is very often the case with purchases of new automobiles, where the actual cash price is often impossible to determine with precision. In this type of situation it is often preferable to arrange for a straight cash purchase of the automobile or the appliance and to arrange for the financing independently through one's own credit source. At least, this should help to clarify what is the real price of the car or the appliance, and what is the cost of the credit.

Interest on most small consumer loans (either for cash or to finance a purchase of a major appliance) is computed on an "add-on" basis that permits a mild deception about the effective interest rate. Add-on interest can best be described by an example. A $1,000 two-year loan is stated to be available at 8 percent on an add-on basis. When the actual computation is made, interest of $160 (.08 x 1,000 x 2) is added to the principal amount, and the total ($1,160) is divided by 24 to determine the monthly payment ($48.33). The actual rate of interest on this transaction is 14.67 percent and not 8 percent. Do you see why the effective rate is considerably greater than 8 percent? (Hint: If interest of $160 per month is being added to the loan each month while it is outstanding, what is the average balance outstanding on the loan?) Under federal disclosure regulations the actual as well as the add-on rate must be disclosed. Whether or not this actually helps the average consumer is debatable.

Consumer loans also often involve a variety of small (or not-so-small) charges for credit checks, credit life insurance, or a variety of other financing or handling charges. Often the services or benefits provided by these charges cost considerably less than the amount charged, so that some uncertain portion of these charges also may legitimately be viewed as a charge for the use of money, (i.e., interest).

§1.12 Home Equity Loans

In 1986 Congress enacted major amendments to the federal income tax statute. (See generally Chapter 12.) One change made by this legislation (the "1986 Act") affects consumer lending to a substantial degree. That change eliminated the deductibility of interest on most consumer loans. This change does not affect the middle- or lower-middle-income borrower who does not itemize personal deductions on his or her personal income tax return: That type of borrower uses only the "standard deduction" (see §12.9.2) and does not itemize personal deductions at all.

The borrower who is most affected by the change in tax law is a person who owns his or her residence. The mortgage interest and real estate tax payments due each year in connection with the ownership of a residence usually make itemization of personal deductions advantageous (and the 1986 Act does not affect these deductions). Before the 1986 Act, such a person also was able to deduct the interest paid on loans for a vacation, a new car, a boat, or other expenditures. Indeed the deductibility of the interest on these consumer loans probably increased somewhat the willingness to borrow money for these purposes.

Since most taxpayers who want to deduct consumer interest already are homeowners, the obvious solution for a taxpayer who wishes to buy, say, a new automobile on credit and deduct the interest payments after the effective date of the 1986 Act is to take out a loan using his or her residence as security and use the proceeds to buy the automobile. Thus was born the *home equity loan*.

Once this possibility was recognized, Congress ringed the deduction with limitations. To deduct the interest on the loan on the house to buy the automobile, the taxpayer may borrow only an amount equal to the cash invested in the residence (purchase price plus cost of improvements) and cannot deduct interest to the extent the loan is secured by general appreciation in value of the residence. However, this restriction is eliminated for loans for medical or educational purposes.

Refinancing a mortgage on a home has traditionally been a rather costly proposition since it is viewed as a conveyance of real estate. Home equity loans involve the creation of a line of credit secured by a lien on the value of the home. The line of credit is arranged in advance and can be activated simply by writing a check or even by using a credit card. Of course, the borrower accustomed to using these traditional unsecured credit devices may not realize that the transactions actually involve placing a second mortgage on his or her residence. Nonpayment, or even the failure to make prompt payment, may cause the borrower to lose his or her home, or at least, create significant discomfort and insecurity. (See the discussion of foreclosure of second mortgages in §3.12.) Hence, there is doubt about the wisdom of this new, tax-driven, consumer financing device, the full impact of which is deferred by a gradual "phase-out" of the loss of the consumer interest deduction until 1990.

§1.13 Travelers Checks

Another intriguing aspect of interest involves the widely used and advertised *travelers checks* issued by several banks and other organizations for the use of travelers or vacationers. At first blush, these travelers checks appear to be bargains: For the nominal charge of one dollar for each hundred dollars of checks, the traveler is promised free replacement of lost checks and the convenience of world-wide acceptance. How can a bank possibly make money charging only one dollar per hundred, let alone meeting the cost of expensive radio and TV advertising commonly used to promote the use of travelers checks? The answer is that in general you must pay for the checks immediately but they are not "cashed in" until some time later. In the meantime, the bank invests your funds and earns interest without paying any interest at all to you. Further, since people are constantly buying new travelers checks, the available funds for investment remain reasonably stable, subject, of course, to seasonal variations. The amount available may be a very large sum — running into the hundreds of millions or billions of dollars for the larger companies — and is usually called "the float." The interest on the float is what makes travelers checks profitable for the issuer.

One major issuer of travelers checks has an advertisement in which the announcer suggests that on returning from vacation, "keep your last travelers check in case of an emergency." Might there be an ulterior motive behind this helpful and friendly suggestion?

§1.14 Usury Statutes

Most states have usury statutes that purport to limit the maximum interest rate to 12 or 14 percent. Because of unusually high interest rates during a period in the early 1980s, many of these statutes were amended to raise the maximum rate significantly, or to apply a floating maximum rate that is dependent on some external market rate of interest. As a result, the potential importance of these statutes has diminished with the decline in interest rates from the early 1980s level.

The maximum interest rate permitted by the usury statutes is often significantly lower than the effective interest rates being charged on many consumer loans. In a handful of states the usury statute has created problems for credit card or consumer loans, but in most they have been held inapplicable for two reasons. First, in most states the usury rate is created by statute and may be changed by statute. Small loan companies and pawn shops, for example, operate under special statutes that expressly authorize the charging of high interest rates. It is somewhat ironic that the persons for whom the usury rate was designed — lower- and middle-class citizens — are often able to borrow money only from businesses operating under one of these special statutes that permit interest rates significantly above the statutory usury rate. However, that is often the market reality. Second, the courts in most states have developed a distinction between a "cash sale" and a "credit sale" that permits retailers to avoid usury problems. The cash sale/credit sale distinction allows the seller to establish a higher price for credit sales than for cash sales of the identical goods without the difference being considered interest for purposes of the usury statute. This so-called *time-price differential* has an element of fiction about it but is widely accepted.

The usury statutes of many states are also expressly made inapplicable to all corporate borrowers or to transactions over a certain size. Other states permit a higher maximum interest rate for corporate transactions than for individual transactions. The theory of these provisions is that borrowers in such transactions can take care of themselves. These exceptions provide a device to avoid the usury statute. A person buying a piece of commercial real estate may do so in his or her own name or may form a wholly owned corporation to do so (see §13.6) at only a modestly greater cost. If the proposed interest rate on a loan to finance the purchase of that real estate exceeds the maximum rate permitted by the usury statute, the transaction may be cast in corporate form rather than as an individual transaction.

A fair amount of controversy exists about usury statutes. They are clearly well-meaning consumer legislation: That they have the counterproductive effect of making credit unavailable at above-usury levels but still lower than small loan levels, has been widely suggested. Certainly, if the usury statutes were made broadly applicable to all types of loans and all loopholes or evasions were eliminated, many persons might be entirely unable to obtain credit legitimately; such persons may be driven to loan sharks or worse, to obtain essential loans.

§1.15 The Importance of Interest in Commercial Transactions

Chapter 19 describes numerous vehicles for investment available to persons with excess capital, either on a short-term or long-term basis. Many of these investment vehicles permit the earning of interest on a daily basis. In reflecting on the concept of interest as compensation for the use of funds, it should be apparent that it is uneconomic to leave large amounts of capital in noninterest-bearing form for any period of time. The most common example of a noninterest-bearing form is the simple checking account. Other examples are cash in a sock, a mattress or safe deposit vault, or investments in jewels, works of art, or gold. Of course, one needs to retain cash in a checking account to pay current bills and to avoid bank service charges, but in this day of electronic fund transfers and flexible investment vehicles, as a general proposition excess cash should be earning interest rather than lying idle in some form. It is not uncommon for businesses to have an average daily balance in the tens or hundreds of thousands of dollars: In such cases, more effective cash management may permit a steady interest income to be developed where none presently exists.

It is also important to recognize that even one day's interest on a large sum of money involves enough dollars to dictate careful planning. Assume, for example that your client has successfully negotiated the sale of his solely owned business for $25,000,000 in cash, payable by bank certified check at the closing. The closing should be scheduled early enough in the day to permit investment of the $25,000,000 the same day. To schedule a closing at 4:00 p.m. after local banks are closed will result in the loss of something like $5,000 in interest for one day. That may sound astonishing, but it is true: Large sums generate an appreciable amount of interest each day. Similarly, to set up a 30- or 45-day escrow account for $10,000,000 without providing for investment of the escrowed amount and a clear statement as to who is entitled to the interim interest is so negligent as to border on malpractice. Of course, clients with access to very large sums of money are usually well aware of the cost of leaving funds idle for even short periods of time and will insist on appropriate investment provisions.

Where *very* large sums are involved, even payment schedules are apt to become a matter of negotiation, since interest may be earned on interest payments and the creditor should seek payments quarterly or even monthly to take advantage of this fact. Correspondingly, the debtor may opt for semiannual or even annual payments, if he or she can. Assume, for example, that your client owns a large hotel and apartment complex on the beach, complete with swimming pool and 18-hole golf course. He has negotiated a sale of the entire property for $100,000,000 on the following terms: $10,000,000 down with the balance payable over 5 years, $15,000,000 per year at 6 percent compound interest per year. Your client proposes that payments of principal and interest be made quarterly each year; the buyer is equally adamant that there be a single $15,000,000 payment plus interest payable on each anniversary date only. Do you appreciate that this apparently minor issue really involves a fairly large sum of money? If your client can earn more than 6 percent in alternative investments (which as of late 1987 he certainly could in several extremely conservative investments), quarterly payments permit prompter investment at the higher rate than an annual payment. Even a 1 percent additional yield on investments above the 6 percent rate makes the quarterly payment plan worth $30,000 more than the annual payment plan in the first year alone. Since the purchaser can also earn more than 6 percent per year on alternative investments, it is to his or her decided advantage to place the funds to be used to make payments in those alternative investments, leave them there as long as possible, and make payments as late as possible.

§1.16 The Bewildering Variety of Interest Rates

How are interest rates established in the real world? If one compares banks and other lending institutions and reads the financial press it quickly becomes apparent that there is a jungle of inconsistent rates all simultaneously existing side by side. To take some examples:

(1) "I am fortunate. I have a 4¾ percent loan on my house." (The speaker is a World War II veteran who bought his house in 1960).

(2) As indicated earlier, credit cards charge 1½ percent a month on the unpaid balance or roughly 18 percent per year.

(3) A bank may make a relatively small loan — say $5,000 — to a good customer in early 1984 at 14 percent per year.

(4) In many states, an unsatisfied judgment earns interest at the rate of 6 percent per year. (In 1981, Florida raised its rate to 12 percent.)

(5) In late 1987, a family desiring to purchase a residence may be charged interest of 10 percent or more on a loan for 75 percent of the cost of the residence.

(6) In September 1979, Utah Power and Light Company, a large investor-owned electric utility, borrowed $65,000,000, with repayment due in 2009, at about 10¼ percent per year, while on the same day Superior Oil Company, another large corporation, borrowed $300,000,000 at 9⅝ percent, repayable in part in 1989 and in part in 1999.

(7) On the same day in September 1979, Austin, Texas borrowed $60,000,000 at interest rates ranging from 5.5 percent for obligations maturing in 1983 to 6.75 percent for those maturing in 2006.

Several factors help to explain the wide diversity in numbers. First, interest rates have varied widely during different historical periods. Many financial transactions — such as many loans to purchase a house — involve fixed interest rates even though they may be outstanding for 25 years or more. Much of the diversity of rates in the foregoing examples simply reflects the historical level of rates when the transaction giving rise to the loan occurred. In recent years devices that permit periodic adjustment of interest rates during the existence of a long-term obligation have been used increasingly, though many long-term, fixed-rate obligations continue to be written. Fixed rates add an element of gambling to transactions whenever fluctuations in interest rates exceed those the market anticipated when the fixed-rate transaction was entered into. This is well illustrated by the fortunate veteran described above who has a 4¾ percent loan on his house when current market rates for new house loans were 10 percent or more. The below-market-value loan is itself a valuable asset that enhances the value of the veteran's home — if he can convey the benefits of that loan to a purchaser of the home. The assumability of that loan is critically important in evaluating whether the veteran can sell that asset or whether it simply disappears when he sells the house. On the other hand, the veteran's asset is the lending institution's albatross. How do you think the lender at 4¾ percent feels today, knowing that it is paying its depositors more than 6 percent to attract deposits and that if it could get the veteran to pay off the balance of his mortgage, the money could be reinvested at more than twice the 4¾ percent rate?

Second, some interest rates described above are established by government fiat and reflect statutory policies rather than market rates. Although their intent is to benefit designated groups, such as veterans buying homes, sometimes a person can take advantage of low statutory rates by deferring payments and investing the capital at higher market rates.

Third, when one considers market rates of interest, wide variations occur because of differences in risk. Other things being equal, an investor demands a higher return from more risky investments than from less risky investments. The difference in rates being paid by Utah Power and Light and Superior Oil Corporation reflects a market difference in risk, though the probability of actual default by either is slight. For many debt securities, independent rating systems exist to determine the degree of risk. Bond rating provided by Moody's and Standard & Poor's are the most widely followed. These ratings assign alphabetical designations to risk categories. AAA refers to the strongest and most secure securities, sometimes called *gilt-edged securities*. More speculative debt securities are assigned successively lower designations, such as AA, A, BBB, BB, B, CCC, and so forth, down to C and D, which are assigned to highly speculative securities that may already be in default or seem unlikely to be repaid. The classification of a debt security in one risk category or another materially affects the interest rate that the borrower has to pay. A guarantee of repayment by the Federal Government obviously significantly reduces the risk that a borrower will default, and therefore reduces the interest cost to the borrower.

Fourth, debt securities issued by state or municipal borrowers are usually exempt from federal income tax. This favored tax status of state or municipal borrowers largely explains why the City of Austin may borrow at a significantly lower rate than large commercial lenders.

§1.17 The Retail Market for Money

There is in the modern American economy a clearly defined market for commercially loanable funds to individuals and enterprises: Interest is the factor that balances the supply and demand for money in this market. In this market the commercial banks are the sellers of money and the individuals and commercial enterprises are the buyers. This is a *retail market* for money to distinguish it from the market from which commercial banks obtain funds — a *wholesale market*. The weather vane interest rate in the retail market is called the *prime rate*. That is the rate that is usually (and not always accurately) defined as the rate large commercial banks charge large borrowers that involve essentially no risk of default. Competition requires large commercial banks throughout the nation to maintain a largely uniform prime rate; however, the rate often changes, and there may be periods of transition in which some banks quote the old rate while others quote the new. If the demand for funds appears to be increasing, one or more banks may announce a quarter-point or even a half-point increase in the prime rate. If other banks believe the higher rate is supportable by the market for funds, they too announce an increase, and the movement becomes nationwide. If other banks do not go along, the innovative banks will probably rescind the increase in order to ensure that their large borrowers do not go elsewhere for funds. A similar pattern appears when the demand for loanable funds appears to be slack and a decline in the prime rate is being considered. At least one major commercial bank uses a formula based on several money market factors to establish a tentative prime rate but competition may force this bank to adjust its rate.

Of course, most commercial borrowers are not candidates for a prime rate loan. However, all such borrowers are affected by changes in the prime rate, since interest rates for less secure commercial borrowers are usually tied — either expressly or in fact — to the prime rate.

For example, a retail bookstore with sales of $10,000,000 per year may have a line of credit of $1,000,000 to finance inventory from a local bank at ¾ of a point above the prime rate. A *line of credit* is a very common kind of open arrangement between a bank and a customer by which the customer — in this case the bookstore — may borrow money as needed up to the stated limit of $1,000,000. To take care of the possibility that there are slightly different prime rates being quoted on the last day of the month, such agreements usually specify which bank's quotations of prime rates should be looked to. In this arrangement, of course, the interest rate is flexible and varies with the prime rate — and therefore the market price for bank-made commercial loans — over time. If the business is cyclical, the store may need the line of credit for only part of each year. If not, the store may have loans under the line of credit close to or at the maximum all year round.

Similarly, a small store owner may obtain a signature loan of, say, $5,000. A *signature loan* is also a very common arrangement between a commercial bank and an individual with a good credit rating: It is simply an unsecured loan made solely on the borrower's signature. Two years ago the store owner borrowed the same amount and was charged 7½ percent interest. This time, the interest rate is 11 percent. "After all," the friendly banker apologetically explains, "two years ago the prime rate was 6½ percent; today it is 10 percent." The storeowner is in effect being charged one point over the prime rate.

§1.18 The Federal Government and Interest Rates

The federal government uses interest rates and the supply of money in commercial banks as devices to fight inflation and unemployment and to encourage a high level of economic activity. (The fact that these may be partially conflicting goals need not detain us.) This control is exercised principally by the Federal Reserve System through several devices, the most important of which are (1) open market transactions in federal securities, (2) reserve requirements, (3) federal debt management transactions, and (4) the discount rate.

These controls work efficiently on state-chartered as well as federally chartered institutions.

A detailed discussion of how reserve requirements, open market transactions, and similar devices by the Federal Reserve System indirectly influences the supply of money and the prime rate is beyond the scope of this book. These devices all operate generally by increasing or decreasing the amount of funds banks have available to lend to customers. The fourth, the *discount* rate, is more visible since it is an interest rate charged by the Federal Reserve System on loans to commercial banks. The discount rate is set by the Federal Reserve System partly on political and partly on economic considerations: Changes in this rate receive as much publicity as changes in the prime rate. The relationship between the discount rate and the prime rate can be most simply visualized as ormer being the wholesale rate and the latter being the retail rate for money. This, of course, is from the bank's perspective. The spread between the discount and prime rate is usually about two percentage points. If the Fed raises the discount rate, the prime rate also rises.

CHAPTER 2
PRESENT VALUES OF FUTURE PAYMENTS

§2.1 Introduction

One of the most fundamental financial concepts is that money to be paid in the future is not worth as much as money to be paid today. Relatively simple formulas permit a direct comparison of the value of amounts to be paid at different times. This chapter discusses this concept, which underlies practically all of modern financial theory and much of current business practice. The process by which amounts payable at different times are made comparable is usually referred to as *discounting future payments to current values* or to *net present values*. The word *discounting* in this context simply means reducing. Another phrase that describes this process is determining the *time value of money*.

§2.2 The Basic Concept

What is the right to receive $1,000 a year from now worth today? Assuming that there is no risk that the payer will default, is it not clear that the right is worth something less than $1,000? For if one had $1,000 today, one could invest it for a year in a riskless investment and thereby earn one year's interest in addition to the original $1,000. Thus, $1,000 payable a year from now has to be worth somewhat less than $1,000 in hand today. How much less? One way that such a question can be answered is to approach it from the point of view of a hypothetical investor: If that investor can make 12 percent per year on his or her money in a riskless investment, how much should he or she pay today for the right to receive that $1,000 in a year? So phrased, the issue becomes an algebraic calculation:

$$X + .12X = 1,000$$

$$1.12X = 1,000$$

$$X = 1,000/1.12 = 892.86$$

To such an investor, the right to receive $1,000 a year from now is worth precisely $892.86. But, it may be rejoined, why choose a 12 percent return? Why not, say, an 8 percent return, in which case the calculation becomes

$$X + .08X = 1,000$$

and the value of the right to receive the $1,000 in 12 months becomes $925.93? The difference between these two amounts is significant. Of course, there is no one single rate of return that is correct in an absolute sense. But that element of uncertainty as to what the correct value is should not hide certain basic truths revealed by these simple examples: (1) since interest rates are positive, a dollar in the future is *always* worth less than a dollar today, and (2) the higher the interest that can be earned on a riskless investment, the lower is the current value of a right to receive a future payment. In other words, there is an inverse relationship between interest rates and current values of future payments. This leads to yet a third basic truth: (3) the riskier the investment, the lower the current value of a right to receive the future payment.

The present value of a future sum is the reverse of the future value of a present sum invested at the same interest rate. For example, assume that one plans to buy a $1,000 stereo a year from now; how much do you have to put aside today in an account earning 12 percent per year to have $1,000 in one year? The answer, of course, is the now familiar amount, $892.96; determining that the present value of $1,000 payable one year from now is $892.96 is simply looking at the same transaction from a different perspective. Compare the example relating to funding the cost of law school tuition in Chapter 1.

When speaking of the earning power of a present amount over time, one usually speaks of the *interest rate*. When going the other way and computing the present value of a future payment, one usually speaks of the *discount rate*. However, it is the same rate, since the present value of a future sum and the future value of a present sum involve precisely the same calculation, examined from opposite perspectives.

§2.3 Present Value Calculations over Multiple Periods

Following the same line, what is $1,000 payable *two* years in the future worth today? If we again assume a 12 percent interest rate, it turns out that a $797.19 investment today grows to $892.86 after one year and to precisely $1,000 after two years. Thus, the present value of $1,000 payable two years from today is $797.19 at 12 percent interest. This involves a compound interest calculation, since the comparison is with a $797.19 investment today that is left untouched until the end of the two-year period. (The concept of compound interest is discussed in §1.5 of the previous chapter, and this discussion should be reread if you are not certain how compound interest differs from simple interest.) A formula to determine present values of future payments over multiple periods, derived from the formula for compound interest, is:

$$PV = \frac{FV}{(1 + i)^n}$$

Table 2-1

Number of years	Value of $1,000 at 12%	Value of $1,000 at 6%
1	892.90	943.40
2	797.20	890.00
3	711.80	839.60
4	635.50	792.10
5	567.40	747.30
10	322.00	558.40
25	58.80	233.00
50	3.50	54.30
100	0.01	2.94

where PV = present value; FV = future value; i is the interest rate; and n the number of periods. The simple calculations of one-year present values set forth in §2.2 are obviously special applications of this formula.

Despite the apparent mathematical certainty of the formula, it is important to recognize that the precise calculation of the present value of a future sum over a specified period depends not only on the applicable interest or discount rate but also on the number of subperiods within the period over which interest is compounded. In other words, in order to get mathematical precision, one must know both the applicable discount rate and whether interest is compounded quarterly, annually, or over some other set of subperiods during the two-year period in question. In the foregoing calculations, it is assumed that interest is compounded only annually so that the number of periods is two. In most calculations like this, involving relatively short time periods, the number of subperiods used does not change the results significantly. For example, if one calculates a 12 percent discount rate compounded quarterly over the two-year period, interest is compounded eight times at 3 percent per quarter, and the present value of $1,000 payable two years from now is $789.41 as compared with the $791.19 obtained above on the assumption that interest is compounded only annually. Do you see why increasing the number of subperiods *reduces* the present value of a future payment?

§2.4 Examples of Present Value Calculations

Table 2-1 indicates what $1,000 payable at various times in the future is worth today at 12 percent and at 6 percent. Several fundamental relationships described in this table should be emphasized:

First, as one should intuitively expect, the longer the period before the payment is to be received, the smaller the value.

Second, the present value of the right to receive even large sums of money in the far distant future is not worth very much, if anything. For example, how much should you pay for the right to receive $100,000 in a lump sum one hundred years from now? Not very much: According to the above tables, you should pay no more than one dollar at a 12 percent discount rate and $294 at a 6 percent rate. Since practically no one living today will be living when this payment is due, even these numbers are suspect. Indeed the entries in the above table for all payments to be made in the distant future — 25 years or more — are so theoretical and subject to so many contingencies that little credence can be given to them.

Third, in making these present value computations, the discount rate that is chosen has a tremendous effect on the outcome of the calculation. One can manipulate answers obtained by superficially minor changes in that number. Section 2.8 of this chapter speculates briefly on how this rate should be selected in real-world calculations.

Table 2-2 shows the present values of one dollar payable at various time periods in the future at most plausible interest rates. It will be noted that the numbers in Table 2-2 are all decimals less than one while in Table 1-1 all the entries are one or larger. That is because each entry in Table 2-2 is the reciprocal of each entry in Table 1-1.

$$\text{Entry in Table 2-2} = \frac{1}{\text{Entry in Table 1-1}}$$

The mathematically inclined may easily satisfy themselves that this reciprocal relationship indeed exists. The formula actually used to generate the entries in Table 2-2 is set forth on page 33.

A simple illustration of the use of Table 2-2 is the hypothetical set forth in §1.8, of a person planning to set aside a sum of money today to provide $10,000 of law school tuition five years from now. The problem further stipulates an interest rate of 6 percent compounded semiannually. One simply has to look up the discount factor for 3 percent over ten periods in Table 2-2, which yields 0.7441, and multiply by $10,000 to get $7,441.00, the same answer obtained by a division by a decimal in Chapter 1.

The decimal numbers in Table 2-2 are sometimes called *discount factors* because they can be added together to determine the present values of future payments. Most people find it easier to add and multiply decimals than to divide by decimals.

§2.5 A Preliminary Look at Annuities

An annuity is a stream of constant payments to be made at fixed intervals. Commercial annuities are the subject of Chapter 5. This section provides a preliminary examination of the underlying concept.

The present value of the right to receive $1,000 each year, beginning next year and continuing for five years at 12 percent compounded annually can be computed in a couple of ways. First, one could simply add up the present values of each of the first five payments in the table at the beginning of §2.4. The sum is $3,604.80, the present value of the right to receive an aggregate

Table 2-2
Present Value of $1 Payable After n Periods in the Future

No. of periods	2%	3%	4%	5%	6%	7%	8%
1	.9804	.9709	.9615	.9524	.9434	.9346	.9259
2	.9612	.9426	.9246	.9070	.8900	.8734	.8573
3	.9423	.9151	.8890	.8638	.8396	.8163	.7938
4	.9238	.8885	.8548	.8227	.7921	.7629	.7350
5	.9057	.8626	.8219	.7835	.7473	.7130	.6806
6	.8880	.8375	.7903	.7462	.7050	.6663	.6302
7	.8706	.8131	.7599	.7107	.6651	.6227	.5835
8	.8535	.7894	.7307	.6768	.6274	.5820	.5403
9	.8368	.7664	.7026	.6446	.5919	.5439	.5002
10	.8203	.7441	.6756	.6139	.5584	.5083	.4632
11	.8043	.7224	.6496	.5847	.5268	.4751	.4289
12	.7885	.7014	.6246	.5568	.4970	.4440	.3971
13	.7730	.6810	.6006	.5303	.4688	.4150	.3677
14	.7579	.6611	.5775	.5051	.4423	.3878	.3405
15	.7430	.6419	.5553	.4810	.4173	.3624	.3152
16	.7284	.6232	.5339	.4581	.3936	.3387	.2919
17	.7142	.6050	.5134	.4363	.3714	.3166	.2703
18	.7002	.5874	.4936	.4155	.3503	.2959	.2502
19	.6864	.5703	.4746	.3957	.3305	.2765	.2317
20	.6730	.5537	.4564	.3769	.3118	.2584	.2145
21	.6598	.5375	.4388	.3589	.2942	.2415	.1987
22	.6468	.5219	.4220	.3418	.2775	.2257	.1839
23	.6342	.5067	.4057	.3256	.2618	.2109	.1703
24	.6217	.4919	.3901	.3101	.2470	.1971	.1577
25	.6095	.4776	.3751	.2953	.2330	.1842	.1460

Table 2-2 (cont.)

Present Value of $1 Payable After n Periods in the Future

No. of periods	2%	3%	4%	5%	6%	7%	8%
26	.5976	.4637	.3607	.2812	.2198	.1722	.1352
27	.5859	.4502	.3468	.2678	.2074	.1609	.1252
28	.5744	.4371	.3335	.2551	.1956	.1504	.1159
29	.5631	.4243	.3207	.2429	.1846	.1406	.1073
30	.5521	.4120	.3083	.2314	.1741	.1314	.0994
31	.5412	.4000	.2965	.2204	.1643	.1228	.0920
32	.5306	.3883	.2851	.2099	.1550	.1147	.0852
33	.5202	.3770	.2741	.1999	.1462	.1072	.0789
34	.5100	.3660	.2636	.1904	.1379	.1002	.0730
35	.5000	.3554	.2534	.1813	.1301	.0937	.0676
36	.4902	.3450	.2437	.1727	.1227	.0875	.0626
37	.4806	.3350	.2343	.1644	.1158	.0818	.0580
38	.4712	.3252	.2253	.1566	.1092	.0765	.0537
39	.4619	.3158	.2166	.1491	.1031	.0715	.0497
40	.4529	.3066	.2083	.1420	.0972	.0668	.0460
41	.4440	.2976	.2003	.1353	.0917	.0624	.0426
42	.4353	.2890	.1926	.1288	.0865	.0583	.0395
43	.4268	.2805	.1852	.1227	.0816	.0545	.0365
44	.4184	.2724	.1780	.1169	.0770	.0509	.0338
45	.4102	.2644	.1712	.1113	.0727	.0476	.0313
46	.4022	.2567	.1646	.1060	.0685	.0445	.0290
47	.3943	.2493	.1583	.1009	.0647	.0416	.0269
48	.3865	.2420	.1522	.0961	.0610	.0389	.0249
49	.3790	.2350	.1463	.0916	.0575	.0363	.0230
50	.3715	.2281	.1407	.0872	.0543	.0339	.0213

Table 2-2 (cont.)
Present Value of $1 Payable After n Periods in the Future

No. of periods	9%	10%	11%	12%	13%	14%	15%
1	.9174	.9091	.9009	.8929	.8850	.8772	.8696
2	.8417	.8264	.8116	.7972	.7831	.7695	.7561
3	.7722	.7513	.7312	.7118	.6931	.6750	.6575
4	.7084	.6830	.6587	.6355	.6133	.5921	.5718
5	.6499	.6209	.5935	.5674	.5428	.5194	.4972
6	.5963	.5645	.5346	.5066	.4803	.4556	.4323
7	.5470	.5132	.4817	.4523	.4251	.3996	.3759
8	.5019	.4665	.4339	.4039	.3762	.3506	.3269
9	.4604	.4241	.3909	.3606	.3329	.3075	.2843
10	.4224	.3855	.3522	.3220	.2946	.2697	.2472
11	.3875	.3505	.3173	.2875	.2607	.2366	.2149
12	.3555	.3186	.2858	.2567	.2307	.2076	.1869
13	.3262	.2897	.2575	.2292	.2042	.1821	.1625
14	.2992	.2633	.2320	.2046	.1807	.1597	.1413
15	.2745	.2394	.2090	.1827	.1599	.1401	.1229
16	.2519	.2176	.1883	.1631	.1415	.1229	.1069
17	.2311	.1978	.1696	.1456	.1252	.1078	.0929
18	.2120	.1799	.1528	.1300	.1108	.0946	.0808
19	.1945	.1635	.1377	.1161	.0981	.0829	.0703
20	.1784	.1486	.1240	.1037	.0868	.0728	.0611
21	.1637	.1351	.1117	.0926	.0768	.0638	.0531
22	.1502	.1228	.1007	.0826	.0680	.0560	.0462
23	.1378	.1117	.0907	.0738	.0601	.0491	.0402
24	.1264	.1015	.0817	.0659	.0532	.0431	.0349
25	.1160	.0923	.0736	.0588	.0471	.0378	.0304

Table 2-2 (cont.)
Present Value of $1 Payable After n Periods in the Future

No. of periods	9%	10%	11%	12%	13%	14%	15%
26	.1064	.0839	.0663	.0525	.0417	.0331	.0264
27	.0976	.0763	.0597	.0469	.0369	.0291	.0230
28	.0895	.0693	.0538	.0419	.0326	.0255	.0200
29	.0822	.0630	.0485	.0374	.0289	.0224	.0714
30	.0754	.0573	.0437	.0334	.0256	.0196	.0151
31	.0691	.0521	.0394	.0298	.0226	.0172	.0131
32	.0634	.0474	.0355	.0266	.0200	.0151	.0114
33	.0582	.0431	.0319	.0238	.0177	.0132	.0099
34	.0534	.0391	.0288	.0212	.0157	.0116	.0086
35	.0490	.0356	.0259	.0189	.0139	.0102	.0075
36	.0449	.0323	.0234	.0169	.0123	.0089	.0065
37	.0412	.0294	.0210	.0151	.0109	.0078	.0057
38	.0378	.0267	.0190	.0135	.0096	.0069	.0049
39	.0347	.0243	.0171	.0120	.0085	.0060	.0043
40	.0318	.0221	.0154	.0107	.0075	.0053	.0037
41	.0292	.0201	.0139	.0096	.0067	.0046	.0032
42	.0268	.0183	.0125	.0086	.0059	.0041	.0028
43	.0246	.0166	.0112	.0076	.0052	.0036	.0025
44	.0226	.0151	.0101	.0068	.0046	.0031	.0021
45	.0207	.0137	.0091	.0061	.0041	.0027	.0019
46	.0190	.0125	.0082	.0054	.0036	.0024	.0016
47	.0174	.0113	.0074	.0049	.0032	.0021	.0014
48	.0160	.0103	.0067	.0043	.0028	.0019	.0012
49	.0147	.0094	.0060	.0039	.0025	.0016	.0011
50	.0134	.0085	.0054	.0035	.0022	.0014	.0009

amount of $5,000 in increments of $1,000 per year over the next five years. It seems odd that the right to receive $100,000 in a lump sum one hundred years from now, also discounted at 12 percent, is worth only one dollar while the right to receive only $1,000 per year over the next five years is worth thousands of times as much. Yet that is the magic of the time value of money.

A second way to calculate the present value of the same annuity is to add up the first five discount factors in Table 2-2 under 12 percent (.8929 + .7972 + .7118 + .6355 + .5674 = 3.6048) and multiply the product by $1,000. Of course this process works only if the payments are identical in amount and evenly spaced.

An even simpler method exists. Table 2-3 is a table of the *present values of annuities* (payable at the end of each period). To get the present value of the 12 percent, five-year annuity one simply looks up the "five year" row and "12 percent" column to find the number 3.6048. Obviously, Table 2-3 may be obtained from Table 2-2 by a process of systematic summing of amounts.

For those mathematically inclined, a nice complex formula to derive the present value of a stream of constant payments in the future is:

$$PV = \frac{P(1 - (1 + i)^{-N})}{i}$$

where P = the recurring payment; and PV, i, and n all have the same meanings as in the previous section.

In recent years, handheld calculators have been programmed to compute present and future values of annuities directly. For the current generation, that may be even easier, but one should understand the underlying theory.

§2.6 The Value of a Perpetual Annuity

Let us take a leap of fancy and assume that an annuity will continue forever — $1,000 per year forever. That must be worth an infinite amount, mustn't it, because the number of payments are infinite?

For simplicity, let us assume that an appropriate discount rate is 12 percent, so that we know that the first five years of the annuity is worth $3,604.80. If you turn back to the table at the beginning of §1.4, it appears that the "infinity" answer may be wrong because the present value of future payments drops off dramatically. Similarly, if one looks at Table 2-3 under the 12 percent column, the value of a 5-year annuity is $3,604.80; a 10-year annuity, $5,650.20; a 15-year annuity, $6,810.90; a 20-year annuity, $7,469.40; a 25-year annuity, $7,843.10; a 30-year annuity, $8,055.20. The present value of the five $1,000 payments from 25 years to 30 years is only $212.00. The present value of a 45-year annuity is $8,285.00; of a 50-year annuity, $8,3045. From the 45th to the 50th year, the five years of payments increase the present value by only $22. Clearly the value of a perpetual annuity is not infinite.

Table 2-3
Present Value of an Annuity of $1 Payable at the End of Each Period for n Periods

No. of periods	2%	3%	4%	5%	6%	7%	8%
1	.9804	.9709	.9615	.9524	.9434	.9346	.9259
2	1.9416	1.9135	1.8861	1.8594	1.8334	1.8080	1.7833
3	2.8839	2.8286	2.7751	2.7232	2.6730	2.6243	2.5771
4	3.8077	3.7171	3.6299	3.5460	3.4651	3.3872	3.3121
5	4.7135	4.5797	4.4518	4.3295	4.2124	4.1002	3.9927
6	5.6014	5.4172	5.2421	5.0757	4.9173	4.7665	4.6229
7	6.4720	6.2303	6.0021	5.7864	5.5824	5.3893	5.2064
8	7.3255	7.0197	6.7327	6.4632	6.2098	5.9713	5.7466
9	8.1622	7.7861	7.4353	7.1078	6.8017	6.5152	6.2469
10	8.9826	8.5302	8.1109	7.7217	7.3601	7.0236	6.7101
11	9.7868	9.2526	8.7605	8.3064	7.8869	7.4987	7.1390
12	10.5753	9.9540	9.3851	8.8633	8.3838	7.9427	7.5361
13	11.3484	10.6350	9.9856	9.3936	8.8527	8.3577	7.9038
14	12.1062	11.2961	10.5631	9.8986	9.2950	8.7455	8.2442
15	12.8493	11.9379	11.1184	10.3797	9.7122	9.1079	8.5595
16	13.5777	12.5611	11.6523	10.8378	10.1059	9.4466	8.8514
17	14.2919	13.1661	12.1657	11.2741	10.4773	9.7632	9.1216
18	14.9920	13.7535	12.6593	11.6896	10.8276	10.0591	9.3719
19	15.6785	14.3238	13.1339	12.0853	11.1581	10.3356	9.6036
20	16.3514	14.8775	13.5903	12.4622	11.4699	10.5940	9.8181
21	17.0112	15.4150	14.0292	12.8212	11.7641	10.8355	10.0168
22	17.6580	15.9369	14.4511	13.1630	12.0416	11.0612	10.2007
23	18.2922	16.4436	14.8568	13.4886	12.3034	11.2722	10.3711
24	18.9139	16.9355	15.2470	13.7986	12.5504	11.4693	10.5288
25	19.5235	17.4131	15.6221	14.0939	12.7834	11.6536	10.6748

Table 2-3 (*cont.*)
Present Value of an Annuity of $1 Payable at the End of Each Period for n Periods

No. of periods	2%	3%	4%	5%	6%	7%	8%
26	20.1210	17.8768	15.9828	14.3752	13.0032	11.8258	10.8100
27	20.7069	18.3270	16.3296	14.6430	13.2105	11.9867	10.9352
28	21.2813	18.7641	16.6631	14.8981	13.4062	12.1371	11.0511
29	21.8444	19.1885	16.9837	15.1411	13.5907	12.2777	11.1584
30	22.3965	19.6004	17.2920	15.3725	13.7648	12.4090	11.2578
31	22.9377	20.0004	17.5885	15.5928	13.9291	12.5318	11.3498
32	23.4683	20.3888	17.8736	15.8027	14.0840	12.6466	11.4350
33	23.9886	20.7658	18.1476	16.0025	14.2302	12.7538	11.5139
34	24.4986	21.1318	18.4112	16.1929	14.3681	12.8540	11.5869
35	24.9986	21.4872	18.6646	16.3742	14.4982	12.9477	11.6546
36	25.4888	21.8323	18.9083	16.5469	14.6210	13.0352	11.7172
37	25.9695	22.1672	19.1426	16.7113	14.7368	13.1170	11.7752
38	26.4406	22.4925	19.3679	16.8679	14.8460	13.1935	11.8289
39	26.9026	22.8082	19.5845	17.0170	14.9491	13.2649	11.8786
40	27.3555	23.1148	19.7928	17.1591	15.0463	13.3317	11.9246
41	27.7995	23.4124	19.9931	17.2944	15.1380	13.3941	11.9672
42	28.2348	23.7014	20.1856	17.4232	15.2245	13.4524	12.0067
43	28.6616	23.9819	20.3708	17.5459	15.3062	13.5070	12.0432
44	29.0800	24.2543	20.5488	17.6628	15.3832	13.5579	12.0771
45	29.4902	24.5187	20.7200	17.7741	15.4558	13.6055	12.1084
46	29.8923	24.7754	20.8847	17.8801	15.5244	13.6500	12.1374
47	30.2866	25.0247	21.0429	17.9810	15.5890	13.6916	12.1643
48	30.6731	25.2667	21.1951	18.0772	15.6500	13.7305	12.1891
49	31.0521	25.5017	21.3415	18.1687	15.7076	13.7668	12.2122
50	31.4236	25.7298	21.4822	18.2559	15.7619	13.8007	12.2335

Table 2-3 (*cont.*)

Present Value of an Annuity of $1 Payable at the End of Each Period for n Periods

No. of periods	9%	10%	11%	12%	13%	14%	15%
1	.9174	.9091	.9009	.8929	.8850	.87723	.8696
2	1.7591	1.7355	1.7125	1.6901	1.6681	1.6467	1.6257
3	2.5313	2.4869	2.4437	2.4018	2.3612	2.3216	2.2832
4	3.2397	3.1699	3.1024	3.0373	2.9745	2.9137	2.8550
5	3.8897	3.7908	3.6959	3.6048	3.5172	3.4331	3.3522
6	4.4859	4.3553	4.2305	4.1114	3.9975	3.8887	3.7845
7	5.0330	4.8684	4.7122	4.5638	4.4226	4.2883	4.1604
8	5.5348	5.3349	5.1461	4.9676	4.7988	4.6389	4.4873
9	5.9952	5.7590	5.5370	5.3282	5.1317	4.9464	4.7716
10	6.4177	6.1446	5.8892	5.6502	5.4262	5.2161	5.0188
11	6.8052	6.4951	6.2065	5.9377	5.6869	5.4527	5.2337
12	7.1607	6.8137	6.4924	6.1944	5.9176	5.6603	5.4206
13	7.4869	7.1034	6.7499	6.4235	6.1218	5.8424	5.5831
14	7.7862	7.3667	6.9819	6.6282	6.3025	6.0021	5.7245
15	8.0607	7.6061	7.1909	6.8109	6.4624	6.1422	5.8474
16	8.3126	7.8237	7.3792	6.9740	6.6039	6.2651	5.9542
17	8.5436	8.0216	7.5488	7.1196	6.7291	6.3729	6.0472
18	8.7556	8.2014	7.7016	7.2497	6.8399	6.4674	6.1280
19	8.9501	8.3649	7.8393	7.3658	6.9380	6.5504	6.1982
20	9.1285	8.5136	7.9633	7.4694	7.0248	6.6231	6.2593
21	9.2922	8.6487	8.0751	7.5620	7.1016	6.6870	6.3125
22	9.4424	8.7715	8.1757	7.6446	7.1695	6.7429	6.3587
23	9.5802	8.8832	8.2664	7.7184	7.2297	6.7921	6.3988
24	9.7066	8.9847	8.3481	7.7843	7.2829	6.8351	6.4338
25	9.8226	9.0770	8.4217	7.8431	7.3300	6.8729	6.4641

Table 2-3 (*cont.*)
Present Value of an Annuity of $1 Payable at the End of Each Period for n Periods

No. of periods	9%	10%	11%	12%	13%	14%	15%
26	9.9290	9.1609	8.4881	7.8957	7.3717	6.9061	6.4906
27	10.0266	9.2372	8.5478	7.9426	7.4086	6.9352	6.5135
28	10.1161	9.3066	8.6016	7.9844	7.4412	6.9607	6.5335
29	10.1983	9.3696	8.6501	8.0218	7.4701	6.9830	6.5509
30	10.2737	9.4269	8.6938	8.0552	7.4957	7.0027	6.5660
31	10.3428	9.4790	8.7331	8.0850	7.5183	7.0199	6.5791
32	10.4062	9.5264	8.7686	8.1116	7.5383	7.0350	6.5905
33	10.4644	9.5694	8.8005	8.1354	7.5560	7.0482	6.6005
34	10.5178	9.6086	8.8293	8.1566	7.5717	7.0599	6.6091
35	10.5668	9.6442	8.8552	8.1755	7.5856	7.0700	6.6166
36	10.6118	9.6765	8.8786	8.1924	7.5979	7.0790	6.6231
37	10.6530	9.7059	8.8996	8.2075	7.6087	7.0868	6.6288
38	10.6908	9.7327	8.9186	8.2210	7.6183	7.0937	6.6338
39	10.7255	9.7570	8.9357	8.2330	7.6268	7.0997	6.6380
40	10.7574	9.7791	8.9511	8.2438	7.6344	7.1050	6.6418
41	10.7866	9.7991	8.9649	8.2534	7.6410	7.1097	6.6450
42	10.8134	9.8174	8.9774	8.2619	7.6469	7.1138	6.6478
43	10.8380	9.8340	8.9886	8.2696	7.6522	7.1173	6.6503
44	10.8605	9.8491	8.9988	8.2764	7.6568	7.1205	6.6524
45	10.8812	9.8628	9.0079	8.2825	7.6609	7.1232	6.6543
46	10.9002	9.8753	9.0161	8.2880	7.6645	7.1256	6.6559
47	10.9176	9.8866	9.0235	8.2928	7.6677	7.1277	6.6573
48	10.9336	9.8969	9.0302	8.2972	7.6705	7.1296	6.6585
49	10.9482	9.9063	9.0362	8.3010	7.6730	7.1312	6.6596
50	10.9617	9.9148	9.0417	8.3045	7.6752	7.1327	6.6605

The present value of a perpetual stream of fixed payments is precisely equal to the reciprocal of the discount rate:

$$\frac{1}{\text{discount rate}}$$

In the above hypothetical,

$$\frac{1}{.12} = 8.3333;$$

the present value of the right to receive $1,000 per year forever (at a 12 percent discount rate) is $8,333.33. This should become intuitively obvious when you realize that $8,333.33 invested at 12 percent yields almost $1,000 per year ($8,333.33 × .12 = $999.99), year after year, forever. Since the present value of a 50-year annuity on those terms is $8,304.50, it follows that the present value of the right to receive every payment, from the 51st on, to infinity, is only $25.50. When one values a long term annuity, a simple way to approximate its value is to assume that it is infinite, and multiply by the reciprocal of the discount factor.

§2.7 Valuing Variable Future Payments

Skill in discounting future payments to present value is useful in a variety of contexts. Clients are sometimes faced with selecting the most attractive of several offers that involve payments at different times and in different amounts, or choosing between two or more strategies that involve payments of various amounts at various times under various assumptions. In order to avoid the common mistake of comparing oranges and apples, that is, of comparing dollars payable at different times without taking into account the time value of money, it is necessary to reduce all future payments to current values. In doing this one must select one or more interest rates: If all the payments are to be made by the same entity under apparently constant circumstances it is customary to use a single interest rate for all calculations. Consider the following example: Your client owns a valuable piece of real estate. He is considering three offers that involve the following terms:

a) $90,000 cash;
b) $10,000 down, $1,000 per month for 120 months;
c) $25,000 down, $1,200 per month for 72 months.

The total payments to be received under the first offer are $90,000. Under the second the total payments to be received are $130,000 ($10,000 plus 120 times $1,000). The contract presented by the hopeful purchaser to your client ignores the interest component entirely and states, as the purchase price, the full $130,000. Under the third alternative, the total payments are $111,400 ($25,000 plus 72 times $1,200). However, because of the time value of money, this comparison of gross amounts to be received is misleading. Calculation shows that at a 9 percent interest rate, and ignoring income taxes, the present value of $1,000 per month for 120 months is $78,941.69 and the present value of $1,200 per month for 72 months is $66,572.22. Thus the present values of the three offers are:

a) $90,000;
b) $88,941.69;
c) $91,572,22.

Even though the second alternative yields the largest gross amount, it has the smallest present value. This occurs because the immediate down payment in alternative b is rather small and periodic payments continue over ten years rather than six years, as in the third alternative. On the other hand, since the present values of the three offers are very close, most persons would probably recommend that the all-cash offer be accepted on the theory that there is some advantage in being disentangled from a property immediately. However, it certainly is not intuitively obvious that this is the most sensible solution.

In this hypothetical, different conclusions may be reached if a different discount rate is chosen. For example, if one computes the present value of the three payment options using a discount rate of 6 percent rather than 9 percent, the results are as follows:

a) All cash — $90,000;
b) $10,000 down, balance at $1,000 per month over 120 months — $95,366;
c) $25,000 down, balance at $1,200 over 72 months — $94,990.

Suddenly, the payments to be spread out over a period of time have become more attractive. Reflection shows that this is a result of the fact that the present value of future payments is higher at lower discount rates, so that at the lower discount rate the future payments become relatively more valuable compared with the down payments than when a higher discount rate is used. As noted before, there is an inverse relationship between value and discount rates: The higher the rate, the less a future payment is worth.

§2.8 What Discount Rate to Use in Calculating Present Values

In light of the foregoing discussion, certainly, a reasonable question at this point is why was the interest rate of 12 percent used in most of the above calculations? Why, in the last example comparing three different payment schedules, were the rates compared unexpectedly changed to 9 percent and 6 percent? Where do rates in the real world come from anyway?

Unfortunately, there is no simple answer to the question of which discount rate to use in all circumstances in the real world. It depends on what the question is, the current level of market interest rates, and the investment alternatives available to the parties. As described above, the differences in results reached vary significantly depending on the rate chosen, though the differences between choosing a 6 percent or a 6.5 percent rate is nowhere near as substantial as the difference between choosing between 6 percent and 12 percent, as Table 2-1 illustrates. However, that does not give much guidance as to whether a 6 percent or a 12 percent rate should actually be used.

Most real-life problems in determining present values come down to a choice between one of the four following rates:

1. The market interest rate for essentially risk-free investments, the yield on short-term debt securities issued by the federal government, for example.

2. The highest interest rate that a person could obtain for a deposit within his or her means at a local financial institution.

3. The lowest interest rate that a person would be charged in order to borrow funds of the same magnitude as the transaction involves.

4. The return that a business has determined it must make on an investment in order to be willing to enter into a transaction.

In instances where a person of doubtful wealth has the obligation to make a future payment, an appropriate upward adjustment may be made to the discount rate. Of couse, the greater the risk, the higher the discount rate will be (and concomitantly, the lower the present value of that payment will be). In most instances, however, the calculations are made using one of the four basic rates set forth above without express adjustment in the discount rate for the risk of nonpayment. Rather, that risk is taken into account in a subjective way in deciding whether or not to enter the transaction at all, even if the calculation shows the value of the transaction to be attractive.

§2.9 Capital Budgeting by Businesses

Traditional books on finance used in business schools present considerably more sophisticated models for financial decision-making by businesses than those described here. The problem is generally addressed in terms of a business facing alternative investment choices, each of which involves certain *outflows* (or payments) and *inflows* (or receipts). The problem addressed is for the business to select, on a rational basis, which projects it should pursue and which it should not. The size of outflows and inflows may be fixed or they may be uncertain (though some way must be found to quantify the uncertainty).

If outflows and inflows occur over various periods of time, the calculation of capital budgeting can become complex even if the element of uncertainty is absent. However, the underlying theory is directly based on the time value of money described in this chapter. There are two widely accepted methods of capital budgeting.

The *internal rate of return* is defined as a discount rate that equates the present value of the expected cash outflows with the expected cash inflows. Assume, for example, that a business is faced with an immediate cash outlay of $20,000 that is expected to yield inflows of $6,000 per year over each of the next five years thereafter. The internal rate of return is that discount rate that makes the present value of the future inflows equal to the present value of the outflow. In this instance, that rate is approximately 15 percent. If similar calculations are made for each of the alternative projects the business is considering, the business should select those with the highest internal rate of return. The calculation of internal rates of return may involve successive estimations, or *iterations*, of the appropriate rate: They have been simplified by the development of computer programs to solve such problems. Comparison of internal rates of returns of alternative ventures provides a useful means of determining which ventures are most attractive for a business.

The *net present value* technique involves establishing a minimum rate of return on projects that the business has determined is necessary for its financial health. When this discount rate is established, all outflows and inflows are reduced to present values using this discount rate and outflows are subtracted from inflows: The project is attractive if the net present value is positive; if it is zero or negative, the project is unattractive.

These capital budgeting theories, as well as many other present value calculations, often contain a hidden assumption that may affect the accuracy of the calculation. That assumption is that interim payments to be received may be reinvested at the same interest rate as was applicable when the transaction was originally entered into. The following simplified example makes this point: Assume that you are the financial vice president of an insurance company with $100,000 to invest. You know that five years from now you must have on hand $190,000 to pay anticipated life insurance claims. A reliable borrower offers to borrow that $100,000 for five years, with annual interest payments at 14 percent per year. In other words, each year he will pay you the amount of the interest due for that year. If one simply calculates the future value of $100,000 at the end of five years at an interest rate of 14 percent, that value is $192,541. There is, however, a critical assumption hidden in this example: this calculation assumes that your company will be able to invest consistently the $14,000 annual interest payment each year also at the steady rate of 14 percent per year. That assumption, of course, may not be correct; if interest rates decline, you may be able to invest some interest payments at only 8 percent, say, and your company then will not have the $190,000 available as expected. While this problem of reinvesting interim payments may seem to be self-evident after it is pointed out, it is an implicit assumption in many capital budget calculations that is not always fully appreciated.

II

$\diamond$

APPLICATIONS

CHAPTER 3

THE CREATIVE USE OF DEBT: REAL ESTATE

§3.1 Introduction

The purchase and sale of real estate are among the most common and the most important commercial transactions. They typify many other modern commercial transactions since they are complex business transactions that almost always involve money borrowed from third persons or from the seller to finance the purchase price. This is true of both residential and commercial real estate, but this chapter concentrates on financing arrangements that are primarily applicable to commercial transactions.

Chapter 4 deals specifically with many aspects of modern residential real estate conveyances. Many of the financing techniques discussed in this chapter are used for residential real estate, discussed in Chapter 4, as well as commercial, and most of the conveyancing practices described in the following chapter are applicable to commercial real estate as well as residential. These chapters consider real estate from the standpoint of land ownership. They do not discuss the relationship of landlords and tenants or the rights and duties of tenants.

While this chapter deals only with the financing of commercial real estate transactions, many of the matters discussed here are also applicable to commercial transactions involving the purchase and sale of whole businesses, of components or segments of businesses, of individual business assets, of controlling shares of stock in corporations, and of valuable personal property.

§3.2 Commercial Real Estate Investments Yield Cash Flows

Commercial real estate transactions differ in several respects from residential transactions. They tend to be much larger than residential real estate transactions, often involving large tracts of land and construction of large and expensive buildings involving millions of dollars. But by far the most important difference is that commercial real estate generates funds on a recurring basis, usually in the form of rentals paid by commercial or residential tenants, or by the subdivision and sale of parts of the tract, while homeowners receive no such income.

49

It should be pointed out in passing that some commercial real estate investments do not fit into the general description of the previous paragraph. For example, a person speculating in commercial real estate may purchase a tract of land and simply hold it, hoping for appreciation in values in the future; such an investment usually has no positive cash flow until the property is sold. Or a person may buy land and build houses, apartments, or other structures on it, planning to resell the real estate as improved. Houses or apartment complexes built on this basis are usually referred to as *spec* (for "speculative") houses or units. The cash flow in this situation is likely to be sporadic and unpredictable. Or a business may buy or develop a commercial real estate tract to use for its own purposes — say, as its manufacturing plant or to house its own offices — thereby hopefully reducing costs the business would otherwise incur if it rented equivalent space. Such an investment does not create an identifiable cash flow since the benefits generated by a business through the use of its own real estate are usually not segregated on the books of the business as arising specifically from the use of the commercial real estate. Rather, they are viewed as part of the overall profitability of the business.

§3.3　Cash Flows Are Not Identical to Income or Loss

The funds generated by a commercial real estate project are universally referred to as its *cash flow*. The cash flow may be computed on a gross basis without taking into account necessary payments that are required to keep the project current, such as monthly mortgage payments or management costs that are applicable to the project. More commonly, however, the cash flow of a project is computed on a net basis, taking into account the necessary payments that must be made to carry the property. If the project produces more cash than the out-of-pocket disbursements necessary to operate the project, it is said to have a positive cash flow. Projects with positive cash flows are self-supporting and do not need infusions of capital from time to time. If disbursements exceed the receipts, the project has a negative cash flow. A negative cash flow means that the cash being generated by the project is not sufficient to cover its cash needs — and that is usually bad. In some new ventures, however, a negative cash flow may be anticipated in the first few years of operation and provision may be made for the additional capital infusions in the original planning. The situation where a positive cash flow is projected but does not materialize is most serious since the investor then faces the painful and unexpected choice of making an additional unplanned capital investment or permitting the project to go into default.

A simplified cash flow projection for a duplex might look as follows:

Duplex — Purchase 12/31/83

Purchase price: $120,000
Mortgage: $100,000
Closing costs: $4,000

Table 3-1
Cash Flow

	1983	1984	1985	1986
Gross receipts	-0-	$10,260	$10,773	$11,312
Less expenses		2,500	2,625	2,756
Net operating income (NOI)		7,760	8,148	8,555
Less mortgage payments (PI)		11,850	11,850	11,850
Cash flow before tax		(4,090)	(3,702)	(3,294)
Income tax saving (from Table 3-2 below)		8,351	7,595	6,826
Cash flow after tax	$(24,000)	$ 4,261	$ 3,893	$ 3,532

Table 3-2
Calculation of Tax Saving

	1983	1984	1985	1986
Net operating income (NOI)		$ 7,760	$ 8,148	$ 8,555
Mortgage interest		(11,501)	(11,457)	(11,407)
Depreciation		(12,960)	(11,880)	(10,800)
Net gain (loss) (NOI − interest − depreciation)		(16,701)	(15,189)	(13,652)
Tax saving on other income (50% bracket)		$ 8,351	$ 7,595	$ 6,826

Table 3-3
Mortgage Analysis

	1983	1984	1985	1986
Mortgage payments (PI)		$ 11,850	$ 11,850	$ 11,850
Interest		11,501	11,457	11,407
Principal reduction		$ 349	$ 393	$ 443

Table 3-1, "Cash Flow" is the critical one. Table 3-2, "Calculation of Tax Saving," shows how the sixth line of the Table 3-1 — "Income tax saving" — is calculated. Table 3-3 "Mortgage Analysis," reconciles the entries "mortgage payments" in Table 3-1 and "mortgage interest" in table 3-2. "Net operating income" in Table 3-2 is calculated in the third line of Table 3-1. In Tables 3-1 and 3-3, "Mortgage payments (PI)" is the monthly payment on the mortgage: Its composition is discussed in §3.8. The meaning of "PI" is discussed in §4.14. Table 3-3 will be more understandable after you read §3.8 below.

Most investors are accustomed to income or profit-and-loss statements that show the earnings (or lack thereof) of a venture on an annual or monthly basis. Such statements are discussed in some detail in Chapters 7, 8, and 9. The net cash flow statement set forth in Table 3-1 is not an income or profit-and-loss statement in the traditional sense (though the calculation of taxable income in Table 3-2 is a form of income statement): It is a cash-in and cash-out analysis which simply compares the dollars coming in with the dollars going out. It differs from a profit-and-loss statement in several respects:

1. Principal payments on a mortgage (the amount that each monthly payment reduces the balance due on the mortgage) reduce the cash available from the venture and therefore negatively affect the cash flow statement for that period, but do not affect the income statement, since the repayment of a loan, in the eyes of an accountant, is a reduction in a liability but not an expense of doing business. (See Chapter 7.) Thus, the reduction of principal of $349 in 1984, $393 in 1985, and $443 in 1986 all affect the cash flow statement but not the income statement.

2. Some expense items such as depreciation are considered to be expenses for profit-and-loss purposes, but since they do not involve any cash payments by the project, they do not affect the net cash flow statement. Depreciation may be thought of for this purpose as amounts subtracted from income in order to reflect the gradual using up of the building. See §8.6. It may be an expense appropriately taken into account in determining profit and loss, but it does not involve any payment of cash.

The hypothetical duplex above reflects a common pattern of commercial real estate projects. It shows a loss on the income statement but a positive cash flow after taxes. An investor in a project with negative income (loss) can, for tax purposes, utilize the negative income on his or her federal income tax return as a tax deduction to shelter the taxable income from other real estate projects from tax. Before 1987, such negative income could be used to shelter income of all types from tax. This led to numerous real estate investments (like the duplex in the hypothetical) by high-income individuals in order to get tax deductions without additional investment, a practice that was sharply limited by the 1986 tax amendments (See Chapter 12). The cash flow table (Table 3-1) ends with 1986 because these 1986 Tax Act limitations began to go into effect in 1987.

In the hypothetical, the duplex is an attractive investment only because the income tax savings significantly exceed the negative cash flow from the duplex itself. It assumes that the owner is consistently in the 50 percent tax bracket each year from 1984 through 1986, a high-income taxpayer indeed. Of course, the investor has invested $24,000 in the duplex in 1983 and the total after-tax cash flows from 1984 through 1986 do not equal that amount. However, the investor owns the duplex (subject to the mortgage) and should recoup all or most of this investment when the property is sold.

To repeat, "cash flow" and "income" are not synonymous. Income assumes there is some matching of income and expense in an accounting sense, while cash flow is a pure checkbook concept. Any kind of cash receipt increases cash flow and any kind of cash payment decreases it.

§3.4 The Purchase of Commercial Real Estate

The goal of a person purchasing commercial real estate differs from that of a person considering the purchase of residential real estate. The goal in purchasing residential real estate is largely personal satisfaction, finding a good place to live given the constraints of the person's financial resources. In contrast, the goal of a person purchasing commercial real estate is usually purely economic, based on the hoped-for financial return in light of the required investment, and is usually (though not always) unrelated to personal considerations of taste or aesthetics.

The ability of commercial real estate to generate gross cash flows usually makes a "bootstrap" acquisition possible: By borrowing most of the cost of the land and improvements, the developer of the property may use the later cash flows to repay the loans and thereby pay for the land and improvements with no further personal investment. When acquiring commercial real estate it is customary to persuade a lender to lend money to finance the project primarily by developing estimates of the later cash flow that show that it will be sufficient to repay the loan. These estimates may be in the form of computer-generated *spread sheets* or documents with titles such as "projected cash flow" or "pro forma cash projections." The hypothetical cash flow projection set forth in the previous section might well have served to convince a lender.

Because commercial real estate loans are typically made or refused primarily on the basis of projected cash flows, analysis of these projections is usually vital to the success of a contemplated project. The question asked by a commercial real estate developer is not primarily "Is this a good project?" but rather "Can I persuade a lender that this is such a good project that they should make a large loan on it?" To a very substantial extent, decisions whether or not projects will go forward are made by the sources of possible financing, not by the developer itself. For this reason, the developer of commercial real estate often seeks to obtain letters of intent from potential tenants — particularly the major tenants (*anchor tenants*) — in order to improve the reliability of the cash flow projections in the eyes of possible lenders. Such letters are usually not binding in a legal sense, but are indications of interest in the project.

There is no traditional minimum cash down payment required for a commercial real estate project. If the cash flows are high enough, a developer may be able to persuade one or more lenders to lend one hundred percent, or even more, of the acquisition and development cost of the project. Generally it is in the interest of the developer to obtain the largest loan possible since that makes the project self-sufficent and reduces the amount of personal capital the developer initially has to invest in the project. After all, the duplex purchaser in the previous section had to come up with $24,000 in cash; he doubtless would have preferred to invest a smaller amount. The way to do that is to get a larger mortgage. If a loan for 80 percent of the purchase price is desirable, then a 90 percent loan is usually preferable, and a 100 percent loan may be ideal from the standpoint of the investor. In the 100 percent mortgage case, the developer of course owns a project with essentially a zero capital investment. However, even where a capital investment is required of the developer, if the cash flows develop as planned or, even better, if they exceed the original estimates, the developer may be able to recoup his or her original investment in a relatively brief period of time. He or she will then own a project (subject of course to the lender's interest) that may be worth millions of dollars with a zero capital investment. It is like magic — making money for oneself using other people's money. Many real estate fortunes have been made on the basis of the simple principle of borrowing as much as possible and then making the project a success.

Most lenders are concerned that the developer does not get a totally free ride and they therefore do not usually give 100 percent mortgages. The total cost of constructing the project is therefore usually a cap on the maximum amount of loans that may be obtained. On the other hand, projected cash flows from a commercial project are often sufficient to justify more than a single mortgage on the project. Junior mortgages from different sources, often called second or third mortgages depending on their priority, may permit a developer to approach or exceed 100 percent financing in specific situations even if the senior lender refuses to fund more than 70 or 80 percent of the anticipated cost of the project. Because the junior mortgages in this type of situation are risky, a junior lender may insist on receiving a percentage of the ownership as a condition to making his or her loan.

The only safe generalizations are that down payments on commercial real estate purchases usually comprise a lower percentage than that required on residential real estate purchases, and that the amount of capital that a developer must invest in a commercial project is inversely dependent on the attractiveness of the cash-flow projections.

The possibility that the cash generated by a project may not cover the costs of the loans, leading to default, and the possible personal liability of the developer on these various mortgages, is discussed in §3.7 below.

§3.5 Permanent and Interim Loans for Real Estate Development

In many situations, a person plans to use the proceeds of a loan to construct improvements on the raw land that he or she already owns. In other instances, a single loan may cover both the acquisition of the raw land and the construction of the improvements, in which case the lender will usually advance the land acquisition cost separately from the funds needed to construct the improvements.

Where loan proceeds are to finance construction it is quite common for two different lenders, providing basically different services, to participate in the transaction. These two lenders are usually called the *interim* or *construction lender* and the *permanent lender*, respectively. They are usually different institutions performing quite different functions.

The interim lender advances funds as construction proceeds to enable the contractor to complete the construction; in advancing these funds, the interim lender relies on architects' or engineers' certificates as required by the interim loan agreement to ensure that work to date has been performed properly and that a designated stage or percentage of completion has been attained. The loan made by the interim lender is often referred to as the *construction loan*, and payments by that lender are often called *progress payments*. When the project is completed, the construction loan is usually paid off in full with the proceeds of the permanent loan. The interim lender therefore usually makes no investigation of the economics of the completed project; rather it relies on the unconditional commitment of the permanent lender to make the permanent loan upon completion of the project. If there is no commitment from an acceptable permanent lender, there is usually no construction loan available.

It is of course theoretically possible that a contractor could build improvements with his or her own resources, or borrow on his or her own personal credit without involving the owner. As a practical matter, these possibilities almost never occur. There are virtually no contractors in business that have the financial resources to construct a major commercial building without using borrowed funds, even if they were willing to use their funds in this fashion. Also, lenders view loans secured by liens on improved real estate as more secure than signature loans and therefore real estate loans are available at more favorable interest terms. The result is that virtually all construction lending is secured by liens on the property.

The permanent lender in effect agrees to make the long-term loan on the property when the project is completed. In other words, the permanent lender examines the cash flow projections submitted with the loan application, and determines the viability of the project. It performs the functions of the lender described in the preceding sections in assessing the long-term economics of the project and the financial strength of the borrower. In the balance of this chapter, "lender" refers to the permanent lender and not the interim lender.

In some instances, the same lending institution may serve as both the interim and the permanent lender; typically, however, such a lending institution has two staffs, one skilled in the responsibilities of an interim lender and the other skilled in the responsibilities of a permanent lender.

§3.6 Real Estate Loans Are Secured by Liens

A loan made to enable the borrower to purchase or develop real estate is represented by a promissory note that is usually on a standard printed form. The obligation to pay is routinely secured by a lien on the real estate that is the subject of the transaction itself. The lien is actually created in a separate document, either a mortgage or deed of trust which is also executed at the closing. The terms of these documents are so standardized that printed forms are usually used with a few blanks filled in. (Typed-in clauses referring to special terms such as prepayment privileges are also sometimes added.) These standardized forms are typically prepared by the lender, who usually resists making changes in them. A *deed of trust* differs from a *mortgage* in only minor respects: The type of instrument used in a particular state or community depends more on tradition or convention than on the differences between the two forms of instruments. Hereafter, the word *mortgage* will be used to refer to both types of instruments.

The lien created by a mortgage covers the entire property that is the subject of the transaction. It covers the improvements as they are constructed as well as the land itself. Liens have both a geographic and a temporal aspect. If the transaction involves a commercial development that includes the installation of streets and utilities followed by a sale of lots, it is necessary to arrange, in the mortgage, a procedure by which the developer is able to obtain the release of individual lots from this lien when they are sold. Otherwise, the purchasers of the lots purchase subject to the lien of the mortgage covering the whole project and will be unable to arrange first lien financing to construct improvements on the lot. Similarly, temporal rights, such as the rights of a lessee under a ten-year lease, are subject to the lien of the mortgagee, though usually in the event of a default it does not want to try to dispossess tenants. In some cities rent control laws may limit the power of owners to dispossess tenants even when they wish to do so.

§3.7 Is Anybody Liable on the Real Estate Loan?

The promissory note secured by a real estate mortgage is, of course, a promise by the person signing it to pay the amount set forth. In most commercial real estate transactions (and practically all residential real estate transactions), the developers or owners are required to sign the note individually so that they have personal liability (as well as the threatened loss of the property) if a default occurs. In commercial real estate, however, it is not unknown for the lender to agree to look solely to the property as the source of payment and not require the developer to assume personal liability. This may be done by having some third person (a *straw party*) or a corporation without substantial assets sign the note. The same result may be reached by a provision in the note limiting the power of the holder to recover from the maker in the event of default. This is often referred to as a *non recourse loan*. In the case of such a loan, the developer then is faced with the loss of the property, including whatever equity he or she has in the property, if there is a default, but is not personally liable for the debt.

Even where the developer is personally liable on the note, individual investors may not be. It is quite common for developers to sell participations in a project through the medium of a corporation or a limited partnership in which the individual investors risk their original investments but have no personal liability in excess of that amount.

Finally, individual liability on real estate notes may be discharged through the bankruptcy process if the individual is insolvent. (See Chapter 10.)

§3.8 The Economics of the Traditional Real Estate Mortgage

This section begins with the classic level-payment real estate loan, widely used for both commercial and residential real estate financing. It then considers the numerous variations that have arisen since 1970.

A traditional real estate mortgage is for a long term — 25 or 30 years —

at a fixed interest rate established at or close to the market rate of interest at the time when the loan is made. Monthly payments are required, and interest is computed on the unpaid balance each month. The loan is amortized over the period of the loan by these monthly payments, which are fixed in advance and remain constant throughout the life of the mortgage. The words *amortize* and *amortization* are fancy terms that simply mean the loan is set up so that a portion of each monthly payment is applied to principal as well as interest: In the classic mortgage of this type the monthly payment is computed so that the final level payment — the 360th in a thirty-year mortgage — reduces the loan balance to zero. The mortgage used in the hypothetical in §3.2 is a traditional mortgage of this type.

The first payment on a traditional mortgage represents virtually all interest with a few dollars being applied to principal; the second payment consists of a tiny bit less interest (since the first payment reduced the principal slightly) and therefore a tiny bit more is available to be applied to reduce principal. This process continues over the life of the mortgage, with each payment representing a somewhat larger amount of principal and smaller amount of interest than the previous one.

To illustrate: on a $75,000 9 percent loan for 30 years, the level monthly payment is $603.47 over the 30 years. The first payment reduces principal by $40.97 (the remaining $562.50 is interest); the second payment reduces principal by $41.27 (the remaining $562.19 is interest); and so on. The 12th payment reduces principal by $44.48; after this payment the principal has been reduced to $74,487.60. The payment made on the fifth anniversary of the mortgage (the 60th payment), reduces principal by $63.66 and the mortgage then has been reduced to $71,910.10. Obviously, only a small amount of the unpaid balance is amortized in the early years of the mortgage. After 10 years, the principal has been reduced to $67,072.31; after 15 years, it has been reduced to $59,497.86; after 20 years to $47,638.70; after 25 years to $29,071.04. During the last five years, most of each payment is principal and upon making the 360th payment, the principal is reduced to zero.

It may seem difficult to set up the amount of the monthly payment so that everything comes out exactly even 25 or 30 years later. But these things need be worked out only once mathematically for each plausible interest rate (e.g., by ¼ percentage points) and for each plausible time period — e.g., 10 years, 15 years, etc., up to 30 years) in order to create a set of tables providing the monthly payment per $1.00 of loan for specified interest rates over specified periods. The monthly payment required for a specific transaction can then be computed simply by multiplying the figure shown in the table by the size of the contemplated mortgage. Other tables permit a person to determine precisely what part of each payment on any loan represents principal and what part represents interest.

The fixed-interest, level-payment loan described here is so common and so widely used that it is sometimes referred to as a *conventional loan*. (The term *conventional* is also sometimes used in a different context to describe residential real estate loans made by a savings and loan association or other lender in contrast to loans guaranteed under federal programs such as FHA or VA.) Until the late 1970s the level-payment loan was the only mortgage arrangement available for residential real estate and was used almost universally in commercial real estate as well. With the very high interest rates that occurred in the late 1970s, a number of alternative mortgages were created that depart from the level-payment structure. Some of these alternative mortgages are widely used today in connection with commercial real estate mortgages.

The basic premises underlying the level-payment mortgage appear to be (1) that the person making payments on the mortgage has a level income over the term of the mortgage, (2) that interest rates are going to remain relatively stable over the term of the mortgage, and (3) that there is no inflation in the system. These premises obviously have not been true in the recent past, and seem particularly inappropriate for commercial real estate with its open-ended potential for producing cash flow. Indeed a very common cash flow pattern in commercial real estate is relatively small gross receipts in early years followed by gradual improvement as the project becomes established and successful. It would seem sensible to structure mortgage payments for commercial loans not on a fixed level over the term of the mortgage, but on a basis that increases over time. Once lenders escaped from the traditional thinking underlying the level-payment mortgage, several variations were commonly offered:

1. The simplest pattern involves *interest-only payments* for a period of several years followed by an increase in the payments to permit amortization of the principal over the balance of the mortgage when the interest-only period ends. This results in an abrupt increase in the size of the payments when amortization of the principal begins.

2. There is no inherent reason why the initial payments should fully cover the interest costs of the initial years so long as the payments are thereafter increased sufficiently to pay off the whole mortgage when it is due. So-called *negative amortization* loans provide initial payments below the interest-only level with the unpaid interest added to principal so that the outstanding balance of the mortgage increases in the early years of the mortgage. Later payments obviously must increase in amount to cover both the negative amortization in the early years and the regular amortization of the principal in the remaining years. Payments often increase gradually, so as to ease the impact on cash flow in later years.

3. There is no inherent reason why the interest rate on a mortgage should be fixed for the life of the mortgage. The *adjustable rate mortgage (ARM)* provides for adjustments to the effective interest rate on the mortgage yearly or semiannually based on changes in some widely publicized market interest rate. Usually, these adjustments are reflected by changes in the amount of the monthly payment on an annual or semiannual basis.

4. Another real estate financing technique involves *balloon notes*. A balloon note is basically a very simple idea: It is a note that requires periodic payments but the unpaid balance comes due long before the payments amortize the borrowed amount. In the real estate context, a balloon note might come due in 5 or 10 years but the periodic monthly payments are computed based on a 25- or 30-year amortization schedule. Such a note might be described as a five-year balloon with payments based on a 25-year 10 percent amortization schedule. This means that monthly payments are computed on the 25-year 10 percent table, but the loan itself comes due in 5 years. When it comes due, there is, of

course, a huge final payment due — the balloon — since the monthly payments have mostly gone to the payment of interest and the principal has been reduced only slightly. Because most borrowers do not have the funds to pay the balloon in cash when it comes due, the property is often resold or refinanced. Refinancing may involve a second balloon note, which in turn may lead to a third. If interest rates have risen or fallen when the balloon comes due, the new mortgage covering the balloon is written at the then-current market rate. A balloon note, in other words, is not unlike the ARM discussed above in ultimate economic effect. Most balloon notes are probably carried by sellers of property, though a number of financial institutions also accept short-term balloon notes. Many balloon notes appear as part of second mortgages in creative financing transactions discussed below.

5. There also exist a wide variety of short-term mortgages that are known as *bridge loans*, *mezzanine financing*, or simply *short-term interim financing*. Such loans usually provide for interest-only payments with no reduction of principal for periods as short as one year, but often running three to five years. Like the balloon note, such loans usually result in refinancing of the project when the note comes due, since rarely is the cash flow sufficient in the early years of the project to retire the bridge loan when it comes due. Sometimes these short-term loans may be unsecured.

In the modern world of commercial real estate financing, these various types of mortgage terms may be combined in a variety of ingenious ways.

§3.9 Junior Mortgages

Many commercial real estate transactions involve second, third, and sometimes even more junior mortgages. The rights of junior mortgages in case of default are described in §3.12. This section describes why purchasing commercial real estate often involves such financing.

Many financial lenders are constrained by statute, regulation, or internal policy to make only first lien mortgages that cover a designated fraction or less of the value of the project. The difference between the amount of the mortgage and the estimated cost of the project has to come either from the developer as a large capital investment or from other lending sources. These first mortgage lenders are commercial banks, savings and loan associations, and other lenders subject to some degree of state or federal regulation. The usual pattern of commercial real estate financing is to obtain a first mortgage from one of these lenders. This mortgage may be a traditional fixed-interest rate, level-payment mortgage, or it may be an ARM or some other type of innovative financing. Nevertheless it is for a long term and provides only a fraction of the needed financing.

Junior mortgages usually provide most of the remaining financing needed to develop the project. The junior mortgages carry significantly greater risk of nonpayment if the project does not work out as well as the developer projects: As a result they usually carry higher interest rates. In addition, the most risky of them may carry an *equity kicker*, the right of the holder to purchase a portion of the developer's interest in the project at a bargain price.

An example may be helpful. Assume that Jones, a real estate speculator and developer, owns a piece of property that is suitable for apartment development: She bought the land two years ago for $15,000 cash and now has an independent appraisal that the current value of the land is $26,000. She plans to build a 45-unit apartment on the land that she estimates will cost $950,000 after making due allowance for all contingencies. She does not wish to invest (a short-hand phrase usually meaning "she does not now have and cannot easily raise") additional capital over and above the value of the land. After a fair amount of effort and discussion with possible lenders, Jones works out the following financing arrangements:

1) A 75 percent (of $950,000) first mortgage from a savings and loan association for 30 years at 10 percent. This first mortgage provides $712,500 of the cost.

2) A $150,000 second mortgage, from a commercial lending company engaged in speculative but not unduly risky investments, for 10 years at 14 percent, adjustable after 3 years on the basis of an index based on the average discount rate on 26-week Treasury Bills as announced by the U.S. Treasury Department following sale of these securities. (Treasury bills and discount rates are discussed in §18.18 below; simply assume for present purposes that this average rate is a reliable indication of market interest rates for commercial first mortgage loans.)

These two mortgages leave Jones $87,500 short of the $950,000 she needs (950,000 - 712,500 - 150,000 = 87,500), well within striking distance. She obtains a *bridge loan* for this amount from a privately owned investment firm that specializes in high-risk loans. The bridge loan carries an interest rate of 16 percent, with monthly payments of interest only for three years. At the end of three years the $87,500 of principal is due. In addition Jones is required to give the investment firm the option to purchase a 25 percent interest in the project for $87,500 at that time. If the project is successful, the holder of the third mortgage will probably exercise its option, which will precisely cancel the principal payment due on the third mortgage. The holder thereafter will not get interest but will have a substantial equity participation in the project. If the project is not sufficiently successful, the holder of the third mortgage will not exercise its option and Jones will (1) have to come up with $87,500 cash, (2) negotiate with the holder of the third mortgage for an extension of that mortgage, or (3) suffer a default and likely foreclosure on that mortgage. If the option is not exercised, the renegotiation alternative is probably the most likely.

On the basis of the foregoing, Jones has invested $26,000 in the form of the value of the land and has borrowed $950,000 to finance the improvements. Her equity investment is therefore about 3 percent, a not unusual figure for commercial projects in real life.

Calculations will reveal that for the first three years after the completion of the project the required monthly cash flow to service the indebtedness is $9,749.37: $6,252.70 on the first mortgage, $2,329 on the second, and $1,166.67 on the third. This is only $216.65 per apartment. Of course, there are other items of disbursement in addition to debt service, and it is possible that if the discount rate on treasury bills rises, the second mortgage payments may increase. If the project appears to be successful and the holder of the third mortgage exercises its option to purchase 25 percent of the project, the payments will drop to $8,581.70 per month after three years, or about $190.70 per apartment. To continue with the mathematics of this example, at the end of three years the first two mortgages will have been paid down to $699,330.48 and $124,279.50 respectively or a total of $823,610. The decision by the holder of the third mortgage whether to exercise its option must be based on his or her estimate of the difference between the value of the project and this indebtedness.

§3.10 Economic Equivalents to Mortgages

A complicating factor in modern real estate financing is that there are many different interests in land that are not formally designated as mortgages but have the same economic effect as mortgages. Most of these transactions involve sales of the real estate coupled with simultaneous long-term leasebacks. "Long-term" in this context usually means a period that exceeds the expected economic life of improvements constructed on the land, 99 years being a popular period for some obscure reason. For example, a person planning to develop a tract of land may sell the land to an investor for a lump sum and take back a long-term ground lease for 99 years. The lump sum received by the developer is similar to mortgage proceeds and the obligation to pay rent for 99 years on the ground lease is analogous to monthly payments on a mortgage. In the event of non-payment, cancellation of the lease is analogous to foreclosure of a mortgage. From the standpoint of the investor, shares in the ownership of the land subject to the ground lease may then be sold to investors who participate in the yield from cash flow as well as possible appreciation in the value of the land. Further, the developer may thereafter place one or more conventional mortgages on the lessee's interest in the ground lease; these mortgages in effect are second or third mortgages (because the lease payments on the ground lease are superior to the rights of the nominal first mortgage on the lessee's interest in the leasehold).

If the property has existing improvements, one may be able to sell the land but not the improvements to one investor and the improvements but not the land to a second investor, in both cases taking back long-term leases. As long as the improvements lease exceeds the expected economic life of the improvements, one or more conventional mortgages may then be placed on the lease-holds. Transactions in which land interests are in effect carved up among several layers or tiers of sales and leasebacks and then mixed with traditional mortgages on the developer's interests may be exceptionally complex, ingenious, and difficult to analyze. Indeed, it may sometimes be difficult to establish the precise priorities of lenders in the various tiers.

In the following discussion, the possibility that one or more layers of financing may be represented by sale and leaseback interests is ignored; the assumption is that only traditional mortgages are involved in order to simplify the analysis.

§3.11 "Creative Financing" of Commercial Real Estate

The term "creative" in the title of this section (and in similar contexts) usually implies a higher degree of speculation and risk than "standard" financing. Thus, the term "creative" is not necessarily a term of praise but rather often implies skirting close to a line of impropriety or unacceptability. On the other hand, creative financing often illustrates the genius of persons in manipulating ideas and practices in order to achieve a specific goal.

Much of the creative financing currently used in commercial real estate financing today involves in one form or another a *participation loan* (or an *equity participation loan*, as it is sometimes called). In such a loan, the basic trade-off is that the lender receives some percentage of the developer's equity in the project in exchange for a reduction in the terms of the pay-back of the mortgage. In a sense, the third mortgagee in Jones's apartment house described above was engaged in creative financing, since, in the absence of the option to repurchase, it is likely that it would have insisted on a considerably higher interest rate to reflect the risk of the third mortgage.

Some modern creative financings take the form of joint ventures or limited partnerships. Others involve straightforward loan/equity transactions. For example, a lender may give a developer a 9 percent mortgage when the normal market rate is 12 or 13 percent if the developer grants it a 20 to 40 percent ownership interest in the property. If the project works out profitably, the lender will get a lower interest rate but should more than make it up by receiving its share of the rental income, and ultimately on the sale or refinancing of the project, a sizable profit as well. If the project starts out more slowly then expected, the lower interest rate may make it possible for the developer ultimately to succeed in the project; if the development had been financed through a straight loan transaction, the higher interest payments from the start could have sunk the project. Somewhat similar variations are deals in which the lender receives some fraction of the cash flow above a specified figure and so-called *shared appreciation mortgages*, in which the lender does not participate in cash flow but does share in the increase in value upon the sale or refinancing of the project.

The sale-and-leaseback described in the previous section is itself a kind of creative financing.

§3.12 What Happens if There Is Default?

Everyone intuitively knows that a second or third mortgage is more risky than a first mortgage. Why should this be? What happens to junior mortgages (i.e., second or third mortgages) when there is a default on a first mortgage? Answers to these questions can be best developed by considering what might happen if the apartment hypothetical described in §3.9 does not work out as projected.

What happens if Jones defaults on one or more of these mortgages? In the first place, it is important to recognize that not all defaults lead immediately to foreclosure on the property and suits brought to recover missed payments. Loan instruments often provide for grace periods in which missed payments may be made up, often upon the payment of an additional charge. In addition, legal action is expensive, and taken only as a matter of last resort. It is not uncommon for lenders to threaten foreclosure, and even post property for sale under the procedures set forth in the mortgage without completing the threatened action. Alternatively, a foreclosure may well lead to the lender purchasing the property at the foreclosure sale. What does it do with it then? If the developer could not make a go of it, will the lender be able to do any better? Probably not, and it may very well do even worse. Also many lenders have to worry about their own bottom line. If a lender forecloses on property that cannot be resold at a high enough price to cover the unpaid portion of the loan, it must recognize the difference as a loss. A troubled lender may therefore prefer to retain *problem loans* or *noncurrent loans* in its portfolio rather than closing them out by foreclosure. Indeed, many lenders have *work out* groups that may temporarily take over a project and try to work out the loan by rigid control over disbursements to persons other than the lender. See §10.5. For these various reasons, defaults often lead to negotiation between the lenders and the developer in an effort to work out on a mutually acceptable basis a revised schedule of payments that is realistic under the circumstances. The final steps of foreclosure described below usually occur only after all these preliminary solutions have been tried out and prove unworkable.

Secondly, in considering what happens upon a default, one must separately examine what happens to the collateral (the apartment house) and what happens to Jones personally. So far as Jones herself is concerned, it is possible that she may not be personally liable on the mortgages (see §3.7); if she is not, she can walk away from the project, sacrificing only her initial investment. In the case of the apartment building, if Jones is not personally liable on the mortgages, she can abandon the project if she is willing to give up the value of the land she originally contributed to the project. If, as is more commonly the case, Jones is personally liable on the mortgages, she cannot extricate herself so easily, but all is not necessarily lost. For one thing, Jones may be insolvent or judgment proof. Often, if one project owned by a developer goes bad, other projects have or will also: Liabilities therefore may greatly exceed assets. In addition, if Jones is pursued vigorously in an effort to collect from her personal assets, she may always take refuge in the federal bankruptcy courts. Further, as a practical matter, Jones is liable only for any deficiency between the realized value of the collateral (the apartment building project) and the amount of the indebtedness. Foreclosure may take several months; suit must then be brought on the "deficiency" (the amount by which the proceeds of the sale net after expenses are less than the unpaid balance on the mortgage), and only then must the developer be concerned about his or her liability on the notes.

What happens to the property is quite different. An uncorrected default on monthly payments permits the lender on that loan to declare the entire unpaid balance due and seek to recover it from the property or from Jones individually. Further, a default on a senior mortgage also is a violation of covenants in junior mortgages, so that a default on the first mortgage usually triggers defaults on all three mortgages. On the other hand, a default on a junior mortgage usually does not affect senior mortgages.

A default on a mortgage leads to a foreclosure and ultimately the public sale of the property, that is, by auction after public announcement. The procedures to be followed are set forth in the mortgage itself; usually no judicial order is required before the sale may be made by the trustee or by the sheriff. The proceeds of the sale, after deduction of expenses, are applied to the mortgages in default. Two critical rules about the effect of a foreclosure of one mortgage on other mortgages are: (1) a foreclosure of a junior mortgage does not affect a senior mortgage and the purchaser at the foreclosure sale takes the property subject to the senior mortgage, and (2) the sale of the property following foreclosure of a senior mortgage automatically wipes out the liens of all junior mortgages. Thus, if Jones defaults only on the third mortgage, the rights of the first two mortgagees are unaffected, and the purchaser at the foreclosure sale takes the property subject to the prior rights of the holders of the first and second mortgages. If that purchaser fails to make the payments necessary to keep those mortgages current, another foreclosure may occur. However, if Jones defaults on the first mortgage, all junior mortgagees are in imminent danger of losing their interest in the apartment building.

Let us assume that the apartment project fails to meet the cash-flow projections, and that after one year Jones does not have the necessary cash to make all three payments. Knowing that she is going into default, she does not make any further payments on any of the mortgages. At this time, the unpaid principal balances on the three mortgages are approximately as follows:

First mortgage	$708,500
Second mortgage	$142,500
Third mortgage	$ 87,500
Total loans	$938,500

Let us assume further that the holder of the first mortgage declares a default and the property is put up for sale at foreclosure. What happens at the sale depends on what the net value of the property after deduction of foreclosure expenses is; while this value is almost always uncertain and subjective, assume for purposes of discussion that its value is known precisely. At the public foreclosure sale, each of the creditors and Jones herself may bid on the property. In addition, opportunistic third persons hoping to find a bargain may also enter bids. If we assume first that the value of the property is $950,000 (exceeding the sum total of the three mortgages of $938,500), the foreclosure of the first mortgage should lead to some spirited bidding at the sale. The holder of the first mortgage, knowing that the value of the property exceeds its interest in the property, bids the amount of the unpaid balance of the first mortgage: $708,500. If it gets the property at this price, fine, but it is not benefitted if the price goes higher: If it bids any higher than the amount of its debt, the surplus goes not to it but to holders of the inferior mortgages or to Jones. The holder of the second mortgage bids up to $851,000 in order to protect its interest in the property and then stop: If it acquires the property it will have to pay the first mortgagee $708,500 to pay off the first mortgage, and therefore it should bid another $142,500 to cover its own debt. If it bids any more, the surplus goes not to it but to the holder of the third mortgage or to Jones. The holder of the third mortgage has a similar motivation to bid up to $938,500 but no more: $708,500 to pay off the first mortgage, $142,500 to pay off the second, and up to $87,500 to protect its own interest. If it bids any more, the surplus simply goes to Jones.

Since Jones has a positive equity in the property of $11,500 (the hypothetical value of the property, $950,000 minus the unpaid balances on the mortgages, $938,500), she should, theoretically, bid on the property to preserve her equity (i.e., the difference between the mortgages and the market value of the project). Of course, if Jones could not meet the monthly payments, she probably also will not be able to raise $938,500 to pay off the loans in cash at the foreclosure sale. As a result, whatever equity she has in the project is, as a practical matter, probably gone. An opportunistic third person should theoretically bid $938,501: He or she will then outbid the holder of the third mortgage and get Jones' $11,500 equity for $1. It would be an unusual opportunistic third person, however, who could come up with $938,501 in cash, or who would be willing to invest $938,500 in a problematic venture in order to secure the equity ownership of an interest worth $11,500. Where the owner's equity is larger, however, it is quite possible that an opportunistic third person or the defaulting owner may be able to raise the necessary funds through a short-term loan that may thereafter be paid off when the foreclosure purchaser refinances or resells the property. One thing is clear: If the owner has a substantial equity in the foreclosed property, he or she must scramble: If he or she does not, someone else will obtain a bargain at his or her expense — either one of the lending institutions or an opportunistic third person, since each will naturally bid the smallest amount necessary to purchase the property.

If the hypothesized market value is only $650,000, no one other than the holder of the first mortgage will bid, since the value of the property is less than the first lien balance of $708,500. The security for the second and third mortgages as well as Jones' equity is simply gone upon the foreclosure sale. If the hypothesized market value is $750,000, the holder of the second mortgage should end up purchasing the project.

Of course, these examples are somewhat unrealistic because it is usually impossible to estimate the fair market value of a defaulted project with any degree of exactness. It is therefore not uncommon for mistakes to be made, for junior lienholders to bid to obtain the property because they are uncertain whether the value of the property exceeds the senior liens. Some things can be said with confidence, however. While it is theoretically possible to obtain real bargains on foreclosure in the absence of perfect knowledge, in the real world, in the normal foreclosure the secured debts significantly exceed the market value. Furthermore, there is no positive equity, and the only bidders are the representatives of the lenders.

Assuming that the property is worth $650,000 and the balance on the first lien is $708,500, how much should the first lien holder bid? The fair market value of the property, the amount of the loan, or something in between? If the lender hopes to collect the deficiency from the developer, the lender probably should bid low in order to preserve its rights against the developer. Where the developer is not personally liable on the mortgage, or is insolvent, the lender is likely to bid the full amount of the mortgage. As long as the bid is less than $708,500, in one sense it does not matter if the bid is above market value because the holder of the first lien is in effect paying itself back out of the purchase price. However, estimates of fair market value are always uncertain, and the lender may wish to defer recognition of any loss on its own financial statements until the property is finally disposed of. The most likely scenario therefore is that the lender bids precisely $708,500 even though it believes the property is worth less.

Once the holder of the first lien acquires the property, what happens to it? The new owner is unlikely to dispose of it at a fire sale price; after all it has $708,500 invested in it and does not want to take a loss. It may manage the apartment complex on its own or it may try to find someone willing to buy it at $708,500. This may be practical because the new owner was also the original lender and may grant the new purchaser favorable financing terms (e.g., no money down and interest partially deferred for a year or so). Selling the property at $708,500 to a new developer on such terms and taking back 100 percent of the purchase price in the form of a new mortgage does not involve the investment of new money (i.e., money in addition to the $708,500 already invested in Jones' defaulted mortgage). If things do not work out, the original holder of the lien may have to foreclose again, but it is not significantly worse off than if it owns the defaulted project. And in the meantime it does not have the headache of managing an apartment complex.

§3.13 The Use of Debt Creates Leverage

As indicated in an earlier section, developers of commercial real estate usually want to finance the real estate with the largest possible loan. See §3.4. The reason that the largest possible loan is usually the most desirable revolves around the concept of *leverage*, a basic characteristic of the use of debt in all commercial enterprises. Jones's apartment building described in the preceding sections provides a clear illustration of the concept of leverage.

The total cost of the apartment house, including the land contributed by Jones, is $976,000. Under Jones's cash flow projections, the apartments should rent for $400 each, and 100 percent occupancy can be expected. (While as a practical matter it is likely that brief vacancies may occur from time to time during changeovers of tenants a 100 percent occupancy rate simplifies and does not materially affect the calculations.) Since there are 45 units, the monthly gross cash flow is $18,000 and the annual cash flow is $216,000, from which operating expenses, real estate taxes, insurance, upkeep, and similar items, must be deducted. Let us assume that Jones' projections estimate that these negative cash flow items (exclusive of mortgage loan payments) will be approximately $27,000 per year. Of course, as with all cash flow projections by developers, these are on the optimistic side and should be discounted to some extent. However, accepting their accuracy for purposes of discussion, one can investigate the cash-flow return Jones will receive on the basis of various assumptions about financing:

1. If Jones builds the project entirely with her own cash and obtains no loans at all, she will have invested a total of $976,000, from which there will be a positive annual cash flow of $189,000 per year ($216,000 gross cash flow minus $27,000 of expenses, real estate taxes, insurance, etc.). On the $976,000 that she invested, Jones will receive a return of about 19 percent on a cash-flow basis without any allowance for federal income taxes.

2. If Jones builds the project with only the first mortgage as financing (face amount of $712,500 and monthly payments of $6,252.70) she will have invested a total of $263,500 and the expected cash flow will be reduced to $113,967.60 for a yield on each dollar invested by Jones of about 43 percent on a cash flow basis. (The $263,500 figure is obtained by subtracting from $976,000 the amount of the first mortgage ($712,500); the $113,967.60 cash flow is obtained by taking the $189,000 cash flow from an all-cash investment and subtracting the annual payments on the first mortgage; again no account is taken of income taxes.)

3. If Jones builds the project with both the first and second ($150,000 face amount and monthly payments of $2,329) mortgages as financing, her cash investment will be reduced to $113,500 ($263,000 minus $150,000) and her annual cash flow will be reduced to $86,019 ($113,967.60 minus $27,948 (12 x $2,329)). Even so, this increases the yield on each dollar invested by Jones to 76 cents on a cash-flow basis.

4. If Jones builds the project with all three mortgages, as she originally contemplated, her cash investment is reduced to $26,000 (the fair market value of the land), and the cash flow will be reduced to $72,019. This is a 277 percent return on each dollar invested; while Jones has a large payment coming due on the third mortgage in a couple of years, the cash flow being generated in this hypothetical should be ample to cover it.

Leverage reflects the fact that the more Jones borrows, the higher the percentage cash-flow return is on each dollar that she has invested. In the foregoing example, every dollar invested in the project yields a cash flow of about $0.19 each year. When Jones borrows on the first mortgage, she is borrowing a dollar at an interest cost of $0.10 per year and receiving $0.19 on that dollar. The additional $0.09 is additional return on the dollars that Jones actually invests. Hence her return on each dollar she invests is improved by each additional dollar she borrows. No wonder borrowing is attractive under such circumstances. Indeed, if Jones can obtain loans for 100 percent of her cost at an interest rate of less than 19 percent per year, she should do so; she then has a zero investment in the project and an infinite return on that investment. The secret of leverage is that if a borrowed dollar yields a greater cash flow than the cost of borrowing it, you should borrow it. The excess is then allocable to the dollars you do invest, increasing the return, often dramatically. Leverage, in short, involves the productive use of other people's money.

§3.14 The Danger of Debt

Leverage is a two-edged sword. By increasing the number of dollars "working" for the developer, the rate of return on the dollars he or she actually invests may be greatly increased. So long as the per dollar return from the venture exceeds the interest cost, it appears to be sensible to borrow. On the other hand, these assertions take no account of the possibility that the developer may miscalculate and the per dollar return may be *less* than the interest cost. If this occurs, the leveraged transaction may be a disaster for the investor because the fixed interest costs must still be met in any event. Indeed, most of the spectacular collapses of real estate ventures have been the result of excessive leverage and a miscalculation by the developer of the return from a venture.

In the hypothetical based on Jones's apartment complex discussed in §3.12, a number of calculations were based on optimistic cash flow projections: rents of $400 per apartment, out-of-pocket costs of $27,000 per year, and 100 percent occupancy rates. Assume, however that because of an unexpected economic downturn in the local economy a large surplus of apartments develops, and Jones finds that she actually has a 60 percent occupancy rate and an average rent of $360 per month per apartment; costs other than financing, furthermore, turn out to be close to $3,000 per month, or a total of $36,000 per year rather than the $27,000 projected. These are dramatic shortfalls in the projections, but in real life it is not uncommon for rosy cash-flow projections to turn bleak in such a dramatic fashion. These misfortunes bring the net cash flow from the project before financing costs to $77,400 per year rather than the projected $189,000.

In the unleveraged transaction (Jones investing all $976,000 in cash) the result is extremely disappointing but not disastrous: Rather than the project showing the expected 20 percent return on a cash-flow basis, the return is a little under 8 percent. Similarly if Jones takes out the first mortgage and invests capital of $263,500 the result is again disappointing but not disastrous: The interest payments on the first mortgage consume virtually the entire cash flow, reducing it to only $2,367 per year, and Jones is receiving a cash-flow return of less than 1 percent on her $263,500 investment. If, however, she has "leveraged up" the project, the results become increasing disastrous: If she takes out the first two mortgages and invests $113,500 in cash, the project has a negative cash flow after financing costs of over $25,000 per year. In other words, she has the choice of watching her $113,500 disappear without a trace or come up with an additional $25,000 per year, with no end in sight unless the apartment rental market improves dramatically. If she leverages out to the hilt, and takes out three mortgages involving monthly cash payments of over $9,000 per month, both she and the project are in deep trouble: The negative cash flow increases to nearly $40,000 per year. At this point the critical question becomes whether Jones is personally liable on those three mortgages. If she is, Jones' personal wealth may well be drawn down the drain: If she is not, she can walk away from the project losing only the original land value she contributed to the project. She can also count herself as one of the lucky ones.

§3.15 Leverage in the Modern Business World

In the remaining chapters of this book, we will encounter the concept of leverage in a number of different guises. In many transactions involving commodities and securities, for example, a portion of the purchase price may be borrowed *on margin*. Such transactions are leveraged because the investor is buying (or selling) a larger amount of the commodity or security in question than he or she could without borrowing. The investor is in effect gambling that the price movement in the securities or commodities in question will more than offset the interest cost of the borrowing. As a result, any change in the price of the commodity or security has a correspondingly greater effect on a borrowing investor than on one who invests the same amount of capital but does not borrow in order to increase the size of the investment. Similarly, a corporation is utilizing leverage whenever it finances expansion of its productive capacity by issuing bonds or debentures that carry fixed interest rates rather than selling additional shares of common stock. Do you see why? There are many other examples of business transactions involving the borrowing of capital in order to improve the overall profitability of the transaction.

CHAPTER 4

RESIDENTIAL REAL ESTATE TRANSACTIONS

§4.1 Introduction

This chapter continues the discussion of real estate transactions begun in the previous chapter. It focuses on residential real estate practices, including title assurance and conveyancing. The purchase of a home is the largest single commercial transaction ever made by most persons. Financing techniques used in modern residential real estate transactions are often similar to those used in the commercial real estate transactions discussed in the preceding chapter, but there are a sufficient number of differences to justify a separate discussion of residential transactions. Of particular importance, in both residential and commercial transactions, is the widespread practice discussed in this chapter of conveying real estate subject to outstanding encumbrances. Equally important, the basic pattern of residential real estate conveyancing — a two-step transaction consisting of the execution of a contract of sale followed at a later time by a formal closing of the transaction — is typical of most important commercial transactions.

This chapter discusses the traditional residential real estate transaction in which title passes immediately to the purchaser (subject to a mortgage to a commercial lender) at the closing of the transaction. In many states there exists an alternative method of conveyancing: an *installment sales contract* or *contract for deed*, as it is often called. In this type of transaction, the buyer enters into a contract agreeing to make specified payments over a period of years in return for which he or she is entitled to immediate possession and use of the property. However, title to the property is conveyed to the purchaser only after the last required payment is made. Often used for low income and speculative resort properties, the contract for deed transaction has its own problems and peculiarities, which are often considered in real property or conveyancing courses. They are not discussed further here.

This chapter generally discusses the roles, perspectives, and objectives of modern facilitators of traditional real estate transactions: brokers, title assurers, lending institutions, and others.

§4.2 Sources of Funds for Acquiring Residential Real Estate

Relatively few persons or families buying a personal residence today have the necessary capital to purchase their home with cash. In this connection a "home" includes cooperative apartments and condominiums as well as traditional urban, suburban, or rural residential real estate. A home is the largest single purchase ever made by most persons, who typically have difficulty scraping up the minimum down payment required by a lender, let alone the entire purchase price. As a result, most of the purchase price of a residence is almost always borrowed: Because of the size of the transactions, home loans are the largest single liabilities ever incurred by most persons.

Unlike commercial real estate, residential real estate does not have a cash flow from which payments on loans may be made in the future. Rather, the payments must come from the future earnings of the owners of the real estate. As a result, eligibility for a residential real estate loan is largely based on the earning capacity of the purchasers. In the event of default, attempts to collect a judgment from financially troubled families are not likely to be successful or cost-justifiable. As a result, relatively large down payments are required for residential property because the lender is necessarily relying primarily on the resale value of the property being purchased as security for its loan and desires to have a cushion between the amount of the loan and the value of the property securing it. The minimum down payment actually required for a loan to purchase residential property varies with the type of lender and the economic conditions at the time of the transaction, but the amount required is much more standardized than the down payment for commercial real estate. There are two traditional sources for residential real estate financing: conventional loans made by savings and loan associations, commercial banks, and possibly other types of organizations as well, and government guaranteed loans (usually guaranteed by the Veterans' Administration (VA) or the Federal Housing Administration (FHA).

The terms of conventional loans are largely dictated by market forces, but the down payment required is traditionally 20 percent of the purchase price: In some circumstances lenders may accept a somewhat smaller down payment, perhaps 15 percent or even less. If private *mortgage insurance* is available, lenders accept an even lower down payment — perhaps as low as 5 or 10 percent — but the purchaser then has to pay a monthly insurance premium. Mortgage insurance is available only for families with relatively high and secure income. In concrete terms, to purchase a $100,000 residence using a conventional loan, the purchaser must come up with $20,000 in cash for the down payment. (It should be noted that the possibility exists that a portion of the down payment may itself be borrowed through a second mortgage or borrowed from a short-term commercial lender on an unsecured basis.)

The terms of VA and FHA loans are largely circumscribed by federal regulation: They typically are available only for smaller or less expensive properties and the down payment required is under 10 percent. Because of the governmental guarantee of payment, the lender does not have the same concern about having a cushion.

In addition to the down payment itself, the purchaser must be prepared to meet a variety of additional costs, called *closing costs*, that may easily add several thousand dollars to the amount of cash that is required "up front." These costs may include *points*, a concept discussed in §4.13.

Persons buying a residence may have liquid funds (available from a modest inheritance, for example), and yet be concerned whether their income can comfortably support the monthly payments required by the mortgage. Such persons may reduce the size of the mortgage by increasing the down payment, thereby reducing future monthly payments and the total interest cost of the loan needed to finance the purchase of the residence.

On the other hand, even in the rare case where a purchaser of a residence has the capital necessary to purchase it entirely for cash, he or she often prefers for personal reasons to borrow a substantial part of the purchase price. For one thing, it is important for every individual to retain readily available funds for emergencies or contingencies, and capital invested in a home is typically hard to get at and certainly cannot be obtained quickly. In a word, capital invested in a residence is *illiquid*. For another, a person with substantial capital is usually interested in *diversifying* his or her investments; diversification is simply another word for the commonsense principle of not putting all your financial eggs in one basket. Putting a large amount of capital into a residence usually decreases diversification, though in the case of extremely wealthy individuals, this decrease may not be viewed as serious. Finally, the purchaser may prefer to borrow most of the purchase price of the residence to leave his or her capital free for speculation or commercial investment. A loan secured by residential real estate may be on more attractive terms than the purchaser could obtain if he or she were to invest capital in a residence and then borrow funds for outside investments through normal commercial channels. Since interest rates on mortgages are relatively high, however, most persons would be better off (contingency and diversification concerns aside) investing the capital in the mortgage rather than in more traditional investments.

The enactment of the 1986 tax amendments has led to the development of so-called *home equity loans*, which enable homeowners to borrow relatively easily on the equities in their personal residences on a tax-advantageous basis. (See §1.12.) The availability of home equity loans may make persons with available liquid capital more willing to use it to increase the size of down payments than they have been in the past.

Of course, the purchase of a residence is also an investment. Most persons and families own several homes at one time or another during their lifetimes, usually selling one home in order to purchase the next one; the sales proceeds from the old home usually provide all or much of the purchase price for the new one. In the past, there has been a general inflation of residential real estate values in many areas, so that people usually profited from buying a residence, living in it a few years, and then selling it in order to buy a new one. In some cases, individuals may have profited so substantially from this speculation in residential real estate that the sales price for the old residence will buy the new one without additional financing. The federal income tax law encourages this practice since it permits a person who sells his or her principal residence and invests the proceeds in a new principal residence within two years to "roll over" the proceeds without paying tax on the gain on the sale of the old residence to the extent that the cost of the new residence equals or exceeds the sales price of the old. In addition, gain of up to $125,000 on residential real estate is exempt on a one-time basis by a person over 55 years old. Much of this exempt gain may arise from earlier "rollovers" in which no gain was recognized. See §12.18.

In some areas of the United States, the pattern of steadily increasing residential real estate values is continuing, though in many areas the prices of residential real estate has stabilized or even begun to decline.

§4.3 How Much Is a Residence Worth?

A person thinking about the purchase or sale of residential real estate has to answer the question of how much the residence is worth. As described in the preceding chapter, valuation of commercial real estate often involves estimates of future cash flows: The same technique is generally not available for residential real estate.

Of course, the owner of real estate is familiar with the property, its advantages, its idiosyncrasies, and its defects, and usually has some idea as to its value. When the property is put up for sale, the owner must put an asking price on that property. That price, however, is not a reliable indication of value since owners often put inflated and unrealistic asking prices on their properties. Since it is quite common for some negotiation over price to occur in connection with residential real estate, a slightly inflated price may be justified in the owner's mind as providing some room to negotiate over price while keeping the price within an acceptable range. Not all sellers use this tactic, however. Some simply set what they view to be a realistic or acceptable price and refuse to negotiate at all over price. As a result, an asking price is not a reliable indication of value or even of what the seller thinks the value is.

A second source of information is the appraised value of the residence for local real estate taxation purposes. Most taxing authorities maintain appraisal offices that are skilled at estimating values of properties within their jurisdictions. Their valuations usually may be obtained simply by a telephone call. The usefulness of this information is limited, however. For one thing, tax appraisals are often not current; they may be redetermined once every few years (or even less frequently), with some kind of automatic adjustment made in the intervening years. More seriously, however, many jurisdictions do not appraise properties for tax purposes at 100 percent of market value. Assessments may be generally set at two-thirds, one-half, or some smaller fraction of estimated value. In the absence of specific knowledge about the practices followed by the local assessment office, these tax valuations should not be viewed as reliable indicators of value.

The most reliable method of estimating value is to employ an independent appraiser who is skilled in the techniques of appraising market values and is familiar with properties in the community. Of course, the question remains: How does such an appraiser estimate the value of residential property?

The most widely used method estimates the market value of the residence based upon recent sales of similar nearby properties — *comparables*, as they are usually called. This comparison is obviously best suited to appraising homes that are substantially similar to other homes in the immediate neighborhood and is less reliable for residences that are unique. Examination of sale prices of other homes will create a range of prices and terms: The appraiser must then adjust these figures, either up or down, to take into account the specific residence's features and deficiencies. It is at this point that the appraiser's judgment and skill is most important. Most residential real estate valuations are based on this method.

Another method of appraisal involves an estimate of the replacement cost of the residence. Appraisers estimating the replacement cost of a residence usually rely on appraisal handbooks that give current construction costs for various materials; this approach often involves long and complicated calculations. Replacement cost may be relied upon as the principal method of valuation if the property is unique and there are no comparable properties for which independent sales data are available.

Finally, the appraiser may consider the sales history of the property in question. If the present owner purchased the property in the recent past, the price he or she paid may be indicative of the current value. This information, however, may not always be easy to obtain. Further, it is always possible (a) that the present owner obtained the property at a bargain price or (b) that recent market trends show that the historical price is no longer an accurate estimate of current value. As a result, most appraisers place less weight on historical data than on recent sales of similar properties in the community. On the other hand, if a property has been on the market for several months at a specified price but has not sold in an active real estate market, that is a quite reliable indication that the market value of the residence is less than the asking price.

In making a formal appraisal, a skilled appraiser may estimate value on more than one basis, and then compare values obtained by using different approaches. In some cases, the appraiser may average the values obtained by these different methods, but a more accepted practice is to select a value that appears to be representative and ignore other approaches that lead to divergent values.

The methods of valuation outlined here are often considered in the appraisal of the value of commercial properties along with cash-flow projections. In other words, in estimating the value of a commercial apartment complex of the type hypothetically owned by Jones in the previous chapter, an appraiser might consider the prices paid for other comparable apartment complexes in the area and the estimated cost of replacing the current structures, as well as the cash-flow data.

§4.4 How Much to Pay

The two variables that determine how expensive a house a specific family can afford are (1) the amount of the down payment the family can or is willing to make and (2) the size of the loan that a lender will make to the family based on its expected income. Lenders have rules of thumb which provide a variety of different guides for the benefit of potential home purchasers, though the guides vary. It must also be recognized that these are only guides, and that lenders are often flexible in granting loans in close cases, depending on the demand for real estate loans. Often a lender will decline to make a specific loan on a specific property at the requested interest rate but will offer to make the loan at a somewhat higher rate to compensate for the perceived riskiness of the loan.

Assuming a 20 percent down payment and a conventional loan at 10 percent interest, a widely followed rule is that the purchase price should not exceed 2½ times the family's gross income. A somewhat different rule is that the monthly mortgage payments for principal and interest should not exceed 25 percent of the family's take home pay. Under these rules of thumb, a family with a median income of $28,000 has sufficient income to purchase a house selling for between $70,000 and $80,000. Of course, that family has to come up with the required down payment either from savings, from inheritances, from family gifts, or the like. Another commonly used rule is that aggregate monthly housing costs should not exceed 40 percent of take-home pay, though many families have demonstrated that one can survive a much higher percentage — over 50 percent — if there are no unexpected emergencies. In comparing these various rules it should be noted (a) that aggregate monthly housing costs are significantly greater than the payments of principal and interest on a mortgage (the major additional items are taxes, insurance, and repairs), and (b) that take-home pay is significantly smaller than gross earnings.

Of course, the larger the down payment a family can pay the more expensive the residence that can be acquired.

§4.5 The Structure of a Real Estate Purchase

The purchase of real estate is usually a two-step process that resembles most substantial commercial transactions. The first step is the execution of a contract of sale, setting forth the terms of the transaction. There then follows a period, often lasting a month or more, during which each party prepares to perform his or her obligations under the contract. Usually the most important responsibility of the purchaser during this period is arranging the necessary financing; another important matter (which may be the responsibility of either the purchaser or the seller, depending on the conventions followed by local realtors) is establishing that the seller has *marketable title* satisfactory to the purchaser. *Marketable title* is a title that a reasonable attorney in the community should accept. The second step is the *closing*, at which the formal steps required to complete the transaction take place. Of course, upon the execution of the contract the parties are legally bound to complete the transaction; the closing is where this actually occurs.

The two-step transaction described here is the pattern for virtually all significant commercial transactions, whether the sale of a business, the purchase of an automobile, or the purchase or sale of securities. This same pattern occurs where the purchaser has an "option" and is not committed to complete the purchase; after the formal exercise of the option a closing is scheduled at the mutual convenience of the parties.

§4.6 The Role of Real Estate Brokers

Most purchases and sales of both residential and commercial real estate involve real estate brokers. The description that follows primarily applies to residential real estate. Often neither the purchaser nor the seller of real estate are skilled at such large financial transactions. In addition, they often lack the services of a lawyer. Real estate brokers routinely guide such persons through the intricacies of buying and selling properties. In contrast, purchasers and sellers of commercial real estate typically have considerably greater sophistication, are accustomed to dealing with lawyers, and may deal directly with each other, thereby limiting the role of the brokers.

The first question that an owner of real estate who wishes to sell must face is whether to list the property with a broker or seek a purchaser directly. A broker is, of course, a professional in selling real estate; the major disadvantage of using a broker is the cost of his or her commission, which typically runs 5 or 6 percent of the aggregate selling price, and in the case of unusual or difficult properties may run higher. This commission, it is important to emphasize, is payable independent of the amount of effort exerted by the broker and is computed on the aggregate selling price, not on the amount of cash that changes hands: on a $120,000 property for which the purchaser is to pay $20,000 in cash and assume an existing $100,000 mortgage, the commission is nevertheless $6,000 or $7,200, exactly the same as if the purchaser was paying all cash for the property. It is usually not possible to negotiate with a broker over the amount of the commission, at least with respect to the average residential property, since the broker usually states firmly that the demanded commission is standard in the community and refuses to consider any change in the commission rate.

Many owners of residential property at least initially seek to sell their properties on their own to avoid the cost of the broker's commission. They may advertise in local newspapers and place signs on the property. This is often unsuccessful because the seller may be unfamiliar with the real estate market and set an unrealistic price on his or her property even without a commission. Also, most brokers refuse to show unlisted properties, and many potential purchasers immediately contact a real estate broker rather than trying first to find a suitable unlisted property. Many properties initially offered for sale by the owner (a phrase that usually implies that no brokerage commission is involved) are later listed with a broker.

Properties listed for sale with a real estate broker are referred to as *listings*.

Most brokers refuse to accept listings unless they are given an *exclusive* for at least a limited period of time. The wording of exclusive clauses varies, but usually the seller's broker is entitled to a commission if (a) the property is sold to anyone during the period of the exclusive, or (b) is sold at any time to a person who was shown the property during the period of the exclusive. Real estate brokers in most communities have a multiple listing system, that is, a centralized system that gives all participating brokers access to all (or most) current listings that have been placed with all other participating brokers. In most communities, brokers also have systems by which participating brokers can obtain access to keys for the property so that it may be shown in the absence of the owner and the broker for the seller.

A potential purchaser usually consults a broker to help him or her locate a suitable property. This broker could be, by chance, the same broker that has the original listing, but usually it is not. If different brokers are involved in a successful transaction, they will share the commission on some predetermined basis that may vary over time, depending on the market for real estate in the community. The division may be 50/50, or two-thirds/one-third, or on some other basis. The brokers' commissions are typically paid solely by the seller out of the proceeds of the sale: The purchaser may not be aware that the very helpful broker showing him or her around, seemingly out of graciousness, is motivated at least partially by the fact that he or she will receive a portion of a substantial commission payable by the seller upon the purchase of a residence shown by the broker.

Everyone familiar with the real estate industry has heard stories of brokers that earned full commissions on the basis of practically no effort. The broker accepts the listing one morning; that afternoon, the telephone rings and it is a person just dying to purchase the just-listed property. If the sale goes through, the broker will have earned perhaps a $7,200 commission for two telephone calls. One must balance stories about such windfalls with stories about the broker that conducts an open house every weekend for six months, advertises the property in the newspaper, and takes unusual steps to try to sell a specific property. Also, a broker representing a purchaser may show a potential purchaser 50 different houses and then fail to earn even a partial commission when the purchasers then stumble on the perfect house on their own. The hard-luck stories are probably more common than the former: One does not hear of real estate brokers retiring rich after a few years' of sales efforts.

§4.7 Negotiation of the Contract of Sale

After locating a suitable property, the potential purchaser makes a bid, or offer, on the property. This usually takes the form of a proposed contract of sale, which in the case of residential real estate is usually prepared by the purchaser's broker (on a standard form contract that is typically more favorable to the broker than to either the purchaser or the seller), setting forth the terms on which the purchaser hopes to purchase the property. This contract covers the basic terms of the sale, the price, the terms of financing hoped to be obtained, the time when possession is to be transferred, what personal property is included in the sale, and so forth. Many unsophisticated purchasers may not appreciate the potential binding effect that this document has on their rights in connection with the proposed purchase, for if the seller simply accepts the proposed contract, the purchaser is bound in accordance with its terms. Because this initial document is so important, a lawyer should examine it on behalf of the purchaser before it is submitted, but brokers usually do not suggest this, and the purchaser may not be sophisticated enough to insist on it. In any event, it is quite common for real estate brokers to draft contract language for their customers' offers.

After the proposed contract of sale is completed with the assistance of the purchaser's broker, it is signed by the potential purchasers, delivered by the purchaser's broker to the seller's broker, and then presented by the seller's broker to the seller. A nominal down payment or *earnest money* payment in the form of a check is attached to the document. A typical down payment on a $120,000 transaction might be $1,000 or $2,000. Brokers usually prefer to act as intermediaries between the potential purchaser and seller throughout the negotiation rather than to allow them to negotiate directly. (The brokers' expressed concern is that a direct confrontation may lead to a breakdown in the negotiations: There may also be concern that, if there is direct negotiation, the purchaser and seller will get along too well and may try to work out a private deal that does not include the brokers' commission.) The seller may make a counteroffer by changing the terms of the contract of sale, perhaps by increasing the price or by requiring the buyer to increase the size of the down payment upon acceptance, and the revised form of contract is returned to the purchaser's broker who then presents this counteroffer to the purchaser. In the process, the brokers tend to act as facilitators of the sale, urging the seller to come down and the purchaser to go up, rather than as true agents or representatives of one party or the other.

If the purchaser is represented by an attorney, the attorney prepares a formal contract of sale that is usually not based on the standardized contract used by real estate brokers. This contract probably represents the purchaser's interests more effectively than does the standard brokers' contract.

§4.8 The Closing

The second step of the process is the closing, which occurs when the title has been examined and the necessary financing arranged. Subsequent sections of this chapter outline some aspects of these intermediate steps. The contract of sale usually contains a time period during which the closing is to occur, but in practice the time is usually set by the availability of the financing commitment and the convenience of the parties.

The closing usually occurs at the offices of an attorney, or the title company, or the lender. When closings take place in the office of a title company or lender, an officer or employee of the title company or lender usually acts as the closing officer: In an attorney's office, the attorney is the officer. It is at this point that the formal deeds, promissory notes, mortgages, etc. are executed, the cash to be paid by the purchaser and the loan to be made by the new lender are paid in, and all the necessary documents to effect a transfer of title to real estate are executed. All checks are usually made payable to the closing officer or to the company he or she represents. All the documents are executed and left along with the checks *in escrow* with the closing officer. *Escrow* is a fancy word that describes the status of documents (and money) that have been delivered to a disinterested third person (here the closing officer) with instructions to deliver documents and disburse funds to specified persons only upon the occurence of specified conditions or events. Escrow is a convenient device for any type of closing transaction that requires a series of steps to be taken in a specific sequence yet virtually instantaneously. Pursuant to the escrow instructions, the closing officer first makes sure that all checks have cleared and the funds deposited in a special trust account. He or she then records in the local land records in the proper sequence the release of the old mortage, the new deed, and the new mortgage executed by the buyers. Funds are then disbursed to the various parties in accordance with the agreed upon settlement sheet and the recorded documents are delivered to the persons entitled to them: the promissory note originally executed by the sellers is marked "paid" and delivered to them. This disbursement of funds and delivery of documents takes place a few days after the closing, the seller receives the portion of the purchase price to which he or she is entitled, the brokers receive their shares of the commission, the old mortgagee receives the entire unpaid balance of its loan, and the purchaser receives the deed, and, shortly thereafter, the payment or coupon book reflecting his or her obligation to make payments on the new mortgage. Possession of the property is often also transferred at the closing by the delivery of keys, but this is a matter of agreement between the parties, and possession may be transferred either before or after the closing.

§4.9 Allocation of Closing Costs

Before the closing, the closing officer prepares a proposed *settlement sheet* showing charges allocable to the purchaser, charges allocable to the seller, and the disposition of all cash held in or to be received by the closing escrow. Federal law requires copies of this preliminary settlement sheet to be distributed to the purchaser and seller for their preliminary review. Even with this advance disclosure, settlement sheets tend to be rather complicated, and many purchasers or sellers probably "trust in God" and do not fully analyze or understand these important documents. The Department of Housing and Urban Development has prepared a pamphlet entitled "Settlement Costs and You" that is helpful.

An examination of a proposed settlement sheet shows that a number of charges are imposed on the purchaser and a number imposed on the seller. Some of the charges relate to the costs of preparing and filing the basic documents in the public land records; others relate to items required by the lender, such as an appraisal, a credit report, "loan origination fees," "points," and other vague charges; still others relate to the costs of obtaining title assurance and a survey. These charges add up to substantial amounts, several thousands of dollars at a minimum even in a routine transaction. A copy of a standard HUD-approved settlement sheet appears at pages 82–84 as Figure 4-1.

At first glance, the allocation of certain charges to the purchaser and others to the seller seem quite arbitrary. If one asks the closing officer how these responsibilities are split he or she will probably respond "custom of the community" or "contract provisions." In fact, a careful reading of the printed boilerplate in the form real estate contract shows that it does contain language that allocates most or all of these costs to one party or the other. The line between custom and contract in this connection is rather blurred because of the widespread use of standard form contracts in most communities. At least theoretically there is no reason why the potential purchaser in the original contract of sale cannot include provisions shifting some or most of these costs to the seller, or vice versa. This is not the norm, however, in part because this must be done at the time the original contract is prepared, and as indicated above, this is usually prepared by a broker rather than a lawyer. Even lawyers, however, may be reluctant to change the customary allocation of costs, since the amounts are relatively small in light of the purchase price of the house, and an attempt to shift the responsibility for these costs may make the contract unacceptable to the seller.

It is important to recognize that practices with respect to the allocation of significant costs vary widely from community to community. For example, on the basic matter of title insurance premiums, it is the custom in some communities for this to be a charge to the seller (on the theory that he or she has to provide acceptable proof of title). In others it is customary for this to be charged to the purchaser (on the theory that this is in part a cost of obtaining a loan).

§4.10 Title Assurance

Title assurance procedures and techniques are an important part of many law school courses on real property and conveyancing. The purpose of this section is to give a brief introduction to the subject and consider only conveyancing by deed.

Virtually all states provide that documents relating to interests in land are binding on third persons only if publicly filed and recorded in the land records of the county or other local governmental unit. The public records are usually filed in the order in which they are received, and the filing office usually maintains *grantor-grantee* and *grantee-grantor* indexes. Unfortunately, it is practically impossible to find out the status of the title to a piece of real estate using records in this form. Instead, in these states a private industry, the members of which may be referred to as *title companies*, *abstract companies* or *title plants*, maintain private summaries of the same records organized on a much more useful tract index basis. To obtain a current and accurate picture of the title of a tract without incurring excessive search costs, one must use the services of one of these private companies, which update their title records daily on a tract basis to reflect all documents filed every day in the public land records.

In some areas public records may be maintained on a tract index basis.

Figure 4-1

HUD-1 REV. 8/76   FORM APPROVED OMB NO. 2502 C 0265 (EXP. 12/31/86)

A.

B. TYPE OF LOAN

1. ☐ FHA   2. ☐ FMHA   3. ☐ CONV. UNINS.

4. ☐ VA   5. ☐ CONV. INS.

6. FILE NUMBER: 7. LOAN NUMBER:

SETTLEMENT STATEMENT
U.S. DEPARTMENT OF HOUSING AND URBAN DEVELOPMENT

8. MORTGAGE INSURANCE CASE NUMBER:

C. NOTE: This form is furnished to give you a statement of actual settlement costs. Amounts paid to and by the settlement agent are shown. Items marked "(p.o.c.)" were paid outside the closing; they are shown here for informational purposes and are not included in totals.

D. NAME OF BORROWER   **E. NAME OF SELLER:**   **F. NAME OF LENDER:**

G. PROPERTY LOCATION: **H. SETTLEMENT AGENT:**   **PLACE OF SETTLEMENT**

I. SETTLEMENT DATE:

J. SUMMARY OF BORROWER'S TRANSACTION		K. SUMMARY OF SELLER'S TRANSACTION	
100. GROSS AMOUNT DUE FROM BORROWER:		**400. GROSS AMOUNT DUE TO SELLER:**	
101. Contract sales price		401. Contract sales price	
102. Personal property		402. Personal property	
103. Settlement charges to borrower (line 1400)		403.	
104.		404.	
105.		405.	
Adjustments for items paid by seller in advance		*Adjustments for items paid by seller in advance*	
106. City/town taxes to		406. City/town taxes to	
107. County taxes to		407. County taxes to	
108. Assessments to		408. Assessments to	
109.		409.	
110.		410.	
111.		411.	
112.		412.	
120. GROSS AMOUNT DUE FROM BORROWER		**420. GROSS AMOUNT DUE TO SELLER**	
200. AMOUNTS PAID BY OR IN BEHALF OF BORROWER:		**500. REDUCTIONS IN AMOUNT DUE TO SELLER:**	
201. Deposit or earnest money		501. Excess deposit (see instructions)	
202. Principal amount of new loan(s)		502. Settlement charges to seller (line 1400)	
203. Existing loan(s) taken subject to		503. Existing loan(s) taken subject to	
204.		504. Payoff of first mortgage loan	
205.		505. Payoff of second mortgage loan	
206.		506.	
207.		507.	
208.		508.	
209.		509.	
Adjustments for items unpaid by seller:		*Adjustments for items unpaid by seller:*	
210. City/town taxes to		510. City/town taxes to	
211. County taxes to		511. County taxes to	
212. Assessments to		512. Assessments to	
213.		513.	
214.		514.	
215.		515.	
216.		516.	
217.		517.	
218.		518.	
219.		519.	
220. TOTAL PAID BY/FOR BORROWER		**520. TOTAL REDUCTION AMOUNT DUE SELLER**	
300. CASH AT SETTLEMENT FROM/TO BORROWER		**600. CASH AT SETTLEMENT TO/FROM SELLER**	
301. Gross amount due from borrower (line 120)		601. Gross amount due to seller (line 420)	
302. Less amounts paid by/for borrower (line 220) ( )		602. Less reductions in amt. due to seller (line 520) ( )	
303. CASH (☐ FROM) (☐ TO) BORROWER		**603. CASH (☐ TO) (☐ FROM) SELLER**	

Figure 4-1 *(cont.)*

L. SETTLEMENT CHARGES

		PAID FROM BORROWER'S FUNDS AT SETTLEMENT	PAID FROM SELLER'S FUNDS AT SETTLEMENT
700.	**TOTAL SALES/BROKER'S COMMISSION** based on price $ @ % =		
	Division of Commission (line 700) as follows:		
701.	$ to		
702.	$ to		
703.	Commission paid at Settlement		
704.			
800.	**ITEMS PAYABLE IN CONNECTION WITH LOAN**		
801.	Loan Origination Fee %		
802.	Loan Discount %		
803.	Appraisal Fee to		
804.	Credit Report to		
805.	Lender's Inspection Fee		
806.	Mortgage Insurance Application Fee to		
807.	Assumption Fee		
808.			
809.			
810.			
811.			
900.	**ITEMS REQUIRED BY LENDER TO BE PAID IN ADVANCE**		
901.	Interest from to @ $ /day		
902.	Mortgage Insurance Premium for months to		
903.	Hazard Insurance Premium for years to		
904.	years to		
905.			
1000.	**RESERVES DEPOSITED WITH LENDER**		
1001.	Hazard insurance months @ $ per month		
1002.	Mortgage insurance months @ $ per month		
1003.	City property taxes months @ $ per month		
1004.	County property taxes months @ $ per month		
1005.	Annual assessments months @ $ per month		
1006.	months @ $ per month		
1007.	months @ $ per month		
1008.	months @ $ per month		
1100.	**TITLE CHARGES**		
1101.	Settlement or closing fee to		
1102.	Abstract or title search to		
1103.	Title examination to		
1104.	Title insurance binder to		
1105.	Document preparation to		
1106.	Notary fees to		
1107.	Attorney's fees to		
	(includes above items numbers:)		
1108.	Title insurance to		
	(includes above items numbers:)		
1109.	Lender's coverage $		
1110.	Owner's coverage $		
1111.			
1112.			
1113.			
1200.	**GOVERNMENT RECORDING AND TRANSFER CHARGES**		
1201.	Recording fees: Deed $; Mortgage $; Releases $		
1202.	City/county tax/stamps: Deed $; Mortgage $		
1203.	State tax/stamps: Deed $; Mortgage $		
1204.			
1205.			
1300.	**ADDITIONAL SETTLEMENT CHARGES**		
1301.	Survey to		
1302.	Pest inspection to		
1303.			
1304.			
1305.			
1400.	**TOTAL SETTLEMENT CHARGES** *(enter on lines 103, Section J and 502, Section K)*		

We, the undersigned, identified as Borrower in section D hereof and Seller in section E hereof, hereby acknowledge receipt of this completed Uniform Settlement Statement (pages 1 & 2) on   19

Borrower: Seller:

_____   _____

_____   _____

This form provided by

Figure 4-1 (*cont.*)

ADDENDUM TO HUD-I
SETTLEMENT STATEMENT

G.F. No. _____

I have carefully reviewed the HUD-I Settlement Statement and to the best of my knowledge and belief, it is a true and accurate statement of all receipts and disbursements made on my account or by me in this transaction. I further certify that I have received a copy of the HUD-I Settlement Statement.

_____   _____

_____   _____

Borrowers   Sellers

The HUD-I Settlement Statement which I have prepared is a true and accurate account of this transaction. I have caused or will cause the funds to be disbursed in accordance with this statement.

_____   _____

Settlement Agent   .   Date

WARNING: It is a crime to knowingly make false statements to the United States on this or any other similar form. Penalties upon conviction can include a fine and imprisonment. For details see: Title 18 U. S. Code Section 1001 and Section 1010.

Also, some areas have adopted the *Torrens system*, which is a form of direct title registration. The discussion below does not deal with these systems of title assurance.

In most urban areas today, title assurance is provided by *title insurance*, though in some areas lawyers' opinions of title based on studies of *title abstracts* may still be used. Title insurance is normally written by specialized companies that maintain tract indexes: companies involved in writing life or casualty insurance usually are not involved in title insurance. Title insurance is an unusual type of insurance in a few respects. For one thing, it is not a recurring policy: There is only a single premium, and a title insurance policy written on behalf of an owner theoretically remains outstanding forever to protect him or her from claims asserted by others. It is more similar to an indemnification agreement than to an insurance policy. For another, title insurance companies generally do not take risks that they know about. If the title search shows that a risk exists, the company will exclude that risk from the coverage of the policy. If a title search reveals a trivial potential defect (such defects are often called *flyspecks*), the company is nevertheless likely to include an express exception not providing protection against that defect. Also, it is to the interest of both the purchaser and the lender to try to persuade a title company to eliminate as

84

many exceptions of this nature as possible. It is sometimes possible to do this by arguing, for example, that the excepted defect was cured by the statute of limitations or that an exception, for example, for an unconveyed dower interest arising from a marriage that took place in 1912 is unlikely to be a real defect today simply because of the passage of time. A third unusual aspect of title insurance is that the premium is based solely on the purchase price of the property and is not dependent on what problems there are in the title. As indicated above, a major problem in the title is excepted from the coverage if it is known, though presumably a title company may decline to issue a policy at all if it concludes that the potential seller does not in fact have title to the property.

Title insurance does protect against some things even if the title company expressly excepts every risk that it is aware of: forged deeds, misfiled deeds, and the like. As a practical matter, however, the risk involved in the average title insurance is not very great, though occasionally one hears of cases where the title company is compelled to acquire land or cover losses incurred by insureds.

Before issuing a title policy, a title company sets forth the results of its title search in the form of a *binder, commitment to insure* or *title report*. This is an important document that every purchaser should examine carefully since his or her title is subject to the exceptions set forth in that document. If a substantial defect appears, the purchaser may reject the title, that is, refuse to complete the transaction on the ground the title is not marketable. What should be done, however, if the report shows a "defect" that is unlikely to affect the purchaser's use and enjoyment of the residence but the title company refuses to remove it? There is a risk in simply ignoring the problem and completing the purchase of the property that may not be self-evident. That risk is that presumably the same defect will reappear when the purchaser tries to resell the property in the future, and the new purchaser (or his or her lawyer) may take a less charitable attitude toward the problem and reject the title. In other words, the concern is as much whether the purchaser will be able to resell the property subject to the defect as whether the defect is one that may hinder the purchaser's use and enjoyment of the property. Where a defect such as this appears, the purchaser may be able to negotiate a reduction in the agreed purchase price if he or she agrees to purchase subject to the defect.

Title companies offer a *mortgagee policy* and an *owner's policy*. The first protects the lender up to the extent of the unpaid balance of the mortgage and is the only policy required by the lender as a condition to making the loan. The second protects the purchaser both with respect to his or her equity in the property and, more importantly, against subrogation claims that might be brought by the title company against the owner on the mortgage note or on his or her warranties of title in the mortgage if a claim is made on the mortgagee policy. *Subrogation* means stepping into the shoes of another: The title company pays off the mortgage, takes an assignment of the mortgage note, and then sues the owner for the unpaid balance of the full amount of the mortgage note as subrogee of the mortgagee's interest. The cost of the owner's policy is not great (when purchased in connection with the mortgagee policy), and a purchaser should always be advised to acquire the owner's policy as well as the mortgagee policy.

A final word should perhaps be added about warranties of title. There are three basic types of deeds: *general warranty deeds*, *special warranty deeds*, and *quit claim deeds*. (In some areas of the country general or special warranty deeds may be known by different names.) The first, as its name implies, includes a general warranty by the seller that his or her title is valid as against the world. The second warrants title as against any act of the seller but does not warrant good title against the world, and the third simply conveys whatever title the seller possesses without any warranty of any kind. These title warranties may serve as a basis for litigation by the grantee against the grantor if there is a title defect. (This is an additional reason to insist that purchasers acquire the owner's title policy since that policy insures against such warranty claims made by a subsequent purchaser as well.)

The type of warranty deed that must be tendered at the closing of a routine real estate transaction is also part of the custom of the community. In most areas, general warranty deeds are the custom, though in some areas the custom is to convey by special warranty deed. If a seller refuses to give the customary type of deed used in the community, that is a powerful warning that there is some title defect somewhere. In particular, if a seller is willing only to give a quit claim deed in a community in which warranty deeds are the custom, that is almost a guarantee that there is something fundamentally wrong with the title to the property, and the purchaser is probably buying a lawsuit.

§4.11 The Survey

Lenders often require a reasonably current survey of the property as a condition for making the loan. The cost, which is usually not great, is usually allocated to the purchaser. Even where a current survey is not required by the lender, lawyers often recommend that the purchaser obtain a new survey for his or her own protection. If it should turn out that the fence at the back of the lot was put up after the last survey and is six inches on the neighbor's land, the purchaser typically has no recourse. Title warranties and title policies are expressly or impliedly subject to whatever state of facts an accurate survey would show; as a result, the cost of a survey should be viewed as a relatively inexpensive "peace of mind" insurance in most cases.

§4.12 Mortgagor Life Insurance

Many mortgage companies offer a type of life insurance to purchasers of real estate that at first glance appears attractive. For a relatively small additional monthly payment, this policy guarantees that upon the unexpected death of the borrower, the insurance policy will provide an amount sufficient to pay off the mortgage in full. As described more fully in Chapter 6, this is a *declining balance* term life insurance policy, and its cost should be evaluated along with other term life insurance policies offered by commercial companies generally. An investigation will usually reveal that the cost of this insurance is high given the amount of protection that is afforded by the policy, though an offsetting feature is that adding the payment to the monthly mortgage payment makes the carrying of this insurance relatively painless.

§4.13 Points

A later section in this chapter discusses the substantial increases in interest rates that occurred in the 1970s and early 1980s. One important consequence of this development was the institutionalization of the practice of lenders of charging *points* in connection with the making of long-term loans for residential and commercial real estate. A *point* (or a *discount point* as it is sometimes called) is simply a charge equal to 1 percent of the loan amount; a lender who charges 3 points on a $100,000 loan in effect imposes an additional $3,000 fee at closing. Originally, points were charged to the borrower as a device to keep real estate loans from exceeding nominal state usury ceilings or to keep quoted interest rates more in line with other competitive rates. So, if a purchaser of real estate "borrows" $100,000 at 11 percent for 30 years but then is immediately required to pay 3 points (or $3,000) back to the lender at closing, he or she is really borrowing only $97,000, but is paying back $100,000 on the regular amortization schedule for that amount. The effect of charging three points on this loan is to increase the effective interest rate on the $97,000 actually borrowed from the 11 percent quoted figure to 11.38 percent without calling attention to it.

The economic effect of charging points against the borrower is so obvious that the federal government in its guaranteed loan programs generally prohibits the evasion of maximum ceiling rates on interest by charging the borrower points. However, both the Veteran's Adminstration and the Department of Housing and Urban Development generally permit points to be charged against the *seller* on the theory that this does not increase the borrowing cost to the purchaser. However, it seems evident that the probable effect of charging the seller points is to cause sellers to increase the price of the property by the amount that they expect they will have to pay to allow the borrower to get the federally guaranteed loan. As a result, points that are charged against the seller probably are in fact paid by the purchaser over the lifetime of the loan through larger payments.

The practice of charging points in loan closings is practically universal today in both commercial and residential real estate transactions. Many additional fees that may not be described as points but, say, as a "loan acceptance fee" or "loan origination fee," are economically equivalent to points if they are received by the lender and do not reflect the actual cost of providing services. For reasons discussed below, purchasers and sellers of residential real estate often agree between themselves in advance to share in some predetermined ratio the cost of the points that almost certainly will be charged at closing.

§4.14 Insurance and Taxes

This section deals with a major post-closing charge that is usually added by lenders to the monthly payment on residential real estate mortgages. The discussion in the rest of this chapter assumes that you understand the concepts underlying the traditional long-term level-payment mortgage described in §3.8 of the previous chapter.

For reasons discussed earlier, lenders who make residential real estate loans tend to rely more on the value of the property as security than on the personal promise to pay the note made by the purchaser. In order to preserve their principal security (the residence), lenders must assure themselves that real estate taxes are paid when they are due and casualty insurance (e.g., fire or storm), is kept up. Together or separately, taxes and insurance are rather big ticket items for many families, and to ensure that funds are available when needed, lenders usually require the purchaser to pay, each month, an additional amount equal to one-twelfth of the estimated cost of insurance and taxes. These amounts are held in escrow by the lender and disbursed more or less on a timely basis directly to the insurer and the taxing authorities to pay the insurance premium and the tax bill.

The internal treatment of these escrow funds varies from area to area. In some areas the lenders collect the escrow amounts, but do not pay interest on them. Since a lender may have hundreds or thousands of mortgages outstanding, the amount of interest-free money may be quite substantial and provides a significant additional return to the lender who, of course, is free to invest these funds profitably until they are needed. Where interest is not paid on escrow funds, knowledgeable purchasers feel there is a rip-off by lenders. Where negotiation with a lender is possible (and often it is not), attorneys should seek to eliminate the tax and insurance escrows completely or to work out an arrangement by which escrow payments earn interest. It should be noted, however, that there are two sides to this issue. The handling of these escrowed funds and paying taxes and insurance involve some cost to the mortgagee (though this cost is probably far less than the earnings on these funds), and in a sense is a convenience to the mortgagor. The issue of whether interest should be paid on escrowed funds has been the subject of litigation in several states. In some communities, escrow payments are treated as reducing the principal of the mortgage and payments of taxes or insurance premiums as increasing the mortgage. In effect, this pays interest on escrow funds at the rate of the mortgage. While such treatment affects the mathematical accuracy of the amortization schedule, that is relatively unimportant since the overall effect is small.

The monthly payment needed to amortize the borrowed amount is sometimes referred to as the *PI* (*principal* and *interest*) payment. The full payment including tax and insurance escrows is referred to as the *PITI* payment. When monthly mortgage costs are discussed with purchasers, only the PI amount is usually quoted because there is no current information about the TI portion of the payment. Some naive purchasers have relied on a PI quotation of the monthly cost of a mortgage of a specified amount and later discovered to their dismay that PITI is considerably larger than PI.

Independent of the escrow arrangement in future years, it is customary to allocate taxes (and insurance, if a new policy is not to be written) between purchaser and seller in the year in which the sale occurs on the basis of the fraction of the year each owned the property.

§4.15 Modern Trends in Residential Real Estate Pricing and Financing

Prior to about 1970, the financing of residential real estate purchases was fairly straightforward. Conventional financing required a down payment of 20 percent and a 25- or 30-year mortgage at the going rate of approximately 5-7 percent a year. All mortgages were of the conventional level-payment type that amortized the unpaid principal over the period of the mortgage. Special financing — FHA or VA — permitted favored purchasers even more favorable terms as to minimum down payment and interest rates, though the level payment schedules were rigorously followed in connection with such loans as well. In effect, the federal government was subsidizing the favored purchaser by making the down payment requirement easier to meet.

It is a little hard to recreate today the attitudes of the post-World War II and pre-1970 era towards real estate ownership. The 1950s and early 1960s were periods of unprecedented prosperity in the United States. It was the era of the tract home with a choice of brick, stone, or redwood facades; of cars with tail fins; of hope and optimism. The notion that every middle-class family could own its own home seemed to be an accepted fact since residential real estate was relatively inexpensive in most areas during this period, and most middle-class American families could find financing that enabled them to purchase housing.

For example, in the 1960s an average upper-middle-class house cost approximately $30,000. A more modest house in a standardized subdivision might sell for half that, and the median price for homes was even lower. A family purchasing the $15,000 house might need a $3,000 down payment (though veterans could obtain such a house with no down payment) plus a $12,000 mortgage at 6 percent over 25 years. The monthly payment PI on such a mortgage is only $71.95 per month, and on a PITI basis the payment might be $100 or $110 per month. The purchase of the much larger $30,000 house might require a $7,500 down payment plus a $22,500 mortgage at 6 percent per year for 30 years. The monthly payment on such a mortgage was only $134.90 per month, PI, and about $200 to $225 per month, PITI. Thus, the payment for housing out of a family budget was relatively modest and well within the means of most of the middle class. Of course, the purchasers of the more expensive house would have to scrape together the down payment plus closing costs either from savings, family gifts, inheritances, or loans from family or other sources. Many families had small nest eggs based on World War II military service and the special VA or FHA governmental programs often provided for reduced or even zero down payments for those who did not.

Beginning in the 1970s, two changes greatly complicated the acquisition of residential real estate by persons of fairly modest means. The first was a sudden increase in the level of interest rates. Mortgages carrying interest rates of 13 or 14 percent per year were the norm in the late 1970s and early 1980s, and in some periods and areas mortgages carrying rates as high as 16 or 17 percent per year were written. Even in 1988, after several years of prosperity, growth in the economy, and general declines in interest rates, interest rates for residential real estate are hovering at or above 10 percent per year. The effect of such an increase in interest rates is very substantial over a long-term mortgage. For example, a 30-year, $50,000 mortgage at 11 percent requires a monthly payment of $476.16 per month, PI, or $176.38 per month more than a 6 percent mortgage. Over 30 years, the *increased* interest charged is about $64,000, considerably more than the original amount borrowed.

A second factor has been the inflation of real estate values and construction costs in many areas. This has been most notable and most persistent in areas such as southern California, the San Francisco Bay area, Washington, D.C., and New York City, but it is to a significant extent a national phenomenon. In 1986, the median price, nationwide, for a used home was about $80,000, a fivefold increase in about 20 years. Of course, rates of inflation and family incomes have also increased significantly during the same period, but housing costs are such an important component in determining inflation rates that it is probably more meaningful to say that inflation rates reflect largely the increase in housing costs than vice versa. Real estate values in specific areas have increased much more rapidly than the national figures, consistently increasing as much as 20 or 25 percent per year, depending on location, the shortage of housing, and other factors. In these areas, construction costs have increased at roughly the same rate. As such costs rise, the cost of existing housing tends to increase proportionally. A house in a Washington, D.C., suburb that cost $35,000 in 1965 was priced at $105,040 in 1975, $200,000 in 1979, and roughly $300,000 in 1986. A conventional loan to acquire such a property now involves "big bucks:" perhaps a down payment of $50,000 and a 30-year 10 percent mortgage for $250,000. That mortgage requires a monthly payment of $2,193.93, PI. In addition, real estate tax valuations reflect market values so that the escrow for that item also has tripled. Similarly, fire insurance rates reflect the replacement cost of structures and have increased along with inflated real estate values. The consequence is that a house that required a down payment of perhaps $10,500 in 1965 with PITI payments of about $250 per month now requires a down payment of $50,000 and PITI payments of over $2,700 per month. Of course, incomes have also increased but often not proportionately to this tremendous increase. And, it is important to repeat, we are talking about the same house.

One major consequence of the increase in housing costs has doubtless been to increase the number of wives in the work force; the two-income family is an economic necessity to purchase housing that a generation ago could readily be purchased on a single income.

Who can afford to buy large houses today except for the very rich? To apply the traditional rules of thumb, a purchaser of a $300,000 house should have a monthly take-home pay of over $8,000 a month. That is not a very large group of Americans, even including two-income families. Certainly, one group that often can afford such costs comprises families fortunate enough to have purchased homes before 1970. Having benefited from the rise in residential real estate prices, they can often put the proceeds into a much larger down payment with correspondingly lower monthly payments. Families moving at the request of their employers sometimes receive substantial housing assistance, both in selling the old home at an attractive price and in helping the employees finance new ones. Without these advantages, however, the young family just starting out on a single income with no family money cannot buy a home.

To some extent the rules of thumb have bent to economic necessity. For example, 10 percent down payments are now common on more expensive properties, and lenders are often willing to accept borrowers that devote a relatively large fraction of their disposable income to housing. However, lower down payments increase the amount of the loan and the size of the monthly payment. Much more promising are changes in the traditional structures of mortgage repayment schedules that tend to defer much of the ultimate cost of the purchase to the future. During periods of inflation this makes obvious sense from the standpoint of the borrower since loans today are being repaid with depreciated dollars in the future. The other major development has been the increased use of creative financing techniques similar to those used in commercial real estate, as well as other innovative ideas. These developments form the subject of the following sections.

§4.16 New Types of Residential Real Estate Mortgages

Because of the changes in the economics of residential home buying since the 1970s, novel types of mortgages have been created. These are used primarily in residential real estate transactions but are also used in commercial transactions. Indeed, they were briefly described in §3.8 of the previous chapter. The principal alternative mortgages are described in the following paragraphs. Several important caveats should be noted at the outset. (1) Nomenclature is not always uniform and some of the instruments described below may have different names in some areas. (2) There are a great many variants and hybrids of alternative mortgages, perhaps as many as 500 in all, though most of them differ in only minor respects, such as the type of index used to calculate adjustments in interest rates or differences in maximum changes in any one year. (3) Some of the variants described below may not be offered by lending institutions in some areas.

The conventional, level-payment long-term mortgage described in §3.8 is usually referred to as the *fixed rate conventional mortgage* or FRCM.

1. *Graduated Payment Mortgage (GPM)*. A graduated payment mortgage has a fixed interest rate and a fixed time for repayment like an FRCM. However, rather than having level payments over the life of the mortgage, the monthly payments for a GPM start out at a lower level than those called for by the FRCM, but rise usually in three or four steps in later years, for example, at the end of the third, fifth, and seventh years of the mortgage. Obviously, payments in later years must be higher than the payment schedule of an equivalent FRCM in order to make up for the reduced payments in earlier years. The graduation rate, the term of graduation, and the interest rate are all fixed throughout the life of the loan.

The theory behind a graduated payment mortgage is that the purchaser's income is likely to be lower in the first years after the purchase of the residence and is likely to increase thereafter, enabling the purchaser to make the larger payments in later years. In effect, a GPM attempts to match mortgage payments with the borrower's anticipated future income stream. The interest cost of a GPM is larger than the cost of a fixed-payment conventional mortgage since the loan is paid off at a slower rate in the early years of the mortgage.

A GPM carries a significant capacity for deception of or misjudgment by a marginal purchaser of residential real estate. Even though the purchaser is warned that mortgage payments will increase in later years, household budgets are usually calculated on current receipts and current expenses. The sudden significant increase in monthly mortgage payments may come as a cruel blow to the household budget if hoped-for increases in salary or take-home pay have not materialized, or additional expenses caused by illness or increase in the size of the family have been incurred. Indeed, GPMs are often advertised by heavily emphasizing the low payments in the initial years, often showing them as a percentage of the loan amount, with only a footnote in fine print warning the reader that the mortgage is a GPM and later payments will be much higher. The rates shown in these ads are often called *teaser rates*.

2. *Deferred Interest Mortgage (DIM)*. The DIM is a type of GPM, with a fixed interest payment and a fixed date of maturity; however, initial payments for the first few years are fixed at such a low level that they do not cover the original monthly interest cost of the loan. The result is *negative amortization*, that is, in the early years the unpaid portion of the interest is added to the principal of the mortgage each month so that the amount of the loan increases rather than decreases after each payment. After perhaps the second step in the graduated payments — the fifth year — the payments are large enough to cover the full interest cost and begin the amortization of the principal. Later payments must be fixed at a higher rate than a regular GPM in order to cover the unpaid interest of the earlier years.

3. *Pledged Account Mortgage (PAM)*. A pledged account mortgage is simply a DIM or GPM in which a fund is created at the closing which is used to finance the lower initial payments. A not uncommon arrangement requires the purchaser to pay points at the closing, and the points form the fund to finance the lower initial payments. In some instances the seller of the property may be persuaded to place a portion of the sales price into the fund for this purpose; presumably, the price of the residence is inflated by the amount of this payment. The seller is willing to do this in order to permit the sale of the property; it is a kind of creative financing. This arrangement is sometimes called a *buydown option*.

4. *Adjustable Rate Mortgage (ARM)*. The interest rate on an ARM is not fixed at the market interest rate when the loan is created but is tied to some index that reflects changes in market rates of interest. Thus, future monthly payments are not precisely known when the loan is originated. A variety of different indexes are used to determine the amount of adjustment in the rates: (1) indexes based on six-month, one-year, three-year, or five-year treasury securities; (2) indexes based on actual mortgage rates, such as the national average mortgage contract rate on the purchase of previously occupied homes calculated by the Federal Home Loan Bank Board; or (3) the average cost of funds to federally insured savings and loan associations in the area, the state, or nationally. All of these indexes are readily available and widely used. Most ARMs provide for the adjustment in rates to be made every six months, but some provide for adjustments annually or over even longer periods.

If there are significant increases in interest rates, it is possible that an ARM may lead to very large increases in monthly payments over a relatively brief period. Many borrowers initially objected to the open-endedness of these mortgages. To increase their attractiveness, many ARMs currently limit both the maximum change in interest rate that can occur in the ARM over the life of the mortgage (usually not more than a 5 percent increase) and provide caps on the maximum change in monthly payment that may occur because of a rate adjustment. If the indexed change is greater than the cap, the excess is added to the principal of the loan much like in a DIM.

Of course, interest rates may go down as readily as they go up, and indeed real estate mortgage rates have declined significantly since the early 1980s. The holder of an ARM has therefore seen his or her payments decline: Of course, this decline does not help the holder of a GPM.

An ARM is also sometimes called a *variable rate mortgage* or *VRM*.

5. *Graduated Payment Adjustable Rate Mortgage (GPARM)*. Two of the above features, a graduated payment and an adjustable rate, may be combined in a single real estate mortgage. Payments go up over time to amortize the principal and the payments are simultaneously adjusted to reflect changes in interest rates. The acronym of such a mortgage often includes a slash: GP/ARM.

6. *"Rollover Mortgage (ROM)*. The ROM (currently used extensively in Canada) is a long-term loan for which the interest rate and monthly payments are usually renegotiated every five years. The rate adjustment is based on an index or formula that reflects current market conditions, with a maximum increase of five percentage points over the life of the mortgage.

7. *Price Level Adjusted Mortgage (PLAM)*. In a PLAM the interest rate and the term of the mortgage are fixed, but the outstanding balance is adjusted periodically in accordance with changes in some agreed-upon price index. In other words, the payments may increase as the value of the underlying property increases.

8. *Reverse Annuity Mortgage (RAM)*. A RAM is in effect an annuity purchased by an increasing loan against the accumulated equity in a residence. It is designed for the elderly and the retired who have a large equity in their home because of inflation and need to use the equity to support themselves. Basically, it enables the owners of an appreciated residence to continue to live in the family home, receiving a monthly payment which reduces their equity in the house. The loan becomes due either on a specific date or when a specified event occurs, such as the sale of the property or the death of the borrower. If the loan becomes due on a specified date, and the owners are still alive, the residence will probably have to be sold, with considerable discomfort to the owners.

It is not necessary to remember all of these modern variants to the traditional fixed rate conventional mortgage. If one is faced with a mortgage with an unfamiliar name, ask what it is. All of the variations are spin-offs from the conventional fixed-rate mortgage: There is nothing mysterious or incomprehensible about them.

§4.17 The Background of Creative Financing

As interest rates and property values increased, a number of innovative financing devices developed that enabled persons to acquire residential properties that they could never have afforded under traditional standards. These practices are generally referred to as creative financing of residential real estate transactions; for a brief discussion of the meaning of the word "creative" in this context, see §3.11.

A critically important factor underlying almost all creative financing of residential real estate is that owners of appreciated property who desire to sell are often as distressed by the inability of potential purchasers to finance the purchase as the purchasers are themselves. It is wonderful to own a house that cost $35,000 a decade before and is now appraised at $200,000, but who can afford to buy it? Often sellers who hope to get all-cash offers (as was routinely the case ten or so years earlier when most mortgages were refinanced upon the sale of the property) find that their property remains on the market for extended periods of time, or that they receive offers that stipulate that they do not receive the entire purchase price immediately. Usually, a small reduction in the asking price by sellers in this situation is fruitless: The problem is much more than a few thousand dollars. Furthermore, the current market price usually reflects a substantial profit component for the seller. For example, a house that cost $30,000 a decade ago now is on the market for $200,000; the mortgage has been paid down to $18,000, and the owner's original $7,000 equity will grow to about $180,000 if someone pays the asking price. However, after watching a few unsuccessful attempts by purchasers to finance the $200,000 asking prices, the seller may conclude that it is sensible to put a portion of his or her potential profit at risk for a period of time in order to help the purchaser finance the transaction. A seller, for example, might be willing to take a balloon note for a portion of the purchase price that represents unrealized profit; why not take a chance as long as the balloon note will require refinancing or sale in five years?

In any event, once the seller recognizes that a straightforward, all-cash sale is not likely to occur, the stage for creative financing is set.

A second fundamental factor in the development of creative financing is increasing recognition that because of the rise in interest rates, older fixed-rate mortgages at low interest rates are attractive assets if they can be transferred to a potential purchaser of the house. If interest rates are at 11 percent, the opportunity to "borrow" a portion of the purchase price by taking over an outstanding mortgage at 6 percent is obviously attractive, since the payments on an 11 percent loan may be hundreds of dollars per month higher than those on a 6 percent loan. Furthermore, an assumption costs the seller relatively little: The real losers are the lending institutions that have older 6 percent loans outstanding. Lenders would naturally prefer that they be paid off when the property is transferred so that they can then make a new loan with the proceeds at the effective market rate of 11 percent. Thus, before considering the nature of creative financing for residential real estate, an examination of the rules governing assumptions of mortgages must first be made.

§4.18 Assumptions and Refinancings of Mortgages

This section assumes that there are no contractual restrictions on assumptions of loans. The effect of these contractual provisions is discussed in the following section.

When a person or family decides to buy a residence on which there is already a mortgage, there are theoretically several ways of handling the transaction, and it is helpful to consider the factors affecting the choice of which method is to be followed. The first alternative is for the new purchaser simply to obtain outside financing for the entire purchase price (over and above the down payment) from independent sources. To use the example from the previous section, the purchaser applies for a new first mortgage at 11 percent; a major portion of this loan will in effect be applied to paying off the old 6 percent mortgage on the property. This is called a *refinancing* and was the pattern usually followed when interest rates were low and stable.

An alternative transaction is an *assumption*. In this transaction the buyer simply pays the owner the difference between the mortgage and the sales price and agrees to make the monthly payments on the mortgage being assumed. Suppose, for example, that there is a $70,000 mortgage on a house that the owner has advertised for sale at $100,000. The purchaser has available $30,000 in cash. If the transaction is refinanced, the purchaser places a new mortgage for, say, $75,000. The proceeds of that mortgage, and $25,000 of the purchaser's outside capital, are used to pay off the $70,000 mortgage and give the seller his $30,000 of equity. In an assumption, the buyer simply pays the owner his equity of $30,000 and also agrees to make the payments required on the $70,000 mortgage.

In the absence of an interest rate differential, both the purchaser and the seller will usually prefer that the existing mortgage be refinanced. The seller who signed the original note for the existing mortgage usually wants the purchaser to refinance since the seller has a contingent liability on the original mortgage. In an assumption, the purchaser agrees to make the required payments on the assumed mortgage. If the purchaser defaults on this promise, the lender will go after the seller as the person who originally signed the note and who therefore remains personally liable on it. Purchasers often also prefer to refinance in the absence of an interest rate differential because an assumption transaction may be more difficult to work out and often requires simultaneous payments on two mortgages. If we assume, for example, that we are talking about a $100,000 purchase price, and there is an outstanding first mortgage with an unpaid balance of $60,000, somehow the purchaser must come up with $40,000 to make up the difference. If the purchaser were to refinance the mortgage, he or she could presumably get an 80 percent mortgage and thus would have to come up with only $20,000 in cash. If the purchaser wishes to assume the existing mortgage but has only $20,000 in cash, he or she will have to take out a second mortgage for $20,000 and will end up making two monthly payments rather than one for a period of several years. Payments on two mortgages totalling $80,000 will usually be significantly higher than the payment on one mortgage for $80,000 because: (1) the interest rate on a second mortgage is higher because of the greater risk, (2) the purchaser will be amortizing the principal of two mortgages simultaneously, and (3) second mortgages usually mature within a shorter period, requiring larger principal payments to amortize the unpaid balance.

Another factor sometimes affecting the decision whether or not to refinance an existing mortgage is differences in closing costs. Many lending institutions impose *prepayment penalties* for an early retirement of the mortgage. This penalty, usually fixed at 1 or 2 percent of the unpaid balance, is nominally a charge for the cost of repaying prematurely the loan and redeploying the funds into another mortgage; in fact, prepayment penalties are simply another way of modestly increasing the profitability of the lending business since in periods of stable interest rates, most mortgages are refinanced when properties are sold and relatively few of them continue in existence for the full term of 25 or 30 years. Prepayment penalties, of course, tend to encourage assumptions, other things being equal.

Where a loan is to be refinanced, the lender who made the original loan may be willing to refinance the transaction charging no prepayment penalty, lower closing costs, and possibly some small reduction in interest rates, over what would be charged if a new loan were made by a third party.

If the purchaser is to take over the seller's mortgage, there are two alternative forms that the transaction may take. The most common is for the purchaser to *assume and agree to pay* the mortgage. The other is for the purchaser to *take subject to* the mortgage. If the purchaser takes subject to the mortgage, the purchaser thereafter makes the payments on the seller's mortgage but is not personally liable on it. The purchaser has not promised the lender to make the monthly payments or pay the amount of the loan. Such a purchaser, theoretically at least, is free to walk away and abandon the property at any time; the incentive to remain and make the payments arises from the fact that he or she will lose whatever cash payment and mortgage reductions made before the mortgage is foreclosed. The seller, of course, remains personally liable on the loan, a disagreeable fact that the seller may regret if economic conditions change dramatically and the purchaser in fact exercises his privilege and "walks."

Alternatively, if the seller requires the purchaser to assume and agree to pay the mortgage, the purchaser makes a promise to the seller that he or she will make all the payments the seller is obligated to make, and if he or she fails to do so, becomes personally liable to the seller. The original lender may also have the right to sue on the purchaser's promise to assume the mortgage on a theory of third-party beneficiary, though as a practical matter this question does not come up very often. The seller who originally signed the note, of course, remains personally liable on the loan, but the seller has some protection if the purchaser walks, because the purchaser is liable on the mortgage and can be sued by the seller if he or she is compelled to pay it. On the other hand, this right to sue may not be very valuable if, as is often the case, the purchaser walked because he or she was unable to keep up the payments.

Considering the exposure of the seller in both subject to and assumption transactions, it might seem plausible for the seller to request the lender to accept the new purchaser in his or her place and release the seller from his or her obligation on the mortgage. This type of transaction is usually called a *novation* since it constitutes the substitution of one debtor for another with the consent of the creditor. Most commerical lenders simply refuse to even consider accepting a novation or releasing the original borrower from that obligation. This position is understandable because there is no benefit to the lender in releasing anyone, and in any event the lender usually prefers that the loan be refinanced so that it can collect the prepayment penalty and current market interest rates. Certainly the lender will not consider releasing the original borrower if the purchaser of the property does not appear to be as creditworthy as that borrower.

Assuming that the seller does not approach the lender for a novation, in both assumption and subject to transactions, the lender is usually unaware that the property has been sold and that some new person is making payments on the mortgage. One might think that it would learn of the transaction because it suddenly starts receiving checks from a different payee; most lenders, however, are large bureaucratic organizations that are concerned about receiving a payment but pay no attention to its source. A lender is more likely to learn of the transaction when it receives an inquiry from the purchaser who explains during the course of the conversation that he or she is now making the payments on the outstanding mortgage.

§4.19 Restrictions on Mortgage Assumptions

The increase in interest rates that occurred in the late 1970s greatly changed the dynamics of refinancing and assumptions. Lenders who were often indifferent to the identity of the person making the payments when interest rates were stable, became much more sensitive about trafficking in mortgages that carried less than market interest rates and began to insist whenever they could that outstanding mortgages should be refinanced when the property was sold. A refinancing, of course, would be at current market rates. During this period, many savings and loan associations were losing money hand-over-fist: In order to attract funds in an increasingly competitive capital market, they were forced to pay investors market rates of interest that were sometimes as high as 14 or 15 percent, while at the same time they were receiving 1960s level interest rates of 6 percent or so on their old fixed-rate mortgages. Compulsory refinancing of these older mortgages became a matter of survival rather than profitability to many associations.

Whether or not the lender's approval of an assumption or subject to transaction is required depends at least initially on the terms of the mortgage. Many older form mortgages conditioned an assumption of the mortgage on the consent of the lender, a provision that apparently had been included to ensure protection of the security in some vague way. Some mortgage forms contained specific and express clauses automatically accelerating the entire unpaid portion of the loan on any sale of the property (a so-called *due-on-sale* clause). Lenders quickly began to use these clauses to try to persuade the purchaser and seller to refinance, or at least to agree to raise the interest rate on the mortgage being assumed toward current market levels. In other words, these clauses were often not used as a total veto of any assumption or a mandatory refinancing, but rather were used as a lever to increase the effective interest on the mortgage. The screams of anger by both purchaser and seller as they saw the asset of the below-market interest rate loan disappear could be clearly heard throughout the country and such clauses rapidly became a political issue in many states. Several states prohibited such clauses either by legislation or by judicial decision but they are permitted by federal law in connection with federally insured mortgages, and the Supreme Court held that state legislation prohibiting such clauses was preempted by the federal rule under the Supremacy Clause.

Of course, it is one thing to include a due-on-sale or consent-to-assignment clause in a mortgage: It is quite another to locate the transactions when both parties realize the importance of not calling the attention of the lending agency to an assignment. At one time, some lending agencies were scrutinizing recent filings in the land records in an effort to locate unapproved assumptions. Further, even when a transaction in violation of such a clause was discovered, the lender often found it difficult to compel the unwilling parties to recognize the rights of the lender. Litigation is costly, and courts and juries are seldom sympathetic with the lender's claim that even though they are receiving promptly each payment when it is due, they are entitled to negotiate considerably higher payments because the parties did not obtain the consent of the lender as required by the boiler-plate language of the mortgage.

The issues discussed in this section arise almost exclusively in connection with fixed-interest-rate mortgages. They are unlikely to be a problem with the alternative mortgage instruments discussed in §4.16.

§4.20 Techniques of Creative Financing

The purpose of creative financing is to enable the purchaser, with the cooperation and assistance of the seller, to buy a residence that the purchaser could not afford using the traditional technique of conventional mortgage financing. With the decline in mortgage interest rates since the early 1980s, these techniques have become less widely used, though they are well understood in the real estate financial community and may be used in specific situations.

Perhaps the simplest form of creative financing involves situations in which there is no first mortgage or the unpaid balance of the outstanding first mortgage is so small that the seller can use the down payment to pay it off. Under these circumstances, the seller may make a first mortgage loan himself or herself, typically at an interest rate or on terms that are more favorable to the purchaser than terms that would be available from commercial real estate loan sources. A first mortgage loan may be salable in the market for real estate mortgages, but typically the specially negotiated terms of a creatively financed mortgage makes the loan unattractive as a commercial investment. Hence this technique is usually practical only where the seller is willing to hold the mortgage for a substantial period of time. Of course, the seller then has to find a place to live (or own a second home that he can move into). Whether or not the seller comes out ahead in following this strategy depends on a host of unknowable and unpredictable factors: the terms of the new first mortgage, future changes in interest rates while the seller owns the mortgage, the strength of the market for outstanding first liens on real estate in the community, and, if the purchaser decides to resell the property, what terms can be worked out for the resale. One suspects that in most situations, the seller ends up losing if he or she agrees to take a privately negotiated first mortgage, though the loss may be mitigated if interest market rates thereafter decline.

Somewhat similar is a short-term first mortgage, which serves as a stopgap for the seller and reflects the willingness of the purchaser to live dangerously. When the purchaser is unable to come up with acceptable traditional financing, the seller may offer to carry a first lien on the property on an interest-only basis for a short time, perhaps two years. This mortgage may be for 80 percent or more of the agreed sales price with the seller paying cash for the balance. It is understood that the purchaser will either find acceptable permanent financing in the interim or resell the property. The purchaser is living dangerously, since he or she is gambling on being able to either resell the property on favorable terms or work out acceptable financing in two years when it is not possible today. If neither alternative is feasible, a default on the short-term loan is inevitable, and the purchaser has lost all the cash invested in the property. The seller, of course, gets the property back, but his or her disappointment is assuaged by the down payment made by the purchaser, which the seller retains.

A much more common type of creative financing is for the purchaser to assume (or take subject to) the below-market-rate first mortgage and for the seller to agree to accept a second mortgage for a short term. Assume, for example, that the parties have agreed upon a price of $100,000 for a residence on which there is a first mortgage that has a current balance of $40,000, payable at the rate of $350 per month, PI, at 9 percent interest. This mortgage was placed on the property eight years earlier to secure a $43,500 loan taken out by the present seller. Current market interest rates are 15 percent per year. The purchaser has $20,000 for the down payment but cannot afford to pay $1,011 per month PI on a conventional $80,000 mortgage. If the first mortgage can be assumed or transferred, the seller may offer to take back a $40,000 second mortgage, also at 9 percent, over 10 years. The payments on this second mortgage are $507 per month, which when added to the $350 first mortgage payment, total $857 per month, a monthly payment that is feasible. A number of variations may occur at this point. The seller may agree to accept interest-only payments for the second mortgage, in effect making it a long-term balloon note, or seek a shorter term for repayment, or a higher interest rate, offset by smaller payments in earlier years. These variations are unpredictable because the terms are entirely the subject of negotiation between two private persons who may reach whatever terms they find mutually acceptable.

If the first mortgage is not assumable and the purchaser must obtain a 15 percent, current-market-rate mortgage, the seller may agree to buy down the purchaser's monthly payments of $1,011 by agreeing to pay points or to contribute a portion of the purchase price to an escrow held by the lender. Presumably, either the points or the contribution are in effect added to the sales price of the residence. These techniques are sometimes called equity sharing. This arrangement is a PAM. See §4.16.

Lease-purchase option arrangements may also be used as creative financing devices. A purchaser faced with unacceptable market interest rates may lease a residence for a period of one or two years with an option to buy. The parties agree that the option to buy at a price set forth in the lease will be exercised; indeed, the purchaser may contractually commit to exercising the option. Even though the formal arrangement is landlord/tenant the parties view it as purchaser/seller. The purchaser may be required to pay a substantial sum for this option, a payment that will be lost if he or she does not complete the purchase. The lease payments in part, as well as the option payment in full, may be credited by the purchaser against the purchase price when the option is exercised. The amount of the lease payments before the option is exercised are usually affected by the size of the outstanding mortgage being carried by the seller as well by the fact that interest and taxes are deductible for federal income tax purposes by the seller during the term of the lease while the payments of "rent" are not deductible by the purchaser.

Creative residential financing also may involve obtaining multiple mortgages on the property in order to finance its acquisition. The techniques are similar to those used with commercial real estate, but there are substantial differences in effect, which may be traced to the difference between a potential open-ended cash flow in the case of commercial real estate, and a much more limited income potential for most purchasers of residential real estate. A not entirely hypothetical case may help to make this difference clear. In 1973 a law school teacher had accepted the position of a senior government bureaucrat in Washington, D.C., a notoriously expensive area for residential real estate. He had six or seven children and a government salary of $47,000. He obviously needed a large and expensive house. In 1974, he bought a $175,000 house in a Washington suburb, substantially on the following basis: (1) A down payment of $20,000 and an $80,000 first mortgage by a savings and loan association for 30 years at 9½ percent, with a monthly payment PI of $672; (2) A second mortgage for $25,000 repayable over 10 years, interest (11 percent) only for 5 years, with the principal to be paid in equal installments over 5 years. The lender was an unregulated commercial lending corporation. For five years the payment was $229 per month; thereafter the payments would jump to $543 per month; (3) A third mortgage for $50,000 was held by the seller on terms of 12 percent per year, payable at the rate of $100 principal per month for five years followed by a single balloon payment of $44,000. For five years the monthly payment on this mortgage was $600 per month ($500 per month interest plus $100 principal).

When the monthly payments were added up, the bureaucrat's housing costs were $1,500 per month, PI, or $1,900 per month, PITI. Approximately 42 percent of his salary was spent on housing. He actually had a modest amount of outside income so that his housing costs were about 35 percent of his actual income. Since virtually all of his monthly payments in the first few years constituted interest that was deductible on his federal income tax return, Uncle Sam assisted him significantly. But what would happen at the end of five years when $44,000 cash must be raised to pay off the third mortgage? The answer is simple: There is no way the bureaucrat could afford to live in the house after the fifth year. At the time he decided to buy the house, he knew he must resell or refinance it at the end of five years, if not before. If inflation continued in the Washington, D.C. area, the appreciation in the value of the house should permit him to meet his obligations without difficulty, and if he resold the house at that time, he might pay off all the obligations and have a profit besides which, presumably, would be invested in another, and potentially even larger, house. If prices continued to increase, he probably could refinance on more satisfactory terms in light of hoped-for governmental salary increases. What actually happened: Real estate values in the area continued to increase substantially, and after three years he resigned his government position, sold the house promptly for $205,000 and moved out of the Washington, D.C. area. His down payment for his next house had increased from $20,000 to about $35,000 as a result of living in Washington. Not too bad, in retrospect.

§4.21 Wraparound Mortgages

A *wraparound mortgage* is an assumption-related device that was originally designed for use in financing commercial real estate but turned out to be ideal for the quiet assumptions of mortgages on residential real estate as well. A wraparound mortgage sounds mysterious but is really not. It is described most easily by an example.

Assume that a residence is for sale for $120,000. There is presently a $70,000, 8 percent loan that has 28 years to run. Current mortgage rates are 12-13 percent for a new first mortgage. The purchaser has $25,000 in cash, which is enough for the required 20 percent down payment. If the property were refinanced with the purchaser paying the $25,000 down and taking a $96,000 mortgage for 30 years at 13 percent, the monthly payment would be $1,061.95, PI. That is more than the purchaser feels he or she can afford to pay on a monthly basis for housing. The purchaser therefore proposes that he or she assume the first mortgage and the seller carry a second mortgage of $26,000 for 10 years at 5 percent. The monthly payments on the first mortgage are $513.64 PI; the payment on the second mortgage is $275.77, for a total expected monthly PI payment of about $790. Seller responds by offering the purchaser a single wraparound mortgage of $96,000 at 9.5 percent over 30 years, with the seller continuing to be responsible for and making the payments on the $70,000 first mortgage. The payment on the wraparound is $807, roughly what the purchaser is willing to pay. The wraparound mortgage is a junior lien, since the first mortgage remains unaffected with payments continued to be made by the seller. Everyone but the lender benefits from this arrangement. The purchaser has bought the desired residence for a down payment and monthly payment that he or she can afford. The seller receives the $24,000 down payment in cash as well as the right to receive $807 per month, out of which $513 per month must be taken to make the payments on the "wrapped-around" first mortgage. After making this payment, he or she keeps $287 per month. This is a 13 percent return on the $26,000 actually borrowed by the purchaser from the seller.

The reason a wraparound is attractive financially to the seller is that the purchaser is in effect paying the seller 9.5 percent interest on the $70,000 mortgage which is actually costing the seller 8 percent. The extra 1.5 percent on this amount results in the dramatic increase in the effective interest rate on the portion of the purchase price being financed by the seller. It is analogous to leverage obtained through the borrowing of working capital by a business. The difference between the 9.5 percent wraparound rate and the 8 percent rate of the first mortgage is usually referred to as the *spread*.

Two further comments are appropriate. First, in a wraparound, the seller remains involved with the property and is not out cleanly. Second, the wraparound mortgage cannot be readily sold in the open market, since it is a second mortgage at less than current market rates of interest for such mortgages.

The wraparound concept violates due on sale clauses but may not violate prohibitions against assignment of the mortgage, since the transaction does not technically involve an assignment of the first mortgage.

CHAPTER 5

COMMERCIAL ANNUITIES AND RETIREMENT PLANS

§5.1 Introduction

A stream of payments payable at specified intervals in the future is called an *annuity*. Annuities significantly affect the lives of most persons in the United States at some time, even though many persons have never seen the word and may not know what it means. Rather, annuities are better known as pensions, retirement benefits, or in-service benefits. Modern annuities form an essential part of retirement plans for employed and self-employed persons, often supplementing social security and related public benefit programs. Almost all of these modern annuities arise directly from the employment relationship and constitute a type of deferred compensation for personal services. They may be referred to in employment manuals or brochures as fringe benefits of employment.

This chapter introduces the real-world modern annuity in a logical but indirect way, dealing first with simple and somewhat artificial examples, and then progressing to present-day retirement annuities.

§5.2 Commercial Annuities in General

Some annuities are actually purchased in the marketplace, usually from life insurance companies. If payments are of fixed amounts for a fixed period, the determination of the present values of such payments is a straightforward application of the time value of money, that is, the principle of discounting future payments to present values, applying an appropriate discount rate to each payment to determine the present value of each payment and then adding up those present values. This subject was introduced in §2.4, and an actual example is given in §5.3.

Most commercial annuities are designed not to make payments for a fixed period but rather to continue for the lifetime of one or more persons. The pricing of such annuities requires an estimate of the probable life-spans involved, which in turn involves reliance on mortality or life expectancy tables.

Indeed, if the word annuity conjures up any image at all to the average person, it is probably to an elderly person receiving a payment each month for the balance of his or her life. Mortality and life expectancy tables are discussed briefly in §6.5. To an increasing extent, modern retirement programs utilize commercial annuities, usually by the purchase of a lifetime annuity shortly before the retirement of the employee. An annuity for the life of a person is in a sense the converse of life insurance on the life of that person: The annuity pays for the lifetime of the person and ends upon his or her death, while life insurance becomes due and payable on death and provides for the period following the death of the person.

In the discussion of commercial annuities below, the person creating the annuity is often referred to as the *creator* or the *contributor*. The person receiving the annuity is referred to as the *annuitant*; the annuitant and the contributor can, of course, be the same person. The person or entity agreeing to make the payments is referred to as the *seller* or *writer* of the annuity: Often the seller of an annuity is a life insurance company that is also in the business of selling annuities.

§5.3 Single-Premium Fixed Annuities

It is easiest to begin with a specific example of the simplest kind of annuity that does not involve any mortality calculation. Your client, a rather well-to-do elderly widow, is considering the purchase of an annuity. For $100,000 cash paid to a large life insurance company, the company will agree to pay her, or her estate, $1,200 per month each year for ten years. The $100,000 represents the bulk of her current liquid resources: It may have resulted from a lifetime of incremental saving, from life insurance proceeds on the life of her deceased spouse, or from a variety of other sources. The theory behind the ten-year provision is that in ten years she will begin receiving retirement income from other sources: social security payments and a lifetime annuity from an employee pension plan. The ten-year annuity is thus a stopgap. There is no gambling on the death of your client in this example; payments are guaranteed for ten years, whether or not your client is alive. If she dies within the ten years, the payments will continue to be made to her estate or to whom she directs in her will for the balance of the ten-year term. At the end of ten years, the obligation of the writer of the annuity ends.

It should be obvious in this example that each monthly payment received by your client consists partly of return of her principal and partly of interest earned on the balance of the money. Without taking into account the time value of money, it appears that she is investing $100,000 and receiving back a total of $144,000 ($1,200 per month times 120 months). However, the discussion in Chapter 2 should make clear the fallacy of that approach. The reason that this is economic from the standpoint of the life insurance company is that each month it is earning interest on that portion of the $100,000 that it has not yet repaid to your client. In other words, each payment except for the last has an interest component as well as a return of principal component. A computation (difficult with pencil and paper but easy with a preprogrammed handheld calculator) reveals that your client is actually receiving a 7.75 percent return on her $100,000 investment over ten years. In other words, the sum of the present values of the 120 payments of $1,200 each computed at 7.75 percent is almost precisely $100,000. Mathematically, at 7.75 percent, the first monthly payment of $1,200 (the first annuity payment) constitutes $645.83 of interest on the $100,000 and $554.17 return of principal. The second payment consists of $642.25 of interest (one month's interest on $99,445.83 ($100,000 − $554.17)) and $557.75 return of principal; the third payment consists of $638.65 of interest (one month's interest on $98,887.88 (99,445.83 − 557.75)) and $561.35 of principal. And so on, for each of the remaining payments until the last $1,200 payment, which consists almost entirely of principal and finally exhausts the original $100,000 of principal. In each month the remaining principal is calculated by subtracting the amount of principal repaid the previous month. (If these figures look vaguely familiar, compare the analysis of the conventional level-premium mortgage in §3.8. From the mortgagee's perspective, an "annuity" is being received from the mortgagor.)

If the current market rate for riskless investments is 9 percent at the time of the proposed purchase, this annuity at first glance does not appear to be a very attractive deal. Your client would apparently be better off simply investing the money in a federally insured bank account at the higher market interest rate of 9 percent, and withdrawing each month the accumulated interest and a portion of principal necessary to yield her $1,200 each month. In the discussion below this will be referred as a "do-it-yourself annuity." The economic difference between the life insurance company's product and the do-it-yourself variety of annuity in this example can be made graphic by considering the composition of the first few payments. If the same amount were invested at 9 percent, the first month's interest would have been $750, and only $450 would have had to be drawn from principal to make the $1,200 payment. The life insurance company only gave your client credit for interest of $645.83 and repaid her $554.17 from her principal. At 9 percent the interest for the second month would be $746.63 and the amount of principal that would would have to be drawn out would be $453.38. Corresponding figures for the life insurance company annuity are $642.25 of principal and $557.75 of interest. In each month thereafter the performance of the do-it-yourself annuity is superior, reflecting the fact that the dollars are invested at a 9 percent annual rate rather than at a 7.75 percent annual rate. At the end of the ten-year pay-out period, the bank account would still have $12,918 in it while the commercial annuity would have been exhausted.

Why might a person be interested in buying a commercial annuity at apparently disadvantageous terms rather than simply investing the money in a bank? There are several possible advantages. For one thing, there is a certain amount of convenience in simply receiving a check each month, rather than going down to the bank and withdrawing $1,200 each month. There is also the matter of self-discipline. Does your client have the mental resolve to follow the routine each month without taking out "a little extra, just this time"? Third, an elderly person with a large bank account may be defrauded by a smooth-talking swindler; investment of funds in an annuity provides protection to the annuitant against such unwise dissipations of assets. These factors may not appear to be of great importance in this simple example, but in individual cases they may well justify the decision to purchase a commercial annuity rather than to simply turn over a large sum of money to a beneficiary who must rely on that sum over a long period of time to provide his or her livelihood.

A much more substantial advantage of the life insurance company annuity from the standpoint of your client is that the return of 7.5 percent is guaranteed for the next ten years; someone opening the bank account implicitly assumes that the 9 percent market rate will remain stable for that period, obviously a very dubious assumption. If the market rate of interest were to drop to 6 percent a year after the annuity arrangement was created, your client would have been considerably worse off electing to "do-it-herself." Correspondingly, if interest rates go up, the life insurance company gets fat from investing your client's funds at 15 percent, say, while continuing to make fixed payments at a rate of 7.75 percent. It obviously suffers if interest rates drop and the insurance company earns 5 percent on invested funds while being required to pay your client 7.75 percent. In effect, the insurance company takes the risk of market fluctuations in the interest rate. It is able to do this profitably because it can diversify against this risk since it enters into many different arrangements and many different investments of varying maturities and varying yields at different times. It probably would be difficult or impossible for your client to find a riskless 10-year investment that would be guaranteed to continue to pay 9 percent and would also permit monthly withdrawals. In a word, the insurance company provides an important service in packaging the investment to meet your client's needs.

A countervailing factor is the possibility of insolvency: The do-it-yourself annuity is invested in insured savings accounts, but the right of your client to receive payments from the insurance company under the commercial annuity is not secured in any way and is dependent on the continued solvency of the insurance company. This may seem to be theoretical because life insurance companies rarely go under, but in the early 1980s one major company writing single-premium annuities became insolvent after it had promised annuity payments at higher interest rates than it could maintain.

A second countervailing factor to consider is the possibility that your client may become ill and need a significant portion of her principal back immediately rather than in bits of $1,200 per month. This, of course, is not a problem with the do-it-youself annuity. Most commercial single-premium annuities allow cancellation of the annuity and a refund of most of the remaining unpaid principal. While cancellation may be relatively expensive, it at least permits most financial emergencies to be met.

A fixed-return annuity can provide a considerable amount of convenience and security at the cost of some loss of yield. One way of looking at this transaction is that for a premium of 1¼ percent, the insurance company is assuming the administrative costs of handling the transaction as well as the risk that interest rates may decline during the next ten years.

Other legal devices exist that may be a substitute for a commercial single-premium annuity. For example, you might consider creating an inter vivos trust for the benefit of your client that would invest and disburse the $100,000. The relatively small amount involved, however, and attendant fees and expenses probably would make this alternative unattractive.

§5.4 Single-Premium Deferred Annuities

The example set forth in the preceding section is not typical of most modern single-premium annuity transactions, since the annuity commences immediately following the payment. Much more representative is a single-premium annuity that does not begin to involve payments to the contributor/annuitant for a period of years.

Assume that a contributor makes a single, lump sum payment of $100,000 when he is 35 years old, for an annuity commencing at age 65. In effect this person is seeking to fund or supplement his or her retirement by making a long-term investment. Originally, most annuities of this type provided a fixed dollar return beginning at the age of 65. In other words, both the interest rate being paid on the $100,000 contribution over the 30 years before the first payment comes due and the interest rate that determines the amount of the annuity to be paid each month thereafter are in effect set forth in the original contract. Typically, a series of elections is provided so that before the annuitant reaches the age at which the first payment is due to be made, he or she could select a *payment option*. Typical options are payments for the balance of the contributor's life, for the lives of the contributor and his or her spouse, or for the contributor's life with a guaranteed period of payments in the event he or she dies shortly after retirement.

The growth that naturally occurs over the 30-year period between the time the annuity is purchased and the time the first payment is due is called the *buildup*. Mathematically, the buildup over 30 years on $100,000 is very substantial: If the insurance company agrees to pay 4 percent per year, the amount available at age 65 would be $331,349.80; at 6 percent, it is $602,257.22; and at 8 percent, $1,093,572.96. Thus, if the contributor can afford to put aside a substantial sum at a relatively young age, there is quite a pot at the end of the rainbow.

Thirty years is of course a long time. A similar investment over ten years shows results that are not as spectacular, but are still substantial. A $100,000 investment made at age 55 with payments to begin in ten years grows to $149,083.27 at 4 percent; to $181,939.67 at 6 percent; and to $221,964.02, at 8 percent.

§5.5 The Concept of Tax Deferral

In §5.3, a commercial annuity was compared with a do-it-yourself annuity providing essentially the same benefits. The do-it-yourself possibility, while viable for a single-premium annuity with payments to commence immediately, is not attractive when compared with a deferred annuity such as the one described in §5.4. The reason for this is the difference in the income tax treatment of an annuity on the one hand and a savings account on the other.

If our hypothetical 35-year old in §5.4 were to try to create a do-it-yourself annuity, he would presumably create a savings account and deposit $100,000 in it, planning to allow it to accumulate for 30 years. However, he would have to pay income taxes each year on the interest earned on that account, whether

107

or not any amount was withdrawn from the account. Assuming that the creator was in the 28 percent bracket, the interest income each year would have to be reduced by 28 percent in evaluating the benefits of a do-it-yourself annuity. As a practical matter, if the contributor created a do-it-yourself annuity, it is likely that he would not actually reduce the account by the 28 percent tax but would simply pay the taxes out of other earnings or other assets, allowing the account to grow unchecked or unconstrained. But it should be obvious that from a total net worth standpoint these tax payments must be viewed as part of the cost of the do-it-yourself alternative since the interest on the commercial annuity is not taxed as it is earned.

In the case of the commercial annuity, no income tax is due from the contributor on the interest on the savings until that person actually begins to receive the annuity payments at age 65. In other words, a deferred annuity offers tax deferral whereas the savings account does not. Because of the 28 percent tax rate differential, an 8 percent do-it-yourself deferred annuity accumulates at about the same rate as a 6 percent commercial deferred annuity. This advantage, however, is not permanent. The tax deferral under the annuity continues only during the period of the buildup. Once payments on the annuity commence, a significant portion of each payment becomes subject to income tax. On the other hand, the person creating the do-it-yourself annuity has been paying taxes all along, and a much smaller proportion of each subsequent payment will be subject to tax.

The underlying concept of tax deferral (which applies to many different kinds of transactions) does not mean that the 30 years of buildup escapes tax forever. It is merely put off until the time the contributor receives his or her first payment under the annuity after reaching the age of 65. At that time, taxation of the buildup begins. Each payment under the annuity is viewed as having two different components: Part of the payment is a refund of a portion of the $100,000 contribution made by the contributor and part of the payment represents a distribution from the buildup. The first portion of each payment is viewed as a tax-free return of capital and the second portion is taxed as ordinary income. The ratio is called the *exclusion ratio* and the Internal Revenue Code and the regulations issued thereunder contain precise rules for calculating it. That ratio, however, is calculated only once at the time of the first payment and is thereafter applied to each payment. Assuming that the exclusion ratio is properly computed; all the contemplated payments are made as scheduled; the annuity is for the lifetime of the contributor; and he or she lives to his or her life expectancy, than the contributor ultimately pays income taxes on every dollar of the buildup.

A single-premium annuity with payments to commence immediately is taxed in precisely the same way as a deferred annuity. Thus even though the creator of the do-it-yourself annuity does not defer taxes during the buildup, an exclusion ratio is created to reflect the interest component earned after the annuity begins paying out.

Investors in commercial annuities gain tax deferral, not tax avoidance. Ultimately, the buildup is subject to tax; the only difference between it and the taxation of a do-it-yourself savings account is that the income is taxed immediately. Why is tax deferral so advantageous if — come the millenium — the contributor's tax position is unchanged? Basically, it comes down again to the time value of money. Where tax deferral is available, the contributor has the use of the funds otherwise needed to pay taxes in order to earn additional interest for an extended period. A dollar today is always worth more than a dollar in the future. A dollar not paid in tax today is worth more than the same dollar paid in tax in 30 years. For this reason alone, tax deferral is almost always advantageous. Furthermore, since the tax deferral in an annuity usually extends over several years, the buildup occurs at an accelerated rate since subsequent earnings on prior years' tax deferrals is also tax deferred. Tax deferral offers other possible advantages as well. For example, tax rates may be lower by the time the tax payments must begin than they were during the buildup. Because of the significant reductions in rates in the 1986 Tax Act, however, this is unlikely to be an important factor in the immediate future: Tax rates are now more likely to go up than to go down, particularly for high-income taxpayers. Another possible advantage is that after retirement, persons may be in a lower tax bracket then they were when employed (though again this seems less likely to be important given the rate structure of the 1986 Tax Act), and thus the deferral may again result in the application of lower tax rates. These differences were obviously more important in earlier years than they are today following the 1986 Tax Act, but in some individual cases advantages remain. The tax rates applicable to income under the 1986 Tax Act are discussed in §12.10.

The favored tax deferral treatment of annuities is usually rationalized on the ground that Congress desires to encourage private savings and private arrangements to provide retirement income.

§5.6 Variable Annuities

The fixed-rate annuities described in the previous sections lost much of their attractiveness during the period of high interest rates in the late 1970s and early 1980s. Even with the advantage of tax deferral, an investment yielding perhaps 4 percent per year is unattractive when compared with riskless market investments yielding 12 or 14 percent per year, as was the case in the early 1980s. A person who has invested in such a fixed annuity will naturally seek to suspend or terminate the annuity, even at a sacrifice if necessary, in order to invest the remaining proceeds at the higher market interest rate. Secondly, the relatively high level of inflation during this period made fixed-rate annuities extremely unattractive: The contributor was making a payment with 1965 dollars, say, in order to receive an annuity of a fixed amount in deflated dollars starting in 1995. These two problems are related since higher inflation levels tend to cause higher interest rates; together they make any long-term, fixed-payment investment relatively unattractive.

There is no inherent reason why the company writing an annuity must create an interest rate and inflation gamble. The gamble arises from the decision to pay interest at a fixed rate established in advance. Why not let the company put all payments for future annuities into an investment fund and have the amount of the ultimate annuity depend on what the company actually earns from this fund? This proposal eliminates much of the gamble on interest rates that inevitably occurs whenever a long-term investment is made at a fixed interest rate. On the other hand, this arrangement makes retirement planning less precise because the amount of the ultimate annuity to be paid becomes expressly dependent on the investment success of the fund. Commercial annuities of this type are called *variable annuities*.

The earliest versions of variable annuities date back to the 1950s. They eliminated the fixed-return feature, but assumed that the premium would be invested in traditional fixed income investments. The "variable" feature resulted only from changes in yields of such fixed investments over the years. However, once the variable annuity concept is recognized, it is a relatively small additional step to relax the requirement that investments be in long-term interest-yielding investments: Any kind of equity or debt investment might be appropriate for the investment fund. Further, it is also only a relatively small additional step for the company to create several different funds with different investment goals, and permit the contributor to designate which fund or funds he or she would like the $100,000 to be placed in, and to permit changes in the investment mix from time to time. The final step in increasing flexibility is to allow contributors to borrow back a portion of their initial contribution whenever they want. Now that the amount of the ultimate annuity is not fixed but is dependent on investment results, such borrowing is essentially a matter of indifference to the issuer of the annuity. If the loan is never repaid, the annuity is simply reduced appropriately. If the loan is repaid, it reduces principal for the period it is outstanding, which reduces the amount of the buildup but does not affect the long-term obligation of the company.

At this point, it is useful to step back and look at what the annuity has become. The power to make decisions as to the investments to be made during the buildup period and the power to withdraw contributions makes the plan not terribly different from an income-producing bank deposit. Yet tax deferral is still available. During the 1970s, the Internal Revenue Service resisted the argument that such an account should be subject to deferred taxation as an annuity, but eventually the IRS lost that argument. As a result, the earnings are still tax deferred (since the transaction is cast in the form of an annuity), and human ingenuity has created an investment vehicle that competes with other savings plans but retains tax deferral. Needless to say, this type of investment quickly became very attractive in the early 1980s because of this feature.

Of course, there are administrative costs associated with all annuities. It has been estimated that the yearly administrative costs associated with the management of a variable annuity are about 2 percent of the contributions and buildup.

A successful tax-oriented device often leads to a legislative response in order to protect the federal revenue base. And so it has with variable annuities. In recognition of the tax avoidance motive that was becoming increasingly predominant in this type of investment, Congress during the 1980s tightened up the annuity rules significantly. Today, any borrowing from an annuity is viewed as being a distribution from the buildup rather than a loan out of the original contribution; other changes in the tax treatment of annuity payments themselves were also made to reduce further the attractiveness of deferred annuities from a tax standpoint. As a result, much of the bloom has gone from this rose.

§5.7 Multiple-Premium Annuities

Consider the situation of a 35-year-old person who lacks the resources to make the $100,000 investment described in an earlier section but who strongly feels that some provision should be made for retirement in 30 years. Commercial insurance companies have long offered annuity plans that are designed precisely to meet the needs of such a person. They involve monthly payment plans under which the contributor gradually builds up a nest egg; the payments accumulate and are converted into an annuity shortly before retirement.

Perhaps the person under discussion feels he or she can contribute $5,000 per year toward ultimate retirement. Traditionally, a fixed interest rate was involved, so that the amount accumulated after the 30 years of payments can be calculated mathematically. For simplicity, let us assume that each payment is made at the end of the year, that the person plans to retire at the end of the thirtieth year, that interest is compounded annually, and that the insurance company guarantees a 7 percent annual return. The value in 30 years of the stream of $5,000 payments is then equal to the future value of $5,000 over 30 years plus the future value of $5,000 over 29 years plus the future value of $5,000 over 28 years, and so forth. This calculation is made much simpler by the development of tables for the *future value* of annuities (which in effect is what is involved). Table 5-1 is such a table. To determine the amount that will be available in this example for the purchase of an annuity in 30 years, one need merely look in the 30 row and 7 percent column of Table 5-1. The number (94.4608) is simply multiplied by $5,000 to determine that the amount available for the retirement annuity will build up to $472,304 in 30 years. At today's prices that amount should yield a reasonably comfortable retirement.

Three important points should be made about the accumulation aspects of this kind of transaction. First, any kind of regular contribution made over a long period of time builds up to a large amount in absolute terms over 30 years. Whether or not this is considered advantageous, however, depends on what assumptions one makes about inflation over 30 years. If inflation remains low, a comfortable retirement may be expected; under the worst inflation scenarios, $472,304 may be only the cost of a haircut in the year 2020. Second, the interest rate that is used in the accumulation phase has an immense impact on the amount of the ultimate annuity. Third, if the build-up phase involves *monthly* payments and *monthly* compounding of interest (rather than annual payments and compounding, as in the previous hypothetical), the amount of the buildup is significantly increased. Do you see why?

This kind of annuity seems to be precisely the type envisioned by the Internal Revenue Code when it granted the advantages of tax deferral described in §5.4. The earnings from the investment of the $5,000 payments accumulate without taxation until the annuity becomes due; at that point an exclusion ratio is calculated and a portion of each payment is subject to taxation and a portion

Table 5-1
Future Value of a Stream of $1 Payments Made at the End of Each Period After n Periods

No. of periods	2%	3%	4%	5%	6%	7%	8%
1	1.0000	1.0000	1.0000	1.0000	1.0000	1.0000	1.0000
2	2.0200	2.0300	2.0400	2.0500	2.0600	2.0700	2.0800
3	3.0604	3.0909	3.1216	3.1525	3.1836	3.2149	3.2464
4	4.1216	4.1836	4.2465	4.3101	4.3746	4.4399	4.5061
5	5.2040	5.3091	5.4163	5.5256	5.6371	5.7507	5.8666
6	6.3081	6.4684	6.6330	6.8019	6.9753	7.1533	7.3359
7	7.4343	7.6625	7.8983	8.1420	8.3938	8.6540	8.9228
8	8.5830	8.8923	9.2142	9.5491	9.8975	10.2598	10.6366
9	9.7546	10.1591	10.5828	11.0266	11.4913	11.9780	12.4876
10	10.9497	11.4639	12.0061	12.5779	13.1808	13.8164	14.4866
11	12.1687	12.8078	13.4864	14.2068	14.9716	15.7836	16.6455
12	13.4121	14.1920	15.0258	15.9171	16.8699	17.8885	18.9771
13	14.6803	15.6178	16.6268	17.7130	18.8821	20.1406	21.4953
14	15.9739	17.0863	18.2919	19.5986	21.0151	22.5505	24.2149
15	17.2934	18.5989	20.0236	21.5786	23.2760	25.1290	27.1521
16	18.6393	20.1569	21.8245	23.6575	25.6725	27.8881	30.3243
17	20.0121	21.7616	23.6975	25.8404	28.2129	30.8402	33.7502
18	21.4123	23.4144	25.6454	28.1324	30.9057	33.9990	37.4502
19	22.8406	25.1169	27.6712	30.5390	33.7600	37.3790	41.4463
20	24.2974	26.8704	29.7781	33.0660	36.7856	40.9955	45.7620
21	25.7833	28.6765	31.9692	35.7193	39.9927	44.8652	50.4229
22	27.2990	30.5368	34.2480	38.5052	43.3923	49.0057	55.4568
23	28.8450	32.4529	36.6179	41.4305	46.9958	53.4361	60.8933
24	30.4219	34.4265	39.0826	44.5020	50.8156	58.1767	66.7648
25	32.0303	36.4593	41.6459	47.7271	54.8645	63.2490	73.1059

Table 5-1 (*cont.*)

Future Value of a Stream of $1 Payments Made at the End of Each Period After n Periods

No. of periods	2%	3%	4%	5%	6%	7%	8%
26	33.6709	38.5530	44.3117	51.1135	59.1564	68.6765	79.9544
27	35.3443	40.7096	47.0842	54.6691	63.7058	74.4838	87.3508
28	37.0512	42.9309	49.9676	58.4026	68.5281	80.6977	95.3388
29	38.7922	45.2189	52.9663	62.3227	73.6398	87.3465	103.9659
30	40.5681	47.5754	56.0849	66.4388	79.0582	94.4608	113.2832
31	42.3794	50.0027	59.3283	70.7608	84.8017	102.0730	123.3459
32	44.2270	52.5028	62.7015	75.2988	90.8898	110.2182	134.2135
33	46.1116	55.0778	66.2095	80.0638	97.3432	118.9334	145.9506
34	48.0338	57.7302	69.8579	85.0670	104.1838	128.2588	158.6267
35	49.9945	60.4621	73.6522	90.3203	111.4348	138.2369	172.3168
36	51.9944	63.2759	77.5983	95.8363	119.1209	148.9135	187.1021
37	54.0343	66.1742	81.7022	101.6281	127.2681	160.3374	203.0703
38	56.1149	69.1594	85.9703	107.7095	135.9042	172.5610	220.3159
39	58.2372	72.2342	90.4091	114.0950	145.0585	185.6403	238.9412
40	60.4020	75.4013	95.0255	120.7998	154.7620	199.6351	259.0565
41	62.6100	78.6633	99.8265	127.8398	165.0477	214.6096	280.7810
42	64.8622	82.0232	104.8196	135.2318	175.9505	230.6322	304.2435
43	67.1595	85.4839	110.0124	142.9933	187.5076	247.7765	329.5830
44	69.5027	89.0484	115.4129	151.1430	199.7580	266.1209	356.9496
45	71.8927	92.7199	121.0294	159.7002	212.7435	285.7493	386.5056
46	74.3306	96.5015	126.8706	168.6852	226.5081	306.7518	418.4261
47	76.8172	100.3965	132.9454	178.1194	241.0986	329.2244	452.9002
48	79.3535	104.4084	139.2632	188.0254	256.5645	353.2701	490.1322
49	81.9406	108.5406	145.8337	198.4267	272.9584	378.9990	530.3427
50	84.5794	112.7969	152.6671	209.3480	290.3359	406.5289	573.7702

Table 5-1 (cont.)
Future Value of a Stream of $1 Payments Made at the End of Each Period After n Periods

No. of periods	9%	10%	11%	12%	13%	14%	15%
1	1.0000	1.0000	1.0000	1.0000	1.0000	1.0000	1.0000
2	2.0900	2.1000	2.1100	2.1200	2.1300	2.1400	2.1500
3	3.2781	3.3100	3.3421	3.3744	3.4069	3.4396	3.4725
4	4.5731	4.6410	4.7097	4.7793	4.8498	4.9211	4.9934
5	5.9847	6.1051	6.2278	6.3528	6.4803	6.6101	6.7424
6	7.5233	7.7156	7.9129	8.1152	8.3227	8.5355	8.7537
7	9.2004	9.4872	9.7833	10.0890	10.4047	10.7305	11.0668
8	11.0285	11.4359	11.8594	12.2997	12.7573	13.2328	13.7268
9	13.0210	13.5795	14.1640	14.7757	15.4157	16.0853	16.7858
10	15.1929	15.9374	16.7220	17.5487	18.4197	19.3373	20.3037
11	17.5603	18.5312	19.5614	20.6546	21.8143	23.0445	24.3493
12	20.1407	21.3834	22.7132	24.1331	25.6502	27.2707	29.0017
13	22.9534	24.5227	26.2116	28.0291	29.9847	32.0887	34.3519
14	26.0192	27.9750	30.0949	32.3926	34.8827	37.5811	40.5047
15	29.3609	31.7725	34.4054	37.2797	40.4175	43.8424	47.5804
16	33.0034	35.9497	39.1899	42.7533	46.6717	50.9804	55.7175
17	36.9737	40.5447	44.5008	48.8837	53.7391	59.1176	65.0751
18	41.3013	45.5992	50.3959	55.7497	61.7251	68.3941	75.8364
19	46.0185	51.1591	56.9395	63.4397	70.7494	78.9692	88.2118
20	51.1601	57.2750	64.2028	72.0524	80.9468	91.0249	102.4436
21	56.7645	64.0025	72.2651	81.6987	92.4699	104.7684	118.8101
22	62.8733	71.4027	81.2143	92.5026	105.4910	120.4360	137.6316
23	69.5319	79.5430	91.1479	104.6029	120.2048	138.2970	159.2764
24	76.7898	88.4973	102.1742	118.1552	136.8315	158.6586	184.1678
25	84.7009	98.3471	114.4133	133.3339	155.6196	181.8708	212.7930

Table 5-1 *(cont.)*

Future Value of a Stream of $1 Payments Made at the End of Each Period After n Periods

No. of periods	9%	10%	11%	12%	13%	14%	15%
26	93.3240	109.1818	127.9988	150.3339	176.8501	208.3327	245.7120
27	102.7231	121.0999	143.0786	169.3740	200.8406	238.4993	283.5688
28	112.9682	134.2099	159.8173	190.6989	227.9499	272.8892	327.1041
29	124.1354	148.6309	178.3972	214.5828	258.5834	312.0937	377.1697
30	136.3075	164.4940	199.0209	241.3327	293.1992	356.7868	434.7451
31	149.5752	181.9434	221.9132	271.2926	332.3151	407.7370	500.9569
32	164.0370	201.1378	247.3236	304.8477	376.5161	465.8202	577.1005
33	179.8003	222.2515	275.5292	342.4294	426.4632	532.0350	664.6655
34	196.9823	245.4767	306.8374	384.5210	482.9034	607.5199	765.3654
35	215.7108	271.0244	341.5896	431.6635	546.6808	693.5727	881.1702
36	236.1247	299.1268	380.1644	484.4631	618.7493	791.6729	1014.3457
37	258.3759	330.0395	422.9825	543.5987	700.1867	903.5071	1167.4975
38	282.6298	364.0434	470.5106	609.8305	792.2110	1030.9981	1343.6222
39	309.0665	401.4478	523.2667	684.0102	896.1984	1176.3378	1546.1655
40	337.8824	442.5926	581.8261	767.0914	1013.7042	1342.0251	1779.0903
41	369.2919	487.8518	646.8269	860.1424	1146.4858	1530.9086	2046.9539
42	403.5281	537.6370	718.9779	964.3595	1296.5289	1746.2358	2354.9969
43	440.8457	592.4007	799.0655	1081.0826	1466.0777	1991.7088	2709.2465
44	481.5218	652.6408	887.9627	1211.8125	1657.6678	2271.5481	3116.6334
45	525.8587	718.9048	986.6386	1358.2300	1874.1646	2590.5648	3585.1285
46	574.1860	791.7953	1096.1688	1522.2176	2118.8060	2954.2439	4123.8977
47	626.8628	871.9749	1217.7474	1705.8838	2395.2508	3368.8380	4743.4824
48	684.2804	960.1723	1352.6996	1911.5898	2707.6334	3841.4753	5456.0047
49	746.8656	1057.1896	1502.4965	2141.9806	3060.6258	4380.2819	6275.4055
50	815.0836	1163.9085	1668.7712	2400.0182	3459.5071	4994.5213	7217.7163

is excluded as a return of capital. In calculating this ratio the capital invested is the total amount contributed without adjustment for the time value of money — 30 payments of $5,000 each.

For the reasons set forth in the preceding section, the fixed interest rate is not an essential aspect of the multiple-premium annuity. The multiple-payment annuity can readily be a variable annuity dependent on the investment results obtained through actual experience in the manner described in the previous section. Indeed, variable annuity plans usually permit contributors to make discretionary payments from time to time.

This example involves a tax deferred annuity but the tax advantages of this plan are not as attractive as the tax benefits available through the device of retirement plans, discussed in §5.8.

§5.8 Employee Retirement Plans: Before-Tax and After-Tax Dollars

The preceding section considered an example in which a person agreed to make annual payments of $5,000 per year to fund a retirement annuity. It was implicitly assumed that the payments would be made voluntarily each year, presumably by a check drawn on the contributor's available funds. Such a plan has some of the disadvantages of a do-it-yourself annuity in that payments require a degree of mental discipline and willpower on the part of the contributor. It also suffers, however, from a more fundamental problem.

Let us assume — as will usually be the case — that the contributor plans to make the payments out of his or her current earnings from employment. This plan is financed with after-tax dollars. This means simply that the contributor must pay income tax on the dollars he or she earns, and then must make the contribution to fund the annuity out of the dollars that remain. In other words, if the employee is in the 28 percent bracket, each dollar earned only leads to a $0.72 contribution to the retirement plan.

If the contributor's employer has created a pension or profit sharing plan that meets the requirements of the federal Employee Retirement Income Security Act (ERISA) and the Internal Revenue Code, contributions may be made by the employer directly for the employee's retirement program *without the contributions being included in the employee's tax return and without affecting the deductibility of the contributions from the standpoint of the employer*. A plan that meets the requirements of these federal statutes is referred to as a *qualified* plan. Such a plan provides for a much greater degree of tax deferral than the plan financed with after-tax dollars, since no tax is imposed on either the employer's contribution, or on the buildup from such contributions, until the employee retires (or in some circumstances, leaves the employer's employment). At the same time, the employer continues to deduct currently on its federal income tax return the gross amount of salary paid to the employee plus the amounts contributed by the employer for his or her benefit to the qualified plan.

A qualified plan requires that the employer in some way physically set aside the funds to be used for retirement purposes. Usually the employer makes contributions directly to a trust or other entity which invests the funds for the benefit of employees, and, upon their retirement, the fund may either pay annuity benefits directly or may purchase a commercial retirement annuity for the employee. Some employers may take advantage of a simplified plan that does not require the creation of a separate trust but provides direct payments for employees' commercial retirement annuities.

In some qualified plans, the employee is required to make a contribution as well as the employer; in others, the employer funds the entire plan. The former is called, logically enough, a *contributory* plan, the latter, a *noncontributory* plan. If the plan is a contributory plan, the portion contributed by the employee is usually with after-tax dollars and the portion contributed by the employer is with before-tax dollars. Employees in some limited occupational groups may make contributions to retirement plans with before-tax dollars — in other words they may take a tax deduction for their contribution to the plan.

Federal law imposes a number of very specific requirements on qualified retirement plans. These requirements include *vesting* (which deals with the question whether the retirement benefits will be paid if the employee quits before retirement), and *nondiscrimination* (which ensures that lower paid as well as higher paid employees are covered by the plan). It is not necessary to describe these technical requirements: the important point is to recognize the significant degree of additional tax deferral that results from the creation of a qualified retirement plan.

In a qualified plan, everyone appears to gain at the expense of Uncle Sam. The obvious justification for these significant tax benefits is that they provide employers with an incentive to make adequate provision for the retirement of their employees, supplementing the social security system. And, indeed, qualified retirement plans are an important source of retirement income for most working people today.

Qualified retirement plans are divided into *defined benefit* and *defined contribution* plans. In a defined benefit plan, the size of the employer's contribution is determined on an actuarial basis to provide employees with designated benefits: an example might be a defined retirement benefit equal to 2 percent of the employee's average salary over the last three years of his or her employment multiplied by the number of years of employment. Thus, an employee with 30 years of service would receive a retirement benefit equal to 60 percent of his or her average three-year preretirement salary. The military retirement plan is a well-known defined benefit plan.

A defined contribution plan, on the other hand, does not establish the amount to be paid by the employer on the basis of the benefits ultimately to be conferred on employees. Rather the amount is established by reference to extrinsic information during each period, such as the employer's profits, or the actual salary paid to the employee during the period in question. For example, a defined contribution plan might provide an annual contribution by the employer equal to 7 percent of the employee's salary each year. The employee receives 100 percent of his or her salary. The employer contributes an additional 7 percent of this amount to the qualified plan and claims as a deduction for tax purposes 107 percent of the employee's salary. The 7 percent each year builds up in a fund until retirement. The amount in that fund upon retirement cannot be ascertained until retirement: Whatever the amount is, it will then be used to purchase a commercial annuity for the life of the retired employee. The amount of that annuity is determined solely by the amount in that employee's fund.

Qualified plans may also be subdivided into *pension plans, profit-sharing plans,* and *stock bonus plans.* Qualified profit-sharing and stock bonus plans involve contributions based on a percentage of profits earned by the employer during the period. A qualified pension plan may be either a defined benefit plan or a defined contribution plan. In the case of all these retirement plans, federal law limits the maximum contributions that may be made in order to cap the maximum tax benefits.

The tax sheltering of the benefit payments in a qualified plan is in addition to the tax deferral of buildup that occurs within the fund or trust to which the contributions are made. Thus, the employee not only excludes the employer contributions from his or her taxable income but also excludes investment earnings from prior years' contributions. This also involves tax deferral because the retirement benefits, when actually received, are taxable.

§5.9 Self-Employed Retirement: Keogh Plans

For many years, the significant tax benefits provided by qualified employee retirement plans could not be obtained by self-employed individuals, who, like the 35-year-old providing a do-it-yourself retirement plan, could only fund retirement plans with after-tax dollars. Today, this discrimination against the self-employed has been eliminated by amendments to the tax laws.

Self-employed persons may create devices called *Keogh plans* (also known as *H.R. 10 plans*) that basically allow self-employed persons to set up a retirement trust or retirement account and make contributions to it that may be deducted from the self-employed person's individual income tax return. Tax penalties are imposed for premature withdrawals. Keogh plans are defined contribution plans. For many years the maximum allowable deductable contribution to a Keogh plan was significantly lower than the amount an employer could provide its employees under a qualified retirement plan, but this discrimination against the self-employed has been largely eliminated.

Where a self-employed person can incorporate his or her own business, he or she can also obtain retirement benefits as an "employee" of the corporation. (As discussed in §13.6, there is generally no reason why the same person cannot be both the sole shareholder and an employee of a corporation.)

§5.10 Individual Retirement Accounts (IRAs)

There is yet another class of workers who cannot take advantage of either qualified retirement plans or Keogh plans. These are persons who are employed but the employer has not elected to create a qualified retirement plan. *Individual retirement accounts,* usually referred to as *IRAs,* were originally designed to permit these persons to obtain some parity in tax treatment. They permitted employees to create special retirement accounts with banks and other financial institutions into which they could make periodic contributions and then deduct the payments from their federal income tax returns. Like Keogh plans, maximum deductions and contributions are specified and a tax penalty is imposed if funds are withdrawn prematurely. In 1981, the IRA concept was broadened to permit *any* employee (including those covered by employer-sponsored retirement plans) to create an IRA and make a contribution of up to $2,000 ($2,250 for an employee and a nonworking spouse) each year. As a result of this change, IRAs quickly became a tax-deferred savings account primarily utilized by the relatively affluent rather than by the persons for whom they were originally designed. In 1986, Congress largely closed off this tax-deferred savings loophole for the well-to-do by limiting IRA deductions to persons not covered by other plans and those below specified income levels.

§5.11 Private Annuities

Finally, brief mention should be made of a device that has some limited usefulness in certain family-related or tax-oriented transactions. A *private annuity* is created by the transfer of property to a person in exchange for a promise by that person to make fixed periodic payments for the life of the transferor. The rights must be unsecured and the transferor cannot be in the business of writing annuities. In other words, it is an annuity based on the credit of a private individual not in the business of writing annuities. Such private annuities may offer tax benefits by deferring the taxation of the transaction.

§5.12 Annuities for One or More Lifetimes

Most annuities are payable for the life or lives of one or more persons. Such annuities involve actuarial calculations as well as estimates of the time value of money. *Actuaries* determine rates, returns, and the like on the basis of recorded data, particularly records of mortality that show numbers of persons of various ages and occupations who die each year. These records form the basis for the widely used tables of life expectancies of persons of various ages that in turn form the backbone of both the life insurance industry and the annuity industry. The Internal Revenue Service also has published a table of life expectancies to be used for the calculation of the tax consequences of transactions involving annuities and lifetime interests.

Let us assume that a client of yours has reached the age of retirement after participating for many years in one or more plans that provide tax deferred benefits arising upon retirement. Specifically, the employer has contributed to a noncontributory qualified pension plan on behalf of your client for 25 years. The plan is a defined contribution plan; the most recent statement from the plan shows that the tax deferred savings credited to the employee's account is $200,000. Now 67, your client has decided to retire, as he is entitled to do.

He must now choose what to do with the $200,000 "nest egg." The plan provides your client the following alternatives upon retirement:

(a) Take the total accumulation in cash;

(b) Elect a single life annuity payable for his life;

(c) Elect a life annuity for the life of the employee with payments for ten years guaranteed; that is, if he dies within ten years, payments will continue to be made to his beneficiary;

(d) Elect a life annuity for the combined lives of the employee and his spouse; that is, the payments are to continue while either the employee or his spouse are alive;

(e) Elect a life annuity for the combined lives of the employee and his spouse with a guaranteed ten-year period; or

(f) Elect a life annuity for the combined lives of the employee and his spouse with a further election that if the employee dies first,

   (i) the annuity drops to two-thirds the level at which it was paid while both are alive; or

   (ii) the annuity drops to half the level at which it was paid while both are alive.

In the case of each of the various lifetime annuity options, the plan assumes that the amount credited to the account of the retiring employee on the date of retirement is used to purchase a commercial annuity. The complete selection from the list of elections must be made before the actual date of retirement, and the selection, once made and payments commenced, is usually irrevocable.

At first glance, these choices may seem confusing and complicated, but they really are not. They are familiar to persons who give financial advice to employees contemplating retirement. Choice (a) is obvious and the simplest, though often not the most advantageous; since the plan was noncontributory, the employee has made no contributions into the plan and the entire amount of $200,000 will be taxable to him upon the date of receipt. When the federal income tax rate structure was strongly progressive, this lumping of income into a single year tended to increase the tax cost of electing an all-cash option, but with the present 28 percent maximum rate, the tax cost has been significantly reduced. More seriously, if the employee elects this option, he then faces the problem of providing for himself and his spouse; there is always some risk that on a do-it-yourself retirement plan, the money may run out while one or both of the beneficiaries are still alive.

Choice (b) requires knowledge of two factors: the life expectancy of a 67-year-old man and the interest rate used by the commercial insurance company in calculating the amount of a lifetime annuity for a single person of a specified age. Table 5-2 is the old Internal Revenue Service table showing the expected return on an ordinary life annuity. It will be noted that Table 5-2, like most nongovernmental mortality tables, expressly takes the sex of an annuitant as well as his or her age into account. Since females live longer on the average then males, a contribution of a fixed amount made for the benefit of a female annuitant leads to a smaller monthly payment under this table than if the same payment were made for the benefit of a male. In 1986, the IRS adopted a revised "unisex" table (Table 5-3) that governs present annuity calculations.

In the present example, one may determine the life expectancy of a

Table 5-2
Pre-1986 Internal Revenue Code Table:
Ordinary Life Annuities — One Life — Expected Return Multiples

Ages			Ages			Ages		
Male	Female	Multiples	Male	Female	Multiples	Male	Female	Multiples
6	11	65.0	41	46	33.0	76	81	9.1
7	12	64.1	42	47	32.1	77	82	8.7
8	13	63.2	43	48	31.2	78	83	8.3
9	14	62.3	44	49	30.4	79	84	7.8
10	15	61.4	45	50	29.6	80	85	7.5
11	16	60.4	46	51	28.7	81	86	7.1
12	17	59.5	47	52	27.9	82	87	6.7
13	18	58.6	48	53	27.1	83	88	6.3
14	19	57.7	49	54	26.3	84	89	6.0
15	20	56.7	50	55	25.5	85	90	5.7
16	21	55.8	51	56	24.7	86	91	5.4
17	22	54.9	52	57	24.0	87	92	5.1
18	23	53.9	53	58	23.2	88	93	4.8
19	24	53.0	54	59	22.4	89	94	4.5
20	25	52.1	55	60	21.7	90	95	4.2
21	26	51.1	56	61	21.0	91	96	4.0
22	27	50.2	57	62	20.3	92	97	3.7
23	28	49.3	58	63	19.6	93	98	3.5
24	29	48.3	59	64	18.9	94	99	3.3
25	30	47.4	60	65	18.2	95	100	3.1
26	31	46.5	61	66	17.5	96	101	2.9
27	32	45.6	62	67	16.9	97	102	2.7
28	33	44.6	63	68	16.2	98	103	2.5
29	34	43.7	64	69	15.6	99	104	2.3
30	35	42.8	65	70	15.0	100	105	2.1
31	36	41.9	66	71	14.4	101	106	1.9
32	37	41.0	67	72	13.8	102	107	1.7
33	38	40.0	68	73	13.2	103	108	1.5
34	39	39.1	69	74	12.6	104	109	1.3
35	40	38.2	70	75	12.1	105	110	1.2
						106	111	1.0
36	41	37.3	71	76	11.6	107	112	.8
37	42	36.5	72	77	11.0	108	113	.7
38	43	35.6	73	78	10.5	109	114	.6
39	44	34.7	74	79	10.1	110	115	.5
40	45	33.8	75	80	9.6	111	116	0

Table 5-3
1986 Internal Revenue Code Table
Ordinary Life Annuities — One Life — Expected Return Multiples

Age	Multiple	Age	Multiple	Age	Multiple
5	76.6	42	40.6	79	10.0
6	75.6	43	39.6	80	9.5
7	74.7	44	38.7	81	8.9
8	73.7	45	37.7	82	8.4
9	72.7	46	36.8	83	7.9
10	71.7	47	35.9	84	7.4
11	70.7	48	34.9	85	6.9
12	69.7	49	34.0	86	6.5
13	68.8	50	33.1	87	6.1
14	67.8	51	32.2	88	5.7
15	66.8	52	31.3	89	5.3
16	65.8	53	30.4	90	5.0
17	64.8	54	29.5	91	4.7
18	63.9	55	28.6	92	4.4
19	62.9	56	27.7	93	4.1
20	61.9	57	26.8	94	3.9
21	60.9	58	25.9	95	3.7
22	59.9	59	25.0	96	3.4
23	59.0	60	24.2	97	3.2
24	58.0	61	23.3	98	3.0
25	57.0	62	22.5	99	2.8
26	56.0	63	21.6	100	2.7
27	55.1	64	20.8	101	2.5
28	54.1	65	20.0	102	2.3
29	53.1	66	19.2	103	2.1
30	52.2	67	18.4	104	1.9
31	51.2	68	17.6	105	1.8
32	50.2	69	16.8	106	1.6
33	49.3	70	16.0	107	1.4
34	48.3	71	15.3	108	1.3
35	47.3	72	14.6	109	1.1
36	46.4	73	13.9	110	1.0
37	45.4	74	13.2	111	.9
38	44.4	75	12.5	112	.8
39	43.5	76	11.9	113	.7
40	42.5	77	11.2	114	.6
41	41.5	78	10.6	115	.5

67-year-old person under the current IRS expected return schedule. Tables actually used by a writer of an annuity may vary from the IRS table. From Table 5-3 one sees that in effect your client's life expectancy is an additional 18.4 years. Basically, the plan is purchasing a single-premium annuity commencing immediately and continuing for the life of the employee, but in determining how much is to be paid, the writer of the annuity assumes that the annuitant will precisely live out his life expectancy. This type of annuity is therefore basically the same as the ten-year annuity described in §5.3. If we assume that an interest rate of 6 percent is used (a reasonable assumption), a $200,000 payment for 18.4 years yields a monthly payment of $1,495.54 per month. It is important to recognize that the payments in this amount continue for the balance of the employee's life, no matter how long or how short that life in fact turns out to be. A particularly long-lived annuitant causes a loss to the insurance company, while one who dies tomorrow gives the company a windfall. From the standpoint of the insurance company that writes the annuity, however, the use of reasonably accurate mortality tables eliminates virtually all of the underlying risk, since if many annuities are written, in the long run on the average the longer-lived lifetime annuitants are balanced and cancelled out by the shorter-lived.

Choice (c) is like choice (b) except that payments are guaranteed for ten years. This also involves an actuarial computation. A moment's thought should reveal that the $200,000 payment will purchase a smaller monthly payment under option (c) than under option (b). The reason is that the premature death of the annuitant under option (c) does not benefit the writer of the annuity as it does under option (b); as a result, the total obligation of the writer of the annuity is increased. In the above example, the monthly payment under choice (c) will be approximately $1,400 per month, the $95 difference from the annuity payable under option (c) compensating the writer of the annuity for the possibility that the annuity must continue for a full ten years even if the annuitant dies before then.

Choice (d) is obviously somewhat more complicated since payments are to continue while either the annuitant or his spouse are alive. Tables 5-4 and 5-5 are portions of the "ordinary joint life and last survivor annuity" tables published by the Internal Revenue Service. Table 5-4 is the old table taking the sex of the joint lives into account, while Table 5-5 is the unisex table in current use. In order to ascertain the amount of the monthly payment if this choice is elected, one must know the age of the spouse as well as of the principal annuitant. If we apply the current table and assume an age of 60 for the wife and 67 for the husband, the expected duration of the annuity is 27.0 years (from Table 5-5). This table is read by selecting one annuitant's age from the horizontal axis and the other annuitant's age from the vertical axis. At 27.0 years of expected return, the monthly payment (at 6 percent) is $1,246.73. Obviously, the difference between this amount and the $1,495.54 that would be payable for the life of the husband alone (option (b)) is likely to affect significantly the lifestyle of the retirees. The reduction is large because of the younger age of the wife. Under the pre-1986 tables, younger wives had an even greater impact on their husbands' annuities.

Choice (e) is a compromise between preserving current lifestyles in the immediate post-retirement period and not leaving the surviving spouse, most

Table 5-4
Per 1986 Internal Revenue Code:
Ordinary Joint Life and Last Survivor Annuities — Two Lives — Expected Return Multiples

Ages Male		61	62	63	64	65	66	67	68	69	70	71	72	73
Male	*Female*	66	67	68	69	70	71	72	73	74	75	76	77	78
35	40	39.4	39.3	39.2	39.1	39.0	38.9	38.9	38.8	38.8	38.7	38.7	38.6	38.6
36	41	38.5	38.4	38.3	38.2	38.2	38.1	38.0	38.0	37.9	37.9	37.8	37.8	37.7
37	42	37.7	37.6	37.5	37.4	37.3	37.3	37.2	37.1	37.1	37.0	36.9	36.9	36.9
38	43	36.9	36.8	36.7	36.6	36.5	36.4	36.4	36.3	36.2	36.2	36.1	36.0	36.0
39	44	36.2	36.0	35.9	35.8	35.7	35.6	35.5	35.5	35.4	35.3	35.3	35.2	35.2
40	45	35.4	35.3	35.1	35.0	34.9	34.8	34.7	34.6	34.6	34.5	34.4	34.4	34.3
41	46	34.6	34.5	34.4	34.2	34.1	34.0	33.9	33.8	33.8	33.7	33.6	33.5	33.5
42	47	33.9	33.7	33.6	33.5	33.4	33.2	33.1	33.0	33.0	32.9	32.8	32.7	32.7
43	48	33.2	33.0	32.9	32.7	32.6	32.5	32.4	32.3	32.2	32.1	32.0	31.9	31.9
44	49	32.5	32.3	32.1	32.0	31.8	31.7	31.6	31.5	31.4	31.3	31.2	31.1	31.1
45	50	31.8	31.6	31.4	31.3	31.1	31.0	30.8	30.7	30.6	30.5	30.4	30.4	30.3
46	51	31.1	30.9	30.7	30.5	30.4	30.2	30.1	30.0	29.9	29.8	29.7	29.6	29.5
47	52	30.4	30.2	30.0	29.8	29.7	29.5	29.4	29.3	29.1	29.0	28.9	28.8	28.7
48	53	29.8	29.5	29.3	29.2	29.0	28.8	28.7	28.5	28.4	28.3	28.2	28.1	28.0
49	54	29.1	28.9	28.7	28.5	28.3	28.1	28.0	27.8	27.7	27.6	27.5	27.4	27.3
50	55	28.5	28.3	28.1	27.8	27.6	27.5	27.3	27.1	27.0	26.9	26.7	26.6	26.5

Table 5-4 (cont.)
Per 1986 Internal Revenue Code:
Ordinary Joint Life and Last Survivor Annuities — Two Lives — Expected Return Multiples

Ages Male	Ages Female	61 / 66	62 / 67	63 / 68	64 / 69	65 / 70	66 / 71	67 / 72	68 / 73	69 / 74	70 / 75	71 / 76	72 / 77	73 / 78
51	56	27.9	27.7	27.4	27.2	27.0	26.8	26.6	26.5	26.3	26.2	26.0	25.9	25.8
52	57	27.3	27.1	26.8	26.6	26.4	26.2	26.0	25.8	25.7	25.5	25.4	25.2	25.1
53	58	26.8	26.5	26.2	26.0	25.8	25.6	25.4	25.2	25.0	24.8	24.7	24.6	24.4
54	59	26.2	25.9	25.7	25.4	25.2	25.0	24.7	24.6	24.4	24.2	24.0	23.9	23.8
55	60	25.7	25.4	25.1	24.9	24.6	24.4	24.1	23.9	23.8	23.6	23.4	23.3	23.1
56	61	25.2	24.9	24.6	24.3	24.1	23.8	23.6	23.4	23.2	23.0	22.8	22.6	22.5
57	62	24.7	24.4	24.1	23.8	23.5	23.3	23.0	22.8	22.6	22.4	22.2	22.0	21.9
58	63	24.3	23.9	23.6	23.3	23.0	22.7	22.5	22.2	22.0	21.8	21.6	21.4	21.3
59	64	23.8	23.5	23.1	22.8	22.5	22.2	21.9	21.7	21.5	21.2	21.0	20.9	20.7
60	65	23.4	23.0	22.7	22.3	22.0	21.7	21.4	21.2	20.9	20.7	20.5	20.3	20.1
61	66	23.0	22.6	22.2	21.9	21.6	21.3	21.0	20.7	20.4	20.2	20.0	19.8	19.6
62	67	22.6	22.2	21.8	21.5	21.1	20.8	20.5	20.2	19.9	19.7	19.5	19.2	19.0
63	68	22.2	21.8	21.4	21.1	20.7	20.4	20.1	19.8	19.5	19.2	19.0	18.7	18.5
64	69	21.9	21.5	21.1	20.7	20.3	20.0	19.6	19.3	19.0	18.7	18.5	18.2	18.0
65	70	21.6	21.1	20.7	20.3	19.9	19.6	19.2	18.9	18.6	18.3	18.0	17.8	17.5
66	71	21.3	20.8	20.4	20.0	19.6	19.2	18.8	18.5	18.2	17.9	17.6	17.3	17.1
67	72	21.0	20.5	20.1	19.6	19.2	18.8	18.5	18.1	17.8	17.5	17.2	16.9	16.7
68	73	20.7	20.2	19.8	19.3	18.9	18.5	18.1	17.8	17.4	17.1	16.8	16.5	16.2
69	74	20.4	19.9	19.5	19.0	18.6	18.2	17.8	17.4	17.1	16.7	16.4	16.1	15.8
70	75	20.2	19.7	19.2	18.7	18.3	17.9	17.5	17.1	16.7	16.4	16.1	15.8	15.5
71	76	20.0	19.5	19.0	18.5	18.0	17.6	17.2	16.8	16.4	16.1	15.7	15.4	15.1
72	77	19.8	19.2	18.7	18.2	17.8	17.3	16.9	16.5	16.1	15.8	15.4	15.1	14.8
73	78	19.6	19.0	18.5	18.0	17.5	17.1	16.7	16.2	15.8	15.5	15.1	14.8	14.4

Table 5-5
1986 Internal Revenue Code Table
Ordinary Joint Life and Last Survivor Annuities
Two Lives — Expected Return Multiples

Ages	55	56	57	58	59	60	61	62	63	64
55	34.4	33.9	33.5	33.1	32.7	32.3	32.0	31.7	31.4	31.1
56	33.9	33.4	33.0	32.5	32.1	31.7	31.4	31.0	30.7	30.4
57	33.5	33.0	32.5	32.0	31.6	31.2	30.8	30.4	30.1	29.8
58	33.1	32.5	32.0	31.5	31.1	30.6	30.2	29.9	29.5	29.2
59	32.7	32.1	31.6	31.1	30.6	30.1	29.7	29.3	28.9	28.6
60	32.3	31.7	31.2	30.6	30.1	29.7	29.2	28.8	28.4	28.0
61	32.0	31.4	30.8	30.2	29.7	29.2	28.7	28.3	27.8	27.4
62	31.7	31.0	30.4	29.9	29.3	28.8	28.3	27.8	27.3	26.9
63	31.4	30.7	30.1	29.5	28.9	28.4	27.8	27.3	26.9	26.4
64	31.1	30.4	29.8	29.2	28.6	28.0	27.4	26.9	26.4	25.9
65	30.9	30.2	29.5	28.9	28.2	27.6	27.1	26.5	26.0	25.5
66	30.6	29.9	29.2	28.6	27.9	27.3	26.7	26.1	25.6	25.1
67	30.4	29.7	29.0	28.3	27.6	27.0	26.4	25.8	25.2	24.7
68	30.2	29.5	28.8	28.1	27.4	26.7	26.1	25.5	24.9	24.3
69	30.1	29.3	28.6	27.8	27.1	26.5	25.8	25.2	24.6	24.0
70	29.9	29.1	28.4	27.6	26.9	26.2	25.6	24.9	24.3	23.7
71	29.7	29.0	28.2	27.5	26.7	26.0	25.3	24.7	24.0	23.4
72	29.6	28.8	28.1	27.3	26.5	25.8	25.1	24.4	23.8	23.1
73	29.5	28.7	27.9	27.1	26.4	25.6	24.9	24.2	23.5	22.9
74	29.4	28.6	27.8	27.0	26.2	25.5	24.7	24.0	23.3	22.7
75	29.3	28.5	27.7	26.9	26.1	25.3	24.6	23.8	23.1	22.4
76	29.2	28.4	27.6	26.8	26.0	25.2	24.4	23.7	23.0	22.3
77	29.1	28.3	27.5	26.7	25.9	25.1	24.3	23.6	22.8	22.1
78	29.1	28.2	27.4	26.6	25.8	25.0	24.2	23.4	22.7	21.9
79	29.0	28.2	27.3	26.5	25.7	24.9	24.1	23.3	22.6	21.8
80	29.0	28.1	27.3	26.4	25.6	24.8	24.0	23.2	22.4	21.7
81	28.9	28.1	27.2	26.4	25.5	24.7	23.9	23.1	22.3	21.6
82	28.9	28.0	27.2	26.3	25.5	24.6	23.8	23.0	22.3	21.5
83	28.8	28.0	27.1	26.3	25.4	24.6	23.8	23.0	22.2	21.4
84	28.8	27.9	27.1	26.2	25.4	24.5	23.7	22.9	22.1	21.3
85	28.8	27.9	27.0	26.2	25.3	24.5	23.7	22.8	22.0	21.3

Ages	55	56	57	58	59	60	61	62	63	64
86	28.7	27.9	27.0	26.1	25.3	24.5	23.6	22.8	22.0	21.2
87	28.7	27.8	27.0	26.1	25.3	24.4	23.6	22.8	21.9	21.1
88	28.7	27.8	27.0	26.1	25.2	24.4	23.5	22.7	21.9	21.1
89	28.7	27.8	26.9	26.1	25.2	24.4	23.5	22.7	21.9	21.1
90	28.7	27.8	26.9	26.1	25.2	24.3	23.5	22.7	21.8	21.0
91	28.7	27.8	26.9	26.0	25.2	24.3	23.5	22.6	21.8	21.0
92	28.6	27.8	26.9	26.0	25.2	24.3	23.5	22.6	21.8	21.0
93	28.6	27.8	26.9	26.0	25.1	24.3	23.4	22.6	21.8	20.9
94	28.6	27.7	26.9	26.0	25.1	24.3	23.4	22.6	21.7	20.9
95	28.6	27.7	26.9	26.0	25.1	24.3	23.4	22.6	21.7	20.9
96	26.6	27.7	26.9	26.0	25.1	24.2	23.4	22.6	21.7	20.9
97	28.6	27.7	26.8	26.0	25.1	24.2	23.4	22.5	21.7	20.9
98	28.6	27.7	26.8	26.0	25.1	24.2	23.4	22.5	21.7	20.9
99	28.6	27.7	26.8	26.0	25.1	24.2	23.4	22.5	21.7	20.9
100	28.6	27.7	26.8	26.0	25.1	24.2	23.4	22.5	21.7	20.8
101	28.6	27.7	26.8	25.9	25.1	24.2	23.4	22.5	21.7	20.8
102	28.6	27.7	26.8	25.9	25.1	24.2	23.3	22.5	21.7	20.8
103	28.6	27.7	26.8	25.9	25.1	24.2	23.3	22.5	21.7	20.8
104	28.6	27.7	26.8	25.9	25.1	24.2	23.3	22.5	21.6	20.8
105	28.6	27.7	26.8	25.9	25.1	24.2	23.3	22.5	21.6	20.8
106	28.6	27.7	26.8	25.9	25.1	24.2	23.3	22.5	21.6	20.8
107	28.6	27.7	26.8	25.9	25.1	24.2	23.3	22.5	21.6	20.8
108	28.6	27.7	26.8	25.9	25.1	24.2	23.3	22.5	21.6	20.8
109	28.6	27.7	26.8	25.9	25.1	24.2	23.3	22.5	21.6	20.8
110	28.6	27.7	26.8	25.9	25.1	24.2	23.3	22.5	21.6	20.8
111	28.6	27.7	26.8	25.9	25.0	24.2	23.3	22.5	21.6	20.8
112	28.6	27.7	26.8	25.9	25.0	24.2	23.3	22.5	21.6	20.8
113	28.6	27.7	26.8	25.9	25.0	24.2	23.3	22.5	21.6	20.8
114	28.6	27.7	26.8	25.9	25.0	24.2	23.3	22.5	21.6	20.8
115	28.6	27.7	26.8	25.9	25.0	24.2	23.3	22.5	21.6	20.8

likely a younger wife, in dire straits following the death of her husband. The amount of the monthly payments under these plans may be readily determined on an actuarial basis, though the calculations are more complex than those set forth above.

The selection of any of these options must take into account the peculiar needs of the retiree and his or her spouse, their ages, their general health, other available assets and insurance, and so forth. These matters are discussed further in the chapter on life insurance.

Retirement plans that offer a variety of lifetime annuity arrangements sometimes describe the effect of the various arrangements as a percentage of a standard benefit. A plan widely used by institutions of higher education to provide retirement benefits for faculty and administrators, for example, estimates the benefit that would be payable on the basis of a life annuity with ten-year guaranteed payments as 100 percent. If the annuitant is 65 at the age of retirement, the election of a lifetime annuity with a 20-year guaranteed payment pays 93 percent of the base annuity. A single life annuity without guaranteed payments pays 104 percent of the base annuity. An annuity for the life of both a 67-year-old husband and his 60-year-old wife, and the survivor of them, with a guaranteed ten-year payment, pays 85 percent of the base amount. These percentages are sometimes more meaningful in the eyes of a person selecting irrevocably among these bewildering choices than dollar figures based on a hypothetical example.

CHAPTER 6

LIFE INSURANCE

§6.1 Introduction

Everyone is generally familiar with the institution of life insurance. In 1984, there were approximately 145,000,000 policyholders in the United States; thus, about two out of every three persons living in the United States have some kind of life insurance. About 45 percent of this insurance is now group insurance, usually provided through employers or membership organizations; the remaining 55 percent is purchased individually, primarily through agents. The average American household had approximately $58,700 worth of life insurance in force in 1984.

Life insurance is an immense industry: In 1984 annual premium payments on life insurance policies exceeded $48 billion and the assets of life insurance companies were nearly $723 billion much of which represented reserves to cover future obligations under insurance policies already in existence. The management, investment, and reinvestment of this huge pool of capital makes this industry an important force in the American economy. The amount of ordinary life insurance in force has increased steadily since the 1930s and in 1984 exceeded $3.625 trillion. Life insurance companies also write annuities and may be involved in other kinds of insurance as well. The discussion in this chapter, however, is limited exclusively to life insurance.

It is probable that a very large percentage of all purchasers of life insurance are not aware of exactly what they have purchased and do not know whether they have purchased what they need.

Until the 1970s, the life insurance industry sold a limited number of products. These traditional products are known as *term insurance* and *whole life insurance*, though there are a number of subvariations of these basic types of insurance. Together they are often described as *ordinary life insurance*. These traditional products were designed basically to provide protection against the unexpected death of wage earners and their spouses and, in the case of whole life policies, to encourage savings in low yielding investments in the guise of providing lifetime life insurance protection. The twin factors of high inflation and high interest rates in the period between the late 1960s and early 1980s shook up the life insurance industry. The traditional policies became less attractive, and new types of life insurance were developed, *flexible premium life insurance* (often called *universal life insurance* or *adjustable life insurance*), and more importantly, *variable life insurance* (often called *single premium insurance*), a type of policy that contains significant tax shelter benefits. Even though tax legislation in the 1980s has generally attempted to eliminate or minimize tax shelter and tax deferral devices, the tax benefits of variable life insurance were not affected by this legislation, and remain as one of the few legitimate tax shelter devices to survive the Tax Reform Act of 1986. Much of the recent growth in the purchase of life insurance products has been fueled by these new, tax-oriented policies.

The first sections of this chapter describe the fundamental relationships and actuarial principles underlying every life insurance contract. The following sections discuss the standard and traditional life insurance products as well as the newer tax-oriented products sold by the life insurance industry today.

§6.2 The Persons Involved in Life Insurance Policies

In addition to the life insurance company that writes the policy, every life insurance policy involves three actors: the insured, the beneficiary, and the owner of the policy. The *insured* is the person whose demise triggers the obligation of the insurance company to pay the face value of the policy, and the *beneficiary* is the person to whom the face value is paid. Often the beneficiary of the policy will be the insured's spouse or children, but it may also be the insured's estate or persons unrelated to the insured. The *owner of the policy* is the person who has the power to exercise a number of options with respect to the policy: to name or change the designation of the beneficiary, to borrow against the policy or pledge it as security for a loan (if it has a cash surrender value), and to surrender the policy or decide to let it lapse for nonpayment. Usually the owner of the policy is the person who pays the premiums. The owner and the insured may be the same person but they need not be, and indeed it is often advantageous from a tax standpoint for them to be different persons. Under the federal estate tax law, if the insured has retained the *incidents of ownership* (e.g., the right to change beneficiaries or to pledge the policy as security for a loan) at the time of death, the policy is includable in his or her estate. This is true even if the beneficiary of the policy is a spouse, other family member, or another individual. See § 6.5 for a brief description of the coverage of the federal estate tax today.

§6.3 Mutual Life Insurance Companies and Stock Companies

Basically there are two types of life insurance companies writing policies today: mutual companies and stock companies. About 40 percent of all life insurance is written today by mutual companies. A mutual company does not have shareholders; its board of directors is elected by its policyholders; and excess earnings of the company are paid to its policyholders in the form of annual dividends. In a broad sense, the "owners" of a mutual life insurance company are the policyholders. One should not put too much weight on this "ownership," however. Policyholders are widely scattered and unorganized and as a result have virtually no voice in how a mutual company is actually managed. Also, most policyholders are indifferent to management issues so long as their individual policies are not adversely affected. Management of a mutual company can therefore run the company with almost complete freedom from oversight by the owners, the only discipline being provided by the need to offer relatively competitive products with those offered by other insurance companies.

The second type of insurance company is a stock company. It is in form a traditional corporation with shareholders who purchase stock in the company and who are entitled to elect the company's board of directors. Dividends in a stock company are paid to the shareholders, not to the policyholders as in a mutual company. In a stock company, policyholders are more analogous to customers of the corporation than to owners.

§6.4 Participating and Nonparticipating Policies

Policies that are entitled to share in dividends are called *participating policies*, and such policies are usually written by mutual companies. In effect, each year when the premium notice is sent, the amount of the dividend is set forth and the owner of the policy may elect to have the dividend credited against the amount of next year's premium. In mutual companies, dividends may be paid on all types of life insurance outstanding or only on specified classes or types of policies. Policies written by stock companies are usually *nonparticipating*, that is, they are not entitled to receive dividends. The amount of the annual premium is fixed and is not subject to reduction by a dividend. In making comparisons between various life insurance policies and the costs of similar policies issued by different companies, it is necessary to take into account whether the proposed policy is participating or nonparticipating. While the amount of a dividend on a participating policy is apt to be rather small in contrast with the amount of a premium, it tends to be stable and reasonably predictable, and a complete assessment of the relative costs of two otherwise equivalent policies should take the dividend into account.

Even though a mutual company pays dividends to policyholders while stock companies pay dividends to shareholders, one should not assume that mutual companies usually offer cheaper products. Both types of companies compete vigorously with each other for the same insurance dollar. It is not uncommon for a stock company to offer a cheaper policy even after the mutual company dividend is taken into account.

§6.5 The Traditional Goals of Life Insurance: Family Protection and Liquidity

Death may strike a person at any age. The most serious family crises are likely to arise from the unexpected death of a person who is the sole or principal income producer for young and dependent children and a spouse who lacks salable job skills. Life insurance obviously provides essential benefits in this type of situation, and as a result it is not surprising that traditionally most life insurance was sold to "breadwinners" in the classic sense. Today, it is not uncommon for both spouses to work even when the children are relatively young, but life insurance may still provide essential protection since the loss of one income may have devastating consequences. Even where one spouse remains home to care for young children, it is increasingly recognized that his or her services are also essential to the family unit and life insurance protection should be purchased for both spouses.

Even where the death of the insured does not create an immediate financial crisis for a family with young children, life insurance is often a desirable component of contingency financial planning because it provides a large degree of immediate liquidity upon the death of the insured. Many persons have assets that may have substantial value if they can be disposed of in an orderly way but relatively little value if they must be sold immediately at "fire sale" or "distress" prices. Good examples of such assets include real estate such as the family home, a wholly owned business, or shares of stock in a family corporation. Also a person's heirs may desire to retain certain assets for their own use after the death of the insured, such as the family home, a cabin in the mountains, or an art collection. Whether or not this is practical may depend on whether the estate has other liquid assets sufficient to cover taxes, expenses, cash bequests, and outstanding indebtedness. If the estate does not, something more must be sold to enable the estate to be administered and closed in a timely fashion, and what is most salable is often precisely what the heirs desire to keep for their own use. Life insurance provides liquidity in the form of ready cash that may be of inestimable value in simplifying the immediate post-death affairs of the deceased person's estate and his or her heirs.

Life insurance that is payable to the estate of the decedent is of course available for the payment of estate obligations, while life insurance that is payable to an individual usually is not. However, the proceeds of an insurance policy are includable in the estate of the decedent for federal estate tax purposes if the policy is payable to the estate of the decedent, no matter who owns the policy. The use of life insurance to improve the liquidity of the estate may therefore increase the taxes imposed on the estate.

The rules about when life insurance must be included in the taxable estate of the decedent for federal estate tax purposes described above and in §6.2 are not as important today as they were a few years ago, because changes in federal tax laws during the 1980s greatly reduced the impact of this tax so that now it affects only the most wealthy individuals. Today there is a $600,000 exclusion applicable to all estates, whereas the exemption was only $60,000 as late as the mid-1970s. Obviously, as a practical matter, with a $600,000 exemption the average estate today does not need to be concerned about federal estate taxes. The federal estate tax law also grants an unlimited deduction for transfers to the spouse of the decedent. Of course, if the spouse dies shortly after the decedent, the estate tax saving that may be obtained in the estate of the decedent by taking advantage of this so-called marital deduction largely disappears because the estate of the spouse who dies second will not have the advantage of a marital deduction and most of the property transferred from the decedent to the spouse will be subject to estate tax upon the death of the spouse. Nevertheless, with proper planning, an aggregate of $1,200,000 (the $600,000 exclusion for the decedent plus the $600,000 exclusion for the spouse of the decedent) may pass tax-free upon the death of both spouses.

§6.6 Gambling, Risk, and Life Insurance

Some people doubtless view life insurance (and perhaps other types of insurance as well) as a form of ghoulish gambling or wagering on the life of a person. In this view, the person buying life insurance is betting that he or she will not live beyond his or her life expectancy while the insurance company is betting that the insured will live to a ripe old age. It is important to recognize, however, that from the standpoint of the life insurance company, life insurance is not gambling at all.

Consider, for example, the situation where a new insured, Jane Doe, aged 30 with three small children, pays her first premium but is hit and killed by a truck ten minutes later while leaving the insurance agent's office. The face amount of the policy is almost certainly due in this situation even though the insurance was in effect for only a brief period because insurance companies universally give their agents authority to *bind* the insurance companies on prospective insurance policies while the companies assess the risk and decide whether to issue a permanent policy. (A *binder*, in other words, is a kind of temporary insurance policy.)

The unexpected demise of Jane Doe does not mean that the insurance company writing the policy lost a gamble. Insurance companies diversify the risk by writing many policies on many different people in many different situations. The whole foundation of life insurance is the existence of reliable mortality tables for members of the population as a whole. The earliest such tables date from the late 1600s and early 1700s, and data have been collected on a regular basis ever since. The translation of this information into tables that permit the determination of theoretical premiums to be charged an average person for a life insurance policy in a specified amount on his or her life is generally the subject of actuarial science. The principal variable is, of course, age, but other more controversial variables that do reliably assist actuaries in predicting mortality rates, such as sex and race, may be used because mortality tables are available for these subgroups of the population. So long as the population of insureds drawn from a specific risk group covered by a specific company resembles the population of that risk group as a whole, and the premiums are established on an actuarial basis to cover not only the risk but also the insurance company's costs and expenses, the element of gambling is largely eliminated. Indeed, in this perspective, the premature death of our unfortunate Jane Doe is not an unexpected event at all. The mortality tables build in the fact that on average a certain number of 30-year-old women of Jane Doe's race will die in motor vehicle accidents each year. From the perspective of the actuary, this tragedy is a predictable statistic.

Table 6-1 sets forth published data on the expectation of life at various ages in the United States both by race and by sex. Table 6-2 describes the historical changes in life expectancies during the twentieth century. Considerably more elaborate tables are of course used by insurance companies to develop premiums applicable to specific applicants, but the general relevance of these tables for purposes of life insurance should be obvious. As long as the individuals being insured by a life insurance company reflect the mortality experience of the population from which they are drawn, premiums may be safely calculated on the basis of available statistics on average mortality tables or life expectancies.

Of course, insurance companies must assess individual risks to make sure that the risk is an average one and not unique in some way. An insurance company must always be careful that risks are randomly obtained and are not self-selected. For example, a life insurance company could easily go broke if it wrote standard insurance policies on a large number of persons with serious heart disease and a large number of persons engaged in ultrahazardous activities like motorcycle racing, skydiving, and bomb disposal. For exactly the same reason property casualty companies generally refuse to write flood insurance since only persons living in flood-prone areas are likely to request such insurance while persons living on top of the hill realize that they do not need the insurance and do not apply for it. It is impossible when writing flood insurance for the persons at risk to avoid self-selection.

The major ways used by an insurance company to ensure that risks are randomly selected are questions on the application form relating to medical histories, occupations, and hobbies; and physical examinations (which are often but not always required). A person who can demonstrate that he or she is in reasonably good health and engages in activities of average risk is said to be *insurable* while a person who cannot is said to be *uninsurable*. These are not black-and-white categories, however. Insurance companies often write *extra-risk* insurance policies for persons with known medical problems, such as apparently controlled cardiovascular disease or a history of successful treatment for cancer. Such policies carry higher premiums, of course, and are written only after careful assessment of the applicant's medical condition. In a sense a person with controlled high blood pressure is insurable on an extra-risk basis because insurance companies have had sufficient experience with mortality rates of persons with that medical condition to permit the writing of actuarily sound insurance.

Persons engaged in hazardous occupations may also often obtain life insurance only upon the payment of a higher premium. Many insurance companies now give discounts for nonsmokers; a "discount" in this situation is simply a reduction in premiums for nonsmokers or, phrased differently, the establishment of a somewhat higher premium rate for insurance applicants who smoke.

Questions on the application form for life insurance are carefully devised to provide the insurer accurate information as to the risks involved. Questions usually relate not only to medical histories and known medical conditions but also involve open-ended inquiries that may lead to further investigation, such as whether the applicant has been denied life insurance in the past or whether the applicant has been under the care of a physician for any reason in the recent

Table 6-1
Expectation of Life of Various Ages in the United States, 1983–1986

Age	1983			1984			1985*			1986†		
	Male	Female	Total	Male	Female	Total	Male	Female	Total	Male	Female	Total
0	71.0	78.1	74.6	71.2	78.3	74.7	71.2	78.2	74.7	71.5	78.5	75.0
15	57.3	64.2	60.8	57.4	64.2	60.9	57.4	64.2	60.9	57.7	64.5	61.1
25	48.0	54.5	51.3	48.2	54.5	51.4	48.1	54.5	51.4	48.5	54.8	51.7
35	38.8	44.9	41.9	38.9	44.9	42.0	38.9	44.8	42.0	39.3	45.1	42.3
45	29.7	35.4	32.7	29.9	35.5	32.8	29.9	35.4	32.8	30.2	35.7	33.1
55	21.4	26.6	24.1	21.5	26.6	24.2	21.6	26.5	24.2	21.8	26.8	24.5
65	14.5	18.6	16.7	14.6	18.6	16.8	14.6	18.6	16.8	14.7	18.9	17.0
75	9.0	11.8	10.7	9.0	11.9	10.7	9.0	11.8	10.6	N.A.	N.A.	N.A.
85	5.2	6.6	6.1	5.2	6.5	6.1	5.0	6.5	6.0	N.A.	N.A.	N.A.

*Data are provisional from the National Center for Health Statistics.
†Data are estimated by Metropolitan Life Insurance Company.
N.A. — Not available.
Sources: National Center for Health Statistics, U.S. Department of Health and Human Services, and Metropolitan Life Insurance Company, *Statistical Bulletin,* July–September 1987.

Table 6-2
Expectation of Life at Birth in the United States (Years)

Year	White			All Other			Total		
	Male	Female	Total	Male	Female	Total	Male	Female	Total
1900	46.6	48.7	47.6	32.5	33.5	33.0	46.3	48.3	47.3
1910	48.6	52.0	50.3	33.8	37.5	35.6	48.4	51.8	50.0
1920	54.4	55.6	54.9	45.5	45.2	45.3	53.6	54.6	54.1
1930	59.7	63.5	61.4	47.3	49.2	48.1	58.1	61.6	59.7
1940	62.1	66.6	64.2	51.5	54.9	53.1	60.8	65.2	62.9
1950	66.5	72.2	69.1	59.1	62.9	60.8	65.6	71.1	68.2
1960	67.4	74.1	70.6	61.1	66.3	63.6	66.6	73.1	69.7
1965	67.6	74.7	71.0	61.1	67.4	64.1	66.8	73.7	70.2
1970	68.0	75.6	71.7	61.3	69.4	65.3	67.1	74.8	70.9
1971	68.3	75.8	72.0	61.6	69.8	65.6	67.4	75.0	71.1
1972	68.3	75.9	72.0	61.5	70.1	65.7	67.4	75.1	71.2
1973	68.5	76.1	72.2	62.0	70.3	66.1	67.6	75.3	71.4
1974	69.0	76.7	72.8	62.9	71.3	67.1	68.2	75.9	72.0
1975	69.5	77.3	73.4	63.7	72.4	68.0	68.8	76.6	72.6
1976	69.9	77.5	73.6	64.2	72.7	68.4	69.1	76.8	72.9
1977	70.2	77.9	74.0	64.7	73.2	68.9	69.5	77.2	73.3
1978	70.4	78.0	74.1	65.0	73.5	69.3	69.6	77.3	73.5
1979	70.8	78.4	74.6	65.4	74.1	69.8	70.0	77.8	73.9
1980	70.7	78.1	74.4	65.3	73.6	69.5	70.0	77.4	73.7
1981	71.1	78.4	74.8	66.1	74.4	70.3	70.4	77.8	74.2
1982	71.5	78.7	75.1	66.8	75.0	71.0	70.9	78.1	74.5
1983	71.7	78.7	75.2	67.2	74.9	71.1	71.0	78.1	74.6
1984	71.8	78.8	75.3	67.3	75.2	71.3	71.1	78.3	74.7
1985*	71.8	78.7	75.3	67.2	75.2	71.2	71.2	78.2	74.7
1986*	72.0	78.9	75.4	67.6	75.1	71.4	71.3	78.3	74.9

*Data are provisional from the National Center for Health Statistics.
Note: Some data are revised.
Sources: National Center for Health Statistics, U.S. Department of Health and Human Services.

past. An applicant for life insurance has every incentive to "fudge" on the application form or to omit reference to medical facts or hazardous activities in order to obtain insurance at favorable rates (or in some cases, to obtain insurance at all). Material omissions or misstatements constitute fraud and, if discovered, usually lead to the cancellation of the policy. On the other hand, insurance companies may be tempted to welsh on policies that have been in effect for a long period of time for nondisclosure of material facts in the original application form. Such a practice might deprive insureds of the benefits of protection and liquidity even though they had dutifully paid premiums for several years and had not sought substitute insurance because they thought the original policy was valid. Modern life insurance regulation prevents insurance companies from cancelling policies for nondisclosure after the lapse of a specified period of time. These so-called *incontestability clauses* are a kind of statute of limitations. They permit life insurance companies only a limited time to raise defenses; after that time has expired, the obligation to insure is binding and cannot be avoided for misrepresentation or nondisclosure in the application. These clauses are mandated by state law: The Texas statute, for example, states that each life insurance policy must contain provisions which state that it and the application form "shall constitute the entire contract between the parties and shall be incontestable after it has been in force during the lifetime of the insured for two years from its date, except for nonpayment of premiums, and which provisions may, at the option of the company, contain an exception for violation of the conditions of the policy relating to naval and military service in time of war."

In addition to the judicious evaluation and acceptance of individual risks, insurance companies may diversify their portfolio of risks by the widespread practice of *reinsurance*, through which an insurance company may transfer certain risks to other insurance companies in exchange for a sharing of the premium. Through this process, imbalances of risks may be distributed throughout the life insurance industry. A specific insured is unlikely to be aware that his or her policy has been transferred through reinsurance to another company.

The previous chapter on annuities pointed out that life insurance and annuities to some extent involve opposite risks, one ceasing on the death of the annuitant and the other commencing on the death of the insured. Much or all of the individual risk assumed by an insurance company when writing insurance on an individual disappears if the insurance company at the same time is asked to write an annuity for the life of that person. This is well illustrated by the early tax case of Helvering v. Le Gierse, 312 U.S. 531 (1941). An 80-year-old woman executed two contracts with the Connecticut General Life Insurance Company less than a month before her death. The first was an annuity contract that entitled the applicant to annual payments of $589.80 for her lifetime; the consideration for this contract was a payment of $4,179. The second was a "single premium life policy — nonparticipating" that provided for a payment of $25,000 to the applicant's daughter on the death of the applicant; the premium for this policy was $22,125. The applicant was not required to take a physical exam or to answer the questions on the insurance application form that other applicants were required to answer. As one reflects on the position of the insurance company on these facts, it seems clear that it was assuming virtually no risk at all. It had the immediate use of $27,125 (the total of the two premiums), subject to the obligation to pay a relatively small annuity during the remaining life of an 80-year-old person plus a single $25,000 payment upon her death. It was a matter of virtual indifference to the company whether the applicant died immediately or lived for another decade. There was no risk. The issue raised by the case was whether the estate of the applicant could exclude the $25,000 life insurance payment from the applicant's estate for federal estate tax purposes; the Supreme Court concluded that this amount was not "receivable as insurance" by the daughter, and therefore was includable in the decedent's estate tax return. It is interesting that the principal argument made by the taxpayer in this case was that the two policies were entirely separate, and that the annuity was written only because it was difficult for

Connecticut General to get a sufficient number of 80-year-old females to apply for similar insurance policies "and thus be brought into the broad average for underwriting purposes."

Tables 6-1 and 6-2 deserve some examination since they provide interesting information that the reader may not be aware of; for example, what is your life expectancy at your present age? Why have life expectancies increased steadily during the twentieth century? Obviously improvements in medical care, the development of antibiotics, and the like largely explain why the life expectancy of a white male born in 1900 was less than 50 years while in 1986 it was over 71.5 years. Average figures, however, have a tendency to mislead. Much of the increase in life expectancy since 1900 has been caused by decreases in infant and child mortality rather than improving the life expectancy of a person who reaches adulthood.

Is it proper or appropriate (or constitutional?) for life insurance companies to use sex-based and race-based tables? The accumulated statistics that support these distinctions provide valid predictors, but they have come under increasing criticism. The reason for this is political more than economic because a longer life expectancy may sometimes be favorable and sometimes not. In 1986 a 65-year-old male had a life expectancy of 14.7 years while a female of the same age had an expectancy of nearly 19 years. If we assume that both the male and the female retire at the same time and have precisely $100,000 to invest in a lifetime retirement annuity which is based on their respective life expectancies, the male would receive monthly payments that are significantly higher than the female: At 7 percent per year, the annuity would be $910.42 for the male and $795.87 for the female. On the other hand, if the transaction contemplates the purchase of life insurance, on the same assumptions the female would be charged a significantly lower premium for the same amount of insurance since she will, on average, be paying premiums for several more years and the insurance company will have the use of her money for a longer period.

§6.7 Term Insurance

Term insurance is a traditional type of life insurance that provides basic life insurance protection. It provides solely death protection for a fixed period of time such as one, five, or ten years. The face amount of the policy is paid only if the insured dies within the time or term stated in the policy. Term insurance is *pure insurance*, based on actuarial data on the probability of death occurring within the fixed period of the policy. As the insured gets older, the probability of his or her death during the current time period obviously increases; thus the cost of term insurance increases with the age of the person involved. At about age 65, the cost of pure term insurance becomes prohibitive. However, for a 35-year-old breadwinner with a nonworking spouse and two or three young children to support — perhaps the prototypical individual needing life insurance — term insurance provides a very large degree of temporary protection at a relatively modest cost.

Even though term insurance is based on actuarial principles, there may be wide variations in price quotations, based on different assessments of risk, different premium structures, different commission rates payable to agents, and so forth. In addition, a variety of options may be offered in connection with a term policy: double payment in the event of accidental death, for example, or an option to convert term insurance at a later date into other types of insurance without a new medical examination.

Term insurance policies usually require a medical examination, though some companies may write term policies for younger persons solely on the basis of written health-related questions. Persons in certain risky occupations or having risky avocations may not be able to obtain term insurance at all, or may be able to obtain it only by paying an additional premium. Term insurance policies are usually renewable for additional terms (at higher premiums) without another medical examination or questionnaire. Many policies provide for level premiums for periods of up to five years, with the level premium during this period being approximately equal to the average of annual premiums over the period for a person of the age in question. Term insurance is also often sold at bargain prices in connection with or as a sweetener for other types of life insurance.

Group life insurance is a type of term insurance usually provided by employers for their employees, and also is offered by a wide variety of different kinds of membership organizations — fraternal organizations, trade associations, social clubs, investment clubs, and so forth — to their members through the organization. The premium for group life insurance is usually lower than the premium for the equivalent amount of term insurance that could be purchased individually for the same persons. There are several reasons for this. The administrative costs of insuring a group may be significantly less than the cost of insuring members individually (since selling and advertising costs are usually nominal and often the employer or organization arranging for the group insurance takes over some of the administrative costs). Second, the risk characteristics for the group in question may be more favorable than for the population generally. For example, a group of accountants may be able to obtain term insurance at more favorable group rates than as individuals because the accountants as a group have a better life expectancy than the population as a whole: They eat better, they are not subjected to employment-related risks that most blue collar workers face, and they are probably less likely to engage in hazardous activities such as motorcycle racing or skydiving. Third, in some cases the insurer may be willing to quote lower rates because the volume of term policies generated improves its diversification of risk or because it wishes to retain important business relationships with the employer.

Term insurance may be either *face amount* insurance (in which event the face amount is constant and the premium increases periodically) or *declining balance* (in which event the premium remains constant but the face amount of insurance coverage declines as the person gets older). A very common kind of declining balance insurance is *mortgage insurance*, sold in connection with a mortgage on a home, or *credit insurance*, required by many lenders when they make small consumer loans. The theory is that for a small additional monthly fixed sum, life insurance equal to the unpaid balance of the loan is maintained to make sure the loan is repaid in the event the borrower dies before the indebtedness is paid. The charges for this type of insurance are often significantly higher than the cost of a straight term policy; many consumer loan organizations maintain relationships with insurers and try to have those insurers write all of this lucrative type of insurance.

Declining balance term insurance is also sold through magazine or newspaper advertisements that promise small amounts of insurance and claim that premiums will not increase before a person reaches some specified age. These policies are usually extremely expensive for the coverage provided. A give-away that declining balance term is being advertised is usually that the amount of the insurance is either not set forth or is described as up to some specified amount.

§6.8 Whole Life Insurance

The most common type of traditional life insurance sold today is known by a variety of different names, such as *ordinary life, permanent life,* or *whole life*. These policies, unlike the tax-oriented variable or universal life insurance policies described in later sections, provide a fixed benefit on the death of the insured. Further, unlike term insurance, the premiums remain level from the date of the inception of the policy until the maturation of the policy upon the death of the insured. They differ significantly from term insurance in three important, indeed fundamental, respects.

First, the premiums for whole life policies for relatively young adults (or rarely, young children) are initially much higher than for term insurance for the amount of insurance protection for a person of the same age. This difference in premiums may be by a factor of 10 or more when the insured is in his or her 30s or 40s. For example, a 35-year-old man will typically pay an annual premium of $15 or $20 per $1,000 of coverage for a whole life policy while a comparable one-year renewable term policy would cost somewhere between $2 and $5 per $1,000. The premiums on term insurance of course increase with the age of the insured. If our hypothetical 35-year-old man retained the same amount of term insurance year after year, he would be in his early sixties before the annual term insurance premium equaled the annual premium for his whole life policy.

Second, even though the premiums remain constant, the face amount of insurance provided by a whole life policy also remains constant. Whole life insurance is unlike declining balance term insurance in this respect.

Third, whole life policies develop *cash values* or *cash surrender values* each year after the policy has been in existence for a couple of years. Much of the initial excess premium over the cost of term insurance goes to building up this value.

The logic underlying a whole life policy is basically very simple. The premiums during the early years of such a policy are much higher than the amount needed to buy only death protection (i.e., term insurance). A portion of this excess is set aside in a kind of savings account for later use by the owner of the policy. A whole life policy, unlike a term policy, thus combines a savings element as well as a life insurance element. This savings element gradually increases as the years go by and more premiums are paid. As described below, this cash value may be borrowed by the owner of the policy, and will be paid to him or her if the policy is surrendered and the insurance lapses. When the insured dies, however, the company pays only the face value of the policy, not the face value plus the cash value. Thus, the payment of the face value of the whole life policy upon the death of the insured in part comes from the savings account inherent in the cash value concept and in part from true life insurance. As the years go by and the cash surrender value increases, the company needs to provide a decreasing amount of pure life insurance protection. Indeed, by the time the insured reaches the ripe age of approximately 85, the savings account reaches the amount of the face value of the policy and the obligation to pay premiums ends. Such a policy is fully paid up since the savings account equals the face value of the policy, and there is no remaining component of life insurance to be paid from premiums.

This description is in some ways an oversimplification. Typically, cash values in a whole life policy build very slowly: There is usually no cash value after one or two years of premiums, and it may be three or four years before the entire cash value equals the amount of the premium due in any single year. Thereafter, the cash value builds more rapidly, fueled in part by the premium payments and in part by earnings on the money already invested. Cancellation of the policy during its first years therefore may involve a substantial financial loss. Furthermore, if a policy lapses and an attempt is made to replace it at a later date, the insured will find that the premium is increased because he or she is placed in an older age group when applying for the new insurance. These costs are often used by insurance agents as arguments against cancelling a whole life policy, or allowing it to lapse, when they learn that an insured is having difficulty making the payments.

At first glance it may seem backward that the buildup of cash value in the earliest years is the lowest, since the pure insurance cost for protection in the earliest years is also the lowest. Several factors help to explain this structure: the administrative costs of writing a policy, including the cost of a medical examination; the commission structure for the life insurance agent (typically one-half or more of the first year's premium goes to the agent as a commission for successfully selling the policy); and the desire to establish a premium structure that encourages retention of a policy rather than surrendering it.

As indicated above, the cash value of a whole life policy increases gradually each year after the first year the policy is in effect. A whole life policy is an investment, an asset of the owner of the policy, much like a bank account or a deposit in a mutual fund. A whole life policy may be assigned to a creditor as security for a loan; the creditor may name itself as beneficiary so that it will receive the proceeds from the policy upon the death of the insured and repay the loan from the proceeds. The remaining balance, if any, presumably belongs to the estate of the insured or his or her heirs. During the lifetime of the insured, the creditor may also surrender the policy for its cash surrender value if a default on the obligation occurs. While loans secured by assignments of life insurance are not uncommon, it is a mark of some desperation by the borrower, since he or she may be depriving the family of needed insurance protection in order to arrange a loan.

While alive, the owner of the policy can also borrow all or part of the cash value from the insurance company. A loan of the cash surrender value does not increase the insurance risk from the standpoint of the insurer, since if the insured dies while a loan is outstanding, the insurer simply subtracts the outstanding loan from the face amount of the policy and pays the beneficiary the difference. Traditionally, the interest rate on such loans is very low, often 5 percent in the case of older policies. It is important to recognize that this is a very peculiar loan because the insurance company is already holding the cash surrender value in order to make a death payment at some future time. Loans of the cash surrender value are more like advances than loans. In one respect, loans of the cash surrender value may adversely affect the insurance company. Its cash flow comes from two sources: premium payments and the return from investments. Loans of cash surrender values reduce the amount available for investment by the insurance company and may reduce its cash flow. This occurs on every such loan whenever the market interest rate on investments is higher than the interest rate charged to the policy owner.

After a whole life policy has been in effect for several years, loans from the cash surrender value may be used to pay future premiums. This practice may permit an insured to keep a policy in effect over long periods without paying premiums, but subject to a gradual reduction of the death benefit that will ultimately be paid. Do you see how this might work?

A study prepared by the Federal Trade Commission in 1979 attempted to estimate the rate of return on a whole life policy viewing its cash value as an investment. This is not a simple computation because a portion of each premium must be allocated to the insurance feature of the whole life policy. The study concluded that the return was negative — that is, the cash value was less than the amount invested — for over 10 years and after 20 years the rate of return was only 2 percent. Thus as a savings vehicle, the whole life policy is inferior to any modern insured savings account. Indeed, a strategy of "buying term and investing the difference" — a phrase used by critics of the traditional insurance industry — usually yields a significantly larger investment after 20 years than buying a whole life policy. This strategy is somewhat similar to the do-it-yourself annuities discussed in the previous chapter, and both suffer from some of the same problems. For example, while the buying term and investing the difference yields superior results, the specific results are based on the assumption that a savings account will yield a definite return, and this cannot be guaranteed. A decline in the rate of interest on the savings component may make the differences much less dramatic. Also, savings through life insurance premium payments is convenient and there is a built-in incentive not to let the insurance lapse. Many persons might lack the discipline to make the same payments into a savings account absent the need to preserve their insurance. Whole life policies also contain some significant options that cannot be replicated in a do-it-yourself plan: A waiver of premiums in the event of disability, for example, is generally available at no additional cost and is tremendously valuable in the rare situation where disability occurs. Other valuable rights may include options to purchase annuity rights, the ability to use the cash surrender value to buy additional paid-up insurance without a medical examination, and so forth. Finally, accumulations in a "buying term and invest the rest" plan are subject to federal income taxes each year while the growth of cash value within a whole life policy is tax deferred.

An argument can be made that it is unrealistic to analyze a whole life policy as being divided into an insurance component and a savings component. One can argue that the whole life insurance contract should be viewed as an undifferentiated whole, and that it consists of buying insurance protection on a level-premium installment plan, in which young people prepay their premiums in the earlier years for protection they will receive many years later when the actual insurance costs greatly exceed the premium then being paid. One basic problem with this analysis is that it gives little weight to the phenomenon of the growth of the cash value within a whole life policy, which is a central feature of whole life insurance. Furthermore, this approach toward whole life raises new questions: It ignores the time value of the money that is prepaid, and also gives no weight to the possibility of inflation and increased earning capacity in later years. If this were the sole explanation of whole life insurance offered to most persons, it is likely that they would opt for term insurance and invest the difference.

§6.9 Endowment and Paid-up-at-65 Policies

In addition to the traditional whole life policy, many other life insurance policies are offered that combine savings and life insurance protection in varying degrees. An *endowment policy*, for example, involves payments for a specified period, perhaps 20 or 30 years; at that point the cash value equals the policy face amount and the insurance is fully paid up. A *paid-up-at-65 policy* is similar except that the period during which payments must be made ends at age 65. Obviously, substantially higher premium payments are required for all types of endowment or "paid-up" policies than for a whole life policy. As a result, these policies enjoy limited attractiveness.

§6.10 Variable Life Insurance

The chaotic economic conditions of the late 1960s and 1970s were marked by high inflation rates and rapidly increasing interest rates. These developments created unprecedented pressures on the traditional forms of life insurance, particularly the whole life policy, the mainstay of the domestic life insurance industry. The prospect of high inflation rates made the savings account feature of cash surrender values relatively unattractive. People realized that they were investing current dollars in exchange for repayments many years later in dollars worth much less because of inflation. Further, the relatively low effective rates of return on the cash surrender value made whole life unattractive when compared with competing, riskless investments. The earliest indication of difficult times ahead for the insurance industry was the increase in cash surrender value loans as policy owners borrowed against cash surrender values at 5 percent per year in order to invest the proceeds in much higher yielding investments in the open market. Furthermore, between 1977 and 1981, whole life policies, while still the largest single selling type of insurance, declined significantly as a percentage of the total amount of ordinary life insurance outstanding, with growth in term insurance accounting for most of the increase. It was apparent from these trends that the insurance industry would have to come up with new products if it wished to prosper.

The first new products developed by the insurance industry were relatively modest. A *variable premium life policy* was offered, which provided that future premiums would be decreased if the company's investment income increased from rising interest rates and inflation. In effect, the company offered to share a portion of the windfall generated by rising interest rates with policyholders by reducing the premium in later years. An *adjustable life insurance policy* was also developed that allowed an individual to switch protection from term to whole life, or back. The policies also offered some flexibility in the timing and amount of premium payments, and provided for periodic readjustments to take into account mortality charges and expenses.

More recently, the insurance industry struck a popular chord when it developed a new life insurance policy that is now generally known as *single-premium variable life insurance*. This policy has significant tax deferral benefits and is sold more for the tax and investment benefits than for the insurance benefits. The policy can be analyzed as containing two interrelated components: a term life insurance component and an accumulation component analogous to the traditional cash surrender value of a whole life policy. The applicant at the outset must deposit a certain amount in an *accumulation account* to finance the insurance component, and may make a larger initial deposit or may thereafter make additional deposits. The accumulation account is virtually an investment account. The applicant may direct how the accumulation account is to be invested within four or five limited alternatives provided by the insurance company or an associated brokerage firm. The choices cover the most popular investment strategies in terms of type of security, degree of risk, and diversification of investments, for example, a stock mutual fund, a bond fund, or a capital appreciation fund. As the accumulation account increases, the amount of insurance that must be purchased also increases, but at a much slower rate. The owner of the policy may also borrow the amount of the excess accumulation account.

The driving principle behind this insurance policy is that, like the accumulation of cash surrender values in a traditional whole life policy, the growth of the accumulation account is not subject to federal income tax so long as the policy remains outstanding. Hundreds of thousands of dollars may be deposited in the accumulation account to grow on a tax exempt basis. Further, the accumulation is exempt from income taxation upon the death of the insured. In other words, this policy is really a tax deferred or tax sheltered investment vehicle packaged as insurance.

The amount of term insurance provided in the package is the minimum amount required by Internal Revenue Code provisions to ensure that the package is taxed as an insurance policy rather than as an investment account. However, in practice the amount of insurance is not the dominant or driving factor but is incidental, determined by the tax laws and the amount the applicant has invested in the accumulation account.

It may be recalled that single-premium annuities also may serve as tax sheltered investment vehicles. (See §5.5.) In 1986, Congress restricted the tax advantages of the annuity by providing that lifetime loans or distributions are deemed to be from the income component of the fund, and therefore taxable to the annuitant when made. At the present time, loans from the accumulation account of the single-premium variable insurance policy are treated like loans from the cash surrender value of a whole life policy and are not viewed as distributions of previously untaxed earnings. In this respect, the insurance vehicle currently has a significant tax advantage over the annuity vehicle. In addition, upon the death of the insured the proceeds may be excludable from the insured's estate for federal estate tax purposes, much as any other type of insurance; that is, if the policy is not owned by the deceased and is not payable to his or her estate.

The disadvantages of this novel type of insurance policy largely revolve around the fees and charges imposed by the insurance company. In addition, premature termination of the policy may result in a significant investment loss, and restrictions are placed on what percentage of the value of an accumulation account may be borrowed by the insured. A further consequence is that the plan necessarily entails the purchase of increasing amounts of term life insurance as the accumulation account increases even though that purchase might not be justified in the absence of the tax deferral aspect of the plan. Finally, there is some lingering concern that Congress may decide to limit the tax deferral advantages of these life insurance policies if they become too popular. Certainly, Congress has consistently tried to limit tax shelters that are believed to be abusive or involve the loss of substantial revenue: The single premium variable life insurance policy may be found to fall within this category in the future.

§6.11 Is Term or Whole Life Insurance Better for Me?

This question cannot be answered in the abstract; the needs of the speaker must be carefully considered.

It seems clear that for most young persons with family responsibilities but no significant assets, term insurance — particularly group insurance — meets a basic need of providing protection at the lowest possible cost. The consequences of an untimely and unexpected death may be so devastating that any trade-off that involves a smaller amount of protection at the same cost would seem unwise. It is surprising that many people in this situation are persuaded to buy whole life policies even though such policies provide significantly less protection for the dollar invested, and the savings account feature of whole life may strain the family's budget in order to provide benefits many years later when they do not need the money as badly. The reason many people are persuaded to buy whole life policies is apparently more a function of the persuasiveness of insurance agents, whose commissions are much higher on whole life policies than they are on term policies, than on rational examination of the alternatives available.

Many people of modest means may buy whole life insurance to ensure that there will be readily available funds for burial and to discharge debts and obligations. Others may purchase whole life because of the savings and tax deferral features of such policies. When all is said and done, however, probably more whole life insurance is sold than objective analysis would justify.

Even though life insurance companies offer reasonably standardized products, there are significant differences in costs from company to company, with the larger, better known, most widely advertised companies usually being at the higher end. Many people apparently do not comparison shop for insurance; rather they apparently deal with a specific agent of some company and buy what he or she sells them.

These comments relate only to the traditional products of term and whole life insurance sold by companies. The development of variable life insurance products is not addressed in this basic choice. Rather, variable life should be viewed as a device to permit tax-free accumulations from large pools of capital.

III

◇

ACCOUNTING, INSOLVENCY, AND VALUATION

CHAPTER 7

FUNDAMENTALS OF DOUBLE ENTRY BOOKKEEPING

§7.1 Introduction

Business and financial transactions are usually recorded in financial books and records as they occur. The results of the operation of the business itself are periodically communicated through financial statements that are themselves usually based on these financial books and records. *Accounting* thus involves the collection, summarization, and reporting of financial data by a business. It also involves the computation of profit and other measures of a business's financial health. The creation and maintenance of financial records are usually performed or overseen by persons with backgrounds in accounting, and the language in which the results of business operations are communicated is typically the language of the accountant. Every lawyer should have working familiarity with this language.

In addition, in order to understand what is being communicated in financial statements, one has to understand not only the underlying principles on which modern accounting systems are based but also the major limitations on, or more accurately, the major policy decisions that underlie, those accounting systems. Since financial statements can be prepared on any number of different accounting systems, one also has to know what principles were followed in the creation of the specific financial statements under consideration, whether they depart from accepted accounting principles, and if they do, the extent to which the differences affect the results being reported. The standard set of accounting principles that forms the norm for financial reporting in the United States is known as *generally accepted accounting principles* (usually abbreviated as *GAAP*). These principles must be followed by most publicly held corporations in the United States in reporting publicly the results of their operations. GAAP is not a canonical set of rules but rather a loose set of rules and principles that outlines a range of reasonable and permissable treatments of many transactions. There is a hierarchy of generally accepted accounting principles: (1) the most authoritative are standards published by the Financial Accounting Standards Board (FASB), a panel created by the American Institute of Certified Public Accountants (AICPA) with the cooperation of the Securities and Exchange

Commission to review accounting issues and promulgate GAAP standards; (2) other accounting standards published by AICPA; (3) general principles that pervade the practice of accounting and the accounting literature; and (4) prevalent customs and usages in the practice of accounting. The Securities and Exchange Commission has legal authority to prescribe mandatory accounting standards to be followed by reporting publicly held companies, but the magnitude of accounting issues has led it to reply primarily on the FASB to establish principles.

Some knowledge of the accounting process is obviously absolutely essential for lawyers in a corporate or business practice, and indeed is useful for all lawyers without regard to the nature of their practice. Furthermore, there is an art to the process of analyzing financial statements with which every lawyer should be familiar.

Law students without business or financial backgrounds may have irrational—almost primordial—fears about accounting principles and concepts. It is true that accounting can become very complex and esoteric; after all, accounting itself is a subject in which people regularly receive advanced graduate degrees and then spend productive lifetimes. On the other hand, one can readily understand the fundamental principles of accounting and learn to read and understand financial statements without becoming enmeshed in these complexities. This and the following two chapters attempt to do precisely this.

§7.2 The Purposes of Accounting

Accounting in a large business involves two basic functions: the entering of records of transactions as they occur, and the subsequent determination and reporting of results of operations on a periodic basis. In a large publicly held corporation, unaudited financial results are usually reported quarterly to the public and audited results are reported annually. These statements are prepared primarily for the benefit of investors: They are widely publicized and are used and relied upon by creditors, regulatory agencies, employees, and others. The preparation of these public reports is usually described as *financial accounting* as contrasted with *management accounting*. A major goal of financial accounting is to ensure that the financial reports are prepared honestly and in accordance with GAAP so that they are comparable with earlier reports and the reports of other companies. The importance of comparability of published financial reports as a concept cannot be overemphasized since innumerable investment and commercial decisions are made on the premise that such reports are comparable with the same company's reports for earlier periods and with published reports of other companies in the same or different industries. On the other hand, in any complex organization numerous discretionary accounting judgments must be made so that variation in treatment is inevitable and total comparability never achieved.

Financial information about corporate affairs is also essential if management of a publicly held corporation is to make informed internal decisions. For internal purposes, financial results may be reported to top management and the board of directors on a weekly or even a daily basis. Financial analyses of specific business alternatives or strategies will also be prepared as the need arises. These internal reports and analyses are usually not prepared in accordance with GAAP since they are not publicly available. They may involve analyses of controls and costs. Their preparation is sometimes called *management accounting* to distinguish this area from the publicly oriented financial accounting described in the preceding paragraph.

The routine recording and summarization of transactions is also essential to ensure that the business always has the proper inventory of raw materials and finished goods on hand, so that its manufacturing operations continue smoothly and that it in fact produces what customers have ordered or are willing to buy. The keeping track of and reporting functions are related since the records utilized in the process of recording transactions as they occur are also used as the basis for the compilation of the results of operations. Modern accounting is a continuing process that permits transactions that are numerous, large, and complex to be accounted for on a routine basis involving relatively low paid and marginally skilled employees. Of course, the original creation of the bookkeeping process for a specific business, the oversight of that process, and decisions as to the manner in which specific significant transactions are to be accounted for within that process require the participation and perceptions of persons who have a broad view of the whole accounting process.

Persons unfamiliar with the accounting process are apt to believe that accounting is a precise science, or at least that there is general acceptance of basic principles as to how transactions should be handled for financial accounting purposes. This is, to a large extent, an incorrect impression. Within the accounting profession, and to a large extent in general business publications, discussions of the most appropriate treatment of specific transactions or of classes of transactions are often heated and the conclusions are controversial. These controversies are fueled by the underlying fact that in the eyes of the financial community the success or failure of an enterprise is largely measured by its reported financial results, and any compulsory change in GAAP that significantly affects (i.e., unexpectedly reduces) the reported results of operations of publicly held companies may have significant and wide-ranging repercussions even though only the manner of reporting the transaction—rather than the transaction itself—has changed. In a fundamental sense, accounting is a language that (like most languages) allows considerable variation in expression; it is not a matter of right and wrong so much as what is useful and comparable and what is not.

Financial accounting gives a deceptive aura of accuracy. Amounts are entered in precise dollars-and-cents figures. Accountants state that accounting principles require a specific treatment of an item. This appearance of accuracy and specificity should not be permitted to hide the fact that there is often room for differences of opinion as to how matters should be treated and presented. Indeed, there is considerable disagreement as to whether the entire edifice of accounting principles described in this and the following chapters is built on quicksand and should be scrapped in favor of a discounted cash flow analysis. See §§9.4 and 11.7.

§7.3 The Fundamentals of Accounting

The starting point of the whole subject of accountancy is a very simple equation:

$$Equity = Assets - Liabilities$$

Equity in this equation has nothing to do with the historical courts of equity or with notions of fairness or simple justice: It means *ownership* or *net worth*. This equation simply states that the net worth of a business is equal to its assets minus its liabilities.

A *balance sheet* is in many ways the most fundamental financial statement: It is simply a restatement of this fundamental equation in the form:

$$Assets = Liabilities + Equity$$

A balance sheet simply is a presentation of this equation in a chart form:

Assets:	Liabilities
	+ Equity

Every balance sheet, whether it is for General Motors or the smallest retail grocery store, is based on this format. As an illustration, Exxon's published 1987 balance sheet is reprinted on page 153 as Table 7-1. The basic construct should be self-evident from a casual examination of this statement, even though it is printed with the liability/equity side immediately below the asset side.

The asset side of a balance sheet is always referred to as the *left hand side* even though it is sometimes printed (as in the Exxon balance sheet) above rather than to the left: Similarly, the liability/equity side is always the *right hand side* even though it is sometimes printed below rather than to the right.

There are four fundamental premises underlying financial accounting that can readily be grasped from this simple introduction. First, *financial accounting assumes that the business that is the subject of the financial statements is an entity.* A person may own several different businesses; if each maintains its own records, it will be on the assumption that it is independent from the person's other businesses. The equity referred to in that business's balance sheet will be limited to the person's investment in that single business. If a person owns two businesses that keep separate financial records, a debt owed by one business to the other will be reflected as an asset on one balance sheet and a liability on the other. Second, *all entries have to be in terms of dollars.* All property, tangible or intangible, shown on a balance sheet, must be expressed in dollars, either *historical cost* or *fair market value* or some other method of valuation. Many "assets" or "liabilities" of a business, however, are not reflected at all. A person's friendly smile may be an asset in a sense, but will not appear on a balance sheet since a dollar value is not normally given to a smile. Intangible assets, such as a debt owed to the company or rights to a patent, on the other hand, are assets

Table 7-1

Consolidated Balance Sheet   **EXXON CORPORATION**

	Dec. 31, 1986	Dec. 31, 1987
	(millions of dollars)	
Assets		
Current assets		
Cash	$ 2,908	$ 1,911
Marketable securities	908	620
Notes and accounts receivable, less estimated		
doubtful amounts	6,784	6,278
Inventories		
Crude oil, products and merchandise	3,603	4,200
Materials and supplies	948	972
Prepaid taxes and expenses	1,169	1,410
Total current assets	16,320	15,391
Investments and advances	2,778	3,822
Property, plant and equipment, at cost, less		
accumulated depreciation and depletion	49,289	53,434
Other assets, including intangibles	1,097	1,395
Total assets	$69,484	$74,042
Liabilities		
Current liabilities		
Notes and loans payable	$ 3,584	$ 2,864
Accounts payable and accrued liabilities	9,515	10,248
Income taxes payable	2,121	2,184
Total current liabilities	15,220	15,296
Long-term debt	4,294	5,021
Annuity reserves and accrued liabilities	5,121	5,902
Deferred income tax credits	10,828	11,863
Deferred income	466	560
Equity of minority shareholders in affiliated		
companies	1,543	1,774
Total liabilities	37,472	40,416
Shareholders' equity		
Capital stock without par value (authorized 2 billion		
shares, 1,813 million issued)	2,822	2,822
Earnings reinvested	37,322	39,476
Cumulative foreign exchange translation adjustment	(196)	1,750
Capital stock held in treasury, at cost (378 million		
shares in 1986, 434 million shares in 1987)	(7,936)	(10,422)
Total shareholders' equity	32,012	33,626
Total liabilities and shareholders' equity	$69,484	$74,042

The information on pages 29 through 36 [in the original] is an integral part of these statements.

that appear in balance sheets. On the Exxon balance sheet, tangible and intangible assets are combined under the entry "other assets, including intangibles."
Similarly, a company may have a reputation for sharp practices or questionable
dealing; while that reputation is doubtless a liability in a sense, it is not the
type of liability that appears on a balance sheet. A liability in the balance sheet
sense is a recognized debt or obligation to someone else, payable either in
money or in something reducible to money. Not all liabilities that in the legal
or lay sense meet this test are recognized as liabilities in the accounting sense.
See §8.2. Third, *a balance sheet has to balance*. The fundamental accounting
equation itself states an equality: The two sides of the balance sheet restate that
equality in somewhat reorganized form. A balance sheet therefore is itself an
equality and the sum of the left hand side of the balance sheet must precisely
equal the sum of the right hand side. Indeed, when accountants are involved
in auditing a complex business, they take advantage of this characteristic by
running *trial balances* on their work to make sure that they have not inadvertently transposed or omitted figures: The mathematical equality of the two
sides of the balance sheet provides a check on the accuracy of the accountant's
labors. In short, if a balance sheet doesn't balance, somewhere there is a mistake.
Fourth, *every transaction entered into by a business must be recorded in at least two
ways if the balance sheet is to continue to balance*. This last point underlies the
concept of that mysterious subject, *double entry bookkeeping*, and is the cornerstone on which modern accounting is built.

Assume that we have a new business, just starting out, in which the owner
has invested $10,000 in cash (for this purpose it makes no difference whether
the business is going to be conducted in the form of a proprietorship, partnership, or corporation; all that is important is that it will be accounted for as an
entity separate from the owner). The opening balance sheet will look like this:

Assets:		Liabilities	-0-
Cash	10,000	Owner's Equity	10,000

Now let us assume that the owner buys a used truck for $3,000 cash. The
effect of this transaction is to reduce cash by $3,000 and create a new asset on
the balance sheet:

Assets:		Liabilities	-0-
Cash	7,000	Owner's Equity	10,000
Used Truck	3,000		
	10,000		10,000

Voila! The balance sheet still balances. Let us assume next that the owner goes
down to the bank and borrows an additional $1,000. This also has a dual

effect: it increases cash by $1,000 (since the business is receiving the proceeds of the loan) and increases liabilities by $1,000 (since the business thereafter has to repay the loan). Yet another balance sheet can be created showing the additional effect of this second transaction:

Assets:		Liabilities	
Cash	8,000	Debt to Bank	1,000
Used Truck	3,000	Owner's Equity	10,000
	11,000		11,000

A couple of further insights should be evident from these two examples: First, *a balance sheet records a situation at one instant in time.* It is a static concept, an equilibrium that exists at one point in time rather than a record of change from an earlier period. Put another way, every transaction potentially creates a different or new balance sheet when the transaction is recorded. Second, *the bottom line of a balance sheet*—$11,000 in this example—*is not itself a meaningful figure,* since transactions such as the bank loan that do not affect the real worth of the business to the owners may increase or decrease it.

§7.4 Accounting for Profits and Losses

The two transactions described above—the purchase of a used truck and a short-term bank loan—involve a reshuffling of assets and liabilities. From an accounting standpoint, the owner of the business is neither richer nor poorer as a result of them. However, most transactions that a business enters into are of a different type: They involve ordinary business operations leading to a profit or loss in the current accounting period. Let us take a simple example: The business involves hauling things in the truck for customers. The day that it opens for business, it hires a truck driver at a cost of $200 per day to drive the truck and pick up and deliver for it. During that first day the truck driver works very hard and for long hours making deliveries for which the business is paid $500. It is simple to create a *profit and loss statement* or *income statement* for the business for the one day of operation. "Profit and loss" and "income" are synonyms for this purpose. The basic formula is:

$$\text{Income} = \text{Revenues} - \text{Expenses}$$

Obviously, the business had income of $300 ($500 of revenue minus $200 of expense for the truck driver) for its first day of operation. There may have been other expenses as well that arguably should be charged to that first day of operation, but for simplicity we are ignoring that possibility.

At first glance the income statement appears to have nothing to do with the balance sheet described in the previous section. However, one should not jump too quickly to conclusions. It is possible to create a new balance sheet to reflect each of these transactions as well:

First, the payment of the $200 to the truck driver involves a cash payment of $200 by the business; it is easy to record that. But where should the offsetting entry be? The balance sheet cannot look like this:

Assets:		Liabilities	
Cash	7,800	Debt to bank	1,000
Used truck	3,000	Equity	10,000
	10,800		11,000

Something is obviously wrong since this balance sheet does not balance. There has to be an offsetting entry. It certainly should not be a reduction of liabilities (since the amount of the bank loan is unchanged) or an increase in value of the truck. Perhaps one could view the services as an asset something like the truck, but that does not make much sense since the services are transient and performed at the time the payment is made. One could perhaps argue that no balance sheet should be created until the payment to the truck driver is offset by whatever he earns during the rest of the day, but that cannot be correct either, because the balance sheet should balance after every transaction, not just at the end of a sequence of transactions. The only possible solution is to reduce "owner's equity" by the payment:

Assets:		Liabilities	
Cash	7,800	Debt to bank	1,000
Used truck	3,000	Equity	9,800
	10,800		10,800

Second, the $500 payment for the services rendered:

Assets:		Liabilities	
Cash	8,300	Debt to bank	1,000
Used truck	3,000	Equity	10,300
	11,300		11,300

Admittedly, these two balance sheets are not very helpful in showing the relationship between the balance sheet and the income statement. What is needed is a segregation of income items *within the equity account* so that the permanent investment and the transient changes are shown separately. If we take as the period of time the one-day period in which the truck driver was

156

hired and his services were performed, the following balance sheet at the end of the period is much more illuminating:

Assets:			Liabilities	
Cash	8,300		Debt to bank	1,000
Used truck	3,000		Original capital	10,000
			Earnings	300
	11,300			11,300

The important point at present is that *the statement of income or profit and loss is itself a right-hand entry on the balance sheet.*

The balance sheet is a static concept showing the status of a business at a particular instant in time while the income statement describes the results of operations over some period of time: daily, monthly, quarterly, or annually. In a sense, the balance sheet is a photograph, the income statement a motion picture. However, the income statement for a period provides the bridge between the balance sheet at the beginning of the period and the balance sheet at the end of the period because positive income items (revenues) increase the owner's equity account while negative income items (expenses) reduce that account. Logically, the balance sheet is the basic document around which all financial statements are constructed while the income statement is a bridge between successive balance sheets.

The balance of this chapter largely considers the problems of the income statement; most investors and creditors look first at the bottom line of the income statement when evaluating financial statements. In practical modern analysis primary emphasis is usually placed on the income statement as reflecting the operations of the business while the balance sheet plays a lesser role.

The concept of profit and loss and accounting periods rests on additional fundamental postulates. First, *accounting assumes the continuing existence and activity of the business enterprise as a going concern*. In other words it is assumed that the business will be around for an indefinite number of future accounting periods. If a business is in such dire straits that its continued existence is unlikely, a totally different set of accounting principles must be adopted. Second, *each business must adopt a fiscal or accounting period and must report the results of operations for that period as a separate accounting unit*. The unit usually chosen is a year, either a calendar year or a *fiscal year*, that is, a reporting period chosen by the business that ends on a date other than December 31 and may vary somewhat in length from a period of precisely twelve months. Third, *in determining the results of operations during an accounting period, some kind of logical relationship must be created between the revenues (incoming dollars) and costs (outgoing dollars) that are taken into account in determining profit or loss for that period*. The principle usually followed is that costs allocable to the creation of revenue should be matched with that revenue. Other costs arising from the passage of time are allocated to the accounting period on the basis of that time and not the time of receipt. Fourth, *some principles must be established as to when revenue is realized.* The usual rule adopted is that revenues are realized when the business becomes unconditionally entitled to their receipt, not when payment is received. In the case of a contract for the sale of goods, for example, revenue may be realized when the goods are shipped, not when the contract was entered into or when payment is made. As a corollary, property of the business that may have appreciated in market value does not give rise to revenue until the gain in value is realized by sale or disposition of the property.

At this point it is necessary to go back and introduce the reader to the way in which the double entry bookkeeping system is used to record transactions as they occur and to permit the development of balance sheets and income statements from those records.

§7.5   Journal Entries

The essence of bookkeeping or double entry bookkeeping is the systematic recordation of every transaction in the offsetting ways described above. For many centuries, the process of recordation involved the manual entry of transactions by persons wearing little green eye shades. In larger businesses, many, many transactions would have to be entered each day, requiring the business to employ many bookkeepers. The development of the modern computer has automated the bookkeeping process as it has so many other areas: In most businesses today, the process involves relatively small inputs of human labor. Computerized accounting programs, however, largely follow the logic of the earlier manual system. In the discussion of fundamentals below, it is assumed that all transactions are entered manually so that the structure can be examined.

The persons recording transactions of the type described above do not normally create a new balance sheet after each transaction; in any business with even minimal activity there are numerous entries each day and a balance sheet is created only periodically. The bookkeeper records each transaction in a "journal" to reflect both sides of each transaction; journal entries to reflect the truck purchase and the bank loan transactions would look like something like this:

Description of transaction	*Debit*	*Credit*
1/1/87 Cash		$3,000
Vehicles	$3,000	
To record purchase of truck		
1/2/87 Cash	$1,000	
Current Liabilities		$1,000
To record 90-day loan from bank		

Now, there may not seem to be any relationship between these two entries, and the two balance sheets set forth above. Because of a couple of ingenious accounting conventions, however, they are reflections of the same transactions, and an accountant can readily go from the journal entries to the balance sheets.

First of all, a word needs to be said about the words *debit* and *credit* in the titles to the foregoing journal entries (titles, incidentally that are so well understood that they do not usually appear on real journal pages). The word *debit* simply means "left hand" and the word *credit* means "right hand." There is widespread popular confusion over the meaning of these two terms. In a lay sense, *debit* is probably associated with *reduction* while *credit* is associated with *increase*. Once the notion of double entry bookkeeping is introduced, however, it is clear that the words require more careful elaboration, for every transaction, in a sense, involves both an increase and a decrease. Further, all journal entries by conventional understanding are positive. The basic accounting convention that ties journal entries to balance sheet items can be simply stated but is rather confusing: a debit journal entry *increases* left hand items on the balance sheet and *decreases* right hand items while a credit journal entry *reduces* left hand items and *increases* right hand items. Thus, in the foregoing examples, an experienced accountant looking at the two entries knows at a glance that the business reduced its cash account by $3,000 when it bought the truck and increased it by $1,000 when it entered into the bank loan. Similarly, an accountant knows at a glance that the credit reflecting the bank loan increased the business's liabilities, since "liabilities" is a right hand account.

A major cause of confusion about the meaning of "debit" and "credit" is that in a two-person transaction, the way one person treats a transaction may be used as a description by both persons. For example, when you deposit $100 in your friendly bank, from the bank's perspective it debits its cash account by $100 (since debits increase left hand items such as cash) and credits the amount owed to you (the debt the bank owes to you in the form of your account with the bank) by $100. When the bank says it has credited $100 to your account you are apt to think, "Aha, I have $100 more in the bank than before" and that credit therefore means increase and debit means decrease, but that is not strictly accurate. When you write a check for $100, and the bank pays it, the bank "credits" its cash account for the $100 payment it has just made and "debits" your account with it to reflect the $100 it has paid at your direction. That is the reason that you may receive from your bank a *debit memo* when a charge, for example, for new imprinted checks, is made against your account by the bank.

Because the income statement may be viewed as part of the right hand side of the balance sheet, journal entries are also used to enter transactions involving the income statement. The basic concept is that revenue items are credits and expense items are debits. (Recall that credits increase right hand items and debits reduce them.) It is no problem at all, therefore, to visualize what the journal entries for the salary payment to the truck driver, Z, as we will call him, and the receipt of the fee for his first effort. They look like this:

1/1/87

Current salaries — expense	$200	
Cash		$200

To reflect Z's salary

Cash	$500	
Fees earned — income		$500

To reflect fee for Z's services

The "current salaries" account is an income statement item (an expense item that reduces earnings, as all debits must do) while the cash account to which it is joined in the journal appears only on the balance sheet; similarly the "fees earned" account is also an income statement item (a receipt item that increases earnings, as all credits must do) while the balance sheet item cash is increased.

The ingenious aspect of the double entry system is that a single set of entries permit the development of both types of financial statements as well as providing the internal controls over transactions that are essential for any large business.

§7.6 Ledger or "T" Accounts

It is theoretically possible to develop a balance sheet and income statement directly from journal entries. However, a moment's thought should reveal that in any business with a large number of transactions, a journal of the type described above, while good for keeping track of transactions individually as they occur, is not very useful in determining where the business stands at any one time. The reason for this is that entries relating to cash and other important accounts on the balance sheet as well as income and expense items are scattered almost randomly throughout the pages of the journal. The obvious solution is to create a separate ledger or page for each of the important balance sheet and income statement entries. These ledger accounts are called "T accounts" because they traditionally are kept on sheets that look like a balance sheet:

Cash
_____
+ entries (debits) | − entries (credits)

All debits go on the left side and credits on the right. Usually there is a separate T account for each item on the balance sheet, and as entries are made in the journal they are also entered on the appropriate T account. They may be entered simultaneously (as occurs in computerized programs), or hourly or daily, depending on the activity in the T account. In connection with the cash account, a person can then determine, by adding each side, then subtracting the right hand side from the left hand side, where the business's cash account stands at any time.

Every item on the balance sheet theoretically has its own ledger or T account. Similarly, separate ledger accounts are created for income and expense entries in much the same way as they are created for balance sheet items. T accounts can best be envisioned as subparts of the balance sheet: The "cash," "notes payable," and "retained earnings" ledgers are shown in the following diagram as a part of the balance sheet:

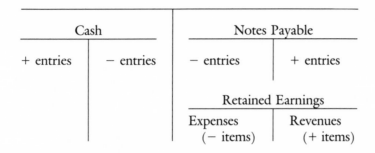

Thus a receipt of cash is a debit to the cash account (itself a left hand entry on the balance sheet) while a payment of cash is a credit to the cash account and goes on the right hand side of the cash account. The cash entry on a balance sheet at any time is the net difference between the debits and credits to cash. Similarly, the payment of an expense reduces the cash account (a credit) and increases the expense account (a debit). The beauty of this system is that it combines the double entry system for recording transactions with a method of developing balance sheets and income statements by following fairly simple and routine processes. If simple rules about recording debit and credit entries for each transaction are regularly followed, one can routinely construct balance sheets and income statements on a relatively mechanical basis as well as providing a method of recording—and thereby keeping track of—routine transactions.

Obviously, the income statement requires its own set of ledger accounts, and many of them are extremely active in any substantial business. Depending on the nature of the business, among these new ledger accounts there are whole families of up-items (receipts, sales, interest, rent, etc.) and down-items (salaries, cost of goods sold, depreciation, advertising, etc.). These income ledger accounts differ from the balance sheet ledger accounts in one respect: Since they reflect transactions occurring during a specific time period, they must be adjusted back to zero at the beginning of each new accounting period. This is done by special journal entries at the close of the prior period that transfer the balances to the balance sheet account, usually called *retained earnings*. Balance sheet accounts need not be closed out after the preparation of a new balance sheet, since balance sheets reflect an instantaneous picture of the business accounts, and the balance sheet at the close of one accounting period is identical with the balance sheet at the opening of the next period.

CHAPTER 8

FUNDAMENTAL ACCOUNTING PRINCIPLES

§8.1 Introduction

This chapter describes the fundamental principles that underlie modern accounting statements. It deals with the accepted methods of treating commonly recurring accounting problems in a complex enterprise. Before turning to a discussion of these major issues, however, it is useful to present a modern income statement and balance sheet for a relatively complex business and describe briefly the items in each statement. The relationship of these two statements to the primitive examples used in the previous chapter should be evident. The purpose of this exercise is primarily to familiarize the reader with the traditional language used in financial statements and give an example of what financial statements look like. The two statements appear on pages 164 and 169.

As is customary, the balance sheet is as of the close of business on the last day of the accounting period covered by the income statement.

§8.2 The Balance Sheet

Table 8-1 shows the left hand side of a balance sheet, which reflects the various asset accounts. It is customarily subdivided into two categories: *current* assets and *noncurrent* assets.

Current assets consist of cash plus other assets that normally may be expected to be turned into cash within a year (or, in a few cases, in a longer period constituting the business's normal operating cycles).

Cash. Cash includes not only funds on deposit in checking accounts, but also cash equivalents. As described in earlier chapters, large sums of money are not normally left idle for even short periods of time (such as a single day). In most publicly held companies, temporarily excess funds are conservatively invested on a daily or short-term basis in riskless securities that are usually not subject to swings in value. In the modern era, such

Table 8-1
ABC Incorporated
Balance Sheet as of December 31, 1987

ASSETS

Current Assets		
Cash	$ 300,000	
Marketable securities at cost (market value $890,000)	460,000	
Accounts receivable: 2,000,000 less $100,000 allowance for bad debt	1,900,000	
Inventories	3,000,0000	
Total currents assets		$5,660,000
Noncurrent Assets		
Fixed assets		
(property, plant, and equipment)		
Land	$ 450,000	
Building	3,600,000	
Machinery	850,000	
Office equipment	95,000	
	$4,995,000	
Less: accumulated depreciation	1,500,000	
Net fixed assets	$3,495,000	
Prepayments and deferred charges		40,000
Intangible assets		
Patents and Copyrights	75,000	
Goodwill	25,000	100,000
Other assets		50,000
Total assets		$9,345,000

LIABILITIES

Current liabilities		
Accounts payable	$ 940,000	
Notes payable	1,000,000	
Accrued expenses payable	300,000	
Federal income taxes payable	290,000	
Total current liabilities		$2,530,000
Long-term liabilities		
5% Debentures, due 2016		2,700,000
Total liabilities		$5,230,000

STOCKHOLDERS' EQUITY

Capital stock		
Preferred stock		
($10 par value, 60,000 shares issued and outstanding)		600,000
Common stock ($5 par value, 300,000 shares issued and outstanding)		1,500,000
Additional capital paid in respect of common stock		700,000
Retained earnings		1,315,000
Total stockholders' equity		$4,115,000
Total liabilities and stockholders' equity		$9,345,000

investments may include United States treasury bills or notes, certificates of deposit, commercial paper, bankers' acceptances, and so-called money market accounts.

Marketable securities. Businesses may have excess or idle cash available for longer periods of time that may be temporarily invested in longer-term marketable securities. The funds may be set aside for business purposes such as long-term capital improvements or real estate acquisition, or they may simply be excess cash that the company does not want to distribute to shareholders in the form of dividends. One of these explanations appears to be the case for ABC Incorporated, since there has been a considerable amount of market appreciation in marketable securities, an indication that the investments are longer term and not of the riskless type described in the previous paragraph.

Accounts receivable are amounts due from customers not represented by promissory notes. Accounts receivable typically arise from the sale of goods on credit. Such amounts are typically due upon billing, possibly with a discount for prompt payment, and possibly with payment terms as long as 90 days. Subtracted from accounts receivable is an *allowance for bad debts* (sometimes more elegantly referred to as an *allowance for doubtful accounts*). The amount of this item is usually estimated based on the prior collection history of the business.

Inventories include several types of goods needed by the business in production of its end product: raw materials, partially finished goods in process of manufacture, and finished goods ready for shipment. The inventory of a retail operation may consist almost solely of finished goods. The manner of valuation of inventory is rather controversial and is discussed in §8.8 below.

Noncurrent assets consist of all assets that are not classified as current, and include a variety of quite different items.

Fixed assets are traditionally defined as property, plant, and equipment. Such items are usually recorded at historical cost; plant and equipment is *depreciated* over its expected life. Hence, the negative item, "Less accumulated depreciation" appears as an offset. This negative item is the total of all prior deductions for depreciation in earlier years. The truck in the simple illustration used in the last chapter to describe basic bookkeeping techniques is an example of depreciable equipment. Land is a fixed asset that is not depreciable. The valuation of fixed assets and the depreciation concept is discussed in §8.6 below.

Prepayments and deferred charges are also sometimes described as prepaid charges. They are discussed in §8.4 in connection with the concept of accrual.

Intangible assets fall into various categories. Traditional intangible assets (those that are usually not controversial from the standpoint of accounting principles) include patents, trademarks, and franchises. These intangible assets are shown at acquisition or development cost. The presence of other intangible assets, particularly "goodwill," "capitalized organizational cost," or "capitalized research and development costs" on a balance sheet should always be a warning sign for careful analysis (see §9.12). These assets may reflect only balancing entries for prior transactions. For example, if a company buys a bundle of assets for more than the sum of their individual fair market values, the excess may be entered as "goodwill." Whether or not the purchase was desirable, not much weight can be given to goodwill as an asset. It is unclear on the face of the balance sheet what the "Goodwill — $25,000" entry represents; it is unlikely, however, that it is an asset in any realistic sense of the word.

Other assets may include a variety of interests, for example, debts owed to the company that mature in more than one year, minority interests in independent businesses that the company plans to retain indefinitely, and the like.

Companies in specialized fields may include additional asset items or different breakdowns of traditional items. Energy companies, for example, present information for energy reserves separately from inventory.

Liabilities in the accounting sense are obligations *that probably will have to be paid in an amount that can reasonably be estimated at the time the balance sheet is prepared.* Material litigation or claims that do not qualify as liabilities in this sense do not appear on the balance sheet itself but should be referred to in the accompanying notes to the financial statements as contingent liabilities.

Current liabilities are those expected to be satisfied out of current assets, usually including all liabilities that become due in the coming year. Their relationship to current assets is an important one for evaluating the financial strength of the business. See §9.9. The most common current liabilities are usually broken down and listed separately.

Accounts payable are amounts owed to suppliers based on deliveries of supplies and raw materials on credit. Sometimes as an inducement for prompt payment, a supplier may give a *cash discount* of, say, 2 percent; if a $1,000 debt is stated with terms of "2 percent in 10 days, net in 30 days," payment of the debt within ten days earns a $20 discount. The debt becomes overdue after the expiration of 30 days.

Notes payable are amounts due to banks and other lenders in connection with loans that mature during the following 12 months. The portion of a long-term loan payable in installments that is due to be paid within 12 months is also included within *notes payable*.

Accrued expenses payable is a catchall for amounts owed to other business creditors that do not fall within either the categories of accounts or notes payable. It may include amounts owed to employees for wages and salaries on the date of the balance sheet, interest on open accounts not reflected as promissory notes, amounts owed to federal, state, or local governments for taxes, fees to attorneys, insurance premiums, required pension plan contributions, and a variety of other current liabilities. Because accountants are (a) conservative and (b) interested in matching costs with revenues, accrued expenses payable may include items that are not yet enforceable legal liabilities.

Long-term liabilities are liabilities due more than one year from the date of the balance sheet. The most common kind of long-term liabilities are mortgages on real property or bonds and debentures issued by the company in order to raise working capital. The debentures shown in Table 8-1 are unsecured debt obligations of ABC, Incorporated, carrying a 5 percent interest rate and not due for repayment for nearly 30 years. The payment date is so far in the future that such debt is realistically viewed as part of the permanent capitalization of the company. See Chapter 15.

Stockholders' equity is, of course, the balancing factor between assets and liabilities on the balance sheet. In the case of partnerships or proprietorships, this part of the balance sheet may be titled *owners' equity*, or simply *capital* or *capital contributed by partners*. Stockholders' equity consists basically of two parts: (1) the permanent capitalization of the business, and (2) retained earnings. Retained earnings, of course, is the item that ensures that balance sheets balance.

Preferred stock is usually a stock with a prior (but limited) claim to distributions ahead of the common shares. Preferred stock also usually has a preferential (but limited) claim upon liquidation. In the case of ABC Incorporated, no information is given on the balance sheet as to the dividend or liquidation preferences of this preferred stock.

Common stock represents the residual ownership of the corporation. In many states it is customary to assign a *par value* to common (and preferred) stock: Par value is an arbitrary amount, a relic of earlier corporation practices. Where par value is used, the virtually universal practice is to issue par value shares for a price higher than par value. Nevertheless, par value stock is entered as permanent capital on the balance sheet at its aggregate par value; the excess amounts paid by the investors over par value when the stock was issued are shown separately as "additional capital paid in in respect of common stock." In other words, the common stock was originally sold for $2,200,000.

See Chapter 15 for a fuller discussion of capital stock and long-term debt on corporate balance sheets.

§8.3 The Income Statement

The items in the income statement are relatively easier to understand than those in the balance sheet since the entries are more self-evident. As described above, it is built on the fundamental notion that

$$\text{Revenues} - \text{Expenses} = \text{Net income,}$$

a relationship that should be immediately apparent from even a cursory examination of the income statement on page 169. The income statement set forth here is for a business primarily involved in manufacturing and selling goods or products. (In the case of a business not involved primarily in selling goods, the revenue side may be titled *operating revenues* and the expense side not broken down between *costs of goods sold* and *other expenses*.) It should be noted that there are six "bottom lines" in this rather elaborate income statement: (1) sales minus cost of goods sold equals *gross margin*; (2) gross margin minus *operating expenses* (i.e., expenses not allocable directly to the goods sold) equals *operating profit*; (3) operating profit plus *other income* (i.e., income from dividends, interest, or rent not connected with the entity's principal business) equals *total income*; (4) total income less interest on long-term debentures equals *income before provision for federal income tax*; (5) income before provision for federal income tax minus income taxes equals *net income for year before extraordinary items*; and finally, (6) *net income* takes into account the extraordinary gain from the settlement of litigation, which is the bottom bottom line. The net income for year before extraordinary items is normally used to compare results with previous years or with other companies. Not all published income statements contain this degree of breakdown: For example, *gross margin* is primarily useful for internal control and projections by management and is not ordinarily separated out. Similarly, interest on bonds or debentures is often not separated out but included as a part of *operating expenses* as a single item *interest expense*, so that the distinction between *total income* and *income before provision for federal income tax* disappears.

Net sales means gross sales minus returns. One of the expenses deducted as *other expenses* from net sales is *depreciation*. This reflects the portion of the original purchase price of each depreciable asset that is allocated to the current year as the cost of gradually using up that asset, and should be distinguished from the *less accumulated depreciation* item in the balance sheet, which represents all prior deductions for depreciation of all depreciable property in the asset account. See §8.6.

Extraordinary items are nonrecurring items that materially affect the operating results. Such items are usually separated out and shown at the very bottom of the income statement after calculating the operating profit, which represents the earnings capacity typical of the firm. Then, an estimate of the taxes that would be due on that profit is determined. Extraordinary items may or may not give rise to accompanying income tax adjustments. For example, an extraordinary item involving the writing off of assets no longer needed in business operations may not be deductible from federal income taxes. Where an extraordinary loss item is deductible for tax purposes in the year in question, the extraordinary loss is shown below the net profit from operations line, reduced by the accompanying tax saving. As a result, taxes payable on regular operations are shown separately from those arising from the extraordinary item, for example:

All of the items in the income statement of course relate solely to the accounting period in question, namely the year ending December 31, 1987. Because you now understand the difference between the income statement and the balance sheet, you should be able to distinguish between the following similar-sounding but quite different items on the balance sheet and the income statement:

(a) The difference between *accounts receivable* on the balance sheet and *dividends and interest* on the income statement;

(b) The difference between *cash* on the balance sheet and *net profit for the year* on the income statement;

(c) The difference between *reserve for depreciation* on the balance sheet and *depreciation* on the income statement;

(d) The difference between *accrued expenses* on the balance sheet and *expenses* on the income statement;

(e) The difference between *prepaid income* on the balance sheet and *other income* on the income statement;

Table 8-2
ABC Incorporated
Income Statement for Year Ended December 31, 1987

Net sales		$10,200,000
Cost of goods sold		7,684,000
Gross margin		2,516,000
Other expenses		
Depreciation	275,000	
Selling and administrative expense	1,325,000	
		1,600,000
Operating profit		916,000
Other income		
Dividends and interest		27,000
Total income		943,000
Less: interest on debentures		135,000
Income before provision for federal income tax		808,000
Provision for federal income tax		365,000
Net profit for year before extraordinary times		443,000
Extraordinary gain — settlement of legal action	123,000	
Less applicable taxes	55,000	68,000
Net income for year		$511,000

Extraordinary loss from confiscation of Iran Properties	$6,000,000
Less tax saving	$2,800,000
Net extraordinary loss	$3,200,000

(f) The difference between *net income for year* on the income statement and *retained earnings* on the balance sheet.

§8.4 The Concept of Accrual

Most individuals and households keep their accounts (such as they are) on a cash basis. Salaries and other income are entered into the checkbook or ledger when they are received; payments for all purposes are entered when they are made. For most people this method of accounting for personal income and expenses is reasonably satisfactory. However, most businesses find this method of accounting inadequate for their purposes, and operate on an *accrual basis*. Indeed, accrual accounting is required by GAAP and by the Internal Revenue Service for most businesses that sell goods.

The basic difference between the accrual and cash methods of accounting lies in the answer to the question, when should transactions be recognized and taken into the accounting system? The cash method of accounting is based on the convention that transactions should be recognized when cash comes in or cash goes out. That system, however, is likely to lead to very erratic results and be easily subject to manipulation in most businesses that maintain an inventory of goods. A large purchase of inventory at a very favorable price in one year should not be treated as an expense for that period. To do so may result in the business showing a loss for the accounting period for that year even though the purchase permitted the business to enjoy high profits in later years. If the accounting process is to reflect accurately what is really happening, that inventory should be treated as an asset and taken into expense only when sales are made from it. Hence the development of accrual accounting.

Second, emphasis on cash payments or receipts ignores the most significant event in the transaction, which is usually doing the actual work or committing oneself to pay for something that is actually used immediately but paid for later.

Third, it is relatively easy to manipulate accounting results if a transaction enters the accounting system only when cash comes in or cash goes out. One can defer receipt or put off paying, whichever happens to be in the interest of the management of the business. (This should not be construed as indicating that manipulation is not possible in the accrual system: As described in §9.14, it is. But it is not as easy.) Businesses in which inventories of physical goods are an important aspect of the operation almost universally operate on the accrual system to avoid distortions of income and expense caused by the timing of raw material purchases and sales on cash or credit. It is for this reason that the Internal Revenue Code requires accrual tax accounting for such businesses.

In any event, the accrual system works on the basis that transactions should be recognized and taken into the accounting system when they have their primary economic impact, not necessarily when cash is received or disbursed. On the revenue side, that time is usually the rendering of service or the sale of goods. In the case of revenue items dependent on the passage of time — say, rent or interest — the critical event is simply the passage of time. As a practical matter, that means such items are taken into the accounts at the end of specific time periods: weekly, monthly, quarterly, or annually. Revenue items accrue (i.e., are taken into the business's accounts) even though they have not been billed and even though there is no right to immediate payment.

Under the accrual system, costs or expenses are taken into the accounts when the benefit occurs, which is typically when the revenues to which they relate are earned. In short, the goal of the accrual system is the matching of expenses with corresponding revenues wherever that is possible. However, a variety of indirect expenses cannot be allocated to specific revenues; these items are accrued over time independent of revenues. Examples of indirect expenses are interest on borrowed funds or rent that must be paid on land that is temporarily idle but will ultimately be used for business purposes.

Cash receipts or payments that relate to income or expenses for accounting periods other than the current one are viewed as creating assets or liabilities on the balance sheet; these assets or liabilities are "parked" on the balance sheet and "written off" (that is, taken as expenses) in the year in which they are recognized for accounting purposes. A few examples of the accrual concept may be useful. In the following examples, assume that the business's accounting period closes on December 31.

(a) The business purchases inventory (goods for resale) on 12/15, paying cash of $500. This transaction affects only the balance sheet, increasing inventory by $500 and reducing cash by the same amount. This transaction is reflected in the form of journal entries as follows:

12/15/87	Cash	$500
	Inventory (goods for resale) $500	
	Purchase of inventory for resale	

The usual bookkeeping practice is to record debits first, but in this and the following illustrations, cash is recorded first to clarify how the transactions relate to the cash account.

(b) On 1/6 the business sells to a retail customer from inventory goods that cost $300; the sales price for the goods is $600, to be paid within 90 days. This transaction increases sales revenue (an income statement item) by $600, it increases accounts receivable (a balance sheet item) by $600; it increases cost of goods sold (an income statement item) by $300, and it reduces inventory (a balance sheet item) by $300. Journal entries would look like this:

1/6/88	Accounts receivable $600	
	Sales revenue	$600
	To record sale of goods on credit	

1/6/88	Cost of goods sold $300	
	Inventory	$300
	To record sale of goods from inventory	

(c) On March 9, 1988, the customer pays her $600 bill. Cash is increased by this amount and accounts receivable are reduced:

171

3/9/88   Cash $600
           Accounts receivable $600
     To record receipt of amount previously billed.

The effect of these various transactions is that the sale of goods is taken into income in January when the sale takes place; the earlier purchase of inventory is parked in the inventory account on the balance sheet until the sale occurs, and then it is moved into the income statement as part of cost of goods sold. The income accounts of the corporation would not be affected if the payment of the account had occurred in 1989, whether the transaction was a cash rather than a credit sale, or whether the customer had made a series of layaway payments in 1987. In each event, the income statement would reflect the sales revenue of $600, the year in which the most significant event — the sale itself — was made.

     (e) *The business opens a new store on December 1: It is required by its new landlord to pay two years' rent in advance.* Transactions of this type require the creation of a new balance sheet asset account, "prepaid rent":

12/1/88   Cash $12,000
            Prepaid rent $12,000
     To record prepayment of rent on store

At the end of one month, $500 is charged to the income statement item, rent, for the December rent, and the same amount is deducted from the prepaid rent account:

12/31/88   Rent $500
             Prepaid rent $500
     To charge rent expense for December

During each month of the following year, the appropriate amount of rent is charged to expense, and the prepaid rent account is reduced. The effect of this treatment is that the prepayment of rent is actually allocated to each time period during which the business has the use of the rented property for income statement purposes. Prepaid expenses are assets, while the receipt of prepaid income creates a liability.

     (f) *The business owns an apartment house; It rents an apartment to X who is required to pay the first and last month's rent of $800 when he enters into the lease on the first day of the tenancy.* A new balance sheet liability account, unearned rent, is created to reflect the receipt of the rent:

9/1/87   Cash $1,600
           Unearned rent $1,600
     To reflect advance receipt of rent

At the end of the first month, rental income is recognized for the first month's rent:

9/30/87	Unearned rent	$800	
	Income from apartment rental		$800
	To reflect September rent		

The unearned rent account remains on the books of the business until the last month of the rental. It is eliminated when the last month's rent has accrued.

In all of these examples there is a common theme: Because revenue is not accounted for until the transaction occurs (or time passes, in the case of rental income), any receipts or payments of cash allocable to other accounting periods are treated as purely balance sheet entries. Prepaid expenses are treated as assets and unearned receipts are treated as liabilities. Thus, the intricacies of double entry bookkeeping make it relatively easy to apply accrual concepts to transactions affecting more than one accounting period. On the other hand, people sometimes find it difficult to accept that the prepayment of an expense item creates an asset while the receipt of unearned income creates a liability. This relationship, however, is required by the structure of the double entry bookkeeping system. It may be appreciated intuitively by noting that the prepayment of an expense is indistinguishable in principle from the purchase of an asset such as a truck. Indeed, in one sense, all assets on a balance sheet other than cash are expenses waiting to be written off in an appropriate future accounting period.

It should also be noted that in accrual accounting, income and expense items are not adjusted for many transactions that intuitively seem to be income- or expense-generating unless gain or loss is recognized. For example, no income is recognized upon the receipt of prepaid rent; that rent can be earned only by the passage of time.

§8.5 Accrual Accounting for Long Lead-Time Businesses

The simple accrual system works best for businesses that have large numbers of profit-making or loss-creating transactions during each accounting period. In other types of businesses, however, traditional accrual accounting results in the bunching of income, making accounting results incomparable from one year to the next.

A classic example of this latter type of business is an airplane manufacturer with a contract to build an airplane that involves two years of design and construction work before the first plane is delivered. An airplane involves a long lead time since costs must be incurred for an extended period before revenues are received. If the contract for the plane involves, say, a $60,000,000 payment when each plane is delivered, the airplane manufacturer, if it follows simple accrual accounting principles, will show no income during the two-year development phase and will record its first revenue with the sale of the first plane in the third year of the contract. If the airplane manufacturer follows conventional accrual principles, it will *capitalize* development expenses (that is, treat them as an asset rather than as expenses) and show zero income for the first two years, followed by profits in the years during which the planes are sold. If it appears likely from the outset that the project will be profitable, however, it is more realistic to allocate a portion of the ultimate profit to each of the two developmental years in which much of the work is done rather than show an erratic and unrealistic zero-profit income statement for two years, followed by years of high income when the airplanes are sold. Much the same pattern may be present in the development of software for computers, the production of motion pictures, heavy construction projects, and other business activities that involve development periods of more than one year.

The application of an accrual accounting system to such businesses is not without controversy. The accountant takes pride in treating recognition issues conservatively, and refusing to recognize income unless it is certain to be earned. The difficulty with our hypothetical airplane manufacturer is that it is usually not possible to determine that the airplane being developed will in fact be salable until after sales begin. In effect, the company is gambling on its ability to design and produce an airplane that will be attractive to customers when it is available, a kind of gambling crucial in an entrepreneurial economy.

Accounting on a basis other than traditional accrual principles is nevertheless well accepted in some industries. For example, many companies engaged in commercial construction report income on a percentage of contract completion basis that spreads anticipated profits over the lifetime of the contract. Sellers of large consumer or commercial equipment on credit over several years may report income on the installment basis rather than using the point of sale as the time of realization of income.

Deciding what is the most appropriate time for revenue recognition is often a matter of judgment. To take one real-life example, the question arises in the trading stamp industry whether revenues should be recognized when the stamps are sold to merchants for distribution to retail customers, or when the stamps are presented for redemption, at which time the costs of providing the redemption goods are known.

§8.6 Depreciation, Depletion, and Amortization

Depreciation, depletion, and amortization in an accounting context all refer to essentially the same process: the allocation of the cost of a long-lived asset to consecutive accounting periods as expenses to reflect the gradual using up of the asset. The word *depreciation* is associated with the process of writing off plant and equipment; the word *depletion* refers to the gradual exhaustion of natural resources through the process of capture and development; while *amortization* involves intangible assets (such as copyrights or patents) and deferred charges (such as organizational expenses, research and development costs, or "dry holes" in oil and gas exploration). In a sense the writing off or expensing of long-lived assets is similar to any prepayment of future expenses: The purchase of a truck, for example, can be seen as a prepayment to ensure the availability of the truck over the balance of its useful life in much the same way that the advance payment of two years' rent creates an asset account — prepaid expenses.

§8.6.1 Depreciation: The Basic Concepts

One of the first transactions discussed in this chapter was the purchase of a used truck for $3,000. This purchase led to the opening of an asset account for the truck with an entry of $3,000, the purchase price (historical cost) of the truck. To calculate the depreciation of this asset following its acquisition requires the following steps: Someone (presumably an accountant) estimates (1) the useful life of the truck and (2) the scrap or resale value of the truck, if any, at the end of that period. Assuming that *straight line depreciation* is being followed, the difference between the original cost and the scrap value is then divided by the number of years of the truck's estimated useful life. That amount is treated as the annual expense of "using up" the truck. For example, if the useful life of the truck is estimated to be five years, and the resale value of the truck at the end of that period is zero, straight line depreciation accounting requires that the business include as an expense, in each of the next five years, $\frac{\$3,000 - 0}{5}$ or $600 per year. At the same time, a new balance sheet account is created, "Less: Accumulated depreciation," that appears as a deduction or offset against the asset account: As each depreciation deduction is taken as an expense, this new account is increased by the same amount. (This type of *negative asset* account is sometimes called a *contra account*.) The journal entry for each annual depreciation deduction is simply:

Depreciation (expense)	$600
Less: Accumulated depreciation (contra)	$600
To record charge for current depreciation	

After two years of depreciation have been expensed, the balance sheet entry will look like this:

Equipment (truck)	$3,000
Less: Accumulated depreciation	$1,200
	$1,800

There are several important points to make about this simple example:

First, the balance sheet item, "Less: Accumulated depreciation" is purely a bookkeeping item. There is no separate fund or separate account in the corporation's assets marked "depreciation account" or "depreciation reserve" that contains $1,200, and there are no funds set aside to help pay for the truck's replacement when it wears out. Rather, the $1,200 is simply the sum of two $600 items taken as expenses; some such entry is necessary in order to make the balance sheet balance. But, mustn't there be an extra $1,200 somewhere? In a sense there is since the two deductions for depreciation made annual earnings smaller than they would have been had no depreciation been claimed. Somewhere in the balance sheet there are offsetting items, but this is not a fruitful line of inquiry since there is no way to say where they are. What is important is that the business has not squirreled away $1,200 in a special account or fund.

Second, the truck will, of course, gradually wear out, and will presumably have to be replaced. However, depreciation deductions do not affect this process in a direct way. The only real economic effects depreciation deductions have on a business are that they (a) reduce reported earnings without being a drain on the business's current cash flow, and (b) reduce the business's tax bill (assuming that the Internal Revenue Code permits the particular depreciation deduction to be calculated and claimed in the way proposed). This tax consequence arises because depreciation is a deductible expense item for tax purposes, and larger depreciation deductions mean lower income subject to tax. Arguments for faster depreciation deductions are usually motivated to some extent by self-interest since faster write-offs mean larger current tax deductions. Even though the accumulated depreciation account is not a fund created to provide for a replacement for the truck when it wears out, one often hears arguments that larger amounts should be deductible from income "to reflect increases in replacement costs because of inflation," or "because the American manufacturing plant is wearing out," or "because the American economy is consuming its own capital." While legitimate arguments (described briefly below) may be made about what kinds of depreciation deductions should be permitted to reflect inflation, most such arguments are based on a selfish unstated premise, namely, that it is desirable from the interests of the speaker for the United States to reduce the amount of income tax it collects from his or her business. Unfortunately, this self-interest colors much of the theoretical debate over depreciation.

Third, after two years, the $3,000 value of the truck has been reduced to $1,800 on the books of the business through two depreciation deductions of $600 each. This $1,800 figure is called the *book value* of the truck (since it is the value of the truck as shown on the books of the business). Is there any relationship between this book value and what the truck is actually worth after two years? The answer is, probably not. If the current market value of the truck is in fact $1,800, it is purely by chance. Trucks do not usually decline in value at a steady rate precisely equal to that originally estimated by an accountant. Furthermore, the starting value for the depreciation calculation was the cost of the truck two years ago: What has happened to the used truck market in the meantime? Indeed, there is no reason to believe that the business originally paid the fair market value of the truck when it bought it: It could have paid too much, or it could have gotten a bargain. But that does not matter. For accounting purposes, the value of the truck when it is purchased is its cost. Certainly, the depreciation calculation takes none of these factors into account. What then does the book value represent? It represents historical cost reduced by some arbitrary number of expense deductions, and not a whole lot more. It may or may not be a reasonable approximation of the resale value of the truck. When the business sells the truck, it probably will be at a price different from its book value; the gain or loss on that transaction is reflected in income or retained earnings at that time.

Fourth, does the truck disappear after its value has been reduced to zero on the books of the business? Of course not. If the truck still has economic value it may continue to be used in the business. In this case, the original estimate of the useful life of the truck was too conservative — the truck was written off more quickly than its useful life actually warranted. Once the truck has been fully depreciated—i.e., reduced to its estimated scrap or resale value—no further depreciation deductions are available to the business for that truck if it continues to be used in the business thereafter.

This traditional way of handling depreciation has one justification: It requires that costs of certain assets be allocated in an orderly and verifiable fashion to different accounting periods. Whether or not the specific allocations to specific periods are accurate may be less important than that they be done on a systematic basis that approximates the useful life span of the asset.

§8.6.2 Accelerated Depreciation Systems

In the foregoing discussion, it has been assumed that annual depreciation deductions will be calculated by dividing the depreciable value of the property by its expected life. This type of depreciation is usually called *straight-line depreciation* since the amount of the deduction for depreciation each year is constant over the life of the asset.

Accelerated depreciation systems involve placing relatively larger amounts of the depreciation deductions in the early years of the asset's life. These systems are to a large extent tax-oriented, because the increased deductions generated by these systems in the early years of the life of the asset, if accepted for federal income tax purposes, create significant tax benefits that are strong incentives to adopt the systems. See Chapter 12. In some circumstances, however, these systems may be independently justified from an accounting standpoint because, by loading most of the depreciation charges in the early years of the asset's life, they more closely approximate actual market values for assets such as automobiles or trucks, which typically depreciate in value very rapidly during their early years of use.

Perhaps the most popular accelerated depreciation system is the *sum of the digits method*. In this method, the depreciation deduction is calculated each year by creating a fraction, in which the numerator equals the number of years of useful life remaining and the denominator equals the sum of all the useful years of life of the asset. For example, for the truck with a five-year useful life expectancy, the denominator is $5 + 4 + 3 + 2 + 1$, or 15; in the first year, the numerator is five (and the fraction is 5/15 or 1/3); in the second year, the numerator is 4 (and the fraction is 4/15); in the third year the numerator is 3 (and the fraction is 3/15 or 1/5), and so forth. The internal logic of this system is not as important as the accelerated pattern of deductions that it creates.

Another popular accelerated depreciation system is the *declining balance method*. In this method, a stable fraction or percentage is applied to the current book value of the asset (historical cost minus previous depreciation deductions), rather than to original cost less salvage value. (Salvage value is not considered when applying the declining balance method.) The fraction or percentage is usually a multiple of the straight-line depreciation rate. Thus, if the asset has a five-year life, the straight-line depreciation rate is 20 percent per year. The *double declining balance* method applies twice the 20 percent rate, or 40 percent per year. For example, a $3,000 truck depreciated over five years by the double declining balance method would lead to the following depreciation deductions in the first five years:

Cost less depreciation	Rate	Depreciation deduction
$3,000	40%	$1,200
(3,000 − 1200) = 1800	40%	$720
(1,800 − 720) = 1080	40%	$432
(1,080 − 432) = 638	40%	$259.20
(638 − 259.20) = 378.80	40%	$151.52

The *150 percent declining balance* method would entail the use of a 30 percent rate on a five-year asset. The declining balance method, like the sum of the digits method, results in very substantial deductions in early years. In the above example, the double declining balance method results in a write-off of 40 percent of the cost of the truck in the first year, compared with the 33 percent maximum write-off obtainable under the sum of the digits method.

Between 1981 and 1986, the Internal Revenue Code permitted the use of the *accelerated cost recovery system (ACRS)*. This depreciation system permitted accelerated depreciation by allowing the adoption of useful lives that are significantly shorter than the useful lives usually adopted for depreciation purposes. Under ACRS, property was divided into four principal categories: three-year, five-year, ten-year, and fifteen-year property. In each instance, the actual useful lives of the assets were significantly longer than the depreciation period. For example, physical plant (buildings, etc.) is usually written off over thirty or forty years under traditional cost accounting: Under ACRS they fell within the fifteen-year category. The 1986 Tax Act generally extended the mandatory lives of assets and repealed ACRS, but still retains a separate set of depreciation schedules that must be used for tax purposes. The result of different depreciation schedules for tax and for general accounting purposes is that businesses must calculate income for tax purposes on a different basis than income for the purpose of reporting results of operations to shareholders and the public. Over the years, the divergence between these two methods of accounting have increased: The 1986 amendments to the Internal Revenue Code impose an alternative minimum tax that in effect imposes a tax upon a portion of accounting income as such.

§8.6.3 Depletion

The calculation of depletion of natural resources is usually made on the basis of estimates of the total recoverable resources in the field or ore body. The original purchase price or cost of the asset is divided by the estimated recoverable resources in the field or ore body to determine the cost per unit (per barrel, per ton, or whatever the appropriate measure is). Then, as each unit is captured and recovered, the cost is shown as "Less: Accumulated depletion" much the same way as depreciation is shown. In effect, depletion allocates the initial cost of the investment in accordance with the recovery from the asset itself rather than over an arbitrary period of years, as is done with depreciation. If the field or ore body contains more resources than estimated, recovery after full depletion of the original cost results in a zero deduction for depletion of the additional units. For many years, depletion of oil or gas reserves was on an income rather than cost basis, but that is now permitted only for smaller unintegrated firms.

§8.6.4 Amortization

The amortization of intangible assets and deferred charges follows a similar pattern, though the issues are considerably more controversial. Relatively few problems are created by traditional intangible assets such as patents, copyrights, and trade names that are purchased or developed internally so that the cost of acquisition or development can be readily established. Serious problems, however, are created by the capitalization and amortization of research and development (R&D) costs, the drilling of "dry holes" in connection with the successful exploration of oil and gas, and start-up expenses for a variety of new businesses or enterprises. If a firm expends funds for R&D, for example, it generally must treat the expenditures as expenses in the year incurred unless it can show that the expenditures will lead to marketable products. If the firm can prove this connection, it may capitalize the expenditures and write them off in future years against those products. While R&D expenditures directed toward a specific product or project probably should be capitalized, basic or general research often cannot be allocated with any precision, and is usually expensed when incurred. The variety of treatment of R&D expenses among publicly reporting companies was so great that in 1974 GAAP were revised to require that most R&D expenditures be expensed currently. While this treatment is not entirely consistent with the basic notion that expenses should be recognized when the revenue to which they relate is recognized, the possibility of manipulation and foul play in financial statements was so great (see §9.14, below), that an objective and relatively bright-line rule was thought appropriate.

The same basic issue is involved in the treatment of "dry holes" in petroleum exploration. A certain number of dry holes may be necessary for the exploration and development of a productive field. Many smaller oil companies capitalize the cost of the dry holes; these companies are known as *full cost companies*, since the reported costs of their reserves include the cost of drilling unsuccessful as well as successful wells. Larger companies usually expense the dry holes immediately; these companies are known as *successful efforts companies*, since the reported costs of reserves include only costs of drilling successful wells. The Exxon financial statement set forth on page 153 is an example of the reporting of costs by a successful efforts company. Its income statement simply sets forth as an expense "Exploration expenses, including dry holes." At the present time, firms may use either accounting system but must disclose the extent of their reserves.

§8.7 An Introduction to Inflation Accounting

Inflation creates several problems for the accounting system. For one thing, accounting assumes that each dollar is worth the same amount. During periods of inflation, this is manifestly not true: A dollar next year will buy less than a dollar this year. Second, artificial profits occur simply when assets are held during inflationary periods. These artificial profits should be distinguished from real profits occurring because of productive activity. Third, in determining the real costs of operation, it may be argued, one should view the business over an entire productive plant replacement cycle. In effect one should view expenses as including all expenditures necessary to keep the productive plant permanently in the strongest possible condition. Income should consist only of the amount by which revenues exceed the expenses so measured.

Most attention has been focused on the third problem, which naturally leads to a consideration of the use of *replacement values* or *replacement cost* rather than historical cost in determining depreciation deductions. Replacement values or costs, as the names suggest, are the estimated cost of replacing the asset in the future when it is used up or worn out. It seems clear that depreciation deductions based on historical cost are unrealistically low during periods of inflation if the replacement cycle is the standard. It is entirely foreseeable that future replacement of assets will have to be at significantly increased prices. If depreciation deductions are too low, it follows that some portion of reported earnings (using traditional depreciation accounting principles) actually represents the cost of replacing capital assets rather than income. This statement is true, but should be considered in context. Traditional depreciation accounting does not disable a business from planning for future price increases for capital equipment. A business may simply preserve sufficient retained earnings to make all necessary capital replacements. If the business is concerned about its ability to replace assets, the company should adopt a conservative dividend policy and not distribute the bulk of its current earnings to shareholders. The issues being addressed are only whether the income reported by the business is overstated because of inflation and, if so, whether a more realistic measure of income can be developed.

During the late 1970s and early 1980s, when inflation was relatively high, attempts were made to devise a system of inflation accounting that would more adequately reflect in income the cost of capital asset replacement, and many companies became unwilling participants in this effort. The effort revealed that inflation accounting involves practical problems and may be confusing to users of financial statements. Companies were required by the Securities and Exchange Commission to create alternative income statements on the basis of *current replacement values* or *costs* (that is, replacement cost measured as of the time the financial statements are prepared without regard to the anticipated future life of the capital asset) rather than historical costs in calculating depreciation deductions. Current replacement cost, of course, comes much closer to the realizable value of the business's productive plant if it were to sell its assets today than do the historical cost figures: Furthermore, one can also assert that the current cost of replacing a set of productive assets is the most sound basis for describing their current value.

On the other hand, there are conceptual problems inherent in the use of current replacement cost. For one thing, the business is not in fact about to sell off its productive plant or to replicate its present plant in a new location, and yet this is what the use of current replacement cost assumes. Thus the proposal can be criticized at the outset for attempting to measure a hypothetical scenario. Also, current replacement cost does not fully meet the theoretical objections to traditional depreciation accounting. A true replacement cost theory would require depreciation to be calculated on the basis of estimated replacement values *at the time when replacement is likely to occur.*

The experiment with replacement cost accounting also revealed formidable practical problems in preparing alternative inflation statements. The most serious problem is that determinations of current replacement cost must involve estimates as to the current market value of many individual productive assets. There simply are not market quotations for many assets; in the case of land or other unique assets, the comparability of what quotations there are may be uncertain. Further, the introduction of *soft* numbers (i.e., numbers that cannot be objectively ascertained and require the exercise of judgment in their development) at least theoretically opens the way to fraud or chicanery in accounting — "cooking the books." One major advantage of historical cost depreciation accounting is that the numbers used are more difficult to tamper with because they are readily verifiable and represent real economic events in the past. Books of the business based on historical cost also provide a complete historical record relating to each particular asset. Of course, the use of historical cost is hardly a guarantee against cooking the books: Current replacement cost accounting, on the other hand, may be so easily subject to manipulation as to invite it. Further, this problem would be even more serious if *ultimate* replacement cost estimates (i.e., the anticipated cost of replacement in the future when the asset is actually worn out or used up) were used. Estimates may have to be made years before the replacement actually occurs and some manner of handling erroneous asset-life expectancies and unanticipated as well as anticipated price increases would have to be created. Such calculations involve numerous assumptions about future price trends, times of replacement, and future changes in technology, and the resulting system would be even more subjective and open to abuse than the experimental current replacement cost standard.

Less attention has been given to the fundamental accounting issues created by inflation. To the extent inflation is relevant to the goals of accounting, the problems are not limited to asset valuations and depreciation deductions. All income figures are inflated to some degree if prices increase generally across the economy. For example, if we assume a 10 percent increase during one year because of inflation, the business's reported earnings will presumably increase by about 10 percent also as sales receipts and expenses both reflect the same percentage increases. It is doubtful, however, whether the owners of the business will feel 10 percent better off even though reported earnings are up by 10 percent. A plausible solution to this inflation problem might be to require all businesses to reduce current earnings by an appropriate inflation index. Then historical comparisons might be more meaningful because all results would be stated in presumably constant dollars. This proposal would not distinguish, however, between real profits and inflation profits arising merely from the holding of assets that appreciate in value, and would indiscriminately discount both for the effects of inflation.

These problems of inflation accounting suggest a couple of final general observations about the traditional accounting system. Earlier chapters of this book addressed the time value of money, and the importance of reducing future payments to current values. Traditional accounting practice is unrealistic in that it does not take into account the time value of money. Debentures carrying low or zero interest rates due in 30 years are reported as liabilities today on the balance sheet at their ultimate face value and no attempt is made to report these obligations at the current value of the future payments. In addition, the accounting system takes no account of past inflation; 1950 dollar amounts and 1988 dollar amounts are sometimes added together within a single account without any recognition that 1950 dollars purchased a lot more than 1988 dollars do. These anomalies can be traced back to the use of historical cost as the core concept underlying modern accounting systems.

§8.8 Accounting for Inventory

Inventory includes (1) all finished goods awaiting sale, (2) all goods in various stages of production beginning with (and including) raw materials, and (3) all goods on hand that are ultimately consumed in the production of goods. Accounting for inventory is complex primarily because tremendous variation exists from industry to industry and from business to business as to the nature and variety of items maintained in inventory.

Control of inventory costs is a major component in determining whether or not a business is successful. Problems of pilferage or shortages are most likely to involve inventory. Unaccountable losses of inventory — whether due to pilferage, failure to maintain adequate records, spoilage, or other causes — are also called, somewhat charitably, *shrinkage*.

Goods that are manufactured or purchased are usually stored (or *parked*) in the inventory account on the balance sheet until they are taken into the expense account of the income statement. Practical considerations, however, require most businesses to adopt artificial conventions for estimating inventory costs since it is not practical or cost justifiable for most businesses to keep track of each inventory item as it wends its way through the manufacturing process and even if it were, this tracking alternative readily lends itself to manipulation. It is usually not practicable or desirable to try to match cost inputs directly with specific sales.

The most widely used inventory systems require businesses to record additions to inventory as they occur on the balance sheet but determine the cost of goods sold only at the end of each accounting period. This determination is usually made in the following way. The cost of goods sold for a period is determined at the close of the period by the following basic formula:

(1)   Cost of goods sold = value of opening inventory +
                additions to inventory − value of closing inventory

The value of both the opening inventory and the closing inventory are determined by taking physical counts of what is on hand at the end of an accounting period and then assigning it a dollar value. In other words, an essential part of the year-end auditing process is a physical count of inventory: The value of the inventory at the end of one period (the *closing inventory*) is, of course, the value of the inventory at the beginning of the next period (the *opening inventory*) so that only one physical count per year is necessary. The manner of placing dollar values on the items counted when inventory additions occur at varying prices is the subject of the remainder of this section. However, before turning to this question, a second formula should be introduced to make clear the critical nature in the income accounting process of the physical inventory count and the manner of valuing that inventory in determining the profitability of the business:

(2)   Gross profit = net sales − cost of goods sold

This formula reveals that every change in the number of dollars attributed to cost of goods sold leads to a dollar-for-dollar increase or reduction in the gross profit of the business. Further, these two formulas are obviously interrelated; one can substitute formula (1) into formula (2) to yield this:

(3)   Gross profit = net sales - value of opening inventory - additions to inventory + value of closing inventory

(Remember your high school algebra about the effect of minus signs on other minus signs.) The implications to be drawn from formula (3) are these: First, every change in the number of dollars attributed to closing inventory also means a dollar-for-dollar change in gross profit. Second, the *higher* the value of the closing inventory, the *lower* the cost of goods sold and the *higher* the gross profit. Correspondingly, the *lower* the value of the closing inventory, the *higher* the cost of goods sold and the *lower* the gross profit.

That the value of closing inventory affects cost of goods sold is a result of the use of a formula to calculate the costs of goods sold: The calculation does not attempt to trace what specific inventory items were actually consumed during the period in question, but simply subtracts the value of closing inventory from all inventory available to the business during the period (opening inventory plus additions to inventory for the period). Since the increase of closing inventory by one dollar increases gross profit by one dollar while the decrease of closing inventory by one dollar decreases gross profit by that amount, the manner of assigning dollar value to closing inventory items significantly affects reported earnings.

Before turning to methods of valuing closing inventory, it may be helpful to consider the nature of the inventory of three prototype businesses. To take the simplest case first, assume that the business involves only the retail sale of new automobiles. The number of inventory items is relatively small and each inventory item — each new car — is clearly identifiable by serial number, and the cost of each item in inventory is readily known. In effect, each inventory item can be "tagged" with its applicable cost, and the process of determining the value of the closing inventory for such a business involves merely identifying which cars are on hand at the close of the period and adding up their costs. At the other extreme, consider a corn oil manufacturer whose inventory consists of raw corn to be processed for the manufacture of corn oil and flour. The corn is stored in a large bin. When the manufacturing process needs more raw material, there are two alternatives: Either someone opens a valve and corn pours out of the bottom into processing kettles or someone opens a trap door and shovels some corn out from the top of the bin. From time to time, additional corn is added, always to the top of the bin. Raw corn varies in price from moment to moment and from day to day, though of course the amount and cost of all the raw corn added to the top of the bin can be readily calculated. Clearly, there is no way that the corn oil producer can physically tag raw corn and determine the cost of the raw materials on hand at the end of the accounting period. It must adopt a more general system. Also, one must question whether the use of a trap door at the bottom or a shovel from the top of a corn bin should be decisive in determining the value of closing inventory. Third, consider a large retail clothing store. It has on hand at any one time thousands of products in hundreds of sizes, styles, and colors. The number of units of each specific type, size, and style of product retained in inventory is relatively small for most items. Again, prices of individual items may vary over time so that, for example, two indistinguishable hats lying side by side may have originally cost different amounts. While it may be theoretically possible to tag each item and determine the actual cost of each item in closing inventory within the store, historically, this has not been very practical or cost-justified. With the development of computerized sales recording and reordering systems for many retail operations, tagging may become more feasible in retail operations in the future, but it is unlikely to supplant the more traditional systems which uses some kind of more general system of valuing closing inventory. These last two prototypes are much more typical of the average inventory problems faced by business than is the tagged inventory of the retail new car business. However, when one considers the problems of the service department of that hypothetical retail new car business: an inventory consisting of replacement parts — boxes of spark plugs, bins of screws and bolts, large cans or barrels of motor oil or transmission fluid, and the like — it should be apparent that even a new car dealer has to adopt generalized accounting procedures for much of its inventory.

The most widely used methods of valuing closing inventory are discussed in the following subsections.

§8.8.1 Specific Identification Inventory Method

Intuitively, the simplest method of assigning values to closing inventory is to keep track of the cost of individual items and assign the cost of an item in closing inventory as the value of that item. The new car inventory of the automobile dealer is a good illustration. This system, however, has basic problems. Assume that the information in Table 8-3 about one inventory item (all the items of which are identical) is available. As in other examples used throughout this chapter, only a skeletal number of transactions is set forth to illustrate the basic principles.

If one can establish, by examining the "tags," that the 400 units on hand at the end of the accounting period consisted of (a) 200 units purchased on

Table 8-3

Date	Purchases		Sales
	No. units	Cost	No. units
On hand	200	$5	
3/1	100	$6	
3/15			200
6/15	400	$7	
7/15			300
8/15	200	$8	
12/10			300
12/15	300	$9	
Close	400	?	

8/15, (b) 100 units purchased on 3/1 and (c) 100 units carried over from the start of the year, one can determine the value of the closing inventory:

$$200 \times 8 + 100 \times 6 + 100 \times 5 = \$2,700$$

Of course, from this number, one can determine the cost of goods sold and the gross profit of the business from the formulas set forth earlier in this section.

One immediate problem with this method of valuing closing inventory is that it may encourage opportunistic behavior by management, since management can increase or decrease gross profit by judiciously selecting which units are sold and which units are carried over into closing inventory. For example, if it wished to increase gross profit, it might sell all the cheaper items and keep in inventory only the items purchased on 8/15 and 12/15, so that the closing inventory value would be:

$$300 \times 9 + 100 \times 8 = \$3,500$$

Similarly if management wished to reduce gross profit, possibly to defer the profit to the next accounting period, it could sell the most expensive items and preserve the cheaper ones in closing inventory. It should be emphasized that even though gross profit may be manipulated in this fashion, the real worth of the business is unchanged by whatever sequence of liquidation of inventory is followed to support the sales during the accounting period. This is so because the number of identical units used up is the same in each case.

§8.8.2 Weighted Average Method

This method determines the weighted average price of every unit of inventory on hand at any time during the accounting period and assigns that average value to every unit. It is a "weighted" average because the number of units at each price is taken into account:

$$\frac{200 \times 5 + 100 \times 6 + 400 \times 7 + 200 \times 8 + 300 \times 9}{1,200 \text{ (the total number of units)}} = \frac{8,700}{1,200} = \$7.25 \text{ per unit}$$

The average cost per unit in the above example is \$7.25; the value of closing inventory is then $400 \times 7.25 = \$2,900$, and the cost of goods sold is $800 \times 7.25 = \$5,800$.

This method is not widely used in part because of its complexity in other than the simplest situations, and in part because the system creates its own anomalies. For example, the purchase of 300 units on December 15 in the foregoing example increased the cost of all goods sold during the year even though all the actual sales of goods occurred before this final purchase.

§8.8.3 First In, First Out Method

One widely used method of closing inventory valuation is to assume that the earliest items in inventory are always sold first. In the foregoing example, the sale of 800 units during the year is assumed to be composed of the earliest items acquired; the 200 items carried over from the prior accounting period and the purchases on 3/1, 6/15, and, in part, on 8/15. Closing inventory would then consist of 300 units at \$9 and 100 units at \$8, for a total value of \$3,500. This method of valuing inventory is universally known as *FIFO*, which stands for *first-in first-out*.

FIFO has certain advantages. For one thing, it actually conforms with the physical inventory practices of many businesses, which follow the principle that because of spoilage, staleness, or obsolescence, the oldest items should always be sold first. That would be true, for example, for our corn oil producer if the corn was always poured from the bottom. Second, it is relatively easy to administer. Third, it eliminates the possible manipulation of gross profit by management that is inherent in any system of assigning varying costs to specific inventory units. Under FIFO it makes no difference whether the corn is taken from the bottom or from the top; in either case it is presumed that the oldest corn is used first. Finally, since inventory is always composed of the last-acquired items, the value of closing inventory on the balance sheet is likely to reflect closely the current market value of inventory items. In this sense, FIFO improves the reliability of the balance sheet since the important inventory item reflects the most current prices at which inventory was actually purchased.

§8.8.4 Last In, First Out Method

The major alternative to FIFO proceeds on the opposite assumption, namely that the last items are always sold first, hence the acronym *LIFO*, which stands for *last-in first-out*. In the foregoing example, the 400 units of closing inventory is assumed to consist of 200 units at \$5, 100 units at \$6, and 100 units at $7, for a total value of $2,300. No account is taken of the sequence of actual subtractions from inventory in applying either FIFO or LIFO. If one chooses LIFO it is assumed that corn is always taken from the top of the bin no matter what the actual practice is. It is probably true that LIFO does not accurately reflect the way in which most businesses in fact consume inventory (i.e. disposing of the last first), but it is certainly true of some businesses.

The advantages of LIFO over FIFO arise because of the general inflationary trends that have persisted in the American economy since World War II. Inventory replacement costs have generally risen and almost never fallen. This is the context in which the choice between FIFO and LIFO must be evaluated. In the last 40 years many companies shifted from FIFO to LIFO for the reasons described below. However, rather paradoxically, some companies continue to use FIFO despite the virtually universal view of accountants and financial management strategists that most companies would obtain significant tax benefits from adopting LIFO.

One major advantage of LIFO is that, since 1939, businesses may use LIFO in calculating their federal income tax liability. By generally increasing inventory replacement costs, LIFO tends to decrease the value of closing inventories, thereby reducing reported income and federal income tax liability. Indeed, if one assumes that inventory costs increase steadily, FIFO maximizes the business's taxes while LIFO minimizes them. The argument has been strongly made that every business should shift from FIFO to LIFO simply because of this tax saving. On the other hand, studies of securities prices of businesses that shift from FIFO to LIFO indicate that the market does not reduce securities prices to reflect the reduced earnings caused by the shift to LIFO. In other words, markets apparently understand that the reduction in earnings caused by a change in accounting for inventory is not a real change in earnings.

The tax savings arising from LIFO are permanent as a practical matter. Theoretically, the tax saving arising from LIFO will be lost when the low-cost LIFO inventory is totally liquidated; at that time FIFO and LIFO should have led to the same total cost of goods sold. This, however, totally ignores the time value of money: The immediate reduction of taxes through LIFO is worth much more than the future increase in taxes when the LIFO inventory is consumed, come the millennium, when the business liquidates. Obviously, most companies go on for years or centuries without totally liquidating inventory: They reduce taxes by the LIFO election immediately and (apparently) permanently.

A second advantage of LIFO is that it tends to cause reported earnings to reflect accurately the most current cost of goods sold, since LIFO uses more current inventory costs in determining cost of goods sold. FIFO tends to make the inventory value shown on the balance sheet relatively current but overstates earnings. LIFO emphasizes the accuracy of the income statement over that of the balance sheet — consistent with modern thinking about the relative roles of the two statements. The major disadvantage of LIFO is that the cost of inventory as shown on the balance sheet tends to become increasingly obsolete if, as is usually the case, the business maintains a stable or increasing inventory over several years. If a stable inventory is assumed, the LIFO inventory will always carry the value it had as of the date on which the LIFO election was made! In other words, it is quite possible that a 1987 balance sheet reflects inventory costs based on, say, 1947 product prices.

A second major problem with LIFO arises when, by reason of a strike or shortage, a LIFO inventory must be partially consumed in a later accounting period to keep up current production or sales. The inventory so consumed is on the books at an artificially low price, so that earnings are inflated solely because of the method of accounting for inventory costs. One possibility is that businesses be allowed to replenish LIFO inventories without adverse accounting or tax consequences when the depletion was in some sense involuntary.

A final observation may be made about the choice between FIFO and LIFO in inflationary periods. Irrespective of the inventory valuation system adopted, profits are going to be inflated during inflationary periods simply from price increases occurring during the period between the time of purchasing inventory and the time of recording it as an expense. The profit recorded by the business is in part its normal operating profit from whatever business it is in and in part an abnormal trading profit caused by price increases during the manufacturing or resale process. LIFO tends to minimize the amount of this artificial profit, but does not eliminate it entirely. Elimination would require a radical shift to a current value system for valuing inventory consumed during the accounting period similar to that discussed in the previous section relating to depreciable plant and equipment. Such a proposal has never been adopted. But LIFO is more sensitive to the effect of inflation on income statements than is FIFO.

Of course, not all goods appreciate in value over time, even during inflationary periods. Changes in technology may lead to price reductions even though prices generally have increased. A good example is the modern personal computer industry which over the last decade has seen product prices decline as product quality and sophistication has improved steadily. Firms in such an industry have no tax reason to adopt LIFO accounting.

§8.9 Why Does the Accountant Use Historical Cost?

The numbers appearing in financial statements are of course in terms of dollars. Nevertheless, the basis on which dollars are assigned to various assets in the accounting system is not a common one. Value usually means the price established by transactions between willing buyers and sellers in a market. It might also mean the value of the asset to the user, or the cost of reproducing or replacing the asset. The one thing it most certainly does *not* usually mean is what the asset cost, perhaps years earlier. And yet that is precisely the definition accounting typically uses. To an accountant, value *means* historical cost. The use of historical cost as the basis for accounting can be justified on several pragmatic grounds: Most importantly, it fits in easily with the intricate systems of accounts created under the principles of double entry bookkeeping. Also, it is objective and easily verifiable. Indeed, the use of historical cost is so basic to the modern accounting system that even assets whose current market values may be determined without difficulty are nevertheless recorded at cost. The value of a portfolio of marketable securities, for example, may be determined by a single telephone call to a securities broker. Yet the value of such securities is always shown at cost on the financial statements though it is customary to show their current market values as a parenthetical addition to the balance sheet as part of the description of the account:

"Marketable securities at cost (market
value 12/31/87, $3,500,000) $2,800,000."

A corollary of the basic historical cost principle is that a business should not record appreciation in the value of assets until that appreciation has been realized by sale or disposition of the asset. In the course of law school, you may run into instances in which a business decided to record (or *book*) unrealized appreciation, and a court decided that it was lawful for the business to do so. The best known example of this is Randall v. Bailey, 23 N.Y.S.2d 173 (1940), where a corporation recorded unrealized appreciation on its books in order to improve its dividend-paying ability. (The booking of unrealized appreciation is quite common today in connection with complex transactions known as *leveraged buyouts*. See §17.16.) Of course, generally accepted accounting principles may not have anything to do with the question of what lawfully may be done. Therefore, cases such as Randall v. Bailey do not really bear on the issues of modern accounting principles. Indeed many statutes embody undefined accounting concepts (such as the dividend statutes) and leave it up to the courts to decide what is and what is not permitted under such statutes. In the absence of legislative direction, one should probably not assume that the legislature intended to require all businesses to follow GAAP in the application of these statutes. In any event, the write up of unrealized appreciation permitted in Randall v. Bailey does not conform to GAAP, but often occurs today in businesses that are not required to prepare GAAP financial statements.

Theoretically, one could develop an alternative accounting system that immediately recorded unrealized appreciation. Abstractly, such a system is neither right nor wrong, neither legal nor illegal. However, it would be a risky accounting system, because asset values that go up can also go down, as was vividly demonstrated by the Great Depression, and there is a serious risk that such asset values might be significantly overstated.

Generally accepted accounting principles do contain a couple of important qualifications to the historical cost principle. The first is that GAAP assumes that the business is a going concern. If an auditor concludes that the business is contemplating liquidation or is otherwise unlikely to survive, he or she should insist that the basis for reporting values be changed from historical cost to liquidation values. As a practical matter, that change usually results in a significant mark-down in values and the elimination of many assets from the balance sheet. For example, organizational expenses may be capitalized and viewed as an asset only if the business is a going concern: It is clear that these expenses have little or no inherent market value if the business is to be liquidated.

Another major qualification is embodied in the principle that assets the firm holds for resale should be valued at the lower of cost or market. In other words, if the market value of inventory or marketable securities is less than their original cost, those assets should be immediately written down to current market value. In connection with inventory, this devaluation of assets may be made either on an item-by-item basis, or by classes of products. With respect to securities, it is customary to net appreciation and depreciation in value of all marketable securities, and make the write-down only if the balance is negative.

The principles outlined in this section are sometimes cited as illustrating the conservatism of the accounting profession in assigning values to assets. This may be so, but it should be recognized that this conservatism has its costs in the form of financial statements that largely reflect historical relationships, not current values. It is likely that using historical costs undervalues assets more often than it overstates them. As a result the accountant's conservatism is more likely to hurt sellers of shares than buyers of shares.

§8.10 Accumulated Retained Earnings and Statement of Source and Application of Funds

The previous discussion has focused exclusively on the balance sheet and the income statement, the most fundamental accounting statements. These statements are usually accompanied by two additional statements, which are described briefly in this section.

The first, the Accumulated Retained Earnings Statement (or Statements of Changes in Retained Earnings, as it is often titled) makes explicit the direct link between the income statement and the balance sheet. Table 8-4 provides an illustration.

It is based on the following self-evident formula:

Retained earnings at beginning of period + income for
period − dividends declared = retained earnings
at end of period

Table 8-4
ABC Incorporated
Accumulated Retained Earnings Statement
for Year Ended December 31, 1987

Balance January 1	$1,022,000
Net income for year	511,000
Total	1,533,000
Less: Dividends paid	
On preferred stock	30,000
On common stock	188,000
Balance December 31	1,315,000

Table 8-5
ABC Incorporated
Statement of Source and Application of Working Capital
1987

Sources of working capital		
Operations		
Net income	$511,000	
Depreciation	275,000	
Amount borrowed from bank	100,000	
Total sources of working capital		886,000
Applications of working capital		
Cash dividends		
Preferred stock	30,000	
Common stock	188,000	
Purchases of plant and		
equipment	305,000	
Increase (decrease) in other assets	(10,000)	
Total applications of working capital		513,000
Net increase in working capital		$373,000

This formula makes explicit the commonsense notion that earnings for the accounting period in question should be reduced by dividends declared during the period in computing the increment to retained earnings from the start of the period. If new permanent capital is raised during the accounting period or shares are issued pursuant to the exercise of conversion rights or options, this information may also appear in the Accumulated Retained Earnings Statement, or it may be described in yet another table usually entitled Statement of Changes in Owners' Equity Accounts.

The second table, usually entitled Statement of Changes in Financial Position or Statement of Source and Application of Funds (or of Working Capital) for the accounting period is a reclassification of accounts that appear in the balance sheet and income statement. It concentrates on the flow of funds or working capital during the accounting period — how a company acquired working capital and what it did with it. A typical funds statement is shown in Table 8-5. There is a considerably greater degree of variation or diversity in this statement than in other GAAP statements. There is little agreement on what is meant by "funds." About half of large publicly held corporations use a working-capital concept of funds, something like that appearing in Table 8-5. The other half may use cash, cash and equivalents, or cash and marketable securities. This diversity sharply limits the comparability and usefulness of these statements. Further, it may be unclear whether or not the flows statement is a true cash flow statement. The variation in and questionable usefulness of the Funds from Operations statements may be a result of accounting preoccupation with the profit and loss statement at the cost of more complete information about actual cash flows. It has been suggested that the funds statement should be standardized and emphasized as a true cash flow statement.

CHAPTER 9

HOW TO READ AND USE FINANCIAL STATEMENTS

§9.1 Introduction

Corporate lawyers are often expected to examine and analyze unfamiliar financial statements on behalf of clients. This process often requires familiarity with the way in which financial statements are prepared, how useful information can be squeezed from them, and recognizing the signs of trouble ahead. This chapter provides an introduction to this rather arcane art.

The analysis of financial statements is usually the responsibility of accountants and other experts trained in financial analysis. Moreover, a lawyer's examination of financial statements for an unfamiliar business may be supplemented by expert advice obtained from nonlegal sources. However, in the routine representation of business clients, lawyers are normally involved in transactions in which the financial position of another entity is important but expert advice cannot practically be obtained. As a result, lawyers must have some knowledge of financial statements.

§9.2 Uses of Financial Statements

When examining financial statements, one must always keep in mind the purpose of the examination. What is your client proposing to do? Likely alternatives your client is considering are: (1) lending money to the business, (2) buying from, selling to, or otherwise dealing with the business, (3) making an investment in the business, or (4) buying the business outright. The attitude you take toward the financial statements must depend to a large degree on what is the nature of the proposed transaction and your client's exposure to loss in the event the other party runs into unexpected financial difficulties or is unable to perform as contemplated.

193

§9.2.1 Short-Term Transactions

If the proposed transaction involves lending money to or entering into commercial transactions with the business on a relatively short-term basis, an extended analysis of financial statements is seldom required. The question usually is simply whether the business is likely to be able to repay the loan or pay for the goods or services being provided. For this purpose, a credit check through one of the commercial credit reporting agencies may provide information about bill-paying history that is more useful than information garnered from financial statements. In addition, useful information about specific companies may be obtained from a variety of publications such as Standard & Poor's Corporation Records, Moody's Industrial Manual, and the Value Line Industrial Survey.

The risk of nonpayment may also be reduced or eliminated by simple protective measures: obtaining a lien or security interest in the debtor's property, requiring the principal shareholders of the debtor to guarantee personally the payment of the debt, or requiring the debtor to provide a letter of credit from a responsible financial institution assuring that payment will be made when required.

If personal guarantees are being relied upon, it is essential to obtain financial statements of the guarantors as well as of the principal debtor.

In deciding what the risk of nonpayment is, the financial statements of the debtor may be examined to determine whether the transaction is of such a magnitude that it may strain the normal resources of the debtor. If so, a relatively short-range cash-flow analysis may be made in order to determine how the debtor contemplates raising the necessary funds to complete the transaction. Even where the risk appears to be a substantial one, your client can protect itself by structuring the transaction so as to limit risk by, for example, providing that your client may suspend performance if payments are not made at specified intervals.

§9.2.2 Long-Term Investments

Decisions on whether or not to make a long-term investment in another business (either of debt or equity) are almost always preceded by an investigation into the nature and quality of the business. Expert analysis of the financial statements is generally a part of this investigation. A long-term investment usually involves a relatively passive interest in the business. Earning potential or longer-term cash flows should be evaluated. Financial statements, prepared on the basis of GAAP or otherwise, may be the principal source of information for this analysis. In this situation, one must always be alert for danger signals indicating that the business is not as financially healthy as the financial statements might indicate. In making a financial analysis, one should always try to obtain financial statements (often referred to simply as *financials*) for at least the last five years to study trends not apparent from current financial statements only. A declining rate of growth or a rate of growth smaller than the industry as a whole are signs of possible trouble. Many danger signals, however, cannot be detected solely from the financial statements themselves. They include unusual turnover of key personnel, changes in auditors, and a gradual slowdown in the rate of payment of liabilities. Additional factors are described in subsequent sections.

§9.2.3 Acquisition of the Business

If your client is proposing to acquire control of the business, a basic question is whether the client wants to acquire specific assets or the entire business (usually through the purchase of shares of stock). Matters of concern are whether the book value of assets significantly overstates their market value, whether the cash flows of the business appear to be sufficient to finance future growth, and whether or not there exist undisclosed or contingent or "off-book" liabilities, such as litigation, the probability of future product liability claims, tax claims, and the like. Obviously, one cannot hope to discover whether such liabilities exist solely from examining the financial statements.

When a business is being purchased, one can often reduce the scope of risk in various ways that involve legal advice and legal principles. For example, it may be possible to require the seller to prove the essential accuracy of the financial statements and that there are no material off-book liabilities. A right to rescind the entire transaction may be negotiated if these warranties turn out to be false after the transaction is closed. It also may be possible to structure the transaction as an asset-purchase transaction that does not involve the assumption of contingent or undisclosed liabilities rather than as a stock-purchase transaction which leaves the purchased business subject to those liabilities. As a general rule, a purchaser of assets alone for fair value is not obligated to assume the seller's business liabilities (unless, of course, the purchaser expressly agrees to do so). However, in some situations courts have insisted that an asset-purchaser also take responsibility for product liability claims despite express provisions that such liabilities are not being assumed by the purchaser. Where shares of stock in a corporation are being acquired by purchase or the corporation itself is being acquired by a merger, the business being acquired (and quite possibly the acquirer as well) remains liable on pre-acquisition liabilities.

Negative factors such as the existence of undisclosed or contingent liabilities may affect only the amount of consideration being paid for the business. In some circumstances, however, the problems discovered may be so significant as to call into question the soundness of the entire transaction.

§9.3 GAAP and Non-GAAP Financial Statements

Publicly held corporations, that is, corporations with securities registered under the Securities Exchange Act of 1934, are required to prepare public financial statements in accordance with GAAP. A major purpose of these mandatory principles is to ensure comparability of public financial statements.

In addition, there are standards for independence of the auditor and the depth of his or her audit that permit a person to deal with such financial statements with some confidence. However, one should not overstate the degree of reliability of financial statements on the basis of a clean certificate by an outside auditor.

Even though GAAP is designed to ensure that operating results reported by different publicly held businesses have a large degree of comparability, it is important to recognize that GAAP, like accounting generally, is not a set of mathematical principles that can be inferred from a limited number of axioms. Rather it comprises judgmental principles established in an effort to make financial statements useful to persons who use them. A fair amount of discretion may exist as to how certain transactions are treated for accounting purposes. Where these transactions are material, a reference to the way they are treated should appear either in the auditor's statement or in the notes to the financial statements. Management rather than the outside auditor usually makes these discretionary decisions, though the outside auditor has a voice in the matter, and in some instances that voice may be decisive. See §9.5. Significant disagreements between a business and its outside auditors as to how a transaction should be treated under GAAP do not occur often, but the fact that they occur at all reveals that even fundamental accounting notions may be subject to challenge and that accounting principles are neither right nor wrong in any absolute sense. Like legal principles generally, the application of GAAP in a specific situation involves exercise of judgment.

Properly read and understood, financial statements created in accordance with GAAP can be used with some confidence. In any event, GAAP statements are the most that normally can be expected. The following sections of this chapter describe more or less standard methods of analysis of financial statements that accept the basic accuracy and comparability of the published figures. These methods of analysis usually may be applied with relative confidence to GAAP financial statements without making an extensive inquiry into what lies behind the figures.

Many smaller businesses and closely held corporations use professional accounting services but do not prepare financial statements on the basis of GAAP. Rather, such statements may incorporate GAAP treatment of some assets or transactions but depart from GAAP in other respects. Such statements also may be useful for analysis; indeed, there is no one right way to present the results of operations of a complex business. Statements that depart from GAAP, however, must be used with circumspection. First of all, one must consider the effects of the deviations from GAAP on both the value of assets and the income statement of the business. Secondly, the comparability of results with corporations that follow GAAP must be investigated to allow comparative analysis. Material adjustments may be necessary in a number of areas in order to reflect income accurately. Of course, considerable variation also exists within GAAP statements in these respects as well.

It should not be assumed that there is a consistent bias in the direction of overstating assets or income in non-GAAP statements. Often closely held corporations adopt accounting principles in an effort to minimize income rather than to maximize it. For example, many closely held corporations follow a policy of expensing as many asset acquisitions as possible, with a view toward reducing stated income and federal income taxes. Excessive salaries payable to the major equity owners of the business who control day-to-day operations may appear as expenses even though comparability may require that much of these salary payments be treated as dividends. Similarly, expense accounts may reflect hidden compensation. In these instances, the reported earnings of the closely held corporation may be significantly understated. Moreover, even the assumption that a single accounting system has been consistently applied by a closely held corporation in the past must be investigated.

Finally, as a kind of ultimate caveat about accounting systems generally, it is important to recognize that all accounting principles, whether or not GAAP, involve not only flexibility and discretion, but also conventions and assumptions about honesty and good faith. Financial statements are usually prepared to put the best possible face on management's performance and management has the preponderant voice on which accounting conventions are adopted. See §9.5. There have been several recent incidents in which outside auditors have given "clean" GAAP opinions on optimistic financial statements even though shortly thereafter the business collapsed from overexpansion or unwise business decisions. Further, no accounting system provides protection against outright fraud or theft. There are many dishonest ways to cook the books even if they are nominally kept on a GAAP basis. A major fraud in 1979, for example, was based on rigging the inventory count at the end of the accounting period by counting four boxes of sutures as 44, three boxes of gauze pads as 33, and so forth. Even though the auditor participated in the physical count of inventory, it did not notice these discrepancies. As described in §8.8, overstating the closing inventory for a period also overstates gross profit for that period. Thereafter, the scheme was to "destroy" the nonexistent inventory thus created, but the scheme collapsed because one of the conspirators went to the SEC in an effort to avoid prosecution. There are many other instances in which even major and massive frauds were being actively pursued unknown to the outside auditor. Obviously, even the finest GAAP financial statements cannot guarantee the honesty and probity of their creation.

§9.4 Cash Flow Financial Projections

In recent years, an alternative method of analysis — a study of expected cash flows — has become popular particularly by investment analysts considering tax-oriented investments. Many persons believe that cash-flow analysis is inherently more reliable than GAAP financial statements in estimating the risks presented by specific investments. This is particularly true with short-term extensions of credit where repayment basically is not dependent on long-term profitability. As described in Chapter 11, present value of a business is ultimately dependent on the ability of the business to produce cash flows in the future, and in a broad sense GAAP financial statements are surrogates for future cash-flow analysis.

Cash-flow statements are usually specific projections of what funds are likely to be available to the business in the future. GAAP statements, of course, reflect what happened in the past, and projections of earnings trends into the future have to be provided by the user of the financial statements.

When one encounters a financial statement or financial analysis that includes projections or cash-flow analysis, they should be examined with care, particularly the bases or assumptions on which projections of cash flow are made. It is very easy to project continued growth and continued improvement in sales, rents, or fees indefinitely into the future, but those projections are rarely realistic. Cash-flow projections that extend far into the future are obviously less reliable than short-term cash-flow projections based on results of operations in the recent past and indeed may be inherently unreliable. Since the early 1980s the Securities and Exchange Commission has permitted good-faith projections and estimates of future cash flow to appear in public disclosure financial documents; good faith, of course, is no guarantee of accuracy.

§9.5 Who Has the Responsibility for Preparing Financial Statements?

The reliability of financial statements is to some extent dependent on their being prepared by or under the direction of independent professionals. As a result, their reliability must be viewed as seriously compromised if they are prepared by persons who are employees of, or somehow dependent on, management.

The preparation of publicly available financial statements prepared in accordance with GAAP is generally viewed as the norm. The preparation of such statements is overseen by outside and independent *certified public accountants* (*CPAs*), who must certify in an auditor's report that the statements have been prepared pursuant to GAAP principles. As a practical matter, in a large and complex business, "overseen" means "spot checked" and the reality is that management largely has the responsibility for preparing the financial statements.

However, sole responsibility for the financial statements is not placed on the internal accounting department of the corporation: An independent accounting entity must make the necessary certification. Most large publicly held corporations use as their outside auditors one of the "big eight" national accounting firms that have offices in all major cities — Price Waterhouse; Deloitte Haskins & Sells; Arthur Young; Ernst & Whinney; Peat, Marwick, Main & Co.; Touche Ross & Co., Arthur Andersen & Co., and Coopers Lybrand. These accounting firms are immense partnerships with hundreds or thousands of partners, though some of them have attempted to segregate out operations in each country from potential liabilities arising from activities in other countries. Smaller accounting firms may be capable of serving as auditors for huge corporations, but an unsystematic sampling of large companies indicate that most of them stick with the "big eight."

The SEC views the selection of the auditor as an important factor in ensuring objectivity in financial statements. Its regulations require the shareholders to ratify the selection of each independent auditor: The SEC has also expressed public concern over corporations that engage in "opinion shopping" by threatening to change auditors if the present auditors prove unwilling to accept the accounting treatment of transactions that management desires.

As indicated above, the actual role of outside auditors in preparing financial statements is more that of overseeing the audit than doing the audit. In a large, publicly held corporation it is not practical for outside auditors to review all transactions or even to review a majority of them. The outside auditor's role has to be more limited: Typically, the outside auditors review the accounting systems used to generate the underlying data, test a substantial number of transactions (a sampling of the largest) to make sure that they are handled in an appropriate fashion, and participate to a limited extent in making physical counts of inventory, cash on hand, and similar matters. The American Institute of Certified Public Accountants, a professional society of CPAs, has established auditing standards that deal with the manner in which CPAs carry out independent examinations of the financial statements of companies. These standards are often referred to as *generally accepted auditing standards* (or *GAAS*). Many auditing firms have developed audit manuals to provide guidelines in various areas and for various problems. Most auditing firms also routinely use forms and checklists in connection with audits. Other mechanisms may involve the periodic rotation of audit partners or peer review, either within the large accounting firms or by outside evaluators. Nevertheless, in the final analysis, it must be recognized that much of the compilation of data used in the outside auditor's report is in fact assembled by the company's own internal accounting staff. Under these circumstances, it is not surprising that routine outside audits often do not catch fraud or theft, particularly fraud or theft hidden by an employee familiar with the accounting practices actually followed by the company. Legislation has been proposed in Congress to require outside auditors to take greater efforts to detect fraud or theft, and it is possible that future legislation may stiffen auditing standards. Of course, such proposals entail additional costs and greater exposure to personal liability on the part of the auditors. Auditing firms often argue that their principal function is to ensure that an acceptable system of accountability is in place and not to uncover fraud or theft. Despite this, auditing firms are often named as defendants in litigation to recover losses caused by undetected fraud or significant misrepresentations as to the prospects of the business. The issues in these cases are whether the auditor performed its audit in accordance with accepted standards for performing audits, and if not, whether that audit would have prevented the losses if it had been performed with customary care. In many states it is unclear whether an accountant owes a duty to exercise customary care to persons who foreseeably may rely on his or her statement, or whether claims based on failure to meet that duty are limited to those with a direct contractual relationship with the accountant.

Several courts have suggested that outside auditors perform a public watchdog role in connection with financial statements of publicly held corporations. Many of these cases in the 1980s have led to settlements under which auditing firms have paid substantial amounts, running into the tens of millions of dollars in individual cases. One consequence of this litigation has naturally been that the cost of liability insurance for auditing firms has increased dramatically.

Where publicly held corporations are concerned, the identity of the auditor is not a guarantee that the financial statements accurately reflect the financial condition of the business, and is certainly no guarantee that a systematic examination has been made in an effort to detect fraud or misconduct. As one moves away from publicly held corporations, the relationship between auditor and corporation becomes more critical. When considering financial statements for a small closely held corporation, one is likely to encounter financial statements prepared by local accounting firms of unknown reputation and quality. In addition, it is likely that the corporation has had close relationships with the auditor for many years, and the auditor's independence may be in serious question. In these situations, inquiry should normally be made about the local reputation of the auditor as well as his or her connection with the corporation in question. Of course, in the last analysis one has to consider whatever financial statements are available. Even financials that were prepared by a person under the control of the owner of the business are better than no financials at all, and therefore still must be examined and analyzed. Issues of auditor independence, in other words, go only to the degree of confidence one places in the reliability of the financial statements. It is almost never practical to require that new audits be performed, though it may be possible to request an auditing firm that your client trusts to review an auditor's report and report any inadequacies in the investigation, and their significance.

§9.6 The Importance of the Auditor's Opinion

The first step in reviewing financial statements is to read carefully the auditor's opinion, the signed statement that appears immediately before the financial statements. A clean opinion on GAAP statements begins with two highly stylized paragraphs that communicate the following basic information: (1) the financial statements were prepared in accordance with GAAP, (2) they present fairly both the financial condition at the end of the year and the results of operations during the period covered, and (3) the accounting principles followed are consistent with those of the preceding year. Typically, the first paragraph describes the company and the financial statements being certified and concludes with this significant statement:

> Our examinations were made in accordance with generally accepted auditing standards, and, accordingly, included such tests of the accounting records and such other auditing procedures as we considered necessary in the circumstances.

The second paragraph should read substantially as follows if the opinion is truly clean:

> In our opinion these financial statements present fairly the financial position of the corporation at December 31, 1987 and the results of its operations and the changes in its financial position for the year ended December 31, 1987, in conformity with generally accepted accounting principles consistently applied.

Any deviation from this language and particularly the inclusion of any additional statements in the opinion should be considered carefully and made the subject of further inquiry. Material changes in the treatment of one or more items may be specifically referred to in the second paragraph, for example, ". . . in conformity with generally accepted accounting principles consistently applied during the period except for the change in 1987 in the method of accounting for foreign currency transactions, with which we concur, described in note 1 to the Financial Statements." The "method of accounting for foreign currency transactions" may not sound very interesting, but it may involve hundreds of millions of dollars. Generally, if the auditor believes an item to be important enough to refer to in its opinion, it is important enough to be considered by users of the statements.

Often the additional information referred to in an auditor's opinion is of fundamental importance. As auditor for Texaco, Arthur Andersen was faced with the issue of what should be said about the 1985 Pennzoil judgment for over 11.5 billion dollars arising out of the struggle for Getty Oil Company. Texaco was vigorously contesting liability under this judgment, and it was therefore not reflected as a liability in the balance sheet. Arthur Andersen decided to add a third paragraph to its opinion on Texaco's 1985 financial statements referring to the Pennzoil judgment. This paragraph stated that the "ultimate outcome of this litigation is not presently determinable," and that Arthur Andersen's certification of the Texaco financial statements was therefore "subject to the effect of . . . such adjustments, if any, that might have been required had the outcome of the litigation . . . been known." That was, all would agree, an important qualification. One can imagine that Texaco was not pleased with this qualified opinion, but its wisdom was attested to when in 1987 the Pennzoil judgment forced Texaco to file for reorganization under Chapter 11 of the Bankruptcy Code.

Basically, if the auditor is unwilling to give a clean opinion, it has three choices. The auditor may give a "subject to" opinion stating that the financial statements fairly present the company's results but are subject to adjustments that are not yet known (e.g., the Texaco qualification). Second, the auditor may give an "except for" opinion that indicates that the auditor was unable to audit certain areas of the company's operations and thus its opinion does not extend to those areas. Such a qualification is rarely seen outside of closely held corporations. And finally, the auditor may disclaim any opinion about the financial condition of the corporation. This can be the most damaging statement of all: "Because of operating losses during 1984 and 1985 no opinion is expressed as to whether the corporation will be able to continue as a going concern."

A qualification of an opinion is a serious matter not made lightly by the auditing firm. It may well cause the corporation, if it feels the qualification is unjustified, to consider changing auditing firms. On the other hand, the failure to qualify an opinion may serve as the basis for subsequent litigation against the auditor by investors or creditors. To repeat, if an auditor qualifies or withholds its opinion, a person using the financial statement should not ignore this clear warning.

§9.7 The Importance of Notes to the Financial Statements

A second source of important information about financial statements is the notes to the financial statements. Some financial statements contain the notation, "The notes are an integral part of these financial statements." (Compare the notation on the Exxon balance sheet that appears on page 153 of Chapter 7: "The information on pages 29 through 36 [in the original] is an integral part of these statements.") Whether or not a statement of this type appears, notes should always be read carefully and their implications considered fully. This is not always easy to do because the carefully prepared language that appears in notes to financial statements is often spare and concise, and the significance of what is being said may not always jump out at the reader. An important disclosure may be stated without any indication of its significance.

To illustrate the importance of notes, consider the following company, whose accounting period ends on December 31. The preparation of financial statements takes some time, and the statements may not actually be released until early March. A not unreasonable question is whether there were important adverse changes in the company's operations between December 31 and early March. If something important has happened after December 31 — for example, the company's business has largely dried up and there is now imminent danger of insolvency — that information will not appear in the year-end financial statements themselves, but the essential facts should be set forth as the first note to the financial statements.

One problem with notes is that they are uneven: some contain additional detail and information about the numbers while others contain significant qualifications to the numbers. The latter is obviously more important than the former, but the notes mix the two together and do not always distinguish between them. In part this is because there is no clear line between explication and qualification. The following areas are usually covered in notes to financial statements:

1. Material adverse post-accounting period developments, alluded to above.

2. A summary of the discretionary accounting policies the company has elected to adopt (e.g., LIFO or FIFO, depreciation schedules, and policies relating to revenue recognition and the capitalization of deferred expenses).

3. The accounting treatment of significant transactions entered into by the company. The notes should indicate, for example, whether the obligations incurred by the company in connection with its employees' pension plan are currently funded and the extent to which the obligation appears as a liability on the balance sheet.

4. Breakdowns of reported amounts that appear as single aggregated figures in the financial statements. A one-page balance sheet often requires the consolidation of numerous accounts into single entries; the notes provide a breakdown in somewhat greater detail. Examples might include breakdowns of long-term indebtedness owed by the company and categories of fixed assets owned by the company. Much of the additional information included in the notes to the Exxon financial statements is of this character.

5. Outstanding commitments not included as liabilities in the financial

statements. Certain commitments entered into by the company may be material but not treated as liabilities under GAAP. Examples include rent obligations for future years under leases that are not cancellable, promises to redeem preferred stock at the option of the holder, and obligations to issue stock pursuant to stock options issued to employees. Material commitments of these types are all usually described in the notes to the financial statements.

6. Contingent liabilities, prospective losses, and unresolved litigation not included as liabilities in financial statements. Under GAAP, contingent items are taken into the accounts only when the outcome of the matter and the amount of the liability can be predicted with a reasonable degree of certainty. (Texaco did not show the Pennzoil judgment as a liability on its financial statements even though the trial court had entered judgment against it because Texaco was appealing and vigorously contesting the claim.) Obviously, some contingent obligations, if they materialize, may overwhelm the company. The notes to the financial statements set forth the nature of material contingencies and an estimate of the possible range of loss.

7. The tax returns for specific years that have been audited by the Internal Revenue Service and the years that are currently open or in audit.

8. A five- or ten-year summary of operations to permit longer-term evaluations of the company.

9. Information on major lines of business and classes of products where the company is a conglomerate involved in activities in unrelated industries.

10. Information on the impact of changes in price and value (i.e., inflation accounting) by large companies. See §8.7. This information adjusts the financial statement's current replacement costs. It (a) restates the financial statement's on a constant dollar basis to reflect changes in general price levels, and (b) reflects current replacement costs of inventory, property, plant, and equipment. Experience with inflation accounting reveals considerable divergence in approach from company to company, and many investors find this information to be confusing and complex and probably of limited value.

11. Management explanations and interpretations relating to favorable or unfavorable trends, changes in product mix, plans to acquire or dispose of major assets or lines of business, and the effect of unusual gains or losses.

§9.8 Traditional Analysis of Financial Statements

This and the following sections describe traditional methods of analyzing financial statements once the numbers in the statements are accepted at face value (or after appropriate adjustments have been made in the numbers). Adjustments to the numbers themselves that might be considered before applying the techniques described in this section are considered briefly in §§9.12 through 9.12.5.

The techniques described below measure different things and are designed for a variety of purposes. The most useful technique in a specific situation obviously depends on the transaction, for example, whether it is proposed to make a loan to the business, to invest in or purchase outright the business, to sell the business, or to engage in one or more commercial transactions with the business.

Most financial statements contain, either as part of the statements themselves or in the notes, historical information or summaries relating to prior accounting periods that are comparable to the information provided for the current period. Significant insights may be gained by considering trends over several accounting periods. Such analysis may show, for example, whether the position of the company is improving or declining over time. Analysis of the single period covered by the most recent statements is usually enriched by historical perspective. When practicable, the ratios discussed below should be computed for several years, and changes in the ratios should be evaluated.

Of course, your client (if on the purchase side) is probably more interested in what the business is projected to do in the future than what it has done in the past. One often must project recent historical trends into the future, but with caution and after considering whether there have been recent changes in the business's prospects and whether there appear to be dark clouds on the horizon. Often the most informed projections are those prepared by management (simply because management is most familiar with the business). Annual reports sometimes contain carefully prepared projections or predictions by management that must be evaluated before they are relied upon. See §9.4. Management is often inclined to make optimistic projections, and one should always be cautious of undocumented general assertions.

The balance sheet and income statement shown in Table 9-1 are the basis of the illustrations used in the following sections. To simplify the calculations in these illustrations, all numbers shown on these financial statements and used in the calculations omit six zeroes (000,000).

§9.9 Balance Sheet Analysis

Several widely used ratios concentrate exclusively on the balance sheet. These tend to be the most traditional analytic techniques.

§9.9.1 Net Working Capital

A basic question is whether a business has sufficient economic strength to continue in operation for a reasonable period. It may be recalled that current assets are those that involve cash, cash equivalents, and assets that should be reduced to cash within a year, while current liabilities are those that come due within a year. A simple measure of short-term stability of the business is to ascertain that current assets exceed current liabilities. The difference is called *net working capital*:

$$\text{Net working capital} = \text{current assets} - \text{current liabilities}$$

X Company has net working capital of $370 - $230 = $140. A negative net working capital indicates actual or potential financial difficulty in the short

Table 9-1
BALANCE SHEET — X COMPANY
December 31, 1987

ASSETS			LIABILITIES		
Current Assets			Current Liabilities		
Cash	50		Accounts payable	75	
Securities	20		Bank note	155	
Accts. rec.	100				230
Inventories	200				
		370			
			Long-term debt		250
			TOTAL LIABILITIES		480
Long-term assets					
Land	30		SHAREHOLDERS' EQUITY		
Plant/equip.	500		Common stock (800 shares)	40	
	530		Retained earnings	380	
		530			420
TOTAL ASSETS		900	TOTAL LIABILITIES/EQUITY		900

INCOME STATEMENT — X COMPANY
Year ending December 31, 1987

SALES		1000
EXPENSES		
Cost of goods sold	600	
Selling costs	170	
Depreciation	60	
Interest	16	
Operating costs		846
PRETAX INCOME		104
Income taxes		44
NET INCOME		60
Dividends		25
Retained earnings		35

term. (See the discussion of insolvency in Chapter 10.) A business with negative working capital may improve its position by raising additional equity capital — selling more stock — or by borrowing long term. Of course, the purchasers of stock or long-term lenders have to assess the possibility that improved working capital will actually have a favorable effect on operational results: It may turn out that additional working capital is only a temporary expedient. If it is, the new capital investment or long-term loan should not be made: It is throwing good money after bad.

A corporation that has adopted the LIFO method of accounting for inventory almost certainly understates its current assets because inventory is carried on the balance sheet at a historical figure that is usually less than current value. Whether or not this is material obviously depends on the circumstances.

§9.9.2 *The Current Ratio*

A widely used measure of the adequacy of working capital is the *current ratio*, which is the ratio between current assets and current liabilities:

$$\text{Current ratio} = \frac{\text{current assets}}{\text{current liabilities}}$$

X Company's current ratio is 370/230, or 1.6 to 1. As a broad rule of thumb, a solid current ratio for an industrial company is 2 to 1. However, lower current ratios may be entirely adequate for many businesses. In general terms, the smaller the inventory levels required and the more easily collectible the amounts receivable, the lower the current ratio that is acceptable. Again, the election of the LIFO method of accounting for inventory may understate the current ratio and give the impression that smaller inventory levels are required than is in fact the case.

§9.9.3 *The Acid Test*

Bankers and others considering short-term loans to a business often rely on quick asset analysis. *Quick assets* are assets that can be used to cover an immediate emergency. They differ from current assets in that they exclude inventories. Quick assets are obviously never greater than current assets.

$$\text{Quick assets} = \text{Cash} + \text{marketable securities} + \text{current receivables}$$

$$\text{Net quick assets} = \text{Quick assets} - \text{current liabilities}$$

$$\text{Quick assets ratio} = \frac{\text{quick assets}}{\text{current liabilities}}$$

The quick assets ratio is usually referred to as the *acid test*. X Company has quick assets of only $170 [$370 - 200]; net quick assets of -$60 [$170 - $230]; and a quick assets ratio of 0.74 to 1 [170/230].

A quick asset ratio of 1.0 or better shows that a company is able to meet its current liabilities without liquidating inventory. Ratios of less than 1.0 do not necessarily signify danger, however. An analysis of anticipated cash flow over the period of the loan may show that the company is able to repay the loan without difficulty despite a ratio of less than 1.0. It all depends on how promptly liquidation or turnover of inventories occurs.

§9.9.4 *Book Value of Shares*

Book value of shares is an important concept that simply means the value of those shares calculated from the books of the company using the values shown on the books. Book value does *not* mean market value. For example, shares of closely held corporations have book value even though the shares have never been bought or sold and no one has any idea of their value. Book value also does not mean liquidation value or "real" value (see $11.7), since the financial statements are constructed on historical cost rather than current market value of assets. See Chapter 8.

Book value of X Company's common shares is computed simply by subtracting liabilities from the book value of assets and dividing by the number of outstanding shares:

$$\text{Book value} = \frac{\text{assets} - \text{liabilities}}{\text{number of shares}}$$

Book value therefore equals

$$\frac{\$900 - \$480}{800} = \frac{420}{800} = \$0.525 \text{ per share}$$

This calculation is relatively simple in this case because X Company has only common shares outstanding. Minor complications may arise when the company has issued more than one class of shares.

Exactly the same mathematical result may be reached in the case of X Company by adding together the capital contributed by the common shareholders and retained earnings, and dividing the sum by the number of outstanding shares:

$$\frac{40 + 380}{800} = \frac{420}{800} = \$0.525$$

Indeed, this should be self-evident once it is understood how the balance sheet is constructed.

$9.9.5 *Asset Coverage of Debt*

X Company has $250 of long-term debt. A measure of how secure the holder of this debt is can be obtained simply by subtracting current liabilities from total assets and dividing by the amount of the debt, all computed at book value:

$$\text{Asset coverage} = \frac{\text{Total assets} - \text{current liabilities}}{\text{long-term debt}}$$

In the case of X Company, each dollar of long-term debt is covered by $2.68 of book assets:

$$\frac{900 - 230}{250} = \frac{670}{250} = \$2.68$$

In this calculation, no account is taken of the interests of the holders of the common shares since the rights of the holders of the long-term debt are senior to those of shareholders, that is, the bondholders must be paid in full before the shareholders get anything.

§9.9.6 Debt/Equity Ratio

The debt/equity ratio recognizes that long-term debt is part of the permanent capitalization of the business; the ratio is computed by dividing long-term debt by the total shareholders' equity in the corporation:

$$\text{Debt/equity ratio} = \frac{\text{long-term debt}}{\text{total equity}}$$

In the case of X Company, the debt/equity ratio is 0.6 to 1 (250/420). The debt/equity ratio gives a picture of what proportion of the company's permanent capital is borrowed and what proportion is contributed (or internally generated as retained earnings). Because borrowed capital carries with it an obligation to pay interest, while dividends are usually discretionary with management, large amounts of debt in the capital structure are more risky than smaller amounts. A company with a high debt/equity ratio is said to be *heavily leveraged*. A heavily leveraged corporation with most of the debt held by the corporation's shareholders is called a *thin corporation* or a *thinly capitalized corporation*.

From the standpoint of a lender, the debt/equity ratio measures the relative size of the equity "cushion" available for repayment of the debt in the case of default. A high debt/equity ratio means that each lender has a relatively small cushion and therefore an increased risk that the debt will not be fully collectible in the event of a default.

Is it appropriate to consider long-term debt as a kind of capital? Debt ultimately has to be repaid. Nevertheless, the treatment of debt as part of the permanent capitalization is certainly reasonable if the repayment date is far distant in the future, or sometimes even if shorter-term debt is involved. Financial statements treat debt as current only if it falls due within 12 months. Debt maturing beyond that time is permanent within the context of the financial statement. Also, debt falling due within two or three years may reasonably be viewed as long-term capital if it is anticipated that new loans will be obtained to repay the debt when it matures, a very common phenomenon in business. This is often referred to as *rolling over* the debt.

Shorter-term debt may be excluded from the debt/equity ratio calculation if its repayment is adequately provided for and no roll-over is contemplated.

§9.10 Income Statement Analysis

For most analytic purposes, information about past earnings and prospects of future earnings is more useful than information about property and assets. An old axiom is that assets are worth only what they can earn. Assets that have no earning capacity are salable only for scrap. Hence, more reliance is usually placed on the income statement ratios described below than the balance sheet ratios described in §9.9. Actually, income statement ratios is not an entirely accurate term, since income statement analysis often involves ratios between items appearing on the balance sheet as well as on the income statement.

§9.10.1 Operating Margin

Perhaps the simplest analytic tool is the *operating* (or *profit*) *margin*: the ratio of pre-tax income to gross sales:

$$\text{Operating margin} = \frac{\text{Pretax income}}{\text{Gross sales}}$$

Interest on long-term debt may be added back to pretax income on the theory that this interest really represents a part of the cost of capital rather than an operating cost. In the case of X Company the profit margin is 104/1000 or 10 percent, if interest is included in the calculation of income, and approximately 120/1000 or 12 percent if interest is excluded from income. The calculation is approximate because a portion of the interest expense of $16 presumably represents interest on current liabilities.

Operating margin is a basic measure of the profitability of a business. Generally, increases in sales cause dramatic improvements in the profit margin since some costs (e.g., rent and main office expenses) are fixed and do not rise or fall in proportion to volume. Correspondingly, a decrease in sales volume may cause a disproportionately large decline in the operating margin.

§9.10.2 Net Profit Ratio

The net profit ratio is simply the ratio between the bottom line and gross sales:

$$\text{Net profit ratio} = \frac{\text{Net income}}{\text{Gross sales}}$$

In the case of X company, its net profit ratio is 60/1000 or 6 percent, not a stellar performance.

§9.10.3 Interest Coverage

Of particular interest to the holders of the long-term debt is the cushion that the holders have between the interest payments on the long-term debt and the total income of the company before payment of interest or taxes. This is usually expressed as a multiple of the amount of interest due on indebtedness:

$$\text{Interest coverage} = \frac{\text{Pretax income} + \text{Interest}}{\text{Interest}}$$

In the case of X company, the interest coverage is $104 + 16 = 120/16$ or 7.5 times the interest cost. The long-term debt of X Company is thus a relatively safe investment, at least so far as the payment of interest is concerned. Ratios of three times or four times the interest cost are generally viewed as acceptable for stable companies in stable industries.

Interest coverage measures that the likelihood that the corporation can meet its periodic interest obligations: The asset coverage of debt (§9.9.5) measures the likelihood of repayment of principal if the debt becomes due immediately.

If X Company had outstanding an issue of preferred shares, one could measure the preferred dividend coverage in an analogous manner.

§9.10.4 Earnings per Share

Another fundamental measure of profitability, which is of particular interest to shareholders, is *earnings per share*, computed as the net income divided by the number of shares outstanding.

$$\text{Earnings per share} = \frac{\text{Net income}}{\text{Outstanding shares}}$$

In the case of X Company, each share of common stock earned $0.075 (60/ 800). Earnings per share is not the same thing as dividends per share; considerably greater weight is given to earnings per share because dividends are discretionary with the board of directors (and because economic theory relating to marketable shares indicates that retained earnings benefit shareholders as much as distributed earnings).

Earnings per share are an important element in the valuation of businesses. See Chapter 11. In this process it is often assumed that earnings per share will either remain stable in the future or increase in a predictable fashion in the future. Earnings per share should therefore be evaluated over a period of years, whenever feasible.

Large publicly held corporations report earnings per share on a dual basis. First, earnings per share are calculated on the basis of the average number of shares outstanding during the period. Second, *fully diluted earnings per share* are computed on the assumption that all options to purchase shares and conversion rights to convert into common shares have been exercised. Fully diluted earnings per share represent what the earnings per share would have been at the worst, assuming all options have been exercised and all conversions have been made. The concept of dilution is discussed further in Chapter 15.

§9.10.5 Relationship of Sales to Fixed Assets

A ratio that helps to determine whether the capital invested in productive facilities is being used efficiently is the ratio between sales and fixed assets:

$$\text{Ratio of sales to fixed assets} = \frac{\text{Gross sales}}{\text{Long-term assets}}$$

X Company's ratio of sales to fixed assets is 1.9 (1000/530). This ratio is particularly valuable as part of a before and after examination of the consequences of a substantial enlargement of productive facilities. The absolute size of this ratio is largely dependent on the nature of the industry in which the company is active. Lower ratios appear in heavy industry—e.g., steel or paper—and somewhat higher ratios (such as X Company's) in industries such as textiles or drugs.

§9.10.6 Inventory Turnover

In a manufacturing or retail business an important — often critical — factor is whether the company's inventory is too large for its level of operations and whether inventory turns over quickly or is sluggish.

Inventory turnover varies widely from industry to industry, and to a lesser extent from company to company within a single industry. Inventory comparisons therefore are most useful on a historical basis for a single company or on an inter-company basis within a single industry.

The most accurate measure of inventory turnover would compare average inventory during the accounting period with cost of goods sold. However, average inventory is not usually available from financial statements, and it is therefore customary to use closing inventory. Unfortunately, the use of LIFO reduces substantially the usefulness of all ratios based on closing inventory, which is carried on the books under LIFO at an artifically low figure. The following ratio is more useful in companies that utilize FIFO or other methods of determining cost of goods sold:

$$\text{Inventory turnover ratio} = \frac{\text{Cost of goods sold}}{\text{Closing inventory}}$$

X Company's inventory ratio is 600/200 or 3.0. A very similar ratio uses gross sales rather than cost of goods sold. This ratio is viewed as the best estimate of whether or not the enterprise is investing too heavily in inventory, and can also be used in connection with financial statements that do not break down cost of goods sold as a separate item.

$$\text{Ratio of sales to inventories} = \frac{\text{Gross sales}}{\text{Closing inventory}}$$

X Company's ratio of sales to inventories is 5.0 to 1 (1000/200).

In general terms, a high or increasing ratio denotes a good quality of merchandise and accurate pricing policies while a low or declining ratio may indicate problems (particularly for a retail sales operation), such as poor merchandising policies, a poor location, or a large amount of "stale" merchandise.

High and low in this context refer to comparisons with comparable businesses, not absolute levels. In making comparisons it is again necessary to exclude companies that have adopted LIFO from both sides of the comparison.

Another widely used ratio to estimate inventory management is inventory as a percentage of total current assets. X Company's inventory is 54 percent of its current assets (200/370). Again this number has little inherent meaning in cross-industry comparisons but may be useful if computed across several accounting periods for a single firm or compared with other firms in the same industry.

§9.10.7 *Return on Equity*

Return on equity is simply the ratio of net income to net worth:

$$\text{Return on equity} = \frac{\text{Net income}}{\text{Net worth}}$$

X Company's return on equity is 14 percent (60/420). This is one of the more widely used ratios since it describes how much the company is earning on each dollar of shareholders' investment. When applied to GAAP statements, it is also broadly comparable from company to company and from industry to industry even though it is affected to some extent by the accounting conventions that have been adopted. It also may be subject to manipulation. Management that desires to preserve a high return on equity may decide to forego current investments that have immediate returns smaller than the current return on equity even though the investments increase the earnings per share and have great potential for future income. These problems may sometimes be discovered by the use of operating margin and net profit ratio as well as return on equity as measures of overall success of operations.

Return on equity is a relatively universal measure of profitability. Information is widely available on the return on equity for thousands of publicly held corporations. In 1986, the composite return on equity for the nation's 1,000 largest companies was 10.9 percent.

§9.10.8 *Return on Invested Capital*

Return on invested capital is analogous to return on equity but treats long-term debt as capital.

$$\text{Return on capital} = \frac{\text{Net income} + \text{interest}}{\text{Net worth} + \text{long-term debt}}$$

X Company's return on capital is 1000/(250 + 420) = 9 percent. This ratio is a broad measure of the effective deployment of capital assets. Like return on equity, when applied to GAAP statements it is broadly comparable from company to company and from industry to industry. Information on the return on invested capital for thousands of publicly held companies is also widely available. In 1986, the composite return on invested capital for the nation's 1,000 largest companies was 10.7 percent.

§9.11 Other Ratios

It is possible to devise additional ratios to measure various aspects of a company's financial statements. For example, the ratio of accounts receivable to average daily sales (total sales divided by the number of selling days in the year) is a technical ratio that provides information as to the turnover rate of accounts receivable. The ratios described in the preceding sections, however, are the most general, the most important, and the most widely used. All of these analytic tools, of course, are not to be used mechanically and their usefulness largely depends on the quality and reliability of the financial statements to which they are applied.

§9.12 Adjusting the Numbers in Financial Statements

It is often desirable to make adjustments in financial statements before (or as part of) the analysis of them. There is nothing magical or correct about numbers simply because they are written down in an official-appearing and certified set of financial statements. Indeed, the reliability and usefulness of financial statements is not improved merely because they appear in an attractive format in an annual report printed in three or four colors and containing a glowing report from management. It is surprising how reluctant many people are to subject attractively printed financial statements to the same skeptical scrutiny they would routinely give typed or handwritten financial statements. The gift wrapping is not important: It is what is inside that counts.

When examining financial statements, it is important to consider the basis on which they were prepared. If the statements are not GAAP statements, both that fact and the manner in which they were prepared should be revealed in the financial statements or the notes. If the contemplated analysis involves comparisons with publicly available GAAP financial statements of comparable companies, adjustments sometimes may be made to make the statements more comparable.

In deciding what adjustments should be made even to GAAP statements, one must always keep in mind the issue that is being addressed. For example, adjustments that eliminate entirely intangible assets such as goodwill from the balance sheet may be entirely appropriate when your client is considering the purchase of the business in order to acquire its physical assets and the question is how much to offer to pay. Similarly, if the financial statements treat as expenses amounts that more appropriately should be viewed as distributions to the shareholders, income should be increased and expenses decreased appropriately if one is using the earning capacity of the business as the basis for deciding how much to offer.

Recurring types of adjustments to GAAP financial statements are described in the following subsections.

§9.12.1 Readjusting Asset Values to Reflect Current Market Values

Assume that you are considering financial statements of a company that has been continuously in existence since 1923. On its balance sheet is the enigmatic entry "Land . . . . $300,000." Such an entry should be a red flag for further investigation and possible adjustment since that $300,000 is a cost figure, and it may reflect either a purchase more than fifty years ago when land was selling for a fraction of what it is today or a purchase last week at or above current market values.

If the company owns marketable securities, the balance sheet should set forth by parenthetical notation a recent estimate of the current market value of the securities. It may be appropriate to substitute these market values for the cost figures for analytic purposes. It may also be appropriate to substitute up-to-date market values for those appearing in the parenthetical notation on the balance sheet (which states figures as of the close of the accounting period).

Other asset adjustments that should be considered include an upward adjustment in value if inventory is calculated on a LIFO basis and a readjustment of the machinery and equipment account if accelerated depreciation schedules that write off these assets more rapidly than market analysis justifies have been used. If accelerated depreciation schedules are being used, an upward adjustment to earnings may also be appropriate. On the down side, the machinery and equipment account may include obsolescent assets that should be written off to zero because their usefulness is exhausted and their resale value non-existent. Inventory is theoretically valued at the lower of cost or market, but additional write-downs may also be appropriate for obsolescent or stale items that have not yet been written down. Adjustments of these types usually require a fairly detailed investigation of specific asset accounts by a person intimately familiar with the type of business involved.

§9.12.2 Elimination of Non-Asset Assets

Balance sheets often contain items that have zero realizable value. The most common items of this type appear in the intangible assets account: "goodwill," "organizational expense," "capitalized promotional expense" or "capitalized development costs." It may be appropriate to eliminate these items entirely from the balance sheet, reducing retained earnings by the same amount.

The problem of non-asset assets is not limited to these intangible asset accounts. Investments in subsidiary corporations or other businesses also may have a zero realizable value. Even traditional asset accounts such as fixed assets or inventory may contain positive values for property that are unrealistic.

214

Usually, a detailed investigation is necessary to determine the extent of over-statement in these accounts.

§9.12.3 Addition of Non-Book Liabilities

Most businesses have at least some material liabilities that are not reflected in the balance sheet. These items include: future obligations under pension and profit-sharing plans, litigation in process, potential future product liability claims, commitments under fixed contracts such as firm long-term leases and employment contracts, and potential tax liabilities arising out of ongoing audits of earlier years' operations. Some of these items may be referred to in the notes to the financial statements: If not, it is usually difficult for an outsider to learn of their existence. It may be appropriate to increase book liabilities to reflect these off-book liabilities or to make an appropriate adjustment to the terms of the contemplated transaction to take account of their existence.

In the modern era of large tort judgments for product defects, a separate inquiry is often made about possible future product liability claims arising from sales of products many years earlier. In many jurisdictions such claims are not barred by the statute of limitations, which begins to run only when the injury occurs. The adequacy of insurance for such risks should also be investigated. Most insurance against liabilities of these types is written on a claims made basis that may require insurance to be maintained indefinitely even if the portion of the business manufacturing the products in question is discontinued.

When a business is being purchased, it is customary to require the sellers to warrant specifically that material unknown liabilities (other than those specifically referred to in the financial statements and notes) do not exist. The absence of such liabilities may also be a condition to closing, so the purchaser may withdraw from the transaction if its investigation reveals the existence of material undisclosed liabilities.

§9.12.4 Reduction of Book Liabilities to Discounted Present Value

Long-term liabilities are shown on financial statements at face value. In other words, a $10,000,000 bond issue is shown at $10,000,000 even though it may not be due to be repaid for another twenty years. Depending on the interest rate on these bonds, their market value may be significantly less than $10,000,000. See the discussion of bond pricing in §18.19. If reacquisition of these bonds by market purchases is feasible, the liability item on the balance sheet may be reduced for analytic purposes to reflect the actual cost of reacquiring and retiring the bonds.

§9.12.5 Adjustments to Income Statements

Because of the central role of the income statement in most analyses, it is important that recent changes in accounting principles or practices do not artificially inflate current earnings. For example, recent changes in the estimated lives of assets subject to amortization or depreciation might be examined for their possible effect on the income statement. Apparent reductions or deferrals of discretionary costs such as advertising or research might be reviewed since that is a relatively easy way to preserve an earnings record despite increases in costs or declines in revenue. Of course, reduction or deferral of such items may be unwise from a longer-term perspective. Professional or expert analysis of the financial statements and the underlying accounting records is usually necessary to determine whether such changes have occurred, and whether they materially affect the results of operations.

In a closely held corporation, accounting policies are often adopted in an effort to minimize apparent income for tax or other purposes. Upward adjustments to reflect income consistently with GAAP principles may be appropriate. The most likely adjustments are to capitalize items that were expensed in the financial statements, to restore to earnings amounts distributed to the owners of the business in the form of excessive salaries or fringe benefits, and to eliminate the effects of excessively rapid depreciation write-offs.

§9.13 Danger Signals

When examining financial statements it is helpful to determine the degree of skepticism that is justified. After all, financial statements are a little like onions; there are deeper and deeper layers, and one can spend almost infinite amounts of time in reviewing such statements. When one or more danger signals are present an increased degree of skepticism is justified and a somewhat greater investment of time warranted.

The quality of financial statements can be gauged by examining estimates or predictions made in earlier years, and then comparing the predictions with the actual financial or operating results for those years. While some optimism is understandable and justified, repeated examples of excessive optimism may require an increased degree of skepticism about the financial statements generally and future predictions in particular.

One common danger signal is a phenomenal growth in earnings in relatively recent accounting periods. It is always possible that the business has dramatically improved the efficiency of its operations and the control of its costs or discovered a new line of activity that produces phenomenal profits. It is also possible, however, that the growth in levels of profits has been helped along significantly by filling a limited demand, or by the use of accounting gimmicks or adjustments that overstate earnings. If earnings growth appears too good to be true, it probably isn't true.

Another danger signal is a company that has changed auditors in the recent past. It is always possible that the original auditor was unsatisfactory for entirely appropriate reasons; it is also possible, however, that the change in auditors was made because the auditor was doing its duty. While any recent change in auditors merits some inquiry, it is definitely a danger signal if it happens more than once. Such a company may well be opinion shopping, seeking to find an auditor who is willing to accept desired accounting treatment of some material items.

Yet another danger signal is a company that has engaged in unlawful conduct in the past or has the reputation for "sharp" business practices. While the conduct may have occurred in the distant past and the reputation may be unjustified, additional caution is justified when examining the financial statements of such a business.

Financial statements of a company that has difficulty in obtaining financing or has accepted significant and unusual restrictions on its management prerogatives in loan agreements should also be examined skeptically. This means that at some earlier time apparently sophisticated lenders declined to deal with the company at all or agreed to lend money to the company only if it accepted unusual and onerous restrictions. There probably was a good reason for the earlier lenders to do this, and the same problem may exist today.

Other danger signals include the use of accounting policies that differ from those prevalent in the industry, changes in accounting policies or principles without apparent justification, and apparently erratic fluctuations in discretionary costs such as advertising or research and development. In each instance, there is some danger that accounting principles or discretionary decisions are being bent to affect the earnings statement rather than having the statement reflect operations. At the very least, investigation is called for when accounting changes appear to have been made without persuasive justification.

§9.14 Flim Flam in the Books

Financial statements nominally prepared in accordance with GAAP are subject to manipulation and may involve outright fraud and misrepresentation. Fraud is often practiced by using fictitious transactions to hide thefts or adopting non-GAAP accounting principles without disclosing them. Income statements may be blatantly overstated by rigging inventory counts, by the creation of fictitious assets, or by omitting liabilities from the balance sheet. Sales to wholly owned affiliates at attractive prices may be booked as sales to independent outside parties. Sales may be booked immediately even though goods have been shipped on approval or subject to buy-back guarantees that are likely to be exercised. Depending on the sophistication of the persons engaged in the wrongful conduct, it may be difficult or impossible to discover that the books have been cooked without tracing specific transactions. Major thefts may often be hidden in the books of a large and complex business in a way that may escape detection for long periods of time. Often, however, successful frauds are based on relatively simple techniques, such as the recordation of non-existent sales or the manipulation of inventory accounts to hide thefts. The development of computerized accounting systems does not prevent the cooking of books; it simply requires a different kind and degree of sophistication to cook them successfully.

Of course, persons who misappropriate business assets or fraudulently misrepresent the financial condition of a business usually face criminal charges at the federal or state level if they are apprehended.

At a higher level of social acceptability are discretionary decisions that have the effect of improving the appearance of profitability and the attractiveness of the business as a financial investment. The goal of management may be to improve the market price of the stock of the company over time; this is furthered by the creation of the appearance of a stable history of growing earnings. Erratic earnings are not as likely to be highly capitalized by the market as steady and predictable increases. A fair amount of smoothing out and improving of earnings may be accomplished by discretionary decisions; for example, by booking income at an early stage of the sales process even though additional costs may later be incurred.

Another common accounting-oriented strategy is "taking a bath" during one bad accounting period. From the standpoint of securities prices and markets it is usually desirable, if a business is going to have a bad year in any event, to lump as many write-offs in that period as possible so that a return to predictable increases in profits becomes possible in the following year. Obviously, it is not ideal to have to issue a press release revealing losses of hundreds of millions of dollars in a single accounting period. However, memories are short, and with all the potential drags on earnings out of the way, the reported earnings in the following accounting periods should show dramatic improvement. Taking a bath in this fashion is a widely followed and attractive strategy for publicly held companies.

Taking a bath involves discretionary decisions to take as many losses as possible within a single accounting period that is going to show losses anyway. Smoothing out income involves discretionary allocations of income and expense items to specific periods to stabilize reported earnings. Many of these decisions may be consistent with GAAP principles because businesses have a considerable amount of discretion when to book transactions and when to recognize losses. For example, businesses often have assets or whole lines of business which can only be disposed of at a loss; the timing of the disposition is discretionary. Similarly, intangible assets or capitalized expenses that can never be fully re-covered may be written off at a time which is to some extent at the discretion of management. Bad debts or obsolete inventory may similarly be written down or off on a discretionary basis. Whenever one reads about a company that unexpectedly announces very substantial losses despite a history of profitability, it is likely that the company is taking a bath.

Companies have sometimes engaged in transactions near the end of their fiscal year primarily in order to improve the closing figures and the current and other ratios described in an earlier section. The company may make big ship-ments from inventories at bargain prices near the close of the accounting period in order to be able to book the sales. In effect the company may be "borrowing" from next year's sales, booking thirteen months of sales in a single year, as it were. Manipulation of the mix of inventory between raw materials and finished products may increase closing inventory (thereby increasing gross margin) at the expense of the following year. A company that has well-publicized cash flow problems may borrow money on December 28 in order to show a large amount of cash on hand at the close of the fiscal year. Of course, that cash is only temporarily resident in the company's accounts and may disappear on January 3. These tactics are known as "window dressing" and shade off into actionable fraud or deception.

CHAPTER 10

INSOLVENCY AND BANKRUPTCY

§10.1 Introduction

This brief chapter deals with issues that may arise when a business or individual is in financial difficulty. Perhaps the two most basic lessons of this chapter are (1) it is not a crime or a sin to be unable to pay one's debts and (2) a lot of people successfully avoid paying their debts even though they have the assets to do so if they wish. The federal bankruptcy law provides a fresh start for most individual debtors and enables one to preserve a portion of one's assets and continue living without hounding and threats by unpaid creditors. A corporation that is unable to pay its obligations is usually liquidated or abandoned: In the absence of misconduct of some kind, the shareholders lose only what they have invested but no more, and the creditors receive whatever assets are available and no more. Creditors thus often have to write off as uncollectible substantial amounts of claims.

Corporations (and sometimes individuals) that are not hopelessly insolvent but are in stressful situations with respect to their creditors may also file for *reorganization* under Chapter 11 of the Federal Bankruptcy Code. Reorganization is basically a time-buying process during which a debtor devises a plan to pay off some or all of its liabilities: The plan must be approved by certain categories or percentages of creditors and the bankruptcy court. During the period the plan is being devised, considered, and approved, the debtor usually continues to manage the assets. In the process of reorganization, some creditors may be compelled to accept partial or deferred payments in lieu of previous obligations. Many corporations that file for reorganization ultimately emerge as successful and profitable businesses.

Individuals with a regular income and with relatively small amounts of debt may take advantage of a somewhat analogous reorganization procedure under Chapter 13 of the Federal Bankruptcy Code. A Chapter 13 reorganization requires court confirmation but not creditor approval.

Detailed analyses of the topics touched on in this chapter appear primarily in third-year law school courses and seminars devoted to bankruptcy, debt collection, and corporate reorganization. This chapter does not go into as much detail as these advanced courses; rather it simply introduces the reader to the modern treatment of the insolvent or financially troubled debtor.

This chapter concentrates on the rights of unsecured creditors and the rights and duties of the debtor: It does not generally deal with the rights of secured creditors with respect to the collateral securing their debts or the rights of creditors to proceed against sureties and others who may have guaranteed the payment of debts to certain creditors.

§10.2 "I Just Lost a Lawsuit. What Happens Next?"

Much of law school is devoted to teaching how one goes about getting a judgment and how one gets it affirmed on appeal. Not very much is taught about how one translates a final judgment into money in the bank.

First of all, the fact that a plaintiff has been awarded a dollar judgment against a defendant does not mean that money flies automatically out of the defendant's bank account and into the plaintiff's account. Indeed, after a judgment has been entered, not very much at all happens. The plaintiff simply has a court determination that the plaintiff should recover a specified amount from the defendant. There is no promise by the judgment defendant to cooperate by voluntarily making the required payment. A judgment defendant that does not want to pay the amount of the judgment can simply sit tight. The next move is up to the plaintiff.

Each state provides procedures for collecting upon a judgment. While the procedures available vary from state to state, the basic remedy is obtaining a writ of execution and having the sheriff seize nonexempt property and sell it at public sale. The proceeds of the sale are paid to the judgment creditor to satisfy its claim, and any excess is paid to the judgment debtor. Every state provides that certain types of property are exempt from execution, which means that they cannot be levied upon to satisfy a judgment. The property that is exempt varies widely from state to state. It may be enumerated by item (e.g. one automobile or horse or certain household furniture) or may be enumerated as an amount (e.g. $5,000 of personal property). Most states have a variety of exemptions, some by category and some by dollar amounts within other categories. In some states, a person's residence (or homestead) may be exempt from execution, either in whole or up to a specified value. A uniform federal exemption effective only in federal bankruptcy proceedings is applicable in about a dozen states.

In addition, a judgment creditor may *garnish* amounts owed to the judgment debtor. A writ of garnishment is served on a person who owes the judgment debtor money and commands that person to pay the amount due to the judgment creditor rather than the judgment debtor. Bank accounts are the most commonly garnished property. States usually limit the kinds of accounts which may be garnished; many, for example, limit or prohibit the garnishment of wages due to the judgment debtor. Federal law also prohibits wage garnishments in excess of 25 percent of disposable earnings of any employee in any work week.

Many states provide, as an alternative method of enforcement, that the entry of a judgment, or the abstracting and recording of judgments in the county records, impresses a lien on real (and in some cases personal) property located within the state or within that specific county. The principal advantage of the lien is that the judgment debtor is thereafter unable to dispose of the property without "clearing up" (i.e., paying off) the judgment lien. The creditor does not have to persuade the sheriff to go out and seize property but can simply sit back and wait patiently for the lien to produce the needed payment.

The execution and garnishment process is relatively costly. Property must be located, care must be taken that the sheriff seizes and sells the right property, and the sheriff may require a bond or indemnification in the event the property he is directed to seize turns out not to be owned by the judgment debtor or to be exempt from execution. Under these circumstances, it is not uncommon for a judgment debtor to offer to make a partial payment in full settlement of the judgment, and for the judgment creditor to accept this offer.

§10.3 State Law: Assignments for Benefit of Creditors

A debtor who is in a hopeless position financially may take advantage of a long established state procedure and make an assignment of property for the benefit of creditors. Such an assignment is to a third person for the benefit of the creditors and is theoretically a voluntary act on the part of the debtor. The theory is that the debtor has recognized the hopelessness of his or her financial situation and has decided to turn the available property over to a trustee for the benefit of creditors to be administered and divided up on an equitable basis. Of course, the reality is usually more complex: Debtors are usually reluctant to throw in the towel and make a voluntary assignment for creditors. Usually such an assignment is made after considerable pressure from the major creditors who argue that the only alternative is a more expensive proceeding in the federal bankruptcy courts. The major creditors may also insist that a specific person be named as the assignee to administer the debtor's property.

Many states have statutes that regulate, in whole or in part, assignments for the benefit of creditors. These statutes generally follow the common law principles developed with respect to such assignments. They may require recording of the assignment, the filing of schedules of assets and liabilities with a court, and the giving of notice to all creditors.

An assignee for the benefit of creditors is viewed as a trustee and is subject to the standard trustee's fiduciary duties. His or her duty is to liquidate the assets of the estate and distribute the proceeds to creditors as expeditiously as possible. The assignee has limited power to set aside recent transactions with specific creditors: The assignee may have power to set aside fraudulent conveyances (discussed in §10.7) and some unperfected liens, but does not have a general power to set aside transactions that may have the effect of giving preferential treatment to some creditors over others. The power to set aside *preferences*, as they are called, does exist in federal bankruptcy court: If a debtor has made one or more voidable preferences, that may make impractical the assignment for benefit of creditors route. Also, a new uniform statute intended for state adoption dealing with fraudulent transfers (see §10.7) does give the assignee for benefit of creditors power to attack certain preferences.

An assignment for the benefit of creditors usually occurs only when the debtor's assets are insufficient to pay off the creditors in full and all of the debtor's nonexempt property is included within the assignment. The receipt by a creditor of a partial payment from the assignee does not discharge the debtor from residual liability on the unpaid balance. As a result, assignments are much more likely to be used by corporate than by individual debtors, who prefer the federal bankruptcy route since a discharge from this residual liability may be available.

An assignment for the benefit of creditors does not need the consent of specific creditors. However, a partial or qualified assignment may be set aside as a fraudulent conveyance. And, creditors who object to an assignment for the benefit of creditors may be able to commence an involuntary bankruptcy proceeding in the federal courts since the execution of an assignment for the benefit of creditors is a basis for ordering relief against the debtor in a creditor-commenced bankruptcy proceeding.

An assignment for the benefit of creditors prevents unsecured creditors from attaching or seizing the assigned property to secure the payment of their debts.

§10.4 State Law: Compositions and Extensions

A *composition* is an agreement between a debtor and two or more creditors by which the creditors agree to accept a partial satisfaction of their claims and forgive the balance. An *extension agreement* is an agreement between creditors and a debtor that gives the debtor additional time to discharge the debts but does not forgive them.

A creditor who is not a party to a composition or extension agreement is not affected by it. Such a creditor may continue to seek to enforce its claims against the debtor and its property by legal or extra-legal means.

A composition differs from an assignment for the benefit of creditors primarily because it is a contractual understanding between the debtor and specific creditors settling their claims. An assignment, on the other hand, is a liquidation arrangement not dependent on the assent of creditors and not involving any release of the unpaid portions of any claims. A composition and an assignment for the benefit of creditors nevertheless may occur simultaneously, as where a debtor agrees to make an assignment for the benefit of creditors and each creditor agrees to forgive the excess by which its claims exceed the amount available for that creditor from the assignment.

§10.5 Workouts

A *workout* is a process by which a leading or principal creditor of a debtor in serious financial difficulty in effect takes over the operation of the debtor's business, or requires the debtor itself to modify business operations in cooperation with lenders, so as to develop the cash flow necessary to repay the outstanding indebtedness. Many banks and commercial lenders maintain work out departments that specialize in this process. It is known as a workout because the goal of the debtor's operations is changed to "working out" the indebtedness over a period of time.

The power of the principal lender to compel a workout may arise from contract — provisions in the loan agreement — or from the debtor's recognition that the only alternative to a workout is bankruptcy in which his or her interest in the business will necessarily be lost.

The workout process involves rigorous control over cash flow and the diversion of the maximum amount of cash consistent with continuing operations to the payment of outstanding indebtedness. The managers during the workout have the sole power to draw on funds of the debtor (or to veto specific contemplated uses of funds); they also have the power to enter into transactions for the primary purpose of raising cash to pay off indebtedness. A workout is obviously not a pleasant process for the debtor, who must accept a process that may entail a partial or virtually complete liquidation of an ongoing business.

§10.6 Bankruptcy and Insolvency

The words *insolvency* and *bankruptcy* are often thrown around loosely. From a legal standpoint the word *insolvent* is much the more precise term even though it has two quite different possible meanings. The most common meaning of insolvency is simply that the debtor is unable to meet its obligations as they come due. This is usually referred to as *equity insolvency* or *insolvency in the equity sense*. The second meaning is that used in §101(26) of the Federal Bankruptcy Code: A debtor is insolvent if "the sum of such entity's debts is greater than all of such entity's property, at a fair valuation" exclusive of exempt property and certain other items. This is usually referred to as *balance sheet insolvency* or *insolvency in the bankruptcy sense*, phrases that are somewhat misleading because the Federal Bankruptcy Code also uses the concept of equity insolvency in a number of different sections. Balance sheet insolvency requires acceptance of some kind of accounting principles, though the phrase "at a fair valuation" obviously assumes that realistic asset values may be substituted for book values.

In real life, the difference between equity and balance sheet insolvency can be very great. Equity insolvency focuses on the *liquidity* of a continuing entity while balance sheet insolvency focuses on the *liquidation* of a terminated entity. A person or entity may well be insolvent in the bankruptcy sense but solvent in the equity sense: A debtor may have sufficient cash flow to enable it to deal with the bills as they roll in, month after month indefinitely, even though its aggregate liabilities greatly exceed its assets. A debtor could have a large slug of indebtedness that does not come due for another three years or so. Similarly, a debtor may lack sufficient liquidity to meet its obligations as they are coming due today and thus be insolvent in an equity sense, but at the same time have illiquid assets and resources with a value far in excess of all of its liabilities, so that it is not insolvent in the bankruptcy sense.

The word *bankrupt* has several varied and loose meanings. In the most technical sense, bankrupt means that a person is the subject of a federal bankruptcy proceeding. At one time it also meant that the person had committed one or more *acts of bankruptcy* (a concept that was eliminated from the Federal Bankruptcy Code in 1978 but continues to be referred to in the literature). It may mean a commercial trader who is insolvent (either in the equity or balance sheet sense). It also may be used as a synonym for "insolvent." Generally, the word should be limited to its technical meaning of someone subject to a federal bankruptcy proceeding, to avoid confusion and uncertainty.

Most state statutes (dividend restriction statutes and the like) use insolvency in the equity sense as the appropriate legal standard. The pattern is not uniform, however, and one must examine the precise language of each specific statute to determine which type of insolvency triggers the specific statute. As indicated above, the Federal Bankruptcy Act relies on both definitions of insolvency. As described in the following section, state statutes relating to fraudulent conveyances usually adopt the equity insolvency meaning of the term.

§10.7   Fraudulent Conveyances

The state law doctrine of fraudulent conveyances (or *fraud on creditors*) is designed to protect creditors from transactions entered into by debtors that have the purpose or effect of hindering or defeating the creditor's ability to collect on the indebtedness. The doctrine has its roots in the statute of 13 Elizabeth enacted in 1570 and is part of the received English common law inheritance in all states. The Commissioners on Uniform State Laws adopted a Uniform Fraudulent Conveyance Act (UFCA) in 1919 that has been adopted by some 25 states. In addition, a complete revision and modernization of this Act was approved in 1984 under the name Uniform Fraudulent Transfers Act (UFTA). The description below is based on the assumption that in the future many states will substitute the UFTA for the old UFCA, and that additional states that did not adopt the UFCA will codify their rules relating to fraudulent conveyances by adopting the UFTA.

One class of fraudulent conveyance covered by the statute involves transfers made with an actual intent to defraud or under such circumstances in which such an intent may be reasonably inferred. Section 4 of the UFTA defines these conveyances in the following terms:

(a) A transfer made or obligation incurred by a debtor is fraudulent as to a creditor, whether the creditor's claim arose within a reasonable time before or after the transfer was made or the obligation was incurred, if the debtor made the transfer or incurred the obligation:

(1) With actual intent to hinder, delay, or defraud any creditor of the debtor; or

(2) without receiving a reasonably equivalent value in exchange for the transfer or obligation, and the debtor:

(A) was engaged or was about to engage in a business or a transaction for which the remaining assets of the debtor were unreasonably small in relation to the business or transaction; or

(B) intended to incur, or believed that the debtor would incur, debts beyond the debtor's ability to pay as they became due.

This is an *actual intent* section. Actual intent may be difficult to prove, but §4(b) makes proof easier by in effect creating a series of presumptions. Section 4(b) states that, when determining whether actual intent to defraud exists, consideration may be given to 11 different factors — for example, that the debtor absconded (factor 6) or removed or concealed assets (factor 7). These factors are usually referred to as *badges of fraud*.

A second category of fraudulent conveyance involves transfers when the debtor is insolvent. Such transfers are actionable without regard to actual intent. The operative language of section 5 of the UFTA is as follows:

(a) A transfer made or obligation incurred by a debtor is fraudulent as to a creditor whose claim arose before the transfer was made or the obligation was incurred if the debtor made the transfer or incurred the obligation without receiving a reasonably equivalent value in exchange for the transfer or obligation and the debtor was insolvent at that time or the debtor became insolvent as a result of the transfer of obligation.

(b) A transfer made by a debtor is fraudulent as to a creditor whose claim arose before the transfer was made if the transfer was made to an insider for an antecedent debt, the debtor was insolvent at that time, and the insider had reasonable cause to believe that the debtor was insolvent.

This section protects existing creditors from asset-depleting transactions when the debtor is insolvent.

The UFTA contains a carefully drafted set of definitions that flesh out many of the general terms used in §§4 and 5. It defines insolvent as "the sum of the debtor's debts is greater than all of the debtor's assets at a fair valuation," but adds that a debtor "who is generally not able to pay the debtor's debts as they become due is presumed to be insolvent." It also defines terms such as *reasonably equivalent value, insider* and *transfer*.

Generally, a conveyance that falls within one of the categories of fraudulent conveyance is voidable at the suit of a creditor, an assignee for the benefit of creditors, or a bankruptcy trustee. Alternatively, the creditor may ignore the transfer and simply proceed against the property by attachment or other private remedy. Protection, however, is given to a transferee who takes the property in good faith and for a reasonably equivalent value. A good faith transferee is also protected to the extent of the value of any improvements he may have made in good faith to the property.

$10.8 An Overview of the Federal Bankruptcy Code

The Federal Bankruptcy Code was enacted pursuant to the constitutional provision authorizing Congress to enact "uniform bankruptcy laws." The current code was enacted in 1978, replacing an earlier statute enacted in 1898.

Substantial amendments to the administrative provisions of the 1978 Act were made in 1984. The 1978 Act made numerous changes in the bankruptcy code, so the pre-1978 literature cannot be safely relied upon.

Major features of federal bankruptcy law that distinguish it from state law are (1) a broad power to avoid prefiling transfers of property — particularly *preferences* — to ensure equality of treatment among creditors of the same class, (2) the existence of an automatic stay against collection efforts by creditors immediately upon filing a bankruptcy petition, and (3) the grant to a bankrupt of a discharge from prefiling debts in most circumstances. The underlying theory of a discharge is that an "honest" debtor should be given a fresh start.

The three major chapters of the Bankruptcy Code dealing with individual and corporate bankruptcies are Chapters 7, 11, and 13. (Because of historical reasons, there are only odd-numbered chapters in the current bankruptcy code.)

Chapter 7 governs traditional or "straight" bankruptcy proceedings for both individuals and businesses. The nonexempt assets of the bankrupt are liquidated under the supervision of a trustee. A Chapter 7 proceeding may lead to a discharge of an individual debtor from most obligations.

Chapter 11 deals with reorganizations of businesses (and individuals): This chapter has been utilized in recent years by Johns Mansville seeking protection from asbestos claimants, A. H. Robins seeking protection from Dalkon shield claimants, and Texaco, Inc., seeking protection from the Pennzoil judgment. Chapter 13 deals with reorganizations by individuals with a regular income with unsecured debts of less than $100,000 (and secured debts of less than $350,000) — most consumer bankruptcies, in short.

Bankruptcy proceedings are generally administered by federal district judges. Judicial districts also have bankruptcy judges to assist the district judges: Bankruptcy judges are not Article III judges. In addition, Chapter 7 cases and Chapter 11 cases will involve a trustee to administer the estate of the bankrupt. A trustee is a private individual (named either by the district judge or by the creditors, depending on the type of case) who is charged with representing the interests of creditors generally in the property of the bankrupt that is available for distribution to the creditors.

Most bankruptcy proceedings are initiated by a voluntary filing by the debtor. Any person with debts may make a voluntary filing; it is not a requirement for filing that the debtor be "insolvent" in either the balance sheet or equity senses. Chapter 7 and Chapter 11 proceedings may also be instituted by creditors seeking the involuntary institution of bankruptcy or reorganization procedures against a debtor. Generally three creditors with unsecured claims totaling at least $5,000 must join in the petition for involuntary bankruptcy, though debtors with less than twelve creditors may be placed into involuntary bankruptcy by a single creditor with an unsecured claim exceeding $5,000. An involuntary petition must allege either that the debtor is not paying debts as they mature (i.e., is insolvent in the equity sense) or that the debtor has made an assignment for the benefit of creditors within 120 days.

The filing of an involuntary bankruptcy proceeding almost always severely disrupts the defendant's activities and adversely affects its reputation. Severe sanctions may be imposed on a creditor who files such a petition in bad faith.

§10.9 Unexpected Consequences of a Bankruptcy

A complete description of bankruptcy proceedings is well beyond the scope of this book. There are certain consequences of a bankruptcy proceeding, however, that should be part of the general knowledge of every lawyer.

From the standpoint of creditors, the filing of a bankruptcy proceeding by a debtor has several unpleasant consequences. First, the automatic stay requires the immediate cessation of collection efforts. This includes attempts to foreclose on liens or security interests in specific property as well as attempts to collect upon unsecured claims. After the petition is filed, the rights of the creditor are to be determined in the bankruptcy proceeding and that may entail delays of two years or more in payment. Except for this delay, liens or security interests in property are respected in bankruptcy. Second, the bankruptcy trustee has the power to disaffirm executory contracts, so that persons with contract rights against the debtor may find that the contract is no longer enforceable and they have an unsecured claim arising under the contract that must be established in the bankruptcy proceeding. Alternatively, the bankruptcy trustee may elect to enforce the contract against the other party for the benefit of the estate. Third, if a creditor has been successful in obtaining payment of an antecedent debt shortly before the bankruptcy proceeding is commenced, that payment may be a voidable preference and the creditor may be compelled to return the payment to the trustee for the benefit of the bankruptcy estate. Preferences may be set aside if made within 90 days before the filing of the bankruptcy petition, or, within one year of the filing if the preference is to an insider, for example, a relative of an individual debtor or the directors of a corporate debtor.

For the individual debtor considering whether or not to file a voluntary bankruptcy petition, the major goal is usually the bankruptcy discharge, which provides for the fresh start that is the justification for federal bankruptcy. However, not all debtors are entitled to a bankruptcy discharge, and even where such a discharge is granted, it does not cover all classes or types of claims. There is thus a two-step inquiry in determining whether a debt is discharged in bankruptcy. First, it must be determined if the debtor is entitled to a discharge at all. Second, if so, it must be determined if the specific debt is covered by the discharge.

1. *Debtors that are not entitled to a discharge.* A debtor is not entitled to a discharge at all if it is determined that he or she engaged in acts of dishonesty or refused to cooperate with the bankruptcy proceeding in specified ways. These grounds include the making of a fraudulent conveyance within a year of filing the bankruptcy petition, failing to keep or preserve financial records, refusing to testify after immunity is granted following the invocation of the privilege against self-incrimination, failing to explain satisfactorily the loss of assets in connection with the bankruptcy proceeding, or making a false claim against the estate. If a debtor is not eligible for a discharge, he or she remains liable on all prefiling debts. As a result, it is customary to investigate carefully the availability of a discharge before the decision is made to file a voluntary bankruptcy petition.

2. *Debts not covered by a discharge.* Even when granted, a bankruptcy discharge does not cover several classes of claims: (1) most federal tax claims, (2) debts for money, property, or services obtained through fraud, false representations, or false financial statements relied upon by the specific creditor, (3) debts that are not scheduled in the bankruptcy proceeding, (4) child support and alimony, (5) tort liabilities arising from "willful and malicious" conduct, (6) fines, penalties or forfeitures payable to governmental entities, (7) educational loans, and (8) claims arising from driving while intoxicated. The exclusions of these items from the bankruptcy discharge are based upon policy and social considerations relating to inappropriate conduct by a debtor. Some of these limitations on the bankruptcy discharge are applicable automatically based on the nature of the debt. Others, particularly item (2) above, must be expressly pleaded by a specific creditor who must then be prepared to establish at a hearing that the conduct of the bankrupt with respect to his or her claim makes the bankruptcy discharge inapplicable to that creditor's claim.

CHAPTER 11

VALUATION OF AN ONGOING BUSINESS

§11.1 Introduction

This chapter deals generally with the question of what a specific business is worth. In this context "business" means any asset or group of assets that promise to produce a flow of cash or income in the future. It may include a piece of commercial real estate, (e.g., the apartment house described in Chapter 3), a manufacturing business, a retail store, a consulting business, a barber shop, or a solo or group legal practice. The definition is broad enough to include a portfolio of marketable investment securities, but the valuation of such securities usually presents few problems because quotations for marketable securities are readily available from brokerage firms.

The words *valuation* and *appraisal* are virtually synonymous and are used interchangeably in this chapter. The appraisal of the value of a business means the same thing as valuation of the business. In corporation law there also exists a narrow statutory *appraisal right* or *right of dissent and appraisal* designed to protect minority shareholders against certain types of potentially abusive transactions specifically defined in the statutes. This statutory appraisal right, described briefly in §17.9.2, has nothing to do with the subject of this chapter.

This chapter deals with both the valuation of the entire business as a whole and the value of interests — usually shares of stock or partnership interests — in a business.

The valuation techniques discussed in the later sections of this chapter require familiarity with concepts discussed in earlier chapters, particularly the time value of money (Chapters 1 and 2), the valuation of real estate (Chapter 3), and the fundamentals of accounting (Chapters 7, 8, and 9).

§11.2 The Standard for Valuation

There is general agreement as to the fundamental standard by which the value of a business is ascertained. Valuation is an attempt to determine the fair market value of the business, which in turn is defined as the price that would be established by a buyer and a seller in an arms-length negotiation for the purchase and sale of the business, with both parties ready, willing, and able to enter into the transaction, each under no compulsion to enter into the transaction, and each having essentially complete information about the relevant factors.

While this fundamental standard is relatively easy to state, it gives little guidance as a practical matter in every case where the business is closely held and there have been no recent sales of the business itself. Indeed, the "ready, willing, and able" test in one sense begs the question because it gives no clue as to what techniques should be used by a hypothetical buyer and hypothetical seller in determining what price to offer and what price to accept for a closely held business that has not previously been the subject of a sale.

Valuation problems arise primarily in the context of a closely held business, that is, a business with relatively few owners. A publicly held business differs from a closely held one in the valuation context primarily because there exists an ongoing market for ownership interests in publicly held businesses — the national securities exchanges or the "over-the-counter" market (see Chapter 18). The existence of this market for ownership interests makes valuation of a publicly held business considerably easier than a closely held corporation since there are always current market price quotations available for ownership interests in publicly held businesses. It should not be assumed, however, that no valuation problems exist in publicly held businesses. See §11.8.6.

§11.3 Expert Business Appraisers

Valuation of a business is a factual and business-related issue, not a legal issue. Many persons and firms call themselves valuation or appraisal experts, familiar with valuation techniques for businesses and competent to estimate values of businesses of various types. These persons are retained regularly to provide opinions or recommendations on questions of valuation, or to serve as expert witnesses in litigation on valuation questions. However, valuation is not an exact science and the conclusions of even sophisticated "experts" can be suspect.

Indeed, it is easy to be cynical when discussing valuation experts. Every person in business is familiar with stories in which valuation opinions were given primarily on the basis of what the person paying for the opinion wanted to hear. The necessary points of view are usually not conveyed by such crass statements as "I want you to come out with a high value," or "I want an opinion that this business is worth between $20,000,000 or $30,000,000," or "I want an opinion that $21 per share is a fair price for the rest of the stock." Rather, they may be effectively communicated simply when the proposed transaction or reason for the appraisal is described to the person retained to give a valuation opinion. After all, it does not take a genius to realize that sellers usually want high valuations and buyers low valuations, or that minimization of taxes is the goal of an estate seeking a valuation of a closely held business. It is also not unknown for a person dissatisfied with one opinion to commission a second opinion from a different, and perhaps more sympathetic, source.

Among the many individuals and organizations that consider themselves competent in business valuation matters are the following:

1. Accountants and accounting firms regularly make valuation studies and recommendations on valuation issues. They may prepare studies and recommendations for the benefit of management decision-making on investment or divestment issues that involve substantial valuation questions. A company, for example, has decided to sell off a line of business on which it is currently losing money but which it believes can be turned around with different management: The price to be placed on that line may be based on a report and recommendation by the company's outside auditors. The company's internal accounting staff probably has essentially the same expertise as the outside auditor and also may make a study and report, or may review the outside auditor's report and make an independent recommendation. The report of an outside accounting firm should be obtained both as a check on the conclusions of the inside auditors and because an internal recommendation may be viewed as being more subject to the domination of management than the same recommendation from the outside auditor.

2. Investment banking firms also regularly make valuation recommendations or give opinions relating to value, particularly with regard to transactions involving the purchase or sale of interests to the general public. The expertise of investment banking firms in the valuation area rises from their historical role of establishing prices for the sale of stock to the general public in connection with raising of capital. The establishment of such public issue prices is tricky: The price must be low enough to attract outside capital and yet not so low as to anger existing shareholders because of the dilution caused by issuing new shares at bargain prices. In recent years, investment banking firms have also been heavily involved in the takeover business, and in that connection have prepared numerous *fairness opinions* that judge whether or not a proposed price for a business is a fair one. These opinions have sometimes been the subject of litigation.

3. Similar valuation expertise may reside in employees of so-called full-service securities brokerage firms, that is, firms that provide a variety of advisory and related services in addition to the simple execution of securities transactions. These firms may provide services similar to investment banking firms; in addition they regularly provide investment advice that necessarily involves valuation questions. These firms also have information immediately at hand to value portfolios of securities.

4. Independent firms that describe themselves as *management consultant firms* also provide valuation services. These firms may employ persons with experience in accounting and auditing as well as management decision-making, areas where valuation expertise is likely to develop.

5. Valuation or appraisals of specific income-producing properties such as commercial real estate may be prepared by real estate brokerage firms or individual real estate brokers. See the discussion in §4.3. Persons actively engaged in buying and selling commercial real estate in the community usually have a feel for the market and are likely to be familiar with prices being paid for other commercial properties in the area and the comparability of those other properties to the property in question.

6. Auction or brokerage firms may specialize in the purchase and sale of substantial commercial assets such as heavy construction equipment, and may provide valuation opinions in some situations. These values may be liquidation values, based on the assumption that the operating assets are to be broken up and sold or auctioned off individually. For some types of second-hand equipment there may be published *blue books* or catalogues used in estimating value.

7. Some brokers, usually working on a nationwide scale, specialize in the listing of existing businesses for sale and in locating persons who are both interested in acquiring such businesses and have the financial resources to do so. Most of the businesses listed are usually relatively small, but that is not always the case: Some very large firms may list themselves (or large specific lines of business they are interested in disposing of) with these brokers. These brokerage firms of course have extensive experience with business valuation matters, though like brokers generally, their principal interest is usually the commission upon the completion of the sale.

§11.4 The Vain Search for the "Actual Value" of a Business

Those unfamiliar with the valuation process often labor under the entirely mistaken apprehension that businesses have a "real" or "actual" value, and that the goal of the valuation process is to find that value. Valuation is not an exact science, nor is it a search for the holy grail of value. Rather it is a study of competing approaches that lead to inconsistent results and of estimates and approximations based on incomplete and sometimes unreliable information. Valuation issues are interesting and challenging precisely because there is no single number that can be pointed to as the value of a business. At best there is a range of possible values that might be assigned, and at worst there are wildly varying approximations as to what an appropriate value is, with the approximations based on quite different approaches as to how value should be measured in the specific case. Intuitively these alternative approaches toward valuation may seem to be equally plausible. Further, the uncertainties of the valuation process are usually so great that high or low valuations may be plausibly argued for even when following the same basic technique of valuation.

A number of different adjectives may be associated with the word "value," for example, fair value, market value, book value, liquidation value, and replacement value. Some of these phrases refer to specific and meaningful concepts — for example, book, liquidation, and replacement value all refer either to specific numbers in connection with a business or to a specific method of calculating a number in connection with that business. Other phrases, such as fair value, real value, true value, and actual value, have no inherent meaning at all. At best, these phrases are merely synonyms for the basic definition of value, namely the price on which a willing buyer and willing seller agree. Basically, there is no objective answer to the question, "What is this business really worth?"

There is some advantage in exploring further unarticulated lay notions of value. Many individuals have had the experience of selling a used car, where value means "resale value" which can be easily approximated simply by looking it up in the "blue book," by going to several used car dealers and asking for price quotations, or by advertising the car oneself and seeing what offers come in. These are appropriate ways to measure the value of goods that are reasonably standardized and are recognized objects of trade. The problem is that businesses are rarely like used cars; they are not at all standardized, each one is unique, there is no authoritative blue book, and there is not an active market with many buyers and sellers. A value may have to be assigned to a business where there are no sales that are even remotely comparable.

A second lay approach toward value is to assume that value really means liquidation value, that is, what the assets could be sold for if the business were closed down and the assets broken up and sold. For an individual, this would be the answer to the question, "What are my worldly assets worth?" or, in more pessimistic terms, "How large would my estate be if I died today?" A business can certainly be valued in this way. However, in almost every situation, liquidation of the business is not contemplated by anyone, and what is being valued is not a mass of isolated assets but something that has value because it produced income or cash flow in the past and has (presumably) greater potential of producing income or cash flow in years to come. The use of liquidation value in most situations is therefore illogical because it values the business in a way that does not address the actual value-producing ability of the business.

Whatever the reason for the notion that a business has a "real" or "actual" value, students regularly rely on this notion in law school classes when valuation issues are first discussed. One also finds traces of it in opinions of presumably sophisticated judges who argue, for example, that a transaction should be set aside because a price for shares of closely held stock was set entirely arbitrarily and did not reflect "real," "actual," or "true" value. Since there is no such thing as "true" value in an objective sense, this reasoning simply is assertion of a conclusion and not analysis. (It does not necessarily follow, of course, that the court was wrong in setting aside the transactions in question in these cases; what is being criticized here is the reasoning, not necessarily the result.)

There are different valuation techniques that may be used to analyze value, and each technique may yield significantly different numbers. These techniques are described in the following sections of this chapter: The point here is that it is considerably more accurate to envision the ultimate "value" of a business as a range than as a specific number. For the same reason, the valuation opinions of even sophisticated individuals with extensive backgrounds in valuation techniques usually may be impeached, or at least shaken, by a lawyer familiar with valuation techniques and their limitations.

§11.5 Valuation Based on Cash Flow or Income

Usually, the value of a business lies in its ability to provide a future stream of net cash. The simplest and most direct way of measuring value therefore is to estimate what this stream will be in the future and assign a value to it, using the techniques described in earlier chapters on discounting future payments back to present value (Chapter 2). A similar process is followed in determining the values of annuities (Chapter 5). Usually, reliable estimates of future net cash flows will not be available, and the only available information will be conventionally prepared income statements for prior accounting periods. Estimates of future income flows, based on the conventional income statements, are widely used instead of net cash flows. Indeed, this method of valuation is usually described as the *capitalization of income* or *earnings*. It is a well-established method of estimating value.

It will be recalled that the valuation of an annuity or a stream of cash payments in the future requires knowledge of two variables: the size of the payments each year, and the appropriate discount or interest rate by which the future payments can be discounted to present value. This rate in turn is a function of two variables: the going or market interest rates for riskless loans in the economy at the time, and the degree of risk presented by the specific transaction. Where constant perpetual payments are involved — that is, the stream of payments is assumed to remain fixed in amount and continue permanently in the future — the present value of the stream is equal to the reciprocal of the interest rate multiplied by the payment:

$$\text{Present value} = \text{Payment} \times \frac{1}{\text{discount rate}}$$

This formula is developed in section 2.6. The reciprocal of the discount rate (1/interest rate) is called the *capitalization factor* or *multiplier*. Table 11-1 shows how one can quickly develop a table of reciprocals that show what the capitalization factor is for a variety of discount rates.

In the context of a going business a value can be obtained simply by estimating the future income or cash flow of the business, selecting a discount rate, and multiplying by the reciprocal set forth in Table 11-1. Thus, if a business's estimated future income is $120,000 per year, and it is determined that an appropriate discount rate is 10 percent, that business is worth $1,200,000 (10 × $120,000 = $1,200,000). If the estimated future income were $90,000 per year, the value would be $900,000. If the business were considerably riskier and the appropriate discount rate were 20 percent, the

Table 11-1

Discount rate	Capitalization factor
100%	1
50%	2
33.33%	3
25%	4
20%	5
16.66%	6
12.5%	8
10%	10
8%	12.5
7%	14
6%	16.7
5%	20

company would be worth precisely half as much: 5 × $100,000 = $500,000. The riskier the business, the higher the discount rate, the smaller the capitalization factor, and the lower the value placed on the stream of income or cash flow. If it were so much less risky that the appropriate discount rate was 6 percent, the business would be worth $1,666,667, and so forth. It is apparent that accurate assessments of both anticipated income (or cash flow) and discount rate are essential if the valuation so obtained is to be reliable. However, it should also be apparent that in real life, information about both variables creates serious problems.

§11.5.1 The Size of Future Payments or Cash Flows

For some businesses, the size of future payments or cash flows can be estimated with a fair degree of reliability. For example, the rental income of a shopping center may be based on long-term leases that provide a reasonable basis for estimating future returns (though the standard practice of charging rent based in part on a percentage of gross sales may be a complicating factor). Much the same thing may be true of a hotel or an apartment house in which vacancy rates can be estimated based on experience or historic patterns. Such businesses, however, probably are unusual; the more common characteristic is that future cash flows or income are highly erratic, uncertain and problematic.

As described in the chapters on accounting, in some instances projections of future income or cash flow prepared by management may be available. (See §9.4). These estimates may be used as the projection of earnings into the future; there is a risk, however, that these estimates may be overly optimistic.

For most businesses, historical information is available as to how the business fared in the recent past. Table 11-2 shows an example of information that may be available in early 1988 as to income for the previous five years. Again a caveat may be necessary: These are "book earnings" and adjustments may be necessary to more accurately reflect the true earning capacity of the business. See §9.12. Assuming that this is unnecessary (i.e., the income stream described above has already been suitably adjusted), can one draw an inference about what future income will be from this historical data? One might take the average earnings over these five years, which is $154,000 (100,000 + 120,000 + 180,000 + 210,000 + 160,000 = 770,000/5 = 154,000), and conclude that this number is a reasonable estimate of the average earnings of the business

Table 11-2

Year	Net income after taxes
1983	100,000
1984	120,000
1985	180,000
1986	210,000
1987	160,000

in the future. One can then choose an appropriate discount rate (e.g., 12.5 percent) and conclude that the value of the business is $1,232,000 ($154,000 × 8). (Where the 12.5 percent discount rate comes from is discussed below.)

It is easy to raise objections to the reliability of this process. First of all, is it realistic to assume that the earnings will average $154,000 per year *forever*? What about the period beginning three years from now? Ten years from now? Certainly, as the time frame lengthens, the uncertainties and inaccuracies of present predictions must also increase. That is true, but there are two plausible countervailing comments. As pointed out in an earlier chapter, mathematically, the contribution to value made by those later years is relatively small in contrast to the contribution of the next few years, where presumably the estimate is more reliable. In other words, most of the overall value is represented by the next five, more reliable years, and a relatively small amount is represented by the assumption that earnings will average $154,000 from 1998 on. (See the discussion in Chapter 2.) Hence one might conclude that the calculation should not be materially changed if the $154,000 assumption were extended to the infinite future or, alternatively, that a different assumption were made about the income in these later years. Secondly, while it is true that uncertainties increase the further into the future we look, it also is as likely that the current estimate will understate future earnings as it is that they will overstate them. If the probability of an upside error and of a downside error are roughly of the same order of magnitude, the current estimate will not be materially changed. Clearly we are engaged in an impressionistic and not a scientific inquiry, and there is a gamble in it from the perspective of both sides.

On the other hand, the seller of the contemplated business (interested, obviously, in a high valuation) might legitimately complain that the $154,000 average figure used in the above calculation gives undue weight to the first two years (1983 and 1984), which are the most remote from the present. After all, in the last three years of the five-year period (1985-1987), earnings never were below $160,000 and yet future earnings are estimated at only $154,000. It is more reasonable, it might be argued, to use only the average earnings of the last three years, which places the estimated earnings at $183,333 per year. The overall value of the business, using a 12.5 percent discount rate, would then be $1,466,664. In response, it might be argued that the significant decline in earnings in 1986 is a warning that conditions giving rise to the steady increase in earnings before 1987 may have changed, and that the average earnings in the future should in no event be viewed as being greater than those in 1987 ($160,000). Along the same line, earnings arguably should be less than $160,000 if the downward trend can be expected to continue. Obviously, analysis of causes of the 1987 decline is of central importance in this debate.

Let us assume a somewhat different pattern of earnings for the period 1983-1987, with no change in average earnings for the period:

1983	100,000
1984	120,000
1985	160,000
1986	180,000
1987	210,000

This rather minor adjustment gives a dramatically difference appearance to the future of the business. The seller might well argue that the estimate of average income in the future should build in a growth factor. For example, the seller might argue that the trend of growth in current earnings should be extrapolated into the future, for example:

1987 (actual)	210,000
1988 (est.)	240,000
1989 (est.)	270,000
1990 (est.)	300,000

If this analysis is accepted, and the average of these four projections ($255,000) is taken as the anticipated income or cash-flow stream, the value of this business at a 12.5 percent discount factor becomes $2,040,000. At the very least the trend might justify the use of the results for 1987, or $210,000, as estimated future income. If the 12.5 percent discount factor is applied to this figure, the value of the business is $1,680,000.

All this may be entirely too subjective for many people. There exists a well-developed theoretical model for analysis of future cash flows under conditions of uncertainty. This analysis essentially involves the assessment of likely future cash-flow outcomes, the assignment of probabilities to each outcome, and the weighting of all possible results with the probability that that result will occur. The end result of this process is a single number that represents the value of the probable outcome given the uncertainties worked into the analysis. This analysis is often presented in the form of a "decision tree" that may help in making sure that major contingencies are not overlooked.

The isolation of possible outcomes and the assignment of specific probabilities to each outcome gives a satisfying specificity to the entire operation. However, even if all major contingencies are isolated in the decision tree analysis (itself a dubious assumption), the assignment of probabilities to them usually involves so much guesswork and is so uncertain that it is doubtful that the use of this technique in real life situations provides a materially improved estimate of future events than the much more impressionistic analysis based on a mixture of historical results and generalized predictions about future trends set forth above. And the danger of assigning hard numbers to estimates is that the conclusion may appear to be more specific, and therefore more reliable, than it actually is.

§11.5.2 Capitalization Factors

Recall that the interest rate used to discount future payments back to present values in effect describes a measure of the risk that the payments will not occur (as well as the general costs of borrowing money in the economy as a whole). The determination of what discount rate to use in valuing a business appears at first glance to involve variables even more uncertain than the determination of the anticipated income or cash flow of the business. Indeed, one might argue that the multiplication of one gross approximation by an even grosser approximation yields only "garbage," that is, a figure that is so unreliable that it should not be used at all.

The capitalization factor is not as bleak as that, however. Usually the discount rate used in valuing a business is established from the actual relationships between average earnings and sales prices of similar businesses in the recent past rather than from a market interest rate plus additional risk assessment. Persons familiar with the purchase and sale of businesses usually are also generally familiar with actual sales prices of businesses that have been sold in the recent past and the estimated earnings used in the negotiations leading to those sales. Statements such as "Companies in which the personal services of the owners are an important income-producing factor generally sell at two times earnings, or less," or "Steel companies generally sell for about eight times earnings," or "Companies developing computer software that have marketed at least one successful product generally sell for at least fifteen times earnings," are all meaningful statements that provide useful signposts for the selection of an appropriate capitalization factor for a noncomparable business in the same or related industry.

In addition, for publicly traded securities there is readily available information about price/earnings ratios. The price/earnings ratio is the ratio between the market price per share and the earnings per share of the publicly held stock for the last available accounting period. See §9.10. The price/earnings ratios are not precisely identical to capitalization factors because the price/earnings ratios of publicly traded stocks reflect a multitude of investment decisions for small blocks of stock not affecting the control of the business, while capitalization ratios assume that control of the business itself is being bought and sold. In other words, the price/earnings ratio of publicly held companies, as usually computed, reflects only the investment value of securities and not any premium that represents the control factor. See §11.8.6. Use of price/earnings ratios as the capitalization factor for valuation purposes for closely held businesses therefore may underestimate to some extent the value of the company being appraised. However, in view of all the uncertainties inherent in the valuation of a closely held business, this concern does not appear to be a serious one. However, the two are related, and price/earnings ratios are routinely used as estimates of capitalization ratios.

In an ideal situation, one may be able to find a publicly held corporation that is similar in most important respects to the closely held business being valued. If the two businesses are roughly comparable, then one can apply the price/earnings ratio of the publicly held stock as a ball park estimate of the appropriate capitalization ratio for the closely held company being valued. Again, it must be remembered that we are not dealing here with precise scientific data but with an impressionistic analysis establishing a range of values.

Unfortunately, however, there is usually no publicly held corporation that is a close match for the company being valued. The most common problem of noncomparability is that the publicly held corporation has substantial business operations in several different industries while the closely held corporation being valued is active in only a single industry. In this situation one may use a composite price/earnings ratio for all the publicly held companies in the industry, if that is available. That composite ratio may be an appropriate capitalization factor for a business active only in the same industry on the theory that the averaging of price/earnings ratios for different publicly held companies tend to cancel out the effect of different multiple operations in different industries. If the notes to the financial statements of one or more of the publicly held corporations may contain sufficient breakdowns and information on the results of operations in the industry in question, it may be possible to obtain a separate price/earnings ratio for those operations alone.

In selecting an appropriate capitalization ratio, it may be appropriate to adjust an industrywide price/earnings ratio to reflect unique aspects of the company. For example, if the company appears to have a more obsolete plant than the comparable company or the industry average, a reduction in the capitalization ratio may be appropriate. The following hypothetical analysis is typical: "The best managed companies in this industry sell for nine times earnings. The company being valued is certainly not among the most efficient. A downward adjustment in the capitalization ratio is therefore appropriate." There are two problems with such an adjustment, however. First, it is relatively easy to say that an "appropriate" adjustment should be made, but there is usually no criterion for determining what that adjustment should be. If the base ratio is 9 times earnings, should the appropriate capitalization ratio for the corporation with a somewhat obsolete plant be 8 times earnings? 8.5 times? 8.75 times? Such differences in the capitalization ratios may have substantial effects on the overall value of the business. The difference between 8.5 and 8 times earnings, for example, may easily involve millions of dollars. The second problem is the risk of double counting a negative factor. If the lack of efficiency is used first to justify a reduction of anticipated future earnings or cash flow, and a second time to reduce the appropriate capitalization ratio, it is likely that the double use of the same negative factor will overstate its importance.

Logically, an adjustment of this nature probably should be made in the expected income determination rather than the discount rate because changes in capitalization rates have more substantial impact on the total valuation figure. Double counting of such an item may in any event be avoided if the analysis follows a standard decision tree approach.

§11.5.3 Valuation Based on Cash Flow or Earnings: Conclusion

What then should be said about the capitalization of earnings or cash flow approach? It is the most popular method of valuation of closely held businesses that are being purchased because of their potential earnings or cash flows. It is also widely used in valuation disputes generally, such as those relating to the value of closely held stock for gift and estate tax purposes. Indeed, despite its drawbacks, the capitalization of earnings or cash flow is generally believed to be the most reliable method of estimating the value of a business anticipated to be in existence indefinitely.

§11.6 Valuation Based on Asset Appraisals

As discussed earlier, a valuation based on what the assets of the business would bring if they were sold may seem to be the simplest and most intuitively acceptable method of valuation of a business. When an individual asks himself or herself, "What is my financial worth?" he or she is likely to think in terms of what the various assets he or she owns would bring if sold. However, in most circumstances this method of valuation is unrealistic since neither the buyer nor the seller contemplates that the liquidation will in fact occur. Typically, what is being bought and sold is an entity that produces earnings or cash flow, not a string of individual, unrelated assets.

Asset valuations nevertheless may enter into the calculation of the value of a business in many circumstances. The most obvious situation is where the goal of the purchaser is in fact to liquidate the business — a "bust-up transaction," as it is sometimes called. Bust-up transactions occur in publicly held corporations when the securities of a corporation are depressed in price and the liquidation value of its assets exceeds its value as a going business as measured in the securities markets. Similar transactions may occur in closely held corporations as well whenever the present owners fail to recognize that the corporation is worth more liquidated than it is as a going entity.

Another situation in which liquidation values may enter into the valuation of a business is where the purchaser's basic goal is obtaining the use of one specific valuable asset or line of business and he or she plans to dispose of the balance of the assets in some way after the sale is completed. In this situation, the buyer is likely to value the business by taking the value of the desired asset or line of business (determined by capitalizing its contemplated cash flow or income) and adding to it an estimate of the liquidation value of the remaining assets.

If the business being acquired has assets that the purchaser believes to be unnecessary for the successful continuation of the business (or if the assets duplicate underutilized property that the purchaser currently owns), the purchaser may again simply add the liquidation value of those assets to the value based on capitalized earnings to determine the total price he or she is willing to offer. Similarly, if the company being valued has cash or marketable securities in excess of its needs, the buyer may increase the price by the amount of the excess cash or cash equivalents which, if the purchase is successful, may be withdrawn without adversely affecting the operation of the acquired business. In effect the buyer is paying cash for cash or cash equivalents.

In many of these situations, the seller may be aware of the existence of the excess assets and will exclude them from the sale (or distribute them as dividends to the owners of the business before the sale takes place).

The calculation of liquidation value becomes very difficult on an asset-by-asset basis for any substantial business. Estimates of net asset value are usually made in such situations by using book values and then making adjustments for assets such as land, marketable securities, and LIFO inventories. When lines of business are salable as units, traditional income or cash-flow analysis may be applied to those lines with the resulting value being treated as net asset values for each particular line.

Assets may also be valued on the basis of an estimate of what it would cost to replicate the plant and operations of the business rather than what the assets of the corporation would bring upon dissolution, an asset valuation based on replacement cost rather than liquidation value. Such a figure is usually estimated when a business is contemplating expanding into a new area of operation, and is choosing between the alternatives of building a plant from scratch or buying an existing company that owns a plant then in operation. However, replacement cost, like liquidation value, is generally not an appropriate way to measure the value of an ongoing business, since normally the purchaser would not view the business as equal in value to what a brand-new plant created from scratch would cost. Indeed, in the case of many mature businesses the replacement cost of a plant greatly exceeds the value based on future net cash flows. The only reliable indication of value in that situation is the capitalization of estimated cash flows.

§11.7 Valuation Based on Book Value

Book value means the value of the residual interest in the business according to the financial records of the business. *Residual* means what remains after subtracting liabilities from assets. It is an accounting concept rather than a true measure of value. Book value is discussed in §9.9.4, where it is pointed out that financial records are normally kept on the basis of historical cost, and that book value therefore usually does not reflect either the earning capacity of the business or the current value of its inventory and capital assets. Furthermore, book value is calculated from the balance sheet, which is sometimes used in accounting as a place to park assets waiting to be written off, a fact that should not inspire confidence in the reliability of book value as a measure of value. See §8.4.

Despite these deficiencies, book value is almost always calculated as part of the valuation process, and may be relied upon to a greater or lesser degree in that process. There are several reasons for this. First, it is always easy to calculate book value from the financial records of the business; second, book value tends to increase with the success of the business so that it is not automatically made obsolete simply by the passage of time; third, shareholders may view book value as a floor under the price for shares and resist proposed sales for less than book value. On the securities markets, a stock that is selling for less than book value is often viewed, somewhat irrationally, as a questionable investment. Even though these attitudes are not strictly logical, they do reveal that book value, based as it is on historical cost, is given some weight in the valuation process.

One problem with book value is that it may be significantly affected by accounting conventions that do not themselves affect the earning capacity or assets of the business. For example, if there are two identical companies, one using LIFO and the other using FIFO to reflect inventory costs, the book value of the FIFO company will usually be higher than the book value of the LIFO company. See §8.8. Thus, if book value is relied upon, adjustments may be necessary to offset the use of these accounting conventions.

§11.8 Valuation Based on Prior Purchases and Sales

This section considers the relevance of prior sales of the business, or more commonly, prior sales of shares of stock or other interests in the business, in determining the value of the business. This discussion sharply distinguishes between a closely held business where there is no regular market for the shares of the business, on the one hand, and businesses whose shares are publicly traded, on the other. The distinction between these two basic functional classifications of modern business is discussed in Chapter 14.

§11.8.1 Sales of the Entire Business

When valuing a business, one sometimes discovers that a negotiated sale of the entire business occurred at some earlier time. A sale of the entire business in the fairly recent past, in an arms-length transaction between sophisticated individuals, is considered practically conclusive evidence of value as of the time of the sale. Indeed, where a retrospective valuation is involved, such as the value of a gift for tax purposes made several years ago, one happily uses an arms-length sale occurring years after the gift was made, as providing a reliable basis for going back and estimating the value of the business at the earlier time when the gift was made. In these determinations, adjustments made to that negotiated sales price are limited to adjustments required by changes that occurred in the business between the time the sale took place and the earlier or later date on which the value is to be ascertained.

§11.8.2 Sales of Stock in General

More commonly, prior transactions involve purchases and sales of shares of voting stock of the company rather than a sale of the entire company. At this point the difference between a closely held corporation and a publicly held one becomes critical. In the case of a publicly held company, purchases and sales of stock usually occur on a daily or hourly basis: Professional analysts keep up with the company and make recommendations about the desirability of its stock as an investment to numerous investors. In closely held corporations, on the other hand, the sales are almost by definition, isolated, infrequent, and few in number. Furthermore, transactions in shares in closely held corporations are usually made without skilled investment advice, and under circumstances in which one party to the transaction is under financial compulsion to sell while the other party may be under little or no compulsion to buy.

Since the abstract test of fair market value is a price established by negotiation between hypothetical buyers and sellers, it should not be surprising that actual sales of small portions of a business are given great weight in the process of making a valuation of the whole business where it seems clear that the earlier transactions were in fact at arms length. Obviously, more recent transactions should be given more weight than older ones. However, in every case the circumstances surrounding a specific sale have to be examined to determine how close the transaction reflects the abstract ideal of the arms-length transaction.

§11.8.3 Sales of Minority Interests in Closely Held Businesses

In a closely held corporation, minority interests in the corporation are unlikely to be salable to outside investors at prices that reflect their allocable portion of the value of the business if sold as a unit. The reason for this is that closely held corporations rarely pay dividends, preferring to disguise distributions as salary expenses and similar payments to shareholders. A minority shareholder therefore has no assurance of any return from his or her investment unless the majority shareholders permit the minority shareholder to be an employee of the corporation at a salary that is comparable with the salaries of other shareholder-employees. Since the minority shareholder cannot assure an outsider of employment with the corporation, it is unusual for a nonshareholder to negotiate independently with a minority shareholder to acquire a minority interest. Where such negotiations occur, the nonshareholder is apt to demand a significant discount to reflect the lack of liquidity of the investment and the risk that the anticipated return may not be forthcoming.

Shares of closely held corporations are usually subject to share transfer restrictions or buy/sell agreements that require a shareholder who dies or who desires to dispose of his or her shares to offer (or sell) the shares to the corporation or to the other shareholders at a fixed or readily determinable price. A very popular price used in these agreements is book value. An option agreement commits the shareholder to sell but does not commit the corporation or other shareholders to purchase; a buy/sell agreement commits the purchaser as well as the seller to the transaction. Binding agreements of these types set a cap on the value that may be placed on the shares for most purposes. If the agreement is a buy/sell agreement binding the purchaser as well as the seller, the shares are usually valued at the contract price; if it is an option agreement where the purchaser has the power to purchase at a designated price but is not committed to do so, the shares may be valued at or below the agreed upon price.

In the absence of a binding option or buy/sell agreement, a minority shareholder desiring to sell his or her shares usually cannot compel the corporation or other shareholders to purchase his or her shares. Rather, the shareholder who desires to sell must seek voluntary transactions either with the corporation or with one or more other shareholders. The corporation is a surrogate for the remaining shareholders in this connection since a purchase by the corporation does not affect the relative holdings of the remaining shareholders. Neither majority nor minority shareholders have a strong incentive to offer the selling shareholder a generous price: Other minority shareholders do not generally improve their position significantly vis à vis each other or the majority shareholder by becoming larger minority shareholders. The majority shareholder, on the other hand, by hypothesis already has a controlling position and does not need the additional minority shares to cement or preserve that control. However, the other shareholders collectively, and the majority shareholder individually, usually do desire to eliminate minority interests if they can do so on an acceptable basis: Minority shareholders are therefore usually able to liquidate their holdings by selling to the corporation or to the majority shareholder if they are willing to accept a low enough price. Even though the situation is not hopeless in terms of finding a buyer, it is certainly not the traditional willing buyer and willing seller exchange.

Where three or more factions exist, none of which individually has a majority of the outstanding shares, the dynamics are quite different. If the shares owned by the shareholder who wishes to sell represent the balance of power if they are conveyed to one of the other factions, spirited bidding by the remaining factions may occur as each seeks to obtain the "swing shares" necessary to acquire the controlling interest in the management of the business. The per share value of the swing block may overstate the aggregate per share value of the business in this situation.

When valuing the overall business, what weight, if any, should be given to a sale of a minority interest — a 10 percent interest, say — that does not involve control considerations by a minority shareholder? This question has no fixed answer: It depends entirely on the circumstances. Such sales should be investigated to determine how closely they meet the valuation ideal (a ready buyer, ready seller, etc.) because they provide the only objective evidence of actual values of interests in the corporation. Thus, a sale between family members under circumstances that indicate a motive for the transaction may have been partially to make a gift is given little or no weight. A sale to the corporation, the majority shareholder, another minority shareholder, or conceivably to an outsider, that appears to be at arms length and not entered into by the seller under financial exigency or pressure, may be presumptively accepted as an accurate valuation of at least a minority interest at the time of the sale. Where the purchaser is the corporation or the majority shareholder, however, it is likely that the minority shareholder was under considerably greater compulsion to sell than the purchaser was to buy. Thus, the circumstances underlying each specific sale have to be examined carefully. For example, an arms-length sale by a 10 percent shareholder to the majority shareholder at a price that was clearly bargained over, would be given some weight even though it might appear that the seller was in some financial distress and needed cash for personal reasons. Absolute perfection in the bargaining process is not required. On the other hand, if it appeared that in a similar transaction (1) there were unsuccessful attempts by the seller to find other potential purchasers, (2) the seller needed cash urgently for personal reasons or to avoid bankruptcy, or (3) the sale took place at a price set by the buyer on a take-it-or-leave-it basis, that sale is not a very reliable indication of value. It all depends on an estimate of how close the actual transaction came to the theoretical ideal described at the beginning of this chapter. In many other contexts, a price negotiated at arms length is given some weight in assessing the fair market value of an asset even though defects existed in the negotiation process. One need only think of transactions taking place at rug bazaars, at country auctions, and in a host of everyday transactions in which it is unlikely that the ideal conditions of perfect knowledge and lack of compulsion are present. The same thing is true of isolated arms-length sales of closely held securities to outsiders, to the corporation, to other minority shareholders, or to the majority shareholder.

When the value of an entire business is estimated from isolated sales of minority shares, an appropriate adjustment should be made to reflect the discounts normally applied to such shares for lack of marketability and the minority status of such shares. See §11.11.

§11.8.4 Sales of Majority Interests in Closely Held Businesses

Prior sales of controlling interests in closely held businesses, unlike sales of minority interests, are usually viewed as very reliable indicators of value. The majority shareholder usually is reasonably sophisticated and knowledgeable about his or her business, and in a position to negotiate effectively. Further, controlling interests are more salable to outside persons than minority interests, since the purchaser immediately has power to manage the business rather than being simply an inactive investor in a business and subject to the majority's whim. As a result, a majority block of shares commands a significantly higher price per share than a minority block, even though the shares are formally indistinguishable. The majority shares are referred to as *control shares*. Minority shares that are not part of the control block sell at significant discounts from the price that control shares command, when they sell at all. It is not uncommon for a person seeking to buy all the outstanding shares of a closely held corporation to offer a significantly lower price per share for the minority shares than for the control shares on a per share basis. In the closely held corporation this distinction between control shares and minority shares is easy to visualize since ordinarily it is permanent: It is not physically possible for minority blocks of shares aggregating 40 percent of the stock, say, ever to outvote the majority's 60 percent block.

The difference between minority shares and control shares in a closely held corporation is sometimes reflected in discounts applied when valuing minority shares. See §11.11.

§11.8.5 Valuation of Small Blocks of Shares of a Publicly Held Business

The mechanics of the great trading markets for common stock are described in Chapter 18. When the common stock of a company is itself publicly traded on one of these markets, the market price conclusively establishes the value of all noncontrol blocks of stock on that date. Indeed, in widely traded stocks, the textbook methods of determining value are to use either the closing price on that date or the mean between the bid and asked offers at the closing.

Many smaller companies are publicly traded on the over-the-counter market, but by reason of their size or the number of shareholders, the volume of trading does not approach that of companies listed on the major exchanges. These publicly held stocks are referred to as being *thinly traded* or having *thin markets*. Prices of trades in thin markets should be examined, since some thinly traded stocks may have more characteristics of closely held corporation than of publicly held corporations.

§11.8.6 Valuation of a Publicly Held Business and the Market for Control

Even when a publicly traded stock has a broad market with numerous transactions each hour, it does not necessarily follow that the total value of the business, if it were sold as a single entity, precisely equals the current market price per share multiplied by the total number of shares outstanding. The outstanding shares of course represent the aggregate equity ownership interest in the corporation: The common stock usually possesses the entire voting power to elect directors. Under these circumstances, it is tempting to view each transaction in a publicly traded common stock as a trade that represents in microcosm the value of the underlying business. If this conclusion were correct, valuation of publicly held corporations would be relatively easy, since one could obtain the current value of the entire business simply by adding up the current market values of all outstanding shares. Many persons do, in fact, use this market value as a measure of the value of the corporation under present management and in current circumstances. Academic writers in the field of law and economics often make this assumption.

Many recent takeover fights, however, have amply demonstrated that the value placed on a business by the securities markets is usually significantly smaller than the amount a purchaser might be willing to pay for the entire business (or all the outstanding stock) if it were in fact put up for sale. In other words, the public market for stock often appears to significantly understate the actual sales price of the entire company when it is put up for sale. This phenomenon has been the subject of considerable speculation since there is a great deal of evidence in other contexts that the public securities markets are efficient in the sense that the price encapsulates all currently available public information about the stock. See §18.2. One plausible explanation, which appears to explain the price variation in some takeovers but not in others, is that the securities markets value the business only on the assumption that current management will remain in office while aggressors in takeovers set a higher value because they plan to replace incumbent management with more effective management that justifies a higher price per share.

Another explanation is based on the fact that the great trading markets for securities described in Chapter 18 are primarily markets for investments, not markets for controlling interests in companies. Almost all transactions on public securities markets involve minute fractions of the total outstanding shares of companies and these transactions individually do not carry with them any meaningful opportunity to affect the business policies of the company. However, where the transactions increase in size so that control of the company may be involved, the purchasers are willing to pay more — usually significantly more — than the prices for smaller blocks of shares that are traded solely as investments. Of course, if one person buys enough small blocks in a publicly held corporation, he or she will ultimately end up with a big block, and quite possibly a majority block. But that is not the way things usually work since only a few persons have the financial resources to assemble such a block of shares, and federal law requires public disclosure of a person who accumulates more than 5 percent of any public corporation's stock. The result is that the market for the whole corporation — the takeover market or market for control, as it is sometimes called — arguably is different from the regular market for investment securities.

Yet a third explanation is that the pricing of an offer for all or a controlling interest in a publicly held corporation is usually not entirely rational since it must be based on publicly available information that may not be accurate or complete. A related explanation is that the prices offered for all or a controlling interest of publicly held corporations are dictated more by the availability of risk capital to finance the acquisition than considerations of value. In the modern era, many acquisitions of publicly held corporations involve the extensive use of debt to finance the purchase. Usually, the business being purchased becomes the ultimate debtor whose cash flow is expected to discharge the debts incurred in the takeover. This type of acquisition is referred to as a *bootstrap acquisition* (the company is in effect purchased with its own assets) or as a *leveraged buyout* (if incumbent management and outside financers end up as the ultimate owners of the business after the transaction is completed). How is the price to be offered for such a transaction ascertained? It must be set higher than the current market price in the investment markets: Indeed, it must be set significantly higher in order to be attractive to investors and to close out possible competitive offers from other sources. One suspects that the decision whether such a transaction is feasible may be based on (1) a crude cash-flow analysis indicating the maximum amount of debt the business can possibly carry and (2) estimates of the amounts for which nonessential assets or peripheral lines of business can be sold for. In the most extreme case, most of the assets of the business may be sold off in order to raise funds to reduce the outstanding indebtedness incurred to finance the purchase price: a bust-up acquisition in the true sense of the word. This explanation is consistent with the fact that some aggressors have publicly admitted that they paid too much for the target.

§11.9 Valuation Based on Subsequent Performance of the Business

When a business is being sold for cash to an independent purchaser, differing valuations of the business may create an impasse: The gap between the lowest price the seller is willing to accept and the highest price the buyer is willing to offer may be unbridgeable by negotiation. This gap is usually traceable to differing assumptions about what the future holds for the business: The parties agree that the price should be ten times future earnings but they disagree on what the future earnings are likely to be: The seller sees a high probability of continuing improvement in earnings or cash flow with relatively little risk, while the buyer, naturally more cautious, sees cloudier skies with greater probability of disappointing results. This impasse threatens to kill the deal entirely, and yet it involves the valuation issue exclusively.

Devices exist that may enable the parties to bridge the gap between these inconsistent expectations and forecasts. These devices basically set the initial contract price at the buyer's price but defer the final determination of the sales price until after the post-sale operations of the business can be evaluated. The buyer commits to the conservative price he is willing to pay and agrees to pay an additional amount at the end of one or two years if earnings exceed an amount stated in the agreement (basically the buyer's conservative prediction). If the operations are more profitable than this stated amount the seller is entitled to an addition to the purchase price computed on the actual post-sale earnings. This contingent payment based on actual post-sale results largely eliminates the impasse over valuation, since if the buyer's more pessimistic forecasts turn out to be accurate, no further payment is due, while if the business is as profitable as the seller expects, the ultimate purchase price will be based on the seller's estimate. These devices are sometimes called *workout agreements* because a portion of the purchase price is earned or worked out after the transaction is closed. They have nothing to do with the workouts in the near-insolvency context. See §10.5. Agreements of this type permit transactions to close immediately without requiring consensus on the true value of the company at the time of the closing. The usual period for the workout is three years or less following the closing, though longer workout periods are of course possible.

Workout agreements involve complex negotiation and complex drafting, particularly where the parties have no reason to trust the other side's good faith. The seller may be unwilling to accept the unsecured promise of the buyer that the additional purchase price will be paid when it becomes due a year or two after the sale has closed. The seller may request that the workout payment be placed in escrow with a stakeholder to assure the seller that the payment will be made promptly if it is earned. The buyer may resist this proposal if he or she proposes to use the cash flow generated during the workout period to pay the additional purchase price. The escrow arrangement, of course, ties up independent funds for a significant period of time. There may also be detailed negotiation over the terms on which the business is to be conducted during the workout period. The most basic concerns are from the seller's standpoint, who wishes to ensure that the purchased business has a fair shot of earning the workout. The two parties must decide whether the buyer or the seller is to manage the purchased business until the workout period ends, how much additional capital is to be provided by the buyer during the workout period, at what times and in what amounts, and a host of other business issues such as limitations on salaries, on interbusiness transactions the buyer may have with the purchased business, and so forth. Usually the seller proposes to run the business during the workout period: If this is acceptable to the buyer, the buyer may nevertheless seek protection against artificial changes in business operations, such as reduction of deferrable expenses, which the seller may quietly institute in order to improve earnings during the workout period and thereby earn the workout payment.

Even though the development of a workout agreement may involve difficult negotiations and complex issues, the advantage of permitting negotiations to come to a settlement without requiring either party to accept the valuation assumptions of the other, should be obvious. The workout concept is practical principally in connection with transactions involving the sale of businesses. It cannot ordinarily be used in other types of transactions to avoid valuation controversies.

§11.10 Valuation Based on a Mixture of Methods

It is customary, when valuing a business, to make estimates of value based on different approaches or assumptions. For example, a person preparing a valuation opinion might assemble the following estimates of value:

1. Straight book value, without adjustment for accounting conventions.

2. Adjusted book value, with adjustments for LIFO accounting convention, appreciation in marketable securities, and elimination of nonasset assets.

3. Capitalized earnings, assuming mildly pessimistic long-term projections for the industry as a whole and average projections for the business's market position within the industry.

4. Capitalized earnings, assuming average growth projections for the industry as a whole but assuming a gradual improvement in market position of the business being evaluated within the industry.

5. Capitalized cash-flow projections eliminating all depreciation deductions and assuming the debt/equity ratio is increased from 25 percent to 60 percent.

6. Estimated resale value of physical assets (obtained by using balance sheet assets excluding intangible assets and making adjustments for inventory valuation, marketable securities, land, and excess depreciation on plant and equipment taken in earlier years).

After making these six calculations, the results may be tabulated and the degree of disagreement considered. If all are within a relatively narrow range, it is likely that a number will be selected within that range and an optimistic report stating that "all signs point to a value within the range of . . ."

If the numbers vary widely, the general rule should be that the most reliable estimate in the eyes of the person doing the study should be adopted. However, it is always tempting to take an average of the values, and view that average as the best estimate of value. This is a somewhat muddled approach because the averaging process involves combining discrete numbers, apples and oranges, as it were. The decision to take the arithmetic mean of book value, liquidation value, and value based on capitalized earnings estimates, for example, has little theoretical justification. The fundamental valuation standard does not appear to contemplate an averaging of different estimates of value, but the temptation to combine disparate figures into a single number is strong. Even if the highest and lowest estimates of value are discarded, and the remaining estimates averaged, the same basic problem exists.

In one area there is judicial support for averaging discretely different estimates of value. In statutory proceedings for the appraisal of the value of shares (discussed briefly in §17.9.2) the Delaware courts adopted a stylized valuation technique that required trial courts to measure value based on three different approaches, and then assign weights to each approach that reflect the court's judgment as to the reliability of the factor. In Gibbons v. Schenley

Industries, Inc., 339 A.2d 460 (Del. Ch. 1975), for example, the court-appointed appraiser valued shares of Schenley common stock as follows:

	Value factors	Weight	Assigned value
market	29.00	35%	10.15
earnings value	52.78	45%	23.75
asset value	49.83	20%	9.97
			43.87

The market value is an estimate based on actual sales of stock of Schenley. The earnings value in this calculation was computed on the basis of averaging five years' earnings with a capitalization factor of 14 based on the price/earnings ratio of an industrywide spectrum of liquor companies, and the asset value was an estimate of the value of Schenley's plants based on expert appraisals. On review by the Chancellor, the weight given to asset value was reduced to 0, the earnings per share were reduced by the exclusion of a nonrecurring transaction and the multiplier was increased to $16.72. The result was that the above table was revised as follows:

	Value factors	Weight	Assigned value
market	29.00	55%	15.95
earnings value	39.79	45%	17.91
asset value	49.83	0%	0.00
			33.86

This is obviously a highly stylized approach toward valuation in which the court's analysis is channeled in narrow directions. In a more recent decision, Weinberger v. UOP, Inc., 457 A.2d 701 (Del. 1983), the court rejected this long established approach toward judicial evaluation on the ground that "to the extent it excludes other generally accepted techniques used in the financial community and the courts, it is now clearly outmoded." The court adopted "a more liberal approach [which] include[s] proof of value by . . . techniques or methods which are generally considered acceptable in the financial community and otherwise admissible in court."

§11.11 Discounts for Lack of Marketability and Other Factors

This section deals primarily with valuation issues as they pertain to the value of specific holdings of common stock, rather than to the overall value of the business itself. At the outset, it assumes that the aggregate value of the business has been established by expert opinion, prior sales transactions, analysis of net present value, or judicial decision.

Once the value of the business itself has been determined, the value per share would appear to be calculable simply by dividing that value by the number of outstanding common shares. This value per share is different from book value per share, which is obtained by dividing the net worth of the business ascertained from its financial records by the number of outstanding shares. Unfortunately, however, life is not that simple.

When valuing shareholdings, there is no inherent reason why the value of a business has to be allocated proportionately to each share. Indeed, the earlier discussion of closely held shares should make it clear that proportional allocation is usually not realistic. The usual manner of handling these differences between otherwise identical shares is not by setting up a dual price structure, but by a system of discounts and premiums that reflect the marketability or value of shares. A discount is simply a justification for knocking off a portion of the per share value: A premium is an additional amount added to one specific block of shares.

There are a large number of discounts that have received some degree of judicial or professional acceptance. These discounts tend to arise during negotiations as arguments over valuation. Since they have some degree of judicial recognition, however, they must be considered. The following listing is not complete, but includes the ones most likely to be encountered in practice.

1. Lack of marketability. This applies to shares that are otherwise publicly traded but the specific shares are subject to significant legal restraints on transferability. (It may also be applied to closely held shares, but a *minority interest discount* is generally used for those shares to describe the same factor.) Otherwise publicly traded stock subject to legal restraint on transferability is called *letter stock*. If a transfer is permitted to a limited number of persons but subsequent transfers by those persons are limited or prohibited without the consent of the issuer, the discount may be for "lack of alienability" rather than "lack of marketability."

2. Minority interest in closely held corporations. For the reasons discussed earlier, minority interests sell at substantial discounts from control shares. The discount from gross per share value for minority interest status may be substantial, ranging from as low as 50 percent to as high as 90 percent.

3. Restrictive agreements. Agreements applicable to shares of publicly held corporations that require the shares to be offered first to the corporation may justify a discount from the market price of shares not subject to the restrictive agreement. The value at which the shares must be offered is likely to be accepted as the value of the shares for valuation purposes without regard to other valuation techniques.

4. Loss of key person.

5. Small company business risk.

6. Inability to obtain financing.

7. Unaudited financial statements.

8. Blockage. In connection with publicly traded stock, large blocks may be more difficult to market than smaller blocks. In a thinly traded market, the dumping of a large block of shares may depress the market significantly. A discount per share for large blocks of publicly traded shares is called *blockage*.

Large blocks of shares may have to be sold through an underwriting process that adds costs to the marketing effort. These costs of distribution may be viewed as an estimate of the blockage discount.

It should be noted that a blockage discount should be limited to non-control blocks of shares. If the block of shares carry with them control, normally no discount is appropriate, and, indeed, a premium may be justified.

The precise character of these discounts is less important than an appreciation of their niche in the valuation process.

§11.12 The Importance of Valuation in Legal Practice

On the basis of the foregoing discussion, valuation of a business appears to be a factual and business-related issue, not a legal issue. Why might a lawyer become involved in such a question? Consider the following contexts:

1. Your client is the sole owner of a business, and she has decided to sell it in order to retire. The issue is what asking price she should place on the business. She has hired an expert appraiser who studied the business and came up with a figure that she thinks is ridiculously high and will scare off possible purchasers. She asks you what she should do. The asking price obviously involves a question of strategy or tactics in a purely commercial context — clearly a pure business issue that does not lie within the expertise of a corporate lawyer. The problem is that your client has come to rely on you for your commonsense business judgment as well as legal acumen. Suitable disclaimers about the appropriate roles of lawyers may be appropriate. But the client still expects you to give her sensible advice as to what price tag she should place on her business.

2. It is equally likely that a lawyer will become involved from the opposite side. Your client has learned that the sole owner of a competitive business has decided to retire. Your client is anxious to buy the business if he can; on the other hand he wants to get the business at the best possible price so he does not want to appear to be too eager. The immediate issue is whether the seller's asking price should be viewed as a firm and nonnegotiable price, whether a lower price should be offered, and, whether, if a lower price is offered, some third person might come along and snap up the business before your client has a chance to offer his top price. The issue again comes down to business issues: an assessment of the reasonableness of the asking price, the willingness of the seller to bargain, and the number of potential purchasers out there. Again, however, your client wants your recommendation on a nonlegal question that revolves at least in part around what a business is worth.

3. For many years you have prepared your client's tax returns and handled various tax matters as they have come up. Your client has now decided to establish a program of making annual gifts of stock in his closely held business to his three children. You are asked to advise the client on the gift tax consequences of gifts of specific numbers of shares each year, whether a gift tax return needs to be filed, and if so, how the gift should be reported on that return. There is an annual exemption from the gift tax (involving gifts of less than $10,000 per year to a single donee), and it is clearly desirable to keep the

size of the gift each year within that limit for each child. The first question you ask is how much is the stock worth; your client hands you a copy of a report by the client's accountant concluding that the value is almost certainly somewhere between $10 and $30 per share, and that $25 per share seems about right. What do you do next? Unfortunately, it is not possible to obtain advance rulings from the Internal Revenue Service on factual issues such as the value of a business. So you are pretty much on your own. Suddenly the valuation issue has become more than a purely business judgment.

4. Your client has died owning a business that comprises a major portion of his estate. You are the attorney for the estate and are preparing the estate tax return. You must assign a value to the business in question for purposes of this return. A conservative value seems desirable as an initial matter since that should result in a lower overall estate tax bill. (In situations where estate taxes are not applicable, a high valuation may be favorable to the taxpayer because of the step-up in basis to fair market value upon the date of death.) However, if a conservative valuation is made and the Internal Revenue Service audits the return (almost a certainty) and questions the valuation, a substantial penalty may be due if it is concluded you significantly underestimated the value. In this context, you commission a valuation study and work closely with the person making it during the course of its preparation. At some point, however, you have to take primary responsibility for the value placed on the business for estate tax purposes.

5. Your client and her spouse have separated and are about to divorce. The business has been operated successfully for several years by your client with some assistance by her husband. The issue of the property settlement is particularly sticky, with the value of the business being at the center of controversy. The opposing lawyer has presented a report by an expert appraiser setting a high value on the business while it is to your client's interest to have a low valuation on the business. What do you do next? Do you get your own appraiser, do you attack the report of your opponent, or do you do both? Do you try to negotiate the issue of value, and, if so, what arguments do you make?

6. Your client is a minority shareholder in a corporation, and a transaction has been proposed that will eliminate entirely his interest in the corporation in exchange for a cash payment. The transaction requires the approval of only two-thirds of the voting shares, and your client has less than that number, so he is unable to block the transaction. Your client believes that the payment being offered is only a small fraction of the real value of his shares. In many states a minority shareholder has a statutory right of dissent and appraisal by which he can reject the offered price and obtain a judicial determination of the value of the shares. You have checked and discover that this statutory right is indeed available to your client. However, litigation over value is notoriously difficult and expensive (see §11.13) and should be pursued only if it is highly likely that the court will establish a significantly higher value than the cash payment originally proposed in the transaction. Should your client pursue the statutory remedy or accept what he has been offered?

7. In either of the last two scenarios, the issue of valuation has led to litigation and you are the lead trial attorney. You must be prepared to take the

deposition of a person designated as an "expert" on the valuation issue, and later to conduct a vigorous cross examination of the methods the expert used to ascertain the value he placed on the business. Other than testing his expertise (i.e., his experience and background in business appraisals), what avenues of inquiry should you pursue?

8. You are counsel for a closely held corporation and have been asked to draft a share transfer agreement that will obligate each shareholder (1) to sell his or her stock back to the corporation (or to the other shareholders) upon death or resignation, and (2) to offer the stock to the corporation before it is sold or transferred to any other person. The issue you face is how the price for that sale is to be determined. The price must be determinable in an objective way not dependent on the cooperation of the potential seller. (Otherwise the withdrawing shareholder or the deceased shareholder's estate could easily defeat the plan by not cooperating or by insisting on a very high price for the shares.) What pricing mechanism should be put in the agreement? In this instance, the lawyer drafting the agreement is creating by contract a mandatory valuation process that will later be used to determine the values of interests in the business. The valuation process, further, must be one the courts would enforce if necessary. And finally, it should lead to a reasonably fair price, since one can never tell which shareholder will be the first to die or resign. Again, knowledge about valuation techniques has moved out of the business realm and into the legal.

§11.13 Valuation Issues in the Litigation Context

Valuation of a closely held business seems to be a purely factual question that can be resolved in the context of litigation in the same manner as any other factual question. Yet experience indicates that not many large valuation cases are pursued in litigation through trial and appeal.

Undoubtedly a major reason for this is concern about the adequacy of the fact-finding mechanisms of ordinary litigation to resolve complex valuation questions. In many states either party may be entitled to a jury trial upon request. How competent would a jury be in resolving such a question? Probably not at all. For that matter, how competent would the average trial or state appellate judge — presumably familiar with criminal cases, tort cases, family disputes, and ordinary contract or commercial disputes — be on this type of issue? Probably somewhat more competent, though one still might have qualms about submitting an important valuation issue to the average judge. When considering litigation as the ultimate solution to a valuation dispute, one must consider the nature and sophistication of the fact-finding process that would be employed. If the case is important enough, a court might be persuaded to refer the issue to an experienced special master to prepare a report and recommendation for its consideration. Nevertheless, all things considered, complex valuation disputes are not the ideal subjects for full-scale judicial adjudication.

One suspects that most valuation disputes are negotiated out rather than litigated. Also, a voluntary submission of the issue to binding arbitration might be attractive in some cases, since the arbitrators selected would probably have a higher degree of sophistication than the average judge, and certainly higher than the average jury. Since valuation reflects a continuum rather than polar alternatives, both settlement and arbitration usually end up by splitting the difference between two competing valuations rather than a complete victory by one party or the other.

IV

◇

FEDERAL TAXATION

CHAPTER 12

FEDERAL TAXATION

§12.1 Introduction

During most of the twentieth century, federal income taxes have had a major influence on virtually all business and financial transactions. Indeed, the Internal Revenue Code probably is the single most important statute ever adopted by the United States in terms of its effect on business and financial transactions, dwarfing other important statutes such as the antitrust laws, the securities acts, and the bankruptcy acts.

In 1986 Congress enacted sweeping changes in the tax laws. The core ideas behind these changes were to (1) cut maximum tax rates, (2) expand the tax base, and (3) minimize or eliminate tax shelter-oriented transactions that are entered into primarily for their effect on one's tax bill. The long-term effects of the 1986 changes obviously cannot be assessed yet, but preliminary indications are that the tax law continues to be a major influence on all business and financial transactions. As a result, every lawyer should have a basic working knowledge of how the tax code operates and how it affects specific transactions.

Because the rules of the tax game changed very significantly in 1986, many of the widely used pre-1986 strategies for reducing taxes are obsolete. Among those that remain effective under the new legislation is the single-premium variable life insurance policy described briefly in §6.10. However, new strategies are being devised and undoubtedly more will be developed in the future. See, for example, the discussion of home equity loans in §1.12.

Because of the 1986 tax law changes, anyone reading the voluminous literature relating to taxes and tax strategies before 1986 should examine the current law and regulations to determine whether the recommended strategies continue to provide tax advantages today. Most of the pre-1986 strategies no longer lead to desirable tax results. In part, the applicability of the pre-1986 strategies may depend on the specific tax year involved. Most of the changes mandated by the 1986 Act went into effect for the 1987 tax year, though some were deferred until the 1988 tax year, and several very important and controversial changes were phased in over several years so that the full impact of the changes will not be felt until 1990 or 1991. So far as rates are concerned, 1987 was a transition year between the higher rates under the old Act and the new, more egalitarian rates of the 1986 Act that went fully into effect for the 1988 tax year.

The Tax Reform Act of 1986 renamed the Internal Revenue Code the "Internal Revenue Code of 1986" even though the 1986 Act was not a recodification in the true sense of the word. The balance of this chapter uses the phrase "the 1986 Act" to refer to the new tax law; the pre-1986 statutes are referred to collectively usually as "the old Act" or as the "Internal Revenue Code of 1954." References to "the old Act" as a single entity are somewhat misleading since numerous substantive amendments to the tax laws were made over the years before 1986, particularly during the period between 1976 and 1984. Thus, there were numerous "old Acts," almost one for each year, at least after 1976. These references should therefore be viewed as being to general principles in effect before the enactment of the 1986 Act rather than to the galaxy of specific rules applicable in any one particular year.

The federal income tax laws are administered by the Internal Revenue Service (the IRS), an agency within the United States Department of the Treasury.

This chapter, like several others in this book, deals with major legal topics that are the subject of advanced law school courses. This chapter has only a limited and modest purpose. It introduces the reader to the broadest concepts, a summary overview as it were, and tries to explain how it is that the tax laws are as complex as they are.

§12.2 The Role of Tax Law in Business and Financial Transactions

The reasons for the preeminent importance of tax law on business and financial transactions can be set forth quite simply: The purpose of business and financial transactions is to earn a profit, and the federal income tax statutes (at least since World War II) require persons who earn profits to share a substantial portion of them — indeed, at times *very* substantial portions of them — with the United States government. Further, the federal income tax is not, and never was, a flat tax imposing the same percentage tax on all income and gains (assuming that were possible), but is composed of numerous distinctions imposing different levels of taxation on different amounts of income, different types of income, and different types of taxable organizations. Different tax rates are also applicable to individuals with identical incomes depending on their marital or filing status. Under the old Act, some dollars of income were taxed at very high rates: as high as 90 percent at some periods shortly after World War II; as high as 70 percent as late as 1980. Tax rates at these levels provide a powerful incentive for devising techniques to avoid their full impact wherever possible. For many years, ingenious minds have been devoted to creating and perfecting such techniques. For example, at the same time that the maximum rates of 70 percent or more were in effect, the maximum tax rate on a different form of income — long-term capital gains arising from the sale or exchange of capital assets held for more than 6 months—was only 25 percent. This dramatic difference in rates created strong incentives to structure transactions or establish long-term strategies so as to transmute ordinary income into long-term capital gain in order to make the 25 percent rather than the 70 percent rate applicable. Several successful strategies were devised, but the 1986 Act invalidates them entirely by applying the same tax rate to both ordinary income and long-term capital gain.

There is, of course, always an incentive to structure transactions and devise strategies so as to reduce taxes no matter what the rates. Thus, the same incentive as always exists under the 1986 Act with its lower rates, though perhaps without the same degree of urgency. It is for this reason that the changes made by the 1986 Act are unlikely to affect the central importance of taxes and tax planning in business and financial transactions generally.

A. COMPLEXITY, SPECIALIZATION, AND AVOIDANCE

§12.3 Tax Specialists and the Complexity of the Internal Revenue Code

The income tax laws (including the regulations issued by the IRS to implement these laws) are exceedingly complex and difficult to understand. Anyone attempting to read the thousand-plus page statute for the first time is almost immediately lost in numerous cross references, defined terms, and opaque and elliptical provisions that appear to form a seamless web with no beginning and no end. The regulations are in many ways even worse: they consist of multiple volumes of fine print that are, if anything, even more opaque and difficult to get through than the statute. The IRS publishes proposed regulations for comment: Such regulations are often included in commercial compilations even though they have only been proposed and may be changed in substantial respects before they are finally adopted. In some instances, regulations may remain in "proposed" form for many years. The standard, multi-volume, loose-leaf tax services that are in every law library and most lawyers' offices attempt to describe and summarize the rules but they contain even more detail than the statute and regulations. Merely using the index volume to these loose-leaf tax services may be a daunting task.

While the tax laws have increased steadily in their complexity since World War II, this complexity has increased significantly in recent years. Beginning in about 1975, new and often fundamental concepts were introduced into the tax laws almost every year. Probably more complexity was introduced between 1975 and 1985 than in the preceding 35 years. Regrettably, the 1986 Act did not improve either the simplicity or clarity of these statutes. Quite the contrary. The 1986 Act did not expressly eliminate or repeal; rather it added a new layer of complex provisions over what was there before. This is particularly true with respect to its provisions relating to tax shelters and the deductibility of non-business interest. It changed the tax rates so as to render obsolete the special tax treatment of long-term capital gains without repealing the elaborate provisions that defined how they were to be calculated. As a result of the 1986 Tax Act, the statute is even longer, thicker, and more difficult to understand.

The natural consequence of complexity on important economic matters is the development of specialists to deal with problems and give advice. And so it has been with a vengeance in the tax area. Today, the complexity of the tax laws are such that sometimes even tax specialists despair of understanding the entire tax structure and fear that they are becoming unable to provide prompt and accurate advice to clients without expensive study and preparation. Twenty years ago most taxpayers filled out their own tax returns: Many lawyers who were not tax specialists advised clients on tax matters and often prepared tax returns for valued clients, either for a nominal fee or as a favor. Increasingly this work is done by accountants, "street front" commercial tax return preparers, and lawyers who specialize in tax law. The complexity of the tax laws has increased so substantially that most taxpayers today obtain professional assistance in filling out their tax returns if they involve the use of the "long form" (and quite often if they involve simple returns as well). Lawyers in general practice have become increasingly cautious about giving tax advice or preparing returns for clients. To be an effective tax lawyer today, one pretty much has to specialize in that subject.

Growth of specialization is in part a result of the increased specificity of Code provisions defining how certain transactions are to be handled. A generation ago much tax advice involved the application of general tax principles to a specific situation. Today there are often very specific provisions that must be located and carefully parsed in connection with each specific situation. The likelihood of overlooking relevant language or other applicable sections is obviously much greater under a very detailed statute than it is under a more general one.

§12.4 Tax Avoidance and Tax Evasion: The Role of Tax Advisers and Tax Attorneys

It is obviously entirely proper to seek to minimize one's taxes by lawful means. Careful planning and judicious structuring and timing of receipts and transactions may permit the same income or gains to be taxed at much lower rates, to be deferred to a later tax year, or in some instances to escape income tax entirely. Thus was born the tax attorney, the tax planner, and the tax adviser. All engage in essentially the same planning activity — to structure transactions and economic activities in a way that takes the maximum legitimate advantage of the various provisions of the Internal Revenue Code — to structure transactions so as to minimize taxes due to Uncle Sam. Of course, these tax specialists engage in other activities as well: They may prepare returns, represent taxpayers before the IRS in administrative proceedings or in litigation against the Service, and so forth.

The services of the most successful tax planners are largely utilized only by the affluent individual taxpayer and by business. These are the only taxpayers that are regularly involved in transactions large enough to support the high fees normally charged for these services. Of course, many taxpayers engage in tax planning on a modest scale.

Every tax adviser must constantly be aware of the basic distinction between legitimate tax avoidance on the one hand and improper tax evasion on the other. Tax avoidance is the structuring of transactions so as to take legitimate advantage of the provisions of the Internal Revenue Code and the regulations existing thereunder. Tax evasion, on the other hand, involves improper or unlawful reduction of tax liabilities by omission, misstatement, misrepresentation, or fraud. To take simple illustrations: For many years the special tax treatment for long-term capital gains was available only for capital assets held for more than six months. Gains from the sale or exchange of capital assets held for less than six months were taxed at the relatively higher rates applicable to ordinary income. A person planning to sell a capital asset at a profit might legitimately wait until the day after the six-month period expired to make the sale. That is simple tax avoidance: The taxpayer takes the economic risk, by deferring the sale, that the value of the capital asset may decline during that period. On the other hand, if the same transaction is agreed upon five months and twenty days after the taxpayer originally acquired the asset, possession of the asset is transferred immediately to the purchaser, and both the sale contract and the payment check are dated and delivered so that the sale appears to have occurred after the expiration of the six-month holding period, there is a significant risk that the IRS, if the circumstances become known, will treat the sale as occurring within the six-month holding period. More serious examples of improper evasion are situations involving "forgetting" to include items of income at all or claiming exemptions for six children when in fact the taxpayer only has three. If such transactions are discovered, civil fraud penalties are usually imposed, and in extreme cases, there may be criminal prosecution as well.

Often, however, the distinction is not as easy or sharp as these two hypotheticals suggest. Many transactions have as their principal purpose the reduction of taxes. The IRS may attack these transactions on very broad grounds: for example, that they are sham transactions without business purpose that should be ignored entirely, that they are step transactions that should be viewed as a single whole rather than as a series of independent transactions, or that the effect of the transactions should be recast so as to clearly reflect income. In some instances a taxpayer may be able to obtain an advance ruling as to how a specific transaction should be treated for tax purposes (a *letter ruling*, as it is usually called), but the IRS declines to give rulings in many sensitive or fact-specific areas. Tax shelters have been a major target of the Service in recent years, and the tax returns of many thousands of taxpayers were ensnarled in this campaign during the late 1980s.

The giving of tax advice is greatly affected by the fact that most returns are not fully audited, and the questionable treatment of a specific item may never be raised. Nevertheless, disclosure of the questionable item in the return is sensible in order to minimize the risk that the Service may later attempt to impose a fraud penalty on the taxpayer or, conceivably, penalties on the attorney involved or on the person who prepared the return. Also, relatively high-income persons with complex or tax-avoidance oriented transactions cannot rely on escaping an audit since the probability of an audit increases substantially as the taxpayer's income increases.

Until relatively recently, most of the taxpaying public was probably unaware of the full extent of the activity by the affluent to avoid and/or minimize taxes. Most Americans are employed and are subject to the tax withholding mechanism that in effect requires all employers to become tax collectors for Uncle Sam. For them, paying taxes involves little discretion (at least if they are honest) and usually is relatively painless. Indeed, since many taxpayers whose sole incomes are salaries or wages end up being entitled to a refund, the process is often almost pleasant.

B. THE BACKGROUND OF THE 1986 ACT

§12.5 The Pre-1986 Progressive Tax Rate Structure

The pre-1986 tax rates for individuals combined high-percentage tax rates with a highly progressive rate structure. This tax structure directly or indirectly caused much of the complexity of the Internal Revenue Code and dissatisfaction with this pattern of tax rates led to the 1986 Act.

A *progressive rate structure* is one in which the rates are fixed so that as taxable income increases, the tax rate on additional dollars also increases. Under a progressive rate structure, additional or last dollars earned by a higher income person are taxed at a higher percentage rate than the same number of additional dollars earned by a lower income person. The progressive rate structures in the pre-1986 tax law can best be illustrated by the tax rates from the year 1980 (the last year before the "Reagan era") to persons filing joint returns:

Taxable income	*Tax*
3,400 or less	-0-
3,400–5,499	14% of income in excess of 3,400
5,500–7,599	294 plus 16% of excess over 5,500
7,600–11,899	630 plus 18% of excess over 7,600
11,900–15,999	1,404 plus 21% of excess over $11,900
16,000–20,199	2,265 plus 24% of excess over $16,000
20,200–24,599	3,273 plus 28% of excess over 20,200
24,600–29,899	4,505 plus 32% of excess over 24,600
29,900–35,199	6,201 plus 37% of excess over 29,900
35,200–45,799	8,162 plus 43% of excess over 35,200
45,800–59,999	12,720 plus 49% of excess over 45,800
60,000–85,599	19,678 plus 54% of excess over 60,000

85,600–109,399	33,502 plus 59% of excess over 85,600
109,400–162,399	47,544 plus 64% of excess over 109,400
162,400–215,399	81,464 plus 68% of excess over 162,400
215,400 or more	117,504 plus 70% of excess.

First, a brief description of how to read the above tables might be helpful: The tax brackets are additive or cumulative. For example, a couple with a taxable income of up to $5,500 filing a joint return and paying a tax under the above schedule would owe .14 × (5,500 − 3,400) = .14 × (2,100) = $294. If the couple's income were $7,600, they would owe the same $294 on the first $5,500 plus 16 percent of the excess over $5,500; the tax would be .16 × (7,600 − 5,500) + 294 = .16 × (2,100) + 294 = $630. As the hypothetical couple's taxable income continues to increase, the tax on the lower levels remains unaffected, but the additional income is subject to increasingly higher percentages. At the very top, the couple would owe 70 percent of each dollar of taxable income earned in excess of $215,400. Looking at this explanation of this table it should be clear that the odd-looking numbers at the beginning of the right hand column of the table are not mysterious at all; they are simply the amount of tax determined cumulatively from the rows of the table above the row in question. The different levels of income subject to different tax rates in the above table are universally referred to as *tax brackets*. The percentage rates set forth in the above table (14 percent, 16 percent, etc. on up to 70 percent) are called *marginal rates* because they apply only to the additional dollars earned above the previous bracket. The marginal rate must be distinguished from the *effective rate* of taxation, which is the percentage that the total tax is of one's total taxable income (or of one's gross income before exemptions and deductions). To illustrate, in 1980 a couple filing a joint return with precisely $35,200 dollars of taxable income is at the beginning of the 43 percent bracket. However, the amount of tax actually due on $35,200 of income is $8,162, or 23 percent of taxable income. Assuming that the person had an average amount of deductions and exemptions, his or her total income before deductions and exemptions was probably about $50,000, so that the effective tax rate on total income would be about 16 percent. That is a large percentage to be sure, but the actual effective tax rate is nowhere near the 43 percent that a superficial examination of the tax rates might indicate to be applicable. Of course, if our hypothetical taxpayer earned additional dollars of taxable income each of those dollars would be taxed at the 43 percent rate until the couple reached $45,800 of taxable income, when the marginal rate would increase from 43 percent to 49 percent.

The effective tax rate is never higher than the marginal rate (since the first dollars of income are always taxed at lower rates than the highest marginal rate), though at very high incomes the two tend to merge. For example, a couple with $300,000 of taxable income in 1980 was comfortably in the 70 percent bracket and owed $176,724 in taxes — 59 percent of taxable income. If the couple were really well off and had $10,000,000 of taxable income, their tax bill would be $6,966,724; this is an effective rate of 69.67 percent of taxable income, still lower than the marginal rate.

For tax planning purposes, the marginal rate is usually more important than the effective rate. This is because most tax planning relates to specific transactions that take place "at the margin"; for example, a strategy that defers tax on a transaction defers the tax that would be due if the gain from that transaction were added to all the other taxable income of the taxpayer. The bulk of the taxpayer's other income, and the tax that will be due on that income, is unaffected by that tax planning.

Under even a progressive tax rate structure with very high marginal rates, it always pays to earn another dollar (so long as the highest bracket is less than 100 percent). Some high-income taxpayers at this time indicated that "it is not worth it" to earn more money because of the tax structure. Take these remarks with a grain of salt. Certainly, if a person earns another dollar, he or she will always keep a part of it even under a progressive tax structure. A more subtle question (which is the point the "not worth it" speakers may have had in mind) is whether a person will engage in risky, entrepreneurial conduct in an effort to earn an extra dollar when he or she is allowed to keep only 30 percent of it.

The high and progressive rate structure also created significant anomalies in treatment for essentially indistinguishable taxpayers. For example, one major consequence of the rate structure described above was that for higher income taxpayers, splitting income among two or more different taxpayers would often reduce the total tax due. Do you see why this was usually so? When high progressive rates were first imposed during World War II, most families consisted of a single, male income earner and a wife who remained at home to care for the family. The first major controversy arose when married couples with a single wage earner who resided in community property states argued successfully that the nonworking spouse should report one half of the community's earnings on the theory that one-half of the earnings was hers under state law. If the couple's income was substantial, this income-splitting created obvious discrimination between otherwise identical families who happened to live in community property and non-community property states. This dispute was resolved by the development of different tax schedules for single individuals and for married individuals filing a joint return, with the latter entitled to use a tax schedule that in effect gave all married couples the advantage of income-splitting that community property residents were entitled to for tax purposes. The 1980 tax schedule set forth above was applicable to married couples filing joint returns. Over the years, the number of separate tax schedules gradually increased; the present pattern is described briefly in §12.10.

With the growth in the number of working wives, the income-splitting tax schedules for families created a new type of discrimination. If one spouse within a family was the sole wage earner, the rates applicable to married taxpayers filing joint returns provided a significantly lower tax than if that same wage earner were unmarried. However, if two persons had equal amounts of income, their total tax bill was significantly higher if they were married and required to file joint returns than it would have been if they were not married and were filing separately. For example, in 1980, if two individuals living together each had precisely $25,000 of taxable income, the tax on their joint return was $14,778 if they were married. If they had remained single and each filed separate returns as unmarried individuals, the tax would have been $5,952 each, or a total of $11,904. This results from the fact that when the two taxpayers are married, the second income is added to the first, and is taxed only at the higher brackets. When the two taxpayers are not married, each gets to take advantage of the very low marginal rates on their first dollars of income. The difference between $14,778 and $11,904 can be viewed as a tax on marriage, or put another way, a bonus of nearly $3,000 per year for living in sin. This discrimination against marriage even led a few married couples to divorce but continue to live together, or to divorce on December 28 and remarry on January 3, in order to save on federal income taxes. (While there is a filing category, "married couples filing separate returns," the tax schedule for this category was created to ensure that couples filing separate returns were subject to the same tax brackets and rates as if they filed jointly; as a result the "marriage tax" could not be avoided simply by filing separate returns.) An attempt was made to lessen this discrimination during the 1980s by giving a special deduction of up to $3,000 per year for a married couple when both work; this lessened but did not eliminate the discrimination. The 1986 Tax Act repealed this special deduction for two-income families on the theory that the changes in rates minimized this discrimination, though it does not eliminate it entirely. This is one of the few instances in which the 1986 Tax Act actually simplified the system.

High-income taxpayers also found it profitable from a tax standpoint to give income-producing property to infant children in order to permit the income to accumulate for college expenses at lower tax brackets than if the parent retained the property, paid tax on the income from the property, and then used the remainder to pay for college. Indeed, a number of tax-oriented trust and custodial devices were invented in order to enable high-income taxpayers to minimize the effect of the sharp progressivism of rates. This strategy was largely foreclosed by provisions in the 1986 Act that basically require the unearned income of children under the age of 14 to be taxed at their parent's top rates (except for the first $500 of income). Unlike the repeal of the working couple deduction, this change greatly complicates the tax structure, requiring many children to obtain social security numbers and file returns; it also creates potential complications and anomalies when the minor child works for all or, more likely, part of the year.

The progressive structure of rates also had one other significant effect. It caused tax revenues to increase automatically during periods of inflation. Whatever was happening at the high-income level of the spectrum, millions of taxpayers whose sole income was from wages and salary were paying taxes under a progressive tax structure that built in progressivism at a relatively low level. During periods of inflation, as individual incomes increased along with price increases, taxpayers were pushed into higher marginal brackets, and the revenues of the United States government increased dramatically even though the taxpayers were probably not better off economically from the increased wages. The large number of brackets at relatively low levels of income reflect the brackets originally established when income levels were perhaps one-third of what they were in 1981. As inflation continued, the progressive income tax rates became an effective money machine for government. Perhaps no feature of the progressive tax structure infuriated the Reagan administration more than this automatic increase in governmental revenues due purely to the interaction between inflation and progressive tax rates.

§12.6 The Successful Attack on Progressivism and High Tax Rates

The sharply progressive tax structure and relatively high marginal rates illustrated by the 1980 tax rates was a basic philosophical underpinning of tax policy for more than fifty years. The notion that a person who makes more could afford to, and should be required to, pay a higher portion of the extra dollars earned seemed so obvious as not to require extended discussion. The resulting anomalies that were necessarily created between married and cohabiting taxpayers, or between single and married one-income taxpayers, were viewed as an inevitable cost of a progressive system. However, as early as the 1950s, and increasingly during the 1960s and 1970s, serious criticism of the theory underlying high tax rates and a progressive rate structure in the Internal Revenue Code surfaced. Most of the criticism was based on a conservative political agenda embraced by President Reagan.

First and most broadly, there was the belief by conservatives that the federal government was too large and too heavily oriented toward ill-conceived welfare schemes. One naive way to attack big government is based on the quite erroneous belief that reduction of the growth of tax revenues would lead to a reduction in growth of governmental operations. In fact, reductions in the growth of tax revenues, when they occurred during the 1980s, did not produce a corresponding change in governmental activities, but rather simply inflated the federal deficit.

A second, and entirely inconsistent conservative argument was that high taxes and high tax rates were undesirable because they had adverse affects on the economy. Lower rates, it was argued, spur economic activity to such an extent that any loss of tax revenue from reduced rates would be more than offset by revenue increases from improved economic activity. This too has not been borne out by experience.

A more persuasive argument is that the high and progressive rate structure prompted inexorable political pressure by interest groups for special deductions, special exceptions, and special credits for favored activity. By 1980, the Internal Revenue Code, it may be argued, had become so riddled with special interest provisions that it had ceased to be a fair and progressive structure. One perverse result of this constant pressure was that the tax system enabled many high-income individuals quite legally to avoid paying taxes entirely or to pay only very small amounts — often less than a middle-class wage earner. Also, it quickly became clear that the tax changes made in 1981 to encourage and assist business to recover from the deep recession of that period had virtually eliminated the corporate income tax as a factor in raising revenue: Many very large companies ended up owing no tax or even being entitled to refunds of tax from earlier years despite the fact that they were reporting substantial earnings to their investors.

A related charge was that the combination of high progressive tax rates and complex rules led to the development of sophisticated avoidance techniques by affluent individual taxpayers. Congress responded to many of these techniques over the years by special provisions designed to close off specific avoidance techniques. This, however, increased the complexity of the Code and did not solve the underlying problem which was the motivation to create new avoidance techniques caused by the high and progressive rates.

During the early 1980s particular attention was paid to the development and growth of tax shelters, investments whose purpose was not so much to make money as to make tax deductions available to high-income persons to allow them to protect or shelter other income from federal income taxes. An example of a tax shelter is the rental duplex from the cash-flow analysis in §3.2. By 1983 the maximum tax bracket had been reduced from 70 percent to 50 percent, but even at that rate, as that example illustrates, investments may be profitable solely because of the tax savings involved. If a taxpayer is in the 50 percent bracket, the impact of an investment that shows an economic loss before taxes is greatly reduced or even made profitable if the amount of the loss is deductible against other income, and that saving in tax is viewed as a consequence of the tax shelter. (Most tax shelter analysis during this period assumed that at some future time the property could be disposed of profitably at long-term capital gains rates so as to recoup the bulk of the original investment, but that was not an essential aspect of most tax shelters.) During the 1980s, public advertisements of tax shelters increased dramatically. Further, the liberalization of depreciation schedules in 1981 just about assured that every commercial real estate venture had some tax shelter benefits. All this led to the further charge that the Internal Revenue Code appeared to be warping economic activity by placing emphasis on less than maximal economic activity, particularly overinvestment in real estate, oil wells, box cars, and other items. Such shelters were often widely advertised and purported to offer deductions three or four (or sometimes even more) times larger than the amount invested. While most of these publicly advertised shelters have been successfully attacked by the IRS, during the early 1980s it appeared likely that tax avoidance might become commercially available to everyone. In other words, it appeared that the high tax rates and sharp progressivism of the system had generated a counterattack that blunted the force of the tax system.

Finally, there was the belief that the special tax treatment of long-term capital gains gave unwarranted tax benefits to high-income taxpayers who used complex strategies to transmute ordinary income into capital gains and who used capital gains treatment as the device ultimately to bail out of tax shelters.

The 1986 Act made sweeping changes in the tax structure. The 14 or 15 brackets of prior law were swept away and a two- (or three-) bracket structure — 15 percent and 28 (and 33) percent for individuals was adopted. The parenthetical notations in the last sentence indicate that the precise structure of the 1986 rates cannot be easily summarized; a more detailed description of it is set forth in §12.10. Because of the lower, more egalitarian rates applicable to income generally, all special tax benefits for long-term capital gains were eliminated, and such gains receive no special treatment under the 1986 Act. (The elimination of preferential treatment for capital gains was extremely controversial, however, and the rather elaborate statutory mechanism for calculating capital gains was not repealed, but was left in place to guard against the event that Congress may, some time in the future, decide again to give special tax breaks to long-term capital gains, presumably in connection with a decision to raise tax rates generally.)

In order to avoid a massive revenue loss from the reduction in rates, Congress made numerous changes in deductions and exemptions to limit the revenue loss. Nevertheless most individual taxpayers received some reduction in taxes. The 1986 Act tightened up dramatically the tax on corporations, which ended up paying for most of the tax reductions. Further, a major attack on tax shelters was mounted, both by broadening the alternative minimum tax (a special tax designed to prevent taxpayers from escaping their fair share of taxation by the judicious combination of tax benefits), and by imposing restrictions on deductibility of losses from passive investments by individuals. These passive loss limitations, which largely prevent taxpayers in the post-1986 period from taking advantage of tax shelters created in the pre-1986 period to shelter other income from tax, are discussed in §12.11. The alternative minimum tax (an idea originally introduced into the tax law during the Carter Administration) is described in §12.12.

§12.7 Who Were the Beneficiaries of the 1986 Tax Act Rate Reductions?

A comparison of the 1986 Act rates with the 14 or 15 brackets of earlier law shows that the 1986 Act dramatically reduced the progressivism of the tax structure. Now there are only two formal tax brackets with a maximum rate of 28 percent (for taxable income on a joint return in excess of $29,750) rather than a whole string of brackets with rates increasing as high as 70 percent in 1980 and 50 percent in 1986 (the last tax year before the new Act's rates began to go into effect). Looking at these rate changes alone, it would appear that the 1986 Act gives tax reduction benefits primarily to the affluent who were the only ones affected by the highest tax brackets. This, however, is not the case. On the average, the reductions in tax rates for high-income individuals were largely offset by elimination of deductions, the repeal of the preferential tax rate on long-term capital gains, and the broad attack on tax shelters. Overall, considering the high-income portion of the population as a group, the 1986 Tax Act's effect was relatively neutral. The effect on specific wealthy individuals, however, may be spectacular in either a positive or negative direction, depending on the extent to which that individual had taken advantage of deductions and tax shelters in the past.

Further, many low-income taxpayers received tax cuts under the 1986 Act because of the greatly broadened 15 percent bracket, a more generous personal exemption, and a larger standard deduction. Indeed, one important consequence of the 1986 Act is that the more generous personal exemption and larger standard deduction eliminated many individuals at or close to the poverty line from all liability for federal income taxes.

§12.8 How Permanent is the 1986 Tax Act?

The federal income tax structure became a highly charged political issue in the late 1970s and 1980s that ultimately led (to most people's astonishment) to massive changes in structure and rates in 1986. The feat of getting this legislation enacted largely free of special interest influence was so difficult and remarkable that it is unlikely that major changes will be made in this legislation in the near future. Yet, as this is written two years later, there is some uncertainty whether the changes made in 1986 will persist or whether they will be whittled away either directly or through exceptions, qualifications or even more ingenious stratagems. Already suggestions are being raised in the political arena that some of the most wide-reaching changes should be reconsidered (or in some cases deferred or not placed into effect at all). The proposals with the widest support are that higher tax rates be reimposed on high-income persons, that a favorable tax rate for capital gains be restored, and that the impact of the 1986 provisions on real estate transactions be reexamined. What is described below may change in the near future, and may change dramatically.

C. INCOME TAXATION OF INDIVIDUALS

§12.9 Individual Income Taxes

This and the following sections give a broad and somewhat cursory analysis of the present-day individual income tax. The discussion below assumes that the individual in question files Form 1040, the standard full-length individual income tax return and not one of the short forms, 1040A or 1040EZ, that are available to most lower-income taxpayers. In the event you have never seen a real Form 1040, the 1987 form appears at pages 272–273 as Figure 12-1.

The process by which a taxpayer moves from his or her gross receipts to the amount of income subject to tax (or "taxable income") may be shown schematically as follows:

1) Gross receipts
      minus trade and business expenses and expenses directly connected with other gainful, nonemployment activity, equals
2) Total income
      minus "adjustments to income" (employee business and moving expenses, pension plan deductions, and alimony), equals
3) Adjusted gross income
      minus allowable itemized personal deductions (or the standard deduction if one does not itemize) minus the allowance for personal exemptions, equals
4) Taxable income.

Form 1040 Department of the Treasury—Internal Revenue Service **1987** (O)
U.S. Individual Income Tax Return

For the year Jan.–Dec. 31, 1987, or other tax year beginning   , 1987, ending   , 19 | OMB No. 1545-0074

Label

Use IRS label.
Otherwise,
please print or
type.

Your first name and initial (if joint return, also give spouse's name and initial) | Last name | **Your social security number**

Present home address (number and street or rural route). (If you have a P.O. Box, see page 6 of Instructions.) | **Spouse's social security number**

City, town or post office, state, and ZIP code | For Privacy Act and Paperwork Reduction Act Notice, see Instructions.

Presidential Election Campaign
Do you want $1 to go to this fund? . . . . Yes ▨ No
If joint return, does your spouse want $1 to go to this fund?. . Yes ▨ No
Note: Checking "Yes" will not change your tax or reduce your refund.

Filing Status

Check only one box.

1 ☐ Single
2 ☐ Married filing joint return (even if only one had income)
3 ☐ Married filing separate return. Enter spouse's social security no. above and full name here._____
4 ☐ Head of household (with qualifying person). (See page 7 of Instructions.) If the qualifying person is your child but not your dependent, enter child's name here._____
5 ☐ Qualifying widow(er) with dependent child (year spouse died ▶19   ). (See page 7 of Instructions.)

Exemptions

(See Instructions on page 7.)

Caution: If you can be claimed as a dependent on another person's tax return (such as your parents' return), do not check box 6a. But be sure to check the box on line 32b on page 2.

No. of boxes checked on 6a and 6b ▶ ☐

6a ☐ Yourself   6b ☐ Spouse

c Dependents
(1) Name (first, initial, and last name) | (2) Check if under age 5 | (3) If age 5 or over, dependent's social security number | (4) Relationship | (5) No. of months lived in your home in 1987

No. of children on 6c who lived with you ▶ ☐

No. of children on 6c who didn't live with you due to divorce or separation ▶ ☐

If more than 7 dependents, see Instructions on page 7.

No. of parents listed on 6c ▶ ☐

No. of other dependents listed on 6c ▶ ☐

d If your child didn't live with you but is claimed as your dependent under a pre-1985 agreement, check here . ▶☐

Add numbers entered in boxes above ▶ ☐

e Total number of exemptions claimed (also complete line 35) . . . .

Income

Please attach Copy B of your Forms W-2, W-2G, and W-2P here.

If you do not have a W-2, see page 6 of Instructions.

7 Wages, salaries, tips, etc. (attach Form(s) W-2) . . . . | 7
8 **Taxable** interest income (also attach Schedule B if over $400) . . . . | 8
9 **Tax-exempt** interest income (see page 10). DON'T include on line 8 | 9 |
10 Dividend income (also attach Schedule B if over $400) . . . . | 10
11 Taxable refunds of state and local income taxes, if any, from worksheet on page 11 of Instructions . . | 11
12 Alimony received . . . . | 12
13 Business income or (loss) (attach Schedule C). . . . . | 13
14 Capital gain or (loss) (attach Schedule D) . . . . | 14
15 Other gains or (losses) (attach Form 4797) . . . . | 15
16a Pensions, IRA distributions, annuities, and rollovers. Total received | 16a |
b Taxable amount (see page 11) . . . . | 16b
17 Rents, royalties, partnerships, estates, trusts, etc. (attach Schedule E) . . . . . | 17
18 Farm income or (loss) (attach Schedule F) . . . . | 18
19 Unemployment compensation (insurance) (see page 11) . . . . | 19
20a Social security benefits (see page 12) | 20a |
b Taxable amount, if any, from the worksheet on page 12 . . . . | 20b
21 Other income (list type and amount—see page 12) . . . . | 21
22 Add the amounts shown in the far right column for lines 7, 8, and 10–21. This is your **total income** ▶ | 22

Please attach check or money order here.

Adjustments to Income

(See Instructions on page 12.)

23 Reimbursed employee business expenses from Form 2106 . . | 23
24a Your IRA deduction, from applicable worksheet on page 13 or 14 | 24a
b Spouse's IRA deduction, from applicable worksheet on page 13 or 14 . . . | 24b
25 Self-employed health insurance deduction, from worksheet on page 14 . | 25
26 Keogh retirement plan and self-employed SEP deduction . . . | 26
27 Penalty on early withdrawal of savings . . . . | 27
28 Alimony paid (recipient's last name _____ and social security no. _____) . | 28
29 Add lines 23 through 28. These are your **total adjustments** . . . . ▶ | 29

Adjusted Gross Income

30 Subtract line 29 from line 22. This is your **adjusted gross income.** If this line is less than $15,432 and a child lived with you, see "Earned Income Credit" (line 56) on page 18 of the Instructions. If you want IRS to figure your tax, see page 15 of the Instructions . . . ▶ | 30

Figure 12-1

From taxable income one calculates the tax due on the taxable income reflected in the return either from tax tables (if taxable income is less than $50,000) or by the calculation described in the following section. See Form 1040, lines 36-37, at page 273.

Following the calculation of the income tax due and its entry on line 37 of Form 1040, the second page of the Form 1040 systematically goes through

272

	31 Amount from line 30 (adjusted gross income)	**31**

Tax Compu-tation

32a Check if: ☐ **You** were 65 or over   ☐ Blind;   ☐ **Spouse** was 65 or over   ☐ Blind.
Add the number of boxes checked and enter the total here . . . . ▶ | **32a** |

b If you can be claimed as a dependent on another person's return, check here . . ▶ **32b** ☐

c If you are married filing a separate return and your spouse itemizes deductions, or you are a dual-status alien, see page 15 and check here . . . . ▶ **32c** ☐

33a **Itemized deductions.** See page 15 to see if you should itemize. If you don't itemize, enter zero. If you do itemize, attach Schedule A, enter the amount from Schedule A, line 26, **AND** skip line 33b . | **33a** |

Caution:
If you
checked any
box on line
32a, b, or c
and you
don't
itemize, see
page 16 for
the amount
to enter on
line 33b.

◀— **b** **Standard deduction.** Read **Caution** to left. If it applies, see page 16 for the amount to enter.
If **Caution** doesn't   { Single or Head of household, enter $2,540
apply and your filing   { Married filing jointly or Qualifying widow(er), enter $3,760 } . . . . | **33b** |
status from page 1 is: { Married filing separately, enter $1,880

34 Subtract line 33a **or** 33b, whichever applies, from line 31. Enter the result here . . . . . . | **34** |

35 Multiply $1,900 by the total number of exemptions claimed on line 6e or see chart on page 16 . . | **35** |

36 **Taxable income.** Subtract line 35 from line 34. Enter the result (but not less than zero) . . . . | **36** |

Caution: If under age 14 and you have more than $1,000 of investment income, check here ▶☐ and see page 16 to see if you have to use Form 8615 to figure your tax.

37 Enter tax. Check if from ☐ Tax Table, ☐ Tax Rate Schedules, ☐ Schedule D, or ☐ Form 8615 | **37** |

38 Additional taxes (see page 16). Check if from ☐ Form 4970 or ☐ Form 4972 . . . . . | **38** |

39 Add lines 37 and 38. Enter the total . . . . ▶ | **39** |

Credits
(See
Instructions
on page 17.)

40 Credit for child and dependent care expenses (attach Form 2441) | **40** |

41 Credit for the elderly or for the permanently and totally disabled (attach Schedule R) | **41** |

42 Add lines 40 and 41. Enter the total . . . . | **42** |

43 Subtract line 42 from line 39. Enter the result (but not less than zero) . . . . | **43** |

44 Foreign tax credit (attach Form 1116) | **44** |

45 General business credit. Check if from ☐ Form 3800, ☐ Form 3468, ☐ Form 5884, ☐ Form 6478, ☐ Form 6765, or ☐ Form 8586 | **45** |

46 Add lines 44 and 45. Enter the total . . . . | **46** |

47 Subtract line 46 from line 43. Enter the result (but not less than zero) . . . . ▶ | **47** |

Other Taxes
(Including
Advance EIC
Payments)

48 Self-employment tax (attach Schedule SE) . . . . | **48** |

49 Alternative minimum tax (attach Form 6251) . . . . | **49** |

50 Tax from recapture of investment credit (attach Form 4255) . . . . | **50** |

51 Social security tax on tip income not reported to employer (attach Form 4137) . . . . . | **51** |

52 Tax on an IRA or a qualified retirement plan (attach Form 5329) . . . . | **52** |

53 Add lines 47 through 52. This is your **total tax** . . . . ▶ | **53** |

Payments

Attach Forms
W-2, W-2G,
and W-2P
to front.

54 Federal income tax withheld (including tax shown on Form(s) 1099) | **54** |

55 1987 estimated tax payments and amount applied from 1986 return | **55** |

56 Earned income credit (see page 18) | **56** |

57 Amount paid with Form 4868 (extension request) . . . . | **57** |

58 Excess social security tax and RRTA tax withheld (see page 19) | **58** |

59 Credit for Federal tax on gasoline and special fuels (attach Form 4136) | **59** |

60 Regulated investment company credit (attach Form 2439) . | **60** |

61 Add lines 54 through 60. These are your **total payments** . . . . ▶ | **61** |

Refund or Amount You Owe

62 If line 61 is larger than line 53, enter amount **OVERPAID** . . . . ▶ | **62** |

63 Amount of line 62 to be **REFUNDED TO YOU** . . . . ▶ | **63** |

64 Amount of line 62 to be applied to your 1988 estimated tax . . ▶ | **64** |

65 If line 53 is larger than line 61, enter **AMOUNT YOU OWE.** Attach check or money order for full amount payable to "Internal Revenue Service." Write your social security number, daytime phone number, and "1987 Form 1040" on it . . . . | **65** |
Check ▶ ☐ if Form 2210 (2210F) is attached. See page 20.   **Penalty: $**

Please Sign Here

Under penalties of perjury, I declare that I have examined this return and accompanying schedules and statements, and to the best of my knowledge and belief, they are true, correct, and complete. Declaration of preparer (other than taxpayer) is based on all information of which preparer has any knowledge.

▶ Your signature	Date	Your occupation
▶ Spouse's signature (if joint return, BOTH must sign)	Date	Spouse's occupation

Paid Preparer's Use Only

Preparer's signature ▶	Date	Check if self-employed ☐	Preparer's social security no.
Firm's name (or yours if self-employed) and address ▶		E.I. No.	
		ZIP code	

★ U.S.GPO:1987-0-183-082

Figure 12-1 (*cont.*)

another set of calculations to determine the amount that should be paid with the return:

1)   The tax due on the taxable income reflected in the return minus credits (lines 40-47) (i.e., amounts that are subtracted directly from the tax bill as contrasted with "deductions" that are subtracted from gross income to determine taxable income)

273

2) plus "other taxes" due on income tax related taxes (lines 48-53)

3) minus payments made under the "pay as you go" system of tax collection described in §12.13 and certain other payments that may be treated as payment of federal income tax (lines 54-61).

4) equals the amount of the additional payment or refund that is due from the taxpayer (lines 62-65).

This logical structure of the Form 1040 can be most easily appreciated by examining carefully the front and back of the Form as set forth on pages 272–273. There is, however, a large amount of background and nuance in these lines of the Form 1040 that is described in the following subsections.

§12.9.1 The Calculation of Total Income

The federal income tax is a tax on income, not gross receipts. Thus, from the very outset, it was recognized that the costs and expenses of a business must be subtracted from receipts by the business in order to arrive at an income figure on which income taxes may be calculated. An individual engaged in an individual trade or business is thus entitled to these deductions to the same degree as a corporation. An individual who operates a retail hardware store, for example, may deduct the costs of inventory, rent, advertising, etc. These expenses are deductible on a separate schedule, Schedule C, that is similar to a profit and loss statement for any business. After deducting these expenses, only the net amount of income is transferred forward to line 13 of the first page of the Form 1040. A copy of Schedule C appears at pages 275–276 as Figure 12-2. Much the same pattern of deduction of business expenses from gross receipts before the calculation of total income also appears in Schedule E (Figure 12-3) (income from "rents, royalties, partnerships, trusts, etc.") and Schedule F (Figure 12-4) (farm income). In effect, Schedules C, E, and F permit deduction of trade and business expenses before the calculation of total income. (See the Form 1040, Schedule C, set forth at page 275, and lines 13-22 on the first page of the Form 1040). The test for whether specific trade or business, rental or farming expenses are deductible is whether they are "ordinary and necessary" for the business and "paid or incurred" during the taxable year in question. Expenses that provide a benefit over several taxable years, (e.g., the purchase of a truck) must be capitalized and depreciated (or amortized) over the useful life of the asset. Depreciation schedules for most major assets are set by the statute rather than by individualistic estimates of useful life.

The 1986 Act added a major wrinkle to the deductibility of business expenses when it created three classes of income: active business income, investment income, and passive income, and limited the deductibility of expenses to that from the last two categories. See §12.11.

§12.9.2 The Calculation of Adjusted Gross Income

A second category of business-related expenses that are treated differently from "trade or business" expenses involves "employee business expenses," "ex-

Profit or (Loss) From Business or Profession

(Sole Proprietorship)

Partnerships, Joint Ventures, etc., Must File Form 1065.

Department of the Treasury
Internal Revenue Service (0)   ▶ Attach to Form 1040, Form 1041, or Form 1041S.   ▶ See Instructions for Schedule C (Form 1040).

OMB No. 1545-0074

1987

Attachment
Sequence No. **09**

Name of proprietor	Social security number (SSN)

A Principal business or profession, including product or service (see Instructions)	**B** Principal business code (from Part IV) ▶
C Business name and address ▶	**D** Employer ID number (Not SSN)

E Method(s) used to value closing inventory:

    (1) ☐ Cost   (2) ☐ Lower of cost or market   (3) ☐ Other (attach explanation)

		Yes	No
F Accounting method: (1) ☐ Cash (2) ☐ Accrual (3) ☐ Other (specify) ▶			
G Was there any change in determining quantities, costs, or valuations between opening and closing inventory? (If "Yes," attach explanation.)			
H Are you deducting expenses for an office in your home?			
I Did you file **Form 941** for this business for any quarter in 1987?			
J Did you "materially participate" in the operation of this business during 1987? (If "No," see Instructions for limitations on losses.)			
K Was this business in operation at the end of 1987?			
L How many months was this business in operation during 1987? ▶			

M If this schedule includes a loss, credit, deduction, income, or other tax benefit relating to a tax shelter required to be registered, check here.   ▶ ☐

    If you check this box, you **MUST** attach **Form 8271**.

Part I Income

1a Gross receipts or sales		**1a**		
b Less: Returns and allowances		**1b**		
c Subtract line 1b from line 1a and enter the balance here		**1c**		
2 Cost of goods sold and/or operations (from Part III, line 8)		**2**		
3 Subtract line 2 from line 1c and enter the **gross profit** here		**3**		
4 Other income (including windfall profit tax credit or refund received in 1987)		**4**		
5 Add lines 3 and 4. This is the **gross income** ▶		**5**		

Part II Deductions

6 Advertising		**23** Repairs	
7 Bad debts from sales or services (see Instructions.)		**24** Supplies (not included in Part III)	
8 Bank service charges		**25** Taxes	
9 Car and truck expenses		**26** Travel, meals, and entertainment:	
10 Commissions		**a** Travel	
11 Depletion		**b** Total meals and entertainment	
12 Depreciation and section 179 deduction from Form 4562 (not included in Part III)		**c** Enter 20% of line 26b subject to limitations (see Instructions)	
13 Dues and publications		**d** Subtract line 26c from 26b	
14 Employee benefit programs		**27** Utilities and telephone	
15 Freight (not included in Part III)		**28a** Wages	
16 Insurance		**b** Jobs credit	
17 Interest:		**c** Subtract line 28b from 28a	
a Mortgage (paid to financial institutions)		**29** Other expenses (list type and amount):	
b Other		....	
18 Laundry and cleaning		....	
19 Legal and professional services		....	
20 Office expense		....	
21 Pension and profit-sharing plans		....	
22 Rent on business property			

30 Add amounts in columns for lines 6 through 29. These are the **total deductions** ▶	**30**	

31 **Net profit or (loss).** Subtract line 30 from line 5. If a profit, enter here and on Form 1040, line 13, and on Schedule SE, line 2 (or line 5 of Form 1041 or Form 1041S). If a loss, you **MUST** go on to line 32 | **31** | |

32 If you have a loss, you **MUST** answer this question: "Do you have amounts for which you are not at risk in this business?" (See Instructions.) ☐ Yes ☐ No
    If "Yes," you **MUST** attach **Form 6198.** If "No," enter the loss on Form 1040, line 13, and on Schedule SE, line 2 (or line 5 of Form 1041 or Form 1041S).

For Paperwork Reduction Act Notice, see Form 1040 Instructions.   Schedule C (Form 1040) 1987

Figure 12-2

penses for the production of income," and a limited number of other deductions that share the common characteristic that Congress has decreed that they shall be deducted before the calculation of "adjusted gross income." These expenses fall into several categories:

1. Expenses relating to the production of income or wages by an employee not directly related to a trade or business: unreimbursed moving expenses and employee business expenses such as union dues, uniforms (where required by

Part III Cost of Goods Sold and/or Operations (See Schedule C Instructions for Part III)

1	Inventory at beginning of year. (If different from last year's closing inventory, attach explanation.)	1
2	Purchases less cost of items withdrawn for personal use	2
3	Cost of labor. (Do not include salary paid to yourself.)	3
4	Materials and supplies	4
5	Other costs	5
6	Add lines 1 through 5	6
7	Less: Inventory at end of year	7
8	Cost of goods sold and/or operations. Subtract line 7 from line 6. Enter here and in Part I, line 2	8

Part IV Codes for Principal Business or Professional Activity

Locate the major business category that best describes your activity (for example, Retail Trade, Services, etc.). Within the major category, select the activity code that identifies (or most closely identifies) the business or profession that is the principal source of your sales or receipts. **Enter this 4-digit code on line B on page 1 of Schedule C. (Note:** *If your principal source of income is from farming activities, you should file* **Schedule F** *(Form 1040), Farm Income and Expenses.)*

Construction

Code

0018 Operative builders (building for own account)

General contractors
0034 Residential building
0059 Nonresidential building
0075 Highway and street construction
3889 Other heavy construction (pipe laying, bridge construction, etc.)

Building trade contractors, including repairs
0232 Plumbing, heating, air conditioning
0257 Painting and paper hanging
0273 Electrical work
0299 Masonry, dry wall, stone, tile
0414 Carpentering and flooring
0430 Roofing, siding, and sheet metal
0455 Concrete work
0471 Water well drilling
0885 Other building trade contractors (excavation, glazing, etc.)

Manufacturing, Including Printing and Publishing

0612 Bakeries selling at retail
0638 Other food products and beverages
0653 Textile mill products
0679 Apparel and other textile products
0695 Leather, footware, handbags, etc.
0810 Furniture and fixtures
0836 Lumber and other wood products
0851 Printing and publishing
0877 Paper and allied products
0893 Chemicals and allied products
1016 Rubber and plastics products
1032 Stone, clay, and glass products
1057 Primary metal industries
1073 Fabricated metal products
1099 Machinery and machine shops
1115 Electric and electronic equipment
1313 Transportation equipment
1339 Instruments and related products
1883 Other manufacturing industries

Mining and Mineral Extraction

1511 Metal mining
1537 Coal mining
1552 Oil and gas
1719 Quarrying and nonmetallic mining

Agricultural Services, Forestry, and Fishing

1917 Soil preparation services
1933 Crop services
1958 Veterinary services, including pets
1974 Livestock breeding
1990 Other animal services
2113 Farm labor and management services
2212 Horticulture and landscaping
2238 Forestry, except logging
0836 Logging
2279 Fishing, hunting, and trapping

Wholesale Trade—Selling Goods to Other Businesses, Government, or Institutions, etc.

Durable goods, including machinery, equipment, wood, metals, etc.
2618 Selling for your own account

Code

2634 Agent or broker for other firms— more than 50% of gross sales on commission

Nondurable goods, including food, fiber, chemicals, etc.
2659 Selling for your own account
2675 Agent or broker for other firms— more than 50% of gross sales on commission

Retail Trade—Selling Goods to Individuals and Households

3012 Selling door-to-door, by telephone or party plan, or from mobile unit
3038 Catalog or mail order
3053 Vending machine selling

Selling From Store, Showroom, or Other Fixed Location

Food, beverages, and drugs
3079 Eating places (meals or snacks)
3095 Drinking places (alcoholic beverages)
3210 Grocery stores (general line)
0612 Bakeries selling at retail
3236 Other food stores (meat, produce, candy, etc.)
3251 Liquor stores
3277 Drug stores

Automotive and service stations
3319 New car dealers (franchised)
3335 Used car dealers
3517 Other automotive dealers (motorcycles, recreational vehicles, etc.)
3533 Tires, accessories, and parts
3558 Gasoline service stations

General merchandise, apparel, and furniture
3715 Variety stores
3731 Other general merchandise stores
3756 Shoe stores
3772 Men's and boys' clothing stores
3913 Women's ready-to-wear stores
3921 Women's accessory and specialty stores and furriers
3939 Family clothing stores
3954 Other apparel and accessory stores
3970 Furniture stores
3996 TV, audio, and electronics
3988 Computer and software stores
4119 Household appliance stores
4317 Other home furnishing stores (china, floor coverings, drapes, etc.)
4333 Music and record stores

Building, hardware, and garden supply
4416 Building materials dealers
4432 Paint, glass, and wallpaper stores
4457 Hardware stores
4473 Nurseries and garden supply stores

Other retail stores
4614 Used merchandise and antique stores (except used motor vehicle parts)
4630 Gift, novelty, and souvenir shops
4655 Florists
4671 Jewelry stores

Code

4697 Sporting goods and bicycle shops
4812 Boat dealers
4838 Hobby, toy, and game shops
4853 Camera and photo supply stores
4879 Optical goods stores
4895 Luggage and leather goods stores
5017 Book stores, excluding newsstands
5033 Stationery stores
5058 Fabric and needlework stores
5074 Mobile home dealers
5090 Fuel dealers (except gasoline)
5884 Other retail stores

Real Estate, Insurance, Finance, and Related Services

5512 Real estate agents and managers
5538 Operators and lessors of buildings (except developers)
5553 Operators and lessors of other real property (except developers)
5710 Subdividers and developers, except cemeteries
5736 Insurance agents and services
5751 Security and commodity brokers, dealers, and investment services
5777 Other real estate, insurance, and financial activities

Transportation, Communications, Public Utilities, and Related Services

6114 Taxicabs
6312 Bus and limousine transportation
6338 Trucking (except trash collection)
6510 Trash collection without own dump
6536 Public warehousing
6551 Water transportation
6619 Air transportation
6635 Travel agents and tour operators
6650 Other transportation and related services
6676 Communication services
6692 Utilities, including dumps, snowplowing, road cleaning, etc.

Services (Providing Personal, Professional, and Business Services)

Hotels and other lodging places
7096 Hotels, motels, and tourist homes
7211 Rooming and boarding houses
7237 Camps and camping parks

Laundry and cleaning services
7419 Coin-operated laundries and dry cleaning
7435 Other laundry, dry cleaning, and garment services
7450 Carpet and upholstery cleaning
7476 Janitorial and related services (building, house, and window cleaning)

Business and/or personal services
7617 Legal services (or lawyer)
7633 Income tax preparation
7658 Accounting and bookkeeping
7674 Engineering, surveying, and architectural

Code

7690 Management, consulting, and public relations
7716 Advertising, except direct mail
7732 Employment agencies and personnel supply
7757 Computer and data processing, including repair and leasing
7773 Equipment rental and leasing (except computer or automotive)
7914 Investigative and protective services
7880 Other business services

Personal services
8110 Beauty shops (or beautician)
83'8 Barber shop (or barber)
8334 Photographic portrait studios
8516 Shoe repair and shine services
8532 Funeral services and crematories
8714 Child day care
8730 Teaching or tutoring
8755 Counseling (except health practitioners)
8771 Ministers and chaplains
6882 Other personal services

Automotive services
8813 Automotive rental or leasing, without driver
8839 Parking, except valet
8854 General automotive repairs
8870 Specialized automotive repairs (brake, body repairs, paint, etc.)
8896 Other automotive services (wash, towing, etc.)

Miscellaneous repair, except computers
9019 TV and audio equipment repair
9035 Other electrical equipment repair
9050 Reupholstery and furniture repair
2881 Other equipment repair

Medical and health services
9217 Offices and clinics of medical doctors (MD's)
9233 Offices and clinics of dentists
9258 Osteopathic physicians and surgeons
9274 Chiropractors
9290 Optometrists
9415 Registered and practical nurses
9431 Other licensed health practitioners
9456 Dental laboratories
9472 Nursing and personal care facilities
9886 Other health services

Amusement and recreational services
8557 Physical fitness facilities
9613 Videotape rental stores
9639 Motion picture theaters
9654 Other motion picture and TV film and tape activities
9670 Bowling alleys
9696 Professional sports and racing, including promoters and managers
9811 Theatrical performers, musicians, agents, producers, and related services
9837 Other amusement and recreational services

8888 Unable to classify

Figure 12-2 *(cont.)*

the employer), unreimbursed travel expense, the expense of maintaining an office in the home, and unreimbursed entertainment expense.

2. Expenses for the production of income, including rental fees for safe deposit boxes, accountants' fees for keeping books of income-producing property, insurance charges to protect merchandise held by the taxpayer for resale as an investment, investment advisers, and the like.

Supplemental Income Schedule

(From rents, royalties, partnerships, estates, trusts, REMICs, etc.)
▶ **Attach to Form 1040, Form 1041, or Form 1041S.**
▶ **See Instructions for Schedule E (Form 1040).**

OMB No. 1545-0074

1987
Attachment
Sequence No. **13**

Name(s) as shown on Form 1040

Your social security number

| **Part I** | **Rental and Royalty Income or (Loss)** | **Caution:** Your rental loss may be limited. See Instructions. |

1 In the space provided below, show the kind and location of each rental property.

2 For each property listed, did you or a member of your family use for personal purposes any of the properties for more than the greater of 14 days or 10% of the total days rented at fair rental value during the tax year? Yes No

3 For each rental real estate property listed, did you actively participate in the operation of the activity during the tax year? (See Instructions.) Yes No

Property A .... ▶
Property B .... ▶
Property C .... ▶

Rental and Royalty Income		**Properties**			**Totals** (Add columns A, B, and C)
		A	B	C	
4 Rents received					4
5 Royalties received					5

Rental and Royalty Expenses

			A	B	C	
6 Advertising	6					
7 Auto and travel	7					
8 Cleaning and maintenance	8					
9 Commissions	9					
10 Insurance	10					
11 Legal and other professional fees	11					
12 Mortgage interest paid to financial institutions (see Instructions)	12					12
13 Other interest	13					
14 Repairs	14					
15 Supplies	15					
16 Taxes (Do **not** include windfall profit tax here. See Part V, line 40.)	16					
17 Utilities	17					
18 Wages and salaries	18					
19 Other (list) ▶						
20 Total expenses other than depreciation and depletion. Add lines 6 through 19.	20					20
21 Depreciation expense (see Instructions), or depletion (see Publication 535).	21					21
22 Total. Add lines 20 and 21	22					
23 Income or (loss) from rental or royalty properties. Subtract line 22 from line 4 (rents) or 5 (royalties)	23					
24 Deductible rental loss. **Caution:** Your rental loss on line 23 may be limited. See Instructions to determine if you must file **Form 8582,** Passive Activity Loss Limitations	24					

25 **Profits.** Add rental and royalty profits from line 23, and enter the total profits here 25

26 **Losses.** Add royalty losses from line 23 and rental losses from line 24, and enter the total (losses) here . 26 (   )

27 Combine amounts on lines 25 and 26, and enter the net profit or (loss) here 27

28 Net farm rental profit or (loss) from Form 4835. (Also complete Part VI, line 43.) 28

29 Total rental or royalty income or (loss). Combine amounts on lines 27 and 28, and enter the total here. If Parts II, III, IV, and V on page 2 do not apply to you, enter the amount from line 29 on Form 1040, line 17. Otherwise, include the amount from line 29 in line 42 on page 2 of Schedule E 29

For Paperwork Reduction Act Notice, see Form 1040 Instructions.

Schedule E (Form 1040) 1987

Figure 12-3

These income-generating expenses are deductible only to the extent that they exceed 2 percent of total income. This calculation appears on Form 2106 rather than on the Form 1040. In other words, the amount entered on line 23 of Form 1040 has already been reduced by 2 percent of the amount shown on line 22. There are two justifications for this 2 percent "floor." First, concern

Name(s) as shown on Form 1040. (Do not enter name and social security number if shown on other side.) | **Your social security number**

Part II Income or (Loss) from Partnerships and S Corporations

If you report a loss below and have amounts invested in that activity for which you are **not at risk**, you MUST check "Yes" in column (e) and attach Form 6198. Otherwise, you must check "No." See Instructions.

	(a) Name	**(b)** Enter **P** for partnership; **S** for S Corporation	**(c)** Check if foreign partnership	**(d)** Employer identification number	**(e)** Not at-Risk? Yes | No
A					
B					
C					
D					
E					

	Passive Activities		**Nonpassive Activities**		
	(f) Passive loss allowed from Form 8582	**(g)** Passive income from Schedule K–1	**(h)** Nonpassive loss from Schedule K–1	**(i)** Section 179 deduction	**(j)** Nonpassive income ● from Schedule K–1
A					
B					
C					
D					
E					
30a Totals					
b Totals					

31	Add amounts in columns (g) and (j), line 30a. Enter total income here	**31**
32	Add amounts in columns (f), (h), and (i), line 30b. Enter total here	**32** ( )
33	Total partnership and S corporation income or (loss). Combine amounts on lines 31 and 32. Enter the total here and include in line 42 below	**33**

Part III Income or (Loss) from Estates and Trusts

	(a) Name	**(b)** Employer identification number
A		
B		
C		

	Passive Activities		**Nonpassive Activities**	
	(c) Passive deduction or loss allowed from Form 8582	**(d)** Passive income from Schedule K–1	**(e)** Deduction or loss from Schedule K–1	**(f)** Other income from Schedule K–1
A				
B				
C				
34a Totals				
b Totals				

35	Add amounts in columns (d) and (f), line 34a. Enter total income here	**35**
36	Add amounts in columns (c) and (e), line 34b. Enter total (loss) here	**36** ( )
37	Total estate and trust income or (loss). Combine amounts on lines 35 and 36. Enter the total here and include in line 42 below	**37**

Part IV Income or (Loss) from Real Estate Mortgage Investment Conduits (REMICs)—Residual Holder

(a) Name	**(b)** Employer identification number	**(c)** Excess inclusion from Schedules Q, line 2c (see Instructions)	**(d)** Taxable income (net loss) from Schedules Q, line 1b	**(e)** Income from Schedules Q, line 3b

38	Combine columns (d) and (e) only. Enter the total here and include in line 42 below	**38**

Part V Windfall Profit Tax Summary

39	Windfall profit tax credit or refund received in 1987 (see Instructions)	**39**
40	Windfall profit tax withheld in 1987 (see Instructions)	**40** ( )
41	Combine amounts on lines 39 and 40. Enter the total here and include in line 42 below	**41**

Part VI Summary

42	TOTAL income or (loss). Combine lines 29, 33, 37, 38, and 41. Enter total here and on Form 1040, line 17 . . . . ▶	**42**
43	Farmers and fishermen: Enter your share of GROSS FARMING AND FISHING INCOME applicable to Parts I, II, and III (see Instructions) **43**	

☆ U.S. GPO: 1987-183-102

Figure 12-3 (*cont.*)

about revenue loss arises because many of the expenses in this category historically have been subject to abuse in the sense that taxpayers have claimed deductions to which they are arguably not entitled. These deductions are also claimed by millions of lower- and middle-income taxpayers so that widespread cheating entails a very substantial revenue loss. Second, the floor also simplifies the preparation of returns for many lower-income taxpayers whose deductions

Farm Income and Expenses

▶ Attach to Form 1040, Form 1041, Form 1041S, or Form 1065.

▶ See Instructions for Schedule F (Form 1040).

OMB No. 1545-0074

1987

Attachment
Sequence No. **14**

Name of proprietor	Social security number (SSN)

A Principal Product (Describe in one or two words your principal crop or output for the current tax year.)

B Agricultural Activity Code (from Part IV) ▶

C Accounting Method: ☐ Cash   ☐ Accrual

D Employer ID number (Not SSN)

E Did you make an election in a prior year to include commodity credit loan proceeds as income in that year? . . . . . ☐ Yes ☐ No

F Did you "materially participate" in the operation of this business during 1987? (See Instructions for limitation on losses.) . . ☐ Yes ☐ No
If "No" and you have a loss on line 37, you must attach Form 8582.

G Are you electing not to capitalize certain preproductive period expenses? (New rules apply to these expenses, see Instructions.) ☐ Yes ☐ No

Part I Farm Income—Cash Method—Complete Parts I and II
(Accrual method taxpayers complete Parts II and III, and line 12 of Part I.)
Do not include sales of livestock held for draft, breeding, sport, or dairy purposes; report these sales on Form 4797.

1	Sales of livestock and other items you bought for resale	**1**
2	Cost or other basis of livestock and other items you bought for resale .	**2**
3	Subtract line 2 from line 1	**3**
4	Sales of livestock, produce, grains, and other products you raised	**4**
5 a	Total distributions received from cooperatives (from Form 1099-PATR) . .	**5a**
b	**Less:** Nonincome items	**5b**
6	Net distributions. Subtract line 5b from line 5a	**6**
7	Agricultural program payments:	
a	Cash	**7a**
b	Materials and services	**7b**
8	Commodity credit loans under election (or forfeited)	**8**
9	Crop insurance proceeds. If election attached to include in income in year following damage, check here ▶ ☐	**9**
10	Machine work (custom hire) income	**10**
11	Other income, including Federal and state gasoline tax credit or refund (see Instructions)	**11**
12	**Gross income.** Add amounts on lines 3, 4, 6, and 7a through 11. If accrual method taxpayer, enter the amount from Part III, line 52 . . . . ▶	**12**

Part II Farm Deductions—Cash and Accrual Method (Do not include personal or living expenses such as taxes, insurance, repairs, etc., on your home.)

13	Breeding fees		24a	Labor hired	
14	Chemicals.		b	Jobs credit	
15	Conservation expenses (you must attach Form 8645)		c	Net labor hired (subtract line 24b from line 24a)	
16	Depreciation and section 179 expense deduction (from Form 4562)		25	Machine (custom) hire	
17	Employee benefit programs other than on line 26		26	Pension and profit-sharing plans . .	
18	Feed purchased		27	Rent of farm, pasture	
19	Fertilizers and lime		28	Repairs, maintenance	
20	Freight, trucking.		29	Seeds, plants purchased	
21	Gasoline, fuel, oil		30	Storage, warehousing	
22	Insurance		31	Supplies purchased	
23	Interest:		32	Taxes	
a	Mortgage (paid to financial institutions)		33	Utilities	
			34	Veterinary fees, medicine	
b	Other		35	Other expenses (specify):	
			a	------------------------------	
			b	------------------------------	
			c		

36	**Total deductions from Part II.** Add amounts in columns for lines 13 through 35c . . . . . ▶	**36**
37	**Net farm profit or (loss)**. Subtract line 36 from line 12. If a profit, enter on Form 1040, line 18, and on Schedule SE, line 1. If a loss, you **MUST** go on to line 38. (Fiduciaries and partnerships, see Instructions.)	**37**
38	If you have a loss, you **MUST** answer this question: "Do you have amounts for which you are not at risk in this business?" (See Instructions.) . . . . ☐ Yes ☐ No
	If "Yes," you **MUST** attach **Form 6198**. If "No," enter the loss on Form 1040, line 18, and on Schedule SE, line 1.

For Paperwork Reduction Act Notice, see Form 1040 Instructions.   Schedule F (Form 1040) 1987

Figure 12-4

are likely to be less than the floor. On the other hand (and this illustrates that many simplifying changes may cause increased complexity in individual returns), in the case of a joint return, this 2 percent floor is calculated on the combined income of husband and wife; where both spouses have income but only one has expenses subject to the floor, the filing of separate returns may

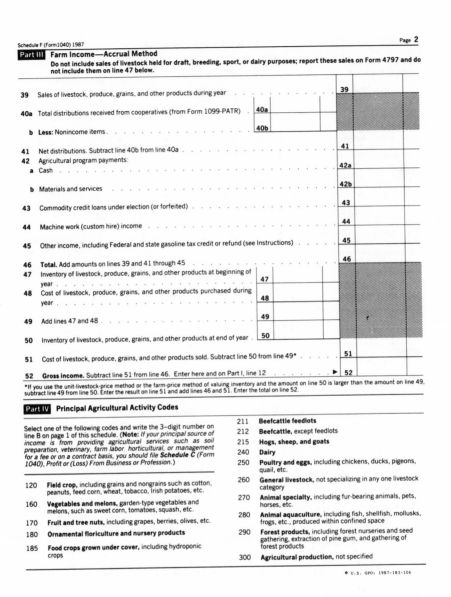

Part III **Farm Income—Accrual Method**

Do not include sales of livestock held for draft, breeding, sport, or dairy purposes; report these sales on Form 4797 and do not include them on line 47 below.

39	Sales of livestock, produce, grains, and other products during year	39	
40a	Total distributions received from cooperatives (from Form 1099-PATR)	40a	
b	**Less:** Nonincome items	40b	
41	Net distributions. Subtract line 40b from line 40a	41	
42	Agricultural program payments:		
a	Cash	42a	
b	Materials and services	42b	
43	Commodity credit loans under election (or forfeited)	43	
44	Machine work (custom hire) income	44	
45	Other income, including Federal and state gasoline tax credit or refund (see Instructions)	45	
46	**Total.** Add amounts on lines 39 and 41 through 45	46	
47	Inventory of livestock, produce, grains, and other products at beginning of year	47	
48	Cost of livestock, produce, grains, and other products purchased during year	48	
49	Add lines 47 and 48	49	
50	Inventory of livestock, produce, grains, and other products at end of year	50	
51	Cost of livestock, produce, grains, and other products sold. Subtract line 50 from line 49*	51	
52	**Gross income.** Subtract line 51 from line 46. Enter here and on Part I, line 12 ▶	52	

*If you use the unit-livestock-price method or the farm-price method of valuing inventory and the amount on line 50 is larger than the amount on line 49, subtract line 49 from line 50. Enter the result on line 51 and add lines 46 and 51. Enter the total on line 52.

Part IV **Principal Agricultural Activity Codes**

Select one of the following codes and write the 3–digit number on line B on page 1 of this schedule. (**Note:** *If your principal source of income is from providing agricultural services such as soil preparation, veterinary, farm labor, horticultural, or management for a fee or on a contract basis, you should file* **Schedule C** *(Form 1040), Profit or (Loss) From Business or Profession.*)

120	**Field crop,** including grains and nongrains such as cotton, peanuts, feed corn, wheat, tobacco, Irish potatoes, etc.
160	**Vegetables and melons,** garden-type vegetables and melons, such as sweet corn, tomatoes, squash, etc.
170	**Fruit and tree nuts,** including grapes, berries, olives, etc.
180	**Ornamental floriculture and nursery products**
185	**Food crops grown under cover,** including hydroponic crops

211	**Beefcattle feedlots**
212	**Beefcattle,** except feedlots
215	**Hogs, sheep, and goats**
240	**Dairy**
250	**Poultry and eggs,** including chickens, ducks, pigeons, quail, etc.
260	**General livestock,** not specializing in any one livestock category
270	**Animal specialty,** including fur-bearing animals, pets, horses, etc.
280	**Animal aquaculture,** including fish, shellfish, mollusks, frogs, etc., produced within confined space
290	**Forest products,** including forest nurseries and seed gathering, extraction of pine gum, and gathering of forest products
300	**Agricultural production,** not specified

✿ U.S. GPO: 1987-183-106

Figure 12-4 (*cont.*)

yield a lower tax since the 2 percent floor is then calculated only on the income of the spouse that has the expenses subject to the floor.

    3. IRA and Keogh plan contributions (see §§5.9 and 5.10).

    4. Penalties on early withdrawal of savings from retirement plans.

    5. Alimony.

These last three deductions (and a very small number of other itemized deductions) are not subject to the 2 percent floor.

§12.9.3 The Calculation of Taxable Income

In addition to business- or income-oriented expenses, the Internal Revenue Code has always allowed, as a matter of policy, the deduction of certain classes or types of personal expenses. Historically, the most important of these were state income, property and sales taxes, interest on personal debts and on real estate mortgages, medical and dental expenses, charitable contributions, and casualty losses. The reasons underlying these deductions obviously vary: encouraging charitable contributions, lessening the financial burden on the unfortunate family struck by a major casualty loss or catastrophic medical expenses, and so forth.

The policies underlying some of these deductions have often been viewed as suspect by tax theorists, since they involve personal rather than business expenditures; however, from a political standpoint some of them are immensely popular. These personal expenses have also involved a fair amount of petty cheating by large numbers of taxpayers. In the 1986 Act, Congress took several steps to limit the widespread use and misuse of these deductions. The most important substantive changes were that it limited the deduction of state taxes to income and real estate taxes, excluding state sales taxes, and limited the deduction of interest on nonbusiness loans basically to those arising from the purchase of residential real estate or, to a limited extent, loans secured by liens on such real estate.

The Internal Revenue Code has adopted several devices to limit the availability of personal deductions. First, the most important device is the availability to all taxpayers of the "standard deduction" that may be used in lieu of the itemization of all personal deductions. The size of the standard deduction varies with the filing status of the taxpayer discussed below. In 1988 the amounts are as follows:

Single persons, $3,000;
Heads of households, $4,400
Married persons filing jointly, $5,000
Married persons filing separately, $2,500.

In 1989 and later years, the standard deduction is also indexed for inflation. The standard deduction applies only to personal deductions: It does not affect the deductibility of employee business expenses or expenses incurred in the production of income. Also, as indicated above, the standard deduction is not a floor (like that applied to employee business expenses) but an amount that is available to and may be claimed by every taxpayer as an alternative to itemization. If the standard deduction is generous enough, most persons of course do not itemize but simply elect to take the standard deduction. This has multiple advantages from the standpoint of the system: It eliminates petty cheating, it simplifies the preparation of returns for many taxpayers, and it improves intertaxpayer general equity since more taxpayers compute their taxes on precisely the same basis.

The second important device designed to limit personal deductions to extraordinary or unusual situations (and possibly also to prevent petty cheating) is the imposition of a floor on specific types of expenses similar to that imposed on employee business expenses. The oldest such floor is on medical expenses, where Congress originally attempted to distinguish between ordinary medical expenses and extraordinary ones by limiting their aggregate deductibility to medical expenses that exceed 3 percent of adjusted gross income. This floor was raised to 7.5 percent in the 1986 Act, thereby eliminating deductions in all but extraordinary situations given the amount of available income. A similar floor was placed on casualty losses in the 1960s because of perceived abuses of claimed losses that were minor in character and often not of the true "casualty" type. Currently, any claimed casualty loss must be reduced by (a) $100, and (b) 10 percent of adjusted gross income, and only the excess is deductible. Again the policy of limiting the deduction to extraordinary losses given the amount of available income is clear. In both instances, only the deductible portion of medical or casualty losses is taken into account to determine whether the standard deduction is advantageous.

A final approach is to require specific documentation about claimed deductions to be filed with the return. This is required, for example, for charitable deductions claimed for contributions of noncash property, where valuation is likely to be overoptimistic.

§12.9.4 Personal Exemptions

Personal exemptions are entirely different from personal deductions. Exemptions permit the subtraction of arbitrary amounts for the taxpayer and spouse (if a joint return is filed), and for each dependent relative (defined precisely in the Code). Additional exemptions were long provided for persons over 65 and for blind people, but the 1986 Act eliminated these exemptions in favor of a limited increase in the standard deduction for the aged and blind. The personal exemption for the 1989 tax year is $2,000 for each allowable exemption.

As a result of the combination of personal exemptions and the standard deduction, a family of four pays no tax if its adjusted gross income is $13,000 or less ($8,000 of personal exemptions and $5,000 of standard deduction).

The 1986 Act adds a new twist on personal exemptions by providing a gradual phase-out of the benefit of the exemptions for high-income taxpayers. This is accomplished by adding an extra 5 percent tax bracket for taxpayers earning more than $149,250 on a joint return until the advantage of all personal exemptions is eliminated. In other words, the high income taxpayer begins to lose all tax benefits from personal exemptions when his or her income exceeds a specified amount.

§12.10 The Calculation of the Tax Due on Individual Returns

Once taxable income is calculated, the next step is the calculation of the actual tax that is due. This is done either from a set of tables (for persons with

Table 12-1

	If taxable income is:	
Over-	*but not over-*	*The tax is:*

1) Married taxpayers filing joint returns and surviving spouses

0	29,750	15% of taxable income
29,750	71,900	4,462.50 + 28% of excess over 29,750
71,900	149,250	16,264.50 + 33% of excess over 71,900
149,250		28% of taxable income.*

2) Heads of households

0	23,900	15% of taxable income
23,900	61,650	3,585 + 28% of excess over 23,900
61,650	123,790	14,155 + 33% of excess over 61,650
123,790		28% of taxable income.*

3) Single taxpayers

0	17,850	15% of taxable income
17,850	43,150	2,677.50 + 28% of excess over 17,850
43,150	89,560	9,761.50 + 33% of excess over 43,150*
89,560		28% of taxable income.

4) Married individuals filing separate returns

0	14,875	15% of taxable income
14,875	35,950	2,231.25 + 28% of excess over 14,875
35,950	74,625	8,132.25 + 33% of excess over 35,950
74,625		28% of taxable income.*

* Taxable income is subject to an extra 5 percent surcharge until the effect of personal exemptions is eliminated.

incomes of less than $50,000) or by a mathematical calculation. Since the lower income tables are themselves simply a reflection of the mathematical calculation, this discussion concentrates on the formulas. The formulas set forth in Table 12-1 apply to the 1988 and later tax years. The 1986 Tax Act does not expressly create the 33 percent brackets set forth in each of the foregoing tables. It does provide, however, for the first time, that upper-income taxpayers should gradually lose the benefit of the lower brackets as their income rises. Thus it tacked on an additional 5 percent surtax applicable to higher-income taxpayers to eliminate the effect of the 15 percent bracket. In other words, a couple filing a joint return with income in excess of $71,940 begins to pay an extra 5 percent tax on the income in excess of that amount in order to phase out the 15 percent bracket. This occurs at precisely $149,250. To illustrate: For the married couple filing a joint return the calculation is $(149,250 - 71,900) \times .05 = 3,867.50 = 29,750 \times (.28 - .15)$. The size of the 33 percent bracket in the above tables is set precisely at a level to eliminate the difference between a 28 percent rate and the 15 percent rates on the taxable income in the lowest bracket.

And that is not all. The 1986 Tax Act added yet another twist as well. After the elimination of the benefit of the 15 percent bracket, a second 5 percent special tax rate kicks in as long as is necessary to eliminate the tax benefit of the personal exemptions claimed on the return. Thus, a married couple with two children — a total of four dependents — with a very high income continues to pay at a 33 percent rate above $149,250 until the additional 5 percent rate yields the tax saved from having $8,000 of exemptions in 1988. In the case of four exemptions the additional 5 percent continues to apply until the taxable income of the couple exceeds $194,050 [.05 × (194,050 − 149,250) = 2,240 = 8,000 × .28]; only then does the tax rate revert back to 28 percent.

These two additional 5 percent surtaxes create an unprecedented regressive feature in income tax rates. For the first time, the marginal tax rate on additional dollars of income actually drops at one point in the tax scale.

There are four different categories of individual taxpayers with different sized brackets depending on marital or family status. These multiple categories, of course, are an inheritance from the earlier era of 14 or 15 narrow brackets and are typical of the complexity of the modern tax law system and the failure of the 1986 Tax Act effectively to simplify the system. The three basic categories of taxpayers are (1) a married couple filing jointly or a surviving spouse (defined as a person whose spouse has died within the previous two years), (2) a "head of household" (defined as an unmarried person who is not a surviving spouse and who maintains a home for a dependent child or relative) and (3) a single person. The fourth category, married taxpayers filing separately, is created by simply halving every entry in the joint return category and thereby ensures that married couples with two incomes cannot take advantage of the single person tax schedule but remains on a tax parity with families in which one spouse is the wage earner and the other is a homemaker. See §12.5 for a further discussion of how these categories of individual taxpayers evolved.

§12.11 Limitations on the Deductibility of Passive Losses and Investment Interest

The 1986 Act develops a classification of interest and passive loss deductions primarily to eliminate excessive deductions from tax shelters. See §12.6. Unfortunately, in doing so, Congress again significantly increased the complexity of the individual income tax system.

The basic idea is not very complicated. *Investment interest*, for example, is basically interest on obligations incurred to buy or carry investment property. That interest is to be deductible only to the extent the taxpayer has income from the investments. The purpose of this provision is to prevent a taxpayer from borrowing funds to acquire deferred income investments and deducting the interest immediately, thereby sheltering other current income from tax. If one does incur interest in a year when it is not deductible because of the absence of investment income, that deduction is not lost but may be carried over indefinitely and deducted in a later year when the taxpayer does have available investment income in excess of investment interest.

The 1986 Act also establishes a similar pattern by creating a class of losses and credits, called *passive losses*, that can be deducted only to the extent that there is income from passive activities. *Passive activities* are defined to include essentially all rental activities and trade or business activities in which the taxpayer does not materially participate. Investment activity is not passive activity. The ownership and rental of commercial or residential property is expressly included in the definition of passive activities, and participation by owners in decisions on matters such as who should be tenants does not take the activity out of the passive category. Virtually the only nonpassive commercial real estate activity is owning and operating a hotel. The purpose of this provision, phased in over five years, is to eliminate most tax shelters, particularly tax shelters involving the direct ownership of commercial or rental residential real estate. As a result of this provision, the investor who acquired the duplex described in Chapter 3 gradually loses after 1986 the benefits of the tax losses that made the duplex an attractive investment originally, unless he can show net profits from other passive activities sufficient to cover the operating losses shown on the cash-flow statement. However, there are exceptions to this rigid treatment of passive activity, including the right to deduct up to $25,000 of passive losses for taxpayers with adjusted gross incomes of $100,000; this deduction is itself gradually phased out at higher incomes until all deduction is prohibited for taxpayers with adjusted gross incomes in excess of $150,000. If the investor in the duplex was in the 50 percent bracket in 1985, and his income remains stable, he will lose some or all of this special $25,000 dispensation. Passive losses that cannot be taken advantage of in any year because of the lack of passive income also do not disappear but may be carried over to later years in which there is passive income in excess of passive losses.

Losses and credits arising from a trade or business in which the taxpayer materially participates are fully deductible. *Materially* means that the taxpayer is involved in the operations of the activity on a regular, continuous, and substantial basis. If the activity is not material, the business becomes a passive activity. Thus, the 1986 Tax Act creates a threefold classification of individual profit-making activity in order to eliminate tax shelters and related activities. Except for real estate activities that are clearly defined as passive activities, difficult problems of classification at or near the boundaries between these three categories are sure to arise. Indeed, the mere reporting of activities in each category significantly increases the complexity of the schedules to Form 1040.

§12.12 The Alternative Minimum Tax

The alternative minimum tax attacks the proliferation of preferential provisions in the Internal Revenue Code and limits the ability of a taxpayer to avoid all taxes by using these provisions, either singly or in combination. It is applicable only to taxpayers with taxable incomes in excess of $50,000. The alternative minimum tax essentially requires a second tax calculation on an entirely different set of computational rules. If the alternative minimum tax is greater than the tax computed in the normal manner, then the taxpayer must add to the tax due on the normal computation an amount equal to the difference between the normal tax and the alternative minimum tax. In simpler terms, if the alternative minimum tax exceeds the normal tax, the taxpayer's total tax liability is based on the alternative minimum tax rather than on the normal computation of tax.

The alternative minimum tax is a flat 21 percent of an amount computed as follows: One starts with the adjusted gross income of the taxpayer computed on the normal basis, and adds back in specific *tax preference items* claimed by the taxpayer in the calculation of adjusted gross income. From this amount one subtracts (1) $40,000, and (2) allowable deductions for charitable contributions, interest on mortgages on the personal residence of the taxpayers, and investment interest. The alternative minimum tax is 21 percent of the amount so computed.

The tax preference items that must be added back into income for the computation of the amount subject to the alternative minimum tax includes accelerated depreciation on property, capital gains deductions, portions of incentive stock options excluded from income, and percentage depletion.

The alternative minimum tax provision is an effort to overcome the deficiencies of the normal income tax structure by overlaying a separate tax schedule on most loopholes. As the alternative tax rate (21 percent) approximates the normal tax rate (28 percent or 33 percent) the normal rate dwindles in significance for upper-income taxpayers. The alternative minimum tax obviously complicates the tax returns of all high-income taxpayers.

§12.13 The Collection Process

The Internal Revenue Service has the responsibility for collection of federal income, gift, estate, and excise taxes. The discussion here is limited to the process of collection of income taxes.

Income taxes are collected on a highly efficient "pay as you go" basis. For most Americans, the "pay as you go" system means simply that employers must withhold from each paycheck an amount that approximately covers the employee's tax liability by the end of the year. Probably every reader has had some contact with this withholding system, involving the filing of a Form W-4 with one's employer declaring the number of exemptions claimed, and the receipt from the employer each January of a W-2 Form showing the amounts actually withheld during the previous calendar year. The withholding schedules and tax rates are structured so that if a person accurately declares the number of exemptions and uses the standard deduction, he or she ends up having more deducted from paychecks than the amount of tax actually due. Most taxpayers therefore receive refunds every year. Of course, these refunds are paid in effect from funds painlessly collected over the course of the preceding year from the taxpayer by his or her employer, without interest. The fact that most people are entitled to refunds each year materially increases the political acceptability of the system. The arrangement is attractive to the federal government as well: The collection process is painless and does not give rise to large amounts of resentment, the government has the interest-free use of funds for nearly a year, and tax collections are spread around the year and not bunched in a single month.

The employer is required to pay over to the IRS the amount withheld from employees at the end of each calendar quarter. Even though the Internal Revenue Code requires that these withheld funds be placed in a separate account, most employers do not segregate the funds but simply use them as part of general working capital until the check is written to the IRS. Of course, from time to time a business may become insolvent without having forwarded the money withheld from employees to the Service. There is a 100 percent penalty against an individual with the responsibility for these funds who fails to pay them over to the Service. In other words, the corporate treasurer or individual with analogous responsibilities is personally liable for the amount withheld if it is not in fact paid over. Like other claims arising under the Internal Revenue Code, this liability is not discharged in bankruptcy. Whether or not the Service successfully collects the withheld taxes from the employer, however, the employee is entitled to credit against his or her taxes of the amounts shown as withheld on statements reported to the IRS.

If persons have income or gains not subject to withholding, they may be required to file quarterly declarations of estimated tax, which are intended to provide a "pay as you go" system to taxpayers with substantial amounts of self-employment activity, personal investments, and other sources of nonwithheld income such as gambling or stock market trading. Quarterly declarations are due April 15, June 15, September 15, and January 15, and must be accompanied by a proportional amount of the estimated tax that is shown to be due on the estimate. A person subject to withholding is theoretically required to file a quarterly declaration whenever taxes withheld are less than 90 percent of taxes due, but such persons may avoid this filing if they increase the amount of withholding so that the estimated tax for that quarter is shown to be zero. The obligation to file quarterly declarations of estimated tax, and to pay the proportional amount of tax due, is enforced by penalties applied when the final return is filed for the year showing substantial underpayment of tax. What is substantial in this context is defined in the Tax Code very specifically: if the amount paid by withholding and quarterly estimates is less than 90 percent of the actual tax shown to be due on the return. The 1986 Act imposes a stiff penalty if the total "pay as you go" payments fail to equal 90 percent of the actual tax; in earlier years a smaller penalty was due only if the payments were less than 80 percent of the actual tax due. There are also other bases on which this penalty may be avoided.

D. TAX ACCOUNTING AND FINANCIAL ACCOUNTING

§12.14 Tax Accounting in General

The Internal Revenue Code obviously requires the utilization of accounting concepts for determining in which years items of income and deduction should be reported. Tax accounting differs materially from traditional income accounting in numerous specific respects. Tax returns are not prepared on GAAP principles so that income for tax purposes and income for accounting purposes may vary substantially.

§12.15 Cash Basis Accounting

Most individual taxpayers are on the cash basis, reporting income when it is received rather than when it is earned and taking advantage of deductions when they are paid rather than when they are incurred or when they are due. This permits some income and deduction shifting from one year to another. For example, a doctor who does not bill for November or December services until January takes the income arising from those services into his or her tax return for the second year, not the first. It is almost always advantageous to defer taxes even if tax rates are identical because of the time value of a deferred payment. Prior to 1986, year-end planning might also permit a taxpayer to shift income from a high-income year to a lower-income year to be taxed at lower marginal rates. Similarly, a taxpayer may be able to shift two years' real estate property taxes into a single year by paying one year's taxes in January and prepaying the next year's taxes in December of the same year. Combining two years' taxes into a single year may be advantageous if the standard deduction is claimed for the year in which no payments of real estate tax are made. While strategies of this type offer some modest degree of tax saving, they have become significantly less important since the 1986 Act with its lower overall tax rates and limited number of tax brackets.

There are some exceptions to the straight cash basis of individual taxpayer accounting. The doctrine of *constructive receipt* does not permit a taxpayer to defer reporting income items that are within his immediate control. One cannot defer an income item, for example, merely by not depositing a check until the following year. There are also special rules relating to receipt of interest: Interest on financial instruments such as zero coupon bonds purchased at a discount from face value (see §18.21) must be reported as it is earned rather than being deferred until the instrument is paid. Similarly, interest paid by a taxpayer in a lump sum to cover several accounting periods cannot be deducted in the year of payment but must be accrued and deducted ratably over the relevant periods. Restrictions also are imposed on the deductibility of prepaid amounts. These various qualifications to the general cash method of accounting reflect pragmatic judgments designed to limit revenue loss from tax-minimizing transactions.

§12.16 Accrual Accounting and Financial Accounting

It has long been an observable fact of corporate life that many publicly held corporations reflect substantial earnings in their GAAP financial statements and reports to shareholders but pay little or no federal income tax. Undoubtedly, much of this difference is due to tax benefits intentionally given to business, such as the accelerated cost recovery system for calculating depreciation deductions and investment tax credits. However, in part the difference is due to differences in accounting principles.

The Internal Revenue Code prohibits corporations and specified other types of businesses from adopting a cash basis of accounting for tax purposes. A form of accrual accounting, roughly analogous to GAAP accounting, is required for most businesses. However, the purpose of tax accounting and financial accounting differ: The primary goal of financial accounting is to provide useful information to management, shareholders, creditors and others properly interested while the primary goal of the income tax system is to protect the public fisc. The test of tax accounting is that the method clearly reflect income. These differences in purpose result in many differences in detail. The tax system, for example, generally requires that receipts of cash be included in income immediately while financial accounting may require that they be parked on the balance sheet until the services have been performed or the goods delivered. See §8.4. Similarly, GAAP may call for the creation of reserves and deducting amounts allocated to them from book income; it is unusual for such deductions to be recognized for income tax purposes.

The differences between tax accounting and financial accounting is a specialized area of interest primarily to accountants and attorneys who represent businesses in tax matters. They are the outgrowth of basic differences in the purposes of the two accounting systems. Because the systems are different, businesses must usually keep tax books and financial books separately.

The 1986 Act introduces a controversial and novel accounting-related concept. It requires corporations to include a fraction of the difference between their taxable income and their net book income as reported to shareholders in the calculation of the alternative minimum tax for corporations. The purpose of this provision is to ensure that corporations that show substantial book earnings in reports to shareholders also pay a reasonable amount of tax. However, it is uncertain how important this provision will be in practice, since the manner of calculating a corporation's alternative minimum taxable income already takes into account the impact of some of the most important corporate tax preferences, such as ACRS.

E. SALES AND EXCHANGES OF PROPERTY

§12.17 Sales and Exchanges of Property in General

A major area of tax law deals with gains and losses from the sale or exchange of property. At the most basic level, a sale or exchange of property gives rise to taxable income. Say a farmer swaps a side of beef for a bolt of cloth from the local dry goods store. The exchange is a taxable transaction and each participant should report gain or loss from the transaction on his or her federal income tax return. Obviously, in the barter economy that quietly exists in many communities there is a lot of tax evading going on since it is likely that few, if any, transactions of this type are reported.

Of course, in the barter of the beef for the cloth, both parties are swapping goods that involve their trade or business. But that is not essential. If you sell your secondhand car at a profit, the gain should be reported to the IRS as income. Similarly, if you swap your car for a motorcycle or a used computer, the gain should be reported. (Losses from such personal transactions are not deductible at all, and hence need not be reported.)

The calculation of the amount of the gain from sales or exchanges involves the use of technical language that is fundamental to any understanding of the tax laws:

a. *Basis* is the investment the seller of the property has in the property. It is the cost or purchase price of the property paid or incurred by the seller in acquiring the property. In the case of property acquired by gift, the basis in the hands of the donee is usually the same as the basis in the hands of the donor (a *substituted basis*); in the case of property acquired by inheritance, it is generally the fair market value of the assets on the death of decedent (a *stepped up basis*).

b. *Adjusted basis* is the basis of the property, (1) plus capital improvements made by the seller, purchase commissions originally paid by the seller, legal costs for defending or perfecting title, and so forth, and (2) minus returns of capital, particularly depreciation claimed as tax deductions, depletion, deducted casualty losses, insurance reimbursements, and the like.

c. The *amount realized* includes the cash received for the property on a sale or the fair market value of the property received in exchange for the property. Selling expenses, including brokerage commissions paid by the seller, reduce the amount realized. In the case of property subject to a mortgage, the amount realized also includes the amount of mortgage debt which the seller is relieved from paying as a result of the sale. For example, if an owner of real estate that is encumbered by a $50,000 mortgage sells the property for $10,000 cash over and above the mortgage, which the buyer agrees to assume and pay, the amount realized from the sale is $60,000, not $10,000. If the property is sold with the seller giving the buyer $5,000 for assuming the mortgage of $50,000, the amount realized is $45,000.

c. *Gain* on a transaction equals the amount realized minus the adjusted basis. If the adjusted basis is greater than the amount realized, the difference is the loss.

§12.18 The Concept of "Recognition" of Gain or Loss

In order to be taxable, a gain or loss must be recognized as well as realized. *Realized* means that the transaction is closed and the sale or exchange has occurred. *Recognized* means that the gain or loss is also to be taken into account as a taxable transaction. If a realized gain or loss is not recognized, it is deferred to a later year.

Generally, gain or loss is recognized whenever property is sold or exchanged, but there are significant exceptions: exchanges of like kinds of property, involuntary conversions of property, sales of residences followed by a rollover of the purchase price into a new residence, sales between related persons, and many transactions by a corporation involving its own stock.

A gain on the sale or exchange of the property may be recognized even though a loss on the sale of the same property is not deductible. This includes, for example, a sale of personal assets such as the family home. The loss is not recognized in the case of personal assets because it is considered a result of the personal consumption involved in living in a home rather than an economic loss.

The recognition concept is particularly important in connection with transactions relating to the formation and reorganizations of corporations. Many corporate transactions would be economically impractical if gains or losses from the transaction were recognized. For example, consider the problem of investors in a new corporation planning to contribute not cash but property in exchange for its stock. Assume further that the property has a fair market value today of $25,000 and a basis in the hands of the investor of $16,000. The stock being received also has a fair market value of $25,000. In the absence of a nonrecognition provision, the exchange of the real estate for the stock would result in the realization of gain in the amount of $9,000 (the difference between the fair market value of the property being received in the exchange and the basis of the property being exchanged). The result would be that the investor would owe some $3,000 in tax as a result of making the investment. Fortunately, the Internal Revenue Code permits the transfer of assets to a corporation controlled by the transferor (or a group of which he or she is a member) without recognition of gain if the investors in the corporation are in control of the corporation after the transaction. In this context, control means ownership of at least 80 percent of the voting stock of the corporation and at least 80 percent of all other classes of stock. If this provision applies, the investor does not recognize any gain from the exchange of stock for property, and the basis of the stock received is $16,000, the basis of the property exchanged.

Gain may be recognized, however, if the transferor takes back cash, property other than stock, or his or her debt is assumed in the transfer. For example, if in the above transaction, the investor is contributing real estate with a fair market value of $25,000 and a basis of $16,000 which is subject to a $19,000 lien that the corporation is to assume, the difference between the basis ($16,000) and the amount of the lien ($19,000) must be recognized as gain from the transaction. The basis of the stock received is then $19,000.

Another very important nonrecognition area in the law of corporations deals with different kinds of reorganization transactions — statutory mergers, acquisitions of all the assets of one corporation in exchange for stock of another corporation, etc. These provisions are among the most complicated in the Code, and significantly different tax consequences may follow, depending on how the transaction is structured.

§12.19 Special Tax Treatment of Long-Term Capital Gains and Losses

The 1986 Act imposes the same tax rate on long-term capital gains and losses as on income generally. This represents a change in longstanding tax policy that continues to be controversial and may be reversed in the future. Furthermore, the elaborate definition and classification of capital gains was not eliminated by the 1986 Act, and certain portions of the treatment continue to be applicable under that Act. Hence an examination of the pre-1986 rules is appropriate.

§12.19.1 The Pre-1986 Approach to Capital Gains and Losses

Under the 1954 Code, gains and losses from sales or exchanges of property were generally taxable in the same manner as any other income. However, gains and losses from the sale or exchange of capital assets were subject to special rules and limitations.

A *capital asset* is any property held by a taxpayer other than inventory, property held primarily for sale to customers, depreciable and real property used in a trade or business, and several other less important items. A taxpayer's personal residence is thus a capital asset, but if the same property were used in a trade or business it would not be a capital asset. Depreciable property used in a trade or business (such as the residence), however, is often entitled to special treatment that is even more favorable to the taxpayer than if it were a capital asset.

Shares of stock in a corporation are capital assets; interests in a partnership are also capital assets (except for designated assets such as accounts receivable and appreciated inventory). On the other hand, an interest in a proprietorship is not a capital asset but a composite of individual assets.

A *capital gain* or *capital loss* arises from the sale or exchange of a capital asset. Historically, a distinction was also made between long-term and short-term capital gains and losses, the dividing line usually being a holding period of six months. In some years between 1954 and 1986, the holding period was as long as 12 months. Long-term capital gains were subject to special treatment that in effect imposed a maximum tax of 25 percent on them when other income was being taxed at progressive rates up to 70 percent. Long-term capital losses were also subject to special treatment, but that treatment was usually disadvantageous to the taxpayer since long-term losses were deductible against ordinary income only to a limited extent and in many years not on a dollar-for-dollar basis.

The actual calculation of the amount of gain or loss that qualified for long-term capital gain or loss treatment was complicated because a single taxpayer often had both short- and long-term gains or losses in a single tax year. Basically the tax law required a netting of short-term gains and losses separately from long-term gains and losses, then netting the two categories, with only the ultimate difference being categorized as long- or short-term.

If a taxpayer's return showed a net long-term capital gain, that gain was entitled to special tax treatment. Mechanically, the taxpayer was permitted to exclude a specified percentage (50 or 60 percent, depending on the year the transaction occurred) of the net long-term gain entirely from the tax computation, and only the remaining portion of the net long-term gain was included in ordinary income. When the maximum tax bracket was 50 percent, exclusion of half of the gain in effect meant that the maximum tax rate applicable to long-term capital gains was 25 percent. When the exclusion was 60 percent, the maximum tax rate on long-term capital gains was 20 percent (only 50 percent of the remaining 40 percent was subject to tax). When the maximum tax bracket was 70 percent, the exclusion of half the gain might theoretically lead to a tax rate higher than the 25 percent applicable to long-term capital gains, but in those years, a maximum 25 percent rate on long-term capital gains was also specifically mandated.

Long-term capital losses were also treated differently from ordinary losses. Losses from capital assets that were for personal use (such as a residence or an automobile) were not deductible at all. Other long-term capital losses (after the netting process described above) were deductible against ordinary income only up to the amount of $3,000, and long-term capital losses counted for only one-half, so that $6,000 of long-term losses were needed to obtain a $3,000 deduction. The precise treatment of net capital losses varied somewhat depending on the year in question.

Short-term capital gains (after the netting process described above) were includable in ordinary income in their entirety, while short-term capital losses were deductible in full against ordinary income.

In these pre-1986 years, it was generally desirable to structure sales and exchanges so that the taxpayer showed either a net long-term capital gain or a short-term capital loss, or even better, an ordinary loss.

To complicate matters further, the sale of depreciable properties used in a trade or business that do not fall within the definition of "capital asset" may nevertheless be entitled to the best of both worlds: to long-term capital gain treatment in the case of a gain and ordinary loss treatment in the event of a loss. Such gain, however, in some circumstances might be recaptured and subject to ordinary income treatment. Similarly, other capital asset transactions were made subject to other complex recapture provisions, all designed to limit the ability of taxpayers to transmute ordinary income into long-term capital gain. Again the precise rules applicable to these situations vary somewhat, depending on the year in which the transaction occurred.

§12.19.2 Evaluation of the Treatment of Capital Gains and Losses Under the 1986 Act

As indicated above, the 1986 Tax Act eliminated all special treatment of long-term capital gains after 1987. The application of the $3,000 maximum deduction for long-term capital losses nevertheless continues to apply after 1987, but the old two-for-one rule is eliminated.

Certainly one advantage of the 1986 Act is that the elimination of the differential favorable rate for long-term capital gains eliminates the significance of much of the elaborate embroideries of tax provisions on an already complex tax structure. These embroideries, nevertheless, were not repealed for future years, so that the traditional capital gain/capital loss treatment may be restored simply by Congress reimposing a differential rate on long-term capital gains.

A second argument that a special rate for long-term capital gains is unnecessary under the 1986 Act tax rates is that the principal justification for the special rate was to avoid squeezing an incremental gain over several years into a single year when the capital asset is sold or exchanged. This was particularly unfair when the pre-1986 progressive tax structure was applicable, but it is unlikely to be unfair under the two- or three-bracket tax structure mandated by the 1986 Tax Act.

On the other hand, it has been feared that the complete elimination of special tax treatment for long-term capital gains may lead investors to stress current income at the expense of risk-taking in new ventures promising higher growth returns in the future. It is difficult to assess how much of these fears are based on a self-interest in the favorable tax rate and how much on a genuine concern that the 1986 Tax Act in this regard may have counterproductive consequences. Most industrial countries tax long-term capital gains at low rates or not at all. One commentator's initial examination of the 1986 tax reform was that it is somewhat pro-consumption and short-changes savings and investment. He concluded, however, that "only time will tell whether there is need for corrective action."

Raising the tax on capital gains for the transition year 1987 did cause a burst of sales at the end of 1986. Perhaps those that did not liquidate unrealized long-term capital gains in existing investments in 1986 may feel locked in to existing investments, and hold them to await more favorable treatment of long-term capital gains in the future. If this "locking in" phenomenon occurs, it may slow the flow of capital to more efficient uses and, ironically, will reduce tax receipts in later years.

F. OTHER TYPES OF TAXPAYERS

§12.20 Partnerships and Corporations

Corporations are generally treated as separate taxable entities under the Internal Revenue Code with their own sets of rules and own tax schedules. Partnerships, on the other hand, are not treated as separate taxable entities. Rather, partnerships file information returns showing the results of operations and allocating the profit or loss among the partners. The partners then must include the income or loss in their own personal returns, whether or not any monies are in fact distributed to them. This method of taxation is usually called *pass through* or *conduit* taxation. The limitations on deductions of passive losses and investment interest discussed earlier are applicable to investment interest or passive losses incurred by the partnership: In other words, the same individual limitations on deductibility exist whether the investment is made individually or in the form of a partnership.

§12.20.1 Corporation Tax Rates

Unlike a partnership, a corporation is viewed by the Internal Revenue Code as a separate legal entity and separate legal taxpayer. Under the 1986 Act, corporations are subject to tax on income at the following rates:

Taxable income	Tax rate
Not over $50,000	15%
Over $50,000, under $75,000	25%
Over $75,000	34%

An additional 5 percent surtax is imposed on a corporation's taxable income in excess of $100,000 to phase out the lower graduated rates for income under $75,000. This additional 5 percent tax is similar to that imposed on high-income individuals. The effect is that corporations with incomes from $100,000 to $335,000 pay at the rate of 39 percent; above $335,000, all corporations pay a flat tax at a 34 percent rate for all of their income.

In addition, there is an alternative minimum tax for corporations that taxes at a flat 20 percent a corporation's alternative minimum taxable income. This income is computed by taking the corporation's regular taxable income and increasing it by specified tax preferences: accelerated depreciation on real and personal property, rapid amortization, and (in a novel provision described in §12.16) 75 percent of the difference between the taxpayer's adjusted net book income and its alternative minimum taxable income.

§12.20.2 The Double Taxation of Corporations

The income of a corporation is subject to a *double tax*. This double tax arises because the corporation income tax is not in lieu of the personal income tax but in addition to it. Thus, if a corporation has earnings, those earnings are subject to the corporate income tax at the above rates. If the corporation then distributes all or part of its income that remains to its shareholders, the amount received by the shareholders is a taxable dividend and subject to the individual income tax at whatever rate is applicable to the individual share-holders. The result is that doing business in the corporate form, accompanied by a policy of distributing excess earnings in the form of dividends is the most expensive possible way, tax-wise, to conduct the business.

In small corporations, it is often possible to avoid the double tax by paying the income to shareholders in the form of salaries, rent, interest, or other payments that are deductible by the corporation. It is also possible in many situations to avoid the double tax problem by conducting business in the form of a partnership or limited partnership, or by the corporation electing S corporation treatment, as described below. See also Chapter 13.

The tax schedule for corporations described above should be compared with the tax schedule in §12.10 for individuals. For businesses that produce large amounts of income and have owners in the highest tax brackets, the highest effective corporate rate of 34 percent (or 39 percent if the special 5 percent corporate surcharge is applicable) is higher than the maximum individual rate of 28 percent (or 33 percent with the special individual surcharge). This pattern is a reversal of the traditional relationship between individual and corporate rates that existed before the 1986 Tax Act. Under these rates, it is more desirable from a tax standpoint to conduct business in a form that permits a noncorporate method of tax treatment than in the traditional corporate form.

When starting a new business, the organizers usually have the choice of forming a corporation or conducting the business in the form of a partnership. One consequence of choosing one over the other is the tax schedule the participants elect to have the business profits be taxed under. However, nontax considerations are also often important in making the selection of business form, and one cannot conclude that simply because of the tax provisions now applicable, one form is necessarily more desirable than another. These matters are discussed in greater detail in Chapter 13.

§12.20.3 S Corporation Election

The taxation of corporations is further complicated by the existence of another important election for corporations with less than 35 shareholders who are all individuals (or estates of deceased individuals). Such a corporation may elect to be taxed under Subchapter S of the Internal Revenue Code, which results in the corporation being taxed essentially like a partnership even though it possesses corporate characteristics. Under the 1986 Tax Act, this election is extremely popular since it permits small corporations with relatively few shareholders to combine the corporate advantages of limited liability and structured management with the tax advantages of avoiding both the higher corporate income tax rate and the double taxation problem. This election is also discussed in Chapter 13 in connection with the most appropriate business form for a new business enterprise.

A corporation that has elected to be taxed under Subchapter S is called an *S corporation*. All other corporations are called *C corporations* since they are taxed under Chapter C of the Internal Revenue Code.

§12.21 Income Taxation of Trusts and Estates

Trusts and estates are also separate taxpayers for purposes of the federal income tax law and must file income tax returns and often pay income taxes. This responsibility is independent of, and different from, the possible responsibility of such entities for gift and estate taxes.

The tax schedule shown in Table 12-2 applies to the taxable income of trusts and estates. Estates and trusts file income tax returns on Form 1041. Both estates and trusts, however, may largely avoid the payment of income tax by making distributions of income to the beneficiaries entitled thereto. The

Table 12-2

If taxable income is:	*The tax is:*
Not over $5,000	15% of taxable income
Over $5,000, under $13,000	$750 plus 28% of taxable income over $5,000
Over $13,000, under $26,000	$2,990 plus 33% of taxable income over $13,000
Over $26,000	28% of taxable income

beneficiaries must then include those distributions in their tax returns as income. See Line 17 of the Form 1040 reprinted on page 272, supra.

§12.21.1 The Tax Consequences of the Death of a Taxpayer

When a person dies, his or her representative must file a final return in the decedent's name for the period ending with death. The estate must then file an estate income tax return for the period beginning the day after the date of death and ending on a date selected by the fiduciary for the estate. Annual returns from the estate may be necessary thereafter. The income items included in the return of the estate may include investment income from assets owned by the estate, gains from the sale or exchange of estate property, and by the receipt of post-death income items attributable to services of the decedent, such as fees for services provided by the decedent before death if payment is received after death. These latter items are called *income in respect of a decedent*.

In calculating taxable income, an estate may claim expenses in much the same manner as an individual. An estate is also entitled to a single $600 personal exemption.

An important rule affecting the income tax consequences of the death of a person is the step-up in basis of property that automatically occurs upon the death of the owner. The basis of all property owned by the decedent automatically becomes its fair market value on the date of death. This principle often results in elderly or ill individuals refraining from selling or disposing of appreciated properties during the remainder of their lifetimes. The appreciation in value during the lifetime of the decedent escapes taxation entirely.

§12.21.2 Trusts

The taxation of trusts is considerably more complicated than the taxation of estates and cannot be adequately summarized in a brief comment. A taxpayer may create numerous trusts and each will be a separate taxpayer unless the Service determines that tax avoidance was a principal factor in their creation and the beneficiaries are substantially identical. In addition, trusts may be created in which the trustee has authority to distribute income or accumulate it for long periods. Further, a grantor of a trust may reserve substantial powers of management and control, and may also retain a reversionary interest in the trust. All of these arrangements are dealt with in some detail in the Tax Code.

Certain revocable trusts and short-term trusts are not recognized as separate taxpayers. The income from such trusts is taxed directly to the creator.

V

◇

THE PRINCIPLES OF BUSINESS
ORGANIZATION

CHAPTER 13

SELECTING THE FORM OF A BUSINESS ORGANIZATION

§13.1 Introduction

One of the most important topics covered in traditional law or business school corporations or business organization courses is the selection of the most appropriate business form for a new venture. The choices that are usually considered are: general partnership or proprietorship, limited partnership, and corporation. The corporate form may be further subdivided on the basis of an important tax election, between a *C corporation* and an *S corporation*. See generally §§12.20.2 and 12.20.3 for a discussion of the importance of this election from a tax standpoint.

The important economic, legal, and tax differences between these forms of organization that largely dictate which form is best for a specific business are presented in Table 13-1 on pages 324-325 of this chapter. In functional terms, when considering which form of business is most suitable for a specific enterprise, the following factors are the most significant ones:

1. Considerations of internal efficiency, operational cost, and organizational convenience;

2. Considerations of limited liability and the responsibility of the owners of a business for its debts;

3. The minimization of federal income taxation; and

4. Considerations relating to the ease of raising capital in the future.

Traditional corporation texts also discuss the differences between the forms of business organization partially in terms of legal differences (i.e., "continuity of life," "centralization of management," and "free transferability of interest"). These factors are also discussed below, but they are less important than the functional differences listed above because they are not truly unique characteristics of a specific form of business enterprise. By suitable advance planning a considerable degree of "continuity of life," "centralization of management," and "free transferability of interest" may be granted to, or withheld from, any form of business organization.

There are only a limited number of organizational forms suitable for most modern businesses, and each form combines in a unique way the considerations discussed above.

A. FORMS OF BUSINESS ENTERPRISE

§13.2 Proprietorships

Consider first a business that is to be operated by a single person. Perhaps it is a service business, for example, an accountant going into business on her own, an attorney hanging out a shingle, or a person good with his hands putting up a sign offering to do odd repair jobs. In these simple situations, it is almost always convenient to conduct the business as a *proprietorship*. A proprietorship is simply a business individually owned by a single person.

In the very simplest cases there may be little or no distinction between the affairs of the business and the affairs of the individual owner. However, most proprietors find it necessary or desirable to keep a fair degree of separation between the business and the owner for accounting and record-keeping purposes. At the very least a set of books is maintained independent of the personal accounts of the individual owner. This simplifies the preparation of tax returns and permits the owner to identify the profitability of his or her endeavors. It also permits ready identification of property that is formally devoted to the business. In addition, a proprietorship today normally has its own bank account, stationery, and other distinguishing characteristics that indicate the separation of business transactions from personal ones.

Whether the degree of separation between the owner's personal and business affairs is large or small, it is useful to discuss the owner (the proprietor) and the business (the proprietorship) as though they were separate entities.

A proprietor may conduct business either in his or her own name or in a trade or assumed name. Many states have assumed name statutes that require a public disclosure of the identity of a person conducting business in an assumed or trade name, but that is a simple and straightforward process. Often proprietorships do business and enter into contracts in the form "John Jones dba Jones Construction Company." *Dba* (or *d/b/a*) stands for "doing business as." In this way both the proprietor and the trade name under which he or she is conducting business appear on most business transactions. There are few restrictions on the use of trade or assumed names: As long as the name is not misleadingly similar to the name of a competing business or otherwise used in a fraudulent or deceptive manner, a person may conduct business in any name he or she wishes. However, a few words, such as *corporation*, *Incorporated*, or *Inc.* may not be used because they falsely imply that the business is incorporated. The word *company* does not carry this implication.

The owner of a proprietorship may act individually or employ one or more agents, employees, or managers to act on his or her behalf. As a result, the proprietor can delegate business-related activity and decisions freely to subordinates or employees and may take a vacation without the business shutting down if there are agents he or she trusts. Thus, the benefits of efficiency and flexibility that arise from specialization and separation of functions are as readily available in a proprietorship as they are in other forms of business enterprise.

The owner of a proprietorship is entitled to the fruits of the business, that is, its income and cash flow (after making due provision for its debts), without any formality or difficulty. For example, a proprietor may simply empty the cash drawer of the business to pay for his personal vacation if that does not disrupt business operations and appropriate records are maintained.

For legal purposes, a proprietorship is not a separate entity. For example, the owner of a proprietorship is liable for all business debts. A proprietor of a business may borrow money on his or her personal credit either for personal use (e.g., a family vacation) or for use in the business. If such a loan is unsecured, the creditor may levy upon either personal or business assets if there is a default without regard to whether the loan was originally used for business or personal purposes. Loans may also be obtained solely in the name of, and on the credit of, the proprietorship but the proprietor is individually liable on such loans whether or not his or her name appears on the note or whether he or she actually negotiated the loan and signed the note. Often a proprietorship purchases inventory, supplies, or machinery in its assumed name on credit secured by a lien or security interest in the property being purchased. The owner of the business is personally liable on these obligations as well, though the creditor in these situations may as a practical matter look only to the property securing the loan or to the assets of the business itself in determining whether or not to extend credit.

Similarly, if the business becomes involved in litigation, the proprietor is the appropriate plaintiff; if the business is sued, the proprietor is the proper defendant. In litigation involving a proprietorship it is customary in many jurisdictions to use the "dba" designation when describing the party suing or being sued.

A proprietorship is not a separate taxable entity and no separate federal income tax return is filed, though the proprietor must file a schedule C with his or her personal return showing revenues and expenses of the business. The proprietor must also obtain an employer's identification number from the IRS. The business may also have to obtain local permits to engage in specific businesses or occupy space for commercial purposes. Again, these permits are usually issued in the "dba" form. If it is a law, medical, or accounting practice, of course, the owner must be a licensed professional.

If the proprietorship opens an office in a different state, there are no additional formalities or consents required other than those applicable to any-one engaging in that business in the new state.

§13.3 General Partnerships

A partnership is a logical extension of a proprietorship where there is more than one owner. A partnership (sometimes called a *general partnership* to distinguish it from the *limited partnership* discussed in §13.5) is the operation of a business by co-owners. It can be formed simply by a handshake. There is generally no need for a written agreement and no public filing of any document other than an assumed name certificate that may be required if the business is conducted under a trade name and not the names of the partners. With respect to local permits and qualifications, interstate operations and the like, generally the same rules are applicable to partnerships as to proprietorships.

Some additional complexity is created, of course, simply because there is more than one owner. In a proprietorship, the owner calls all the shots. In a partnership, there is more than one owner, and some principles must be established for determining how decisions are to be made and how the rights of individual partners are to be ascertained. Most of the law of partnership that is discussed in law school courses deals with the rights and duties of partners among themselves rather than with the relationship of the partnership to the outside world.

§13.3.1 Sources of Partnership Law

The law of partnership is largely codified in the Uniform Partnership Act (UPA) that has been adopted by virtually every state, though some areas of partnership law are still governed by common law principles.

The UPA recognizes that the primary source of law relating to a specific partnership is the partnership agreement. Indeed, partners are able to structure their relationships by appropriate provisions in the partnership agreement to a considerably greater extent than participants in other forms of business enterprise. The partnership agreement is often called the "law" of that particular partnership. The UPA departs from this consensual model in two important respects:

1. The UPA includes a variety of *default provisions* that govern aspects of the partnership relation in the absence of express agreement on those aspects. These default provisions are most likely to be applicable to "handshake partnerships" without formal written partnership agreements and partnership arrangements entered into by nonlawyers without legal assistance. However, even carefully drafted partnership agreements sometimes do not cover all matters. These default provisions sometimes create problems because they are not always the provisions that would have been selected by businesspeople for the specific situation if the possibility of that situation arising had been brought to their attention at the time the partnership agreement was being negotiated. It is generally desirable to agree explicitly on basic rights, powers, and duties rather than to rely on these default provisions.

Most of the default provisions in the UPA can be identified by the presence of the phrase "unless otherwise agreed" somewhere in the statutory provision.

2. The UPA also contains several mandatory provisions governing the relationships among partners that probably cannot be varied by the agreement among partners. These mandatory provisions include a broad fiduciary duty that exists among all partners, the power of every partner to dissolve the partnership by his or her express will at any time, the unlimited liability of every partner for partnership obligations, and the apparent authority of partners to bind the partnership to obligations within the apparent scope of the corporate business. These mandatory provisions largely codify common law partnership principles.

In 1988, the Commissioners on Uniform State Laws announced a project to revise and update the UPA.

§13.3.2 Control and Management

In the absence of an agreement to the contrary, the partners in a partnership have equal rights to participate in the management of the business, which can be conducted with whatever degree of informality the partners desire. If a vote is taken on specific matters each partner has one vote and the majority decision controls in the absence of an agreement to the contrary. Where financial contributions are unequal, the normal assumption by businessmen is that votes should be weighted in accordance with relative financial interests rather than being on a per capita basis, but this is not the case unless the partners so agree.

The partnership agreement may create classes of partners with different voting and financial rights. For example, classes of "junior" or "senior" partners may be created or a "managing partner" or "managing committee" with designated rights and responsibilities may be established. Many law firms utilize classes of partners in this fashion to ensure that the senior partners have power to govern the affairs of the partnership.

Partners also have apparent and actual authority to bind the partnership to obligations relating to the business of the partnership. In the absence of knowledge by the third party, a partner may bind the partnership on obligations he or she was not authorized by the partnership to create. The partner so acting is presumably in breach of his or her obligations under the partnership agreement, but the partnership is nevertheless bound by the commitment entered into by the partner.

§13.3.3 Financial Provisions

Partners may share profits and losses in any way they agree and they may agree to share losses in a different way than they share profits. Profits may be shared on a flat percentage basis, in proportion to the relative financial investments in the partnership, on a sliding scale based on receipts attributable to each partner's efforts, or on some other basis. One or more partners may be paid a fixed salary which the agreement requires to be viewed as an expense of the business (i.e., deducted from revenues before calculating distributable income). Alternatively, the agreement may provide that the salary is to be charged against the partner's distributive share with the proviso that no refund is required in any year in which the salary exceeds that partner's distributive share for the year. This arrangement is usually called a *guaranteed payment.* In the absence of an agreement about how profits are to be shared, the default provision of the UPA is that partners share profits equally. Where relative contributions of the partners are unequal it is unlikely that the parties would desire profits to be shared equally. In the absence of an agreement as to how losses should be shared, the default provision is that losses are shared in the same proportion as profits are shared. It is often desirable to share losses on a basis different than profits are shared.

Since profits are determined on an annual basis, *drawing accounts* or advances may be authorized so that each partner may draw specified amounts monthly or weekly against the ultimate distribution of profits for living purposes during the year. Many partnership agreements provide for three different ownership accounts for each partner: a *capital account*, reflecting amounts invested by each partner in the business, an *income account* to which is credited income as it is ascertained and allocated among the partners, and the drawing account described above. The drawing account is usually closed out against the income account on an annual basis. Income earned in excess of distributions may be paid to each partner in a lump sum shortly after the close of the accounting period, or may be added to the capital account in whole or in part to be retained by the partnership or withdrawn by the partner at a later time. In partnership practice, a distinction is drawn between allocations of *income* and allocations of *cash available for distribution.* Allocations of income determine tax liability while allocations of cash determine how much a partner can withdraw and is based on the cash flow within the partnership.

Each partner is unlimitedly liable for the debts of the partnership. This unlimited liability is independent of whatever agreement exists among the partners as to how losses should be shared. In other words, any partner may be called upon to pay a specific partnership debt at any time by a creditor. If a partner does so, he or she then has a right to reimbursement from the partnership or from the other partners in accordance with the agreed-upon loss-sharing ratio. If one or more partners are insolvent or unable to pay their agreed-upon share of partnership losses, the solvent partners must do so.

A distinction is also made in partnership law between *partnership* obligations and *personal* obligations of individual partners. The distinction is basically between business debts of the partnership and personal or individual debts of a partner. A personal creditor of a partner cannot attach or seize partnership assets: Such a creditor must proceed against the interest of the partner in the partnership through the device of a *charging order*. The protection of partnership assets against seizure by individual creditors reflects the fact that all partners have interests in partnership assets and that a partnership business should not be disrupted because of the financial problems of an individual partner. Partnership creditors, on the other hand, may proceed directly against either partnership assets or the personal assets of any partner.

§13.3.4 *Contributions of Property or Services*

The contributions of one partner to a partnership may differ from the contributions of other partners either in amount or in kind. For example, it is very common for one partner to contribute his or her services, primarily or exclusively, while one or more other partners contribute capital or property, primarily or exclusively. In effect the service partners are managing a business financed by the capital-contributing partners.

Elements of bargaining and negotiation are inevitably involved in the formation and operation of such partnerships. In negotiating a partnership agreement that involves dissimilar contributions, interests may conflict; a single lawyer should be very cautious about agreeing to represent different interests simultaneously in such a situation. Each partner should be encouraged to have individual legal representation.

Where one partner is contributing services over a period of time for a partnership interest, and another partner is contributing capital immediately, difficult issues may arise as to when the service partner should be deemed to have "earned" his or her interest, what the value of the contributed services is, and what the responsibilities of the respective partners are if the partnership incurs losses. The default provisions of the UPA are unhelpful in this regard since they simply provide that in the absence of agreement, (a) partners are not entitled to compensation for services rendered on behalf of the partnership and (b) as among themselves, each partner must contribute toward losses in accordance with his or her share of the profits.

In law partnerships, when an associate is made a partner, provision may be made for the new partner to make a capital contribution to the partnership; as a practical matter this contribution must usually be in the form of reduced cash distributions for a limited period of time.

§13.3.5 Dissolution, Winding up, and Continuation of the Business

A basic principle of partnership law is that a partner has the power to compel dissolution by his or her express will at any time. In addition, a partnership may be dissolved in a variety of other circumstances set forth in the UPA, including the death of a partner, but the unique feature of partnership law that distinguishes it from corporation law is that each partner has inherent power to dissolve the relationship at any time.

The power to dissolve a partnership at any time may not be free, however. The partnership agreement may provide that the partnership is to continue for a specified term or until the occurrence of a specified event. A dissolution by a partner before the expiration of the term or the occurrence of the event is a breach of the partnership agreement and opens the dissolving party to liability for breach of contract. On the other hand, if the partnership agreement does not set forth a specified term, it creates a *partnership at will* which may be dissolved at any time without liability by the express will of any partner. Informal partnerships are almost always partnerships at will and many formal partnerships are also. A partnership that is to continue for a specified term or until the occurrence of a specified event is usually called a *partnership for a term*.

Partnership agreements often provide that upon the death or withdrawal of a partner, the partnership continues and the withdrawing partner or his or her estate is entitled to receive the value of the partnership interest as specified in the agreement. The agreement often specifies how the value is to be calculated and the period over which it is to be paid. Provisions of this nature are binding on the withdrawing partner and his or her estate in accordance with the general principle that the partnership agreement is the law of that partnership. In the absence of an agreement, the default provisions of the UPA provide that upon the dissolution of a partnership, the withdrawing partner or his or her estate may compel the partnership business to be wound up and liquidated, or alternatively may permit the partnership business to continue and be entitled to receive the value of the partnership interest at the time of dissolution plus either interest or a continuing share of the profits until payment is made, at the election of the withdrawing partner or the estate.

Where the partnership continues, a question sometimes arises as to whether a new partnership has been created following the dissolution of the old, or whether the old partnership continues, at least with respect to the partners who remain in the business. This appears to be purely a conceptual question on which no substantive issue turns.

§13.3.6 Fiduciary Duties

The relation between partners is one of trust and confidence. This follows necessarily from the agency powers of each partner to bind the partnership to obligations as well as the concept of cooperative enterprise inherent in a partnership. The relation of trust and confidence is enforced judicially through the recognition of a broad fiduciary duty each partner owes to the other in connection with all matters relating to the partnership. This duty may require voluntary disclosure of relevant information. It continues to exist even though the partners are antagonistic to each other and are in the process of dissolving their relationship; it also covers all activities relating to the use and distribution of partnership property.

§13.3.7 The Partnership as an Entity

A long and rather sterile debate exists as to whether a partnership should be viewed as a separate legal entity or whether it is, like a proprietorship, simply an extension of the individual partners without separate legal status. The distinction is usually phrased in terms of whether a partnership is an *entity* or an *aggregate* of the partners. The UPA contains internal evidence of both theories: Much of the early case law adopts the aggregate theory, but the modern view strongly tends to treat the partnership as a separate legal entity. The characterization may be important when analyzing issues not specifically addressed in the UPA.

A partnership is not a separate taxable entity under the Internal Revenue Code. Under the federal income tax law, a partnership must prepare an information return each year that shows partnership income and expenses, and allocates the income or loss of the partnership to the individual partners in accordance with the partnership agreement. Each individual partner must then include in his or her personal income tax return the amount of the income or loss so allocated. See §12.20. It should be observed that a positive allocation of income to a specific partner for tax purposes often occurs even though the partnership may not in fact make any distributions of cash or property to that partner with respect to the year in question. Similarly, a partnership may have a loss for tax purposes in one or more years even though it makes substantial capital distributions during those years to the partners.

A partnership is also not an entity for purposes of most state statutes requiring foreign corporations to register if they transact business in the state. It is usually viewed as an entity for purposes of litigation (though rules differ from state to state). In most states, for example, it is possible to sue a partnership without suing individually any of the partners, and partners may be held individually liable only if the complaint or other process expressly states that recovery is being sought from their individual assets. These rules about procedure and civil process, of course, do not affect the basic responsibility of each partner for the debts of the partnership if they are made defendants in the litigation on an individual basis.

§13.3.8 Miscellaneous

Abstractly, it seems obviously desirable not only to have an agreement dealing with the various rights of partners but also to have it reduced to writing so that rights and duties are explicitly defined and known not only to the partners themselves but also to their heirs and assignees. The preparation of such an agreement usually requires the services of a lawyer and thus increases the costs of formation. Even in situations in which cost is no problem, a surprisingly large number of partnerships, including some law partnerships, operate successfully for many years without a written agreement. Of course, the partners may have verbal or implicit understandings as to how the business should be conducted. The major problems likely to arise in this scenario are falling outs that may occur between partners and the problem of succession upon death or retirement.

Whether or not there is a formal written agreement, a partnership is inherently a more complex and expensive manner of conducting business than a single person running a proprietorship. Nevertheless, it is usually less expensive than alternative forms of business operation involving several owners, and is often the most convenient form of operation for many small businesses if the unlimited liability of each partner for partnership obligations is not a matter of serious concern to any partner.

§13.4 Joint Ventures

Many cases involving partnership-like relations describe the relationship as a *joint venture* rather than a partnership. If there is any difference, it is that a joint venture involves a more limited business purpose than a partnership — perhaps a partnership for a single transaction. Most partnership rules are applicable to joint ventures, the major difference being in the scope of the actual and apparent authority that each joint venturer possesses to bind the venture.

There is some tendency for courts to accept the categorization of the agreement itself—e.g., an arrangement that is created pursuant to a joint venture agreement is likely to be referred to as a joint venture rather than a partnership by the courts. However, there appear to be relatively few practical differences in the legal principles applicable to a partnership and to a joint venture.

§13.5 Limited Partnerships

A limited partnership differs from a general partnership in that there are one or more partners, called *limited partners*, who are not personally liable for the debts of the partnership and who are not expected to participate in the day-to-day affairs of the partnership. In effect, limited partners stand to lose what they have invested in the enterprise but no more. Partners who are not named as limited partners are called *general partners* and are unlimitedly liable for the debts of the business. If a limited partner does take part in the control of the business in more than nominal ways, he or she may lose the shield of limited liability and become personally liable on some or all of the partnership debts. Under the statutes of many states, a limited partner may also lose the shield of limited liability if his or her surname is part of the partnership name or if he or she makes contributions to the limited partnership in the form of services rather than cash or property. The reasons for all of these restrictions on limited partners are obscure, though it appears probable that they are based on the assumption that these activities are likely to mislead third persons into believing that the limited partner is really a general partner.

Unlike the law of partnership, there is apparently no common law of limited partnerships. The limited partnership is a form of business created exclusively by state statute: In the absence of statute, all partners presumably are general partners no matter what they are called in the partnership agreement. State laws recognizing limited partnerships are largely based on the Uniform Limited Partnership Act of 1913, the Revised Uniform Limited Partnership Act of 1976, or a 1986 revision of the 1976 Act. Since a number of states have adopted modifications to these uniform acts, the degree of diversity in state limited partnership statutes is considerably greater than in the case of general partnership statutes.

Limited partnership statutes deal with a variety of matters. A limited partnership is created by the public filing of either the partnership agreement itself or of a *certificate*. The certificate must include designated financial and other information about the business and the general and limited partners. Unlike a general partnership, a limited partnership cannot be created simply by a handshake. (An attempt to create a limited partnership by a handshake will probably result in the creation of a general partnership.) There must be a public filing that sets forth prescribed information. The modern trend is to reduce significantly the amount of information required, but many statutes require full disclosure of the amounts of all contributions by limited partners. The name of a limited partnership must contain the word "limited" or a similar word indicating that some participants have limited liability. Foreign limited partnerships may have to register or qualify as foreign entities if the benefits of limited liability are to be available for transactions entered into by them in the jurisdiction. Where limited partnership agreements are silent, the general law of partnership supplements the limited partnership statute.

A major problem with the limited partnership as a business form is uncertainty over what powers the limited partners may retain consistently with the statutory admonition that they not take part in the "control of the business." Older statutes simply state the "control" test without indicating which actions involve taking part in "control" and which do not. Modern statutes address this problem in various ways. Some statutes contain a list of activities that limited partners may engage in without losing their shield of limited liability. This is a kind of safe harbor statute, but it casts serious doubt on whether limited partners can ever engage in unlisted activities without losing their shield of limited liability. Other statutes provide that isolated acts not involving general participation in the business by a limited partner create liability only with respect to creditors who are aware of the acts. Nevertheless, uncertainty over specific activities continues to be a problem, and this uncertainty is an important deterrent to the routine use of the limited partnership form of business for many ventures.

In some rare situations, limited partners may be willing to accept the risk of unlimited liability in exchange for management powers. This usually occurs where general partners have acted improperly but have disappeared or become insolvent, or where the limited partnership is insolvent but some limited partners believe something may be salvaged. General partners often insert in limited partnership agreements affirmative prohibitions against limited partners assuming management roles in the business, though the efficacy of these provisions in extreme situations is doubtful.

§13.5.1 Limited Partnerships in Modern Practice

The modern limited partnership often bears little resemblance to a traditional partnership, or presumably to the type of small and local business originally envisioned by the draftsmen of the original Uniform Limited Partnership Act. The reason is that the limited partnership is an ideal business form for tax shelters since it permits a combination of factors unavailable in any other business form: limited liability of investors without limitation as to their number plus partnership tax treatment for them for federal income tax purposes. See Chapter 12, particularly §§12.6, 12.11, and 12.20.

The modern limited partnership has also been shaped by another development. Until the middle of the twentieth century, the rule was universally accepted that a corporation could not be a general partner in a partnership since the duties of corporate management to the shareholders were viewed as inherently inconsistent with the fiduciary duties a partner owed to its copartners. A corporate general partner therefore created insoluble conflicts of interest. Statements to this effect may still appear in some treatises, but the modern view, accepted today in virtually all states, is now precisely the opposite: Corporations may act as general partners without limitation. Most tax shelter limited partnerships created today take advantage of this rule and have only a corporation as a general partner. Thus, the typical modern limited partnership consists of a single general corporate partner and hundreds or thousands of limited partners whose principal motivation for investing is to obtain tax benefits in the form of deductible losses or tax-sheltered income.

The use of a corporate general partner apparently results in a partnership in which no individual is personally liable for the partnership obligations. The IRS recognizes these organizations as eligible for partnership taxation only if the corporate general partner has substantial assets invested in the partnership.

Because the modern limited partnership is a tax-oriented investment vehicle, provisions relating to distributions and allocations of income, loss, and excess cash flow are often extremely complex. Limited partnership agreements may provide, for example, for the allocation of income or loss on one basis and the allocation of excess cash on a different basis. These ratios may shift after the limited partners have received a return of their cash investments in order to increase the shares allocable to the corporate general partner which is owned by the original entrepreneurs.

§13.5.2 Master Limited Partnerships

In the 1980s, publicly held limited partnerships were developed. These organizations issue limited partnership interests that are readily marketable and traded either over-the-counter or on securities exchanges much as though they were shares of stock. See §§18.3 and 18.11. This public trading is technically trading in depository receipts for limited partnership interests rather than in the interests themselves. A *master limited partnership* is the organization issuing these publicly traded interests.

A master limited partnership is more attractive than a corporation as a business form only for tax reasons. The theory of master limited partnerships is that investors benefit from a "pass-through" of tax characteristics of income in certain types of businesses (e.g., extraction of natural resources), and as a result the financial return to investors is improved if the business is conducted in the form of a master limited partnership rather than a corporation. In 1987, Congress restricted the ability of new master limited partnerships to provide these desirable tax characteristics to investors, and it is therefore likely that the growth of this form of business has ended.

§13.6 Corporations

A corporation is a relatively complex form of business that plays a vital role in modern American society. Aspects of financial concepts relating to corporations are discussed at length in Chapters 14 through 17 of this book, and trading in securities issued by corporations is discussed in Chapters 18 through 20. This introductory section only describes the most fundamental aspects of corporateness.

§13.6.1 What Is a Corporation?

A corporation is usually viewed as a fictitious legal entity separate from its owners, the shareholders. The fictitious entity is created by a public filing with the secretary of state (or other designated public official in the state) and the payment of a filing fee. In comparison to proprietorships and general partnerships, this is a relatively expensive form of business organization, since legal assistance is usually involved not only in its creation but also in its continued operation. Tax costs at the state level are relatively high since all states impose annual franchise or stock taxes on corporations. Further, corporations engaged in business in several states may have to qualify to transact business in each state and thereby becomes subject to taxes in each state.

The nature of the fictitious entity that is a corporation is never precisely defined. A corporation can be envisioned as an artificial person having most of the same powers, rights, and duties that an individual has. This artificial person has no flesh, no blood, no eyes, or mouth but it may nevertheless do many things that real people do: it may sue and be sued, enter into contracts, purchase property, run a business, and so forth.

In considering what it really means to conduct business in the corporate form, it is useful to consider the one-person corporation, that is, a corporation in which one single individual owns all the outstanding shares of the corporation. In effect, the business is an incorporated proprietorship. One should understand precisely what the notion of a fictitious entity means in this situation. In practical and economic effect, the shareholder runs the business much as though it were a proprietorship. He or she decides what business the corporation should be in, whether it should enter into specific contracts, what price to charge for its products, and so forth. The shareholder in a sense also owns the entire corporation since he or she owns all the outstanding shares. Indeed, the combination of total ownership and total control in this situation often leads the shareholder to believe that he or she owns the corporation's business and property much as though the business were conducted in the form of an unincorporated proprietorship. "I own this business," he or she may proudly say. While in an economic sense this is true, in the legal sense it is not at all true. If a business is incorporated, the assets of the business are owned by the corporation, not by the person who owns the shares in the corporation. The shares are property but they are not the corporate assets. Further, the shareholder exercises control over corporation activities not through ownership of business assets but by serving the corporation basically as its sole agent. Manifestly a fictitious entity can only act through agents. Assume that a sole shareholder decides she wants to be employed by the corporation and receive a salary. Acting as agent on behalf of the corporation she offers herself employment with the corporation at a salary in a specified amount, and acting as an individual she may then accept the corporation's offer. This is not a sham transaction for most purposes: the IRS, for example, unhesitatingly recognizes the validity of such transactions if the compensation is reasonable in amount, giving the corporation a deduction for salaries paid, requiring the corporation to withhold for federal income taxes, FICA, and the like, and requiring the shareholder to include as wages the amount paid to her under this arrangement.

Where does the sole shareholder in this example obtain the authority from the fictitious entity to act as its agent and offer herself the employment contract? That is the subject of corporation law: The corporation's affairs are managed by a board of directors elected by the shareholders; the sole shareholder thus elects the board of directors (which may consist of only herself in most states), and the board of directors then appoints a president or other officer (who again may be the sole shareholder) to negotiate the employment contract on behalf of the corporation. It is a bit incestuous.

The corporation provides limited liability for the shareholders because all obligations are entered into in the name of the corporation rather than in the names of the individual owners, and the corporation is a separate legal entity. Further, an agent (who may or may not be a shareholder) who commits the corporation to a transaction giving rise to liability is not personally liable on obligations negotiated on the principal's — the corporation's — behalf under accepted agency principles. The result is that a corporation, unlike a general partnership, provides (at least in theory) limited liability for its owners, and, unlike the limited partnership, the persons with limited liability in a corporation may participate freely in its management and control so long as they stay in their proper role as agents of the fictitious entity. Sophisticated creditors are unlikely to be willing to deal with a small corporation with limited assets unless the shareholder or shareholders agree to give personal guarantees to pay the corporate debt. Thus, as a practical matter, the protection against unlimited liability provided by the corporate form is not as important as might first appear.

There is obviously an element of play-acting in closely held corporations because the formalities that must be followed do not reflect the reality that the business is actually being owned and operated by individuals; the theory assumes that the same individuals assume different roles as shareholders, directors, or agents, and act according to the appropriate role. But there is a serious aspect to these formalities. A failure to follow them may result in the court "piercing the corporate veil" — and holds shareholders personally liable on corporation debts.

Since a corporation may have only one shareholder, a sole proprietor may decide to incorporate his or her business without losing control and without having to cut other people in on the action.

§13.6.2 Sources of Corporation Law

The major source of corporation law is state corporation statutes, the provisions of which of course vary from state to state. The variation is considerably wider than the statutes relating to partnerships or limited partnerships, though there is a surprising core of uniformity in these statutes. Part of this uniformity may be traced to an important model statute drafted by a committee of the American Bar Association; part may be traced to the leadership of the state of Delaware in developing significant principles of corporation law. Part may be traced to the natural tendency of one state to copy statutes that embody good ideas developed by other states.

State corporation statutes deal with issues of formation, corporate purposes and powers, internal organization (the roles of shareholders, directors, and officers), permissible securities that corporations may issue in order to raise capital, mergers and consolidations of corporations, foreign corporations, and dissolution. In addition, states may require annual reports as well as franchise tax returns and other reporting requirements. These state statutes thus largely deal with the internal relationships within a corporation, but they also may affect other important aspects of corporation behavior.

State corporation statutes are largely technical in nature and generally not the subject of extensive debate in state legislatures. Many proposed changes in corporation statutes are developed by committees of the state bar association, though these provisions must run the same legislative gauntlet as any other proposed legislation.

In the United States there is no federal or national corporation statute. Every domestic corporation, no matter how large, is incorporated under the statute of some state — usually Delaware in the case of the largest corporations. Two New Deal-era federal statutes — the Securities Act of 1933 and the Securities Exchange Act of 1934 — provide a substantial degree of federal regulation, particularly for large corporations with more than 500 shareholders of record.

In addition to state corporation statutes, all states have adopted *blue sky laws* that regulate the public sale of corporate securities within the state.

§13.6.3 The Internal Structure of a Corporation

Basically, the internal organization of a corporation consists of three levels or tiers: shareholders, directors, and officers.

Shareholders are persons who own shares in a corporation. Shares represent the ultimate ownership interests in the corporation. See Chapter 15. Shares may be divided into two or more different classes with different financial and voting rights. As described above, one individual may own all the shares of a corporation; at the other extreme, there is no limit on the number of shareholders or the number of shares that may be issued by a corporation, so that a corporation may have thousands or even millions of shareholders. Despite the wide gulf between a corporation owned by one person and a corporation with hundreds of thousands of shareholders, the two corporations are largely governed by the same theoretical organizational structure.

The board of directors has the responsibility of managing, or overseeing the management of, the corporation's business. Historically, the traditional statute required a board of directors to consist of three directors; today, in most states, a board of directors may consist of a single director, though in some states the privilege of having a board of one or two members is limited to corporations with one or two shareholders. In a few states, three directors are still required; in these states a sole proprietor planning to incorporate his business must find two loyal persons to serve as directors with him.

The board of directors selects corporate officers to execute the decisions of the board and conduct the business on a day-to-day basis. Traditional officers are a president, one or more vice presidents, a secretary, and a treasurer, though some modern statutes do not require designated offices. Most modern statutes also permit a single person to hold more than one office simultaneously, though a fair number of statutes require the corporate president and secretary to be different persons. Corporate officers may also have discretion to appoint additional assistant officers and employees. In large, publicly held corporations the corporate officers — often collectively referred to as "management" — may have considerable discretion in fact on both routine and extraordinary matters. The theory, however, is that the ultimate power of management and control rests in the board of directors, not the officers of the corporation. See generally Chapter 14.

There is no requirement that officers or directors also be shareholders, though such a requirement may be imposed voluntarily by appropriate provisions in the governing documents of the corporation. In some states, special close corporation statutes give small corporations the option of adopting management principles much as though they were general partnerships.

§13.6.4 The Documents Governing Internal Corporate Matters

The two basic documents within every corporation are the articles of incorporation and the bylaws. The articles of incorporation are filed with the appropriate state agency to form the corporation and are the basic constitution of that particular corporation. Terminology in this respect is not uniform from one state to another: In some states this basic constitutional document is known as the *charter* or the *certificate of incorporation* or by other names. Amendment of articles of incorporation generally requires approval by a specified vote of the shareholders as well as approval by the board of directors.

The bylaws constitute an internal set of rules for the governance of a corporation. It deals with such matters as elections, notices, size of board of directors, restrictions on the transfer of shares, and similar matters. The bylaws may usually be amended by the board of directors acting alone, or by the shareholders.

Many provisions relating to the internal affairs of the corporation may be placed either in the articles of incorporation or the bylaws, at the option of the management of the corporation. Provisions placed in the articles of incorporation become a matter of public record: Where the number of shareholders is large, they may be more difficult to amend. Many lawyers prefer that important and unusual governance provisions appear in the articles of incorporation rather than the bylaws because the provisions are then a matter of public record.

§13.7 Professional Corporations

Certain professions — law, medicine, and dentistry, primarily — are prohibited by ethical considerations from conducting business in the traditional corporation form. The *professional corporation* is a specially designed business form that enables such persons to obtain the benefits of incorporation and meet ethical requirements. Originally the professional corporation was developed to take advantage of special tax rules applicable to corporations, particularly the right to create more attractive pension and profit-sharing plans for employees (including shareholders) than proprietors can provide for themselves or partnerships can create for partners. These tax advantages have been largely eliminated, but modest fringe benefits are still available on a before-tax basis that cannot be claimed by proprietors or provided by a partnership to its partners. See §5.8 for a general discussion of before-tax and after-tax benefits. The continuing popularity of the professional corporation now rests primarily on the limited liability benefits discussed in §13.8 that such corporations may provide its owner in many (but not all) states.

B. COMPARATIVE ANALYSIS

§13.8 Limited Liability

As indicated above, a business that is conducted in the corporate form provides limited liability to shareholders. The shareholders may lose what they have invested in the corporation but cannot be called upon to pay debts that the corporation itself is unable to pay. This results from the fiction that a corporation is a separate legal entity and it is the corporation rather than the individual owners who has entered into the corporate obligations and is liable for the corporation's debts. While this fiction is generally accepted, it is important to recognize that it is a fiction. If a corporation is used in a way as to injure creditors in some unfair manner, a court may "pierce the corporate veil" and hold the shareholders, or some of them, personally liable to the creditors. A corporation formed by a single person who is the sole shareholder is nevertheless a separate legal entity and the sole shareholder is not automatically liable for corporate debts.

A limited partnership provides limited liability to the limited partners at the cost of prohibiting the limited partners from taking part in control of the business. A limited partner who does take part in control of the business becomes liable as a general partner to some or all of the debts of the business.

A professional corporation may provide some advantages of limited liability in specific states. Professional corporation statutes are often less than clear on the issue, but in many states the rule appears to be that the shareholders (i.e., the professionals) in a professional corporation are liable for their own malpractice, or the malpractice of employees that they supervise, but are not liable for the malpractice of other shareholders. They also may not be personally liable in many states for debts of the professional corporation not related to professional practice, such as leases of office space or purchase obligations for capital equipment. In partnerships, joint ventures, and proprietorships, the owner participants are personally liable on all the debts of the business.

As one reflects on the importance of limited liability, the first reaction of law students is usually that protection against unlimited liability is of great significance, and that in terms of selecting an appropriate business form, one should always opt for this protection. Of course, there is clearly some value in protection against unexpected liability that the corporate or limited partnership forms of business provide, but one should not overstate its importance.

First of all, large creditors often decline to deal with small corporations unless the owners (or some of them) voluntarily agree to guarantee the payment of the obligations by the corporation. Large creditors are sophisticated and understand that limited liability means that the creditor can only look to the assets of the business: They may (and usually do) decline to do business with a corporation without substantial assets unless the shareholders voluntarily guarantee repayment of the debt. Where shareholders are called upon to make personal guarantees, the value of limited liability is obviously significantly diminished.

One benefit of limited liability from the standpoint of shareholders is that there are some significant kinds of contract claims in which it is not customary or practical for the creditor to require the shareholders to give personal guarantees of the payment of the debt. An obvious example is employee wage and salary claims. Usually, the economic bargaining power of employees is such that they are in no position to ask for or obtain such guarantees. Small creditors also may not request guarantees simply because the cost of requesting and obtaining them exceed the amount of the credit they expect to extend. Other creditors may be satisfied with a purchase money security interest or other type of lien, and may not request personal guarantees. Thus, the protection of limited liability in these areas may have some favorable practical consequences from the standpoint of shareholders.

When one turns to tort liabilities, it should be immediately clear that corporations should purchase liability insurance to protect their assets from being consumed by a tort judgment. This insurance normally protects the owners of the business as well as the corporation's assets from tort claims. It is possible, of course, for a tort judgment to exceed the amount of liability insurance available, but that is at best a remote risk. One can purchase insurance against excess liability, so-called umbrella policies, for relatively small cost. The difference in annual cost between $100,000 of coverage and $10,000,000 of coverage, for example, is usually not very great.

There are some tort claims for which insurance protection is simply not available. Intentional torts fall into this category. However, the probability of such liability actually arising in a commercial context is quite small for most businesses. Further, where true intentional torts are involved, the possibility of liability being imposed through agency principles or by piercing the corporate veil of at least small, closely held corporations is probably fairly high.

There are other types of claims not falling clearly into either the contract or tort category that also may be affected by limited liability. Some tax claims, for example, may only be the responsibility of the corporation or limited partnership; presumably shareholders or limited partners are not personally liable for such claims, while general partners or sole proprietors are liable. If so, limited liability again provides some significant benefits.

If one weighs the advantages and costs of limited liability from a realistic perspective, a fair conclusion is that limited liability is a definite but limited benefit from the standpoint of the owners. Its advantages are not so overwhelming that it should be insisted upon in every case. Obviously, some individuals are more risk-adverse than others: The more risk-adverse, the more important limited liability is apt to appear.

§13.9   Federal Income Taxation

In considering the effect of federal income taxation on the various forms for doing business as a small venture with relatively few owners, it is essential to review briefly the tax schedules for individuals and for corporations set forth in §§12.10 and 12.20.1. It is also important to understand the essential difference between the tax treatment of a C corporation and an S corporation. See §12.20.3 In the following discussion it is assumed that all individual participants in the venture are filing joint returns and that in each instance their taxable income exceeds $29,750 so that all individual taxpayers are in either the 28 or 33 percent brackets. (If the significance of these amounts of income and tax brackets is not clear, one should also review §12.10.)

Since virtually all types of businesses now may incorporate, the election to be taxed as a C corporation or an S corporation is open to most businesses with less than 35 owners. Some businesses with less than 35 shareholders may not be eligible for the S corporation election since they may not meet other requirements for the election (see §13.9.3), but they usually have the option of conducting business in partnership form in order to achieve much the same result. Businesses with more than 35 owners usually are incorporated and, since the S corporation election is not available to them, they have no choice but to accept C corporation status for tax purposes. In some instances, however, such a business may be able to conduct business as a limited partnership and thereby obtain pass-through tax treatment.

In the discussion below it is assumed that the business has less than 35 owners and the S corporation is available to it.

§13.9.1   Taxation as a C Corporation

The first issue to be considered is whether it is desirable ever to create an entity that is taxed as a C corporation, that is, to create a corporation and not make an S corporation election. A C corporation is subject to the tax rates set forth in §12.20.1: a marginal tax rate of 15 percent for income under $50,000; 25 percent for income between $50,000 and $75,000; 34 percent for income between $75,000 and $100,000; 39 percent for income between $100,000 and $335,000, and, finally, a reduced tax rate of 34 percent for income in excess of $335,000. The alternative to C corporation taxation is taxation as a proprietorship, partnership, limited partnership, or S corporation, all of which involve no separate tax at the business level and a pass-through of business income directly to the individual tax returns of the owners of the business. See §13.9.2.

In addition, it will be recalled that a C corporation involves a potential double tax problem. See §12.20.2. The corporation is subject to a direct tax on its earnings at the above rates, and, if there are future distributions of these earnings in the form of dividends by the corporation to the shareholders, there is a second tax on the same earnings when the dividend is received by shareholders and included in their tax returns. This double tax can be minimized or eliminated through the distribution of earnings in the form of salary or other tax deductible payments by the corporation to the shareholder. If deductions arising from such payments totally eliminate all taxable income to the corporation, that income is said to be *zeroed out*. However, zeroing out is not always practical, since only "reasonable" salaries or other business expenses are deductible by the corporation.

Assuming that the owners (or shareholders) are already in the maximum 28 or 33 percent brackets, C corporation tax status immediately begins to create a tax disadvantage whenever the taxable income of the corporation is above $75,000 even without taking the double taxation problem into account. At that level of income the corporate marginal tax rate is higher than the maximum individual tax rate. As business income rises above this amount, taxation as a C corporation becomes increasingly disadvantageous. This is a relatively low level of income for most businesses; any business that is even modestly successful should reach this level of income in a relatively brief period of time. Thus, the basic rule is that C corporation tax treatment should generally be avoided for corporations with substantial income, if possible.

The Tax Act of 1986 dramatically changed the structure of the rates for both individuals and corporations. Prior to 1986, the tax rates were generally lower for corporations than for individuals at practically all levels of income. As a result, profitable corporations taxed under the C corporation schedule usually ended up paying less tax than if the same income were allocated directly to individuals. Under pre-1986 rates, therefore, a common strategy was to plan for a long-term accumulation of excess undistributed earnings at lower corporate tax rates (and unrealized capital appreciation of assets) within the corporation, followed by a later liquidation or sale of the corporation's stock or its assets in a transaction that qualified for long-term capital gain treatment and permitted the accumulation to be obtained by the shareholders at favorable tax rates. Until the sale occurred, the corporation had the use of funds saved by taking advantage of the lower corporate tax rate. This pattern was usually called the *accumulation/bail out strategy*; it is no longer generally attractive because of the changes in tax rates.

It is true that a modest amount of tax sheltering is still possible on the $0-75,000 range of corporation income. Nevertheless, this is a very narrow window in which the election of C corporation tax status might be marginally advantageous. Unfortunately, even if modest amounts of corporate income are accumulated within this range at a lower tax cost than on a pass-through basis, the bail-out on favorable tax terms has been made impossible by two other tax changes in the 1986 Act: the elimination of the special tax treatment of long-term capital gains and the requirement that corporations upon liquidation must recognize gain from appreciation in value of assets (the repeal of the so-called General Utilities Doctrine). Thus, there is now no readily available method for bailing out earnings at a later date by a liquidation or sale of stock on a favorable tax basis. If favorable long-term capital gains tax treatment is restored in the future, modest accumulation/bail out strategies may again become advantageous from a tax standpoint. Nevertheless, given the tax rates in the 1986 Tax Act, it appears that C corporation tax treatment should be avoided whenever it is possible to do so.

A corporation that is not eligible for S corporation status may sometimes reduce the total tax bill for itself and its shareholders by following the strategy of zeroing out its income in whole or in part. See section 12.20.2.

§13.9.2 Taxation as an S Corporation, Proprietorship, or Partnership

The other major forms of business organization — proprietorships, general partnerships, limited partnerships, and S corporations — involve a pass-through or conduit form of tax treatment by which income or loss is taxed directly to the owners. See §§12.20, 12.20.3, 13.2. This form of tax treatment has always been generally advantageous if the business expected to show a loss and this continues to be true under the 1986 Tax Act. In addition, this form of tax treatment is, for the reasons set forth in §13.9.1 also generally advantageous if the business expects to show a profit (except possibly for the narrow window of business income up to $75,000.)

Ventures that appear likely to show operating losses for a period — perhaps a new venture that is likely to show losses in its early years of operation — should elect to be taxed in a manner that permits the owners of the business to take advantage of the losses immediately on their personal income tax returns. A loss corporation that adopts pass-through tax treatment is a tax shelter since it shields a portion of the shareholders' other income from tax. Under the pre-1986 tax laws these losses were deductible in their entirety; under the 1986 Act their deductibility may be limited to some degree by the investment interest and passive loss limitations on deductibility of losses. (See §12.11 for a discussion of these limitations.) Even though the advantages of pass-through tax treatment for loss corporations have been limited in certain situations by the 1986 Tax Act, they are still available for immediate tax sheltering in many situations.

§13.9.3 S Corporation Election Compared with Partnerships or Limited Partnerships

Both the subchapter S election by a corporation and the general treatment of partnerships or limited partnerships lead to essentially similar pass-through or conduit tax treatment. However, the two choices differ dramatically in other respects. Subchapter S election is a tax election: It does not affect nontax corporation attributes. Thus it is possible to combine the S corporation election with limited liability for, and direct participation by, all owners in the management of the business as directors, officers, or employees. A general partnership does not provide limited liability at all, while a limited partnership does not permit active participation in the business by limited partners. In some states, however, limited partners may be able to participate in management by serving as officers or directors of a corporate general partner without losing the shield of limited liability.

The major disadvantage of the S corporation election is its strict eligibility rules: no more than 35 shareholders, all of whom must be individuals or estates. An S corporation also may not itself have subsidiaries. Other, less important restrictions on eligibility for the S corporation election also exist, particularly those making corporations with trusts or aliens as shareholders ineligible for the election. Because of these strict eligibility rules, there is a risk that dissatisfied shareholders in an S corporation may seek to cause a loss of the election by transfers of shares to ineligible persons. This may usually be prevented by carefully drafted share transfer agreements.

§13.10 Ease of Raising Capital in the Future

For small businesses the choice of business form is not likely to have much effect on the ability to raise capital. The willingness of lenders or investors to provide funds to a business depends more on the perceived economic strength and promise of the business itself than the legal form the enterprise takes. Personal guarantees of corporate indebtedness by major shareholders are almost routinely required for major debt financing of such businesses.

In the United States the dominant business form for more than a century has been the corporation. Lenders and investors are accustomed to deal with this business form and with the securities corporations issue. As a result, a corporation is the preferred business form when it is anticipated that capital may be raised in the future through a broad public offering of securities. In some instances it may be practical to use a limited partnership form to effect a public offering: It is not practical to use a general partnership because of the risk of unlimited liability.

The S corporation election is almost never available after a public offering in light of the 35-shareholder limitation for that election. Thus, in a corporation that is contemplating "going public" by sale of equity interests in the future, one must be prepared to accept ultimate C corporation tax status.

When considering public sales of securities of any form — whether in general partnership interests, limited partnership interests, shares of corporate stock, bonds, debentures, or evidences of indebtedness — one must always take into account the possible applicability of the Federal Securities Act of 1933 and the state securities laws (the blue sky laws). Compliance with these statutes by businesses for the first time is expensive and sometimes difficult since they require significant disclosure and the preparation of audited financial statements. Failure to comply with these requirements may lead to broad rights of recission by investors, and the imposition of civil and possible criminal liability on the participants. While exemptions from the registration requirement may be available in some circumstances, securities law is complex and technical; outside expert assistance may be necessary to determine whether a specific exemption is in fact available.

§13.11 Centralized Management

A corporation has the attribute of centralized management: The management of corporate affairs is vested in the directors and officers who may consist of all or some of the shareholders or of persons having no financial interest in the corporation. A partnership on the other hand is pluralistic in theory: Its affairs are managed by the partners. Each partner possesses authority to bind the partnership and a right to participate in management. However, a considerable degree of centralization of management may be provided in a general partnership by carefully drawn contractual provisions in the partnership agreement. Indeed, all powers of management may be vested in one or more managing partners and substantial liquidated damages may be imposed on nonmanaging partners who interfere with management.

In a limited partnership the general partners are vested with the power to manage the partnership affairs and, as among the general partners, power to manage the affairs of a limited partnership is pluralistic as in a general partnership. Limited partners usually do not participate in management; if they do, they lose the shield of limited liability and assume the obligations of a general partner. A major uncertainty about limited partnerships is to what extent limited partners may participate in management decisions without losing that shield. Many modern limited partnership statutes grant limited partners the right to vote on certain fundamental changes without loss of the shield of limited liability. As in a general partnership, classes of managing and nonmanaging partners may be created by agreement.

In general, centralized management is unlikely to be a controlling factor in selection of a business form because contractual provisions may create or limit the power to manage in any form of business.

§13.12 Continuity of Life

Corporations are usually formed with perpetual existence. This simply means that the corporation continues indefinitely, that the death or withdrawal of a shareholder does not terminate the corporate existence, and that a minority shareholder does not have the power to compel or force a dissolution. A partnership's existence is more flimsy. Numerous events automatically cause the dissolution of a partnership, and each partner has the inherent power to dissolve the partnership at any time, though in some circumstances such a dissolution may constitute a breach of contract. In a limited partnership, the general partners have the dissolution powers of a partner in a general partnership, while the limited partners usually have no power to compel dissolution except by decree of court.

Again, however, contractual provisions may generally provide what the law of partnerships or corporations does not. It is possible to create by contract a power of dissolution in a corporation that is not essentially different from the power possessed by partners in a partnership. Contractual provisions in a partnership agreement may also make the power of dissolution so expensive to exercise that essentially it can be exercised — like in a corporation — only by a judicial decree finding substantial misconduct or oppression.

§13.13 Free Transferability of Interest

In the absence of contractual restriction, shares of stock of a corporation may be freely sold, assigned, or otherwise disposed of by the owner. A purchaser of a share of stock becomes a shareholder in the corporation with whatever rights pertain to that status. In contrast, the holder of a partnership interest can only convey limited rights to an assignee or purchaser of the partnership interest unless the other partners agree to accept the assignee or purchaser as a partner. General partners in a limited partnership have no more power to dispose of their interest than do partners in a general partnership, while a limited partner's interest usually is made assignable by appropriate provision in the limited partnership agreement.

Again, however, these differences are more theoretical than real. Transfers of shares in a closely held corporation are usually restricted by agreement, and in any event, it is unlikely that there are very many people interested in buying them. Conversely markets may exist for partnership interests — particularly limited partnership interests — and all partnership interests may be made freely transferable by appropriate provisions in the partnership agreement.

§13.14 Summary

The most desirable form of business for a specific venture cannot be selected in the abstract. It depends on the nature of the business, the future plans of the participants, the risk-adverseness of the participants, and the potential income-generating and liability-generating features of the business. In this context, tax considerations point to conducting business in partnership form or under an S corporation election. Future changes in the present tax law are a real possibility and may affect this conclusion. The following generalizations appear to be reliable as of 1988:

First, when in doubt, keep things simple. Small, marginal businesses with limited capital usually benefit by limiting organizational expenses and devoting capital to operations and inventory rather than to lawyers. Simplicity also means that the owners may concentrate on business matters and not be saddled with unessential organizational details.

Second, limited liability is generally advantageous, but is not of critical importance in most ventures. If unlimited liability for business obligations exists in a business form, care should be taken that adequate liability insurance coverage is available to protect the participants.

Third, taxation as a C corporation should be avoided. If limited liability is desired when the venture is small, the S corporation election should be

Table 13-1

Form of venture	Liability	Tax status	Flexibility	Source of law
Proprietorship	unlimited	individual	maximum	agency
Partnership	unlimited	conduit	maximum	UPA
Limited Partnership	limited (some partners only)	conduit	medium	ULPA RULPA
C Corporation	limited	dual tax	medium	Bus. Corp Acts
S Corporation	limited	conduit	low — 35 shareholder maximum	Bus. Corp Acts

exercised. However, the S corporation election is not always available to small corporations and is never available to corporations with more than 35 individual shareholders. Limited liability combined with conduit tax treatment may sometimes also be obtained in ineligible corporations through the use of a limited partnership with a corporation as the sole general partner. In this event, however, it is essential that the corporation be more than nominally capitalized following the guidelines adopted by the IRS in determining when such an entity should be taxed as an "association" (i.e., as a C corporation), or as a partnership. Tax laws may be tightened further in the future with respect to the tax treatment of large limited partnerships and limited partnerships with corporate general partners.

Table 13-1 summarizes the current principal consequences of the selection of alternative forms of business for a new venture.

C. THE DEVELOPMENT AND FINANCING OF A BUSINESS VENTURE

§13.15 The Stages of Development and Growth of a Business

Most newly formed and ultimately successful businesses go through several different stages of development. The financing and managerial needs of the business vary significantly depending on the stage of development. Obviously not all businesses go through each of these stages, but they are sufficiently typical to justify discussion. The three stages discussed here may be described as the start-up stage, the established business stage, and the publicly held stage.

In the following subsections, the word *entrepreneur* is used to describe the owners of a business. It should be understood that this may include several owners as well as a single owner. The phrase *chief executive officer* (or *CEO*) is used to identify the senior manager of a publicly held corporation; the CEO may have been the entrepreneur that built up the business at an earlier stage, but more likely he or she is a professional manager who never was the principal owner of the business.

§13.15.1 *The Start-Up Business*

As the name suggests, a start-up business is a new business just getting underway, usually in the form of a proprietorship or a small partnership. The prototype start-up business is the entrepreneur with a good idea attempting to translate it into a viable and profitable business. Several individuals may be involved, each making a unique contribution to the success of the business. One individual may have the basic idea, a second may provide the start-up capital, and the third may provide the services — the "sweat equity" — to make the business a success.

In the prototypical start-up business, the entrepreneur is actively involved in the provision of the goods or services that are the backbone of the new business. If the business develops a good reputation for reliability and quality, it is the consequence of the energy and skill of the entrepreneur. Quality control may not be a problem since the entrepreneur is personally involved in the business. If employees are hired and trained, their activities are closely overseen by the entrepreneur. Equipment is purchased by the entrepreneur, the product is priced by the entrepreneur, and if customer problems develop, the entrepreneur is there to work them out. The success or the failure of a start-up business, in short, depends on the personal abilities of the entrepreneur in providing the goods or services of the business.

Most start-up businesses ultimately fail, usually because of the lack of economic viability of the underlying business concept, lack of sophistication of the entrepreneur, failure to control avoidable costs, or lack of capital sufficient to develop the business concept on a profitable basis.

§13.15.2 *The Established Business*

The second stage of a business to be discussed is an established business of moderate size. This is a business that has been in existence for at least several years and has had substantial growth. If the business, when it started up, had sales of perhaps one or two hundred thousand dollars per year, the same business, when established, will have sales perhaps ten or twenty times as large. If the business involves the production and sale of specific lines of goods, it may own one or two plants, a warehouse for inventory, and ten or so retail outlets. Businesses of this type are usually incorporated; their shares are owned by a relatively few persons, often including the original entrepreneur and several other persons. Usually a business of this type has not made a public offering of its shares.

The role of the entrepreneur in a business of this size is quite different from his or her role in a start-up business. In a larger business, the entrepreneur is primarily a manager and a planner and usually not personally involved in the routine provision of goods and services. Indeed, there is a quantum leap between a start-up business in which the entrepreneur is personally involved in all aspects of the business, and the established business in which routine transactions are handled entirely by employees. The start-up business is a personal service business from the standpoint of the entrepreneur: The established business is a bureaucracy in which the entrepreneur has little or no direct involvement with most employees, customers, or suppliers. The owner of the established business may be involved in the development of new products, unusual or extraordinary transactions, short- and long-term planning, capital investment, meeting the future capital needs of the business, and so forth.

This difference in role is reflected throughout the enterprise. One might consider such matters as inventory, accounting and auditing functions, delegation of managerial responsibility, the selection of employees, and controls over funds, including mundane (but essential) matters such as the simple question of who has authority to sign checks.

It is important to recognize that the path from a start-up business to an established one is not smooth. Rather, there are critical points in the growth of a business at which very substantial infusions of capital are required and entirely new management skills must be developed. It is quite possible for a business to be successful, indeed to have more potential customers than it can handle, and yet fail. Every owner of a successful business recognizes that these critical points exist, where a new plant becomes absolutely essential if the business is to continue to operate in an efficient manner, where the owner finds it impossible to ensure high quality control by personally being involved in every job or project, or where he or she learns that more sophisticated accounting systems for inventory are essential if production is to continue smoothly and theft or shrinkage is to be avoided. If these critical points are not surmounted, the ability of the business to provide high-quality goods and services declines, inexplicable delays occur, billings are not made promptly, accounts receivable are ignored, costs increase, and the business suffers. Probably everyone has had dealings with a small business that originally provided quality goods and services on a personal basis, but then suffered growing pains as matters began to slip. Unless corrected, such problems may doom the business. "The business just grew too fast," the entrepreneur may say ruefully, as he or she surveys the wreckage of a once promising enterprise.

From a managerial standpoint, probably the two most critical points are, first, when the business has grown to the point where the entrepreneur recognizes that he or she can no longer personally ensure that quality control has been maintained for every transaction, and, second, when the business has grown to the point where the entrepreneur is compelled to delegate substantially all routine operating functions to others (e.g., plant managers, warehouse managers, and store managers), and ceases to be a manager of day-to-day affairs. These transitions are difficult since the entrepreneur is required to change roles from what he or she has previously been accustomed to doing in the past and to delegate essential managerial functions to subordinates. The failure to develop a "managerial style" in a larger enterprise may have serious consequences: For example, delays may occur because the entrepreneur is trying to oversee too much. If lines of responsibility are not clearly established and respected, morale suffers and the cardinal principle of responsibility for consequences of decisions may be lost.

§13.15.3 The Large Publicly Held Business

In a large publicly held business, the role of top management is as different from that of the established business as the role of the entrepreneur in the start-up business differs from his or her role in the established business.

A large publicly held business may have hundreds of plants or offices, profits of hundreds of millions of dollars per year, and sales in the billions of dollars. Its business is usually international in scope. Virtually all such businesses are incorporated. Further, the corporation has had one or more public offerings of securities. Most of its stock is owned by members of the general public, while top management (the CEO and other senior officers) own a minute fraction of the shares issued by the corporation (though the absolute value of these holdings may be larger than the total net worth of the established business as described in the previous subsection).

The organization of such a massive entity involves virtually complete delegation of authority over whole areas of business to departments or divisions or subsidiaries that are autonomous in virtually all business matters. It is a private bureaucracy built on the lines of organizational charts and targeted goals. The home office or central organization takes responsibility for selection of top divisional managers and review of their performance; the oversight and investment of excess funds generated by divisions; the provision of auditing and legal services; the raising of capital; and the long-term direction of the enterprise.

Many established businesses never make the transition from an established business to a large publicly held one. There does not appear to be a single explanation of why some businesses do and others do not. It clearly helps to be in an industry that is undergoing continued, explosive growth. During the 1970s and 1980s the computer and computer software industries displayed this type of growth; indeed, several businesses in this industry went from start-up businesses to large publicly held corporations in a relatively brief period. Alternatively, the entrepreneur may possess the peculiar genius of being able to produce growth through acquisition, management and restructuring of diverse businesses in stable industries — an ability that few persons possess.

In a publicly held corporation, the top management — the chief executive officer and other top managers — usually have quite different roles than the entrepreneur in an established business. The most important difference is that the entrepreneur is still the primary owner of the business and the principal beneficiary of successful operations and the principal loser if things do not go well. That is not true in the typical publicly held corporation. The CEO is working for a large and diffuse number of public shareholders whose composition is changing every day. The CEO, of course, is driven by selfish and personal considerations as well when he or she strives to make the business as profitable as possible; there is a great deal of prestige in being the CEO of a successful corporation and it is not something to be given up lightly. Further, the CEO's salary probably is in the high six or low seven figures, and usually tied to some extent to the success of the business. However, he or she is still principally a manager of a business largely owned by others. The CEO perhaps is more risk-adverse and cautious than the entrepreneur who is still the principal owner of an established business; whether or not this is true, he or she certainly must recognize the importance of keeping happy many shareholders who are purely passive short-run investors interested in a large immediate return on their investment.

A second important difference is that, unlike the entrepreneur in an established business, the CEO always has to be concerned about his or her tenure. He or she is evaluated periodically by the board of directors which usually has some degree of independence from the CEO. The chance of a CEO being fired is not very great so long as the business is profitable, but it is at least possible and it does occur sometimes. Even where this possibility is remote, the CEO must deal effectively with the board of directors in a way that the entrepreneur in an established business usually does not. In addition, the CEO of a publicly held corporation must always be aware of the possibility that an outside entity or group may make a cash tender offer for the business, threatening the continued tenure of the CEO, and indeed the tenure of the board of directors itself. See Chapter 17.

Third, a publicly held corporation has substantial disclosure obligations that closely held corporations do not have. These obligations arise because of the existence of public investors and the public market in the shares of the corporation.

Fourth, as discussed below, the large publicly held corporation has sources of capital and the power to raise funds that are not available to smaller businesses.

§13.16 Sources of Capital for Businesses

Virtually every business must rely on capital provided by persons or entities other than the entrepreneur if it is to be successful. The basic question, when discussing the capitalization of any business, small or large, is always whether the provider of capital is making a loan to the business or whether it is acquiring an ownership interest in the business. This basic question may be phrased in different ways. Is the capital being supplied debt capital or equity capital? Is the provider of capital a creditor or a partner or shareholder? Generally, a mix of debt and equity in the capitalization of a business is more desirable than pure equity. The combination of debt and equity in a single capital structure gives rise to the phenomenon of leverage. See §13.18.

A second important question with respect to the use of debt capital is whether the debt is current debt or long-term debt. See §8.2. Current debt should be utilized as necessary to provide adequate working capital for day-to-day operations; long-term debt is more analogous to an equity investment in the sense that it is part of the permanent capitalization of the business. See §9.10.8.

It turns out that at the margin the distinction between debt and equity is blurred. Because suppliers and users of capital are largely free to structure their relationship as they wish, it is possible to create debt instruments that have some equity characteristics, and vice versa. In some instances, it may not be possible to classify such hybrid instruments as either debt or equity. See §13.17.

§13.16.1 Financing the Start-Up Business

The most common financial problem of start-up businesses is inadequate capital for the needs of the new business. The amount of working capital may be inadequate for the conduct of the business at a profitable level or the permanent capital available to the business may be insufficient to permit it to develop suitable facilities. Commonly, both short- and long-term capital is inadequate. Inadequate capitalization prevents the business from taking full advantage of its natural success: Growth is hampered and the entrepreneur is compelled to devote appreciable portions of time to raising funds to permit the business to continue.

There are basically four sources of financing for a start-up business.

1. The entrepreneur may use his or her personal funds to finance the business. This may involve prior savings or current earnings from unrelated employment or activity to finance the new business. It is not uncommon for an entrepreneur to invest all available family funds in the new business: savings set aside for a rainy day, for medical expenses, for education of small children, for vacations, for the purchase of a new home, and for what-have-you. Where the business ultimately succeeds, this strategy usually maximizes the value of the business to the entrepreneur. However, where it does not, the entrepreneur's personal and family financial picture will certainly be adversely affected to some extent, and may be devastated.

Modern portfolio theory recommends that investments generally should be diversified. The owner of a typical start-up business rarely is in a position to diversify investments — indeed, the investment of all available funds in the new business is the opposite of diversification. Funds contributed by the entrepreneur constitute, of course, equity capital. In some circumstances, entrepreneur-contributed funds may be treated for internal purposes as a loan by the entrepreneur to the business. This is particularly likely where the business is conducted in corporate or partnership form, and there are partners or shareholders in addition to the entrepreneur and his or her immediate family. Entrepreneur-contributed funds may be treated as loans for tax reasons (where the S corporation election is unavailable) or where special payments are to be made to the entrepreneur to adjust the relative rights of investors in the business among themselves.

2. A second major source of financing for a start-up business is capital borrowed by the entrepreneur from commercial sources. The entrepreneur may be able to borrow funds on the basis of a signature loan from a bank or commercial lending agency. More likely, security will have to be given for such

a loan, perhaps a second mortgage on the family residence. The cash surrender value of ordinary life insurance policies may be borrowed to invest in the new business. Some start-up entrepreneurs rely on personal credit cards to obtain additional loan funds at interest rates in excess of 18 percent per year. Such an entrepreneur may have eight or ten bank credit cards each with an independent line of credit that in the aggregate may provide borrowing power in excess of $25,000 in a single month. Credit cards are an expensive source of borrowed capital, and it is likely that this source is used only by the most marginal business unable to obtain more conventional financing. A friend or a relative may be persuaded to act as surety for the entrepreneur to raise additional capital through commercial loans.

Once the business is underway, a fair amount of credit can usually be raised through anticipation of the receipts of the business itself. Inventory may be purchased on credit to be repaid (hopefully) out of the sale of the inventory. Accounts receivable may be assigned as security for a continuing loan arrangement. Of course, the entrepreneur is usually personally liable on this debt, but the issue under discussion here is not what happens if the business fails, but how the business is to get the capital desperately needed for it to stay in business.

Since the liquid assets of the entrepreneur are often limited, most of the capital of the start-up business may be in the form of debt. Most of this debt is short-term, carrying relatively high interest rates and short repayment dates. The business must generate a sufficient cash flow to service this debt which may be a major obstacle to future growth, though if the business appears to be a success the debt may usually be rolled over by borrowing new debt to pay off the old when it matures.

3. The third major source of financing for a start-up business is from relatives, friends, and acquaintances. Sometimes individuals involved with the business as satisfied customers, suppliers, or employees may express an interest in investing in, or be prevailed upon to invest in, the business. The major problem with this type of financing is apt to be uncertainty as to the precise legal relationship between the provider of the capital and the proprietorship. When nonrelatives invest in a business, they usually intend to purchase an interest in the ownership of the business and not simply make a loan to a business. The entrepreneur, on the other hand, is not happy at the idea of giving up a part of his or her business. Since these arrangements are often informal, entered into without the advice of a lawyer, there may be no definitive resolution of the underlying disagreement as to whether the transaction is a loan or a purchase of an interest in the business. Where a definitive understanding is reached that the investment involves an equity interest, the entrepreneur should normally insist on a provision that permits the reacquisition on a reasonable basis of that interest if there is a disagreement as to goals or policy. Otherwise, the entrepreneur may find it necessary to pay a premium price (largely caused by the entrepreneur's efforts) to reacquire the equity interests granted at an earlier time.

Much the same uncertainty may exist as to funds supplied by relatives, though it is more likely that an indefinite loan, or even an outright gift, was intended than is the case with capital provided by nonrelatives. In this context, an indefinite loan is one in which there are not definite terms of repayment: Typically there is a vague understanding that the loan is to be repaid when the business is able to do so.

4. The final source of funding for a start-up business is the venture capital industry discussed in greater detail in the following section. While venture capital funds usually invest in more established businesses, some funds may seek out promising start-up businesses, particularly those in the high-tech area or where, because of the proven track record of the entrepreneur, the probability of success seems high. Indeed, in the most attractive high-tech start-ups, the entrepreneur may discover that he or she has more venture capital funds offered to the business than can be effectively utilized.

§13.16.2 *Financing an Established Business*

An established business has sources of debt and equity financing not available to a start-up business. Because it has a credit history and a credit rating, it usually may borrow funds on its own credit without involving the shareholders. In addition, new sources of debt and equity capital may be open to the business with an established track record.

1. *Internally generated funds.* A successful and established business has the capacity of generating significant amounts of funds internally. Earnings may be set aside and accumulated over a period of several years to finance expansion or the development of new manufacturing facilities. However, a significant positive cash flow may be generated even without substantial earnings if the corporation claims accelerated depreciation or other deductions that do not require cash outlays. Internally generated funds represent equity capital.

2. *Lines of credit.* An established business may create lines of credit at one or more commercial banks that provide access to working capital as needed for the day-to-day activities of the business. Lines of credit are established in advance, up to specific maxima, and may be drawn upon simply by writing checks. Interest is payable only on funds actually drawn upon. Similarly, an established business may enter into regular inventory financing plans, assignments of accounts receivable, and the like, which permit the business access to cash immediately rather than tying up working capital in accounts receivable and inventory.

3. *Government assistance or government guaranteed loans.* In some instances, an established business may be eligible for governmental assistance, perhaps in the form of direct loans or, more commonly, loan guarantees. The sources may be local, state, or federal. The United States Department of Commerce and its Small Business Administration have a variety of loan and loan guaranty programs that may be available for specific businesses.

4. *Venture capital funds.* An important source of capital for developing businesses that have economic promise are venture capital funds. These funds pool equity or risk capital from a variety of sources in order to provide capital to promising small businesses. These funds actively seek out promising businesses in which to make substantial equity/debt investments. For many businesses struggling to develop sufficient capital resources to expand, joint venture funds are the answer, since the relationship is a continuing one, and the joint

venture fund may provide additional capital at a later date. The cost of this type of financing is not cheap, however. Venture capital funds normally charge commercial interest rates and in addition demand the right to acquire a significant slice of the equity of the business — 50 percent or more in some cases. They may acquire a package of debt instruments combined with common shares purchased at a nominal price or debt instruments combined with rights or options to purchase common shares at a fixed price that may remain in effect for long periods of time. Or they may acquire debt instruments that may later be converted into equity: convertible debentures. The theory underlying each of these arrangements is that the entrepreneur should retain working control of the enterprise but the venture capitalist may "cash in" if there is a public offering of equity (see below), or the business is sold outright to third parties.

Venture capital funds are a major provider of capital to smaller businesses. During the 1980s, many institutional investors such as pension funds have set aside small portions of their immense pools of funds for venture capital investments in an attempt to diversify and improve their overall investment return. It is estimated that private investors provided $4.2 billion to venture capital funds in 1987, about half of which was provided by institutional investors.

As the capital available to venture capital funds has increased, they have moved beyond their traditional investments into more risky service-oriented businesses such as caterers and funeral homes. Some venture capital funds also invest in leveraged buyouts and recapitalizations. See $17.16.

The policies of a fairly typical publicly held venture capital fund have been described as follows:

> [The Fund] . . . invests in all stages of business development from start-up companies to established companies with renewed growth potential.
>
> *Start-up* Financing provided to companies to develop a new product or service.
>
> *Early stage* Financing made available to initiate commercial production and initial sales.
>
> *Expansion* Funding of companies to expand production and sales, more rapidly introduce improved products, or enter new markets.
>
> *Leveraged Buyouts* Funding provided to acquire a division or major portion of an existing company, usually in cooperation with the present operating management.
>
> *Special Situations* Financing of special investment opportunities, including investments in public companies. . . .
>
> The [Fund] . . . seeks to invest in companies that combine the following critical elements:
>
> - A competent management team with expert knowledge of its business and the ability to work well together.
> - A large and growing market with favorable competitive characteristics.
> - Innovative products or services, proprietary technology, or specialized expertise.
> - Compatibility with our own skills and resources to allow us to provide meaningful support to the management team.

5. *Private placements of debt*. Well-established businesses may be able to borrow large amounts of funds from a small number of institutional investors

such as insurance companies, pension funds, and similar organizations. These loans are usually secured by liens on real estate or substantial machinery or equipment, or on all of the assets of the corporation. They are known as *private placements* since they are effected without registration of the securities for public sale under the Securities Act of 1933 or state blue sky laws. These loans may be for very long terms: They may provide for adjustments in interest rates based on market rates or permit the institutional investor to convert into an equity position if the business goes public.

A company that is sufficiently established to raise funds through a private placement is unlikely to be interested in dealing with venture capital funds, since such funds usually insist on receiving a major portion of the company's equity as the price for providing capital.

6. *Private sales of equity interests.* An established company may raise equity capital by sales of common stock to a limited group of investors. However, direct sales of corporate shares to investors located by officers or directors of the corporation may be inefficient and distracting: The loss of executive time and attention from the business must be factored in. Further, such attempts run a significant risk of inadvertant violations of federal or state securities laws. As in the case of private debt placements, such sales must be carefully structured to avoid registration under the Securities Act of 1933 and state blue sky laws. The principal exemption under this statute is "Regulation D." Substantial amounts of capital may be raised under this exemption by private sales of equity securities to *accredited investors* (defined precisely in the regulations in an effort to determine which investors possess sufficient sophistication that they can take care of themselves and do not need the protection of the registration provisions of the 1933 Act). In some limited circumstances, a public offering may also be exempt if offers are made only to persons living within a single state.

A registered public sale of securities will usually involve the use of professional securities underwriters and securities firms to distribute the securities to the investing public. An underwriter is a person or organization that acquires shares for resale or who arranges the direct sale of shares by the issuer. Investment bankers and securities firms regularly underwrite new securities issues on a commercial basis. Large issues are "syndicated" or broken up among a number of securities firms and sold by them to investors. There is a precept in the securities business that "shares are sold not bought" and that professional selling assistance is essential for most successful floatations of new securities. The flip side, of course, is that underwriting fees and sales commissions add significantly to the cost of the public offering. Nevertheless professional assistance may be a bargain in the long run, since a do-it-yourself public offering may not raise enough capital.

7. *Registered public offerings of equity securities.* An established business may consider going public to raise capital by selling equity securities to members of the general public. This is a serious and substantial step that should be taken only after careful consideration.

There are significant advantages to a public offering. A successful public offer may create a market for the shares of the corporation: The entrepreneur may later use this market to liquidate a portion of his or her investment in the business. Further, very large amounts of capital may be raised through a public offering, and, as discussed in the following subsection, once a corporation is publicly traded, new sources of capital are available to it.

There are significant disadvantages as well. The cost of a public offering for an "unseasoned" company (one that has not previously made a public offering) is so substantial that a public offering of at least $10,000,000 is necessary to justify the expense. Further, there are substantial disclosure obligations with respect to previous transactions that the entrepreneur may prefer not be made public. Finally, a public company takes on disclosure and other legal obligations that add to the cost of operation and limit the amount of information about future developments that may be kept confidential. Whether or not these disadvantages outweigh the advantages cannot be answered in the abstract.

§13.16.3 Sources of Capital for Publicly Held Corporations

A publicly held corporation has a wide variety of financing sources available to it. The decision as to which source to pursue is a function of *cost* and *dilution*. Almost never is the problem a shortage or lack of capital: The most common problem is overcapitalization, that is, liquid assets in excess of the business needs of the enterprise.

Large publicly held corporations have general access to debt capital in a variety of forms. The choice of which form to utilize comes down primarily to economic cost, and to a lesser extent, business need. Available forms include:

Short-term loans with maturity dates ranging from overnight to one year.
Lines of credit bearing interest only to the extent drawn upon.
Inventory or accounts receivable financing.
Private placement of long-term debt securities in very large amounts — sometimes hundreds of millions of dollars.
Public offerings of investment grade bonds and debentures, again in very large amounts.
Public offerings of *junk bonds*. See §§18.20, 17.17.3.
Public offerings of *zero coupon bonds* and *deep discount bonds*. See §18.21.
Public offerings of convertible debentures.

The ability of large publicly held corporations to raise huge amounts of debt capital is well illustrated by actions of aggressors in takeover battles, who have consistently demonstrated the ability to raise billions of dollars to acquire another business. See §17.17.

Large publicly held corporations also have the ability to raise large amounts of equity capital through public offerings or privately negotiated sales of stock. In start-up and established small corporations, the sale of equity is a matter of concern because it reduces the equity ownership of the entrepreneur. The same concern is not present in publicly held corporations, in which by definition the general public already owns most of the outstanding equity shares and the CEO and senior managers own relatively small percentage interests. Rather, the principal concern is *dilution*, that is, the effect on existing shareholders of issuing new equity interests.

§13.16.4 Dilution of Existing Shares When Issuing New Equity Securities

Outstanding shares have both a market value (as reflected in the price of the shares on the securities market) and a book value. See §9.9.4. The issue of additional shares to third parties for cash is not apt to give rise to serious dilution problems since the issue price and the market and book values of outstanding shares may be immediately compared. Of course, dilution occurs if the corporation issues shares for less than the market or book values, but corporations rarely issue bargain-priced shares to third parties. Where it is desired to issue new equity shares for cash at a price less than book or market value, one can avoid dilution by offering to sell the new securities proportionately to existing shareholders rather than to third parties.

The issuance of shares for property or as compensation to managers for services raises more serious dilution problems because of the difficulty of valuing the consideration received by the corporation. Dilution may also arise through the issue of convertible securities, options, warrants, or rights to purchase shares that continue for long periods of time at a price fixed at the outset. Again, this possible dilution may be avoided by offering the new securities to existing shareholders proportionately. Dilution may also be minimized if the corporation purchases its own shares in the open market and uses those shares to acquire property or as compensation for services.

§13.16.5 Overcapitalization

Publicly held corporations usually have strong cash flows that permit the accumulation of large amounts of capital from internal sources. Recourse to commercial lending sources or the equity capital markets is therefore unnecessary except in rare situations. Indeed, capital may be generated so easily from internal sources that the corporation may have liquid funds in excess of its present or foreseeable needs: overcapitalization, as it were.

Excess capitalization in publicly held corporations is not viewed as good or as sound, conservative management. On the contrary, excess capital is viewed as a sign of management weakness, the inability to deploy available assets efficiently. Excess capital may also attract takeover bids, since the excess capital may be used to effect a bootstrap acquisition or leveraged buyout. See §17.16. As a result, an accepted pre-offer defense tactic is to dispose of excess capital, perhaps by an extraordinary dividend to shareholders.

§13.17 The Distinction Between "Debt" and "Equity"

Securities issued by a corporation may be broadly classified as either *equity securities* or *debt securities*. In theory, equity securities refer to all securities that represent ownership interests in the corporation, while debt securities, such as bonds or debentures, represent interests that must eventually be repaid. Common shares, of course, are the ultimate equity security since they represent the basic residual ownership of the corporation.

Initially, the distinction between equity and debt seems sharp. A debt is something that must be repaid: It is the result of a loan, and if periodic payments are made, they are interest. On the other hand, equity represents an ownership interest in the business itself. One thinks in terms of shareholders, shares of capital stock, voting, and dividends rather than interest. The fact is, however, that the distinction between debt and equity is not at all clear in many marginal situations. For example, a 100-year debt instrument with interest payable solely from income if and when earned, with repayment subordinate to all other debts of the business is much more like an equity security than a debt security. Corporations sometimes create mixed or hybrid securities which have some of the characteristics of debt and some of equity. Despite the lack of clear distinction between debt and equity in these situations, legal consequences vary substantially depending on how a particular hybrid security is classified. A hybrid security may be treated as a debt security for some purposes and as an equity security for other purposes, (e.g., income taxation, rights on bankruptcy or insolvency, and the right to participate in management).

§13.18 The Mix of Debt and Equity in Capitalizations: Leverage

The *capital structure* of a corporation refers to the mix of debt and equity in the permanent or near-permanent capitalization of the corporation. The first chapters of this book gave numerous examples of the effect debt has on the profitability of commercial enterprises. See particularly Chapter 3. Increasing the amount of debt capital in a capital structure has somewhat the same effect on corporate profitability.

A capital structure that has large amounts of debt capital is said to be a leveraged capital structure. A process by which debt capital is substituted for equity capital (e.g., by distributing equity capital and then borrowing long-term funds to replace them) or by which the debt component in a capital structure is increased (e.g., by borrowing funds and distributing them to shareholders in the form of a dividend) is sometimes described as *leveraging up* the capital structure.

A useful way to encapsulate the relationship of debt and equity in a capital structure is the debt/equity ratio, the ratio of long-term debt to equity. See §9.9.6. For example, a corporation with $2,000,000 of long-term debt and $1,000,000 of equity has a debt/equity ratio of 2/1. In calculating debt/equity ratios, it is customary to classify interests in a traditional manner. Thus, a class of preferred shares is usually viewed as equity even though it is redeemable and has many of the characteristics of debt. Similarly, debt interests may have some of the characteristics of equity and yet be considered debt in determining the initial debt/equity ratio. It is also customary to exclude short term debt (i.e.,

Table 13-2

ALTERNATIVE A

Assumed net earnings	$25,000	$100,000	$150,000	$200,000
Number of shares	50,000	50,000	50,000	50,000
Earnings per share	$0.50	$2.00	$3.00	$4.00

ALTERNATIVE B

Assumed net earnings	$25,000	$100,000	$150,000	$200,000
Interest on bonds (8% on $250,000)	$20,000	$20,000	$20,000	$20,000
Earnings allocable to common	$5,000	$80,000	$130,000	$180,000
Number of shares	25,000	25,000	25,000	25,000
Earnings per share	$0.20	$3.20	$5.20	$7.20

debt that is to be paid within a year). While this ratio is a convenient descriptive tool of the capitalization of a corporation, it should be apparent that it is hardly a complete description of the way in which a corporation is capitalized.

Leverage arises from the use of debt capital when the corporation is able to earn more on the borrowed capital than the cost of the borrowing. The entire excess of earnings over costs is allocable to the equity accounts of the corporation, thereby increasing the rate of return on the equity invested in the corporation. An example may help to make this clear. Assume that a corporation has total invested capital of $500,000. Let us consider the earnings per share on two alternative assumptions: (A) all this capital is invested as common stock, say, 50,000 shares sold at $10.00 per share, and (B) half is borrowed on a long-term basis at 8 percent per year, and the other half is common stock, e.g., 25,000 shares sold at $10.00 per share. The two alternatives are illustrated in Table 13-2.

In alternative B, interest payable on the bonds represents a fixed cost, a charge for obtaining the use of $250,000 of capital. Thus, the $20,000 interest cost must be deducted as an expense before calculation of income allocable to the common shares in alternative B. When earnings are low, debt service takes up most of the earnings: In the hypothetical above, if earnings drop below $20,000, alternative B will show losses while alternative A continues to show modest profits until earnings drop to zero. When earnings increase above $20,000, however, the per share earnings under alternative B rise much more rapidly than alternative A even though the shares are otherwise identical. In effect in alternative B the common shareholders are getting $500,000 to work for them even though they contributed only $250,000 at the cost of the fixed interest charge, which they must meet out of their own capital if necessary. Thus, leverage in the capital structure context is essentially the same phenomenon that makes commercial real estate development a potential boom or bust industry. (See Chapter 3.)

One question discussed in finance courses is whether the total value of a business is increased by a leveraged capital structure. The question, in other words, is whether the aggregate market value of the stock in alternative (A) would be less than the sum of the aggregate market values of the bonds and the stock in alternative (B). The Miller-Modigliani theorem states (with certain simplifying assumptions, including elimination of the tax advantage of debt) that the aggregate value of a corporation's securities is independent of the amount of debt in the corporation's capital structure. In other words, in a perfect world any enhanced value of common stock in alternative (B) because of the advantages of leverage is precisely offset by a reduced market value of the bonds. The above illustration shows leverage in its simplest form in a capital structure.

CHAPTER 14

A SURVEY OF CORPORATIONS LARGE AND SMALL

§14.1 Introduction

Most economic activity in the United States is conducted in corporate form: As a result, a study of corporation law is an important aspect of legal education. It is sometimes not fully appreciated that corporations differ widely in form and structure; they are not all cast from a single mold. Throughout the legal literature relating to corporations there are references to two different corporate forms: *publicly held corporations* and *closely held corporations*. These two corporate forms are quite dissimilar in most important attributes. The only aspects that they have in common are that both are created under the same set of state statutes (the state corporation laws) and both have the same internal tripartite structure described in §13.6.3: shareholders, a board of directors, and corporate officers. As a result, they share a common core of legal principles despite the very different economic and social environments in which they operate.

This brief chapter explores what is meant by publicly held and closely held corporations. It also points out that there are many thousands of corporations that do not fit these extremes, corporations that, in other words, share some characteristics of both types of corporations.

§14.2 Publicly Held Corporations

A *publicly held corporation* is one that has outstanding shares held by a large number of people. While there is no minimum number that defines when a corporation is publicly held, corporations with shares traded on the securities exchanges, or shares for which there are published price quotations (see Chapter 18), are clearly publicly held. Corporations with more than $5,000,000 of assets and an outstanding class of securities held by more than 500 shareholders of record are subject to special regulation under the Federal Securities Exchange Act of 1934 (1934 Act), including requirements that the corporation register that class with the SEC and make public periodic financial information. Corporations with securities registered with the SEC under the 1934 Act (often called, not surprisingly, *registered corporations*) are all publicly held corporations. However, there are also corporations that are considered publicly held even though they have less than $5,000,000 of assets or securities held by fewer than 500 people.

Publicly held may also be defined in terms of whether a corporation has ever made a public offering of its securities. The Federal Securities Act of 1933 (the 1933 Act) and state statutes (called blue sky laws) provide that corporations may not sell securities to the public unless a registration statement has been filed with the SEC or state security commissions (or both) and reviewed and approved. A *public offering* under the 1933 Act is defined in terms of the sophistication of the people being solicited, not their numbers. In some circumstances, an offering to a very small number of unsophisticated potential investors may be a public offering under the 1933 Act. Most state statutes employ a numerical minimum for defining a public offering. A common provision is that an offering to less than 35 persons is not a public offering; an offering to a larger number is a public offering, as is any offering involving public advertising or solicitation.

Corporations may have to register both an issue of securities under the 1934 Act and a proposed offering under the 1933 Act. In the case of corporations that are already registered under the 1934 Act, registration of a public offering under the 1933 Act is usually relatively simple, since a corporation may incorporate its 1934 Act filings into its 1933 Act registration.

When an unregistered corporation is planning to make its first public offering, the 1933 Act registration is an important and often difficult step, requiring full disclosure and careful planning. Usually an unregistered corporation that makes its first public offering files a 1934 Act registration shortly after the public distribution is completed.

Many publicly held companies are quite large. The so-called *Fortune 500* — the 500 largest corporations as determined by Fortune magazine — is composed almost entirely of publicly held companies. These companies each have billions of dollars of assets and annual sales, thousands of employees, and usually tens or hundreds of thousands of shareholders. They possess tremendous economic and political power merely from their size and their importance to the economy of communities, cities, and indeed, whole states. However, size alone is not a reliable criterion for the definition of a publicly held corporation: A few closely held corporations rival publicly held corporations in size.

The most important distinguishing features of publicly held corporations are: (1) the existence of a public market for their shares so that investors can buy and sell relatively easily, and (2) the wide availability of relatively current information about their activities.

§14.3 Closely Held Corporations

A *closely held corporation* is one with relatively few shareholders. Again there is no definite maximum number, but everyone agrees that a corporation with less than 15 shareholders is a closely held corporation, and one may argue that a corporation is still closely held if the number of shareholders is as large as, say, 35 or 50. Typically a closely held corporation is one in which (1) the number of shareholders is small, (2) there is no outside market for its shares, (3) all or most of the principal shareholders participate in its management, and (4) the free transferability of shares is restricted by agreement. A closely held corporation is almost always one that has never had a successful registered public offering of securities and certainly is not registered with the SEC under the 1934 Act. Obviously, most closely held corporations are small and most publicly held corporations are large, but that is not universally true.

The absence of a market for shares is the most important single characteristic of a closely held corporation. Because there is no market for shares, there is a substantial risk that minority shareholders may be locked in with no avenue to sell their shares if they become alienated from the majority shareholders. See §11.8.3. As a result, outside investors are usually reluctant to make equity investments in closely held corporations, and do so only if contractual commitments are entered into under which the shares of minority shareholders will be purchased by the corporation, or more rarely, by the other shareholders under specified circumstances.

Where a closely held corporation is involved one should never assume that a market for the shares exists or that a dissatisfied minority shareholder has the option of selling his or her shares at a fair price. See Chapter 11.

§14.4 Management of Closely Held and Publicly Held Corporations

The corporate model that appears in state incorporation statutes assumes that shareholders are the ultimate owners of the enterprise and that they elect directors to manage the affairs of the corporation. The directors in turn select officers to implement the board's policies. This is an idealized model that is not tailored specifically either for the closely held corporation or for the publicly held corporation. It is a model that is sufficiently broad and generalized that large portions of it are appropriate for both the very large and the very small.

Despite this common core of legal principles, management of publicly held and closely held corporations in actuality usually have little in common.

§14.4.1 Closely Held Corporations

In a closely held corporation, the principal shareholders in the corporation are usually actively involved in management. Decisions are apt to be made informally and without formal meetings or votes. The corporation may have elected S corporation treatment to minimize the business's aggregate tax cost. Most of the earnings may be distributed informally in the form of salaries, interest, or rent to specific shareholders rather than distributed to the shareholders generally in the form of dividends. A minority shareholder may easily be frozen out from financial participation merely by the remaining shareholders' refusing to allow him or her to participate in management decisions or to receive salary or other payments from the corporation.

About a dozen states have also supplemented their general corporation statutes with optional special statutes designed to provide relaxed rules of mangement for closely held corporations.

§14.4.2 Publicly Held Corporations

In a publicly held corporation the management structure is entirely different from both the theoretical management structure contemplated by the corporation statutes and the actual management structure of closely held corporations. In a publicly held corporation, shareholders are large in number, disorganized, and diffuse; usually no individual or group has direct voting control. Management recommendations are usually accepted by most shareholders. Consider, for example, the role of the small shareholder in selecting directors in such a corporation. He or she is presented with a list of candidates selected and recommended by the current managers of the corporation. The shareholder may vote for them or withhold his or her vote; rarely does he or she have a choice among competing directoral candidates. Further, since the overwhelming majority of the shareholders are going to vote in favor of the persons proposed by management, it really does not make much difference whether or not the small shareholder exercises the franchise or pitches the proxy solicitation form into the nearest trash basket.

For purposes of locating the real source of selection of directors, one must usually look not to the election process, but to some earlier point where an internal decision within the corporation was made as to which names should be presented to the shareholders as the management's candidates. This decision may have been made by the chief executive officer individually, or it may have been made by a committee composed of members of management or of the board of directors. However it was made, this is usually the critical point at which the actual selection of directors occurs. The actual role of shareholders in publicly held corporations is to merely ratify this selection.

Most shareholders routinely accept management's recommendations. For one thing, they often have only the choice of voting in favor of management or not voting at all. For another, many of the issues on which shareholders vote are routine and not controversial, though it may be hard to tell since shareholders rarely hear competing points of view from within management. Rather, management formulates its decision or recommendation and presents it as the experienced voice of those actually managing a complex business; usually no hint of possible internal disagreement or other independent voice is heard through the corporate machinery. Further, it is difficult for either shareholders or outsiders to communicate with each other or address the shareholders as a body. The managers control the *proxy solicitation machinery*. They have the list of shareholders, and are not likely to make that list available to outsiders without a court proceeding. Persons seeking to challenge incumbent management on most issues coming before the shareholders for a vote thus face formidable, if not impossible, obstacles.

Another important reason for the pro-management bias of shareholders is that there is natural self-selection by shareholders. The presence of an active market in shares means that shareholders dissatisfied with the management of a corporation may exercise the "Wall Street option" and sell their shares and invest the proceeds elsewhere rather than fight city hall. Thus, by a process of self-elimination, shareholders unhappy with management tend to disappear, and the remaining shareholders tend to be pro-management, or at least not anti-management. The increased importance of institutional investors described in §14.5 has also helped to solidify incumbent management. Institutional investors own large numbers of shares and usually vote as management recommends.

Management control, however, is not limitless. The exercise of the Wall Street option is in a sense a vote. A poor operating performance by management results in depressed share prices and may lead indirectly to the ouster of management. See Chapter 17.

§14.5 The Growth of Institutional Investors

For many years the small shareholder described in the previous section was thought to epitomize the public shareholder. The predominant view was that share ownership of publicly held corporations was almost atomistic, and that as a result management had virtually a free hand. "Ownership" had become separated from "control." This was the position put forth by A. Berle and G. Means in their influential book of 1932, *The Modern Corporation and Private Property*, and was not seriously questioned until relatively recently. It is doubtful that this view was ever entirely correct, but since World War II a development has occurred that puts quite a different complexion on share ownership patterns. A new type of public investor has grown tremendously in importance — the *institutional investor*. Institutional investors mainly collect and invest other people's money. They include life insurance companies, pension funds, investment companies (mutual funds), bank trust departments, and similar organizations. Assets managed by institutional investors have grown spectacularly, often by factors of 100 or more in the last 40 years. These institutional investors invest only in publicly held corporations, and often only in the largest and most widely traded companies. Overall, they invest huge amounts of capital in a large variety of securities traded on the major securities exchanges. As a group they are now the largest single owner of publicly held corporations; their holdings in the aggregate are in excess of 40 percent of all the outstanding shares of listed publicly held corporations, and, in specific corporations, the percentage may run over 50 percent.

Since funds invested by institutional investors ultimately belong to members of the general public in the form of pensions, life insurance proceeds, savings, or financial investments, their growth can be viewed as increasing the broad base of ownership of the means of production in modern society. However, in terms of power and potential control, the growth of institutional investors represents a concentration of the base. Now only a relatively few persons — the managers of and investment advisers for the institutional investors — determine where huge investments are to be placed and how large blocks of shares are to be voted.

Institutional investors often have the power, if they band together, to effectively dominate and control many large publicly held corporations. Most institutional investors, however, view their role as purely investors and eschew any interest in managing or exercising control over the business and affairs of corporations. This attitude partially explains why institutional investors usually vote their shares in favor of management: If they are dissatisfied with management, they prefer to sell their shares rather than engage in a struggle for control. In a relatively recent development, however, some institutional investors have felt compelled to take affirmative action in opposition to management in connection with the adoption of defenses against takeover attempts by outsiders.

Even though institutional investors view themselves as passive investors, their sheer size raises unique market problems. For example, if an institutional investor decides to exercise its Wall Street option and sell its shares, the block may be so large that only other institutional investors have the capacity to absorb the shares. Large institutional holdings may therefore increase the volatility of share prices since an independent decision by several large institutional investors to dispose of their shares may markedly depress short-run prices because there is not enough demand to absorb the shares being dumped on the market.

Institutional investors often owe fiduciary duties to pension beneficiaries or beneficial owners of investment company shares, which require that the institutional investor maximize its short-run market gains. It has been feared that this concern for short-run return by the largest and most important shareholders may in turn compel corporate management to concentrate on maximizing its short-term earnings to the possible detriment of longer-range profitability. Whether or not this fear is justified is uncertain.

§14.6 Many Corporations Are "In-Between" Corporations

The dichotomy between closely held and publicly held is so sharp and clearly etched that most discussion tends to view all corporations as belonging to one category or another. There are, however, substantial numbers of corporations that have some of the characteristics of both types.

There have been several attempts to describe the corporate population. Table 14-1 shows a breakdown developed by Professor Melvin Eisenberg in 1976.

The table reveals that as of the early 1970s, closely held corporations were by far the most numerous, that all traditional publicly held corporations probably numbered under 10,000, and that there were about 25,000 "in-between corporations" with between 100 and 500 shareholders. Another study prepared about the same time by Professor Alfred Conard based on 1970 Internal Revenue Service data also broadly supports the view that there are thousands of corporations that have more shareholders than a traditional closely held corporation but which are also unlike the average publicly held corporation with shares listed on the New York Stock Exchange. There may be limited

Table 14-1

No. of Shareholders	Approximate No. of Corporations
1-10	1,630,000
11-99	70,000
100-499	26,500
500-1,499	5,000
1,500-2,999	1,700
3,000-10,000	1,200
Over 10,000	600

Source: M. Eisenberg, The Structure of the Corporation (1976) at 42.

trading markets for the shares of many of these in-between corporations, but if there are, they are probably "thin" and relatively inactive.

More current data is available on the number of large publicly held corporations. A study published by the American Law Institute's Corporate Governance Project in 1984 divides publicly held corporations into tiers. Tier One consists of corporations with at least 2,000 record holders of equity securities and $100 million of assets. The Project estimates that there are between 1,500 and 2,000 corporations in Tier One. Tier Two consists of corporations (other than Tier One corporations) with at least 500 record holders and $3 million of assets. The Project estimates that there are between 5,500 and 6,500 corporations in Tier Two. If these estimates are reasonably accurate it appears that the number of corporations with more than 500 record holders has not increased appreciably in the last 15 or 20 years. This data probably cannot be safely generalized to make current estimates of the number of in-between corporations, that is, those with more than 100 record holders but less than 500 holders.

Because the asset holdings of publicly held corporations are immense, they have tremendous economic importance, far greater than their numbers would indicate. In 1984, the 100 largest industrial publicly held corporations alone owned nearly 49 percent of all manufacturing company assets; the 200 largest owned over 60 percent.

CHAPTER 15

CORPORATE SECURITIES

§15.1 Introduction

Perhaps no other area of corporation law is more confusing to persons without prior business backgrounds than corporate securities such as shares of stock, bonds, and debentures. The language is new and unfamiliar, the concepts seem mysterious and sometimes illogical, and everything seems to build on historical concepts of dubious relevance today. This chapter should help to dispel this mystery. The rights given to security holders by statute or by contract build on simple principles. Words such as *cumulative* or *convertible* may sound difficult and confusing, but the concepts are not.

This chapter is largely directed toward publicly traded securities issued by large, publicly held corporations. This chapter therefore provides important background for the following chapters of this book (Chapters 16-20) dealing with dividend policies, takeovers, securities markets, and investment strategies.

§15.2 Common Shares

Shares of common stock are the fundamental units into which the proprietary interest of the corporation is divided. If a corporation issues only one class of shares, they may be referred to by a variety of similar names: *common shares*, *common stock*, *capital stock*, or, possibly, simply *shares* or *stock*. Whatever the name, they are the basic proprietary units of ownership and are referred to here as simply common shares.

The two fundamental characteristics of common shares are (1) they are entitled to vote for the election of directors and on other matters coming before the shareholders and (2) they are entitled to the net assets of the corporation (after making allowance for debts and senior securities) when distributions are to be made, either during the course of the life of the corporation or upon its dissolution.

The fundamental incorporating document of every corporation must state the number of shares of common stock the corporation is authorized to issue. This number is known as the corporation's *authorized capital* or *authorized shares*. In states with older statutes, that document must also set forth the *par value* of the authorized shares or a statement that the shares are without par value. Par value is an arbitrary number without economic significance that, in older statutes, determines the amount of permanent capital and *capital surplus* in the original capitalization of the corporation. See §16.3.

Corporations usually authorize more common shares than they currently plan to issue. Additional authorized shares may be useful if it is decided, for example, to raise capital in the future by selling additional shares, to provide economic incentives to executives or key employees by granting them options to purchase shares at favorable prices, to create an Employee Share Ownership Plan for all employees, or to issue debt or senior classes of securities that have the privilege of being converted into common shares.

The capitalization of a corporation is based on the number of shares actually issued and the capital received therefor, not on the number of authorized shares. Capital received in exchange for shares is usually referred to as the corporation's invested capital (or sometimes its contributed capital) and from an accounting standpoint (though as §16.3 demonstrates, not necessarily from a legal standpoint) is viewed as being invested in the corporation permanently or indefinitely.

§15.3 Reporting of Earnings per Share

Publicly held corporations report publicly their earnings each year on an aggregate basis and on a per-share basis. Earnings per share equal net earnings divided by the number of shares outstanding. See §9.10.4. Publicly held corporations almost always have outstanding commitments to issue, or have granted rights in third persons to acquire, additional shares either by purchase, option exercise, or conversion of convertible securities. These are potential shares since the privilege of acquiring the shares has not yet been exercised: The number of potential shares may be large in comparison with the number of actually issued and outstanding shares. The question then arises, what should be done about potential shares when reporting earnings. Should earnings per share be calculated on shares actually outstanding or on shares potentially outstanding? The solution adopted by the Securities and Exchange Commission is very sensible. When the number of potential shares is material, earnings per share must be reported on both an *actual share basis* and a *fully diluted basis*, that is on the assumption that all options and rights to acquire additional shares have been exercised. Table 15-1 is an example of such reporting for the quarterly earnings of Circle K Corporation, a corporation whose common shares are traded on the New York Stock Exchange.

Table 15-1
Circle K Corporation
Earnings for the Quarter Ending July 31

	1987	*1986*
Sales	$678,530,000	$585,302,000
Net income	17,756,000	18,634,000
Avg. shares	52,634,983	a45,805,748
Shr. earns (primary):		
Net income	.32	.38[a]
Shr. earns (fully diluted):		.31[a]
Net income	.29	

a. Adjusted to reflect a two-for-one stock split paid in September 1986.

§15.4 Preferred Shares

Preferred shares differ from common shares in that (1) they usually have limited rights, and (2) one or more of those rights has a preference over the rights of common shares. Preferential rights are almost always financial in character. Most preferred shares have preferential rights over common shares both in connection with the payment of dividends and in connection with distributions of assets in voluntary or involuntary dissolution of the corporation. A dividend preference means that the preferred shares are entitled to receive a specified dividend each year before any dividend may be paid on the common shares; a preference in liquidation means that the preferred shares are entitled to receive a specified distribution from corporate assets in liquidation (after provision has been made for corporate debts) before the common shares are entitled to receive anything. However, some preferred shares may have only a dividend preference and no liquidation preference, or vice versa.

The rights of preferred shareholders are defined in the corporation's articles of incorporation (or other incorporating document), bylaws, or directors' resolutions filed with the articles of incorporation (in the case of series of preferred shares). If an existing corporation wishes to create a new class of preferred shares, it must usually formally amend its articles of incorporation. Collectively the provisions in these basic corporate documents describing and defining the terms and rights of preferred shareholders are referred to as the *preferred shareholders' contract* with the corporation. Basically, this usage reflects that rights of preferred shareholders are generally limited to those set forth in this contract and that preferred shareholders have relatively few rights outside of those granted expressly to them by that contract.

A single corporation may have outstanding several different classes of preferred shares with varying rights and preferences. While a specific class of preferred may have subordinate rights to another class of preferred, both are still preferred shares since they both have preferences over the common shares. The dividend preference may be described either in terms of dollars per share (the "$3.20 preferred") or as a percentage of par or stated value (the "5 percent preferred"). A dividend preference does not mean that the preferred is entitled to the payment in the same way that a creditor is entitled to payment from his or her debtor. A preferred dividend is still a dividend, and may be made only if the corporation has available surplus from which a preferred dividend may be made. See generally §16.3. Further, even if there are funds legally available from which a preferred dividend may be paid, the directors may decide to omit all dividends, common and preferred. The incentive to pay a preferential dividend comes from the principle that if it is omitted all dividends on the common shares must also be omitted. The preference feature of preferred shares technically means that it is entitled to be paid its dividend first from any amount set aside by the board of directors for the payment of dividends.

§15.4.1　Cumulative and Noncumulative Dividends

Shares preferred as to dividends may be *cumulative*, *noncumulative*, or *partially cumulative*. If cumulative dividends are not paid in some years, they are carried forward and both they and the current year's preferred dividends must be paid in full before any common dividends may be declared. Noncumulative dividends disappear each year if they are not paid. Partially cumulative dividends are usually cumulative to the extent of earnings, that is, the dividend is cumulative in any year only to the extent of actual earnings during that year. Unpaid cumulative dividends are not debts of the corporation, but a continued right to priority in future earnings.

An example may help to illustrate the concept of cumulative, noncumulative, and partially cumulative dividends. Assume that a preferred stock has a preferential right to a dividend of $5 per share per year, but the directors, as is their right, decide to omit all dividends for two consecutive years. In the third year they conclude that the corporation is able to resume the payment of dividends. If the preferred shares' preferential right is cumulative, the board of directors must pay $15 on each preferred share ($5 per share for each of the two years missed plus $5 per share for the current year) before any dividend may be paid on the common shares in the third year. If the preferred shares' preferential right is noncumulative the preferences for the two omitted years disappear entirely, and a dividend on the common shares may be paid after the $5 preferred dividend for the third year is paid. If the dividend is cumulative to the extent earned, the earnings of the corporation in each of the two years in which dividends were omitted must be examined, and the dividend is cumulative each year only to the extent the earnings cover the $5 preferred dividend: If the corporation had a loss in one of those years, the preferred dividend for that year would be lost much as though the dividend were entirely noncumulative.

In evaluating dividend policies with respect to preferred shares, one should normally start with the assumption that the board of directors is elected by the common shareholders and will normally maximize the dividends payable on common shares at the expense of preferred shareholders to the extent they lawfully may do so. A noncumulative preferential dividend right therefore leaves the preferred shareholders quite exposed, because the common shareholders' position is improved in the future whenever a preferred dividend is omitted.

Indeed, a policy of paying dividends erratically once every few years materially improves the position of the common with respect to the noncumulative preferred. Do you see why? Such a policy, however, may be subject to legal attack as a breach of the directors' fiduciary duty to treat fairly all classes of outstanding shares.

Cumulative dividends provide preferred shareholders considerably greater protection than noncumulative or partially cumulative dividends. But cumulative dividends are not a complete answer either, because the board of directors may defer the payment of all dividends indefinitely in an effort to depress the price of the preferred which may then be acquired on the open market. On the other hand, it is customary to provide that preferred shares may elect a specified number of directors if preferred dividends have been omitted for a specified period, and the presence of one or more directors elected by the preferred shareholders may minimize the possibility of such overtly unfair strategies.

§15.4.2 Participating Preferred Shares

The distribution rights of most preferred shares are limited to specific preferential amounts set forth in the preferred shareholders' contract. They are thus entitled to the specified dividend before anything is paid on the common, but they will never be paid anything more irrespective of how large the earnings of the corporation become. Indeed, an attempt by directors to pay a dividend to preferred shareholders in excess of their limited dividend right may be enjoined by common shareholders as a violation of their rights.

Participating preferred shares are shares that are entitled to the original preferential dividend, and after the common receives a specified amount, they may share with the common in any additional distributions. Such shares are quite rare; they are sometimes referred to as "Class A common" or a similar designation reflecting that their right to participate is open-ended. Preferred shares are participating shares only if their rights are so defined in the preferred shareholders' contract.

§15.4.3 Convertible Preferred Shares

Preferred shares may be made convertible at the option of the preferred shareholder into common shares at a specified price or a specified ratio. When convertible shares are converted, the original preferred shares are turned in and cancelled, and new common shares are issued. The conversion price or ratio is fixed and defined in the preferred shareholders' contract: The conversion ratio is usually made adjustable for share dividends, share splits, the issuance of additional common shares, and similar transactions affecting the underlying common shares. The provisions requiring such adjustments are usually called *anti-dilution provisions*. See §15.6.

The determination of the conversion ratio, that is, how many shares of common stock a preferred shareholder receives upon the exercise of the conversion privilege, may involve negotiation between the corporation and a potential investor. Convertible preferred stock may be issued to a venture capital fund or other investor in a closely held corporation to reflect a limited equity investment in the enterprise. Convertible preferred stock may also be issued by publicly held corporations, and the convertible preferred stock may itself be publicly traded. Typically, when both the common and the convertible preferred are publicly traded, the original conversion ratio is established so that the common must appreciate substantially in price before it becomes attractive to convert the preferred into common. A rather detailed illustration of the application of these principles appears in §§15.5 and 15.6 of this chapter.

§15.4.4 Redeemability of Preferred Shares

Preferred shares are usually made redeemable at the option of the corporation upon the payment of a fixed amount for each share. Such shares are called *callable* or *redeemable shares*. The redemption price may be a matter of negotiation between the corporation and an investor. Redemption prices are established in the preferred shareholders' contract; they are usually established at a level somewhat higher than the consideration originally paid by the investor for the preferred shares.

The power to redeem preferred shares is usually applicable only to the entire class or series of preferred as a unit. However, the preferred shareholders' contract sometimes provides that redemptions of a portion of a class or series are permitted; such provisions may also include rules for determining which shares are to be redeemed. If a convertible preferred is called for redemption, the conversion privilege continues after the announcement that the shares will be called for redemption until the shares are actually redeemed.

§15.4.5 Sinking Fund Provisions

Some classes of preferred may have the benefit of *sinking fund provisions*. Such provisions require the issuer to set aside a specified amount each year to retire a portion of the shares of the class that are outstanding. The retirement usually may be made by redemption or by the repurchase of the shares on the open market.

§15.4.6 Series and Classes of Preferred Shares

Articles of incorporation may also authorize preferred shares to be issued in series. The articles of incorporation in effect create a class of shares without any substantive terms and authorize the board of directors to create series from within that class from time to time and to vary any of the substantive terms of each series. Where preferred shares are to be sold by a corporation from time to time to raise capital in substantial amounts, the privilege of allowing the board of directors to set financial terms simplifies financing since the price, dividend, liquidation preference, sinking fund provision, voting rights, and other terms of each series may be tailored to then-current market conditions without incurring the expense of a proxy solicitation and the holding of a special shareholders' meeting to approve the terms of the class. Shares of different series have identical rights except for the specified business terms, which may be varied.

During the 1980s the power to create series of preferred shares was utilized by boards of directors of publicly held corporations fearing a takeover to create "poison pills" without shareholder approval. See §17.13.

There is little or no difference between a series or a class of shares except their manner of creation — by amendment to the articles of incorporation in the case of a class and by action of the board of directors, acting alone, in the case of a series.

§15.4.7 Novel Types of Preferred Shares

The high interest rates of the early 1980s led to the development of novel financing devices, many of which involved preferred shares. For example, many corporations issued preferred stock that was redeemable at the option of the holder, or that became redeemable upon the occurrence of some external event, such as a change in interest rates or the lapse of a specified period of time. Still other corporations issued preferred shares with floating or adjustable dividend rates that depended on interest rates or some similar measure. Most of these novel preferreds were designed to give corporate holders of the preferred the tax benefits of the exclusion for intercorporate dividends, while at the same time giving the holders most of the benefits of traditional debt.

§15.5 Market Price of Simple Preferred Shares

Many preferred shares are publicly traded on the major securities exchanges. Many are listed on the New York Stock Exchange. (If you are not sure you understand what these statements involve you should read §18.3.) Most publicly traded preferreds are straight preferred shares that have fully cumulative limited dividend rights. As a practical matter, in the case of most of these preferred shares, there is virtually no chance that a dividend will ever be omitted. In effect, these securities provide a permanent cash flow in a fixed amount. The value placed on these shares in the market represents little more than the present value of this discounted future cash flow. Yields on high-quality straight preferred shares (the return per dollar invested in the shares) were between 10 and 12 percent in the fall of 1987. At the same time, the yield on investment quality bonds was between 9 and 10 percent. Preferred shares priced on this basis are described below as straight preferreds or pure preferreds. See also §18.9.

§15.5.1 Market Price of Convertible Preferred Shares: Arbitrage

The pricing of a convertible preferred is considerably more interesting and more complex than the pricing of a straight preferred. A rather involved example should be useful. Assume that a publicly held corporation has out-standing several million shares of common stock traded on the New York Stock Exchange. The current market price of the common is $20 per share, and management believes that it is likely to trade in the $20 - $30 range for the indefinite future. A regular dividend of $1 per share has been paid on the common shares for the last three years and management anticipates that this regular dividend will be continued at that rate for the indefinite future. In order to raise additional working capital, the corporation decides to make a public offering of a new convertible preferred stock with the following rights: It is to be entitled to a cumulative dividend of $6 per share per year and will be offered initially to the public at $54 per share in order to yield an initial investor an 11 percent return, the approximate yield of similar convertible preferred shares. There is no appreciable risk that the $6 dividend will be omitted in any year in the foreseeable future. The preferred share is convertible into two shares of common stock at any time at the option of the holder and is callable by the corporation at any time for $65 per share. It is anticipated that the preferred will also be publicly traded on the New York Stock Exchange. The basic financial characteristics described in this paragraph may be summarized:

	Preferred shares	*Common shares*
Market price	$54	$20
Dividend	$ 6	$ 1
Convertibility	Into common 2:1	no
Callability	$65	no

When the preferred is issued, it begins to trade on the New York Stock Exchange at between $52 and $60 per share. At that price, no one exercises the conversion privilege: After all, why give up something worth between $52 and $60 in order to acquire two shares of stock that can be bought on the New York Stock Exchange for $40? Similarly, the corporation probably will not give serious consideration to calling the preferred at $65: If the corporation wishes to retire some preferred shares, it may buy them on the open market for $52 to $60; why pay $65 for them?

Now consider what happens to the price of the preferred when the price of the common begins to creep up. When it reaches $27.50 per share, the value of the conversion security (the security into which the preferred may be converted) has risen to $55, and the preferred must rise in price and remain at or above $55 per share. If it drops below $55 (to $53, say), speculators who closely follow the market will realize that they can buy the preferred at $53 and immediately convert it into common shares that can be immediately sold for $55 per share, making an instant $2 riskless profit. This type of transaction is known as *arbitrage*, a fancy term for the process of profiting on small differences in market prices of two different but equivalent securities (as here) or in the market prices of the same security in two different markets or available at two different times.

Assume now that the price of the common rises further to $32 per share. The floor under the preferred is now $64, and every purchaser of the initial preferred at $54 has made a tidy *paper profit* of at least $10 per share. (It is only a paper profit because it has not been realized either by the sale of the preferred or by its conversion into common and the sale of the common.) More importantly, when the common is at $32, the preferred is no longer priced in the market as a straight preferred. Rather, its price is now directly tied to the price of the common in accordance with the conversion ratio: If the common declines in price by $1 per share, the preferred will decline by about $2 per share; if the common goes up by $3 per share to $35, the preferred will go up by about $6 per share. If there is a major market sell-off and the price of the common plummets, the preferred will follow the common down (at a $2 decline per preferred share for each $1 decline in value of the common) until the preferred reaches a price that reflects its market value as a pure preferred stock; at that point it will again trade much as a straight preferred.

Assuming that the common is at $32 per share, what price will the market place on the preferred? Will it be $64 or will it be even higher? A moment's thought should indicate that it must be higher than $64: if two shares of common with an aggregate two-dollar dividend sells for $64, a stock with the same market characteristics but with a six-dollar dividend is going to be worth more. How much more? One might expect it would be the present value of the stream of the four-dollar difference between the two dividends. However, it will be much less than that because it is unlikely that the difference in dividend rates will continue indefinitely: The corporation may call the preferred at some time in the future and the $32 price may itself reflect the market anticipating an increase in the common dividend rate. (The second factor is relevant because the preferred's dividend can never exceed $6 per share so that an increase in the common dividend reduces the $4 advantage the preferred now enjoys.) It is not possible to calculate mathematically the values to be assigned to these variables and thus what the price of the preferred should be, except to conclude that it must be higher than $64, perhaps $67 or $68.

Another interesting question is this: should a holder of the preferred convert when the common is at $32 if he believes that the price of the common will go even higher? A moment's thought should reveal that that would be an unwise decision. Why give up a six-dollar cumulative dividend in order to obtain two common shares with a combined dividend of two dollars per share? There is no risk that the expected increase in price of the common will escape the owner of the preferred because, as described above, the price of the preferred is now directly tied to the price of the common. In short, there is nothing to be gained and much to be lost by converting immediately.

$15.5.2 Redemption of Convertible Preferred Shares

Finally, let us consider the strategic considerations that relate to the corporation's power to call the preferred shares for redemption at $65 per share at any time. A critical point is that the corporation must announce an impending redemption in advance, and the privilege to convert continues to exist after the announcement and up until the instant the redemption becomes effective and the shareholder ceases to be a shareholder and is entitled to the $65.

What happens after a call for redemption is issued depends essentially on the price of the underlying common shares at the time the redemption actually occurs. If the market price of two shares of common stock is less than $65 per share at that time, shareholders should not convert their preferred shares into common stock, but rather permit the shares to be called at $65 per share. Thus, if the corporation calls the shares for redemption at a time when the price of the underlying common is $32.50 or less, it should end up redeeming the entire issue for cash and having to pay $65 per share for every share of preferred. On the other hand, if the market price of the common is above $32.50 per share at the time of redemption, the shareholders should exercise the conversion privilege shortly before the call becomes effective and convert the preferred into the more valuable common. For example, if the common is at $35 per share, the choice is between permitting the shares to be called for a payment of $65 or converting them into shares of common stock worth $70. Such a conversion is called *forced* since the economics are such that a rational investor has no choice but to exercise his power to convert (or to sell the preferred, in which case the purchaser will convert).

Of course, in the real world, things do not work perfectly. Preferred shareholders are scattered around the country and may not be able to select the best option at the very last minute. Some must decide several days in advance of the final date, and a last-minute price movement of the common may mean that some make the wrong decision. Also, a few may simply act too late, and find that their shares were redeemed when they intended to exercise the conversion privilege. Still others may be ill, out of the country, or unaware that they own the shares of preferred stock, and make no decision at all. Their shares, of course are all redeemed. But the great bulk of shares will be handled in a rational fashion.

Why do corporations compel forced conversions? From the standpoint of the cash flow of the corporation, the substitution of two shares of common for every share of preferred causes a reduction in dividend payments from $6 to $2 for every share of preferred. This reduction in dividend payments is pure gravy since there is no capital outflow to eliminate the more expensive preferred shares. A forced conversion may also appeal to notions of equity as between holders of the common and of the preferred, since the preferred receives the full benefit of run-ups in the price of the common but enjoys three times the dividend and has some protection against price declines on the down-side. Also, the elimination of the preferred shares simplifies the capital structure of the corporation and improves the appearance of the corporation's balance sheet.

If the directors call a convertible preferred for redemption, they are required to give the holders of the preferred accurate information about the reasons for the redemption. The corporation may not withhold from the preferred shareholders information as to developments that would affect the decision whether or not to convert the shares.

§15.6 Protection of Conversion Privilege Against Dilution

In the example discussed in the last section, each share of the preferred stock is entitled to be converted at any time into two shares of common stock. What happens if the board of directors decides to split the common shares three-to-one — that is, it decides to issue each shareholder a new certificate for two additional shares for every share he or she originally owns so that now each shareholder has three shares where before he or she had one? Let us further assume that the dividend rate on each new share is one-third the rate on the old share so that each new share sells for almost exactly one-third of the price of each old share — about $10 per share if before the split the old shares sold for approximately $30 per share. What does this do to the conversion privilege of the preferred?

The black letter rule is very simple: If the drafters of the preferred share-holders' contract did not take this possibility into account, the conversion privilege is not adjusted for the share split. Each preferred share continues to be convertible into only two shares of common stock and the conversion privilege has lost two-thirds of its potential value. Provisions guarding the conversion privilege against changes of this type in the conversion security are called *anti-dilution provisions* and should always be included in preferred share-holders' contracts when there is a conversion privilege. Drafting an anti-dilution clause is tricky because the courts are not going to help the draftsman out if he or she overlooks some possibility. Significant dilution may occur because of a variety of transactions, such as mergers, share dividends, executive compensation plans, and the like, and it is often controversial as to which issuances of new common shares the anti-dilution clause should protect against. But nevertheless the basic principle seems clear and straightforward, at least so far as shares splits are concerned: The drafters of the preferred shareholders contract should insert a clause providing that if the common stock is split, the conversion privilege should be adjusted so that each share of preferred is convertible into the number of new common shares that two shares of the old common stock became upon the split.

§15.7 Classified Common Stock

State statutes give corporations broad power to create classes of common shares with different rights or privileges. For example, the rights of two classes of shares may be identical except that one class is entitled to twice the dividend per share of the second class. Or, shares of each class may have identical financial rights per share but each class of common shares regardless of the number of shares is entitled to elect one director (thereby assuring equal class representation on the board of directors even though the number of shares in the two classes are unequal). Classes of shares are widely used in closely held corporations to govern the control relationships between two or more shareholders. Such classes are usually designated by alphabetical notations: Class A common, Class B common, and so forth.

Classified common shares are rarely used by publicly held corporations. The New York Stock Exchange has historically refused to list shares of a corporation if the corporation also has a class of nonvoting shares or one or more classes with fractional or multiple votes per share. In the 1980s, several publicly held corporations in which specific families had long been associated in a control capacity sought to combat potential takeover attempts by creating special classes of shares with "super" voting rights per share to be issued solely to family members. The terms of these special classes provided, for example, that they had ten votes per share but lost their special voting privilege if they were sold or conveyed to a person who was not a family member. In 1988 the SEC adopted Rule 19c-4 that in effect outlawed new classes of such shares for publicly traded corporations.

§15.8 Transferable Warrants and Rights to Purchase Shares

Some corporations have issued warrants or rights to purchase common shares. If the common shares are publicly traded, the warrants or rights may themselves also be publicly traded.

Warrants are transferable long-term options to acquire shares from the corporation at a specified price (that usually is fixed for the life of the warrant). Warrants have many of the qualities of an equity security since their price is a function of the market price of the underlying shares and the specified issuance price. Of course, warrants have no dividend rights while the underlying shares normally do receive some dividend. Warrants frequently are issued as a sweetener in connection with the distribution of a debt or preferred stock issue: They may be issued in connection with a public exchange offer, or as compensation for handling the public distribution of other shares. Sometimes they are issued in a reorganization to holders of a class of security not otherwise recognized in the reorganization. Warrants issued by a number of corporations are traded on the New York Stock Exchange or other exchanges.

Rights are short-term warrants, expiring within one year. They may also be publicly traded and listed on securities exchanges. Rights are often issued in lieu of a dividend, or in an effort to raise capital from existing shareholders. The price relationship between a warrant or right and the underlying security is a rather complex one. For example, if the underlying security is selling at $10 per share, and the warrant can be exercised (and the underlying security purchased) for $12 per share, one might expect that the warrant would have no value. After all, who wants a right to purchase for $12 per share what can be bought immediately on the open market for $10? In fact it would have some value (perhaps less than $1 per warrant) because of the possibility that the underlying security may rise in price above $12 during the life of the warrant. If the security does rise above $12 per share, the market price of the warrant will also rise in value virtually on a dollar-for-dollar basis. Whether it would be sensible to exercise such a warrant before its expiration depends on the income foregone on the capital necessary to exercise the warrant compared with the dividends likely to be declared on the underlying security. See the discussion of options trading in §20.2.

The value of a warrant or right may be divided into two components: an *intrinsic value* and a *time value*. In the foregoing example, the warrant when the stock is selling at $10 per share has no intrinsic value but has some time value. When the underlying stock is selling at $12 per share, the warrant has an intrinsic value of $2 per share as well as a time value.

§15.9 Bonds and Debentures

The two types of debt instruments most commonly classed as securities are *debentures* or *bonds*. These types of securities may be publicly traded and have close economic similarities to publicly traded preferred stock.

Both bonds and debentures are debt instruments: They reflect unconditional obligations to pay specific sums at a date in the future and usually to pay interest in specified amounts at specified times in the interim. Technically a debenture is an unsecured corporate obligation while a bond is secured by a lien or mortgage on specific corporate property. However, the word "bond" is often used to mean both bonds and debentures and is so used hereafter. The presence or absence of security for these marketable debt interests is not as important as might be first supposed, because if there is any chance that a secured holder will seek to foreclose on corporate property, the corporation will obtain protection from the federal bankruptcy court. See §§10.8 and 10.9.

A bond is usually a long-term debt security: Long-term may mean 50 years or more in some cases, though many marketable bonds and debentures mature in ten years or less. By tradition, bonds are bearer instruments, negotiable by delivery, with interest payments represented by coupons that are periodically clipped and submitted to the issuer for payment. Registered bonds are also widely used: They are bonds made payable to a specific payee with the coupons removed. Interest is payable to the registered owner of such a bond in much the same way as dividends are payable to the registered owner of shares of stock. Transfer of a registered bond is effected by endorsement rather than by mere physical delivery of the piece of paper. Article 8 of the Uniform Commercial Code makes registered bonds negotiable just like any other security. The Internal Revenue Code now requires virtually all new bonds to be registered securities, transferable only by endorsement, so that in future years, it is likely that registered bonds will become more common and bearer bonds rarer.

Interest payments on debt securities are usually fixed obligations, due in any event, and expressed as a percentage of the face amount of the security. However, so-called income bonds, in which the obligation to pay interest is conditioned on adequate corporate earnings, also exist. See §13.17. Somewhat rarer are so-called participating bonds, where the amount of interest payable on the bonds increases with corporate earnings. Such securities are known as hybrid securities since they have some characteristics of an equity security. In recent years debt securities with variable interest rates — based on market interest rates — have also been created.

Debt securities are usually subject to redemption, which means that the corporation has reserved the power to call in and pay off the obligation before it is due, often at a slight premium over the face value of the debt security. Unlike redemption of preferred shares, some bonds may be redeemed without redeeming the entire issue. Securities chosen for redemption may be chosen by lot or by some other system. In a sense redemption of part of a debt issue is partial disproportionate prepayment rather than redemption, but the principle is the same. Many debt securities require the corporation to create sinking funds, to redeem a part of the issue each year or to accumulate to pay off the entire issue when it matures. Similar provisions are also common in connection with issues of preferred stock.

Debt securities, like preferred stock, may also be made convertible into equity securities, almost always common shares, on some predetermined ratio. The conversion privilege for bonds operates in a very similar manner to conversion privilege for preferred shares discussed above. Like convertible preferred, the conversion ratio is set by the creating documents and usually protected against dilution by adjustments for share splits, dividends, etc. When convertible debentures are converted, they, and the debt they represent, disappear and new equity securities (the conversion securities) are issued in their place. Convertible debentures themselves are treated as equity securities for some purposes; in calculating fully diluted earnings per share, for example, the common shares that would be issued upon conversion are taken into account in the calculation.

The interaction between the power of the corporation to call convertible debentures and the power of the holder to exercise the conversion privilege is similar to that of preferred shares. If a convertible debenture is called for redemption, the conversion privilege continues until the debentures are actually redeemed. If the value of the conversion securities exceeds the redemption price, it is obviously to the holders' advantage to convert following an announcement that the debentures will be called for redemption on a specified date. Such a conversion is usually described as forced. A conversion of debentures cleans up the balance sheet by substituting equity for debt, reducing the debt/equity ratio and otherwise appearing to improve the financial health of the business. The same is not true of conversions of preferred stock.

When debt securities mature, the issuer may borrow funds (perhaps by creating a new debt issue maturing far in the future) to pay off the maturing obligations. This process is known as rolling over the debt.

The way in which publicly traded debt securities are priced in the market is discussed in Chapter 18. In most economic respects, long-term debt securities are analogous to preferred shares described in §§15.4 thru 15.6, but there are some important differences. Table 15-2 sets forth the most important similarities and differences between these two types of securities.

Table 15-2

Characteristic	Preferred stock	Bonds
Manner of creation of new classes or issues	Amendment to articles of incorporation	Action by directors alone without shareholder approval
Maturity date	No	Yes
Voting	Usually only if dividend omitted	Rarely (prohibited in most states)
Treatment on balance sheet	Equity	Debt
Interim payments	Dividend	Interest
Amount	Fixed (usually)	Fixed (usually)
Omission of	No default; carries over if cumulative	Default
Tax effect on issuer	Not deductible	Deductible
Tax effect on recipient	Taxable, but dividend credit if recipient is corporation	Taxable
Callable	Usually	Usually
Convertible	Optional	Optional
Effect of conversion into common	Does not affect capital or debt/equity ratio; reduces dividend rates by difference between common and preferred rates; increases number of common shares	Reduces debt and increases equity; affects debt/equity ratio; eliminates interest payments; increases number of shares

CHAPTER 16

DIVIDENDS AND DISTRIBUTIONS

§16.1 Introduction

This chapter deals with dividends and distributions in connection with common stock. (Section 15.4 of the previous chapter briefly discussed preferred share dividends in connection with the description of the rights of holders of those types of securities.) The topics discussed in this chapter are usually considered at some length in law school courses dealing with corporations and corporation finance. The discussion below does not attempt to replicate this detailed coverage of a confusing and complicated subject; rather it concentrates only on the most fundamental financial concepts underlying the problems of dividends and distributions. Some of the material in this chapter requires a working knowledge of how accounting statements are constructed as described in Chapter 7.

The word *distribution* in corporation law is a general term referring to any kind of payment (in cash, property, or obligations of indebtedness) by the corporation to one or more shareholders on account of the ownership of shares. The word *dividend* is usually understood to be a narrower term referring to a special type of distribution: a payment to shareholders by the corporation out of its current or retained earnings. An example of a distribution that is not a dividend is a partial payment to shareholders by a solvent corporation in the process of liquidation. In that situation, one would naturally refer to a liquidating distribution, not a liquidating dividend.

Payments to a shareholder in the form of salary, interest, or rent are not normally viewed as distributions at all since they are on account of services rendered or property supplied to the corporation by its shareholders rather than on account of the ownership of shares. However, if the payments are so large as to bear no reasonable relationship to the value of the nominal transaction to which they are attached, all or part of the payment may be viewed as a disguised or informal dividend or distribution.

§16.2 Types of Distributive Transactions

Several different and superficially unrelated transactions have the effect of making distributions to shareholders. In some states with older statutes different legal rules may be applicable in determining the lawfulness of a distribution depending on the type of transaction involved. More modern statutes, however, seek to apply a single legal standard to all distributions without regard to their form. The following transactions constitute distributions.

§16.2.1 Direct Payments of Money or Property

The most common and best-known kind of distribution is a simple payment of money by the corporation to each shareholder, the amount of which is proportional to the number of shares owned by each shareholder. A corporation may also make a distribution of property other than cash, though such distributions often create practical problems if the corporation has more than a handful of shareholders. Property, unlike money, is usually not divisible into readily usable and discrete units. A distribution of undivided interests in a piece of improved real estate, for example, is likely to create problems of management and control thereafter. Further, undivided interests in property — for example, a 3/25ths or a 91/26,875ths interest in an apartment house — may be difficult to sell except to other owners of undivided interests in the property who may be interested in reassembling the ownership into a salable form. Distributions of undivided interests in property are nevertheless sufficiently common for the corporate literature to distinguish between cash dividends and property dividends.

§16.2.2 Repurchases of Stock by the Corporation: Treasury Shares

An important type of distributive transaction is the purchase by the corporation of its own stock. Superficially, a purchase of stock by the corporation may not be thought of as involving a distribution at all. It appears to be the purchase of an asset rather than the making of a distribution. That analysis, however, confuses transactions in which the corporation repurchases *its own stock* and transactions in which it purchases stock *issued by another corporation*. The former is a distribution, the latter is an investment.

When a corporation buys back its own stock, it does not receive anything of value in the hands of the corporation. The remaining shareholders continue to own 100 percent of the corporate assets (now reduced by the amount of the payment used to reacquire the shares). A corporation cannot treat stock in itself that it has purchased as an asset any more than it can treat its authorized but unissued stock as an asset. One cannot own 10 percent of oneself and have one's total worth be 110 percent of the value of one's assets. This point is so fundamental that it may be well to reread the last few sentences. Stock issued by another corporation is entirely different. That does not create the same circularity problem. Shares of corporation B have value based on the assets owned by corporation B; if shares of corporation B are purchased by corporation A they are an asset in the hands of corporation A.

The fact that a repurchase of shares constitutes a distribution can be most easily appreciated by considering a proportionate repurchase of stock by the corporation from each shareholder. Assume that three persons each own 100 shares of stock in a corporation, its entire outstanding stock. The shareholders decide that each of them will sell 10 shares back to the corporation for $100 per share, or a total of $1,000 each. When the transaction is completed, each shareholder continues to own one-third of the corporation (now represented by 90 shares rather than 100 shares), the corporation is $3,000 poorer and the shareholders are each $1,000 richer. Clearly there has been a distribution even though the transaction was cast in the form of a repurchase of stock rather than a direct distribution.

Under most state statutes, the 300 shares reacquired by the corporation in the previous example are called *treasury shares* and may be held by the corporation in a sort of twilight zone until they are either retired permanently or resold to someone else in the future. Treasury shares are not an asset even though they are salable and may be sold at some later time. Exactly the same thing can be said of every share of authorized but unissued stock. Assume that the corporation in the above example decides to resell the treasury shares to X (a nonshareholder) for $3,000. The interests of each of the three original shareholders have been diluted: There are now four shareholders owning shares in the ratio 90-90-90-30. The corporation could have paid the original shareholders a cash dividend of $1,000 each and then sold 33 shares of authorized but unissued stock to X for $3,000 with exactly the same economic result. (In this variation, the shares are owned 100-100-100-33 rather than 90-90-90-30; the percentage ownership interest, however, is as a practical matter, identical.)

The difference between treasury shares and shares issued by other corporations is reflected in the accounting treatment of transactions in shares. When corporation A buys shares in corporation B, the transaction is reflected solely on the left hand side of the balance sheet: The journal entry shows a reduction of cash and an increase in an asset account "investments in other corporations." However, when a corporation buys its own shares, the reduction of cash on the left hand side of the balance sheet is offset by a reduction in one or more right hand shareholders' equity accounts. The precise account to be debited may vary depending on the status of the accounts themselves; the important point is that the transaction is reflected by adjustments to the right hand shareholders' equity accounts. A straight cash dividend is treated for accounting purposes in the same way: A reduction of the cash account on the left hand side of the balance sheet is offset by a reduction in retained earnings or similar account on the left hand side of the balance sheet.

A repurchase of shares by the corporation is a distribution even if the corporation purchases only shares owned by one shareholder rather than proportionately from each shareholder. Such a transaction is a disproportionate distribution (i.e., one not shared proportionately by all shareholders). The corporation has made a distribution to a single shareholder equal to the purchase price it paid for the shares. This transaction is not all bad from the standpoint of the other shareholders, however, since it simultaneously increases their percentage interest in the corporation. For example, if the corporation with three shareholders in the above example repurchased all 100 shares owned by shareholder A for $10,000, the interests of shareholders B and C in the corporation are each increased from 33.3 percent to 50 percent. The assets of the corporation are reduced by the $10,000 purchase price paid to shareholder A to eliminate his or her interest in the corporation.

Distributions in the form of repurchases of shares are very common in real life. In closely held corporations, the elimination of one shareholder's interest in a corporation is almost routinely effected by a repurchase of shares by the corporation. Such a transaction permits the use of corporate rather than personal assets, has favorable tax consequences, and does not affect the relative interests of the remaining shareholders.

Publicly held corporations also often go into the securities market to repurchase their own shares for a variety of possible uses, for example in compensation plans for executives or employees, for acquisitions or other corporate purposes, or simply to reduce the number of outstanding shares. A repurchase of a corporation's own shares is often preferred to the issuance of new shares because there is no dilutive effect on public shareholders and a market repurchase tends to protect or increase the market price of shares. In contrast, the use of new shares to purchase assets of uncertain value or to provide incentive compensation for senior executive officers may place downward pressure on the market price of the shares. Targets of takeover attempts may also purchase their own shares in an effort to sop up extra cash that the corporation may have and to drive up the price of their shares to make the competing offer by the aggressor unattractive.

§16.2.3 Distributions of Indebtedness

A corporation may also distribute its obligations to make payments at some time in the future. The simplest way to do this is for the corporation to create instruments of indebtedness and distribute them to its shareholders. More commonly, the debt reflects a portion of the agreed-upon purchase price of shares to be repurchased by the corporation where the corporation lacks ready assets to pay the full purchase price and does not want to borrow funds from a commercial source for this purpose.

Distributions of indebtedness are sometimes made by publicly held corporations in connection with so-called poison pill defenses constructed by corporations to make it appear unattractive as a possible takeover candidate. See §17.13.

If a corporation creates indebtedness as part of a distribution, the question arises whether the indebtedness so created is on a parity with ordinary business or trade indebtedness, or whether shareholders who receive distributions of indebtedness should be subordinated to such indebtedness. At first blush, indebtedness created in a distribution would seem not to be entitled to parity since, after all, it is part of a distribution that should be permitted only if all business creditors are paid first. The Revised Model Business Corporation Act, however, places all such debt on a parity with regular business indebtedness on this theory: The corporation, rather than distributing indebtedness directly to shareholders, could have borrowed funds from a third person and distributed the proceeds to the shareholders. The debt to the third person in that situation would almost certainly be on a parity with general trade indebtedness. The creditors of the corporation are thus no worse off if indebtedness issued to shareholders is given parity with them than if money is borrowed from third persons in order to make the distribution in cash. Further, a shareholder who accepts a distribution of indebtedness rather than insisting on cash should not be in a worse position than one who insists on cash knowing that the corporation has to borrow funds to make the payment being demanded.

§16.3 Legal Restrictions on Dividends and Distributions

All state statutes contain provisions governing and restricting the power of corporations to make distributions or to pay dividends. These statutory provisions are confusing, sometimes internally inconsistent or self-contradictory, and often incomplete, in the sense of not addressing at all some recurring issues relating to distributions. Several factors contribute to this unfortunate state of affairs: the historical development of these provisions, the fact that these statutes serve several different but overlapping policies and some statutes appear to be addressed only to some of these policies, and in part because of the inherent difficulty of the subject.

Modern statutes contain two different types of prohibitions: (1) a capital protection provision that prohibits distributions that in some sense invade or reduce the permanent capital of the corporation, and (2) a provision prohibiting distributions that have the effect of rendering the corporation insolvent in the sense of being unable to meet its obligations as they mature. The first test is usually referred to as the balance sheet test and the second as the equity insolvency test. See §10.6.

§16.3.1 The Balance Sheet Test

Statutes regulate and limit distributions by imposing restrictions on the right hand balance sheet entries that may be debited for the payments. (If you are not clear about what this sentence refers to, please reread §7.3.) An oversimplified balance sheet should make this relationship clear:

Assets			Liabilities		
	Cash	20,000		Bank loans	30,000
	Other	40,000	Owners Equity		
				Common stock	20,000
			Earnings		
				current	3,000
				accumulated	7,000
		60,000			60,000

In the owners equity portion of the balance sheet current earnings represent earnings of the present year while accumulated earnings represent earnings from previous years not distributed in the form of dividends. The common stock entry represents what the shareholders paid for the stock when it was originally issued. Now let us assume that the corporation decides it wishes to distribute $6,000 to its shareholders. The payment of $6,000 will reduce cash by $6,000; the offsetting entry must be a reduction of some right hand entry. The only real choices are current earnings or accumulated earnings. The legality of the distribution depends on what the state's distribution statute says about which right hand accounts may be charged with the distribution and which may not. Since all state statutes permit the payment of dividends out of either current or accumulated earnings, the $6,000 payment is consistent with the balance sheet test in all states. This payment is still a dividend even though it is made in part out of accumulated earnings: Following the payment of a dividend of $6,000, accumulated earnings available for the payment of dividends in future years would be reduced to $4,000 ($7,000 − $3,000, where $3,000 is the portion of the distribution that exceeds earnings for the year in question).

Now let us assume that the corporation wishes to distribute $15,000 to its shareholders. May it do so? It probably can afford it in the sense that even after paying out $15,000, the corporation will have assets of $40,000 and liabilities of only $30,000. That, however, is not relevant under the balance sheet test. What is important under that test is which account or accounts are to be debited for the $15,000. The earnings accounts can be reduced by $10,000 to 0 but the remaining $5,000 must be reflected as a reduction or invasion of capital. Another way of looking at this transaction is that the $15,000 payment represents a distribution of (a) $3,000 of this year's earnings, (b) $7,000 of accumulated earnings from previous years, and (c) $5,000 of capital. As to whether a corporation may invade or distribute capital in this manner, state statutes vary widely, with the most modern statutes permitting distributions of capital down to zero, and older statutes establishing a variety of different standards or tests on whether the distribution is permissible.

This simple example makes two critical points. First, in order to control distributions, one places restraints on which right hand entries may be reduced when a distribution is made. The right hand entries in the balance sheet serve as a kind of valve or control on distributions of assets that appear on the left hand side of the balance sheet. Second, the balance sheet test is not directly concerned with solvency, but rather with the preservation of announced capital. It is concerned with appearances: A corporation that says it has capital of a specified amount on its balance sheet may not make a distribution of all or a portion of that capital to shareholders. This test harks back to an early era of corporation law where the corporation's capital was viewed as a cushion or trust fund for the benefit of subsequent creditors who may be induced to extend credit in reliance on the corporation's balance sheet.

State corporation statutes have gone through at least three distinct phases in developing balance sheet tests regulating distributions. In the earliest statutes enacted in the nineteenth century, provisions addressing distribution policies were primitive. Apparently proceeding on the assumption that all capital contributed to a corporation was a permanent fund for the protection of creditors, these statutes provide either that dividends can only be paid from income or, alternatively, that distributions from capital are prohibited.

In the second phase, developed during the first half of the twentieth century, statutes draw a distinction between permanent capital and surplus capital (with the permanent capital usually being defined as the aggregate sum of the par values of all shares issued by the corporation). Many state dividend statutes are currently of this type. Unfortunately, these statutes can easily be evaded by the manipulation of par value principles. As a result, they are largely ineffective in requiring minimum amounts of capital to be retained as a cushion. Indeed, these statutes give a deceptive picture of how much capital the corporation is required to maintain. Rather than providing protection to creditors, these statutes in fact become primarily rites of initiation for new corporation lawyers: When one learns how to avoid all meaningful restrictions on corporate distributions, one has proved one is a corporation lawyer.

The most modern statutes, largely developed in the last decade, recognize the impracticability of defining minimum amounts of capital, and freely allow the distribution of capital so long as after the distribution assets exceed liabilities plus preferential amounts payable in liquidation to holders of preferred shares. In these most modern statutes, greater reliance is placed on the equity insolvency test described below than on the balance sheet test in order to protect creditors.

No matter what specific tests are established in these balance sheet statutes, they all suffer from one major, indeed fundamental, flaw. If you have read the chapters on accounting principles (Chapters 7-9), it should be apparent that the distinction between capital and income is a most slippery one in practice. Income and capital are not self-defining but are dependent on accounting principles adequate to handle a variety of complex and subtle issues such as the allocation of income and expense items to specific periods, the principles on which assets are to be valued, depreciation schedules, the time of recognition of asset appreciation and contingent liabilities, and the like. Different accounting principles may give widely varying answers as to what the income of the corporation is. The creation of accounting principles by legislative fiat for all corporations, large and small, is a daunting task, and no state legislature has attempted to do so. It is basically up to the courts to decide what accounting principles must be followed. The issues usually arise, furthermore, in suits to surcharge directors for approving improper dividends. That is a particularly brutal kind of litigation from the standpoint of the defendants, who are asked to restore to the corporation the amount of the distribution out of their own personal pockets, even though they may have acted in perfect good faith in reliance on expert legal and accounting advice, and did not themselves receive any more than whatever portion of the distribution their shareholdings entitled them to. It is not surprising that courts tended to find a reason to uphold the legality of specific distributions out of sympathy with the defendants — often men of substance in the community — who were faced with substantial liability.

At one time most state statutes imposed a minimum absolute amount of capital ($1,000 in most statutes, but different amounts in some) that every corporation was required to have upon incorporation. These provisions were also ineffective and have been repealed in most states. Any arbitrary minimum (whether $1,000 or some other amount) suffers from the problem that it is going to be inadequate for larger corporations. More fundamentally, however, a minimum initial capital gives no protection once the corporation begins business and actually incurs its first operating loss.

Recognition that elaborate balance sheet statutes fail almost entirely in their basic purpose is also evident from the behavior of creditors. They pay no attention to the elaborate statutory provisions ostensibly designed for their protection. Rather they protect themselves in different ways: (1) they rely on credit reporting agencies and similar private organizations before extending unsecured credit to businesses, (2) they obtain purchase money security interests when they sell goods on credit to businesses, and (3) in the case of larger transactions, they negotiate elaborate loan agreements with debtors by which they obtain contract protection against unwise or improvident distributions of assets to shareholders.

§16.3.2 Equity Insolvency Test

All state statutes relating to distributions impose an equity insolvency test for distributions in addition to the largely ineffective balance prohibitions described above. The test is that a distribution to shareholders is unlawful if it makes the corporation insolvent, i.e., unable to pay its obligations as they mature in the future. (See §10.6.) At first blush, the equity insolvency test may sound like a variant of the balance sheet test for distributions: In fact it is based on a totally different approach. The balance sheet test is based on financial statements and accounting principles. The equity insolvency test is based on an examination of future cash flows after the distribution. It requires the board of directors to determine whether the corporation has or will have available funds to discharge its future obligations as they come due. This test is easily stated but requires difficult estimates and projections in practice. The board of directors must make an examination of anticipated cash flows and future cash needs arising from the maturation of debts and liabilities to determine whether, after the contemplated distribution, the corporation is solvent in the equity sense.

§16.4 Protection of Preferred Shareholders from Improvident Distributions

State statutes also impose restrictions on distributions to common shareholders in order to protect the liquidation preferences of preferred shareholders. Preferred shareholders are in an anomalous position with respect to dividend restrictions. On the one hand they are viewed as contributors of equity capital rather than as creditors. On the other hand, their financial interest in the corporation is usually limited, and once their dividend preference is honored in any one year, common shareholders are entitled to all future dividends and distributions during that year. From an economic standpoint, the position of the preferred shareholders' liquidation preference is closely akin to a creditor's claim, since substantial distributions to common shareholders may effectively disable the corporation from honoring that liquidation preference. Many modern statutes treat these preferences as a liability for purposes of applying the balance sheet test.

§16.5 Distribution Policies in Closely Held Corporations

The balance of this chapter does not deal with legal restrictions on distributions but rather with the underlying economic and financial considerations that determine distribution policies in corporations.

In closely held corporations that are taxed as C corporations (see §§12.20 and 13.9) distribution policies strongly tend in the direction of informal distributions in the form of tax deductible salary, rent, or interest payments rather than formally declared dividends. The principal motivation is federal income taxation: The payment of a reasonable salary to a shareholder, for example, is deductible by the corporation and to that extent avoids the double tax on income that otherwise increases the tax cost of operating as a C corporation. Such deductions are allowed only to the extent that they are "reasonable," but that standard permits considerable flexibility in distribution policy, often allowing the entire income of the corporation to be zeroed out to avoid all taxes at the corporate level.

Informal distributions of this type open the possibility of unfair treatment of minority shareholders, since they may not receive a proportionate part of the informal distribution. Even where the motive of the majority shareholder is not exclusionary, however, strict proportionality is dangerous, since it may suggest to the auditor in a subsequent tax audit that all or a portion of the corporate salary deductions should be disallowed as informal dividends.

The Internal Revenue Code contains a penalty tax against unreasonable accumulations of surplus which, if applicable, provides a strong tax incentive to pay an immediate dividend in order to avoid the penalty tax. Given the structure of tax rates in the 1986 tax law, it is unlikely that any corporation now finds it rational to accumulate unreasonable amounts of surplus so as to trigger the imposition of this tax.

If a corporation has elected S corporation tax treatment, the corporate income is passed through to the shareholders for inclusion in their individual tax returns. There is no tax advantage in utilizing salary or similar accounts as a substitute for dividends. On the other hand, if the corporation fails to pay cash dividends when it has substantial taxable income, minority shareholders may find it difficult or impossible to pay their personal tax bills swollen by the inclusion of a substantial amount of corporate taxable income. In extreme cases, it may be necessary for minority shareholders to seek to revoke the S corporation election, if that is practical, or if it is not, to bring suit to compel the payment of dividends based on breach by the board of directors of its fiduciary duties to act in good faith and treat all shareholders equally. (See §16.6.)

§16.6 Suits to Compel the Payment of Dividends

The decision whether or not to pay dividends or make distributions involves business judgments by the board of directors as to whether it is prudent to preserve earnings for future needs or whether a distribution should be made and in what amount. Indeed, in many respects the decision whether or not to make a distribution is the classic example of a business judgment: Courts have long recognized that this decision involves sensitive judgments about the future cash needs of the business both in terms of satisfying liabilities and making necessary investments in existing or new productive facilities. As a result, courts are loath to second-guess directors on such decisions, and within a broad range accept the decision of the board on such matters.

Directors also owe fiduciary duties to shareholders in connection with their stewardship of the corporation, and the decision to pay (or more commonly, to omit) dividends or distributions may be evaluated within these broad duties. These duties may be phrased in terms of fair treatment of minority shareholders or of all classes of shares, or in terms of not favoring a class in which members of the board of directors have substantial personal interests. There is obvious tension between these fiduciary duties and the business judgment rule described in the previous paragraph. However, the existence of a relatively large number of cases in which courts have ordered that a dividend be paid illustrates that often the fiduciary duty dominates.

A compulsory dividend is most likely to be ordered where the minority shareholder can demonstrate: (1) actions by the majority shareholder that may be construed as constituting antagonism or bad faith against the minority, (2) liquid assets within the corporation in excess of the apparent needs of the business and apparently available for the payment of dividends, and (3) a policy of informal distributions to favored shareholders through salaries, loans, informal cash advances, and the like. When all is said and done, however, suits to compel the payment of dividends should be viewed as a long shot even in relatively egregious circumstances.

§16.7 Distribution Policies in Publicly Held Corporations

Distribution policies within a publicly held corporation are quite different from the policies within a closely held corporation. The standard operating procedure for a publicly held corporation is to establish an announced or regular dividend and maintain it indefinitely, or at least over several accounting periods. A regular dividend may be paid even though the corporation has suffered a loss in that year; the dividend is paid out of earnings accumulated from prior years. Most shareholders in a publicly held corporation, of course, are inactive investors who come to rely on the regular dividend as part of their regular cash flow. However, the reluctance to change an announced dividend — particularly the reluctance to reduce the dividend in periods of adversity — is not based on concern about shareholders' cash flow. Rather, a change in dividend policy is widely viewed in the securities markets as a signal or communication about management's future expectations with respect to the company. An increase in the announced dividend is viewed as signaling improved prospects. It is a strong signal since it in effect states that the corporate prospects have improved to the point where management feels that an increased dividend rate can be maintained indefinitely. On the other hand, a reduction in the dividend rate is a warning of rough seas ahead. The communication of bad news has a potential for serious adverse market repercussions and is not to be made prematurely or before management is reasonably certain that it is imprudent to continue the present dividend. Certainly, such a signal should not be given because of a temporary dip in earnings.

If a corporation has an unusually good year, or has the good fortune to receive a nonrecurring windfall, it may be reluctant to announce a simple increase in the regular dividend because management may be unsure that the rate can be maintained in the future. In this circumstance it usually declares a special or nonrecurring dividend which is paid on a one-time basis and does not create an expectation that a similar payment will be forthcoming in future years. Some corporations have adopted a policy of declaring "extras" above the announced rate almost every year, but that is not the customary practice.

Rather paradoxically, some corporations as a matter of policy pay no cash dividends at all. Assume that a corporation, recently gone public, has positive (and growing) earnings, but needs all available cash for internal growth purposes. Even though a shareholder receives no immediate cash return, the series of glowing annual reports is likely to cause a steady increase in the market price of the stock. In effect, the market accepts and approves of the policy adopted of deferring cash dividends to foster internal growth, and expects that sometime in the future substantial cash flows will be generated. An investment in that stock may yield substantial returns in the future even though it pays no dividend today. Persons may invest in that stock in order to benefit from increases in the market price of the stock. Until 1986, there were tax advantages in speculating in nondividend-paying growth stocks, since market appreciation was taxed at favorable capital gains rates when the stock was sold, but dividends were taxed at ordinary income rates. Some economic analysts even suggested that it was uneconomic for corporations ever to pay dividends under the tax structure then in effect. They argued that a policy by the corporation of reinvesting earnings coupled with a policy by the investor of selling appreciated nondividend-paying shares from time to time would yield a superior return than investing in a dividend-paying security. There are difficulties with this logic since at some point stocks have market value only because of anticipated future cash flows. Nor is it at all clear that the market price of nondividend-paying stocks increase sufficiently rapidly to out-perform equivalent stocks that do pay dividends. However, even if the premises are accepted, the 1986 Tax Law eliminated one of the basic premises of this argument when it abolished the special capital gain tax rate for long-term capital gains.

§16.8 Share Dividends

Publicly held corporations often pay *share dividends* or announce *share splits*. These two transactions are very similar in principle and effect, and are sometimes not fully understood by investors. The following section deals specifically with splits.

A *share dividend* is a distribution of shares of common stock by a corporation to its shareholders in proportion to their shareholders. Thus, a 10 percent share dividend means that the corporation issues one new share to each shareholder for every ten shares held; a holder of 100 shares will receive 10 new shares when the distribution is made, owning 110 shares in all. Fractional shares are usually distributed in cash. From a purely economic or logical point of view this is not a dividend at all, because the number of shares owned by each shareholder has been increased by exactly the same percentage, and each shareholder's proportional interest in the corporation has not been changed. In other words, a shareholder owning 1 percent of the outstanding shares before the share dividend is paid will own precisely 1 percent of the outstanding shares after it is paid as well: The percentage ownership has not changed even though the number of shares has increased. Despite this inescapable logic, many small shareholders welcome share dividends and many sell them shortly after they are received, perhaps not realizing or not caring that by doing so they have reduced slightly their (already infinitesimal) interest in the corporation. For tax purposes, the gain upon the sale of a share dividend is determined by reallocating the original basis of the shares proportionally over the new shares and the old. It should thus be evident to every shareholder at some point that at least for tax purposes a sale of shares received as a dividend constitutes a net reduction of one's investment in the corporation.

A share dividend does have one favorable consequence if the corporation has a regular or stated cash dividend policy. It is customary to leave the regular or stated dividend unaffected after a share dividend so that following the dividend the corporation's total dividend payout is increased. This results from the fact that the same rate is applied to a somewhat larger number of shares.

Why do corporations pay share dividends at all? The usual reason is that it is a tangible signal to shareholders that the corporation is profitable (despite the absence of a cash dividend) and is investing all available funds into the growth of the business. While unsophisticated shareholders may view such a dividend as a little something that can be sold without reducing one's investment in the corporation, in fact it is nothing but a signal.

§16.9 Share Splits

A *share split* closely resembles a large share dividend. In a 2-for-1 split, for example, the corporation issues one new share for every share held by each shareholder so that each shareholder now owns two shares where before he or she owned only one share. It is customary to reduce the regular or stated dividend rate when a share split is completed; if the regular dividend is halved in connection with a 2:1 split, one would expect the market price of each new share would be approximately one-half of the market price of the pre-split shares. Often, however, the effective dividend rate is increased in connection with a share split: Thus in a 3:1 split where the old dividend rate was $0.90

per share, the dividend rate on the split shares may be set, for example, at $0.35, equal to a rate of $1.05 on the pre-split shares.

Many corporations feel that there is an appropriate trading range for its common shares. The common stock of a corporation may have historically traded in the $20 to $30 range, for example. If the price gradually rises, to $40 say, the corporation may split the stock 2:1 in order to return the price to its historic range. See §§18.9 and 18.10. One advantage of maintaining traditional trading ranges is that if the price of a stock rises significantly to a new plateau but the stock is not split, trading volume may decline from previous levels as a result of the fact that most investors trade in round lots and may feel they cannot afford to invest in higher priced stocks. See §18.4.

A split differs from a share dividend in certain minor respects relating to how the transaction is accounted for in the equity accounts of the corporation. These differences, however, rarely affect the shareholder.

A corporation may also split its stock to *reduce* the number of shares outstanding. This is called a *reverse stock split* and is not really a split at all. Rather the corporation amends its articles of incorporation to reduce the number of authorized shares and the amendment provides that each 10 (or 100 or 1000) old shares are to be exchanged for 1 new share. Reverse stock splits often create fractional shares, and may be used to liquidate the interests of small shareholders by establishing a procedure (authorized in many state statutes) to eliminate all fractional shares thereby created for cash. A few corporations have utilized reverse stock splits to eliminate all public shareholders by establishing the split ratio at a level sufficiently high that all nonmanagement shareholders become owners of fractional interests in a single share, and then by acquiring all fractional interests for a designated amount of cash.

§16.10 Determining Who Is Entitled to a Distribution

Whenever a dividend or cash or stock distribution is contemplated, the question may arise as to who is entitled to the distribution if the shares have been sold or transferred around the time of the declaration or payment. This problem is particularly acute in publicly held corporations where many thousands of shares are traded each day among anonymous persons. The New York Stock Exchange has adopted an *ex-dividend* policy to establish whether the buyer or seller of publicly traded shares is entitled to a distribution.

Table 16-1 is taken from *The Wall Street Journal* of July 26, 1988. It is the standard chart showing dividend announcements made on the previous business day. An examination of this table reveals much about the dividend practices of publicly held corporations and the law relating to dividend declarations. First of all, the table distinguishes between various types of dividends:

1. Regular (pursuant to a publicly announced dividend policy);
2. Irregular (occasional or erratic payments not pursuant to an announced policy);
3. Funds, real estate investment trusts, investment companies, limited

Table 16-1

CORPORATE DIVIDEND NEWS

Dividends Reported July 25

Company	Period	Amount	Payable date	Record date
REGULAR				
AAR Corp	Q	.09	9–6–88	8–8
Acme United Corp	Q	.04	9–9–88	8–15
Amer Greetings clA	Q	.16½	9–9–88	8–26
American Reliance Group	Q	.05	9–9–88	8–17
ArcherDanielsMidland	Q	.02½	8–29–88	8–5
Armstrong World Indus	Q	.25	9–1–88	8–5
Armstrong World $3.75pf	Q	.93¾	9–15–88	8–5
Atlantic Richfield Co	Q	1.00	9–15–88	8–19
AtlntcRchfld $2.80pref	Q	.70	9–20–88	8–19
Atlantic Rchfld $3pref	Q	.75	9–20–88	8–19
Baltek Corp	S	n.05	8–17–88	8–12
n-Commencement of a semi-annual payment schedule.				
Bank of New England	Q	.34	10–20–88	9–30
Baukol-Noonan Inc	Q	.30	9–20–88	9–6
Brown & Sharpe Mfg clA	Q	.08	9–9–88	8–19
C.N.W. Corp $2.125pf	Q	.53⅛	11–15–88	10–25
Colonial Group Inc clA	Q	.10	8–17–88	8–3
Consol Freightways	Q	.24½	8–22–88	8–5
Constar International	Q	.16	9–1–88	8–12
Dauphin Deposit Corp	Q	.32	10–28–88	9–23
Detroit Edison Co	Q	.42	10–15–88	9–20
Detroit Ed 5.50%pf	Q	1.37½	10–15–88	9–20
Detroit Ed 7.36%pf	Q	1.84	10–15–88	9–20
Detroit Ed 7.45%pf	Q	1.86¼	10–15–88	9–20
Detroit Ed 7.68%pf	Q	1.92	10–15–88	9–20
Detroit Ed 9.32%pf	Q	2.33	10–15–88	9–20
Detroit Ed 9.72%pf	Q	2.43	10–15–88	9–20
Detroit Ed $2.28pref	Q	.57	10–15–88	9–20
Detroit Ed $2.75pref	Q	.68¾	10–15–88	9–20
Detroit Ed $3.13pref	Q	.78¼	10–15–88	9–20
Detroit Ed $3.24pref	Q	.81	10–15–88	9–20
Detroit Ed prefB	Q	.68¾	10–15–88	9–20
Everest & Jennings clA	Q	.05	8–19–88	8–5
Everest & Jennings clB	Q	.02½	8–19–88	8–5
First Wisconsin Corp	Q	.25	8–15–88	8–1
FirstWisconsin adjpfB	Q	2.14⅝	8–15–88	8–1
IRREGULAR				
Cardinal Federal Savings	–	.12½	8–15–88	8–1
Charter Fedl S&L Assoc	–	.02½	8–25–88	8–4
Indiana Fedl S&L	–	.05	8–31–88	8–15
Talman Home Fedl S&L	–	.05	9–1–88	8–15
FUNDS–REITS–INVESTMENT COS–LPS				
AARP Grwth & Inco Fd	Q	h.24	7–29–88	7–25
AmerTrCocaCola primes	Q	.28¾	10–13–88	9–15
AmerTrCocaCola units	Q	.28¾	10–13–88	9–15
AmerTrHewlettPckdprms	Q	.07¼	10–24–88	9–22
AmerTrHewlettPckdunts	Q	.07¼	10–24–88	9–22
Bull & Bear Hi Yield Fd	M	h.104	7–29–88	7–25
Circle Income Shares	M	.11	9–2–88	8–19
Circle Income Shares	M	.11	10–7–88	9–23
Circle Income Shares	M	.11	11–4–88	10–21
Circle Income Shares	M	.11	12–2–88	11–18
Dreyfus Strategic Muni	M	.06½	8–19–88	8–12
Health & Rehab Props Tr	Q	.28	8–30–88	8–4
Mission Resource Ptnrs	–	.35	9–1–88	8–15
Putnam High IncoGovt	M	p.10	8–15–88	8–5
p-Payment consists of 2.4 cents from capital gains and 7.6 cents from income.				
PutnmUSGvtGtdSecsInco	M	h.114	8–15–88	8–5
ServiceMaster L.P.	Q	.42	10–31–88	10–5
STOCK				
ArcherDanielsMidland	–	5%	9–16–88	8–22

INCREASED

Company	Period	Amounts New	Amounts Old	Payable date	Record date
Rohm & Haas Co	Q	.28	.23	9–1–88	8–5
Simpson Indus	Q	.15	.14	9–22–88	9–1
SouthwstrnElSvc	Q	.53	.51	9–23–88	9–9

REDUCED

Company	Period	Amounts New	Amounts Old	Payable date	Record date
Howell Corp	Q	.07	.08	9–21–88	9–7

INITIAL

Company	Period	Amount	Payable date	Record date
Ashland Oil Inc new	Q	.25	9–15–88	8–12
FstFedSvgsCharlotteCnty	–	.06	9–6–88	8–15
Sanford Corp new	–	.04	8–31–88	8–12

A-Annual; Ac-Accumulation; b-Payable in Canadian funds; F-Final; G-Interim; h-From income; k-From capital gains; M-Monthly; Q-Quarterly; S-Semi-annual.

* * *

Stocks Ex-Dividend July 27

Company	Amount	Company	Amount
AmericusTrFordunits	1.18¾	Lawrence Ins Group	(c)
AmericsTrFord primes	1.18¾	c-3-for-2 stock split	
Ames Dept Stores	.02½	Learonal Inc	.12
Birmingham Steel new	.07½	NECO Enterprises	.37½
Citytrust Bancorp	.28	Overseas Shiphldg Grp	.12½
Ford Motor Co	.60	Security Pacific Corp	.49
Homestake Mining	.05	Univ'l Med Bldgs L.P.	.12½
ICMPropertyInvestors	.34	ValeroEngy $3.44deppf	.86
		ValeroEngy $2.0625pref	.515⁄8

partnerships (these are special types of investment vehicles, some of which are discussed in Chapter 19);

4. Stock (discussed in previous sections);
5. Increased (discussed in previous sections);
6. Reduced (discussed in previous sections); and
7. Initial (discussed in previous sections).

In addition, another category, "special," may appear in some dividend tables if a company announces a one-time "extra" or "special" dividend in addition to its regular dividend. These are discussed in previous sections. Secondly, there are three dates established by the corporation with respect to each dividend or distribution: (1) The date of announcement; (2) The record date; and (3) The payable date. The announcement date is basically the date of the press release that a cash or stock dividend is to be paid or a distribution is to be made. The record date determines in whose name specific checks or share certificates are to be issued: The check is made out to the order of (or the certificate is made out in the name of) the person or persons who are the holders of record on the books of the corporation at the close of business on the record date. The payable date is the date the checks or certificates are actually mailed; the customary delay of between two to four weeks is necessary for the corporation to go through the mechanical process of making the distribution in the proper amounts to the thousands or millions of recordholders.

The New York Stock Exchange policy is as follows. The *ex-dividend date* is always five business days before the record date. See the very bottom entries in Table 16-1. Ex-dividend means without the dividend. The ex-dividend date convention assigns the dividend to the buyer or seller as follows: A buyer in a transaction that occurs before the ex-dividend date is entitled to receive the dividend and the seller is not; a seller in a transaction that occurs on or after the ex-dividend date is entitled to keep the dividend. The theory behind the five-day gap between the ex-dividend date and the record date is based on the standard settlement practice for stock exchange transactions, which is settlement five business days after the transaction on the exchange. On the settlement date the buyer must pay the purchase price and the seller must deliver the appropriate certificates. A buyer who is entitled to the certificates on or before the ex-dividend date is theoretically able to register the transfer with the corporation and become the record owner before the close of business on the record date for the dividend or distribution. The ex-dividend date is thus established as the last day on which that is possible.

The day a stock goes ex-dividend, its market price should decline by approximately the amount of the dividend, other things being equal, since the day before, every buyer of the stock was entitled to the dividend but on and after the ex-dividend date, buyers of the stock do not receive the dividend. Of course, this relationship may not be precise because market conditions can change overnight.

The ex-dividend date is a convention that is not dependent on whether a buyer actually arranges for certificates to be issued in his or her name on or before the record date. If an owner of shares sells them after a dividend has been declared but before the ex-dividend date, he or she will thereafter receive a check for the dividend but under the ex-dividend convention is not entitled to retain it and must turn it over to the buyer. (As a practical matter, the seller's broker is responsible for withholding from the sales proceeds the amount of this dividend that must be paid to the buyer upon the dividend payment date.) It makes no difference what the buyer actually does with respect to the certificates he or she is entitled to receive.

The ex-dividend convention is not applicable to shares sold directly by one person to another not using the facilities of an exchange or the over-the-counter market. In a face-to-face transaction, the parties may make any agreement they wish with respect to entitlement to declared but unpaid dividends or distributions. The five-day settlement convention for publicly traded shares is also not applicable in a face-to-face transaction: Settlement may be on any date mutually agreed upon. In face-to-face transactions, in the absence of an express agreement as to who is entitled to a dividend, it is likely that a court would conclude that beneficial ownership on the record date determines who is entitled to the dividend. In other words, if the sale has been completed before the record date, the buyer would probably be held to be entitled to the dividend; if the sale occurs after the record date, the seller probably would be held to be entitled to retain the dividend. Case law on this issue is rather scant since in most cases the entitlement to a pending dividend or distribution is a matter of direct negotiation.

CHAPTER 17

MERGERS AND TAKEOVERS

§17.1 Introduction

Since the late 1960s the business world has been simultaneously dazzled and shocked by the takeover movement in which one large economic entity acquires another. The target of a takeover attempt usually resists fiercely, using all political, legal, litigious, and economic resources at its disposal. These battles often become epochal, filling the news columns of business journals, providing grist for endless discussion and speculation, and creating their own colorful vocabulary. This chapter attempts to place this type of economic warfare into perspective and to describe in broadest outline the strategy of takeover battles and the economic and financial forces that lead to them.

The takeover movement has shown a remarkable ability to evolve new offensive tactics, followed by new defenses to cope with, and nullify, the new offensive tactics. As a result, any discussion of specific tactics rapidly becomes obsolete.

In October 1987 stock market prices unexpectedly collapsed, temporarily curtailing takeover attempts. In addition, in early 1988, Delaware adopted a statute designed to make hostile takeovers more difficult: This statute is of particular importance because of the very large number of publicly held corporations that are incorporated in Delaware. It is too early to determine what effect these significant developments will have on takeover activity.

In the discussion that follows, the corporation that is the object of a takeover attempt is referred to as the *target corporation*. The corporation seeking to take over the target is the *aggressor*. Individuals may act as aggressors as well as corporations; however, for purposes of simplicity it is assumed throughout that the aggressor is a corporation.

Perhaps one final word should be added. Most of this book deals with individual or personal transactions involving relatively modest sums of money — perhaps one million dollars or less. This chapter in contrast discusses transactions involving big money, indeed, the largest private transactions the United States has ever seen.

§17.2 What Makes the Current Takeover Movement Different

Before discussing the mechanics of takeover attempts in the present era, it may be useful to put them into historical perspective. There have been several well-documented periods of merger movements in American history. In the late nineteenth century a series of acquisitions and mergers created monopolies in several basic American industries, and gave rise to the Sherman Antitrust Act. A period of similar activity before World War I led to Teddy Roosevelt's famous trust-busting activities and ultimately to the second major antitrust statute, the Clayton Act. A somewhat similar period of merger activity occurred during the 1950s, usually involving *conglomeration*, that is the assembling of a number of unrelated industries within a single corporate enterprise. The takeover movement discussed in this chapter began in the late 1960s and has continued at least into the late 1980s. It is unique in several significant respects from those earlier periods.

§17.2.1 The Means Now Exist to Force a Takeover

Prior merger movements basically involved consensual transactions. Management of a target corporation could usually block a takeover simply by refusing to cooperate. Only when both sides agreed upon the terms could one company acquire another. Thus, takeovers became a matter of negotiation over price, continuity of management, and other factors. That is not at all the case today. Aggressor corporations quite regularly go over the heads of management and pitch their takeover proposals directly to shareholders of the target corporation. The pitch to shareholders, furthermore, usually involves offers of cash on the barrel head that individual target shareholders often find attractive and even may feel compelled to accept to avoid claims of breach of fiduciary duty owed to third parties. The success or failure of a takeover in the modern era often depends on the sum total of a large number of individual decisions by shareholders rather than on a single yes-or-no decision by the managers of the target entity.

§17.2.2 Smaller Corporations Frequently Take Over Larger Corporations

In the past, typical takeover transactions involved large corporations becoming larger by taking over smaller ones. In the present period, smaller corporations or even individuals may successfully take over publicly held corporations that have assets much larger than those of the acquirer.

§17.2.3 Overall Economic Concentration May Not Be Increasing as a Result of Present Takeover Activity

In other periods of merger activity it was generally agreed that economic concentration in many industries was increasing as a result of the transactions taking place. It is not clear that this is true of today's takeover activity. Indeed, increased monopoly power does not appear to be the goal of the most modern takeovers at all. Rather, the process appears to be driven by fundamental economic and financial principles that are unique to the firms themselves, involving the relationship between the value of the business and the market prices of the securities issued by the corporation.

The present takeover movement often leads to the breaking up of large firms into smaller components. Because of the mechanics of modern takeover techniques, the aggressor often ends up with both the target and large amounts of debt. It may be compelled to break up and sell off components of the acquired business to raise additional cash in order to reduce the debt to manageable levels. Rather paradoxically, many modern acquisitions involve bust-up transactions in which many or most portions of the acquired business are put up for sale shortly after the acquisition. Whether or not the degree of concentration is increased or decreased in specific industries as a result of takeover transactions is therefore extremely difficult to evaluate.

Modern takeovers have a secondary effect on industry concentration as well. There is a trend toward voluntary "deconglomeration" by businesses that fear potential takeover attempts. Potential targets attempt to make themselves less attractive targets by voluntarily disposing of unessential assets that a successful aggressor might be expected to sell. These transactions overall probably reduce the degree of concentration in American industry.

§17.2.4 Economists Generally Argue that Present Takeover Transactions Are Economically Desirable

Unlike earlier periods of merger activity where concerns of increased monopoly power were dominant, there is a finely developed economic theory that argues that most of the transactions that have occurred during the present takeover movement are socially desirable and should not be prohibited or regulated. Indeed, there is an impressive degree of unanimity within the economic academic world that shareholders in the aggregate benefit from modern takeover transactions. One theory (1) concludes that the need for further governmental regulation of these transactions has not been established and (2) affirmatively argues that attempts at further regulation would likely be harmful to society as a whole. Whether or not one agrees with these views is beside the point; it is enough to recognize that there is a legitimate academic dispute over the social undesirability of these transactions.

§17.2.5 Local and State Political Forces are Generally Strongly Opposed to Takeovers

Local and state political forces usually view the threatened takeover of a large local enterprise as an unmitigated disaster: They see jobs and major industrial plants disappearing or being moved to other areas of the country if the takeover occurs. Local communities and even entire states therefore often join together with threatened target management to try to defeat takeover attempts. These opponents of takeover activity are potent forces politically, both at the state and federal levels.

§17.2.6 The United States Government Has Been Neutral on Takeover Attempts

Unlike state and local governments, the federal government is basically neutral with respect to the current takeover movement. In part this is a result of the fact that the Securities and Exchange Commission under the Reagan administration was unusually receptive to arguments based on economic analysis.

The federal government does have an important rule in the regulation of takeover attempts. Important federal legislation relating to cash tender offers is usually called the *Williams Act*, and is referred to by that name in the discussion below. The Williams Act was enacted by Congress in 1970 in response to the first wave of tender offers of the current era. Technically it consists of several amendments to §§13 and 14 of the Securities Exchange Act of 1934.

The broad purposes of the Williams Act are to create a level playing field between aggressor and target and to protect shareholders from unfair or deceptive tactics. The important substantive provisions of this legislation impose disclosure requirements on aggressors and targets and establish basic ground rules for the conduct of a cash tender offer. In addition, §14(e) of the Williams Act is an anti-fraud provision relating to tender offers that is patterned after rule 10b-5 promulgated by the Securities and Exchange Commission under the 1934 Act. Attempts were made in the 1970s by defeated offerors to use this provision to obtain judicial review of the tactics used by the successful bidder in much the same way as plaintiffs used rule 10b-5. The United States Supreme Court held, however, that an unsuccessful contestant for control did not have standing to attack the other party's actions under §14(e) since that statute was intended solely to protect independent shareholders. (Piper v. Chris-Craft Industries, Inc., 430 U.S. 1 (1977)) The court did not explain why the defeated offeror, who owned substantial amounts of the target stock, lacked standing in its capacity as a shareholder. Following this decision, federal courts have generally refused to consider the validity of specific tactics under federal law (though they increasingly do so under state law relating to duties of directors), and it now appears to be accepted by federal courts that the ultimate success or failure of a takeover attempt should be determined on the economic playing field rather than on the federal judicial one.

Some economists argue that even the minimal degree of existing federal regulation of takeovers is too much; other persons strongly advocate greater participation by the federal government in regulating the takeover movement. To a large extent, the future of takeover activity is thus a political rather than an economic question.

§17.3 The Ways in Which One Corporation Can Take Over Another

There are presently two basic ways in which one corporation can take over another: with the consent of the target management or over its opposition. In fact, these two ways often work in tandem since consensual takeovers may be the product of proposed or threatened nonconsensual ones. Before turning to such matters, however, it is necessary to first outline the broad strategies of nonconsensual takeovers that shape the current takeover movement.

In the sections that follow, a hypothetical but typical takeover attempt is discussed in detail. Let us assume that a potential aggressor has found what it believes to be a suitable target. The target is a medium-sized publicly owned corporation. From its SEC filings and other publicly available information, it is known that it has outstanding 20,000,000 shares of common stock that are trading at about $30 per share. The market is therefore currently valuing all of the common stock at roughly $600,000,000 ($30 × 20,000,000). Of the 20,000,000 shares outstanding, it is estimated that 40 percent of them are held by some 20 or 25 institutional investors. The extent of institutional ownership is significant because the more concentrated the stock ownership, the relatively easier it is to make direct approaches to the holders of blocks of stock that may be decisive in a struggle for control. Like many other publicly held corporations of approximately this size, its management owns an insignificant fraction of the outstanding stock: less than 100,000 shares. The target is apparently well managed and has been consistently profitable, with earnings per share of about $3.00 in the latest year. At a market price of $30.00 per share, the target's stock is selling for 10 times earnings, a rather low price/earnings ratio for the industry. According to its latest financial statements it has about $50,000,000 of cash (or cash equivalents) on its balance sheet that appears to be in excess of its current operating requirements. The most recent report of the CEO states that funds have been accumulated in order to finance "needed plant expansion and acquisitions of smaller companies that complement" the operations of the target corporation.

The potential aggressor is also a publicly held corporation. It has built up a "war chest" of over $300,000,000 in cash for acquisitions, and it has arranged lines of credit (usable only for takeovers) that enable it to borrow up to an additional $2,200,000,000 to finance one or more takeovers. (The sources of such lines of credit are discussed in §17.17.) Except for the accumulation of cash and the negotiated lines of credit, the size and earnings power of the aggressor is roughly comparable with those of the target. This overall profile is also rather typical of aggressors in the takeover movement.

At the outset, the aggressor knows relatively little about the target since it does not have access to internal corporate information. Since the target is publicly held, the aggressor does have available the basic data and financial information that is publicly filed with the New York Stock Exchange and the Securities and Exchange Commission. It also has available private credit reports and industry and trade information about the operations of the target. It may also have the benefit of a modest amount of information through hearsay, espionage, and rumor. While everything the aggressor learns tends to confirm that it is desirable for it to make a takeover attempt, this conclusion is necessarily based on incomplete and partial information, and a substantial misjudgment as to value is possible.

At this point, the aggressor must decide whether to go ahead and obtain a "toehold" in the target corporation's stock. At the same time, it must make a tentative decision as to how to proceed thereafter: either by a direct appeal to the shareholders through a cash tender offer or by a negotiated transaction with target management. Both alternatives have positive and negative features. A negotiated takeover usually has the advantage of making additional information about the target's affairs available to the aggressor before an irrevocable commitment is made. This additional information should permit a more accurate estimate of the value of the target's business and thereby minimize the danger of paying too much for the business. On the other hand, a proposal for a consensual takeover alerts the target to the threat of a direct appeal to the shareholders and gives it an opportunity to adopt defensive tactics that might make a takeover much more difficult or even impossible. An immediate tender offer has the advantage of surprise and is more likely to succeed, even though it suffers from the disadvantage of having to proceed on the basis of a price based on less reliable information.

§17.4 The Purchase of a "Toehold" in the Open Market

Once the decision to go ahead is made, the first step in practically every takeover attempt is the purchase on the open market of a substantial number of target company's shares by the aggressor. These purchases are made at current market prices on the New York Stock Exchange or other market where the target stock is traded but are disguised: Orders may be placed with different brokers in different cities in a variety of different names. The buy orders may be executed at different times as the brokers try to acquire shares at the most favorable prices while hiding the fact that an accumulation of shares for the benefit of one entity is underway.

An aggressor may purchase up to 5 percent of the outstanding shares of the target without making any immediate public disclosure. For this reason, one often reads stories about aggressors acquiring 4.9 percent of the target's outstanding shares and then holding. These announcements of 4.9 percent holdings are made because the aggressor has the independent responsibility of disclosing to its shareholders that it has made a material investment in another corporation in its periodic reports to the SEC. When ownership breaks through the 5 percent level, the Williams Act requires the aggressor to file a statement with the Securities and Exchange Commission within ten days; during that ten-day "window" it may continue to make open market purchases of the stock. One proposed change in federal law that may be enacted in the future reduces this ten-day window to five days or even less; at the present time, however, an aggressor may accumulate a significant holding above 5 percent before being required to show its hand.

Assembling a block of 4.9 percent or more of the target's stock undoubtedly will drive up the price of that stock, perhaps from $30 per share to $33 or even $35 per share. If the target is at all sophisticated it will have detected the surge of buying interest underlying this price run-up. It should suspect that a potential aggressor is accumulating shares since target management should know whether or not there are pending internal developments to justify the increased interest in the shares or the unexplained 10 percent rise in price (from $30 to $33 per share). While it may surmise that someone is accumulating its shares, it probably does not know who it is. If it has not previously adopted takeover defenses, it may hurriedly do so at this time.

The statement that must be filed with the SEC at the expiration of the ten-day window is known as a 13D statement. The reason for this name is that the statement is required by section 13(d) of the Securities and Exchange Act. This statement must include information about the identity of the acquirer and the reason for the accumulation of shares. If an immediate takeover attempt is planned, that must be disclosed. If the aggressor wishes to keep its options open, it may state that its purpose is to make an investment and that it has no plans to seek control at this time. If a takeover offer is made shortly thereafter, however, a legal attack may be made on the adequacy of the disclosure in the original 13D filing.

Let us assume that at the expiration of the ten-day window, our aggressor has accumulated a total of 8 percent of the target stock and has moved the price of target shares to $35.00 per share. Thus, at the time the aggressor goes public by filing its 13D statement, it has purchased 1,600,000 shares of target stock at prices ranging between $30 and $35 per share. If the average price per share was $34, the total investment of the aggressor in obtaining a toehold is $54,400,000. Let us also assume that its 13D straightforwardly states that it has purchased these shares with a view toward obtaining control of the target.

§17.5 The Dynamics of a Cash Tender Offer

We now assume that the aggressor has resolved to seek majority voting control of the target as promptly as possible without negotiating with management. The usual way to do so is to announce a cash tender offer for 42.1 percent of the stock of the target at or about the time the 13D is filed. (42.1 percent plus 8 percent already acquired in the open market equals 50.1 percent.) Target management may receive informal notification of the offer less than 24 hours before it is announced, or they may receive no notification at all.

Basically, a cash tender offer is an open invitation for shareholders to submit (*tender*) shares for purchase by the aggressor at a specified price. Persons desiring to accept the aggressor's offer must submit their shares to a specified bank depository by a specified date. If enough shareholders tender their shares for purchase the aggressor has achieved its goal: If not enough do, the aggressor may return all the tendered shares and not buy any of them. In this event its investment in the target is limited to the cost of the toehold shares plus the comparatively nominal costs of the unsuccessful offer. If a higher bid then comes in from a third party, the aggressor may tender its toehold for purchase by the new aggressor, making a substantial profit.

To make a cash tender offer, the offeror must set a price, decide how many additional shares to tender for, file a 14D statement (required, not surprisingly, by section 14(d) of the 1934 Act), and publicly announce the offer. For example, in the above hypothetical the aggressor could conclude to make a public offer to purchase 42.1 percent of the shares at $50 per share, the offer to expire in 20 business days (the minimum period permitted under SEC regulation). The 14D statement must disclose, among other things, the source of financing of the purchase price and the plans the aggressor has for the target in the event the offer is successful.

A cash tender offer is most likely to be effective in corporations in which management owns or controls only a small percentage or proportion of the shares. In the modern publicly held corporation, nonmanagement shares are held by institutional investors, brokerage firms, speculators, long-term investors, and others. Many of these shareholders may be willing to sell their shares outright at a price significantly above the current market price (e.g., at $50 per share when the current market price is $35), even though they might hesitate to vote to oust incumbent management if they are to remain as shareholders. By offering an attractive price, the aggressor appeals to the target shareholders over the head of management; the appeal is not "I can do a better job" but rather "do you want to sell at $50 per share?" If the offer is accepted by enough holders, the offer succeeds and the aggressor becomes the majority shareholder.

If the aggressor acquires exactly 42.1 percent of the target stock, it will then own 50.1 percent of the target's voting stock. That is certainly sufficient to elect a majority of the target's board of directors, and is sufficient to elect the entire board of directors if the corporation does not have cumulative voting (which is likely to be the case in a publicly held corporation) or has not staggered the election of the board as a takeover defense tactic (see §17.12.1). In addition, the new majority shareholder may be able to replace the entire board of directors through the majority consent procedure permitted in Delaware and several other states. If the aggressor is able to replace a majority of the board of directors with its own people, it may thereafter replace the old target management with its own people, or it may permit that management to continue to operate the target as a subsidiary of the aggressor, if the incumbent management is willing to do this.

It is important to recognize that even if the aggressor acquires over 50 percent of the outstanding shares and replaces the target's board of directors and management, it does not have a free hand with respect to the target's assets. The target is still a publicly owned company with the public owning 49.9 percent; the presence of this minority interest sharply circumscribes and limits what the aggressor can do with the target's assets. For example, the aggressor may not simply distribute to itself the $50,000,000 excess cash owned by the target or combine a manufacturing division owned by the target with a similar division owned by the aggressor. Transactions of these types would almost certainly be viewed as improper and a violation of the rights of the minority shareholders. Indeed, they might well be enjoined before they could be effected at the request of a minority shareholder. Transactions between the aggressor and its new partially owned subsidiary have to be made at arms length and, even then, there is a substantial opportunity for distracting litigation brought by minority shareholders of the target. Hence there is a strong incentive for the aggressor ultimately to eliminate all minority shareholders and obtain 100 percent of the stock. Once it obtains all the shares, there is then no shareholder to complain if the aggressor, for example, uses the target's $50,000,000 to defray a portion of the cost of purchasing the 8,420,000 shares.

Modern corporation statutes allow minority shareholders to be "cashed out" involuntarily, that is over their objection and without their consent. See §17.9. The second transaction to eliminate the minority shareholders is usually called a *back-end* or *mop-up merger* and is an essential aspect of modern takeover transactions. The terms of a back-end merger may be significantly less attractive than the terms of the original offer.

Say the aggressor decides to make a partial tender for 42.1 percent of the target's stock: 8,420,000 shares. What price should the aggressor offer in that tender? It must be high enough above the current market price of $35 per share to attract a sufficient number of tenders to yield 8,420,000 shares of stock. Also, it should be high enough to discourage other possible bidders who may also be looking at the target. On the other hand, one does not want to throw money away with abandon: The aggressor is offering to purchase for cash 8,420,000 shares, and the decision whether to offer $45 per share or $50 per share involves a cool $43,000,000. Average takeover premiums during the early 1980s ranged from 30 to 50 percent over market price at the time of the offer. On this scale, our aggressor should offer between $45.50 and $52.50 per share; $50 per share seems a reasonable price to offer. If this offer is successful, the aggressor is committing itself to invest another $431,000,000 (8,240,000 × $50 = $431,000,000), in addition to the $54,000,000 invested in the original toehold, in order to obtain control (50.1 percent) of the target. In terms of similar transactions during the 1980s, this near half-billion dollar transaction is a small- or medium-sized transaction.

Cash tender offers have become quite stylized in their terms. In very large offers, the offer itself may be contingent on obtaining financing: That is not necessary in our hypothetical because the aggressor has already lined up $2,200,000,000 of cash or commitments, which is more than ample to pay for the target stock. It is customary, however, to include other conditions to the offer, such as the absence of objections from the antitrust authorities. Some of these conditions may be fairly general (e.g., an absence of material changes in market conditions) so that a tender offer has some of the attributes of an option rather than of a firm offer to be accepted by individual shareholders tendering their shares. It is rare, however, for an aggressor to attempt to invoke these "out" clauses to back out of a successful offer.

In a partial offer, as here, the offer is said to be *over-subscribed* if the total shares tendered for purchase by the deadline exceed 8,420,000 shares. In this event the offeror (aggressor) may either purchase only 8,420,000 shares or, at its option, purchase all the shares that have been tendered. If the aggressor elects to limit its purchases to 8,420,000 shares, it must purchase shares pro rata from each tenderer; it may not adopt a first-come first-served policy under the Williams Act. *Pro rata* means that if 12,000,000 shares are tendered, the aggressor must purchase 8,420,000/12,000,000 of each individual tender. The federal prohibition against a first-come first-served strategy is based on concerns that it might cause shareholders to tender hastily without opportunity for reflection (in order to make sure that the tendered shares are actually purchased) and that it tends to favor centrally located shareholders (principally in New York) at the expense of shareholders who live in more remote locations.

The Williams Act also provides that tendered shares may be withdrawn during specified periods; and in any event after 60 days, if the offer continues for that time. The offer must remain open for at least 20 business days, and the aggressor may extend it for a longer period or increase the price (for example, in response to a competing bid at a higher price). If the aggressor does increase the price, however, it must buy all shares at the higher price. On the other hand, an aggressor may let one offer expire and then immediately make a new offer at a higher price, thereby largely achieving the same result without paying everyone the increased price.

As long as the tender offer is open, the aggressor may purchase shares only through the tender offer: It may not negotiate separately with large institutional shareholders. On the other hand, immediately after the offer expires it may negotiate with shareholders and purchase their shares in private transactions. See §17.8.

All of these rules are part of the basic ground rules for tender offers established by or pursuant to the Williams Act.

§17.6 Open Market Purchases as an Alternative to a Tender Offer

There have been a few instances in which an aggressor sought to obtain a majority of the outstanding shares of the target by a stream of open market purchases without ever making a public tender offer. A 13D statement must be filed when the purchaser breaks the 5 percent level, but no 14D filing is required since no public tender offer is being made. There are problems with this approach, however. For one thing, a stream of purchases of this magnitude may drive the market price of the target stock significantly above the price that would bring forth the same number of shares if a tender offer were made. In other words, a tender offer at $50 per share — a one-shot, limited-time offer — may draw more stock out for purchase at $50 per share than could be obtained on the open market at an average price of $50 per share even if the price began at $35 per share. Shareholders watching a buying campaign that causes a significant rise in the price naturally tend to hold back waiting for even further increases in the stock price. Holding out for a better price is not generally practical; it is in fact very risky, in the case of a tender offer. Second, if the aggressor communicates directly with large investors while actively purchasing shares in the open market, it may be argued that the communications constituted an informal public tender offer (even though made only to selected persons) which is illegal under the Williams Act when it is not made to all shareholders and not made pursuant to a filed 14D statement.

§17.7 Role of Risk Arbitrageurs and Market Speculators in Takeover Battles

When a cash tender offer is made for target shares, the subsequent market activity in the stock strongly influences the outcome of the offer. A major run-up in price usually occurs at or shortly before the announcement of the tender offer. Major run-ups in price *before* the offer probably are caused by information leaks about the contemplated offer followed by insider trading by favored speculators on the basis of such information. In the past there was a large amount of trading in advance of an offer. Criminal prosecutions of many of the individuals involved in this trading have occurred, and it is likely that this type of insider trading is a thing of the past.

Leaving aside the possibility of insider trading, when a tender offer is publicly announced the market price for the target shares jumps almost instantly to or near the offer price. (The price of the aggressor's shares may well decline, but that is another story; see §17.20.) This post-offer market behavior is a result of trading by a group of sophisticated speculators, known as *risk arbitrageurs*. They actively accumulate shares that are offered in the market planning to tender them to the aggressor (or to the highest competing bidder). On the day the aggressor announces its $50 bid, arbitrageurs immediately enter the market, buying target shares at whatever prices they are offered below $50 (and in some cases, above $50 if they have reason to believe the bid will be increased or competing offers will be made). These transactions are not classic arbitrage (see §15.5.1 for a discussion of the traditional meaning of that term) since the success of the offer is not guaranteed and there is therefore a degree of risk involved. One should not overstate the degree of risk, however. Market wisdom is that once a company is "put into play" by a tender offer, its chances of remaining an independent entity are small (see §17.8). In other words, risk arbitrageurs historically have been able to liquidate their positions in target stock on a profitable basis. Indeed, risk arbitrage has been so consistently profitable during the current takeover period that the financial resources of risk arbitrageurs have increased to the point that they are now a major force in takeover battles, well able to absorb hundreds of millions or billions of dollars worth of target shares as they are offered on the market.

The result of risk arbitrage is that upon the announcement of the bid the price of the target stock is quickly driven up from the pre-tender price to the neighborhood of the tender offer price. The precise relationship of the market price of the target's shares following the announcement to the announced tender offer price is a complex one that depends on the answers to several questions: (1) what is the probability that the offer will succeed? (2) If it does succeed (and the offer is a partial one), to what extent will it be over-subscribed? (3) If it is oversubscribed, will the offeror acquire all shares or will the offer be prorated? (4) If the offer is prorated, what are the terms of the proposed back-end or mop-up merger, if any, likely to be? (5) What are the chances that a higher offer may be forthcoming from a different source? (6) What are the chances that management will attempt a leveraged buyout or a reorganization that provides shareholders with more value than the offer? Depending on these variables, the market price may be substantially below, slightly below, slightly above, or substantially above, the tender offer price.

Consider the position of shareholders in the target corporation when the offer is made. Upon the announcement of the offer, they see the market price of their shares advance significantly, usually close to the tender offer price. They then have three plausible choices: (1) they can hold their shares, hoping that the offer fails and incumbent management remains in control, (2) they can tender their shares to the aggressor pursuant to the offer, hoping that the offer succeeds and is not oversubscribed, but with the risk that they may get back some or all of their shares if the offer is prorated, or (3) they can sell their shares on the open market and be out of the situation entirely. The first choice is usually unattractive because, if the offer fails, history shows the market price of the target shares declines to levels that may be even below the pre-offer price; on the other hand, if the offer succeeds, the non-tendering shareholder may be at a serious disadvantage by being remitted to whatever rights he or she may have in the subsequent back-end or mop-up transaction that is likely to occur. See §17.9. The second choice carries the risk that the offer may be oversubscribed and some of the shares returned with the result that the shareholder may again be remitted in part to the back-end offer. Further, tendering involves a mechanical process of complying with the terms of the tender offer and delivery of shares in advance of payment that many shareholders find complex and uncertain. The simplest thing to do is to sell the shares into the market. One thereby obtains the benefit of most of the run-up in price with none of the problems or risks of actually making a tender. The cost of this strategy is that the selling shareholder loses any benefit of subsequent offers by third persons or the benefit of any increase in the offer price by the aggressor.

One thing is virtually certain: If shareholders of the target sell their shares in the open market during the pendency of the offer, they will be acquired by risk arbitrageurs and are going to be tendered to somebody. Open market sales are thus virtually a vote for the aggressor. Put another way, risk arbitrageurs and aggressors are natural allies in the takeover wars.

Institutional investors are under pressure to tender their shares or sell into the market for a different reason. Many of them hold and invest funds as fiduciaries for other groups — employees, insurance policy holders, small investors, and so forth. They have fiduciary responsibilities to obtain the maximum financial return for the current beneficiaries. They may conclude that these fiduciary duties require them to maximize short-run profit by taking advantage of the run-up in price resulting from a tender offer either by tendering shares to the aggressor or by selling them into the market during the offer. In other words, cash tender offers may also encourage large investors to tender, or to sell into the market.

A major advantage of the cash tender offer over alternative methods of takeovers is that the market pressure of the offer encourages many shareholders of the target to desert incumbent management and bail out by selling their shares into the market. Indeed, the market behavior described in this section greatly increases the probability that once a tender offer is made for a target, that offer, or another better offer from another source, will succeed. The market vernacular reflects this fact: A target for which an offer is made is said to be put into play and the generally accepted market wisdom is that once put into play, the target will thereafter disappear as an independent entity, absent the most heroic defensive strategies.

§17.8 "Street Sweeps" Following Unsuccessful Tender Offers

As described in the previous section, when a corporation is put into play, very large market accumulations of stock are made by risk arbitrageurs and other market speculators in anticipation of the target being taken over by another entity. It has sometimes happened that the bidder is unexpectedly stymied by defensive techniques and is compelled to withdraw its offer. At that point there is a risk that there will be no takeover at all and arbitrageurs face massive losses since they have paid high prices for shares that will now decline dramatically in price when the takeover threat disappears.

Even in this situation the risk arbitrageurs have usually avoided substantial losses. Despite the withdrawal of the tender offer, the target remains in a very precarious situation because of the concentration of share ownership in the hands of arbitrageurs and other speculators who are anxious to sell. The percentage ownership of target shares by this relatively small group may approach or exceed 50 percent of the outstanding shares. The target is even more ripe for a takeover than it was before the offer was originally made because of this concentration of ownership in the hands of persons who have no loyalty to the target and who are interested only in an immediate financial return. It is easy for either the aggressor that withdrew its recent offer or an opportunistic third person to contact the risk arbitrageurs directly and offer to buy their holdings of the target shares. The price offered for the shares may be somewhat below the price previously offered in the withdrawn tender offer but certainly above the pre-offer price, since the shares being purchased may determine who has working control of the target enterprise. This practice of purchasing shares directly from arbitrageurs and speculators immediately after an unsuccessful tender offer has come to be known as a *street sweep* (the street being Wall Street).

The Securities and Exchange Commission has unsuccessfully challenged street sweeps as violations of the Williams Act and as being unfair to smaller shareholders who are not offered the opportunity to sell their shares in the sweep. These challenges have been unsuccessful, and the SEC has proposed a rule that would make all street sweeps within ten days after an offer is withdrawn subject to the Williams Act. If this rule is adopted and is upheld, the street sweep may become a thing of the past. Legislation addressing street sweeps has also been proposed.

§17.9 Back-End Transactions

As described in §17.5, most successful aggressors ultimately desire to acquire 100 percent of the outstanding shares of the target. However, it is not possible, as a practical matter, ever to acquire 100 percent of the shares of a publicly held corporation by a tender offer. Even in an irresistibly attractive tender offer for all shares, a few shareholders always fail to tender by reason of inadvertence or inattention, and there always are a few small shareholders who hold out and refuse to accept an offer at any price. A follow-up transaction to eliminate the remaining public shareholders is an essential step in all tender offers where 100 percent ownership is desired. These follow-up transactions by themselves are called *back-end* or *mop-up transactions*. Technically, they are statutory mergers. A back-end transaction is not necessary if the aggressor is willing to accept the status of a majority shareholder in a publicly held corporation with minority shareholders.

In a public cash tender offer the aggressor may make the back-end transaction an affirmative weapon. The aggressor may make a partial tender offer, seeking to acquire a controlling interest less than all of the target's outstanding shares, and at the same time announce, as part of its takeover strategy, the terms of the back-end merger that will eliminate all of the remaining outstanding shares if the original partial offer is successful. Such an offer is known as a *two-tier offer*. The terms of the back-end part of the two-tier offer, moreover, may be less attractive than the terms of the original cash tender offer, thereby encouraging (or coercing) all shareholders to tender promptly to avoid the less attractive terms of the follow-up transaction. Such an offer is known as a *front-end loaded offer*; examples are given in §17.9.3. Section 203 of the Delaware General Corporation Law, enacted in 1988, places major restrictions on back-end transactions. See §17.14.2.

§17.9.1 Cash Merger Statutes

The keys to back-end transactions are modern state merger statutes that permit "cramdown" transactions involving differential treatment of minority and majority shareholders. The phrases "cramdown" and "differential treatment" in the preceding sentence should be noted carefully. "Cramdown" means that a transaction may be imposed on a shareholder over his or her objection; "differential treatment" means that some holders of common shares receive different types or kinds or amounts of property in the merger than do other holders of otherwise indistinguishable common shares; it does not necessarily imply that the property received by one category of shareholders is worth more or less than the property received by another category. The traditional, naive view of a merger is a transaction in which two corporations combine their assets into a single entity with shareholders of both corporations continuing to own shares in the combined entity. That is one type of merger transaction authorized by modern statutes, but there are other types of mergers so authorized as well.

A *cash merger* must involve the combination of two or more constituent corporations. However, not all shareholders of the two combining corporations automatically end up as shareholders of the resulting entity. Some shareholders of the constituent corporations are compelled to accept a specified amount of cash or property for their shares rather than shares in the continuing entity.

Modern merger statutes, furthermore, generally provide for the approval of merger transactions by a simple majority of all outstanding voting shares rather than a two-thirds (or higher) vote required by older statutes. Shares that are treated differently from other shares are not entitled to vote separately on the transaction. In other words, if a corporation has 100 shares outstanding, the affirmative vote of 51 shares approves a merger transaction in which the 49 remaining shares may be treated differently than the 51 shares voting to approve the transaction.

An example of how a cash merger might be utilized to force out the minority shareholders remaining after a successful tender offer has given the aggressor a majority of the stock may be helpful. Assume (as in the foregoing hypothetical) that the aggressor has acquired 50.1 percent of the outstanding shares of the target for a total consideration of $485 million. It has decided to force out the remaining 49.1 percent of the shares for a consideration of a certain amount (x) per share. Precisely what x consists of (i.e., whether it is money, debt, or nonvoting preferred stock of the aggressor, or a combination of the three) and how much of x each minority shareholder is entitled to, is discussed in §17.9.3. The aggressor creates a wholly owned subsidiary and transfers to that subsidiary whatever cash, evidences of indebtedness and preferred stock of the aggressor is necessary to enable the subsidiary to pay x to the holders of the 49.1 percent of the target shares the aggressor does not own. The aggressor then proposes a merger of the target corporation into the subsidiary (i.e., a merger in which the surviving corporation is the subsidiary) under the terms of which the holders of the 49.1 percent minority shares are to receive a consideration of x per share for each of their shares in the target while the shares of the target owned by the aggressor itself are to be exchanged share-for-share for shares of the wholly owned subsidiary that is the surviving corporation in the merger. Approval of this transaction is no problem: the aggressor already owns all the stock of one party to the transaction (its subsidiary) and 50.1 percent of the stock of the other (the target), and since a simple majority of the outstanding shares of each constituent corporation is all that is required to approve the merger, the result of the vote is a foregone conclusion. When the transaction is closed, each minority shareholder receives x per share and the aggressor receives additional shares in its wholly owned subsidiary. All shares of the target are cancelled; since the wholly owned subsidiary is the surviving corporation in the merger, it ends up with the property and business of the target and the aggressor is the owner of 100 percent of the outstanding shares of that corporation. (Essentially the same result may be reached by structuring this transaction in other ways as well, but in every case, the critical step is the ability to provide differential treatment for different shareholders without their individual consent.)

§17.9.2 Protections Against Abuse of Cash Mergers

In this scenario, at first blush, it appears that something is terribly wrong. Apparently, the minority shareholders of the target must be satisfied with whatever pittance the aggressor — the new majority shareholder — decides to give them. In fact, however, there are important safety valves. The first is the statutory right of *dissent and appraisal* available in most states that permits any minority shareholder dissatisfied with the proffered terms (1) to reject them, (2) obtain an independent judicial appraisal of the value of his or her shares, and (3) receive that value in cash in lieu of the consideration offered in the cash merger transaction. This alternative is not really as attractive as it might first appear. There are major practical problems with the right of dissent and appraisal from the standpoint of small shareholders: the cost of maintaining any judicial proceeding, delays (during which the shareholder loses the use of money), and the uncertainty in outcome inherent in any judicial proceeding. Nevertheless, if the new majority shareholder is too stingy with the minority, it will find itself involved in litigation with unhappy minority shareholders over the value of the minority shares, with a contingent obligation to pay the dissenting shareholders immediately in cash whatever amount the court ultimately determines to be the fair value of the minority shares.

A second major safety valve is the recognition by the Delaware Supreme Court that the majority shareholder, when it decides to vote its 50.1 percent of the target's stock to approve the transaction, is engaged in a self-dealing transaction that must meet a standard of "intrinsic fairness." (Weinberger v. UOP, Inc., 457 A.2d 701 (1983).) Intrinsic fairness requires full disclosure of all relevant facts and fair price with the aggressor having the burden of proof. This burden, however, may be met if the transaction is approved after full disclosure by the minority shareholders voting separately — a majority of the minority, so to speak. While such a minority vote is not required under the merger statute, approval by the minority may as a practical matter be necessary if the merger is to withstand judicial scrutiny.

A third safety valve is that Delaware case law permits more powerful defensive tactics by a target against a proposed takeover bid if the target reasonably believes that the proposed back-end transaction makes the entire transaction inadequate or coercive to minority shareholders. (See, for example, the defense described in §17.12.2(4) below.)

§17.9.3 Front-End Loaded Tender Offers

If an aggressor announces a two-tier offer in which the amount offered for the back end of the offer (x in the preceding section) is openly stated to be less than the amount offered in the front-end offer, the offer is called a "front-end loaded" tender offer. Two different examples of such offers are described below.

In one famous case, involving the takeover of Marathon Oil Company by United States Steel in 1981, the aggressor, USS, announced a tender offer at $125 per share for 51 percent of the shares and also announced that if the first offer were successful a back-end transaction would be proposed eliminating the unpurchased shares for a consideration to be paid in the form of bonds worth approximately $76 per share. This offer was successful and the disparate treatment between the two transactions was upheld against judicial attack. Such an offer places economic pressure on all shareholders to tender into the original offer in order to take advantage of the front-end price and avoid the lower back-end price. As a result, a transaction structured in this way is generally viewed as highly coercive, though its use has been defended on abstract grounds by some economists. Their argument is that the true price being offered for the target company is the "blended price" obtained by averaging the front-end and back-end prices: If this blended price is above the pre-offer market price the transaction still creates value for the target shareholders as a whole. This argument assumes implicitly that all shareholders will tender into the front-end offer, as they rationally should do. There is then no harm to any of them since all will effectively obtain the blended price (since all will share proportionately in both the front-end and back-end prices when the oversubscribed offer is prorated). However, these arguments mask a considerable potential for unfairness to individual shareholders, not all of whom may be aware that a rational decision is required or be able to act on a timely basis to accept the front-end offer. Devices such as *short tendering* also exist that allow sophisticated shareholders to obtain the purchase of a larger percentage of their shares at the front-end price than other shareholders.

A second approach toward front-end loaded offers is illustrated by T. Boone Pickens's offers for oil companies larger than the aggressor entity. In the offer of Mesa Petroleum Corporation (a Pickens corporation) for Unocal Corporation, for example, Mesa offered $54 per share in a tender offer for enough shares (an additional 37 percent) to raise its holdings to fractionally above 50 percent of Unocal Corporation, and in the back-end offer, proposed a consideration of "highly subordinated" Unocal debt securities "with a market value of $54." Presumably the "subordination" referred to new bank loans to be obtained by Unocal to assist Mesa in financing the original purchase of the 37 percent of Unocal. Unocal vigorously opposed this transaction, pejoratively describing the debt securities proposed by Mesa as "junk bonds," and proposing a discriminatory exchange offer (to become effective if Mesa's offer succeeded) for all of its remaining shareholders except Mesa that would have provided each shareholder with a substantial amount of senior Unocal debt. This discriminatory offer was upheld by the Delaware Supreme Court (Unocal v. Mesa Petroleum Co., 493 A.2d 946 (Del. 1985)), and ultimately defeated Mesa's offer. Following the *Unocal* opinion, the Securities and Exchange Commission adopted an "all holders rule" to prohibit the kind of discriminatory offer made by Unocal in this case.

As a general proposition, it is difficult to quarrel with the Delaware Supreme Court's categorization of Mesa's offer for Unocal. An all-cash $54 offer is more attractive than an offer of debt and securities "with a market value of" $54 because of the uncertainties of valuation and the possibility that the market may value the debt securities at a lower price than what the offeror optimistically estimates. Further, the ready marketability of the debt may be doubtful, particularly for large holders. Hence, this type of offer appears also to be a type of front-end loaded offer, though perhaps not as blatant as the dual-price offer pioneered by the United States Steel Corporation.

The use of front-end loaded offers has declined dramatically since 1985. The most common pattern today is simply to announce that in the back-end offer the same amount of cash will be paid as in the front-end offer (or to state that no plans for a back-end offer exist). Several factors caused the apparent abandonment of the front-end loaded offer. A number of corporations adopted *fair price amendments* to articles of incorporation requiring back-end transactions to be made at prices at least as favorable as the front-end offer price. Several states imposed similar fair price requirements for such mergers by statute: Maryland was the first state to adopt this type of statute. Finally, the judicial antagonism to such offers, epitomized by the Delaware Supreme Court's categorization of Mesa's offer for Unocal as an "inadequate and coercive two-tier tender offer," indicates a willingness by courts to permit extreme defensive measures to defeat such offers. Aggressors apparently concluded that the coercive advantages of the front-end loaded offer were outweighed by these disadvantages.

§17.10 Other Nonconsensual Takeover Techniques: The Proxy Fight

Historically, the earliest type of nonconsensual takeover technique, long antedating the development of the cash tender offer, was the *proxy fight*. In a proxy fight, the aggressor solicits the target's shareholders with a proposal that they vote for an alternative slate of directors proposed by the aggressor. If holders of a majority of the shares vote for the alternative slate, the aggressor obtains control of the board of directors of the target. Thereafter a cash-out merger with the aggressor may be negotiated or the target may remain in business as a separate entity indefinitely under the new management. The proxy fight is much more of a traditional political campaign than a tender offer; shareholders who vote in favor of the aggressor generally remain shareholders after the change in management occurs. Proxy fights are subject to significant regulation under the proxy rules adopted by the Securities and Exchange Commission. These rules basically require full and open disclosure of objectives and plans.

The proxy fight has not been a popular modern takeover device primarily because the probability of its success is relatively low and because cash is usually available to buy control directly through a cash tender offer. The reason for the low probability of success is that it is difficult to persuade shareholders to vote out incumbent management when they will remain as shareholders in the target corporation after the change in management occurs. Nevertheless, there have been a handful of attempts during the recent takeover movement to use the proxy fight as an auxiliary device to place additional pressure on the target short of making an outright offer to purchase control. This usually occurs when it appears the target is so large, or its defenses seem so impregnable, that it is impractical for the aggressor to mount a cash tender offer.

With the development of powerful takeover defenses by corporations and the enactment of statutes by Delaware and other states that make takeovers more difficult, it is possible that proxy fights may be more widely used in the future than they have been in the recent past.

§17.11 Other Nonconsensual Takeover Techniques: Straight Exchange Offers

During the current takeover activity, a few takeover offers have been based not on offers of cash for target securities but on offers of exchanges of aggressor debt for shares of the target. At one time Ted Turner unsuccessfully attempted to acquire a controlling interest in rival CBS, Inc. by an offer to swap a variety of debt instruments, including several zero coupon notes, for CBS stock. The offer did not succeed, in part because CBS installed substantial takeover defenses that probably would have made it impractical for Turner to utilize CBS assets or cash flow to service any of the additional debt.

Transactions are cast in the form of exchange offers when the aggressor finds it impractical to raise sufficient cash to mount a straight tender offer. Exchange offers suffer from problems of uncertainty over the market value of the proffered debt securities and concerns over the potential lack of marketability of large blocks of those securities. There may also be a substantial risk of default: The aggressor may be unable to satisfy the obligations set forth in the debt securities it is offering, and the market discounts the securities accordingly. These securities are sometimes called "funny money," a phrase that reflects the skepticism of the market about this type of transaction.

An offer of aggressor-issued debt for stock in the target in a sense proposes that the shareholders of the target themselves finance the takeover of their own company. Rather than the aggressor borrowing money from third parties by the issuance of debt and using the money to purchase shares, the aggressor offers the debt directly to the target shareholders. It is not surprising that such offers have not proved to be attractive.

§17.12 Defensive Tactics in General

When the first cash tender offers were made, the targets were virtually defenseless. They were often unprepared for the offer, and a successful purchase of the majority of the outstanding shares often occurred before the simplest defensive measures could be taken. The Williams Act sharply cut down the advantage of surprise by its disclosure requirements and the provision that all tender offers must remain open for at least 20 business days, thereby eliminating pressure on shareholders to tender immediately or lose out.

Today, defensive measures are well understood and practically every publicly held corporation has erected a shield consisting of a number of different types of defenses. Defenses may be usefully classified into two basic types: those put into place before any tender offer is made, designed to discourage the approach in the first place, and those instituted after a cash tender offer has been launched in an effort to defeat an ongoing offer.

§17.12.1 Pre-Offer Defenses

The simplest types of pre-offer defenses involve the utilization of options long provided for in corporation statutes that have the effect of making it more difficult or more expensive to obtain working control of the target even if the aggressor obtains a majority of its outstanding voting shares. These provisions, known as "shark repellants" or "porcupine provisions," may either make more difficult the process by which the board of directors is replaced by a new majority shareholder, or impose additional costs on the corporation in the event of a successful takeover.

A popular defense is to stagger the election of directors so that directors have three-year terms and only one-third of the board is elected each year. At the same time it is necessary to provide that directors may only be removed for "cause" (to prevent a new majority shareholder from calling a meeting of shareholders and simply removing all the directors without cause, as is permitted under most state corporation statutes). The theory of these provisions is that it may take the aggressor two years after obtaining a majority of the shares before it is able to replace a majority of the board of directors with its own designees.

Another popular provision limits the power of shareholders to call special meetings of the shareholders on the theory that the new majority shareholder may be unable to act except at a meeting. In states that permit the shareholders to act by majority consent informally without a meeting (an option that is available in Delaware and a limited number of other states), bylaw or charter provisions may also be adopted defining and circumscribing that power, again with the view of making it as difficult as possible for a new majority shareholder to translate its shareholdings into operating control of the target.

Pre-offer defensive tactics may also involve economic changes designed to make the corporation less attractive as a target. This is a second line of defense independent of the internal corporate changes described above. For example, corporations may grant officers and mid-level employees *golden parachutes* or *tin parachutes* triggered by a takeover of the management of the corporation over the objection of incumbent management. Golden parachutes are lucrative severance contracts for top management whose employment with the corporation may be terminated upon a successful takeover. Tin parachutes are smaller severance contracts for middle-level management. The total payments required under individual contracts may run into the tens of millions of dollars for high-level individual officers: The largest such contract revealed to date was a severance payment of over $30,000,000 to a single CEO. Aggregate payments may be several times larger. Even with large payments, however, it is unlikely that they will seriously deter an aggressor already contemplating a transaction running into the hundreds of millions or billions of dollars. The corporate justification for golden and tin parachute contracts is that they enable management to serve the corporation during the pendency of a takeover bid without concern about their personal economic futures.

Another type of economic defense against unwanted takeover attempts involves restructuring the corporation itself to reduce its attractiveness as a takeover target. Many corporations, for example, have distributed excess cash to its shareholders either in the form of an extraordinary dividend, or, more commonly, in the form of open market share repurchase plans. See Chapter 16. A major share repurchase plan (1) reduces the number of outstanding shares, (2) leaves total earnings per share virtually unchanged (since the cash used is excess and not essential for the operation of the target's business), and (3) thereby increases earnings per share and the market price of the target shares. See §16.2.

The business may also be recapitalized by the sale of unessential lines of business and distribution of the proceeds to the shareholders in the form of extraordinary distributions or a share repurchase program. Large amounts may also be borrowed in order to leverage up the target and increase its debt/equity ratio; the cash is again distributed to shareholders. This makes the target "leaner and meaner" and basically does what a successful aggressor would be likely to do if it obtained working control of the target. Whether or not these transactions are desirable from the standpoint of the economic well-being of the target may be questionable. A series of transactions in which a corporation borrows additional amounts in order to distribute those amounts to its shareholders directly or indirectly is called a *leveraged recapitalization*.

Yet another popular defensive tactic is to make it difficult for a successful aggressor to obtain approval of back-end merger transactions. These provisions may no longer be necessary in Delaware corporations (and corporations formed in states with statutes similar to Delaware's) since a statute now limits such transactions. Corporations formed in other states may adopt *super-majority provisions* requiring approval by more than a majority vote of the shareholders: two-thirds or even a higher percentage vote of the shareholders may be required for approval of transactions between the corporation and a major shareholder. In order to avoid imposing impossible restraints on *desired* transactions with major shareholders, the super-majority provision may be made suspendable by the board of directors or applicable only to transactions with a person who recently acquired a substantial interest in the target's stock. A more radical type of provision grants rights of redemption to minority shareholders at the same price paid by an aggressor who acquires a majority of the outstanding shares. Another provision imposes favorable fair price provisions limiting the power of an aggressor to impose a back-end transaction on terms less favorable than the terms on which the aggressor obtained its controlling interest. Rights of redemption or fair price provisions may impose significant financial obligations on corporations.

Other popular pre-offer defenses affecting the internal management structure of potential target corporations in advance of any takeover attempt are poison pills (discussed in §17.13), and control share acquisition plans (discussed in §17.14.1).

§17.12.2 Defenses After an Offer Has Been Made

Once an offer is made, the nature of defensive tactics changes materially. The object is to defeat the offer by any fair (or not-so-fair) means. The following are typical (though the list is not exhaustive):

1. Acquiring another corporation that creates antitrust problems for the aggressor if it completes the purchase of the target company.
2. Attacking the funding of the offer, usually by direct approaches to the financial institutions named in the aggressor's 14D statement.
3. Driving up the price of the target stock so that it is above the tender offer price. This may be accomplished by making a major distribution (a type of restructuring or recapitalizing), or by entering into a huge share repurchase plan that may reduce the number of outstanding shares by 20 percent or more.
4. Disposing of desirable assets — "crown jewels," they are usually called — to friendly entities on terms that are less than favorable to the target. The object of these transactions is to make the target less attractive as a target. At the most extreme, the target may destroy itself as a viable economic entity to avoid capture, a "scorched earth" tactic.
5. Granting "lock up" options or rights to friendly interests to purchase additional shares of the target's stock at bargain prices. Such transactions increase the number of shares needed to be purchased by the aggressor and therefore increase the capital investment it must make if it wishes to acquire more than a majority of the target's stock.
6. Making a competing tender offer for the aggressor's stock. Often referred to as the "pac man defense," this strategy may lead to the bizarre situation in which each corporation has acquired a majority of the outstanding shares of the other corporation. This strategy has only rarely been attempted.
7. Finding a more congenial suitor — a "white knight" — and arranging a consensual transaction with that suitor.
8. Arranging a leveraged buy-out with a new entity in which incumbent management participates.
9. Adopting poison pill or control share acquisition provisions (discussed in the two following sections) on a crash basis.
10. Changing the state of incorporation to take advantage of more favorable state laws.

Some of these defensive tactics may lead to the defeat of the takeover attempt outright while others tend to encourage bidding contests by introducing new contestants for control of the target.

§17.13 Poison Pills

Poison pills are special types of preferred stock or debt securities issued by potential target corporations with rights that are designed specifically to make unwanted takeover attempts difficult, impractical, or impossible. Poison pills were invented in the early 1980s and have become one of the most popular takeover defenses; they have been adopted by hundreds of publicly held corporations. The phrases *poison pill* and *poison pill preferred* are virtually synonymous since almost all poison pills are created using preferred stock as the vehicle.

Poison pills are usually created by the board of directors acting alone without shareholder vote pursuant to the statutory power to create series of preferred shares if appropriately authorized in the articles of incorporation. See §15.4.6. While a poison pill theoretically could be created by shareholder action, boards of directors usually prefer for tactical reasons not to submit such a sensitive and potentially controversial issue to the shareholders. Because shareholder approval is not obtained, arguments have sometimes been made that the creation of a poison pill constitutes an act of "entrenchment" by incumbent management in violation of duties owed to the corporation and its shareholders. The Supreme Court of Delaware has held, however, that a poison pill adopted in advance of any takeover threat is not of itself an act of entrenchment if the pill is fashioned so as not to prevent all takeovers. The decision whether or not to adopt such a pill then becomes a matter of business judgment. (Moran v. Household International, Inc., 500 A.2d 1346 (1985).)

The unique characteristic of a poison pill is that additional rights are granted to shareholders when an aggressor makes a public tender offer for target shares or acquires a specified percentage of the target shares. Typical triggering events are either a tender offer for 30 percent of the target's shares or the outright acquisition of 20 percent or more of those shares. The additional rights may consist of increased voting rights for shareholders other than the aggressor (e.g., shares owned by persons other than the person triggering the poison pill become entitled to ten votes per share when the pill is triggered, while the voting rights of the triggering person are unchanged), additional financial rights in the target (e.g., the right to acquire additional shares or indebtedness issued by the target corporation at a bargain price if the poison pill is triggered), or rights to purchase aggressor shares at bargain prices in the event of a back-end merger between the target and the person whose acquisition or tender offer originally triggered the poison pill (e.g., the right to purchase $200 worth of the common shares of the tender offeror for $100 in the merger). These three basic types of poison pills are called *voting poison pills*, *flip-in poison pills*, and *flip-over poison pills* respectively. Poison pills usually may be disarmed by management redeeming the poison pill preferred at a nominal price before its rights become vested.

Voting poison pills have been invalidated in two cases (arising under New Jersey law) on the ground that the corporation statute of that state does not contemplate that differential voting rights may be created for some common shares while being withheld from others. Since these decisions do not appear to be based on unique New Jersey law, most creators of modern poison pills avoid voting poison pills.

In practice, poison pills turn out to be negotiating devices more than deterrents. They tend to compel potential aggressors to negotiate with incumbent management for a takeover and are rarely actually triggered by a tender offer. Poison pills are not foolproof defenses. They may be neutralized in the context of an unwanted tender offer in several ways. For example, the aggressor may make a tender offer on condition that the board redeem the poison pill preferred, or the aggressor may tender for both shares and rights under the poison pill preferred, or it may tender and simultaneously solicit consents to replace the board and redeem the rights, or it may acquire over 50 percent of the target shares and then cause the target to self-tender for the rights.

Litigation may also be possible on the premise that the target board of directors may not arbitrarily reject a tender offer or refuse to redeem rights in order to preserve (i.e., entrench) their positions within the corporation.

Section 203 of the Delaware General Corporation Law (see §17.14.2) may largely duplicate the protection that poison pills provide, but as a practical matter it is likely that corporations with poison pill defenses already in place will simply retain them.

§17.14 State Statutes Relating to Takeovers

For reasons discussed in an earlier section, states generally oppose takeovers of corporations with significant local connections. The first attempts by states to slow down takeover activity led to the enactment by virtually all states of registration requirements for cash tender offers. These registration requirements were applicable to publicly held corporations with significant local contacts (usually defined in terms of having property with a specified value in the state, having its principal executive offices in the state, being organized under the laws of the state, or having a specified number of shareholders in the state). In Edgar v. Mite Corporation, 457 U.S. 624 (1982), the United States Supreme Court invalidated all of these first-tier state laws on the ground that the Williams Act preempted state laws in this area. A plurality of the court also concluded that the statutes constituted an unreasonable burden on interstate commerce. Based on this decision, some commentators concluded that the national market for control of publicly held corporations was beyond the scope of state regulation. This, however, did not prove to be the case.

§17.14.1 Control Share Acquisition Statutes

In 1987 the United States Supreme Court upheld an Indiana antitakeover statute called a *control share acquisition statute.* (CTS Corporation v. General

Dynamics Corp. of America, 107 S.Ct. 1637 (1987).) This statute defines a control share acquisition as any acquisition that causes the shareholder to break through the 20 percent, the 33⅓ percent, or 50 percent levels of share ownership. A person making an acquisition of control shares of an Indiana corporation does not obtain the right to vote the newly acquired shares unless a majority of disinterested shareholders (excluding both the shares owned by the acquirer of the control shares and the shares owned by incumbent management) vote to grant voting rights to the acquirer. A proposed acquirer may compel a vote by disinterested shareholders on whether voting rights should be granted upon the acquisition if the acquirer agrees to pay for the cost of the shareholders' meeting. The Supreme Court upheld this statute largely under the traditional power of states to regulate internal affairs of domestically created corporations. Following this decision, states rushed to enact similar statutes, amid dire predictions that the result would be inefficiency and less competent management on a national scale.

The precise impact of the Indiana control share acquisition statute and similar statutes on the takeover movement is difficult to assess in the abstract. These statutes were clearly enacted with the intention of making takeovers more difficult, but it is not clear that they will have this result. Certainly, the possibility of losing the right to vote newly acquired shares despite a major financial investment in those shares may be a serious deterrent to takeover attempts. On the other hand, it may be possible to obtain a vote of the shareholders before the decision to purchase is final. Aggressors may prefer to have a vote in advance on their proposed takeover attempt so they can gauge in advance the degree of support they have from the shareholders. It was in part for this reason that Delaware decided to adopt a different type of statute.

§17.14.2 Regulation of Back-End Transactions

Some 15 or so states have adopted statutes that deter takeovers by regulating the back-end transaction. Many of these statutes are fair price statutes that require the price paid to minority shareholders to be not less than the price paid by the interested shareholder. If this price condition is not met, the transaction requires the approval of: (1) the board of directors in office before the interested shareholder acquired its shares, (2) a supermajority (e.g., 80 percent) of all voting shares, or (3) a majority of the disinterested shares, that is, those owned by shareholders other than the interested shareholder. These statutes, the terms of which vary from state to state, are generally patterned after the Maryland statute.

A second major type of statute prohibits all back-end mergers with an interested shareholder for a specified period of time following the acquisition of shares by the interested shareholder, unless the transaction is approved in one of the ways described in the previous paragraph. Most of these statutes are modeled after the New York statute which prohibits back-end transactions for a period of five years.

Section 203 of The Delaware General Corporation Law, enacted in 1988, is a statute of the New York type. It generally prohibits a wide variety of transactions between the corporation and a shareholder owning more than 15 percent of the corporation's shares within a period of three years after the transaction in which the shareholder acquired the shares. Approval by the board of directors (in office before the acquisition) or by two-thirds of the remaining shareholders permits a transaction to proceed immediately. The transaction may also proceed immediately if the interested shareholder acquires over 85 percent of the corporation's stock.

This section is applicable to share acquisitions after December 23, 1987. Its actual impact cannot be determined yet and there must be a test of its constitutionality, but it appears likely that not only will it significantly reduce abusive two-step offers, but may also increase offers for more than 85 percent of the outstanding target stock.

§17.15 State Regulation of Defensive Tactics

An unusual mosaic of state and federal law governs takeovers and defensive tactics. The Williams Act, a federal statute, largely controls the mechanics and detail of a tender offer itself. Attempts by states to interfere directly with the tender offer through registration requirements applicable to the tender offer itself are foreclosed by the *Mite* decision. Peculiarly, however, the defensive tactics management may employ are largely ruled by state law, with little or no federal contribution. In this regard, decisions by the Delaware Supreme Court have been particularly influential.

Directors of a corporation that is the target of a takeover attempt have a potential conflict of interest: On the one hand, their personal positions of profit and honor within a large public entity may evaporate if the aggressor is successful. (For this reason, basic decisions whether or not to oppose an offer may be delegated to the directors who are not also officers or employees of the corporation.) The accepted state law principles on defensive tactics are that the adoption of such tactics in the good faith belief that the offer is not in the best interests of the target is a matter of judgment subject to review under the common-law "business judgment rule" but that actions involving entrenchment of incumbent management are judged by the more rigorous fiduciary duties relating to self-dealing. The business judgment rule provides a very lenient standard of review while the standard of review for self-dealing transactions is considerably more onerous. The line between these two principles is hardly a clear one, since most defensive tactics can be viewed as either legitimate defense or entrenchment, depending on motives.

The Delaware Supreme Court held that the decision to impose a poison pill takeover defense in advance of an actual takeover is to be evaluated under the business judgment rule (Moran v. Household International, Inc., 500 A.2d 1346 (1985)). Similarly, decisions to oppose a pending takeover offer by extreme means (such as purchasing businesses to create antitrust problems for the offeror) are also evaluated under the business judgment rule if the disinterested directors have made a rational decision that a proposed tender offer is not in the best interest of the shareholders or of the corporation. Similarly, offers which involve unfair or coercive partial tender offers at inadequate prices may be opposed by any available means (Unocal Corp. v. Mesa Petroleum Co., 493 A.2d 946 (1985)). While the Securities and Exchange Commission prohibited the specific defense tactic adopted in this case when it adopted its all holders rule, that rule does not affect the scope of the Delaware holding as to permissible defensive tactics against perceived inadequate or coercive offers.

In a third important decision, the Delaware Supreme Court held that quite a different set of principles becomes applicable once the board has resolved to sell the company. At that point, the duty of the directors shifts to obtaining the best possible price for the shareholders: The board may not favor one contender for control over another except on the basis of maximizing the price obtained by the target shareholders (Revlon v. MacAndrews & Forbes Holdings, Inc., 506 A.2d 173 (1986)). The Delaware Supreme Court has since reaffirmed that this principle applies only after the board of directors has decided to sell the company (Ivanhoe Partners v. Newmont Mining Corp., 555 A.2d 1334 (Del. 1987)).

While the principles relating to defensive tactics have been largely created under Delaware law, federal courts are often called upon to resolve issues relating to defensive tactics in litigation involving federal law issues or diversity of citizenship. Other state courts also have resolved litigation relating to defensive tactics in ways generally consistent with Delaware law. In practice, however, courts have sometimes invalidated takeover defenses on a selective basis on the grounds they involve entrenchment or they fail to meet the lenient standards of the business judgment rule. For example, the Second Circuit invalidated options on crown jewel assets given to one contender for control when it appeared that the options were granted significantly below the market value of the assets involved (Hanson Trust PLC v. ML. SCM Acquisition, Inc., 781 F.2d 264 (1986)). This decision appears to be based solely on state law. Other decisions involving similar transactions have upheld the defensive tactic. There appears to be no overarching principle in this complex area except evaluation of the motives of the directors and the court's view of the overall fairness of the transaction from the standpoint of target shareholders.

§17.16 Leveraged Buyouts and Going Private

In each of several recent takeover battles, one contender has been a group of investors that prominently includes incumbent management. This contender offers to buy all publicly held shares for cash, planning to continue the enterprise as a privately held, unregistered corporation. These transactions were first described as *going private transactions*, and more recently have come to be known as leveraged buyouts.

It obviously takes a great deal of money to offer to buy out all the public shareholders for cash. Incumbent management rarely has immediate access to funds of the required magnitude from personal sources. Rather, they must borrow the bulk of the funds from traditional takeover sources. One brokerage firm has specialized in the financing of management-based bids to take corporations private and eliminate the public shareholders. In these arrangements, a new entity is created in which both individual members of management and outside investors are represented: The new entity obtains unsecured loans for the hundreds of millions or billions of dollars required for the tender offer for public shareholders. Incumbent management may be required to invest relatively small amounts in the new enterprise but their investments are almost trivial — perhaps a few million dollars in a transaction involving hundreds of millions of dollars — with almost all of the purchase price being borrowed. Once the publicly held shares are acquired by the new entity, the target corporation (now a wholly owned subsidiary of the new entity) obtains a new loan secured by a lien on all of its assets. The proceeds of this second loan are upstreamed to the new entity, which uses the proceeds to pay off the unsecured loan. The target thus ends up with the obligation to pay off the loan used to acquire its assets out of its own income or cash flow. These transactions are called bootstrap transactions since the assets of the target corporation are used to pay for its own purchase: They are also highly leveraged since virtually the entire purchase price is borrowed.

Following a leveraged buyout, the target may sell off portions of its business in order to pay down the new indebtedness. Improvements in earnings and cash flow may arise from the savings inherent in not being a reporting publicly held corporation as well as in economic improvements to the target's business. The ideal scenario, from the standpoint of management and its partners in the leveraged buyout, is (1) to reduce the burden of the indebtedness created by the buyout by selling off nonessential portions of the target's business, (2) to improve the profitability of the core businesses that remain, and (3) to arrange a new public offering of shares in the restructured target at a significantly higher price than was paid to take the corporation private to begin with. In a few instances, this pattern of public to private and then back to public resulted in profits of hundreds of millions of dollars to individuals who originally invested only a small fraction of that amount.

By the middle 1980s, leveraged buyouts had become as common as cash tender offers from third party aggressors. Outside offers from third parties were regularly met with a proposed leveraged buyout in which management participated actively. Issues of fiduciary duty in competitive takeover situations are particularly close to the surface in these situations, where one of the competitors is a management-organized leveraged buyout. In these situations, the board of directors may well favor the leveraged buyout offer, thereby increasing both the reality and the appearance of conflict of interest.

§17.17 Where Does All the Money Come From?

One factor that sharply distinguishes the present period of takeover activity from earlier periods can be stated in one word: cash. Lots of cash. Modern takeover acquisitions are fueled by the ready availability of cash to enable aggressors to buy out target shareholders in transactions that in the aggregate often run into the billions of dollars for a single target. Transactions like the ones outlined above involving hundreds of millions of dollars — amounts so large as to be almost unimaginable in a private transaction just two decades ago — are now so routine that they rate mention only on the inside pages of the financial press.

A reasonable question is, where does all the cash come from? Clearly there has been a dramatic growth in the money supply in the domestic economy in the last 20 years: The rate of inflation during this period alone is proof of that. Growth in the amount of money in circulation, however, does not explain how one individual can raise more than 500 million dollars to buy a majority of the outstanding shares of Trans World Airlines or how one oil company can raise more than $13 billion to purchase for cash all the outstanding shares of Gulf Oil Company. Nor does it explain how a group of incumbent managers with limited personal funds at their disposal may arrange a buyout of all the public shareholders of a large corporation involving hundreds of millions of dollars.

§17.17.1 Internally Generated Funds

Funds raised by large corporations to finance their takeover attempts are easier to explain than the apparent ability of single individuals or small groups with limited personal resources to raise large sums to finance takeovers or leveraged buyouts. Many large corporations accumulated substantial funds during the 1980s from internal operations. The favorable tax rules adopted in the early years of the Reagan administration (rules that were largely repealed by 1986), permitted the growth of internally generated war chests of $1,000,000,000 or more that were often used to fuel takeover bids. A second important source of internal funds comes from the sale of unprofitable or non-essential components of large businesses. Over the years most large corporations acquire for one reason or another a variety of odds-and-ends of businesses, usually as a by-product of other transactions. Companies traditionally tend to stick with these small components trying to make them profitable rather than disposing of them on the theory that growth in aggregate sales is a mark of successful business operation. Today, profitability and cash flow are the keys: Unprofitable or marginal businesses are often sold even at bargain basement prices if necessary. These transactions may also generate large amounts of funds available for takeover attempts. A few individuals have also assembled personal fortunes in the hundreds of millions of dollars that are sufficient to enable them to launch takeover bids. Many of these fortunes were the product of earlier successful takeover activities on a modest scale, followed by increasingly large transactions. Some were based on the success of privately owned businesses.

§17.17.2 Traditional Loan Sources

Most of the money used in takeover activity today is borrowed money, not internally generated money. This is true of most third-party offers as well as virtually all leveraged buyouts. The name of the takeover game is leverage, just as in commercial real estate deals and many other businesses. The only difference is there are usually another three or six zeros in most of the figures used in the computations.

In the hypothetical used earlier in this chapter, a middle-sized publicly held corporation was posited as having developed lines of credit for $2,200,000,000. Loans of the same order of magnitude may be obtained by groups of speculators or incumbent management launching proposed leveraged buyouts of a publicly held corporation. Who is willing to lend this kind of money to finance the apparently risky takeovers? Financing commitments running into the hundreds of millions or billions of dollars may come from a variety of sources. The monied institutions — commercial banks, pension funds, insurance companies, investment bankers, large brokerage firms, and the like — traditionally do not engage in speculative commercial loans, but this policy began to change in the 1970s. By the 1980s, these entities often made available substantial amounts to fund takeover attempts in the form of short-term commercial or bridge loans that permitted transactions to proceed with the understanding that longer-term loans — perhaps junk bonds or secured loans in leveraged buyouts — would be obtained to pay off these interim loans. (Some of these sources may also commit large amounts to long-term as well as bridge loans.) A second important source of loan money includes speculators who pool large amounts of funds into trading partnerships in contemplation of engaging in takeover activity. This pool of liquid risk capital has grown steadily as one successful transaction followed another. A third major source of loan funds are foreign lending sources with large dollar accounts arising from the imbalance of foreign trade with the United States. Indeed, foreign corporations have often been aggressors in takeover attempts, relying largely on foreign loan sources for their capital.

§17.17.3 Junk Bonds

One brokerage firm (Drexel & Company) has developed the ability to raise hundreds of millions or billions of dollars through the placement of less than investment grade debentures — *junk bonds* as they are called. This firm developed a large network of financing sources — often masked behind impersonal partnership names — who were willing to advance millions of dollars in funds to finance takeover attempts. Drexel charges fees for obtaining these financing commitments as well as participating with its own funds in many of these transactions.

Junk bonds have been popular investments because of the high rates of return — perhaps 13 or 14 percent while investment grade securities had a return of perhaps 9 or 10 percent. Whether their popularity will survive the first major economic downturn, when defaults are likely to occur on a substantial scale, remains to be seen.

§17.17.4 Where Does All the Money Come From? Conclusion

The growth of financing sources for takeovers is based in part on the realization that investments in these takeover transactions may not be as risky as they first appear. For one thing, financing is based on loan commitments that command substantial commitment fees. If the takeover attempt fails, the potential financier simply pockets the fee and advances no funds. It is thus profitable for the lending sources to make commitments without honoring them. If the proposed takeover is successful, the commitment is called in and funds must be provided, but at that point the assets and cash flow of the target are available to service the loans.

The sources of the large amounts of money needed to fuel modern deals have never been widely publicized. But one thing is clear: If the flow of cash ever dries up, modern takeover activity, as it has evolved over the last 20 years, would die.

§17.18 Profitable Unsuccessful Takeover Attempts

One paradoxical fact about takeover attempts is that it is often profitable from the standpoint of an aggressor for its takeover bid to fail. Indeed, some of the best known corporate raiders are widely believed to be more interested in offers failing than succeeding.

As indicated above, when a target is put into play by a cash tender offer, the probabilities are very high that the target will be taken over by someone. Some aggressors may put a target into play by a tender offer with the hope that a bidding contest may develop. If the target is ultimately acquired by someone else, the unsuccessful aggressor simply sells its toehold investment in the target to the successful aggressor at a price that usually entails a very substantial profit. The unsuccessful aggressor may also receive additional consideration for discontinuing its offer, but most of its profit usually comes from the transactions in the target's shares.

§17.18.1 Greenmail

Another possible source of profit from unsuccessful offers involves what is usually called *greenmail*. After a takeover attempt is launched, negotiations may occur between the aggressor and the target. One possible outcome of this negotiation is that the target agrees to buy out the aggressor's investment at a profitable price (usually a price above market and certainly above the aggressor's cost) and the aggressor agrees to make no further investments in the target for an extended period. In effect the target buys its peace from the aggressor; such payments to an aggressor are usually called greenmail. Greenmail is not illegal, but is viewed as of questionable propriety: Its payment may be prohibited by legislation in the future. In 1987 Congress imposed a nondeductible excise tax on the receipt of greenmail in an attempt to discourage the practice.

§17.18.2 Standstill Agreements

Agreements between a target and an aggressor may also take the form of a *standstill agreement* under which the aggressor agrees not to increase its holding in the target beyond a specified size for a specified period of time, ten years perhaps. Some kind of consideration to the aggressor typically accompanies a standstill agreement. A standstill agreement also usually does not prevent the former aggressor from selling its shares profitably to a third party seeking to obtain control of the target.

The promise by an aggressor accepting greenmail that it will not acquire shares in the target for a specified period of time is a type of standstill agreement (in which the maximum permitted additional acquisition is zero).

§17.19 Consensual Takeovers of Publicly Held Corporations: Bear Hugs

Many consensual transactions occur within the modern takeover movement. Typically, the aggressor obtains a toehold in the target and then arranges for a meeting with representatives of target management to propose an amicable buyout arranged on mutually acceptable terms. In this approach, a veiled or explicit threat may be made that if the target chooses not to negotiate, an unfriendly takeover attempt addressed directly to the target's shareholders may be undertaken. An approach to target management under these circumstances is called a *bear hug* in the vernacular of the takeover community. Sometimes the approach to incumbent management may occur after a tender offer has been announced.

When this negotiation is successful, the transaction often proceeds in the form of a tender offer by the aggressor for any and all shares of the target. The target management announces that its members plan to tender their shares and recommends that all its shareholders do likewise. This tender offer may attract 95 percent or more of all the target shares. However, because no tender offer in a public corporation produces 100 percent of the shares, a follow-up statutory merger is necessary to mop up the small number of target shares that were not tendered. The consensual takeover thus often involves a three-step process: negotiation, a friendly tender offer, and a mop-up merger.

Consensual takeovers may also be effected through more traditional means such as a statutory merger dependent on the approval of the transaction by the shareholders of both corporations.

§17.20 Are Takeovers Economically or Socially Desirable?

There have been numerous attempts to explain the modern takeover phenomenon in economic terms. This concluding section summarizes these various attempts in rather subjective terms; many people might disagree with some or much of what is said here.

There is one point on which there is broad consensus among economists. If the proper measure of social welfare in corporation law is the maximization of economic returns to shareholders as a group, the modern takeover movement improves social welfare. For practically every empirical study of price movements in connection with takeovers reveal that on the average and over many takeover transactions, shareholders of the target corporation enjoy substantial and real increases in value while shareholders of the aggressor may gain slightly or suffer small declines in value; the gains of the target shareholders significantly exceed any losses suffered by the aggressor's shareholders.

Presumably, the loss suffered by the aggressor's shareholders on the average indicates that during the current takeover movement, aggressors sometimes pay too much for their targets.

The reason why the net gains occur is more controversial. One plausible explanation is that target corporations are relatively poorly managed, and that the net gain to target shareholders reflects the improvement in target profitability resulting from the change in management. In other words, before the takeover the securities issued by the target were depressed because of the relatively poor financial outlook of the target. The outlook improves dramatically with the prospect of fresh management, and the price of target shares increases in to reflect this improvement in outlook. This theory is strongly endorsed by members of the "Chicago School," an influential group of conservative economists and law professors whose opinions (on takeovers and mergers particularly) today constitute a distinct school of thought. The theory is both neat and consistent with the efficient capital market hypothesis (discussed in §18.2). The major problem with it is that it seems to explain only a relatively small number of the actual takeovers that occur. During the 1980s, most of the target corporations appeared to be well-managed companies; indeed, the aggressor often announced in advance that it did not plan to make major changes in target management or target operations if the takeover was successful. Furthermore, the most seriously mismanaged companies — those in Chapter 11 reorganization, for example, are rarely the subject of takeover bids.

A second possible explanation is based on the concept of synergy. Two separate businesses may fit together so that the combined value of two together is greater than the sum of the values of the two separately. While it is possible that synergy may explain a few successful combinations, it does not begin to explain most of the transactions that occurred during the 1980s. Indeed, the argument about synergy was most strongly put forward in the late 1960s and early 1970s during the period when many conglomerates were created; the combination of unrelated business was generally so unsuccessful that much of the takeover activity after that period was prompted by busting up the conglomerates back into more atomistic units.

A third possible explanation is that the takeover movement is primarily empire building by a few entrepreneurs who believe that bigger is better. The economist rejects this explanation almost out-of-hand because it is not consistent with basic assumptions that underlie modern economic analysis. A strategy of growth for growth's sake must inevitably fail unless size in some way reflects greater efficiency. Economists argue that an empire building explanation is not consistent with the empirical evidence of real shareholders' gains from the takeover movement.

A fourth possible explanation builds on the theory that the takeover movement is primarily financial in origin, caused by the general failure of the securities markets to reflect accurately the break-up values of corporations. This explanation is at least superficially inconsistent with the efficient capital market hypothesis, but cannot be dismissed out-of-hand. Take a situation in which the aggressor borrowed huge amounts of capital in order to acquire a target in order to break it up and sell off individual business components of the target to satisfy the debt created to buy the target. In some instances the sales proceeds have substantially exceeded the cost of the original acquisition. The simplest explanation of the success of such transactions is the failure of the market to price the target's common stock to reflect the liquidation of break up value of the target.

The most likely explanation of the modern takeover phenomenon is that several factors are at work and no single factor explains all transaction.

VI

SECURITIES AND INVESTMENTS

CHAPTER 18

AN OVERVIEW OF THE PUBLIC MARKETS FOR STOCKS AND BONDS

§18.1 Introduction

This chapter describes the public markets for stocks and bonds, beginning with the New York Stock Exchange (and other securities markets that are patterned on the NYSE), followed by a discussion of the second major market for securities, the over-the-counter market. In recent years, these markets have been supplemented by the development of financial futures and options, primarily through innovative securities introduced by the Chicago Board of Trade and other organizations that historically were involved with commodities trading and commodities futures rather than with securities trading. Commodities trading and futures and these new financial instruments are described briefly in Chapter 20.

The markets discussed in this chapter are primarily secondary markets in which persons who already own outstanding shares and wish to sell them deal with persons who wish to buy them. These markets are usually *not* the place where a corporation desiring to raise new capital through the sale of new securities to the public is likely to go (though in a few recent instances, the facilities of the New York Stock Exchange have been used to float new securities). Rather, the markets discussed in this chapter provide basic liquidity so that persons who invest in publicly traded securities can be confident that they can dispose of them if and when they wish.

In general terms, raising capital through the sale of new issues is accomplished through chains of brokerage firms, offering customers the opportunity to invest in the new issues. These chains of distribution for new issues are usually informal, based on a series of continuing business relationships, and do not involve negotiation over price.

In this and the following chapters the New York Stock Exchange is also referred to as the *NYSE*; the over-the-counter market as the *OTC market*.

§18.2 The Efficient Capital Market Hypothesis

Modern economic analysis has developed a theory that capital markets are efficient: The implications of this theory are both far-reaching and startling. In brief, the efficient capital market hypothesis states that securities prices reflect everything publicly known about the prospect of individual companies and the economy as a whole at any point in time. When new information becomes available, the market absorbs and discounts it instantaneously and efficiently. Furthermore, the market accurately assesses the known information and is not put off or misled, for example, by announced changes in accounting principles that affect book earnings but not the real worth of a business. The efficiency of the market can be traced to the efforts of large numbers of analysts and speculators working independently who follow the market extremely closely and exploit any opportunity to make a profit from temporary deviations of market prices from the prices that reflect all known information. These temporary deviations provide an incentive for these analysts and speculators to continue to search for them, but the deviations are small and their existence is fleeting. The combined and systematic efforts of hundreds or thousands of persons to make profits in the market make the market efficient.

There are several different levels of the efficient capital market hypothesis. The version described above is called the *semi-strong version* and has the widest degree of acceptance. Under the semi-strong version, market prices do not encapsulate information that is not publicly available, e.g., inside information about the issuer, or the unexpected possibility that a specific takeover offer may be made in the future. The hypothesis therefore does not deny that profits may be made on inside information about the issuer or about planned takeover moves, so long as the information is acted upon before it becomes public. Where leaks occur, persons acting on such information are part of the mechanism by which the information is absorbed quickly and accurately into the securities price; if this occurs before the time the information is officially announced, the market is said to have *fully discounted* the information in advance of the announcement.

The implications of the efficient market hypothesis in its semi-strong version are startling. First of all, if this theory is correct, one cannot predict the future movement of stock prices based on presently available information; since all current information is already embedded in a security's price, that price will be changed only by events or information that cannot now be foreseen. (If it could be foreseen it would have been already embedded in the current price.) Second, at any instant in time, the next price movement of a stock is as likely to be down as to be up, irrespective of the direction of the previous price movement. Stock prices move randomly, showing no historical pattern. Third, all historical or technical analysis of previous stock price movements is useless for the prediction of future prices, since all that technical analysis is already embedded in current prices. It is true that many persons successfully charge substantial fees for making precisely this kind of historical or technical analysis, but they are either charlatans or just plain lucky. Fourth, extensive reading and study of historical information about a company is also a waste of time: that information is already embedded in the price. The notion that a very smart and sophisticated person can improve the profitability of one's trading by studying historical information and trends is also essentially erroneous. Fifth, in-and-out trading is a losing strategy since one cannot beat the market in the long run and such strategy simply runs up brokerage costs. Finally, the goal of many money managers and institutional investors to beat the averages in the long run is impossible: An investor can only do as well as the market as a whole.

There is little doubt that many Wall Street traders do not agree with the efficient capital market hypothesis in all of its implications. There are numerous stories always making the rounds of how X has devised a strategy that consistently beats the market. Economic theorists tend to reject such anecdotal evidence on the ground that it merely reflects the laws of chance in operation: After all, someone may be able to guess how ten coin flips will come out once in a while, but will stumble on the eleventh. There are, however, some anomalies that create conceptual difficulties for the theory: Investment strategies that have been empirically tested and appear to produce consistently above-average market returns over long periods. Another serious problem for the theory was the sharp market break that occurred in October 1987. There appear to have been no developments during the period of that decline that can account for a decline of nearly one-third in the value of many stocks. Nevertheless the amount of evidence supporting the efficient capital market theory at least during periods of normal market activity is so great that the evidence supporting it has been described as overwhelming.

Despite some anomalies, the efficient capital market hypothesis is accepted as a reasonably accurate description of modern securities markets by many sophisticated people. For example, as described in the following chapter on mutual funds, the basic premise of many institutional investors has gradually shifted in the direction of accepting the conclusion that their goal should be to try to equal the performance of the market as a whole, not to try consistently to beat it.

One important point about the efficient market hypothesis that is not always appreciated is that the studies tending to show the efficiency of the securities markets are largely based on examination of securities that are widely traded on the largest markets, particularly trading in shares of the largest companies registered on the New York Stock Exchange. Some parts of the OTC market also attract a large amount of interest and probably rival the NYSE markets in efficiency. When one moves into other parts of the over-the-counter market or into local securities traded on regional exchanges, however, there are many fewer analysts following specific stocks, and one would expect the efficiency of the market to be significantly lower than the market for the most widely traded stocks. Indeed, the market for many publicly held securities may be "thin," with trades occurring infrequently and only one or two brokers (whose primary interest is with other stocks) regularly quoting prices. In the market for such a stock, there may be virtually no efficiency in the theoretical sense.

A. THE NEW YORK STOCK EXCHANGE AND SIMILAR EXCHANGES

§18.3 The New York Stock Exchange

The New York Stock Exchange is a place — a building located in the central part of the financial district on Wall Street in New York City. All transactions in shares occurring on that Exchange take place in a large room in this building. This room is called the "trading floor," or simply the "floor of the exchange." You may have seen pictures of the trading floor or even visited the NYSE as a tourist and watched from the balcony the beehive of activity that occurs on the floor during trading hours. The floor consists of a series of desks (or *posts*, as they are called) at which specific securities are traded and around which members interested in specific stocks congregate. There are also numerous computer screens being watched, a *ticker* that displays a continuous record of trading in more than two thousand stocks more or less simultaneously with the transactions themselves, and news tickers running full blast.

Only stocks that are listed on the New York Stock Exchange are traded on that market. To be listed, a company must meet specific size and share ownership requirements; in addition, such a company must enter into a standard listing agreement with the Exchange that imposes certain procedural and substantive obligations on the listing company. Among these obligations is a commitment to make publicly available on a timely basis information about developments affecting the company.

The listing requirements ensure that only the largest and most successful of the publicly held corporations are traded on the NYSE. This is the market for the *blue chip stocks* that are household names: General Motors, IBM, and so forth. However, among the more than 2,200 stocks currently actively traded on the NYSE, there are many that are not widely known.

Not anyone can go down to the New York Stock Exchange building on Wall Street in New York and decide to buy or sell some shares: Only members of the Exchange have the privilege of trading on the Exchange floor. Most members are brokerage firms that deal with the general public; transactions are executed on behalf of members of the general public on the floor of the Exchange by representatives of those brokerage firms. Some individuals (called *floor traders*) also are members of the Exchange. To be entitled to membership an individual or firm must buy a seat on the Exchange that entitles the member (or a broker employed by a member firm) to go onto the floor of the Exchange during trading hours and execute transactions. The number of seats is limited, and a trading market of sorts exists for seats. Since most Exchange members trade on behalf of the public, the value of a seat is partially dependent on market activity in securities. In recent years, seats have sold for several hundred thousand dollars each.

The NYSE retains a hefty share of the order flow and volume of securities trading. Its success is based on several factors: (1) it is the most prestigious exchange and many companies desire to be listed there and have their shares traded there; (2) the NYSE has historically provided a highly successful continuous and orderly market for securities traded there; and (3), perhaps most significantly, the Exchange prohibits members from executing transactions in listed securities other than on the floor of the Exchange. Today the Exchange is a highly computerized operation capable of handling trades of hundreds of millions of shares per day. The following sections describe more fully how this institution operates.

§18.4 A Prototypical NYSE Transaction

Assume that you decide to purchase 100 shares of IBM. On Friday, June 10, 1988, IBM was selling for about $115 per share, and that is the date on which the prototype transaction occurs. To buy 100 shares of IBM requires about $11,500 in cash plus commissions, but you have that amount on deposit with your broker. You therefore call up your broker and instruct him to buy 100 shares of IBM "at the market." This last phrase means that your order will be executed at the market price in effect at the time your order arrives on the trading floor. (You may also give a *limit order*, that is, an order that will be executed only at a price you specify, if the market reaches that price. See §18.5.)

An order for 100 shares is known as a *round lot*, and is the standard trading unit for shares on the NYSE. One can sell blocks of less than 100 shares; a unit of less than 100 shares is known as an *odd lot* and is handled in a different way than round lots. Your transaction, however, involves a round lot.

Under modern NYSE practice, all market orders for less than 2,099 shares are "small" orders and, as described in §18.4.2, are filled automatically by computer. In order to describe the mechanics of the NYSE, however, we will first assume that it will be filled in the traditional manner that existed for all stocks before the 1960s, and continues to exist today for larger orders.

§18.4.1 Noncomputerized Execution

Before the computerization of the Exchange in the 1960s, a transaction would occur as follows. Your broker receives your order and telephones it to its New York office (or to the New York offices of a broker regularly used by your broker to fill orders). The order is then conveyed by telephone to the floor of the New York Stock Exchange where a floor broker receives your order. He or she walks to the post where IBM is traded. Behind this post is the specialist handling IBM. The specialist is a critical component of the market that the NYSE operates for IBM shares. Also, surrounding this post there are a number of other brokers interested in IBM, many with orders of their own to fill. The latest price at which IBM traded, and the current bid-and-asked prices are on computer screens for all to see. These quotations might be "115 bid 115⅛ asked." At this point, either of two things might happen:

1. The broker with your order may signify that he wants to buy 100 IBM at the market. A broker outside the post may have an order to sell 100 IBM

also at the market. A deal may be struck then and there at a price negotiated on the spot, either at the last price, the bid price, the asked price, or in between, whatever is agreed upon. The identities of the buying broker and selling brokers are each noted, and given to a "reporter" who sends information electronically about the transaction to the ticker screen, where the transaction will appear in a few seconds.

2. The broker with your order may not find another broker with an order to sell that precisely matches your order to buy. At this point the specialist may step in and complete the transaction from within the post, normally at the "asked" price. The source of the stock supplied by the specialist may be either of two sources. The specialist keeps a list of limit orders to buy or sell IBM stock at various prices other than the market price at the time the order was entered; your buy order may be used to fill one of the sale entries from this book. Alternatively, if the order cannot be filled from this source, the specialist sells from its own inventory the shares needed to complete your order. Again, the transaction appears on the ticker within seconds of the completion of the transaction.

Having completed the purchase, the closing actually takes place five days later. Five days is a NYSE convention. At that time, the broker pays for the shares and you become entitled to the certificate for the shares. You could direct the broker to obtain a certificate for the shares in your name if you plan to hold the shares for a while, or, if you do not give this instruction, the broker simply records on the next statement of your account with it that you own 100 shares of IBM. A third choice exists: You may arrange to obtain shares registered in your own name but leave them with your broker for safekeeping.

Even though settlement is five days after the transaction, you are the immediate owner of 100 shares of IBM for most purposes. (See §16.10 for a discussion of whether the purchaser or seller is entitled to a dividend.) If you become unhappy with your investment before the five-day period for closing lapsed — even later on the same day — your broker can "close out your position" by entering into a commitment to sell 100 shares of IBM. You would, of course, owe two commissions and if the market declined between the time you purchased and the time you sold, you would lose that amount also.

§18.4.2 Order Execution Under the DOT System

In the 1960s, the NYSE began the computerization of many aspects of its operations. Indeed, the tremendous growth in trading that has occurred in the last 20 years — in the 1960s a routine trading day involved a volume of about 10 million shares while in the late 1980s the average volume was in the neighborhood of 150 million or 200 million shares per day — would not have been possible.

The computerized order execution system of the NYSE is known as *Designated Order Turnaround* or *DOT*. It permits member brokers to transmit orders electronically directly to the specialists' posts without the intervention of a floor broker. If the order is a market order and is smaller than a designated number of shares of a single stock (currently 2,099 shares) the order is automatically executed by computer either from other computerized orders or with the specialist. DOT also automatically notifies the member firm placing the order and the specialist of the price at which the transaction was executed.

DOT also permits much larger orders (currently up to 30,099 shares for some of the most actively traded stocks) to be transmitted electronically to the specialist. These larger orders are not executed automatically but must be handled manually by the specialist.

DOT has a third market order feature that is primarily used by program traders and arbitrageurs (see Chapter 20). The LIST program allows member firms to use DOT to electronically transmit orders to purchase or sell up to 500 different stocks simultaneously for automatic execution.

DOT order routing now accounts for approximately two-thirds of all orders executed on the NYSE. The prototype transaction described in §18.4.1 would, of course be executed through DOT, and is so small that it would create barely a "blip" in that system.

§18.5 Limit Orders

The above example involved an order to purchase 100 shares of IBM at the market. When placing an order, one may specify the price at which it is to be executed, say a purchase of IBM "at 114 or lower" or a sale of IBM at "116 or higher." These are *limit orders* because the authority of the executing broker is limited as to the price at which the transaction may be executed.

Limit orders are handled quite differently from market orders. Today they are largely entered through the DOT system, but the way they are handled can best be understood by describing first the process in the pre-electronic era.

Assume you place a limit order to buy 100 shares of IBM at 114 when the market price is about 115 1/2. When the broker arrives at the IBM post with your order he finds that the market price for IBM is about 1 1/2 points (*points* means dollars when discussing stock prices) above your order price. Obviously no seller is going to sell for 114 under these circumstances. The broker is also not going to wait around at the IBM post for 30 minutes or so to see whether IBM will conveniently drop a point and one-half while he waits. Rather, the broker gives the limit order to the specialist who records it in the limit order book he maintains as an offer to buy at 114. If the price of IBM drops to 114, the purchase orders in the limit order book are filled in the order that they were received by the specialist. Because of this priority in execution, it is possible that the price of IBM may drop briefly to $114 and then rise again, and yet your order might not have been executed.

The limit order books record both offers to buy and offers to sell at various prices. An investor is normally interested in buying at a low price and selling at a high price. Thus most limit orders are of the two types described above, that is, "buy at 114 or lower," or "sell at 116 or higher." Not all limit orders are of these types, however. Another type of limit order is a *day order*: for example, "buy at $114 or better but in any event buy at the close of trading at the market." Another type of limit order is a *stop order* which is an order to *sell* when the price has *declined* to a particular point or to *buy* when the price has *increased* to a particular point. A stop order to sell when a stock declines to a specific price may be placed by a person who wishes to save a profit or cut a loss by selling when a stock breaks in price. Similarly, a person may feel that a stock will continue to go up if it breaks through a particular price; hence a stop order to buy the stock if it reaches or exceeds a specified price may be utilized.

Limit orders (other than day orders) are good until cancelled. In other words they remain on the specialist's books awaiting execution until they are cancelled by the person placing the order. Brokers usually recommend that limit orders that are unlikely to be executed promptly or that have lost their original justification be cancelled.

Limit orders today may be placed through DOT (see §18.4.2) up to a specified maximum number of shares (currently 99,900). Most limit order books in use today continue to be physical books in which limit orders are placed manually. Limit orders placed through DOT destined for these limit order books are printed out on the stock exchange floor printers and entered manually by an employee of the specialist. Gradually these books are being replaced by electronic limit order books that permit DOT-placed limit orders to be printed out directly in the specialists' records.

Limit order books contain important price-sensitive information relating to likely future movements of securities prices. They are therefore carefully guarded against improper disclosure. This is as true of electronic limit order books as it is of traditional physical limit order books.

§18.6 The Role of the Specialist

Specialists have existed on the New York Stock Exchange throughout most of its history. They are charged with the responsibility of making an orderly market for the shares they work with. They are expected to maintain inventories of the shares, and buy when the market is declining or sell when the market is rising to assure a smooth trading pattern. In the absence of specialists, the price of a stock — even a stock as widely traded as IBM — might have erratic fluctuations due to temporary blips in demand or supply arriving at the post. Indeed, it might be possible that there will be brief periods when there might be only buyers and no sellers, or only sellers and no buyers. In the absence of a specialist filling gaps, prices might fluctuate excessively in a manner unrelated to the essential supply and demand for the stock. Specialists are thus supposed to hew to their posts, smoothing out artificial fluctuations by trading against the market when necessary to ensure that the market remains orderly. Specialists are not expected to try to prevent market declines (and indeed usually could not possibly do so, even if they tried). Their objective is to let the market find its proper level, given the supply and demand for the stock that then exists, in an orderly way. The obligation of the specialists to maintain an orderly market is qualified by the phrase "so far as is practical." During the sharp market break that occurred in October 1987, some specialists concluded that buying stock in the face of the massive decline then occurring was futile and could only bankrupt the specialist without improving the orderly flow of the market. They therefore withdrew from the market for brief periods and requested halts in

424

trading until an acceptable price to reopen trading could be established. A price is acceptable in this context when it *clears the market*, that is, when it leads to a balance between shares offered for purchase and shares offered for sale at that price without intervention by the specialist.

At first blush it might seem that specialists are sure to lose money in their trading activities when they trade against the trend. In fact this is not the case. Specialists carry substantial inventories of their stock, much of which may have been purchased at significantly lower price levels in the past. Similarly, while they may purchase stock for their own account during a price decline, they may ultimately profit if the market recovers and they dispose of that stock at higher price levels. Specialists consistently show net trading profits from these activities. Indeed, over 60 percent of specialist net revenue comes from dealer-type transactions.

The second major source of income for specialists is commissions for acting as agent for brokers who place limit orders with them for execution. The specialist earns a commission on the execution of each such order. These commissions aggregate tens of millions of dollars per year since over 12 percent of all NYSE transactions involve limit orders on at least one side.

Over 50 firms are designated as specialists by the NYSE. Some 400 individuals actually perform the functions of specialists on behalf of these firms. There is only one specialist per stock, but with 2,100 listed stocks, obviously specialist firms serve as specialist for many stocks. The largest firm acts as specialist for more than 100 stocks. The individuals who actually perform the specialist functions handle an average of 3.7 stocks each. Specialist firms must meet specified capital requirements and their performance is monitored, particularly during times of market turmoil.

Specialists are *downstairs* brokers since they deal only with members of the NYSE but not with members of the general public. The brokerage firms that deal with the public are known as *upstairs brokers* because their offices are physically located above the trading floor. Upstairs brokers are often many times larger than the downstairs specialist firms, and the question has arisen whether upstairs firms should be permitted to acquire specialists. The major concern is the fear of leakage of sensitive market information to the upstairs firm. Several upstairs firms, however, own specialists on regional exchanges without any apparent leakage of information.

$18.7 Block Trades

Block trades are trades involving large blocks of shares, a minimum of 10,000 shares and often much larger. Only a relatively small number of potential buyers and sellers exist for trades of this magnitude, and almost all of them are institutional investors.

Block trades are an increasingly important part of NYSE activity. In 1986, there were over 665,000 such trades that represented nearly 50 percent of total NYSE trading volume. These startling figures reflect the increasing dominance of institutional traders in the NYSE: In 1965 there were only 2,171 such trades, representing about 3 percent of NYSE volume.

Most of the work of putting a block trade together occurs upstairs, in the institutional trading departments of the member firms. Some of these departments develop expertise in effecting transactions in stocks of certain types of companies (such as utilities or banks). Other departments tend to specialize in stocks of specific companies. Some firms act as *block positioners* and use their own capital to take parts of a block trade that cannot be entirely placed with institutional investors. Block positioners must register with the NYSE and meet minimum capital requirements (currently $1 million).

Salespeople and traders of institutional departments maintain constant communication with hundreds or thousands of institutional investors. Many maintain direct phone lines to the trading desks of the institutions. When a department receives an order to buy or sell a large block of stock, it contacts other institutions to see whether they want to participate on the other side of the trade. There also exists an electronic network connecting about 900 trading desks of institutional investors that may be used for simultaneous inquiries about possible interest in the block. The company itself may be contacted if it has announced a share repurchase program. An inquiry also may be made of the specialist to determine how much of the block might be absorbed by public orders at the contemplated price.

Inquiries of the nature described in the preceding paragraph sometimes generate additional interest on the same side of the transaction as the original block. For example: "No, we are not interested in buying any XCo. at 60. Indeed, we currently have 30,000 shares of XCo. that we would like to sell at 60. Can you place it for us?" The managing firm may thus put together an even larger transaction, involving several buyers and sellers on each side of the transaction. If the managing firm is a block positioner, it may participate in the transaction by acquiring the "stub end," that is, the portion of the block not purchased by other investors.

When the transaction is put together upstairs, it is usually passed through the NYSE floor. Relatively small amounts of shares not otherwise committed may be handled by the specialist or sold to customers of floor brokers present at the post. Passing the transaction through the trading floor also ensures that public orders for the same stock (held either as limit orders by the specialist or by floor brokers) may participate in the offering if it is favorable for them to do so. If the managing firm is a block positioner, taking some shares for its own account, SEC rules require provision be made for the public to participate if the block trade is to be executed at a price above the current offer bid or below the current sale bid.

When a block positioner takes a substantial position in a stock in order to complete a block trade, it may thereafter hedge its position through option transactions. See §20.2. Since these positions are taken not as considered investments but as means to facilitate a larger trade by a customer, they are usually liquidated as promptly as is practical.

Block trades would appear to be logical candidates for computerization. There already exists one electronic system for institutional and non-NYSE member brokerage firms to trade among themselves. This service is provided by Instinet Corporation. In a way it is surprising that this service has not garnered greater attention than it has. Data on Instinet trades is regularly reported in financial newspapers.

The floor of the Exchange is touted as a place where the public can buy stock at the same price as the biggest players. This comes about because virtually all trades, even the big block trades, make a pass before a specialist for execution. If the specialists see that a big block order has been negotiated at a better price than what is available on the floor at that time, the block can be picked apart and portions given over to satisfy orders from the investing public — both on the big board and on the regional exchanges.

§18.8 Regional Exchanges Also Trade in NYSE Listed Stocks

In addition to the NYSE, several regional securities exchanges exist, Philadelphia, Cincinnati, Boston, Midwest, and Pacific being the largest and best known. Regional exchanges may list and freely trade in stocks listed on the New York Stock Exchange. Over 1,000 NYSE stocks are traded on one or more regional exchanges. A computer system called ITS (Intermarket Trading System) provides automated price quotations on these stocks traded in multiple markets and an automated routing system so that orders are sent to the market providing the most favorable price.

The regional exchanges also may actively trade in stocks of companies of local interest and with a regional following.

§18.9 How to Read the Newspaper Reports of NYSE Trading

Your decision to buy IBM was based on some kind of investment decision or estimate of likely future stock prices or market trends. Quite likely it was based on the advice of a broker or by your following trading in IBM for several days, weeks, or months.

The financial pages of a newspaper give considerable information about the trading activity each day on the Exchange, about the trading in specific stocks, and about the specific investment characteristics of each stock traded on the New York Stock Exchange. This section, based on *The Wall Street Journal* reporting system, describes the information that is available.

§18.9.1 The Level of Trading Generally

Table 18-1 shows the breakdown of trading in NYSE listed stocks by market, and on a $\frac{1}{2}$ hourly basis, for Friday, June 10, 1988 (a routine day chosen more or less at random). About 181,000,000 shares were traded, an unexceptional trading day for that period. Trades executed on the regional exchanges are included in the composite figures and are broken down separately. While the NYSE still accounts for the great bulk of trading, the regional exchanges' share of the market for trades involving less than 3,000 shares has gradually increased to close to 30 percent of the trades of that size; of course, when trades of all sizes are concerned, the NYSE still predominates since it executes trades for more than 85 percent of the stock traded on any day.

Table 18-1

Breakdown of Trading in NYSE Stocks

BY MARKET	Fri	Thur	WK AGO	½-HOURLY	Fri	Thur	WK AGO
New York	155,710,000	235,160,000	189,600,000	9:30-10	24,990,000	50,150,000	24,580,000
Midwest	10,998,400	10,420,500	9,287,000	10-10:30	11,650,000	20,610,000	17,000,000
Pacific	5,557,800	5,880,300	4,364,100	10:30-11	9,760,000	19,430,000	26,330,000
NASD	3,240,720	4,861,650	3,432,110	11-11:30	14,100,000	27,100,000	20,050,000
Phila	2,425,800	2,312,400	2,347,400	11:30-12	15,200,000	5,610,000	15,540,000
Boston	2,372,900	2,464,700	2,222,400	12-12:30	9,450,000	14,090,000	7,570,000
Cincinnati	1,075,900	1,910,100	1,234,700	12:30-1	8,390,000	30,530,000	11,930,000
Instinet	200,400	453,100	383,300	1-1:30	9,100,000	10,760,000	5,790,000
Composite	181,581,920	263,462,750	212,871,010	1:30-2	11,040,000	6,670,000	6,760,000
Block trades are trades of 10,000 shares or more.				2-2:30	9,390,000	9,070,000	11,120,000
x-Ex-dividend of Detroit Edison Co. 42 cents lowered				2:30-3	12,370,000	12,540,000	11,530,000
the Utility average by 0.24. This lowered the Composite				3-3:30	10,870,000	13,560,000	13,440,000
average by 0.15.				3:30-4	9,400,000	15,040,000	17,960,000

It will be noted that Instinet (see §18.7) accounts for only a minute fraction of all trading. The entry in Table 18-1 for "NASD" is discussed in a later section.

Table 18-2 is part of *The Wall Street Journal* daily diary that shows overall price movements for all stocks traded on Friday, June 10, Thursday, June 9 and for the full week ending on June 10. Block trades, the last entry, are single trades of 10,000 shares or more. They are, of course, indicative of the degree of institutional investors' market activities. See §18.7.

Table 18-2

Diaries

NYSE	FRI	THUR	6/10 WK
Issues traded	1,974	1,983	2,192
Advances	875	815	1,446
Declines	585	720	490
Unchanged	514	448	256
New highs	36	30	79
New lows	3	5	19
Adv Vol (000)	98,254	72,322	505,677
Decl Vol (000)	38,237	109,589	296,361
Total Vol (000)	155,710	235,160	1,022,070
Block trades	3,110	3,612	17,095

§18.9.2 Information About Active Stocks

Tables 18-3 and 18-4 give information about the most active stocks traded on the NYSE on Friday, June 10, 1988, both from the standpoint of the most active issues and of the largest percentage gainers and losers. It may be noted that IBM was well up in the list of most active issues, but was neither a large percentage gainer or loser. This is to be expected, because almost all large percentage gainers or losers are relatively low-priced stocks.

Table 18-3

Most Active Issues

NYSE	Volume	Close	Change	
Peoples Energy	12,789,900	19⅛	+	⅛
Texaco Inc	2,708,500	51⅞	+	½
Payless Cash	2,006,700	25⅝	+	1⅛
Exxon Corp	1,739,500	45⅞	+	½
Chrysler Corp	1,657,100	23½	+	1
Macmillan Inc	1,508,800	75⅞	+	2⅜
Union Carbide	1,506,200	20½	+	⅝
Amer Express	1,440,000	27¼	+	½
Occidental Pete	1,300,900	26⅝	+	⅛
General Elec	1,296,400	43	−	⅛
IBM	1,285,600	116	+	⅝
AT&T	1,207,900	26½	−	⅛
Detroit Edison	1,203,700	x13	−	⅜
Cmwlth Ed	1,191,400	28¼	+	⅛
Ford Motor Co	1,146,400	51¾	+	⅛

Table 18-4

Price Percentage Gainers . . .   and Losers

NYSE	Close	Change		% Chg.		Close	Change		%Chg.
A M C A Intl	3⅞ +	½ +		14.8	NortonCo	59 −	5 −		7.8
Russ Togs Inc	15⅛ +	1⅞ +		14.2	AmaxGoldInc	24¼ −	2 −		7.6
Allegheny Intl	3⅜ +	⅜ +		12.5	UnitCorp	2 −	⅛ −		5.9
Wilshire Oil TX	5⅞ +	⅝ +		11.9	Oppenheimer	12¼ −	⅝ −		4.9
Fruehauf B	2⅞ +	¼ +		9.5	WesternUnion	2⅝ −	⅛ −		4.5
Lone Star Indus	36 +	2⅞ +		8.7	MDCHoldings	5¼ −	¼ −		4.5
Claire's Stores	13¼ +	¼ +		8.3	UnvlMatchbx	5½ −	¼ −		4.3
Transcon Inc	3¼ +	¼ +		8.3	RaytechCorp	5¾ −	¼ −		4.2
EMC Corp	8¾ +	⅝ +		7.7	KeystoneCons	11¾ −	½ −		4.1
Wyle Labs	10½ +	¾ +		7.7	PublicSvcNH	3 −	⅛ −		4.0

§18.9.3 Information About Specific Stocks

Table 18-5 sets forth *The Wall Street Journal* NYSE table for trading in NYSE stocks that begin with the letter "I" for Friday, June 10, 1988, the day on which you bought the 100 shares of IBM discussed in the previous section. The letter abbreviations in Table 18-5 are explained in Table 18-6. IBM appears about two-thirds of the way down the column. The information about each stock from this table may be summarized briefly.

1. The "52 Weeks: High - Low" data to the left of the names simply reflect the highest and lowest prices during the previous 52 weeks. Prices of the last day's trading are not reflected in the 52-week figure.

2. The "High - Low - Close - Net Change" data to the far right of the table reflect the latest day's trading, in this case Friday, June 10, 1988. IBM traded at a high of 117⅜ and a low of 115½; the final trade was at 116. If the price had broken through either the 52-week high or 52-week low figure (it did not on June 10) a footnote "u" (for up) or "d" (for down) would have been added, and the 52-week figures to the left would have been changed the following day.

A special daily table of new highs and new lows is also printed by *The Wall Street Journal*. See Table 18-7.

The "Net Change" figure represents the change between the closing price on June 10 and the closing price on the previous trading day, which in this case was June 9. The net change figure thus is unrelated to the high and low trading prices during the day.

3. The "Sales 100s" column describes the number of round lots traded on June 10. As indicated above, IBM was one of the most active stocks with just under 12,900 round lots sold. The approximate value of IBM traded in just one routine day was approximately $12,856 \times 100 \times 116$, or something over $149,000,000. And the "I"s represent only a small fraction of all listed stocks; clearly billions of dollars of stocks are traded on the NYSE each day.

4. The entry under "Div" is simply the regular dividend paid by IBM. Most NYSE companies maintain a stable dividend over time; IBM pays $4.40 per year, or $1.10 per quarter.

5. The entry under "Yld" ("Yield") is the approximate current sales price divided into the regular dividend. Thus IBM's dividend of $4.40 per share is a 3.8 percent return on a $116 investment. This number, of course, can be calculated directly from other information shown on this page.

6. The entry under "P-E Ratio" (Price/earnings ratio) is the ratio the current stock price for IBM bears to its earnings per share for the prior reporting period. IBM's price of 116 is 13 times its earnings per share last year. This number, unlike the yield, cannot be calculated from other information appearing on this page; earnings per share for IBM were reported in *The Wall Street Journal* some time earlier and that number is essential for calculating the P-E ratio.

The calculations of yield and P-E ratio are not adjusted daily and are indications of range. Because physical space is at a premium on this page, calculations are not carried out to any degree of precision.

If one looks through the "I"s, one sees that there are companies that show a positive yield but have no P-E ratio. An example is ICM (which stands for ICM Property Investors). How can that be? Another company, InspRs (which stands for Inspiration Resources, Inc.) has a P-E ratio of 41 but no yield. How can that be? Hint: Can a company pay a dividend even though it has no current earnings? Can a company have current earnings and pay no dividend?

Finally, brief mention should be made of the preferred stocks that are

Table 18-5

NEW YORK STOCK EXCHANGE COMPOSITE TRANSACTIONS

52 Weeks High	Low	Stock	Div.	Yld %	P-E Ratio	Sales 100s	High	Low	Close	Net Chg.
			–I–I–I–							
20¼	10¾	IBP n	.60	4.2	14	1678	14¼	13⅝	14¼	+ ½
41¼	22⅜	IC Ind	.96	2.9	15	2554	33⅝	33	33⅛	+ ⅛
15⅜	8	ICM	1.42e	13.4	...	104	10⅝	10⅜	10⅝	+ ⅛
13¾	5⅝	ICN Ph		...	...	207	7	6¾	6¾	– ⅛
25	20⅞	IE Ind	2.02	8.7	10	58	23½	23¼	23¼	– ⅛
34⅝	22½	IMC F n	.37e	1.1	...	941	34½	34	34⅛	...
19½	14⅛	INAIn	1.68a	9.9	...	27	17¼	17	17	– ¼
27¼	17¼	IPTimb	2.72e	11.6	9	104	23¾	23¼	23½	+ ⅛
20⅜	12⅞	IRT	1.40	8.2	12	130	17⅛	16¾	17⅛	+ ⅜
66⅜	41¾	ITT Cp	1.25	2.4	7	7158	51⅞	50⅝	51½	+ ⅞
108⅛	79	ITT pfK	4.00	4.6	...	3	87½	87½	87½	+ ⅞
105½	73½	ITT pfO	5.00	5.8	...	2	86½	86	86½	+ ¾
83	54⅛	ITT pfN	2.25	3.4	...	14	66	65	66	+2
26¼	19	IdahoP	1.80	8.1	19	281	22⅛	21⅞	22⅛	– ⅛
4¼	1⅞	IdealB		...	...	625	3⅛	3	3	– ⅛
27¼	16½	IllPowr	2.64	14.1	6	3238	18⅞	18½	18¾	– ⅛
22½	18¼	IlPow pf	2.04	10.9	...	z200	18¾	18¾	18¾	– ¾
24	19	IlPow pf	2.10	10.9	...	z710	19½	19¼	19¼	...
44¾	34¾	IlPow pf	4.12	10.6	...	z3800	39	38⅞	38⅞	+ ⅜
41	30	IlPow pf	3.78	10.6	...	z600	35¾	35½	35¾	+ 1¼
51	38	IlPow pf	3.80e	9.6	...	30	39½	39½	39½	+ 1½
49½	25¼	ITW	.40	1.0	18	459	40	39¼	39½	...
20⅝	11	ImoDl s	.32	1.7	14	7361	19¾	19	19⅜	+ ⅜
108⅛	66½	ImpCh	3.99e	5.2	9	1071	76⅞	76⅜	76⅝	+ ⅛
16¼	7	ICA	.60	5.3	5	264	11¼	10⅞	11¼	...
32¾	12⅜	INCO	.80	2.4	14	8544	33	u 32⅜	32¾	+ ¼
25	18½	IndiM pf	2.15	9.0	...	44	24	23⅝	24	+ ⅜
26	19¼	IndiM pf	2.25	9.7	...	3	23⅛	23	23⅛	+ ⅛
31¾	23¾	IndiEn	2.20	7.4	8	58	30	29½	29⅞	+ ⅛
45¾	22½	IngerR s	1.04	2.4	19	3197	43⅜	42⅜	42¾	+ ¼
28¼	10	IngrTec	.54	1.9	34	12	28	27⅞	27⅞	– ⅜
35¼	17	InldStl	.25e	.8	13	1810	34⅛	33	33	– 1⅛
65¾	43	InldSt pf	3.62	5.9	...	30	61½	61½	61½	– ½
25¼	14	Insilco	1.00	5.2	...	398	19½	19	19⅜	+ ¼
10⅛	3¾	InspRs		...	41	278	6⅝	6½	6⅝	+ ⅛
9¾	4⅛	Integra		...	27	2317	6	5⅞	5⅞	...
32⅞	14¾	IntgRsc		...	6	401	17⅜	16⅞	16⅞	– ⅜
44⅞	30	IntgR pf	4.25	13.3	...	50	32¼	32	32	– ¼
24	14½	IntgR pf		...	...	3	15⅞	15⅞	15⅞	...
6¾	2⅜	Intlog		...	25	24	2⅞	2¾	2¾	...
15	6¾	IntRFn		...	14	43	10⅝	10¼	10½	– ⅛
22⅝	17½	ItcpSe	2.10	9.7	...	51	21⅝	21⅜	21⅝	+ ¼
54	29½	Interco	1.72	4.0	12	229	43⅞	43	43⅜	...
55	34	Intrlke	1.40	3.0	10	209	46	45¾	46	+ ⅛
34	11⅞	Intmed s	.03e	.1	20	422	33⅜	31¾	32⅝	+ ¾
24¼	15¼	IntAlu	.80	3.5	9	19	23⅜	23⅛	23⅛	+ ¼
175⅞	100	IBM	4.40	3.8	13	12856	117⅜	115½	116	+ ⅝
58	37¼	IntFlav	1.60	3.0	17	1002	53¼	52¼	53	...
53	28	IntMin	1.00	2.2	18	x1047	45½	44⅝	44¾	– ⅛
67	48½	IntM pfA	3.75	6.4	...	x213	59	59	59	–1
39¾	22½	IntMult	1.18	3.7	14	489	32⅜	31½	31½	– ¼
56	27	IntPap	1.30	2.8	11	6929	46½	45⅞	46⅜	+ ½
12⅛	4⅜	IntRect		...	...	202	7¼	7⅛	7⅛	– ⅛
15⅞	1⅞	IT Crp		...	...	1741	3¼	3	3⅛	...
43½	22¾	IntpbG	.80	2.5	14	346	31¾	31⅜	31½	+ ⅛
25½	19⅜	IntstPw	1.96	9.2	14	44	21¾	21⅜	21⅜	– ⅛
27	20¼	InPw pr	2.28	9.5	...	z300	24⅛	24⅛	24⅛	– ¼
11⅞	7	IntSec	.40	4.8	...	51	8¼	8¼	8¼	...
42⅝	33¾	IowllG	3.18	8.6	10	88	37¼	36¾	37	– ⅛
23	15⅞	IowaRs	1.66	9.5	8	83	17½	17⅜	17½	– ¼
24⅝	19½	Ipalco	1.64	7.1	10	285	23⅜	23	23¼	+ ¼
18¾	8	IpcoCp	.36	3.6	40	9	10	9⅞	10	...
79	37¾	IrvBnk	2.42	3.7	...	707	65	64½	65	+ ½
12⅝	6¼	Italy n	.29e	4.1	...	32	7⅛	7	7	– ¼

Table 18-6

publicly traded on the NYSE. Many utility companies have outstanding several issues of preferred shares carrying varying rates of dividends. Illinois Power is a good example; it has five different classes of preferreds that were traded on the NYSE on June 10. Presumably these preferreds reflect different financing by Illinois Power at different times. Some of these are not traded in round lots of 100 shares (the entries marked with a "z" in the sales column). A round lot for these classes of preferred is usually ten shares. It will be noted that no P-E ratio is set forth for preferreds; this is because they are limited participation securities with no claim to increased dividends based on increases in earnings. Their value therefore is determined largely by their distribution rights. The yields for these preferreds issued by a single company may vary substantially, depending on their relative priorities to distributions and other rights of the

Table 18-7

NYSE HIGHS/LOWS

Friday, June 10, 1988

NEW HIGHS — 36

AGS Cptr	ComlMetl s	HarleyDav	PaylessCash
BancoSant n	FedlHmeLn pf	HiltonHtl wi	Pnwlt 1.60pr
Bearings s	FinevstFds n	INCO Ltd	Proler Int
BirminghStl	FstFldBc	Koppers pf	Quanex
Boeing	FtFldBcp pfA	LIL Co	Savin 1.50pf
CRS Sirrine s	FtFldBcp pfB	LIL Co pfl	StrideRite s
Castle Cke	FtFldBcp pfC	MAI Basic	TexasInd
CastlCke pfA	FrptMcMCop	PNC Fn pfC	UnPark Mn
CenturyTel	HannaCo	PNC Fn pfD	Zweig

NEW LOWS — 3

FinCpAm pf   MonarCa pf   Morgan adjpf

s-Split or stock dividend of 25 per cent or more in the past 52 weeks. High-low range is adjusted from old stock. n-New issue in past 52 weeks and does not cover the entire 52 week period.

432

specific class, including conversion and call rights. The yields on the Illinois Power preferreds vary from 9.6 percent to as high as 14.1 percent while the yields on the ITT "k" and "0" preferreds vary from 4.6 percent to 5.8 percent. Why should the yields of ITT preferreds range from 4.6 to 5.8 percent while those of Illinois Power range from 9.6 to 14 percent?

In general terms, preferreds listed on the NYSE are high-quality preferreds on which continued dividend payments are highly probable. As a result, risk of omitted dividends is relatively low and yields and prices are more highly sensitive to interest rates and relative rights than to changes in earnings or prices of common shares. The differences in yields of preferreds of about the same degree of risk are usually based on differences in rights. For example, an unfavorable redemption privilege from the standpoint of shareholders will depress the yield on that preferred.

Market-quality preferred shares are particularly attractive investments for corporations because of the intercorporate dividend-received deduction, which permits a corporation receiving a dividend to deduct 70 percent of it from its taxable income (80 percent if the receiving corporation owns more than 20 percent of the paying corporation). The dividend-received deduction often makes an investment in preferred stock more attractive than a straight loan of funds by one corporation to another. As a result, many "loans" by one corporation to another are cast in the form of a purchase of a special class of preferred stock that may have a variable dividend rate tied to an interest rate index and a contractual obligation on the part of the issuing corporation to redeem the special class of preferred upon demand.

§18.10 The American Stock Exchange

A second important trading market located in the New York area is the American Stock Exchange (AMEX). The AMEX is considerably smaller than the NYSE. The summaries for its operations on June 10, 1988 are set forth in Tables 18-8 and 18-9. It operates in essentially the same way as the NYSE, but there is no cross-listing of individual stocks between the AMEX and NYSE. Some AMEX stocks are also traded on regional exchanges and price quotations for these stocks are reported by ITS. Listing standards for the AMEX are lower than for the NYSE, and most companies listed on the AMEX are smaller and the securities lower priced on the average than for companies on the NYSE. This is well illustrated by Table 18-10, which reflects the "I"s for this smaller exchange. It should be noted that most NYSE stocks sell for more than $20 per share while most AMEX stocks sell for less than $10 per share. These ranges are maintained over long periods by individual stocks through the device of splitting the stock if it rises in price beyond its traditional trading range.

It is relatively common for corporations, as they grow, to be first listed on the AMEX and later, as they continue to grow, to move up to the NYSE. This is a mark of some prestige: One sometimes sees advertisements placed by such companies announcing that in the future their stock will be traded on the more prestigious NYSE.

Table 18-8

Diaries			
AMEX			
Issues traded	832	867	1,035
Advances	320	347	516
Declines	244	253	302
Unchanged	268	267	217
New highs	27	25	46
New lows	6	7	25
Adv Vol (000)	4,835	11,256	37,995
Decl Vol (000)	3,941	3,609	15,770
Total Vol (000)	11,660	16,780	65,100
CompVol (000)	15,025	19,579	78,245
Block trades	168	273	1,072

Most Active Issues			
AMEX			
Damson Oil	1,701,800	$\frac{1}{16}$ −	$\frac{1}{32}$
Dome Pete	1,122,400	$1\frac{5}{32}$ −	$\frac{1}{32}$
Wang Labs B	745,600	$10\frac{7}{8}$ −	$\frac{1}{4}$
Amdahl Corp	640,400	$53\frac{1}{8}$ +	$1\frac{5}{8}$
Texas Air Corp	530,200	$12\frac{3}{4}$ +	$\frac{3}{4}$
Horn & Hardart	475,300	$9\frac{1}{8}$ −	$\frac{1}{4}$
Instrument Sys	362,100	$1\frac{3}{8}$	

B. THE OVER-THE-COUNTER MARKET

§18.11 The Over-the-Counter Market

The over-the-counter market (OTC market) is quite unlike the organized exchanges described in the previous sections. There is no single place or location for the over-the-counter market. Rather it consists of a large number of brokers and dealers who deal with each other by computer or telephone, buying and selling shares for customers. A *dealer* is a securities firm trading for its own account while a *broker* is executing an order for a customer. Large securities firms commonly act both as broker and as dealer in OTC securities, and may act as both a broker and a dealer in the same transaction if suitable notice is given to the customer. Dealers involved in the OTC market are organized into

Table 18-9

Price Percentage Gainers . . .				and Losers			
AMEX							
Direct Action	$3\frac{1}{8}$ +	$\frac{1}{2}$ +	19.0	AmericanCap	$3\frac{3}{8}$ −	$\frac{3}{8}$ −	10.0
Schwab Safe Co	$17\frac{1}{4}$ +	$2\frac{3}{8}$ +	16.0	WarnerCmptr	$5\frac{3}{4}$ −	$\frac{5}{8}$ −	9.8
Verit Industrie	$6\frac{1}{4}$ +	$\frac{3}{4}$ +	13.6	GeniscoTech	$2\frac{3}{8}$ −	$\frac{1}{4}$ −	9.5
Lifetime Corp	$4\frac{3}{8}$ +	$\frac{1}{2}$ +	12.9	EmpireAmFed	$2\frac{5}{8}$ −	$\frac{1}{4}$ −	8.7
Teleconcepts	$2\frac{1}{4}$ +	$\frac{1}{4}$ +	12.5	T2Med.clA	$10\frac{7}{8}$ −	$\frac{3}{4}$ −	6.5

Table 18-10

AMERICAN STOCK EXCHANGE COMPOSITE TRANSACTIONS

52 Weeks High	Low	Stock	Div.	Yld %	P-E Ratio	Sales 100s	High	Low	Close	Net Chg.
				–I–I–I–						
14 7/8	6 1/4	ICH		...	10	1021	7 3/4	7 1/2	7 5/8	– 1/8
18 1/2	9 3/4	ICH pf	1.75	17.5	...	302	10 5/8	10	10	– 1/2
5 3/8	1 3/8	IRT Cp		...	...	21	3 5/8	3 1/2	3 5/8	+ 1/8
19 3/8	6 3/8	ISI Sys	.24	1.6	19	165	15	14 3/4	15	– 1/8
61 5/8	37	ImpOil g	1.80	...	...	236	47 1/2	47	47 1/4	+ 1/4
13 3/8	7 1/2	IncOpor	1.00	10.4	21	39	9 5/8	9 1/2	9 5/8	– 1/8
1/2	1/8	IncOp wt		...	...	1	3/16	3/16	3/16	...
5	1 3/4	Incstar		...	18	47	4 7/8	4 5/8	4 3/4	+ 1/8
17 1/4	8	Insteel	.24b	1.8	6	20	13 5/8	13 5/8	13 5/8	– 1/8
16 7/8	8 1/4	Instron	.12	.8	26	x51	14 7/8	14 5/8	14 7/8	+ 3/8
2 1/4	1	InstSy		...	9	3621	1 1/2	1 3/8	1 3/8	...
98 7/8	89	InsSy pfA	12.50	13.0	...	1	96	96	96	+1
7 7/8	3 1/2	IntlgSy	.90e	22.5	5	50	4	3 7/8	4	...
15 3/8	10 1/8	IntCty g	.72	...	...	x17	13 1/4	13 1/8	13 1/8	+ 1/8
14 1/4	6 3/4	Intrmk	.11	.8	8	9	13 3/8	13 1/8	13 1/8	– 1/4
13 5/8	7 1/8	Intmk pf	.10	.9	...	2	10 5/8	10 5/8	10 5/8	– 1/8
6	2 1/8	IntBknt		...	...	110	4 1/8	4	4 1/8	+ 1/8
1 3/8	1/16	IntBk wt		...	...	200	3/32	1/16	3/32	+ 1/32
		IIP rt		...	...	10	3/16	3/16	3/16	...
19 7/8	10	IntProt		...	20	10	13	12 7/8	12 7/8	...
14	6 1/4	IntlRec		...	28	13	8 3/8	8 1/4	8 3/8	– 1/8
13 7/8	4 1/8	IntTlch		...	...	531	11 7/8	10 7/8	11	– 5/8
3/4	1/4	IntThr		...	...	804	9/16	1/2	9/16	...
3/4	5/16	InThr pf		...	...	27	5/8	5/8	5/8	+ 1/16
10 1/8	4 1/2	IGC n	.60e	8.3	6	50	7 1/4	7 1/4	7 1/4	...
19 1/2	10 3/8	Ionics		...	36	22	19 1/4	18 7/8	18 7/8	– 3/8
19 1/2	6	IvaxCp		...	...	38	10 5/8	10 1/2	10 1/2	– 1/4
23	11 1/2	Iverson		...	15	3	17 5/8	17 5/8	17 5/8	...

a semi-public association called the National Association of Securities Dealers (NASD). The core of the OTC market is the *market maker* in an individual stock. A market maker is a dealer who announces its continued willingness to both buy and sell a specific stock; the price at which a market maker is willing to sell is, of course, somewhat higher than the price at which it is willing to buy. Price quotations by market makers are referred to as *bid-and-asked quotations*. Today most bid-and-asked quotations for OTC stocks appear in a computerized quotation system called NASDAQ (National Association of Securities Dealers Automated Quotations) but many bids and asked quotations for less heavily traded stocks continue to appear in an overnight publication known as the *sheets*. A broker with an order to buy or sell an OTC stock finds the best price quotation from a market maker, either from the NASDAQ screen or by using the telephone, and then places the order with the one with the best price. There may be more than one price in the OTC market since for most stocks there are several market makers. The OTC market thus consists of a web of brokers and dealers dealing with each other by telephone or by computer.

A bit of history is instructive. The over-the-counter market was originally completely unregulated and unorganized. Dealers would make a market in specific stocks simply by announcing price quotations in that stock. The accepted method of communication was through the insertion of representative bid-and-asked quotations in a daily publication called the *pink sheets*. A broker with an order to fill would check the pink sheet to see which dealers were making a market and would then telephone one or more of them seeking the best price. For many years, this market functioned quietly, with virtually no information available as to actual prices at which trades occurred or to actual volumes of transactions in specific shares. Of course, this was before the age of computerization, so that a technology to record transactions and prices in such a large and diffuse market simply did not exist.

With the development of the modern computer, a much more systematic and regularized OTC market developed, described in the following sections.

§18.12 NASDAQ and the National Market System

As mentioned above, NASDAQ is the computerized quotation system at the heart of the modern OTC market. NASDAQ offers subscribers three levels of quotes: Level I provides representative bid-and-asked quotations that enable a person to get a feel for the market. Level II provides access to actual quotations by every market maker in each security listed. Level III allows market makers to input the machine and enter or change quotations.

A second major development in the OTC market was the creation of the *National Market System* for widely traded securities. The principal market makers for these securities now report actual trades and prices, and the reporting of such transactions is superficially indistinguishable from that of the formally organized exchanges. There are over 4,000 stocks in the National Market System. The average national market stock has over 7 market makers, and the most heavily traded ones may have 20 or more. To be eligible for listing in the

Table 18-11

Diaries			
NASDAQ			
Issues traded	4,639	4,637	4,639
Advances	1,079	1,234	1,909
Declines	932	851	1,152
Unchanged	2,628	2,552	1,578
New highs	183	176	218
New lows	32	37	119
Adv Vol (000)	60,866	52,643	311,162
Decl Vol (000)	26,947	39,864	143,021
Total Vol (000)	145,324	143,305	695,158
Block trades	2,353	2,379	11,898

National Market System the issue must trade an average of 600,000 shares per month for 6 months, and sell at a price of $10 per share or more. Companies that have an average volume of 100,000 shares per month over 6 months and a price of $5 or more may elect to join the National Market System voluntarily.

The large national securities firms are major market makers in OTC securities. Some may make markets in more than 1,000 different securities at any one time, ranging from securities traded in the National Market System to securities primarily of regional or local interest.

The National Association of Securities Dealers also maintains an automated small order execution system (SOES) that permits automatic execution at the best available price quotation of orders for national market securities of up to 1,000 shares. SOES accounts for less than 2 percent of the volume of the National Market System, but is involved in about 15 percent of its trades. In addition to SOES, several proprietary automatic execution systems are available on a subscription basis.

Tables 18-11, 18-12, 18-13, and 18-14 reflect the June 10, 1988 activity in the National Market System, and the price quotations for the "I"s in that market.

Reporting members of NASD who are not members of the NYSE may trade in NYSE-listed stocks. These trades, and some block trades arranged by

Table 18-12

Most Active Issues			
NASDAQ			
Lyphomed Inc	2,574,000	11½ +	1¼
M C I Comm	1,934,500	15	
Jerrico Inc	1,865,800	16½ +	1
S H L System	1,777,100	8¾ −	⅛
Intel Corp	1,751,900	34 +	¼
Intergraph	1,641,200	29¼ +	¾
Equitex Inc	1,628,300	¼	

Table 18-13

Price Percentage Gainers . . .				and Losers			
NASDAQ NMS							
Nu-Med Inc	3⁹/₁₆ +	¹³/₁₆ +	29.5	MargoNursery	1¾ −	½ −	22.2
Xyvision Inc	7½ +	1¼ +	20.0	CmwlthS&LFL	4⅛ −	⅞ −	17.5
Amer Passage	4½ +	¾ +	20.0	BankersNote	2 −	⅜ −	15.8
Cable TV Indus	3¼ +	½ +	18.2	ArabianShield	3¼ −	½ −	13.3
Royalpar Ind	3¼ +	½ +	18.2	VikonicsInc	1¾ −	¼ −	12.5

NASD members, are reported in the NYSE composite trading list as NASD trades.

§18.13 Other Levels of the Over-the-Counter Market

There are four levels of the OTC market. The first level is the National Market System described above, for which the National Association of Securities Dealers provides daily information on actual trades and volumes.

The second level is the so-called National List, for which NASD provides representative volume figures but not actual prices. *Bid* and *asked figures* are dealers' quotations of prices, not transaction prices. Securities on the National List are widely traded, active issues that fall below the standards for listing in the National Market System. Table 18-15 shows representative quotations for the National List for June 10, 1988. They are in traditional "bid" and "asked" format but partial volume figures are shown.

The third level is the so-called Supplemental List, for which only traditional bid and asked quotations are supplied: This list is printed in the major financial newspapers (though often not on a daily basis). There are some 2,000 stocks on the Supplemental List. The size of these listings varies on a daily basis. Table 18-16 shows representative quotations from the Supplemental List. These quotations are in the traditional "bid" and "asked" format without any volume information. Traditional OTC market quotations before the electronic era were uniformly in this format.

The fourth and lowest level of the OTC market is the quotations in the daily pink sheets of inactively traded OTC securities. This information generally does not appear in financial newspaper reporting. The pink sheets today consist of hundreds of long, skinny pages of bid and asked quotations for inactively traded securities. They may range from insolvent shells, to solid, old-line companies that have barely enough outside holdings of shares to justify a listing in the sheets. Better quality companies may be quoted only with a bid notation (possibly the company's own) and no shares offered for sale. Many of the companies listed in the sheets have so few shares publicly held that they are not registered with the Securities and Exchange Commission. The pink sheets are published daily, and are the last remnant of the old days of the free-wheeling and unregulated over-the-counter market.

Table 18-14

NASDAQ NATIONAL MARKET ISSUES

4:00 p.m. Eastern Time Prices

Friday, June 10, 1988

365-day High	365-day Low	Stock	Div.	Yld	P-E	Sales (hds)	High	Low	Last	Net Chg.
8	2⅛	InterTelinc A		..	12	15	3½	3⅜	3⅜	− ¼
11¼	4⅝	Interactv Tec		..	17	12	10¾	10¼	10¼	− ⅝
3¾	1⅛	InteractT wt		..	..	27	3½	3½	3½	...
8⅛	4	IntrfacSys	10k	..	10	139	7	6⅞	7	+ ¼
14½	7¼	Interface	.16	1.1	15	1852	14¼	13⅜	14	+ ½
30½	17	Intergraph		..	22	16412	29⅝	28¾	29¼	+ ¾
13⅝	11½	Intergroup		..	13	1	13	13	13	...
3 9-16	1⅛	Interim Sys		..	..	1098	3 1-16	2 15-16	3 1-16	+1-16
24⅛	11¼	Interleaf Inc		..	35	5656	16¾	15⅞	16½	− ⅛
6¼	3⅛	Intrmagn Gen		..	..	112	4¼	4¼	4¼	...
21	8⅞	Intermec Corp		..	23	1040	19½	19⅛	19⅜	+ ⅛
18⅛	8½	Intermet	.20	1.5	13	307	13½	13¼	13⅜	...
6¼	2¼	Intermetrics		..	10	24	3⅞	3⅞	3⅞	− ¼
6	1¼	IntlAm Home		..	5	843	1 15-16	1⅞	1 15-16	+1-16
18⅛	6⅝	Intl Broadcst		..	..	32	8⅞	8⅝	8¾	+ ⅛
8	2½	Intl Container		..	29	71	6	5⅞	6	+ ⅛
2⅜	⅞	IntlCap Eqpt		..	..	330	1 7-16	1⅜	1 7-16	+3-16
38¾	9¾	IntlClinic Lab		..	48	76	36¾	36⅝	36⅝	− ¼
33½	20	IntlDairyQ A		..	18	8	30½	29¾	30½	...
(H)	7⅛	IntlGame Tch		..	26	867	15¾	15	15⅜	− ⅛
6¼	1¾	IntlGene Eng		..	..	24	4½	4⅜	4½	+1-16
16¼	10	IntlHldng	.50	3.6	3	1	13¾	13¾	13¾	− ¾
20¾	8¼	IntlLease	.04d	.2	12	462	16½	16¼	16½	+ ⅜
16¼	4½	ItlMobile Mch		..	..	392	8	7⅞	8	...
35	16⅝	IntlMb pf	2.50	12.	..	3	21	21	21	− ½
8½	1¾	IntlMobM wt		..	..	42	2 5-16	2¼	2¼	+ ⅛
2 7-16	1	IRIS Incorp		..	..	174	1⅛	1	1 1-16	+1-16
12¾	5½	IntlResDev	.36	3.1	15	7	11½	11½	11½	...
10	1½	Intl Robomatn		..	13	19	2⅜	2⅜	2⅜	...
17¾	7⅝	IntlShipHld s		..	..	9	17½	16¼	17½	...
5⅜	1¾	Intl Total Sys		..	22	252	2⅝	2 9-16	2⅝	+1-16
41¾	30¾	Interhome E		..	..	3	38½	38½	38½	+ ¼
15¼	4¾	Interphase		..	23	33	9	9	9	− ¼
15¼	4	Interspec Inc		..	19	45	11	10¾	11	+ ¼
(H)	13¼	InterTAN Inc		..	19	66	31¼	30½	31¼	+ ¾
10⅜	4⅛	Intertrans		..	19	53	9¾	9⅜	9½	+ ⅛
18⅛	7⅜	Intrex FncS		..	..	134	18	18	18	...
10⅛	5	Invacare Corp		..	19	5	8¾	8¾	8¾	− ⅜
14⅞	6⅛	Investr SB	.20	3.1	..	237	6⅝	6⅜	6⅜	...
17¾	6¾	InvestorsT	.04	.6	10	13	7½	7	7	+ ¼
12¾	5	Invest SvCp		..	..	45	5¾	5½	5¾	...
9½	4½	INVG M	.25d	6.7	..	105	7⅞	7½	7½	− ⅜
11⅜	4¾	Invitron Cp		..	..	77	5¾	5⅜	5⅝	− ⅛
4¼	1¼	Iomega Corp		..	..	256	3 13-16	3 11-16	3 11-16	...
30¾	24¾	IaSthrn	2.08	7.9	22	19	27	26¼	26¼	− ¾
3¼	1¼	IPLSystems A		..	9	1	1¾	1¾	1¾	− ⅜
10½	4½	Irwin Magnet		..	14	155	7¾	7½	7⅝	...
(H)	8	Isco Inc	.20	1.1	20	277	18½	17¼	18	+ ¾
9¾	4¾	I S C Syst Cp		..	11	200	6¼	6	6¼	+ ¼
10¾	5⅛	ISOETEC Cm		..	12	281	10¾	10	10¼	+ ¼
8	3⅝	Isomedix Inc		..	52	188	6¼	6⅛	6¼	+ ⅛
26⅞	10⅝	Itel Corp		..	..	1511	20½	20	20⅜	+ ⅜
64	31½	Itel pfB C	3.37	6.1	..	10	55½	55½	55½	+2½
154	82¾	ItoYokao	.29d	.2	59	5	148	148	148	+1¼
21¼	17	IWC Res	1.38	7.1	11	8	19½	19	19½	...
		--I I--								
7⅞	3¼	ICN Bmd	.15d	1.9	..	401	7¾	7½	7¾	+ ⅛
8¼	3	ICOT Corprtn		..	16	137	3⅛	3	3	...
18	10	ICP		..	..	13	11⅝	11¼	11⅝	+ ⅜
15¾	7¾	IdealSchl Sup		..	16	6	11⅝	11⅝	11⅝	...
10⅝	4¾	IEC Elect	.10d	1.0	14	28	10⅜	10⅜	10⅜	...
32	3 7-16	IGI Inc		..	103	536	10⅜	10	10¼	...
5⅝	2⅛	IIS Intel	.16	3.9	..	62	4¼	4⅛	4⅛	− ⅛
7	3½	II-VI Inc		..	..	45	6¾	6½	6¾	+ ⅛
2½	13-32	Imatron Inc		..	..	84	9-16	7-16	9-16	+ ⅛
12¾	4⅜	Immucor Inc		..	32	422	7½	6¾	7⅜	+ ⅜
25⅛	9⅜	Immunex Cp		..	..	334	15¼	14⅞	15¼	+ ⅜
13⅝	4¼	Immunomed		..	..	342	8¼	7⅞	8¼	...
8⅝	2½	Impact Syst		..	15	121	4¼	4⅛	4⅛	...
16½	7¾	ImperlBc	.07	.6	11	60	12¼	12¼	12¼	− ¼
17	15	ImprlHolly wi		..	..	8	15¾	15¾	15¾	...
8¼	2 5-16	IMP		..	14	994	3⅜	3	3¼	...
17⅛	4⅛	Imreg Inc A		..	..	3121	15½	14⅞	15⅛	+ ⅜
11⅛	3¾	Inacomp Cmp		..	12	241	7⅜	7⅛	7⅜	−1-16
35	19¾	IndepBcp	1.16	5.0	9	24	23¼	23	23	...
17¼	9¼	IndBcMa	.21a	1.7	8	20	12¾	12¾	12¾	− ¼
4¾	⅛	Indep Bksh		..	..	5	⅜	⅜	⅜	+ ¼
39½	25	IndInsGrp	1.52	4.6	8	921	33	32½	32¾	...
46¼	23	IndnHdB	1.04	3.0	10	41	35¾	35	35	− ¼
12¾	8⅛	Indiana Fed		..	..	12	12⅝	12⅜	12⅜	...
47	29	IndianaNt	1.28	3.4	17	373	37½	37	37¼	+ ¼
9¼	5½	Ind Accus	.25d	3.2	8	5	7¾	7¾	7¾	...
3	1 11-16	Ind Electrcs		..	..	209	2 9-16	2 5-16	2 9-16	+ ⅛
4½	1 3-16	Indust Resour		..	..	535	4 1-16	3 13-16	3 29-32	+1-32
8	(L)	IndustTrn Cp		..	13	5	5	5	5	− ½
31½	12½	InfintyBrd A		..	131	4516	30¾	30	30⅛	− ⅜
4¾	2½	Infodata Sys		..	11	250	3 7-16	3 7-16	3 7-16	−1-16
32⅜	8	Info Resource		..	..	1013	10⅞	10½	10⅝	− ⅛
14¾	9⅜	Inform Intl	.22	1.7	16	18	13⅛	13⅛	13⅛	+ ¼
2	7-16	Info Science		..	..	120	⅞	13-16	⅞	+1-16
31¼	11½	Informix Cp		..	30	1372	21¾	20¾	21½	+ ¾
12	2½	Infotechnlgy		..	..	270	5⅝	5¼	5⅜	+ ¼
14¼	4½	Infotron Syst		..	..	485	13⅛	12¾	12⅞	+ ⅛
13⅜	6⅝	InglesMkt A		..	13	211	8⅞	8¼	8¾	+ ½
25⅛	13½	Inmac Cp	.08b	.4	20	1358	20⅛	19¾	20	− ¼
14	3	Innovex Inc		..	16	150	5⅛	5	5⅛	...
9	3⅜	Insitfm East		..	21	30	7½	7¼	7¼	− ¼
9¾	1	InsitufmGr wt		..	..	5	5¾	5¾	5¾	− ¼
12¾	3⅛	Insitfm GL		..	..	72	8½	8¼	8½	− ⅛
9	3¼	InsitfmMA A		..	45	21	5½	5	5	...
17¼	4¾	Insituform NA		..	..	250	9⅝	9⅜	9⅜	− ¼
27¼	6	Inspeech		..	357	288	7½	7⅛	7⅛	− ⅛
3	1½	Intech Inc	5k	..	..	2	1¾	1¾	1¾	...
7⅛	3	Integon CP	.16	2.7	6	237	6	5⅞	6	− ⅛
11	7¼	InterFedl SB		..	..	10	9½	9½	9½	+ ½
6⅜	2¼	IntegrtCir	10k	..	11	10	4⅛	4⅛	4⅛	...
16¼	4⅞	Integrt Device		..	34	1476	15⅞	15⅝	15⅝	− ⅛
13⅜	3⅝	Integrt Gene		..	..	97	4½	4⅜	4½	+ ⅛
41¾	13	Intel Corp		..	25	17519	34½	33½	34	+ ¼
20⅜	2⅛	Intel wt88		..	..	4394	7	6⅜	6⅞	+ ⅜
24⅜	6	Intel wt92		..	..	587	14⅞	14⅜	14⅝	+ ⅛
23	6⅞	Intel wt95		..	..	785	15⅝	15⅛	15⅜	+ ¼
6¼	3¼	Intellicall		..	14	90	5 5-16	5⅛	5 5-16	−3-16
10¼	2⅜	IntelliCorp		..	13	160	3	2¾	3	...
12¾	5	Intellgnt El		..	9	21	8	7¾	8	+ ¼

Table 18-15

NASDAQ BID AND ASKED QUOTATIONS

Stock & Div	Sales 100s	Bid	Asked	Net Chg.
AdelphiaCm A	124	17½	18	...
Advatex Assc	10	2⅝	3¼ +	⅛
AFN Inc	50	½	⅝	...
Airsensors	1326	2¼	2⅜ + 7-16	
AJRossLog ut	105	2⅞	3⅛ +	¼
AldenElect A	21	5½	5⅞ +	⅛
All Amer Tel	55	2⅛	2⅜ +	⅛
Allecol Deb	z55	63	65	...
Am Biodynm	100	1½	1⅝	...
Ameribanc	25	16¼	16½	...
AmAircrft s	1283 1	17-32	1 9-16 + 7-32	
ACityB pf1.50	90	14¼	14½	...
Am ConsltgCp	36	3⅝	4¼ −	⅛
AmCont'l pf	9	18¾	19¾	...
AFncl pfF 1.80	z57	15	15½ +	⅛
Am Fncl pf D	3	10¼	10½	...
AmFst P P E	82	16¾	17¾	...
AmGuarn Fnc	204	13-16	15-16	...
Am Natl Pet	65	2 3-16	2⅜ + 1-16	
ARecreatn .13	22	8⅜	8¾	...
Am W Air deb	13	47	48 +	½
Andrews Grp	56	4½	4¾	...
ApolloCm deb	5	101	103 −	½
Arden ItlKitch	37	1¼	1½	...
Artistic Grtg	20	2	2¼	...
Asea AB .92b	47	62½	63 +	⅛
AstecInd wt	10	8¼	8¾	...
Atlantc Grp	z50	8¼	8¾	...
BncOnepfB 3	25	56½	59	...
B&H BulkCr	5	12¾	13¼	...
Bk of SF 10k	16	5¼	6	...
BkMidA ·pf2.50	26	3	3¼	...
Base Ten B	10	5	6¾ −	½
Benafuels .70	40	2½	2⅝	...
BenihanaN A	6	⅞	1⅛	...
BF Enterprise	16	7½	8	...
Big O Tires	800	2⅜	2 7-16 + 1-16	
Biosonics Inc	1184	9-32	5-16	...
BirdIncpf 1.85	15	12¼	12½ +	¼
Blinder Intl	572	11-16	25-32 − 1-32	
Bobbie Brooks	70	1	1 1-16	...
Braniff Inc	1283	6½	6⅝ + 1⅜	
Braniff pf	842	1⅞	2¼ + 7-16	
Bralorne Res	2	⅞	1	...
BrentnB .12d	6	16⅜	16¾	...
BroadNatl Bc	6	28½	31	...
Broadvw Svgs	45	1⅞	2 +	⅛
Builders Dsgn	130	2⅞	3 +	⅛
Builders ut	5	9⅝	10½ +	⅛
Cabarrus SB	10	5¼	5⅝	...
Cadema pf .40	63	2½	2¾	...
Candela Laser	43	8½	9 +	¼
Cannon Exprs	20	4⅞	5¼	...
Card Tel	188	1¼	1 5-16 + 1-16	
Cell Tech wt	1	1⅛	1⅜	...
Centercore	8	2⅜	2½	...
CnBkgSys .40g	239	16½	17 −	1
Central Corp	433	2½	2¾	...
Central PcMin	110 1	23-32	1 13-16 − 1-32	
Ceramics Pr	5	4½	5	...
CtznBcMDs 1	71	22½	23½ −	1
CitzSecG .02d	14	3¾	4⅛	...
CityRes wt	88	7-16	9-16	...

Table 18-16

ADDITIONAL NASDAQ QUOTES

	Bid	Asked
ACS Enterprise	9-16	11-16
Action Staffing	¾	15-16
Admar Grp Inc	⅜	7-16
AdvDisplay Tec	⅜	7-16
AdvPrdctsTc A	⅝	¾
AdvPrdctsTc C	¾	⅞
AdvMedical Pr	1-32	3-32
AdvnNMR Syst	5¾	6
AdvNMRSyst ut	34	35½
AdvNMRSys wt	5⅝	5¾
Advanced Prod	2⅜	2⅝
AdvPrdctTc ut	10½	11½
AdvisorsCp Tc	¼	5-16
Aerosonic Corp	1⅜	1 7-16
AFP Imaging	1 3-16	1⅜
Agouron Pharm	13½	14½
AirshipIntl Ltd	23-32	25-32
AJ Ross Logist	1 5-16	1 7-16
Alaska Apollo	11-16	25-32
Alcide Corp	5½	5⅝
Alcide Corp wt	1⅛	1⅜
Alfa Interntl	3⅞	4⅛
AllAm Semicon	2¾	2⅞
Alpha Solarco	5-16	⅜
Alternatv Hlth	1⅛	1¼
Amer Bionetics	2⅛	2¼
AmerEco Envir	3-32	⅛
Am Business	1 3-16	1¼
AmClaims Eval	3⅝	4
Am Comm Tel	3-32	⅛
Am CruiseLine	½	¾
AmIntl Petrol	1 13-16	2
Am Medical El	10	10½
AmMobile Syst	2¾	3
API Enterprs	17-32	23-32
Am Screen Co	⅜	13-32
AmSolar King	1⅝	1⅞
AmToxxic Con	25-32	13-16
AmVision Cntrs	2	2 1-16
Amnews Holdng	4⅞	5
AnCon Genetics	1⅜	1 9-16
Angel Entrtnmt	1	1⅜
Angio-Medcl	3¼	3⅜
Annandale Corp	¼	5-16
APA Optics Inc	6¾	7¼
Apogee Robotc	1⅝	1¾
Appld DNA Sys	3 3-16	3 5-16
AppldDNA wt	½	19-32
Appld Microbio	2¾	3¼
AppliedMic ut	5¾	6¾
Appld Spectrum	⅛	3-16
AppldSpect wt	1-32	1-16
Aquanautics Cp	21-32	¾
AquaSciences	1	1⅛
AristaInvst ut	4¼	4¾
ARNOX Corp	2⅞	3¼
Artech RecvSys	15-16	1
ASA Intl Ltd	⅛	3-16
ASDAR Group	¼	9-32
Asha Corp	3-32	⅛
Aspen Explortn	17-32	19-32
Austin McDanl	¾	1
AutomdxSci ut	2	2¾
Automedix Sci	⅝	11-16
AutoSpa A Mall	1⅞	1 15-16
AxiomSyst ut	1½	1⅝

Table 18-17

STOCK MARKET DATA BANK							June 10, 1988			
Major Indexes										
HIGH	LOW	(12 MOS)	CLOSE	NET CH	% CH	12 MO CH	%	FROM 12/31	%
DOW JONES AVERAGES										
2722.42	1738.74	30 Industrials	2101.71	+ 8.36	+ 0.40	− 276.02	−11.61	+ 162.88	+ 8.40
1101.16	661.00	20 Transportation	877.39	+ 4.78	+ 0.55	− 152.14	−14.78	+ 128.53	+17.16
213.79	160.98	15 Utilities	x179.11	+ 0.23	+ 0.13	− 24.66	−12.10	+ 4.03	+ 2.30
992.21	653.76	65 Composite	x784.02	+ 3.14	+ 0.40	− 114.64	−12.76	+ 69.75	+ 9.77

C. STOCK MARKET INDEXES

§18.14 The Dow Jones Industrial Average

Stock market indexes or averages attempt to measure the general level of stock prices over time. Of these the best known is the Dow Jones average, which is actually four different averages: of 30 industrial companies, 20 transportation stocks, 15 utilities, and a composite average of the 65 stocks. The Dow Jones dates back to the end of the nineteenth century and the index numbers purport to be comparable to those in earlier years.

Table 18-17 is the June 10, 1988 Dow Jones averages as they appear in the June 13 *Wall Street Journal*, which is itself published by Dow Jones & Co., Inc. This company also owns the *broad tape*, which is the major teletype news service covering financial, business, and national news.

The 65 stocks that make up this average are set forth in Table 18-18, as is the method of calculation of the indexes themselves. In one sense, the Dow Jones Industrial Average is narrowly based, reflecting the price movements of only 30 stocks; it is a "blue chip" average since the 30 companies are among the largest and most influential in the country. Because of this emphasis on the largest companies, it is not uncommon for the Dow Jones Industrial Average to move in one direction while the broader-based indexes described in the following section are moving in the opposite direction.

It is not entirely clear why the Dow Jones Average has achieved the prominence that it has. One advantage is its relative antiquity, going back nearly 100 years. It also has attracted a following because it involves rather dramatic price moves — during the first part of 1987, for example, it rose steadily, breaking "barriers" at 2,300, 2,400, and so forth reaching an all-time high of 2,722.42 on August 25, 1987. These numbers, of course, have only psychological meaning since they are index numbers. Nevertheless there was a wide following of the Dow Jones average as it continued to break new barriers and set new records.

The Dow Jones average also has been widely used to describe the collapse of securities prices that occurred in October, 1987, following the August 25 high. After a period of increasingly volatile prices, the second week of October

Table 18-18

THE DOW JONES AVERAGES ®

High
Close
Low

Industrials

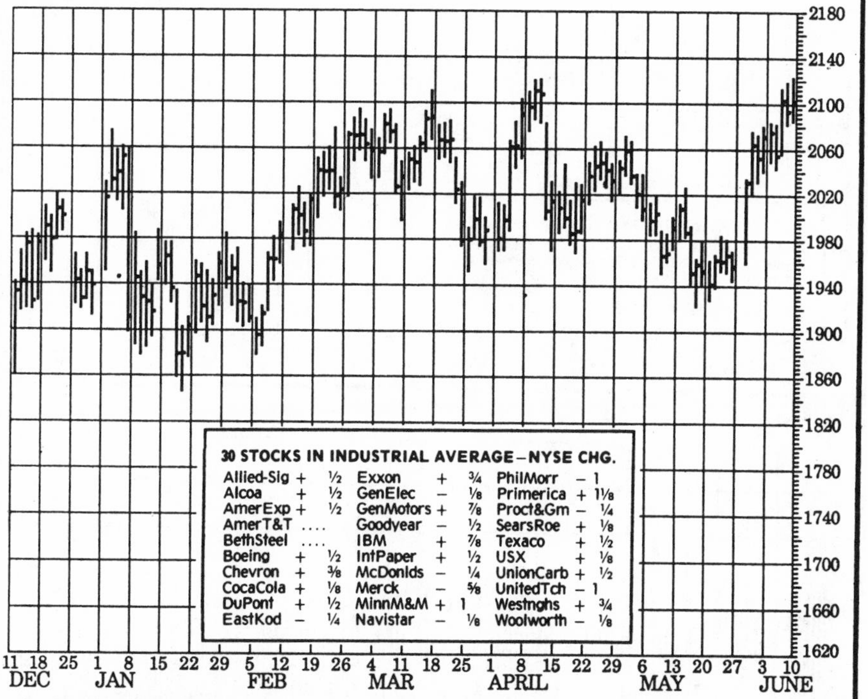
2180
2140
2100
2060
2020
1980
1940
1900
1860
1820
1780
1740
1700
1660
1620
30 STOCKS IN INDUSTRIAL AVERAGE–NYSE CHG.
Allied-Sig + ½
Alcoa + ½
AmerExp + ½
AmerT&T ....
BethSteel ....
Boeing + ½
Chevron + ⅜
CocaCola + ⅛
DuPont + ½
EastKod – ¼
Exxon + ¾
GenElec – ⅛
GenMotors + ⅞
Goodyear – ½
IBM + ⅞
IntPaper + ½
McDonlds – ¼
Merck – ⅝
MinnM&M + 1
Navistar – ⅛
PhilMorr – 1
Primerica + 1⅛
Proct&Gm – ¼
SearsRoe + ⅛
Texaco + ½
USX + ⅛
UnionCarb + ½
UnitedTch – 1
Westnghs + ¾
Woolworth – ⅛
11 18 25 1 8 15 22 29 5 12 19 26 4 11 18 25 1 8 15 22 29 6 13 20 27 3 10
DEC JAN FEB MAR APRIL MAY JUNE

Transportation

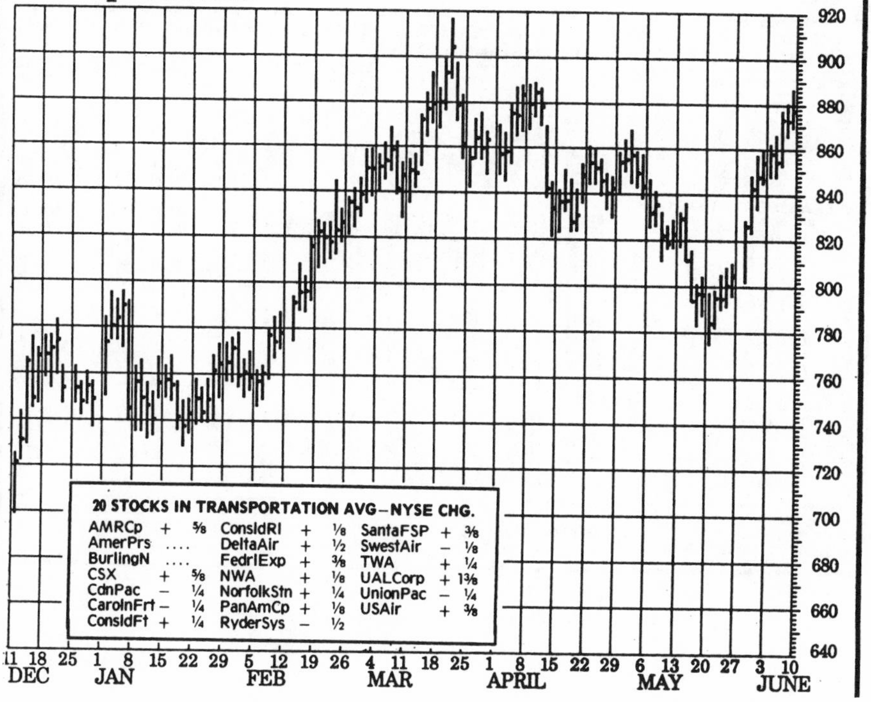
920
900
880
860
840
820
800
780
760
740
720
700
680
660
640
20 STOCKS IN TRANSPORTATION AVG–NYSE CHG.
AMRCp + ⅝
AmerPrs ....
BurlingN ....
CSX + ⅝
CdnPac – ¼
CarolnFrt – ¼
ConsldFt + ¼
ConsldRl + ⅛
DeltaAir + ½
FedrlExp + ⅜
NWA + ⅛
NorfolkStn + ¼
PanAmCp + ⅛
RyderSys – ½
SantaFSP + ⅜
SwestAir – ⅛
TWA + ¼
UALCorp + 1⅜
UnionPac – ¼
USAir + ⅜
11 18 25 1 8 15 22 29 5 12 19 26 4 11 18 25 1 8 15 22 29 6 13 20 27 3 10
DEC JAN FEB MAR APRIL MAY JUNE

Table 18-18 *(cont.)*

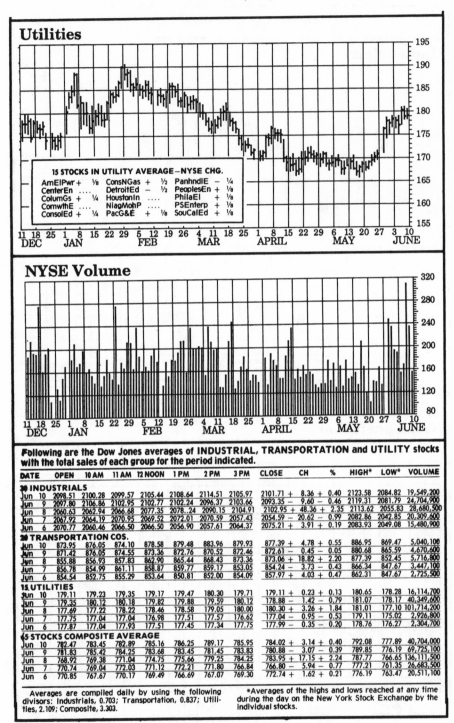

Utilities

15 STOCKS IN UTILITY AVERAGE—NYSE CHG.

AmElPwr +	⅛	ConsNGas +	½	PanhndlE −	¼
CenterEn		DetroitEd −	½	PeoplesEn +	⅛
ColumGs +	¼	HoustonIn +		PhilaEl +	⅛
ComwthE		NiagMohP		PSEnterp +	⅛
ConsolEd +	¼	PacG&E +	⅛	SouCalEd +	⅛

DEC 11 18 25 JAN 1 8 15 22 29 FEB 5 12 19 26 MAR 4 11 18 25 APRIL 1 8 15 22 29 MAY 6 13 20 27 JUNE 3 10

NYSE Volume

DEC 11 18 25 JAN 1 8 15 22 29 FEB 5 12 19 26 MAR 4 11 18 25 APRIL 1 8 15 22 29 MAY 6 13 20 27 JUNE 3 10

Following are the Dow Jones averages of INDUSTRIAL, TRANSPORTATION and UTILITY stocks with the total sales of each group for the period indicated.

DATE	OPEN	10 AM	11 AM	12 NOON	1 PM	2 PM	3 PM	CLOSE	CH		%		HIGH*	LOW*	VOLUME
30 INDUSTRIALS															
Jun 10	2098.51	2100.28	2099.57	2105.44	2108.64	2114.51	2105.97	2101.71	+	8.36	+	0.40	2123.58	2084.82	19,549,200
Jun 9	2097.80	2106.86	2102.95	2102.77	2102.24	2096.37	2103.66	2093.35	−	9.60	−	0.46	2119.31	2081.79	24,704,900
Jun 8	2060.63	2062.94	2066.68	2077.35	2078..24	2090.15	2104.91	2102.95	+	48.36	+	2.35	2113.62	2055.83	28,680,500
Jun 7	2067.92	2064.19	2070.95	2069.52	2072.01	2070.59	2057.43	2054.59	−	20.62	−	0.99	2082.86	2042.85	20,309,600
Jun 6	2070.77	2060.46	2066.50	2066.50	2056.90	2057.61	2064.37	2075.21	+	3.91	+	0.19	2083.93	2049.08	15,480,900
20 TRANSPORTATION COS.															
Jun 10	873.95	876.05	874.10	878.58	879.48	883.96	879.93	877.39	+	4.78	+	0.55	886.95	869.47	5,040,100
Jun 9	871.42	876.05	874.55	873.36	872.76	870.52	872.46	872.61	−	0.45	−	0.05	880.68	865.59	4,670,600
Jun 8	855.88	856.93	857.83	862.90	865.44	868.43	873.36	873.06	+	18.82	+	2.20	877.39	852.45	5,716,800
Jun 7	856.78	854.99	861.11	858.87	859.77	859.17	853.05	854.24	−	3.73	−	0.43	866.34	847.67	3,447,100
Jun 6	854.54	852.75	855.29	853.64	850.81	852.00	854.09	857.97	+	4.03	+	0.47	862.31	847.67	2,725,500
15 UTILITIES															
Jun 10	179.11	179.23	179.35	179.17	179.47	180.30	179.71	179.11	+	0.23	+	0.13	180.65	178.28	16,114,700
Jun 9	179.35	180.12	180.18	179.82	179.88	179.59	180.12	178.88	−	1.42	−	0.79	181.07	178.17	40,349,600
Jun 8	177.69	177.22	178.22	178.46	178.58	179.05	180.00	180.30	+	3.26	+	1.84	181.01	177.10	101,714,200
Jun 7	177.75	177.04	177.04	176.98	177.51	177.57	176.62	177.04	−	0.95	−	0.53	179.11	175.02	2,926,800
Jun 6	177.87	177.04	177.93	177.51	177.45	177.34	177.75	177.99	−	0.35	−	0.20	178.76	176.27	2,304,700
65 STOCKS COMPOSITE AVERAGE															
Jun 10	782.47	783.45	782.89	785.16	786.25	789.17	785.95	784.02	+	3.14	+	0.40	792.08	777.89	40,704,000
Jun 9	781.83	785.42	784.25	783.68	783.45	781.45	783.83	780.88	−	3.07	−	0.39	789.85	776.19	69,725,100
Jun 8	768.92	769.38	771.04	774.75	775.66	779.25	784.25	783.95	+	17.15	+	2.24	787.77	766.65	136,111,500
Jun 7	770.74	769.04	772.03	771.12	772.21	771.80	766.84	766.80	−	5.94	−	0.77	777.21	761.35	26,683,500
Jun 6	770.85	767.67	770.17	769.49	766.69	767.07	769.30	772.74	+	1.62	+	0.21	776.19	763.47	20,511,100

Averages are compiled daily by using the following divisors: Industrials, 0.703; Transportation, 0.837; Utilities, 2.109; Composite, 3.303.

*Averages of the highs and lows reached at any time during the day on the New York Stock Exchange by the individual stocks.

444

was marked by several trading days of increases in trading volume accompanied by moderate decreases in the Dow Jones average. On Monday, October 19, however, the NYSE suffered its largest one-day loss in history as measured by the Dow — 508.32 points. It closed on October 19 at 1,738.40, down one-third from its historic high in August. During the two-week period in October when most of this decline occurred, less than 3 percent of all the outstanding shares registered on the NYSE were traded, but the aggregate loss in value of all NYSE shares was approximately $1 trillion. While much of this loss reflected only the disappearance of appreciation in values during the long price run-up that had never been realized (so-called *paper profits*), many traders and investors suffered devastating losses of capital. All losses, whether of paper profits or of capital, are, of course, felt keenly and have a psychological effect on future economic behavior.

When the Dow climbs, it puts investors in a buying (or "bullish") mood; when it declines, sentiment turns gloomy (or "bearish").

§18.15 Other Indexes

There are several other widely followed market indexes other than the Dow Jones average. Table 18-19 sets them forth as presented by *The Wall Street Journal*. Several of these are broad-based indexes covering hundreds or thousands of stocks. None of them, however, have achieved the wide following of the Dow Jones Industrial Average. All of them reflected the market break that occurred in 1987 indicating that the decline was marketwide and not limited to the 45 blue chip stocks that comprise the Dow Jones averages.

The two most widely followed alternative indexes are the New York Stock Exchange Composite and Standard & Poor's 500 indexes. These indexes differ conceptually from the Dow Jones Average. In the Dow, a dollar change in the price of a single stock in the average has the same effect as a change of one dollar in the price of any other stock in the average. There is no weighting of the individual stocks by the size of the company or the number of shares outstanding. Both the S&P and NYSE Composite are true indexes. They measure changes in total market value of the stocks that make up the index, and the index number is the percentage change compared with a base period. The NYSE Composite is indexed to December 31, 1965 (when the base was 50) while the S&P 500 is indexed to the period from 1941 to 1943 (when the base was 10). The NYSE Composite is based on 1,632 companies traded on that Exchange; S&P 500 is based on 500 stocks, primarily on the NYSE.

The Value Line Composite Index is based on 1,650 stocks, 300 of which are traded OTC and 100 of which are AMEX stocks. The Wilshire 5,000 is even broader, covering 5,000 stocks traded on all the principal securities markets.

An important function of these alternative indexes is to serve as the basis for options and futures trading on indexes. This subject is described in Chapter 21.

Table 18-19

STOCK MARKET DATA BANK   June 10, 1988

Major Indexes

HIGH	LOW	(12 MOS)	CLOSE	NET CH	% CH	12 MO CH	%	FROM 12/31	%
NEW YORK STOCK EXCHANGE									
187.99	125.91	Composite	152.89	+ 0.53	+ 0.35	− 16.96	− 9.99	+ 14.66	+ 10.61
231.05	149.43	Industrials	185.35	+ 0.64	+ 0.35	− 21.15	− 10.24	+ 18.31	+ 10.96
80.22	61.63	Utilities	71.95	+ 0.17	+ 0.24	− 2.42	− 3.25	+ 4.64	+ 6.89
168.20	104.76	Transportation	137.03	+ 0.75	+ 0.55	− 15.95	− 10.43	+ 18.46	+ 15.57
165.36	107.39	Finance	128.88	+ 0.63	+ 0.49	− 26.03	− 16.80	+ 14.31	+ 12.49
STANDARD & POOR'S INDEXES									
336.77	223.92	500 Index	271.26	+ 1.06	+ 0.39	− 30.36	− 10.07	+ 24.18	+ 9.79
393.17	255.43	Industrials	313.62	+ 1.15	+ 0.37	− 35.50	− 10.17	+ 27.76	+ 9.71
274.20	167.59	Transportation	213.12	+ 1.43	+ 0.68	− 38.27	− 15.22	+ 22.95	+ 12.07
121.11	91.80	Utilities	109.62	+ 0.47	+ 0.43	− 3.38	− 2.99	+ 7.50	+ 7.34
32.56	20.39	Financials	24.47	+ 0.13	+ 0.53	− 5.56	− 18.51	+ 2.84	+ 13.13
NASDAQ									
455.26	291.88	Composite	386.25	+ 1.65	+ 0.43	− 39.13	− 9.20	+ 55.78	+ 16.88
488.92	288.30	Industrials	400.21	+ 2.29	+ 0.58	− 52.67	− 11.63	+ 61.27	+ 18.08
475.78	333.66	Insurance	400.26	+ 0.74	+ 0.19	− 35.65	− 8.18	+ 49.20	+ 14.01
510.24	365.63	Banks	451.41	+ 0.86	+ 0.19	− 28.97	− 6.03	+ 60.75	+ 15.55
195.37	124.98	Nat. Mkt. Comp.	167.15	+ 0.72	+ 0.43	− 15.67	− 8.57	+ 24.56	+ 17.22
187.94	110.21	Nat. Mkt. Indus.	155.08	+ 0.89	+ 0.58	− 17.64	− 10.21	+ 23.97	+ 18.28
OTHERS									
365.01	231.90	AMEX	309.33	+ 0.71	+ 0.23	− 26.31	− 7.84	+ 48.98	+ 18.81
1926.2	1232.0	Fin. Times Indus.	1468.2	+ 4.5	+ 0.31	− 299.7	− 16.95	+ 94.9	+ 6.91
28072.02	21036.80	Nikkei Stock Avg.	27920.36	− 151.66	− 0.54	+ 2026.06	+ 7.82	+ 6356.36	+ 29.48
289.02	181.09	Value-Line (geom)	235.57	+ 0.93	+ 0.40	− 32.31	− 12.06	+ 33.95	+ 16.84
3299.44	2188.11	Wilshire 5000	2697.98	+ 11.25	+ 0.42	− 289.44	− 9.69	+ 280.86	+ 11.62

D. MARGIN TRADING AND SHORT SELLING

§18.16 Margin Transactions

A margin transaction simply involves borrowing money from your broker to enable you to buy more shares of marketable securities. By obtaining such a loan, an investor may make a larger investment than he or she could have without the loan. Since the loan is secured by a lien of the securities purchased, it is a relatively riskless loan from the point of view of the broker. Margin trading involves a kind of leverage.

Margin trading is subject to federal regulation because it was believed that excessive margin trading before the collapse of the securities markets in 1929 contributed significantly to the magnitude and severity of that collapse. An analysis of the way margin trading may have contributed to the dramatic collapse of securities prices in 1929 is instructive since it both reflects the dangers of leverage and explains how margined securities transactions work.

The late 1920s was a period of unparalleled optimism in the securities markets. Securities prices were going up and seemed to have no way to go but up even further. (Does this sound like the 1980s?) Many brokers provided purchasers of shares with 90 percent or even higher margin privileges. A person buying 1,000 shares of $10 stock could therefore buy $10,000 worth of stock simply by putting up $1,000 in cash and borrowing $9,000 from the broker. When the price of the stock went from $10 to $12, the investor more than doubled his money: he sold for $12,000 the stock he had purchased for $10,000, returned the $9,000 to the broker and kept $3,000 (minus brokerage commissions and interest) for himself. These transactions occurred time and time again during the 1920s: Buying stock on margin was like finding money. Furthermore, many people pyramided: They would take the potential gain from the run-up in price (without actually selling the stock and liquidating the position) and use that equity to borrow additional margin to buy additional stocks on the 90 percent debt/10 percent equity ratio. To make matters even more dangerous, many persons of very modest means were speculating on margined stocks and pyramiding. This is, of course, classic leverage that is also involved in buying commercial real estate or many businesses. When prices are going up, profits roll in at a fast clip; when prices decline, disaster strikes.

When the first breaks in price occurred in the summer of 1929, many margin purchasers found themselves facing *margin calls*, that is, requests from the broker to put up more collateral since the price of the stock had declined and the broker's loan was not fully secured by the stock. For example, in connection with the $10 stock described above, when the price declined to, say $9 per share, the broker was seriously at risk: The collateral was worth only $9,000 and declining, while the loan was at $9,000 plus accrued interest and increasing steadily (from additional interest charges). Most margin purchasers had no additional capital to deposit with the broker (even if they wished to do so) since all of their resources were already out "on margin" supporting other margin purchases (which were also seriously at risk because of the decline in price). To cut the potential losses, brokers began selling margined shares on a distress basis, if necessary, to recoup as much as they could. The decline began to feed on itself; panic resulted, driving down prices even further as more margin calls were triggered and increasing the sharpness of the market break. In October, 1929 a break in prices of the same order of magnitude as that of 1987 occurred. In the process many brokerage firms were wiped out along with their customers since the customers were insolvent and the firms were unable to cover all of their customers' commitments. Brokerage firm failures then wiped out the assets of solvent customers since all accounts were uninsured, and the customers became unsecured creditors in the broker's bankruptcy proceeding. The bottom of the market collapse did not occur until 1931 and 1932, when many securities prices had declined by over 70 percent. It was not uncommon for the $10 stock sold in 1929 to be be selling for $2 per share or less in 1931.

One lesson learned from the 1929 market debacle was that limits should be placed on the amount of margin customers can borrow on the security of marketable securities of fluctuating value. This regulatory power is vested in the Federal Reserve Board. Over the years, the required margin has varied; for over a decade, however, the requirement has been stable at 50 percent. This means that today an investor may borrow no more than 50 percent of the cost of his purchase. If one has $10,000, and wants to buy a $100 stock, one can borrow an additional $10,000 from a broker, and buy 200 shares — $20,000 worth of the stock. From the broker's standpoint the risk is not very great since the $10,000 loan is secured by stock worth $20,000. Since the stock is collateral for the loan, the broker will of course not let the customer sell the stock or even obtain possession of the certificate, without discharging the loan. In a margin account the securities are restricted to protect the broker. Interest charged on loans in a margin account is relatively inexpensive: about 3½ points above the prime, or 12 percent in 1987. This interest charge in effect provides a spur to margin investors to close out margined positions if the stock does not move upward promptly.

Of course, when stocks go down, persons who have bought on margin are hurting. The effect of the 50 percent margin requirement is in effect to double the consequence of each dollar of decline in the stock over what the consequence would have been in an unmargined investment. As was true in 1929, at some point the decline may be large enough that the broker will feel compelled to make a margin call. A rule of the New York Stock Exchange requires additional margin when the value of the collateral has declined to the point that the amount the investor would have left after selling the shares (and paying off the loan) represents less than 25 percent of the value of the shares. In other words, if one bought 200 shares of a $100 stock on margin (putting up $10,000 in cash and borrowing the remaining $10,000), a margin call would be made when the stock declined to a value of $12,500. The stock would have to decline from $10 to $6.25 for this to occur, a major decline certainly. Many brokers, however, make margin calls before this level is reached; several lending brokerage firms, for example, require additional margin at 30 percent or 35 percent coverage rather than at the 25 percent level. Brokerage firms may also urge the investor to close out the position (by selling the stock) before it reaches this level. Many brokers have published brochures that set forth their policies as to when additional margin will be required.

Technically, *margin* is the amount that must be put up on the original purchase (50 percent currently) while *maintenance* is the point at which a margin call is made to preserve an outstanding position. Both margin and maintenance, however, are usually referred to as "margin."

Margin calls are made on the basis of the value of the entire portfolio of securities maintained with the broker by the customer, not on each individual stock. When the value of the portfolio has dropped so that a margin call is necessary, the broker is expected to telephone the customer no later than the next day; depending on the brokerage firm's policies (and the perceived creditworthiness of the customer) the customer may be allowed a day or two, or as long as a week, to supply the additional capital in the form of either cash or marketable securities. If the additional capital is not received, the securities in the account are sold and the proceeds used to repay the outstanding margin loan.

Margin regulations are also applicable to banks. When a person borrows money from a bank secured by a lien on shares of stock, for example, he or she must sign a statement that the purpose of the loan itself is not to invest in marketable securities.

With the development of standardized options trading (discussed in Chapter 20) one can obtain the same (or greater) benefits by the purchase of call options as can be obtained by margin trading.

§18.17 Short Selling

Short selling is a well-known practice that enables an investor to speculate in a price decline to the same extent as the purchase of shares constitutes speculation in a price increase.

The idea is basically very simple: A short seller borrows shares from his or her broker and sells them immediately. When the price declines, the short seller buys shares in the market in order to replace the shares that he or she borrowed. The difference between the higher sales price and lower purchase price, less commissions, interest, and any dividends paid on the borrowed stock (all of which are the short seller's obligation), is the short seller's profit. At first blush, it may seem unethical to profit on a decline in prices or to sell something one does not actually own. However, that is a bit naive. As long as the person from whom the shares are borrowed consents to the transaction and gets the shares back, who is hurt?

Between 1929 and 1932, several fortunes were made by a systematic campaign of short selling (or "shorting") many common stocks. These campaigns are known as "bear raids." People borrowed shares and sold them, further driving down prices on an already soft market. Profits from successful short sales were used as collateral to borrow more shares and sell them to drive the price down further. In a way this appears to be predatory behavior. In another perspective, these people were simply more accurate in their foresight of what the short-term future would bring than the people who bought shares during this period believing that the worse was over and prices would be going up.

The mechanics of short selling are rather interesting. First of all, where does the borrowed stock come from? There is a large supply of marketable securities floating around the brokerage community that is available for borrowing. These are typically shares registered in *street name* (in the names of Wall Street brokerage firms). While all the shares in the floating supply are owned by someone, there are no specific ownership rights in specific certificates or specific shares. There is thus a floating supply of securities available for use by brokers. The largest source of available shares is shares held by brokerage firms for people who have bought on margin. Margin account agreements specifically authorize brokers to lend out shares in the account. In other words, a brokerage firm may lend a margin buyer 50 percent of the purchase price of stock and then turn around and lend the same stock to another customer (or the customer of another brokerage firm) to sell short. If the original customer decides to close out his or her margined stock position, the broker must come up with shares, either by getting them back from the short seller, or more commonly simply by using other shares in the floating supply until the time the short seller closes out his or her position and returns the shares. Shares are also routinely lent by large stockholders, including pension funds and mutual funds. The incentive for lending is that these loans are collateralized with cash on which no interest is customarily paid to the stock borrower but on which the lender may earn interest. An institutional investor may lend shares in its portfolio simply to earn interest on the collateral. There is no downside cost, because the short seller — the person borrowing the stock and selling it — is responsible to the owner of the stock for any dividends that may be declared on the stock while it is borrowed.

From the standpoint of the short seller, the borrowing of stock is viewed as a margin transaction. The borrower must provide collateral equal to 50 percent of the value of the stock being borrowed. Upon receiving the borrowed stock and selling it, the proceeds are retained in the customer's account and cannot be drawn on if that would reduce the margin protection to the broker. No interest is usually paid on the capital in this account, though it may be possible for large short sellers to earn interest by substituting treasury bills or other interest-earning cash equivalents.

If the short seller guesses wrong, and the price of the stock goes up, he or she may face a margin call much as a margin buyer faces a margin call when the stock price goes down. Indeed, in most respects purchases on margin and short sales are mirror images of the same type of transaction. Theoretically, the liability of a short seller is infinite since there is no maximum limit on the rise of a stock price, while the most a margin buyer can lose is twice the amount of capital invested if the stock drops to zero (assuming a 50 percent margin requirement). These are theoretical maximum losses, however, not realistic ones.

The only situation in which a short seller is really at serious risk is where an investor in the business seeks to obtain a *corner* on the outstanding floating stock so that it becomes increasingly difficult for short sellers to find shares to buy back to cover their short positions. A corner requires the availability of very large amounts of capital to buy up the entire outstanding floating supply of stock, absorbing the short sales made by persons expecting the price to go down further. There have been no attempted corners in recent years in the securities markets, though there have been attempts in the commodities markets. An attempt to corner the floating supply of a stock is sometimes called *squeezing the shorts*.

Financial newspapers publish the *short positions* for many widely traded stocks on a monthly basis. It is relatively easy to determine whether the number of shares sold short (and not covered by repurchases) increased during the current month. An interesting question is this: Assuming that uncovered short sales did increase the previous month, is that a "bullish" or "bearish" sign? (A bullish sign indicates that prices are likely to move up; a bearish sign indicates a downward movement.) An increase in uncovered short positions obviously means that many investors thought prices were going down; that should be bearish. However, most analysts put an opposite twist on the data. All the uncovered short sales reported for the month have been made and absorbed by the market; they will have to be covered in the future. Thus, an increase in uncovered short sales represents a potential increase in demand, and is a bullish sign.

In some instances, an investor may enter into a short sale by borrowing the stock and selling it even though the investor already owns the stock. This is called a *short sale against the box*, the "box" being a hypothetical safe deposit box in which the certificate is stored. This is primarily a tax-oriented maneuver.

Among securities traders, selling shares short while planning to cover in the near future by purchasing shares is as common a market stratagem as purchasing shares planning to resell them in the near future. Indeed, the terminology of traders suggests equivalence: a trader who owns shares is said to be *long* while one who owes shares to the market is said to be *short*. SEC regulations distinguish between regular security sales from a long position and true short sales in one respect. Aggressive short selling has the capacity to depress a security's price to unrealistically low levels, particularly in an already declining market. The SEC requires that short sales be made only on an *uptick* (that is, only after a market transaction that was at a higher price than the preceding transaction) or on a *zero uptick* (i.e., only after one or more trans-actions at a level price if the last previous price movement was an uptick). This provision (dating from the 1930s) is designed to prevent the depressing effect of an unrelieved series of short sales at steadily decreasing prices. During the market decline in October, 1987, however, it appears that some short sales were made in violation of this rule — some short sales were executed despite the fact that the previous transaction was a *downtick* (i.e., executed at a price lower than the transaction preceding it) or a *zero downtick*.

D. MARKET PRICES OF DEBT SECURITIES

§18.18 Short-Term Debt Sold at a Discount from Face Value

Some short-term debt obligations do not carry an affirmative obligation to pay interest by the borrower. Rather, the borrower simply agrees to pay a specific amount — say, $10,000 in 30 days — and then sells this obligation at whatever price it can get at an auction or by a negotiated sale. A person may buy such an obligation for, say $9,930. The $70 difference in price in effect represents both the interest earned by the purchaser and the cost of the bor-rowing to the debtor. The effective interest rate for the 30-day period is a little less than 8 percent per year. That interest is computed by comparing the amount invested ($9,930) and the interest earned ($70). Rather confusingly, interest rates on transactions of this type are often quoted as the percentage the discount bears to the face amount — $70 as a fraction of $10,000 rather than as a fraction of $9,930. The difference is usually not great, but the latter quotation understates slightly the true rate of interest on the investment. Quoted interest rates on short-term discounted debt are usually annualized for convenience of making comparisons.

A major issuer of debt instruments at a discount is the United States government. The United States Treasury issues discount instruments — known as *treasury bills* (also called *T-bills* or simply *bills*) — with maturities as short as three months. Large volumes of discounted bills due in six months or one year are also sold each month. The minimum purchase is $10,000 of face value and a round lot is $5 million of face value. These instruments are viewed as entirely riskless and the price is established solely on the basis of market interest rates in the economy. The higher the interest rates, the greater the discount and, hence, the lower the price a $10,000 bill would command.

Secondary markets in discounted securities are made by securities dealers in all maturities of Treasury issues so that holders may sell securities before they mature. This secondary market also enables persons to make investments in these short-term interests at times when the Treasury is not making a direct offering in the primary market.

Short-term discounted instruments are also sold by state and local governments, corporations, and other entities.

§18.19 The Market Price for Interest-Bearing Debt

Many corporations have outstanding interest-bearing debt that is not due for many years. Such debt is issued in the form of publicly held negotiable certificates in $1,000 units. These certificates are technically *bonds* if the debt is secured or *debentures* if it is unsecured. Hereafter the term *bonds* will be used to describe both secured and unsecured instruments. The federal government, state governments, political subdivisions, and governmental agencies such as the Federal National Mortgage Association also issue huge amounts of bonds to finance their activities. The United States Treasury issues *notes* for maturities of less than ten years and bonds for longer maturities. Notes are usually sold by competitive bid at auctions based on yield or interest rate rather than on price. A round lot for treasury notes is usually $1,000,000 of face value while a round lot for treasury bonds is $25,000 of face value.

Long-term commercial loans may also be privately negotiated and evidenced by promissory notes rather than negotiable certificates. Most long-term bank loans are of this character. This section, however, deals only with negotiable bonds.

Before turning to pricing, it is necessary to first describe the characteristics of the instrument under discussion. Bonds are issued in $1,000 denominations or in multiples of $1,000. Each bond carries with it a right to receive a stated amount of interest every half year (or full year, in some cases). The ratio between this fixed amount and the $1,000 face value is called the *coupon rate*. Historically, bonds were payable to bearer and the right to receive each semiannual payment was reflected by a coupon attached to the bond; every six months or year the owner would clip off the maturing coupon and submit it for payment. Increasingly, bonds are issued in registered form, which means they are issued in the name of a person rather than in bearer form and the interest payments are not represented by negotiable coupons. The issuer simply sends a check to the registered owner every six months for the maturing interest.

The coupon rate is set when the bond is created and is an integral part of the description of the bond. For example, a bond that commits the issuer to pay $45 every six months has a coupon rate of 9 percent: $90 per year is 9 percent of the face value of $1,000. This coupon rate is constant for the life of the bond and the bond is usually described as a 9 percent bond.

When bonds are originally issued, the coupon rate is usually fixed at or very close to the then going market interest rate so that the bond initially sells for approximately $1,000. Sales at the face amount of the bond are said to be *at par* or *at face value*. Once the bonds are issued and sold to the public, a market in them develops. As interest rates and risk of nonpayment change, the bonds sell at various prices determined by the market for debt instruments. The market price is unrelated to par or face value. If interest rates are *higher* than the coupon rate, the bond sells at a discount from par, that is, for less than $1,000. The actual market price is the price that makes the return actually obtained by a purchaser of the bond at that price equal the higher market rate of interest. If market interest rates are lower than the coupon rate, the bond sells at a *premium*, that is, at a price higher than the par value of $1,000.

An illustration may be useful. A small volume of bonds are traded each day on the New York Stock Exchange. Table 18-20 is an excerpt from this table for trading that occurred on June 10, 1988. First, one must learn to read the descriptions of the bonds themselves: "AlaP 8½s01" means that these are bonds issued by Alabama Power and Light Company maturing in the year 2001; the coupon rate is 8½ percent per year, or, in other words, the holder of each bond receives $42.50 every six months. The "s" means that the interest is paid semiannually; bonds that pay interest annually appear without an "s," for example, "AVX 13½00." Trading prices for bonds are quoted without one zero for reasons of space (or what amounts to the same thing, are quoted in $10 units); the 8½ percent Alabama Power bond closed at 91, or $910.00 for each $1,000 face value bond. How could it be that a bond with a face amount of $1,000 and paying $85 per year in interest sells for only $910? That is the market compensating for the fact that the current *market* interest rate for a bond with this Alabama Power bond's financial return and risk characteristics is higher than 9 percent.

What is the actual market interest rate for this bond? The column "Cur Yld" (current yield) gives a strong clue: That shows an entry of 9.3 percent for the Alabama Power bond under discussion. It turns out that the 9.3 percent figure is only an approximation. All interest-bearing bonds have two features. For example, the purchaser who buys the 8½ percent Alabama Power bond for $910 is entitled to receive two things: (1) $42.50 every half year from now until the year 2001, and (2) on a specified day in the year 2001, $1,000 in cash as the bond matures. For this combination of two benefits, a purchaser today pays $910. The 9.3 percent *current* yield in the table reflects only the return on $910 that the $42.50 semiannual payments yield; no account is taken of the fact that some 13 years from now the holder will also receive $1,000 while investing only $910.

The true measure of yield that takes into account both factors is called the *yield-to-maturity*. The yield-to-maturity is the interest or discount rate that in a present value calculation would make all the cash payments over the remaining life of a bond — both interest payments and repayment of principal at maturity — equal to the bond's market value. This calculation assumes that interim interest payments are reinvested at the same yield-to-maturity rate.

Calculations of yield-to-maturity are obviously closely related to present

Table 18-20

NEW YORK EXCHANGE BONDS

Friday, June 10, 1988

Total Volume $29,150,000

	Domestic		All Issues	
	Fri.	Thu.	Fri.	Thu.
Issues traded	662	689	663	692
Advances	365	310	365	310
Declines	165	211	165	213
Unchanged	132	168	133	169
New highs	17	16	17	16
New lows	5	6	5	8

SALES SINCE JANUARY 1

1988	1987	1986
$3,504,302,000	$4,517,655,000	$5,082,326,000

Dow Jones Bond Averages

−1986−		−1987−		−1988−			−1988−		−1987−		−1986−	
High	Low	High	Low	High	Low				Friday			
93.65	83.73	95.51	81.26	91.25	86.92	20 Bonds	88.00	+0.20	87.85	+0.04	89.86	+0.34
95.79	81.85	98.23	79.51	91.88	86.05	10 Utilities	87.69	+0.36	88.71	+0.17	89.54	+0.46
91.64	84.82	93.10	83.00	90.64	86.96	10 Industrial	88.31	+0.05	86.98	−0.10	90.18	+0.22

CORPORATION BONDS
Volume, $29,120,000

Bonds	Cur Yld	Vol	Close	Net Chg.
AVX 13½00	12.9	2	104¼	− ¾
AbbtL 11s93	10.5	4	104⅝	...
Advst 9s08	cv	21	81	+ 1
AetnLf 8⅛07	9.3	15	87⅜	+ 1¾
AirPr 11⅜15	...	15	106	− ½
AlaBn 6¾99t	6.8	8	99¼	+ ¼
AlaP 8½s01	9.3	10	91	+ 1
AlaP 7⅞s02	9.3	13	85	...
AlaP 8⅞s03	9.6	17	92½	+ ½
AlaP 8¼s03	9.5	20	87	+ ⅜
AlaP 8¾407	9.9	93	88¼	+ ¼
AlaP 12⅝10	11.8	49	106¾	+ ¾
AlskH 16¼99	14.3	115	114	...
AlskH 15¼92	14.1	3	108¼	− ⅛
AlskH 10¾493	10.5	4	102½	− ½
vjAlgI 10¾499f	...	4	56½	− ½
vjAlgI 10.4s02f	...	10	54½	...
vjAlgI 9s89f	...	14	61	− 2
AlldC zr92	...	35	69½	+ ⅜
AlldC zr98	...	7	39⅞	+ 2⅜
AlldC zr2000	...	20	31¼	+ ¼
AldC dc6s88	6.1	5	98¹³⁄₁₆	+ ¹⁄₃₂
AldC dc6s90	6.4	1	93⅞	− 2⅛
AlldC zr97	...	50	41⅝	+ ⅛
AlldC zr99	...	10	35⅝	+ ¼
AlldC zr05	...	80	18¾	+ ¼
Alcoa 9s95	9.0	5	99½	− ⅛
AForP 5s30	9.8	1	51¼	...
AFor 5s30r	9.9	1	50½	...
AAirl 4¼92	5.1	3	83⅛	...
AAirl 5¼98	7.5	4	69⅝	...
ABrnd 8⅝90	8.7	15	99⅝	− ⅛
AExC 7.8s92	8.0	5	97	+ ⅜
AmMed 9½01	cv	74	99¾	+ 1
AmMed 11s98	11.0	30	100	...
ATT 5½97	7.2	10	76⅞	+ ⅞
ATT 6s00	8.2	34	73⅜	− ⅜
ATT 5⅛01	7.6	20	67¾	+ ¾
ATT 8¾400	9.2	115	95⅜	+ ¼
ATT 7s01	8.6	10	81	+ ¼
ATT 7⅛03	8.9	41	80⅛	+ ⅛
ATT 8.80s05	9.3	158	94¼	+ ¼
ATT 8⅝s07	9.6	414	90¼	+ ⅛
ATT 8⅝26	9.8	55	88	+ ⅛
Amfac 5¼94	cv	5	110½	− 1½
Amoco 6s91	6.3	10	94½	+ 1
Amoco 6s98	7.3	30	82	+ ⅛
Amoco 9.2s04	9.5	76	97¼	− ¼
Ancp 13⅞02f	cv	11	107½	...
Anhr 8s96	8.7	20	92¼	...

EXPLANATORY NOTES
(For New York and American Bonds)
Yield is current yield.
cv-Convertible bond. cf-Certificates. dc-Deep discount. ec-European currency units. f-Dealt in flat. il-Italian lire. kd-Danish kroner. m-Matured bonds, negotiability impaired by maturity. na-No accrual. r-Registered. rp-Reduced principal. st-Stamped. t-Floating rate. wd-When distributed. ww-With warrants. x-Ex interest. xw-Without warrants. zr-Zero coupon.
vj-In bankruptcy or receivership or being reorganized under the Bankruptcy Act, or securities assumed by such companies.

value calculations of the type described in Chapter 2. For many years these calculations were made by the use of *basis books* that show yield-to-maturity when coupon, bond price, and time remaining until maturity were known. Today these calculations may be most efficiently performed by preprogrammed handheld calculators.

Two debt securities with the same yield-to-maturity may trade at very different prices, depending on coupon rates and maturity dates. To facilitate price comparisons in active trading in debt securities, traders usually refer to *basis points* rather than price. A basis point is $\frac{1}{100}$ of 1 percent in yield. A price movement of 25 basis points is a change in price sufficient to change the yield-to-maturity of a security by $\frac{1}{4}$ of 1 percent.

The current yield is widely used because (a) it is much easier to calculate than the yield-to-maturity and (b) when the payment date is far in the future, the difference between the current yield and the yield-to-maturity will rarely be significant. Recall how small the present values of payments due in the distant future are. See Chapter 2.

The method of calculation of current yield probably explains some apparent anomalies in the table. For example, why does the AAirl (American Airlines) 4¼92 show a current yield of only 5.1 percent while the other AAirl bond shows a yield of 7.5 percent and other bonds are in the 9 or 10 percent range? The reason is that the final payment of $1,000 due in 1992 — approximately four years from the date of the quotation — is a significant component in calculating the yield-to-maturity of the American Airlines 4¼ bond. A person buying this bond pays about $831 for (1) annual payments of $42.50 for four years plus (2) $1,000 at the end of the four-year priod. Clearly the current yield, which takes into account only component (1) significantly understates the true yield-to-maturity of this investment.

When bonds are bought and sold, it is customary to apportion the interest due as of the date of closing. Bonds that are in default, or are significantly below investment grade, may be "dealt in flat," that is, there is no apportionment of interest and each holder is entitled to any payments received without regard to the period those payments represent.

Most bond trading occurs over-the-counter rather than on the New York Stock Exchange. The NYSE has a "nine bond rule" that states transactions involving more than nine bonds may be executed off the Exchange floor. Thus the published quotations in Table 18-20 do not reflect the prices at which the vast majority of bond trades actually occurred: Indeed most publicly traded bonds are not even listed on the NYSE.

Investments in corporate bonds by individual investors may appear attractive because of their relatively high interest rate and relatively low risk of default. There are potential pitfalls for individual investors, however. A rise in interest rates by itself immediately significantly erodes the value of the investment; there is usually no downside price protection for the investor in the event of a rise in interest rates. The price erosion caused by an increase in interest rates is felt more heavily by holders of bonds with longer maturities than those with shorter maturities. For example, a rise of 200 basis points (2 percent in yield) reduces the price of a ten-year bond with a 7 percent coupon rate by about 13 percent. If this bond had a 30-year maturity and a yield of over 8 percent the decline in price as a result of a 200 basis point price movement would be nearly 20 percent.

In addition, there is some danger that the slight risk of default inherent in all corporate bonds may be magnified by corporate changes over which the bondholder has no control. Finally, there may be a lack of liquidity where the number of bonds (less than $25,000 of face value) being purchased is small; over-the-counter traders may not be interested in purchasing bonds in units of less than $25,000 of face value except at a deep discount. This last risk can usually be avoided by investing in mutual bond funds (see Chapter 19) or in investment trusts that hold large amounts of bonds but provide a fair degree of liquidity.

§18.20 Junk Bonds

Junk bonds are bonds that are below investment grade as determined by one or more investment rating services. They have been widely used in recent years to raise very large amounts of capital — billions of dollars in many cases — for takeover bids by outsiders. In these situations, the cash flow generated by the corporation being acquired is usually the source of funds to service the debt represented by the junk bonds. In the relatively short period that junk bonds have been widely used, there have not been significant defaults on them, though obviously the risk of default is significantly higher than on investment grade securities.

§18.21 Zero Coupon Bonds

The bonds issued by Allied Corporation described in Table 18-19 ("AlldC") are examples of zero coupon bonds. These are bonds that are issued at deep discounts from par value and do not pay interest. A "zero" issued by Allied Corporation and due in 1992 can be purchased for about $625 for a $1,000 bond. The entire difference of $375 represents interest that is in effect paid in a lump sum in 1992 when the bond matures. Since zeros by definition do not pay current interest, there is no current yield.

The Allied Corporation zero due in 1992 actually yields close to 17 percent per year. Again at first blush, this would appear to be an attractive investment for individuals. However, the tax rules applicable to such investments are unfavorable: An individual buying a zero must include in his or her tax return each year the amount of imputed interest payable on the investment even though it is not received until maturity. As a result, zeros are attractive investments only for tax-exempt entities, particularly Keogh plans and IRAs owned by individuals. Of course, the risk of default may also be increased by reason of the long period between the time the investment is made and the time of maturity of the obligation.

Deep discount bonds are similar to zeros except that they pay current interest rates well below effective market interest rates. Allied Corporation has also issued two sets of bonds that are classified as deep discount bonds. They are the 6s due in 1988 and 1990.

Brokerage firms create zeros by stripping interest-bearing coupons from United States long-term bonds. They are usually offered under feline acronyms: CATS (certificates of accrual on treasury securities) or TIGRs (treasury investment growth receipts). In response, the United States Treasury has issued its own zeros called STRIPS (Separate Trading of Registered Interest and Principal of Securities). Zeros based on United States securities are attractive because there is no risk of nonpayment at maturity. The same cannot be said for corporate zeros, such as those issued by Allied Chemical Corporation.

Zeros that are publicly traded of course fluctuate in price in response to changes in interest rates. Zeros are very volatile. For example, a 20-year bond selling at par might be stripped of its coupons and sold at $146 per $1,000 bond to yield 9.55 percent to maturity. If the price of the unstripped bond rises from 1,000 to $1,010, the price of the stripped zero would rise about $28, or a price increase of nearly 20 percent over the original $146 price.

§18.22 Municipal Bonds

Bonds issued by states, municipalities, and state-created taxing authorities are usually called *municipal bonds*. They are attractive investments primarily because interest on them is exempt from federal income taxation. Because of this tax-exempt feature, municipals carry significantly lower interest rates than taxable bonds of approximately the same risk.

Some municipals issued by a specific state may also be exempt from state income taxes, and from municipal income taxes as well. These bonds are sometimes referred to as *double-exempt* or *triple-exempt* bonds. Double- or triple-exempt bonds should normally be purchased only by persons who can take full advantage of the multiple tax exemptions.

In the 1986 Tax Act, Congress restricted the purposes for which municipal bonds that are entitled to federal tax exemption may be used. Since tax exemption is an important part of the value of municipals, it is important to obtain reliable advice as to the tax status of specific municipals before any investment is made.

Tax-exempt municipal bonds are predominantly investments for the affluent taxpayer in high tax brackets. The lower tax rates applicable in 1987 and later years under the 1986 Act may limit the attractiveness of holding municipal bonds in the future.

CHAPTER 19

INVESTMENT STRATEGIES FOR THE SMALL INVESTOR

§19.1 Introduction

Today the most sensible strategy for investors is to *diversify* investments and not place one's entire resources at the individualized risk of a single business or single type of investment. This theory of risk taking in connection with investments is often described as *portfolio theory*. A *portfolio* is simply a number of different investments held by a single investor.

A relatively small investor cannot diversify effectively by purchasing small amounts of different publicly traded securities issued by different companies. The trading units for round lots are simply too large for effective investment of small amounts of funds. Brokers' premiums on odd lot transactions make that alternative unattractive. The obvious alternative is investment in one or more *investment companies* or *mutual funds*. This chapter describes a number of essentially risk-free investments available to small investors that provide attractive rates of return. Diversification for the small investor may involve a combination of these various types of investments with mutual funds, limited partnership interests in real estate, and possibly a smattering of other, more risky investments.

§19.2 Investment Companies

A mutual fund is one type of investment company. An investment company is simply a corporation that invests only in marketable securities of other corporations. An investment company therefore has at any given time a portfolio of securities and usually some cash or cash-equivalent assets awaiting investment. Because of the nature of the holdings of an investment company, it is relatively easy to determine the aggregate value of its holdings at any point in time. Valuation is not usually a problem for investment companies.

Investment companies are themselves corporations that issue shares. Investors may purchase these shares and thereby obtain instant diversification, since the shares issued by an investment company in effect constitute investment in the portfolio owned by the investment company. Because the value of the investment company's portfolio is known, it is also relatively easy to determine the net asset value of each share of the investment company's stock. One simply values all the holdings in the investment company's portfolio and divides by the number of outstanding shares.

Not all companies that invest in marketable securities are investment companies. If a company invests exclusively in controlling interests in several operating companies and itself has no other business, it is usually called a *holding company*. A company that itself has business operations and also invests in marketable securities is not an investment company either.

The investment goals of a publicly held investment company — the objective of its portfolio activities — are publicly stated. They may be to maximize long-term capital appreciation, to maximize current income, to invest in a diversified portfolio of public utility stocks, to invest in long-term investment grade bonds, or some combination of these. Modern investment companies generally do not seek controlling positions; most are diversified investors that limit their investments in any one corporation to a small fraction (e.g., less than 1 percent) of the voting shares of each operating company.

Investment companies earn profits from two principal sources: trading profits from buying and selling portfolio securities and dividends or interest from investments. Investment companies that distribute substantially all of their earnings each year to shareholders are not themselves subject to tax. Rather, they are conduits whose income — e.g., capital gain, tax-exempt municipal bond interest — is passed through to the shareholders. Thus, an investor who seeks only tax exempt municipal bond income may invest in an investment company that invests only in such bonds, and the dividends received by the shareholder are exempt from income tax to the extent they represent interest on tax-exempt municipal bonds. Management fees are subtracted from income prior to their distribution to shareholders and are not separately itemized in the distribution process.

An investment company itself has shareholders. It must hold shareholders' meetings, elect directors and officers, and so forth. Most investment companies contract with a brokerage firm or investment banker to obtain investment advice for a fee: The brokerage firm or investment banker may also handle share transfer and other related costs of the investment company operation. Of course fees are also charged for these services.

If an investment company is closely held by a few shareholders it is usually called a *personal holding company*. The investment companies described in the balance of this chapter are all publicly held corporations. Publicly held investment companies are subject to a substantial degree of regulation by the Securities and Exchange Commission under the Investment Company Act of 1940.

Publicly held investment companies are broken down into two broad categories discussed in the two sections immediately following: *closed-end companies* and *open-end companies*. Open-end companies are usually called *mutual funds*.

§19.3 Closed-End Investment Companies

Closed-end companies are the oldest type of investment companies. Their unique characteristic is that they have outstanding a fixed number of their own shares that are traded either on a securities exchange or over the counter. Before World War II, investment companies were generally closed-end; after World War II they fell into a period of eclipse but in the last few years a number of new closed-end funds have been created. Many of these new closed-end funds concentrate in foreign securities of specific countries. Closed-end companies are also known as *publicly traded funds* since their shares are listed on securities exchanges or traded in the OTC market like any other securities.

An investor who decides to invest in a closed-end fund simply places an order with a broker to purchase the desired number of shares wherever the shares are traded. A shareholder who decides to liquidate his interest in the closed-end company places an order to sell the shares in the appropriate market. In either event, investing in a closed-end fund or disposing of such an investment involves merely the payment of the standard brokerage fees for executing the transactions.

The market price for shares issued by closed-end investment companies fluctuates according to market conditions, and may be either higher or lower than the net asset value of the shares. Shares of a closed-end fund are said to trade at a *discount* if the market price for its shares is less than the net asset value per share. Closed-end fund shares are said to trade at a *premium* if the market price of the fund shares is higher than the net asset value. Table 19-1 is a table of the major publicly traded closed-end funds that invest in common shares, and Table 19-2 is a table of the publicly traded closed-end funds that invest solely in corporation bonds. In both tables "Stock Price" is the market price of the shares issued by the closed-end company. These tables reveal that most common stock closed-end funds trade at a discount, while bond funds are more mixed. Where closed-end funds trade at significant discounts, enterprising speculators have sometimes purchased large amounts of the shares on the open market and then successfully forced the closed-end fund to amend its articles of incorporation to become an "open-end" fund (thereby automatically eliminating the discount from net asset value). See §19.4.

The attractiveness of many closed-end funds is that they sometimes trade at deep discounts from net asset value. If the discount narrows, an investor may show substantial capital appreciation. On the other hand, many closed-end companies trade at discounts over long periods, and a seemingly advantageous investment may turn out disadvantageous if the discount remains stable or increases. In 1986 and 1987, on the other hand, a number of new country-oriented or region-oriented closed-end funds consistently traded at significant premiums over net asset value.

§19.4 Open-End Investment Companies (Mutual Funds)

Open-end investment companies are unlike closed-end funds in two respects: First, they do not have a fixed number of shares outstanding but stand ready

Table 19-1

CLOSED-END BOND FUNDS

Tuesday, July 26, 1988

Unaudited net asset values of closed-end bond fund shares, reported by the companies as of Friday, July 22, 1988. Also shown is the closing listed market price or a dealer-to-dealer asked price of each fund's shares, with percentage of difference.

Fund Name	Stock Exch.	N.A. Value	Stock Price		% Diff.
Bond Funds					
ACM Govt Inco Fund	NYSE	10.84	11⅝	+	7.2
ACM Govt Securities	NYSE	10.69	11	+	2.9
ACM Spectrum Fund	NYSE	9.23	9⅛	−	1.1
AMEV Securities	NYSE	10.35	10⅝	+	2.7
American Capital Bond	NYSE	b20.96	20⅝	−	1.6
American Capital Inco	NYSE	e9.22	9⅞	+	7.1
American Govt Income	NYSE	7.26	8	+	10.2
Bunker Hill Income	NYSE	17.64	17	−	3.6
Circle Income Shares	OTC	12.20	12¾	+	4.5
CNA Income Shares	NYSE	11.31	11⅜	+	0.6
Comstock Ptr Strategy	NYSE	9.51	10	+	5.2
Current Income Shares	NYSE	c11.91	12⅛	+	1.8
Dean Witter Govt Inco	NYSE	9.42	9⅜	−	0.5
Drexel Bond-Debenture	NYSE	19.39	19⅛	−	1.4
Dreyfus Strt Gov Inco	NYSE	11.14	11½	+	3.2
Excelsior Inco Shares	NYSE	16.90	14¾	−	12.7
First Boston Inco Fd	NYSE	8.76	8¾	−	0.1
First Boston Strategic	NYSE	11.18	11⅛	−	0.5
Ft Dearborn Income	NYSE	14.62	14½	−	0.8
Hatteras Income Secs	NYSE	16.03	15⅞	−	1.0
High Income Adv Tr	NYSE	9.27	9⅞	+	6.5
High Yield Income Fd	NYSE	9.44	9⅜	−	-0.7
High Yield Plus Fund	NYSE	9.27	9⅜	+	1.1
INA Investments	NYSE	17.83	17	−	4.7
Independence Sq	OTC	16.31	16½	+	1.2
Intercapital Income	NYSE	19.25	21¾	+	13.0
John Hancock Income	NYSE	15.28	14⅜	−	5.9
John Hancock Invest	NYSE	20.62	20¼	−	1.8
Kemper High Inco Tr	NYSE	11.06	12⅛	+	9.6
Kemper Inter Govt Tr	NYSE	9.27	10	+	7.9
Lincoln Natl Dir Place	NYSE	27.67	25⅜	−	8.3
MFS Gov Mkts Inco	NYSE	9.12	10	+	9.6
MFS Inco & Oppor Tr	NYSE	a9.54	10⅛	+	6.1
MFS Intermed Inco Tr	NYSE	9.16	9⅝	+	5.1
MFS Multimkt Inco Tr	NYSE	9.03	10¼	+	13.5
Montgomery Street	NYSE	18.47	18	−	2.5
Mutual Omaha Int Shs	NYSE	13.67	14½	+	6.1
New America Hi Inco	NYSE	8.92	10¼	+	14.9
Oppenhmr Multi-Sectr	NYSE	11.06	11⅜	+	2.8
Pacific Amer Inco Shs	NYSE	b15.38	15¼	−	0.8
Prudential Interm Inco	NYSE	9.24	9⅝	+	4.2
Prudential Strat Inco	NYSE	9.04	9	−	0.4
Putnam Int Govt Inco	NYSE	9.32	9⅞	+	6.0
Putnam Mstr Inco Tr	NYSE	9.44	9½	+	0.6
Putnam Mstr Int Inco	NYSE	9.35	9¼	−	1.1
Putnam Prem Inco Tr	NYSE	8.96	9½	+	6.0
State Mutual Securities	NYSE	10.82	10¾	−	0.6
Transamerica Income	NYSE	22.20	24½	+	10.4
USLIFE Income Fund	NYSE	9.58	9	−	6.1
Vestaur Securities	NYSE	13.53	13⅛	−	3.0
Convertible Bond Funds					
Lincoln Natl Convert	NYSE	13.78	11⅞	−	13.8
Putnam Hi Inco Conv	NYSE	8.49	8¼	−	2.8
International Bond Funds					
First Australia Prime	AMEX	10.79	8⅞	−	17.7
Global Government	NYSE	9.03	9½	+	5.2
Global Yield Fund	NYSE	9.98	9¼	−	7.3
Kleinwort Benson Aust	NYSE	11.62	10¼	−	11.8
Templeton Global Inco	NYSE	9.13	9⅞	+	8.2
Municipal Bond Funds					
Allstate Muni Inco Tr	NYSE	10.17	10¼	+	0.8
Allstate Muni Inco II	NYSE	9.53	9⅜	−	1.6
Colonial Muni Inco Tr	NYSE	8.98	9⅜	+	4.4
Dreyfus Strategic Muni	NYSE	9.82	10	+	1.8
MFS Muni Income Tr	NYSE	9.05	9⅛	+	0.8
Muni Insured Fd Inc	AMEX	a9.76	10	+	2.5
New York Tax-Exmpt	AMEX	9.78	9½	−	2.9
Nuveen Muni Inco	NYSE	11.14	10½	−	5.7
Nuveen CA Muni Inco	NYSE	11.21	11	−	1.9
Nuveen NY Muni Inco	AMEX	11.16	11¾	+	5.3
Nuveen Muni Value	NYSE	9.59	9¼	−	3.5
Nuveen CA Muni Val	NYSE	9.66	9⅞	+	2.2
Nuveen NY Muni Val	NYSE	9.92	10	+	0.8

a-Ex-dividend. b-Fully diluted. c-Thursday's close. e-closing stock
price for July 15 was 8⅛.

Source: Lipper Analytical Services, Denver Colorado.

Table 19-2

PUBLICLY TRADED FUNDS

Friday, June 10, 1988

Following is a weekly listing of unaudited net asset values of publicly traded investment fund shares, reported by the companies as of Friday's close. Also shown is the closing listed market price or a dealer-to-dealer asked price of each fund's shares, with the percentage of difference.

Fund Name	Stock Exch.	N.A. Value	Stock Price	% Diff.
Diversified Common Stock Funds				
Adams Express	NYSE	17.36	16⅞	– 8.55
Baker Fentress	OTC	50.68	41	– 19.09
Blue Chip Value	NYSE	7.37	6	– 18.59
Clemente Global Gro	NYSE	b8.78	6¼	– 28.82
Gemini II Capital	NYSE	16.60	12¼	– 26.20
Gemini II Income	NYSE	9.53	13	+ 36.40
General Amer Invest	NYSE	18.94	15½	– 18.20
Global Growth Capital	NYSE	8.82	8	– 9.30
Global Growth Incme	NYSE	9.51	9½	– 0.10
Growth Stock Outlook	NYSE	9.70	9⅛	– 5.90
Lehman Corp.	NYSE	14.43	12⅛	– 15.00
Liberty All-Star Eqty	NYSE	8.58	7	– 18.41
Niagara Share Corp.	NYSE	16.27	13¼	– 18.56
Nicholas-Applegate	NYSE	8.72	6⅞	– 21.16
Quest For Value Cap	NYSE	10.50	8⅛	– 22.62
Quest For Value Inco	NYSE	11.71	10	– 14.60
Royce Value Trust	NYSE	9.40	8½	– 9.97
Schafer Value Trust	NYSE	8.93	7½	– 16.01
Source Capital	NYSE	38.06	36⅜	– 4.43
Tri-Continental Corp.	NYSE	25.18	22¼	– 11.64
Worldwide Value	NYSE	19.45	15¼	– 21.59
Zweig Fund	NYSE	10.50	10⅞	– 3.57
Closed End Bond Funds				
CIM High Yield Secs	AMEX	9.63	10	+ 3.84
Zenith Income Fund	NYSE	9.33	10	+ 7.18
Specialized Equity and Convertible Funds				
American Capital Conv	NYSE	23.68	21½	– 9.21
ASA Ltd	NYSE	bc53.07	45⅝	– 14.00
Asia Pacific	NYSE	8.63	6⅝	– 23.20
Bancroft Convertible	AMEX	23.14	20½	– 11.40
BGR Precious Metals	TOR	be14.68	11½	– 21.66
Brazil	NYSE	11.63	9¼	– 20.46
CNV Holdings Capital	NYSE	9.86	5	– 49.29
CNV Holdings Income	NYSE	9.58	11¼	+ 17.43
Castle Convertible	AMEX	22.98	21⅞	– 1.53
Central Fund Canada	AMEX	b6.53	6	– 8.10
Central Securities	AMEX	11.95	9⅞	– 17.36
Claremont Capital	AMEX	52.57	49	– 6.80
Couns Tandem Secs	NYSE	7.88	5⅞	– 25.44
Cypress Fund	AMEX	9.80	7¼	– 26.02
Duff&Phelps Sel Utils	NYSE	7.82	8½	+ 8.69
Ellsw Conv Gr&Inc	AMEX	8.63	7⅝	– 11.69
Engex	AMEX	12.80	9	– 29.68
Financ'l News Compos	NYSE	16.45	13½	– 17.93
1stAustralia	AMEX	10.65	8⅞	– 16.67
First Financial Fund	NYSE	8.55	7	– 18.13
First Iberian	AMEX	9.36	9⅞	+ 5.50
France Fund	NYSE	b10.77	9⅝	– 10.60
Gabelli Equity Trust	NYSE	11.19	9¾	– 12.87
Germany Fund	NYSE	7.58	7⅝	+ 0.59
H&Q Healthcare Inv	NYSE	8.20	6¾	– 12.20
Hampton Utils Tr Cap	AMEX	b9.76	2⅛	– 16.58
Hampton Utils Tr Pref	AMEX	b49.16	48½	– 1.34
Helvetia Fund	NYSE	11.35	10¼	– 9.69
Italy Fund	NYSE	b8.82	7⅛	– 19.22
Korea Fund	NYSE	44.03	73¾	+ 67.50
Malaysia Fund	NYSE	9.07	7⅜	– 18.69
Mexico Fund	NYSE	b7.84	6	– 23.47
Morgan Grenf SmCap	NYSE	9.19	8¼	– 10.20
Petrol & Resources	NYSE	27.22	25	– 8.16
Progressive Inco Eqty	NYSE	9.44	7¾	– 17.90
Regional Fin Shrs Inv	NYSE	a7.67	6⅛	– 20.14
Scandinavia Fund	AMEX	8.68	6⅞	– 20.79
Scudder New Asia	NYSE	13.28	10¾	– 19.05
Taiwan Fund	AMEX	b28.25	41¾	+ 47.80
TCW Convertible Secs	NYSE	b8.55	7¼	– 15.20
Templeton Em Mkts	AMEX	b9.16	7⅜	– 19.59
Thai Fund	NYSE	11.73	16⅞	+ 43.86
United Kingdom Fund	NYSE	12.07	9½	– 21.29
Z-Seven	OTC	d14.86	15¼	+ 2.69

a-Ex-dividend. b-As of Thursday's close. c-Translated at Commercial Rand exchange rate. d-NAV reflects $1.73 per share for taxes. e–In Canadian Dollars. z-Not available.

at any time to issue new shares to persons desiring to invest in the fund; and second, they stand ready to redeem any shares at net asset value (or in some cases at a small discount from net asset value) at any time for investors who wish to liquidate their positions. Open-end companies are open-ended because there is no fixed capitalization of the investment company: As it grows in size, the number of outstanding shares grows also. These open-end funds are better known as *mutual funds*.

Open-end funds are not publicly traded on the NYSE or other securities markets. Rather, a person who wishes to invest in a mutual fund deals directly with the fund itself and receives newly issued shares. When a person decides to liquidate his or her interest in such a fund, the investor again contacts the mutual fund and arranges to have his or her shares redeemed. Mutual funds are sold directly or through brokers who may push such investments for small investors.

Table 19-3 is an excerpt from the Monday, June 13, 1988 *Wall Street Journal* showing quotations for many of the mutual funds beginning with "A" for Friday, June 10, 1988. In this table, "NAV" stands for net asset value; since there is no market trading in open-end fund shares, there are no share price quotations as is the case with closed-end funds. "NAV Chg." shows the change in net asset value from the previous day.

The entry under "Offer price" and the enigmatic entry "N.L." require some explanation. Until relatively recently, the fees charged by mutual funds were strictly regulated by the SEC. There were two types of funds: *load funds* and *no-load funds*. A *load* is an additional charge imposed on an investor when he or she invests in the fund; it is sometimes called a *front-end load* since it is usually imposed on the purchase of the mutual fund shares. Historically, the load was about 8 percent above the net asset value for small investments, and decreased gradually for larger investments. Load funds can be easily identified from Table 19-3 since they are the funds that show a dollar entry under the "Offer Price" category. Load funds are heavily advertised and recommended by brokers who receive a commission from the load. For example, the ABT family of funds in Table 19-3 are all load funds. One can purchase shares in the "Emerging Growth Fund" that have a net asset value of $8.37 per share for $8.79 per share; that is about a 5 percent load. An investment in this fund would have to increase about 5 percent before the investment could be liquidated without loss to the investor.

No-load funds are funds that offer to sell shares at net asset value. They are sold without extensive advertising and usually without the intervention of a broker, so that the investor has to locate the desired investment on his or her own and contact the manager of the no-load fund directly. Many investment advisers recommend that investors invest in no-load funds suitable for their investment needs in order to avoid paying the sales load. However, the actual investment performance of the two types of funds does not unambiguously indicate that this strategy leads to a higher net return.

In recent years, the SEC has relaxed the rules relating to sales charges, and many mutual funds have switched to more complex pricing structures. Many funds have reduced their front end loads but imposed a back-end redemption charge on redemptions occurring shortly after the investment is made. Funds

Table 19-3

MUTUAL FUND QUOTATIONS

Friday, June 10, 1988
Price ranges for investment companies, as quoted by the National Association of Securities Dealers. NAV stands for net asset value per share; the offering includes net asset value plus maximum sales charge, if any.

	NAV	Offer NAV Price	Chg.
AAL Mutual Fds:			
Cap Gro	p8.71	9.14+	.04
Income	p9.55	10.03+	.02
Muni Bd	p9.75	10.24	...
AARP Invest Program:			
Cap Grw	23.61	N.L.+	.14
Gen Bnd	14.74	N.L.	...
Ginnie M	15.15	N.L.+	.01
Gro Inc	21.06	N.L.+	.08
TxFr Bd	15.66	N.L.	...
TxF Shrt	15.38	N.L.	...
ABT Funds: ABT Funds:			...
Emrg Gr	p8.37	8.79+	.16
Growth I	p10.36	10.88+	.05
Sec Inc	p8.84	9.28+	.06
Util Inc	p13.64	14.32−	.01
AcornFd r	38.11	N.L.+	.13
Addsn Cp	p14.51	14.96+	.08
Adtek Fd	9.39	N.L.	...
Advnt Gv	p9.53	9.95	...
Advest Advantage:			
Govt r	p8.73	N.L.	...
Growth r	p11.51	N.L.+	.06
Income r	p9.76	N.L.+	.03
Specl r	p9.32	N.L.+	.04
Afuture Fd	9.46	N.L.+	.01
AIM Funds:			
Charter	p5.29	5.55	...
Constel	7.55	7.93+	.07
Conv Yld	p9.65	10.13+	.03
Grnway	p8.92	9.49+	.03
HiYld Sc	p8.69	9.12	...
LMTr	p9.89	10.07	...
Summit	6.75	(z)+	.04
Weingr	9.14	9.60+	.01
AlgrGP r	p10.15	10.15+	.02
Alliance Capital:			
Allnc	p6.11	6.47+	.02
Balanc	p13.02	13.78+	.08
Canada	p6.77	7.16+	.04
Convert	p9.24	9.78+	.02
Cntrpt	p14.53	15.38+	.05
Divdnd	p2.95	3.12+	.01
Govt	p8.50	8.99+	.01
HB TxF	p9.03	9.41	...
Hi Yld	p8.60	9.10	...
HI TxFr	9.13	9.51	...
Ins Cal	11.64	12.13+	.01
Intl	p16.46	17.42−	.02
Mnthly	p11.84	12.53+	.01
Mrtge	p9.15	9.68+	.01
Quasr	p17.59	18.61+	.16
Survyr	p11.17	11.82+	.07
Technol	p23.35	24.71+	.08
AMA Funds:			
Class Gr	p9.15	N.L.+	.03
Globl Gr	p19.86	N.L.+	.05
Glob Inc	p20.19	N.L.+	.01
Glob ST	p10.14	N.L.+	.01
Grw+ I	p18.26	N.L.+	.06
Class In	p8.78	N.L.+	.01
EMT	p12.92	13.56+	.08
Med Tec	p10.52	N.L.+	.01
American Capital Group:			
Comstk	13.43	14.68+	.07
Corp Bd	7.08	7.43+	.01
Enterpr	10.45	11.42+	.06
Exch Fd	65.05	(z)+	.18
Fed Mtg	12.89	13.53+	.02
Fd Amer	11.05	12.08+	.05
Govt Sec	10.23	10.97+	.03
Growth	15.79	(z)+	.04
Harbor	12.59	13.76+	.04
High Yld	9.14	9.80+	.01
Muni Bd	17.78	18.67	...
O T C	6.34	6.93+	.02
Pace Fd	22.38	24.46+	.10
Prov Inc	4.23	4.56+	.02
TxE HY	10.79	11.33	...
TxE Ins	10.57	11.10	...
Venture	11.96	13.07+	.02
American Funds Group:			
Am Bal	10.72	11.72+	.03
Amcap F	10.38	11.34+	.03
Am Mutl	18.58	20.31+	.05
Bnd FdA	13.41	14.08	...
Cap IncB	p22.29	23.65+	.06
Cap Wld	p16.12	16.92+	.05
Eupac	p25.35	27.70−	.05
Fund Inv	14.82	16.20+	.06
Govt	p13.81	14.50+	.02
Gth FdA	18.24	19.93+	.12
HI Tr	p14.16	14.87+	.02
Inc FdA	11.64	12.72+	.04
Int Bd	p13.98	14.68	...
I C A	13.47	14.72+	.04
Nw Econ	20.81	22.74+	.12
Nw Prsp	10.65	11.64	...
TxEx Bd	10.70	11.23+	.01
TxE CA	p13.61	14.29+	.01
TxE MD	p13.51	14.18+	.02
TxE VA	p13.88	14.57+	.01
Wash Mt	12.52	13.68+	.04
Am Grwth	6.74	7.37	...
Am Heritg	1.19	N.L.+	.02
Am Invest	6.35	N.L.+	.01
AmInv Inc	8.73	N.L.+	.06
Amer National:			
Growth	4.60	5.03+	.02
Income	20.17	22.04+	.02
Triflx	15.02	16.24+	.04
API Tr r	10.88	10.88+	.07
AMEV Funds:			
Capital	11.82	12.92+	.05
Fidcr	18.50	19.37+	.06
Growth	15.06	16.46+	.03
Special	18.96	18.96+	.05
TF Nat	9.74	10.20	...
US Govt	9.79	10.25+	.01
Amway Mt	8.45	9.04+	.03
Analytic	12.34	N.L.+	.04
Aquila:			
Haw TF	10.55	10.99	...
TF Ariz	9.44	9.83+	.01
TF Ore	9.58	9.98	...
Armstrng	7.06	N.L.+	.02
Assc Plnr	13.55	14.23+	.07
Avon Gv	9.81	N.L.+	.02
Axe-Houghton:			
Fund B	p7.99	N.L.+	.02
Income	p5.20	N.L.	...
Stock Fd	p5.81	N.L.+	.02

d-Ex-distribution. f-Previous day quotation. x-Ex-dividend. p-Distribution costs apply. r-Redemption charge may apply. s-Stock split. N.L.-No load. z-Not available.

that impose a redemption charge in Table 19-3 are marked with an "r." In addition, an SEC rule allows mutual funds to deduct certain marketing and distribution costs directly from assets; in effect this imposes the costs of distribution on existing fund holders rather than on new investors. Funds adopting this practice in Table 19-3 are marked with a "p." A sales load may also be charged indirectly on reinvested dividends. With a variety of costs being imposed, some in a hidden manner without complete disclosure, the comparison of costs between alternative mutual fund investments has become treacherous, and the formerly sharp line between load and no-load funds has become blurred to some extent.

Table 19-3 shows that mutual fund managers create "families" of mutual funds, each with their own investment objective. The goal is to provide a fund that meets the investment objectives of numerous diverse groups of investors with different short- and long-term goals. Most fund families permit free transfer of investments from one fund in the family to another fund in the same family without service charge. In this way, the manager hopes to retain control over investment funds even when the goal of the investor changes because of changes in individual circumstances.

Most mutual funds are actively managed. That means the fund manager shifts investments aggressively in order to maximize the return to investors. The usual yardstick for performance is whether the fund exceeds the market performance of one of the broad market averages, usually either Standard & Poor's 500 stock index or the New York Stock Exchange Composite Index. The efficient capital market hypothesis (see §18.2) states that fund managers cannot hope to beat the market averages consistently, and indeed most mutual funds have not been able to consistently exceed these market averages. One study in the late 1970s showed, for example, that 90 percent of the managed funds fared worse than the Standard & Poor 500 index over a ten-year period. In recent years there has been a strong trend toward *index funds* that are not actively managed but hold a portfolio that is structured so that it closely mimics the mix of stocks in one or more broad market indexes. An index fund also may be more attractive to sophisticated investors since it involves significantly less trading than a managed fund, and brokerage commissions, investment advice, and other costs are significantly reduced. The tremendous growth in mutual funds in recent years is in part the result of the increased use of index funds by pension plans and other institutional investors who are seeking only a market level return on their investments.

Mutual funds provide instant diversification for the small investor at relatively nominal cost. The major problems with the use of this investment vehicle by the small investor are, first, the difficulty of ascertaining the actual cost of alternative mutual fund investments, and second, the bewildering variety of different families of funds, and the equally bewildering variety of funds with varying investment objectives within each family.

§19.5 Money Market Funds

One unusual type of mutual fund that has become extremely popular is the virtual equivalent of an uninsured savings account: the *money market fund*.

The development of this type of mutual fund is a good illustration of the problems of government regulation when faced with free market forces. For many years the United States government regulated the maximum interest rates that commercial banks and savings and loan associations could pay on savings accounts. The maximum rate was 5½ percent. This created no real problem until the early 1980s, when competitive interest rates rose to 12 percent, or even higher in some areas. At first, regulated banks and savings and loan associations were overjoyed, as they paid 5½ percent interest on deposits which they could lend out at rates as high as 15 or 16 percent. That joy proved to be very short-lived, however, as mutual fund managers, investment banks, and brokerage firms devised a new type of mutual fund that promised market rates of interest for depositors in a virtually risk-free investment. All at once the regulated banks and savings and loan associations were faced with a severe liquidity crisis as millions of savers withdrew funds from regulated savings accounts in order to invest them in these new accounts. The federal government quickly realized that if these long-standing financial institutions were to survive at all, they would have to be permitted to compete effectively with the new-fangled money market funds for savings. Thus, the development of the money market fund was the cause for deregulation of bank interest rates in the early 1980s. The competitive bank and savings and loan programs that were developed in response to the money market fund are described in the following section.

A money market fund is a mutual fund that invests only in short-term, virtually riskless investments. They bear names such as "cash management accounts" or "liquid assets funds." Most money market funds are very large, with hundreds of millions or billions of dollars of assets. They invest in such items as negotiable bank certificates of deposit maturing within six months issued by large commercial banks, bankers' acceptances, commercial paper, short-term time deposits with foreign banks, and U.S. treasury notes and bills. Investments are usually in units of at least $10,000,000, and often in amounts of $100,000,000 or more. Since all of these investments have very short maturities, measured in days rather than months or years, the risk of default or collapse is very low.

One unique aspect of money market funds is that the trading unit is one dollar and earnings are reflected not by increases in the value of the trading unit but by adding more trading units to the account. The result is that an investor who holds, for example, 3,456 shares of a money market fund thinks in terms of having a deposit of $3,456. And the money market fund does what it can to further that impression. Additional trading units are added to the fund in proportion to its size in one dollar units. Depositors are permitted to write checks on the account without limitation, though usually small checks under $100 are prohibited. Whenever a check is presented the required number of trading units are redeemed into dollars. The whole arrangement is indeed very close to a bank account.

Money market funds are not insured against loss by the United States government. There is a theoretical risk of loss, but none has occurred. Investment advisers generally view these investments as cash equivalents, given the gilt-edged nature of the investments that form the portfolios of these funds and the short maturity periods.

Table 19-4 is an excerpt from *The Wall Street Journal* reporting the results of operations of large money market funds. Because of the short-term nature of the investments, yields are reported on alternative annualized "seven-day yield" bases: (1) on the actual yield over the prior seven-day period (the "7 day Yld") and (2) the same yield on a compounded basis (the "7 day EFF" or "e 7 Day yield"). The table also gives the average maturity of the portfolio investments in days and the approximate size of the fund's portfolio. The portfolio size is reported in millions of dollars: "AARP Money Fund" has assets of $213,700,000 while the "Active Asset Government Securities Fund" has assets of $241,100,000.

Money market funds may also have specialized portfolios to a limited extent. Some funds invest solely in short-term tax-exempt municipal anticipation notes or similar securities in order to provide a tax-exempt yield on a pure money market fund investment. Of course, the yield on tax-exempt funds is significantly lower than the yield on taxable money market funds.

§19.6 Insured Money Market Accounts and Certificates of Deposit

Interest-bearing deposits in commercial banks and savings and loans institutions are truly riskless investments to the extent they are insured by the Federal Deposit Insurance Corporation or the Federal Savings and Loan Insurance Corporation. The maximum deposit currently covered is $100,000. These financial institutions now offer a variety of different accounts; the two most widely used are a traditional passbook account that pays perhaps 5½ percent per year and requires no minimum balance, and an account with a minimum balance (often $2,000) that pays floating interest rates that are dependent on market interest rates generally. The latter type of account may be called a money market account, a money market checking account, or a variety of other names that emphasize that it provides a floating interest rate based on market rates; it is the traditional banking institutions' response to the money market fund described in the previous section. Usually a depositor is entitled to write a limited number of checks on the account without penalty or service charge. Some institutions may also provide free transferability from a money market account to a checking account at the same institution, or vice versa. Some accounts provide an automatic periodic transfer of excess funds in a checking account to a money market account. This is sometimes called a *sweep*. Traditional checking accounts are noninterest-bearing and should not be used for the deposit of excess funds.

Banks and savings institutions also offer competitive interest rates on *certificates of deposit (CDs)* that pay somewhat higher interest rates than on passbook or money market accounts. CDs are usually issued in round-number denominations, say, $1,000, $5,000, $10,000, and larger amounts. Interest rates on larger denomination CDs may be somewhat higher than on smaller denominations. A CD differs from a traditional interest-bearing savings account in that the investor agrees to leave the specified amount with the bank for a

Table 19-4

MONEY MARKET MUTUAL FUNDS

The following quotations, collected by the National Association of Securities Dealers Inc., represent the average of annualized yields and dollar-weighted portfolio maturities ending Wednesday, July 13, 1988. Yields are based on actual dividends to shareholders.

Fund	Avg. Mat.	7Day Yld.	e7Day Yld.	Assets
Tecmseh Prime	37	6.70	6.92	275.8
AAL MoneyMkt	34	7.25	7.52	19.1
AARP Money	39	6.14	6.33	213.7
ActvAsst GovSc	35	6.45	6.66	241.1
ActvAsst Money	45	6.82	7.05	2627.9
ActvAsst TxFr	19	4.45		
AlexBCash Gvt	30	6.73	6.95	283.2
AlexBCash Prm	29	6.93	7.17	881.4
Alliance Capital	60	6.58	6.80	1404.7
AllianceGvt Res	59	6.63	6.85	338.5
AllianceTE Res	49	4.53	4.63	663.9
AllianceTE CA	8	4.79	4.91	32.2
Alliance TE NY	31	3.96	4.04	42.1
AMA PrimePrt	76	6.50	6.71	67.0
AMA TreasPort	1	5.82	5.99	15.5
AmCap Resrv a	22	6.69	6.91	423.1
Amer Natl MM	16	6.63	6.85	12.6
AMEV Money	384	6.42	6.33	73.2
ArchFdMM clA	22	7.02	7.27	208.3
ArchFd TE A	91	4.65	4.76	72.1
AT Ohio Tax Fr	37	4.40	4.50	241.1
AutomCash Mgt	37	6.91	7.15	905.2
AutomGvt MTr	34	6.78	7.01	2180.8
Axe Hghtn MM	16	6.68	6.91	108.9
Babson Prime	31	6.58	6.80	74.8
BayshreC Rs	33	7.01	7.26	323.8
BayshreUS T	31	6.76	6.99	42.0
BenhamCal TF	4	4.37	4.47	304.7
BenhamNatl TF	12	4.60	4.71	72.7
BirrWilson MFd	26	6.17	6.36	31.0
Boston Co Cash	50	6.60	6.82	303.1
BostonCo Gvt	51	5.95	6.13	45.9
BostonCo Mass	76	4.43	4.53	147.9
Bull&Bear DRs	78	6.75	6.98	103.2
CalvrtSocInv af	18	6.64	6.86	77.1
CalvertTF Rsrv	47	4.97	5.10	738.2
CAM Fund	16	6.11	6.30	38.0
CapCash MgtTr	18	6.99	7.24	142.3
Cap Preservtn	39	6.28	6.48	2113.8
Cap Preservtn 2	1	6.64	6.86	487.3
Capital T MM	(z)	(z)		
Cap T ins MM	(z)	(z)		
Capitl T TxFr	(z)	(z)		
CardGovt SecTr	28	6.68	6.95	411.5
Cardinal TEMT	21	4.19	4.39	69.2
Carillon Csh	31	7.00	7.25	100.0
CarngieGov Sec	19	6.58	6.79	145.1
CarnegieTax Fr	32	4.54	4.64	319.2
CashAssett Tr	20	6.91	7.15	203.1
Cash Equiv MM	26	6.77	7.00	5895.1
CashEq GovSec	10	6.85	7.08	1326.9
CshMgt TrAm a	17	7.02	7.27	1092.0
Cash Rsv Mgt a	34	7.05	7.30	3129.6
CBA Money Fd	42	6.90	7.14	312.0
Centenl GovtTr	6	6.58	6.80	93.0
CentennIMM Tr	19	6.65	6.88	247.4
Centennial Tax	51	4.46	4.56	542.9
Churchill Cash	21	7.01	7.26	210.2
Cigna Cash Fd	55	6.39	6.59	81.2
CignaMM Fd b	50	6.53	6.75	183.9
Cigna TxEx	58	4.30	4.39	57.5
CimcoMM Trst	33	6.58	6.78	7.9
CMA GovtSec a	37	5.57	5.73	2224.8
CMA MnyFd a	37	6.74	6.97	19831.9
CMA Tax Ex	49	4.53	4.63	7990.9
Col Daily Inc af	27	6.64	6.87	472.1
ColGovtMM Tr	51	6.26	6.45	90.5
ColonialTE M	62	4.79	4.91	54.5
Compass CshRs	33	6.92	7.16	335.7
Compass TxEx	41	4.55	4.65	149.3
Compass USTrs	40	6.57	6.79	94.0
Commn Sen TM	15	6.73	6.96	12.5
Comp Cash M a	33	6.34	6.54	141.7
ConnDaily TF	81	4.28	4.28	248.2
CoreFund CshR	29	7.29	7.56	89.6

specified period (e.g., one month, six months, a year, or longer). Withdrawals before the expiration of the period are usually permitted subject to a forfeiture of a substantial portion of the interest otherwise earned on the CD.

When investing sums in excess of $100,000, the federally insured bank account or certificate of deposit does not provide protection against a partial loss in the event of bank failure. While bank failures may seem to be a remote possibility, when dealing with large sums of money even remote risks should be avoided. If the amount involved is not too large, complete protection can be obtained by making separate $100,000 deposits in different insured institutions or in accounts under different names in a single institution.

When the amount is so large that it is unwieldy to break it into $100,000 units, there are alternative investments that are either riskless or carry such slight risk of default that they are viewed as riskless. These investments include treasury bills or notes (see §18.18) and *high-quality commercial paper*. Commercial paper is unsecured debt maturing on a specific day in the future, usually 30 days or less. Commercial paper issued by large finance companies or major industrial corporations is generally viewed as being a risk-free investment for short-term investments. The yield is somewhat higher than for treasury bills, which are entirely risk-free.

Another investment is *bankers' acceptances* — short-term interest-bearing notes whose payment has been guaranteed by a major commercial bank. Acceptances arise out of commercial transactions, usually large international sales transactions. Payment may also be guaranteed by the parties to the underlying transaction and possibly by a lien on the goods themselves. Like high-quality commercial paper, bankers' acceptances are generally viewed as risk-free; the yield is also somewhat higher than for treasury bills.

A person investing very large sums of money on a short-term basis (over $100,000) may consider repurchase agreements (usually called *repos*). A repo is a loan structured as a sale; a bank "sells" an investor riskless securities — treasury instruments usually — while simultaneously agreeing to buy them back at a later date for a higher price. The difference in price represents interest to the investor. Repos may be overnight transactions or may continue for as long as a year.

Repos are widely used to avoid the risk of bank failure on investments in excess of $100,000. The theory is that if the bank fails while a repo is open, the customer simply keeps the securities sold to it. In this kind of transaction it is therefore important that the securities involved be in some way set aside for the investor, usually through a third-party escrow account. The investor should also get a list of the securities sold, including certificate numbers. Otherwise, the transaction may be viewed as an unsecured loan by a bankruptcy trustee or receiver. Repos generally earn somewhat more than banks pay on insured certificates of deposit for the same period.

A *reverse repo* is a repo from the standpoint of the dealer who is seeking to borrow securities in order to sell them. A dealer wishes to sell securities it borrows when it anticipates a price decline so that it can replace the securities at a lower price. In other words, it wishes to engage in a short sale of the securities that are the subject of the transaction.

§19.7 Investment Strategies for the Small Investor

There are many different investment strategies for the small investor. It is assumed in this discussion that the typical small investor is relatively risk adverse; he or she does not wish to risk the entire pool of capital on success in a single speculation. In most of the strategies described below, the investor's goal is to obtain a better return, either in the form of income or capital appreciation, than can be obtained from a riskless or virtually riskless investment of the types discussed in §§19.5 and 19.6. Obviously, one needs first to establish investment objectives and then diversify investments that are themselves consistent with those objectives. Plausible investment goals include:

1. *Preservation of assets.* When safety is the most important concern, one may simply invest the entire amount in one or more money market accounts, insured bank money market accounts or certificates of deposit (CDs), and short-term U.S. Treasury securities sold at discounts from face value. The selection may depend on relative yields and the likelihood that the investor may require access to his or her funds in the near future.

2. *Investment income.* When the primary goal is to earn investment income at minimal risk to principal, one might choose mutual funds concentrating in longer-term government securities, municipal bonds, quality corporate bonds, and high-income stocks such as utilities. One might also consider investing a portion of the principal in limited partnership interests investing in positive cash-flow-producing types of real estate investments and in open- or closed-end mutual funds that specialize in blue chip and overseas stocks.

3. *Capital appreciation.* When a person is willing to take a greater risk of loss of assets in exchange for the possibility of greater growth of principal assets, one might choose mutual funds that emphasize capital appreciation (though the performance of many of these funds historically has been disappointing) or direct investments in common stocks and real estate investments.

4. *Aggressive capital appreciation.* When a person is willing to assume a high risk of asset depreciation in exchange for higher growth or speculative increase in asset value, one might choose developmental projects such as real estate, investing either through stock or by direct purchases. One might also invest in stocks that are rumored to be candidates for takeover bids.

5. *Shooting for the moon.* An investor willing to risk the entire pool of capital for a large gain may well end up losing his or her capital. Appropriate investments for this strategy are described in the following chapter.

A plausible balanced portfolio for an investor with capital in the range of $100,000 or more today might include 35 percent in money market accounts or CDs, 25 percent in bonds or mutual funds specializing in bonds, 20 percent in stocks with high growth potential or mutual funds specializing in such stocks, 15 percent in real estate or limited partnerships investing in real estate, and 5 percent in individual growth stocks or a growth-oriented mutual fund. These percentages, of course, may change significantly with changes in economic conditions. Decisions whether to invest directly in stocks or bonds or in mutual funds depend on the amount of capital available for investment and the desire for diversification within the categories.

CHAPTER 20

OPTIONS, COMMODITIES, FUTURES, AND OTHER ESOTERICA

§20.1 Introduction

This chapter introduces the reader to a variety of investment vehicles, including standardized option contracts for securities and futures contracts for commodities and securities indexes. Many of these vehicles are extremely high-risk investments: They are attractive from a speculative standpoint primarily because they combine relatively small initial investments with a substantial potential for gain or loss. They are therefore suitable investments only for the sophisticated. In some situations, however, these investment devices may also be used to "hedge" established positions, that is, to protect existing investments from unacceptable declines in value. In this context, they are conservative rather than speculative in character.

The new securities discussed in this chapter are sometimes called *derivative securities* since their value may be based on, or be derived from, price movements in individual stocks (usually NYSE stocks) or on changes in stock indexes that themselves reflect a hypothetical portfolio of publicly traded stocks. See §§18.14 and 18.15. Elaborate computer-based trading strategies have been developed during the 1980s to take advantage of these new securities. These new strategies link the new markets for these derivative securities with the traditional markets for securities and have greatly increased the volatility and volume of trading in those traditional markets. Indeed, these new strategies are widely believed to have been major contributing forces to the October 1987 market decline.

Some of the investments vehicles described in this chapter are of comparatively recent origin. Others, such as trading in commodities futures, have existed for more than a century. They all share the common characteristic of being dynamic, though rather arcane, tools primarily for professional traders and speculators. Traditional stocks and bonds described in earlier chapters are sometimes referred to as "plain vanilla" securities by speculators to distinguish them from the securities discussed in this chapter.

This chapter deals only with the standard options and futures that are traded on established markets. This is the tip of an iceberg. There also exists a vast, and largely unregulated, over the-counter market for a variety of individually created options or rights with respect to securities or currencies. Some of these securities are so new that the risks involved in them may not be well understood even by the persons who create them. No attempt is made to describe the numerous varieties of newly created options or rights that may be available.

§20.2 Standardized Trading in Securities Options: Puts and Calls

Perhaps the easiest way to describe how standardized securities options work is to use a real-life example. Table 20-1 is the portion of the listed options quotations page of *The Wall Street Journal* for June 13, 1988 that contains the Chicago Board of Trade's listed options for IBM common stock for June 10, 1988.

There are two types of publicly traded options: (1) *call options* are options to purchase IBM stock at a fixed price for a limited period, and 2) *put options* are options to sell IBM stock at a fixed price for a limited period. The left hand column of Table 20-1 simply names the stock in question (IBM) and the closing price for that stock on the New York Stock Exchange (116⅛) for reference purposes. The second column, "Strike Price," is the price at which a specific option in question is exercisable. For this reason it is also sometimes called the *exercise price*. The strike price is fixed when the option is created and remains unchanged during the life of the option. IBM options are in the June - July - August expiration cycle, which means that separate options expire at the close of trading on the third Friday of the months of June, July, and August. Options on other publicly traded securities are on a variety of monthly cycles.

The columns under "Calls - Last" and "Puts - Last" are closing market prices for IBM options at the listed strike prices expiring in the month in question. Thus for IBM there are options potentially being traded at 6 different strike prices at 5-dollar intervals between 100 and 125, expiring at 3 different times, or 18 different potential call options on IBM stock. Similarly, there are 18 different potential put options, or a total of 36 different options on IBM in all (though neither put nor call options are traded or written at all the various possible variations). It must be conceded that information about a large number of different options is crammed into a small amount of space in Table 20-1.

Puts and calls are traded in units or blocks of options on 100 shares; the option unit on 100 shares is called a *contract*. The quotations in Table 20-1, however, are on a per-share rather than a per-contract basis.

Put and call options are referred to by the name of the stock, the strike price, the month of expiration, and where necessary, the nature of the option (i.e., a put or a call). For example, the "IBM June 120 call" option refers to the option in the fifth row, third column, of Table 20-1, priced at ¼ at the close on June 10.

Table 20-1

LISTED OPTIONS QUOTATIONS

Friday, June 10, 1988

**Options closing prices. Sales unit usually is 100 shares.
Stock close is New York or American exchange final price.**

CHICAGO BOARD

Option & Strike NY Close Price	Calls—Last			Puts—Last		
	Jun	Jul	Aug	Jun	Jul	Aug
I B M 100	s	16⅜	18¼	s	$3/16$	$11/16$
116⅛ 105	11⅛	12	14	$1/16$	$5/16$	1¼
116⅛ 110	6¼	7½	10½	$3/16$	$15/16$	2⅜
116⅛ 115	2	3⅞	7	⅞	$2 3/16$	4⅛
116⅛ 120	¼	1⅝	4¾	4⅛	5	6¾
116⅛ 125	s	$11/16$	5	s	8	s

r-Not Traded. s-No Option.

§20.2.1 Call Options

On June 10, 1988, the price of the IBM June 120 call option was $\frac{1}{4}$ or $0.25 per share. The price of a contract for this option was therefore $25.00. Obviously, for any significant speculation, a purchase of several hundred contracts would be feasible for even a person with modest means.

A person who purchased an IBM June 120 call contract would have acquired, at a cost of $25.00, the right to purchase 100 shares of IBM at 120 dollars per share at any time between the date of acquisition and the date of expiration on Friday, June 17, 1988. In this particular case, the expiration date is only seven days after the date of acquisition. A call option gets its name from the power of the purchaser to "call away" the stock from whoever granted the option.

Let us assume for the moment that the speculator has reason to believe that there will be a substantial run-up in IBM in the next week. Indeed, she fully expects that the price of IBM will rise 50 points in the next two weeks — from 116⅛ to 166⅛. This may sound unlikely, and indeed it is, but it is not impossible since IBM traded as high as 175 within the preceding 52 weeks (see Table 18-5 in Chapter 18) and similar increases in price commonly occur in takeover-candidate stocks in very short periods of time.

Assume also that our speculator has only about $12,000 to invest. If she were to buy IBM common stock, she can afford to purchase only 100 shares at cost of 116⅛ ($11,612.50 for 100 shares plus commission). If she can arrange a margin purchase, she can buy an extra 100 shares with the funds borrowed from her broker (see §18.16). If the price of IBM in fact rises to 166⅛ as expected and the speculator sells at this price, she will have made $5,000 ((166⅛ − 116⅛) × 100) less commissions on a straight purchase; if she makes a margin purchase, she will make about $10,000 ((166⅛ − 116⅛) × 200) less commissions and interest. These are certainly tidy profits for a 7-day investment.

But consider what happens if the speculator takes $12,000 and buys IBM June 120 call options: She can buy 480 contracts ($12,000 divided by 25.00) of 100 shares each, and thereby control 48,000 shares with those 480 contracts. Now, when the price goes up 50 points to 166⅛ our speculator is able to exercise the call option and buy 48,000 shares at 120 per share and immediately sell them in the open market for 166⅛. The gross profit is about $2,214,000, and the net profit after deducting the $12,000 cost of the options is about $2,200,000, all on a two-week speculation involving a $12,000 investment.

One can obviously get rich quickly on call options if one can correctly predict when a big run-up in price will occur. People who made fantastic profits on inside information during the insider trading scandals regularly used call options to maximize their gains from reliable inside information.

It is not necessary for the speculator to actually exercise the option to purchase the shares at 120 and then immediately resell them; the options themselves are publicly traded and as the options become valuable (usually described as being "in the money"), they can be sold by themselves. Thus, the $2,000,000 gross profit on IBM is obtainable by the speculator whether or not she has the capital to exercise options on 48,000 shares of IBM at 120 —

about $5,760,000. Nor is there any danger that the option writer will welsh upon this calamitous run-up in price of IBM; his or her performance is guaranteed by both the Chicago Board of Trade and the broker who arranged for the option to be written. Nor is there any danger that someone will goof up and a valuable option will go unexercised on the last day; brokerage firms regularly sweep option customers accounts and exercise all options that are "in the money."

There obviously has to be a downside risk to all of this get-rich-quick stuff. And indeed there is. A price run-up of 50 points is pretty unusual for IBM. That is about a 33 percent increase in price within a week. What happens if the speculator is wrong on her timing, and the price run-up does not occur and the price of IBM stock remains stable? If the speculator bought the stock itself, she is about even: IBM has remained stable in price and most of the $12,000 investment can be recovered simply by selling the stock. Even if the speculator had bought an extra 100 shares on margin, she still would come out basically all right. She is paying interest on the margin loan but the bulk of the $12,000 investment is still intact. But if the speculator had bought call options, they would have expired valueless near the end of June, and she would have lost the entire $12,000.

The June 120 IBM call option used in the last example is an "out of the money" option, since IBM would have to rise four points in price before it has any inherent value. The June 115 IBM option, on the other hand, is "in the money," since the stock is selling at 116⅛ and the option has an intrinsic value of 1⅛. This option sold for 2 on June 10: The difference between 1⅛ and 2 represents a premium for the possibility that IBM common stock may increase in price over the next two weeks before the option expires. The difference between 1⅛ and 2 is sometimes called the *time value* of the option to distinguish it from the option's intrinsic value. The purchase of the 115 option gives the buyer a great deal of upward leverage: if the price of IBM rises from 116⅛ to 117⅛ in one day, that is a tiny fractional rise in the stock of less than 1 percent. However, the 115 option will probably rise by a full point also; going from 2 to perhaps 2⅞ or 3 is about a 33 percent increase in a single day. A decline of IBM from 117⅛ to 116⅛ will also cause a much larger percentage decline in the 120 option, but it probably would be less than a full point. Do you see why? Hint: Why is there any value at all in any out-of-the-money option?

As one would intuitively expect, call options that expire in later months sell for more than options that expire in earlier months. While the IBM June 120 call option traded at ¼ on June 10, 1988, the IBM July 120 call option cost 1⅝ and the August 120 call option was priced at 4¾. Do you see why call options with later expiration dates are more valuable than otherwise identical options with earlier expiration dates?

The person who commits himself or herself to sell IBM shares upon the call of the option purchaser is called the *writer* of the option. Who writes call options? Any investor who owns 100 shares of IBM can write a call option on those shares but as a practical matter, most call options are written by substantial investors managing large portfolios. When a person writes an option and sells it on the Chicago Board of Trade, the writer receives the sales price of the option: The writer of the 480 contracts for IBM June 120 calls described above pockets the $12,000 sales price for the options (less a brokerage commission). If the option expires valueless, the writer keeps the $12,000, thereby improving the yield on the portfolio. If IBM unexpectedly moves up in price and the option is exercised, the writer will of course have to sell the shares at 120 (the strike price). The writer still has a profit to the extent of the difference between 116 and 120, but all profits above the strike price inure to the purchaser of the call option. That is what the purchaser of the call options bought for $12,000. Writing call options at above-market strike prices is generally profitable in stable or declining markets, since few or none of them will be exercised. If the market rises, the writer receives the strike price and the option purchaser the entire value of the stock above the strike price.

Some investors write call options without actually owning the shares. This is called *going naked* or writing *naked options*, and obviously is considerably more risky than writing *covered options*, namely options for which the writer already owns the shares. Writing a naked call option on IBM common stock is analogous, in terms of risk, to a short sale of IBM stock. If the price moves in an unfavorable direction, both the short seller and the writer of the uncovered call are required to go into the market to buy IBM stock on unfavorable terms to close out the transaction. Since the broker selling the uncovered call option is responsible for the production of the shares if the call is exercised, from its standpoint it is essential that the writer of an uncovered call post margin and that that margin be increased if the price of the underlying IBM stock rises during the life of the option.

Most writers of uncovered calls are securities firms or professional investors.

Call options may be purchased in order to hedge short sale positions. It will be recalled that a short seller borrows shares and sells them, hoping prices will decline so that he or she can replace the borrowed shares at a lower price. See §18.17. A short seller gets squeezed when prices move up rather than down; if the short seller is concerned about this prospect he or she can cover most of the risk by buying a call option on the same stock. (It is important to recognize that the last paragraph deals with the risk of the *writer* of the option not the *purchaser*; the present paragraph deals with a *purchaser* of the option who is exposed to a price rise because he or she previously sold short.) If the price goes up, the loss on the short sale position will be largely offset by the gain on the call. Whether or not this is desirable depends in part on how expensive the purchase of the call is, since that is the "premium" for this type of insurance.

§20.2.2 Put Options

A *put option* enables the purchaser of the put to profit on market declines. A put is the mirror image of a call option. The *writer* of a put option commits to buy the stock at the strike price for the specified period at the option of the buyer of the option. In a call, the writer commits to sell and the buyer of the call has the option whether or not to buy. In a put, the writer commits to buy and the buyer of the put has the option whether or not to sell.

For example, from Table 20-1 it will be seen that the IBM June 105 put option sold at ¹⁄₁₆ on June 10. If a person bought this put, and the price of IBM declined to 80, say, the holder of the put would show a profit equal to the difference between 105 and 80, minus the cost of the put option. In the vernacular, the holder of the put could "buy IBM at 80 and put it to the writer at 105." That is why it is called a put.

An examination of Table 20-1 shows the inverse relationship between puts and calls. When a call is in the money and has intrinsic value, the corresponding put must, by definition, be out of the money, and vice versa. Thus, the IBM 120 June call is out of the money since the stock price is 116⅛; the IBM 120 June put is in the money selling for 4⅛ dollars per share. It may be noted that this option has an intrinsic value of $3.875 (120 − 116⅛) and a time value of $0.375.

Since the writer of a put option only commits to purchase a stock at a specified price, there is no precisely analogous concept to writing naked call options on the put side. The writing of puts, however, can create devastating losses if there is a sudden strong downward movement in the price of the stock. The risk involved in writing put options is not apparent in a generally rising market (since relatively few out of the money puts are exercised and in the money puts are usually exercised to cut losses rather than to make a profit). Such a market existed from early 1982 through August 1987. Many brokers recommended to relatively unsophisticated clients during this period that the clients write put options to increase the investment yield of their portfolios. It seemed to be a relatively riskless way of increasing investment return. In the abrupt market decline that occurred in October 1987, many of these investors' savings were wiped out as brokerage firms liquidated entire portfolios in order to meet obligations under put contracts, and some ended up owing their brokerage firms substantial amounts as well. The writing of put options in excess of available at-risk capital is sometimes referred to as writing naked put options as an analogy to the risk involved in writing naked call options in a rising market.

It may be noted that the *writer* of a put option can limit future losses by *buying* an offsetting put option with the same maturity and strike price. Considerable protection may also be obtained by purchasing any in the money put option; partial protection may sometimes be obtained by writing call options. In a period of sharp market decline such as occurred in October 1987, the prices of puts advanced so rapidly (and the process of communicating securities orders was often so constricted) that these strategies were, as a practical matter, unavailable to at-risk put writers.

Puts may be purchased to shield portfolio positions from price declines; for example, a person with 100 shares of IBM who fears a short-term decline in the stock but who does not want to sell the shares, may purchase a put option for one hundred shares. If the price does decline, the loss of value in the underlying stock will be largely offset by the rise in value of the put.

§20.2.3 Summary of Options Trading

It is important to note that in options trading, the *purchaser* of a put or call option risks only the money he or she has invested in the option. If the price moves in the wrong direction, the holder of the option simply allows the option to expire unexercised. The *writer* of an option, on the other hand, is much more at the mercy of market forces.

One can speculate simultaneously on upward and downward movements (a strategy known as a *straddle*) by the purchase of options. One may buy, for example, a put on IBM at 115 for ⅞ (0.875) per share and a call on IBM at 120 for ¼ (0.25). The straddle thus costs 1⅛ (1.125) per share plus commissions. One makes money on this straddle if the price of IBM drops below about 113½ or rises above about 121½. One loses only if IBM steadily trades in the range betwen 113 and 121 for the balance of the option period.

Option trading requires a good sense of timing. In order to be profitable, an anticipated movement in stock prices must occur during the period of the option. Similarly, when one has a profit on an options position one must decide whether to take the profit or let the position ride (i.e., remain open) to improve the profitability. The danger, of course, is that the price movement may reverse itself and the profitable opportunity lost.

The following chart may be useful in assessing the relationship between investment strategies and standardized securities options:

To profit on expected fluctuations in securities prices, an investor should:

If the price is going up	*If the price is going down*
1) buy the stock	1) sell the stock
2) buy the stock on margin	2) sell the stock short
3) buy calls	3) write calls
4) write puts	4) buy puts

§20.3 Options on Indexes, Foreign Currencies, and Interest Rates

Options trading — the writing and selling of puts and calls — can be extended to any product that fluctuates in price. Rather than writing an option on a single stock, one can write an option on a bundle of stocks. One can write an option on a stock index. One can write an option on foreign currencies (whose values fluctuate with respect to U.S. dollars). One can write options on treasury notes or treasury bonds (whose values fluctuate solely in response to interest rate changes since they are viewed as riskless investments). The only real requirement is that the price moves.

Indeed, marketable options are traded on all of the nonstock interests referred to in the previous paragraph. Table 20-2 is a partial listing of trading in these nonstock options as reported by *The Wall Street Journal* for June 10, 1988. The variety of indexes and currencies for which options are currently traded is interesting. The only real difference in operation between traditional securities options described in the previous section and these nonstock options is that one cannot usually receive or deliver the underlying indexes when the option is exercised; one has to settle up in cash.

Table 20-2

INDEX OPTIONS

Friday, June 10, 1988

Chicago Board

S&P 100 INDEX

Strike Price	Calls–Last Jun	Jul	Aug	Puts–Last Jun	Jul	Aug
220	....	....	....	....	½	1⅜
225	34⅛	35	37	1/16	11/16	1⅞
230	28½	32	....	⅛	1 1/16	2 11/16
235	23	26	28	⅛	1 9/16	3¼
240	18¼	21½	23½	¼	2¼	4¼
245	13¼	16¾	19½	½	3⅛	5½
250	8⅜	12¼	16¾	15/16	4½	7
255	4½	9	12¼	2¼	6¼	8⅞
260	1¾	6¼	9½	4½	8⅝	11
265	9/16	4⅛	7	8⅜	11½	12⅜
270	3/16	2 9/16	4¾	12½	14¾	16½
275	1/16	1 9/16	3½	....	19⅛	20⅛

Total call volume 135,460 Total call open int. 330,010
Total put volume 103,132 Total put open int. 375,545
The index: High 260.14; Low 257.12; Close 257.95, +0.83

S&P 500 INDEX

Strike Price	Calls–Last Jun	Jul	Sep	Puts–Last Jun	Jul	Sep
210	....	....	....	1/16	....	....
215	....	....	....	....	....	15/16
230	....	....	....	1/16	½	....
235	....	....	....	1/16	¾	....
240	....	....	....	1/16	1	....
245	....	....	33	⅛	1¼	4⅛
250	23½	....	27¾	¼	....	4½
255	18¼	....	25½	⅜	2¾	....
260	11¼	....	....	11/16	....	....
265	7½	11	....	1 5/16	4¼	7¾
270	4	8¾	14	2¾	7	10¼
275	1⅝	....	11¼	6	8⅛	12½
280	⅝	4⅞	8⅜	7⅝	10⅜	....

Total call volume 10,524 Total call open int. 228,277
Total put volume 3,643 Total put open int. 234,708
The index: High 273.21; Low 270.20; Close 271.26, +1.06

American Exchange

MAJOR MARKET INDEX

Strike Price	Calls–Last Jun	Jul	Aug	Puts–Last Jun	Jul	Aug
365	46⅜	....	....	⅛	1¾	....
370	39¾	39½	....	3/16	2	....
375	....	....	....	¼	2¼	5
380	31¾	....	....	⅜	3¼	6½
385	23	....	....	⅝	4¼	7⅛
390	19	27½	....	1	5¼	7⅛
395	16	....	....	1½	6	9⅜
400	9⅝	17⅛	....	2¼	7½	11
405	5⅞	13	18¼	4	10	....
410	3⅝	10½	16¾	6	12⅜	....
415	1 11/16	9½	....	8	....	....

Total call volume 14,126 Total call open int. 29,814
Total put volume 13,191 Total put open int. 38,866
The index: High 411.72; Low 406.56; Close 407.61, +0.96

COMPUTER TECHNOLOGY INDEX

Strike Price	Calls–Last Jun	Jul	Aug	Puts–Last Jun	Jul	Aug
110	....	5½	....	....	....	....
115	....	....	....	....	3¾	....

Total call volume 30 Total call open int. 349
Total put volume 2 Total put open int. 267
The index: High 114.30; Low 112.73; Close 113.21, +0.47

INSTITUTIONAL INDEX

Strike Price	Calls–Last Jun	Jul	Aug	Puts–Last Jun	Jul	Aug
240	....	....	....	1/16	⅞	....
245	....	....	....	⅛	1½	....
250	....	....	....	3/16	....	....
255	....	....	....	7/16	....	....
260	9	....	....	13/16	....	....
265	5	....	....	1⅞	5⅛	....
270	2½	....	....	4⅛	7½	....
275	11/16	....	....	7¼	....	....
280	⅛	3¼	....	....	....	....
285	1/16	2	3⅝	....	....	....

Total call volume 2,643 Total call open int. 39,921
Total put volume 1,770 Total put open int. 42,326
The index: High 270.57; Low 267.41; Close 268.43, +1.02

Philadelphia Exchange

GOLD/SILVER INDEX

Strike Price	Calls–Last Jun	Jul	Aug	Puts–Last Jun	Jul	Aug
95	....	....	....	....	....	1
100	9	....	....	....	....	....
105	4⅜	....	....	....	2⅝	....
110	1	3½	....	2⅝	4½	....
115	¼	....	....	6⅛	....	....

Total call volume 107 Total call open int. 507
Total put volume 68 Total put open int. 993
The index: High 111.51; Low 109.11; Close 109.22, −0.95

VALUE LINE INDEX OPTIONS

Strike Price	Calls–Last Jun	Jul	Aug	Puts–Last Jun	Jul	Aug
205	....	....	....	....	....	⅞
210	....	....	....	....	....	1¼
220	....	....	....	....	....	2⅛
235	....	....	....	⅝	....	....
240	5¼	....	....	....	....	....
245	1¾	....	....	....	....	....

Total call volume 275 Total call open int. 1,556
Total put volume 170 Total put open int. 693
The index: High 241.81; Low 240.26; Close 241.23, +1.0

NATIONAL O-T-C INDEX

Strike Price	Calls–Last Jun	Jul	Aug	Puts–Last Jun	Jul	Aug
220	....	....	....	1/16	....	....
245	11	....	....	....	....	....
250	....	....	....	1	....	....
255	2⅜	....	....	2⅛	....	....
260	⅞	....	....	....	....	....

Total call volume 42 Total call open int. 86
Total put volume 16 Total put open int. 112
The index: High 256.42; Low 253.57; Close 255.69, +1.47

Pacific Exchange

FINANCIAL NEWS COMPOSITE INDEX

Strike Price	Calls–Last Jun	Jul	Sep	Puts–Last Jun	Jul	Sep
165	21⅜	....	....	....	....	....
170	16¾	....	....	....	....	....
175	11⅜	....	....	....	....	....
180	6⅞	9⅜	....	⅝	....	....
185	2½	....	....	1½	....	....
190	⅝	4¼	....	4¼	....	....
195	⅛	....	....	8⅝	....	....
200	1/16	....	....	13⅜	....	....
205	....	....	....	18¼	....	....

Total call volume 1,434 Total call open int. 7,519
Total put volume 297 Total put open int. 4,058
The index: High 187.71; Low 185.28; Close 186.36, +1.08

N.Y. Stock Exchange

NYSE INDEX OPTIONS

Strike Price	Calls–Last Jun	Jul	Aug	Puts–Last Jun	Jul	Aug
130	....	....	....	....	3/16	....
140	....	....	....	....	11/16	....
145	9⅞	....	....	⅛	1¾	2⅝
147½	7⅜	9⅛	....	5/16	....	....
150	4 1/16	7¼	8⅛	½	2 13/16	4
152½	2⅛	5⅜	....	1 7/16	....	....
155	11/16	3⅝	....	2⅞	5	....
157½	5/16	....	....	....	....	....
160	⅛	1¼	....	....	9	9½
165	....	⅝	....	....	....	....

Total call volume 1,490. Total call open int. 11,886.
Total put volume 989. Total put open int. 11,924.
The index: High 153.82; Low 152.35; Close 152.89, +0.53

Table 20-2 *(cont.)*

FOREIGN CURRENCY OPTIONS

Philadelphia Exchange

Friday, June 10, 1988

Option & Underlying	Strike Price	Calls—Last Jun	Jul	Sep	Puts—Last Jun	Jul	Sep
50,000 Australian Dollars-cents per unit.							
ADollr	...79	1.78	r	r	r	r	r
80.75	...80	0.81	1.36	r	r	r	r
80.75	...81	r	0.82	1.22	r	r	r
80.75	...82	r	0.50	r	r	r	r
12,500 British Pounds-cents per unit.							
BPound	155	26.85	s	r	r	s	r
181.98	.170	11.70	s	r	r	s	0.34
181.68	172½	r	r	r	r	r	0.51
181.68	.175	6.70	r	r	r	r	0.90
181.68	177½	4.20	4.50	r	r	r	r
181.68	.180	2.00	r	r	r	1.30	2.65
181.68	182½	0.02	1.65	2.75	0.80	r	r
181.68	.185	r	0.72	1.80	3.25	r	r
181.68	187½	r	0.35	1.15	5.70	r	r
181.68	.190	r	r	r	r	8.20	r
181.68	192½	r	r	r	r	10.65	r
12,500 British Pounds-European Style.							
181.68	.180	1.85	r	r	r	r	r
50,000 Canadian Dollars-cents per unit.							
CDollr	...77	5.01	s	r	r	s	r
82.00	...78	3.99	r	r	r	r	r
82.00	...79	3.01	r	r	r	r	0.32
82.00	...80	1.92	r	r	r	r	r
82.00	.80½	1.44	1.56	r	r	r	r
82.00	...81	1.00	r	1.27	r	0.22	r
82.00	.81½	0.47	r	r	0.02	r	r
82.00	...82	0.02	0.44	r	0.05	r	r
82.00	.82½	r	0.30	r	r	r	r
50,000 Canadian Dollars-European Style.							
CDollar	79½	r	2.33	r	r	r	r
82.00	...80	1.99	r	1.87	r	r	r
82.00	.80½	1.51	r	r	r	0.10	r
82.00	...81	1.04	r	r	r	r	r
82.00	.81½	r	r	r	r	0.32	r
62,500 West German Marks-cents per unit.							
DMark	..52	r	6.29	r	r	r	r
58.09	...54	4.18	r	r	r	r	r
58.09	...55	3.22	r	r	r	r	r
58.09	...56	2.19	r	r	r	r	r
58.09	...57	1.11	1.57	r	r	r	0.41
58.09	...58	0.05	0.80	r	0.01	r	0.75
58.09	...59	r	0.27	0.87	0.94	r	1.24
58.09	...60	r	0.09	0.50	1.86	1.85	r
58.09	...61	r	r	0.30	2.85	r	r
62,500 West German Marks-European Style.							
58.09	...58	r	r	r	0.02	r	r
6,250,000 Japanese Yen-100ths of a cent per unit.							
JYen	...71	9.04	s	r	r	s	r
80.03	...72	8.01	s	r	r	s	0.02
80.03	...73	7.05	s	r	r	s	0.02
80.03	...75	5.05	r	r	r	r	r
80.03	...76	4.05	r	r	r	r	r
80.03	...77	3.00	r	r	r	r	0.21
80.03	...78	2.07	r	r	r	0.12	0.34
80.03	...79	0.96	r	r	r	0.28	r
80.03	...80	0.04	0.89	r	0.05	0.55	r
80.03	...81	r	0.43	1.07	r	r	1.50
80.03	...82	r	0.18	r	r	r	r
6,250,000 Japanese Yen-European Style.							
80.03	...80	r	r	r	0.02	r	r
62,500 Swiss Francs-cents per unit.							
SFranc	..61	8.63	s	r	r	s	r
69.52	...62	7.65	s	r	r	s	r
69.52	...63	6.63	s	r	r	s	r
69.52	...69	r	r	r	r	0.42	r
69.52	...70	0.02	0.72	1.63	0.46	0.84	r
69.52	...71	r	0.41	r	1.31	r	r
69.52	...72	r	0.16	r	2.35	2.56	r
62,500 Swiss Francs-European Style.							
69.52	...72	r	r	r	2.25	r	r

Total call vol.	10,742	Call open int.	579,050
Total put vol.	14,052	Put open int.	540,074

r—Not traded. s—No option offered.
Last is premium (purchase price).

INTEREST RATE OPTIONS

Friday, June 10, 1988

For Notes and Bonds, decimals in closing prices represent 32nds; 1.01 means 1 1/32. For Bills, decimals in closing prices represent basis points; $25 per .01.

Chicago Board Options Exchange

U.S. TREASURY BOND—$100,000 principal value

Underlying Issue	Strike Price	Calls—Last Jun	Jul	Sep	Puts—Last Jun	Jul	Sep
9⅛% (ybl) due 5/2018	100	....	....	....	0.10	....	....

Total call vol. 0	Call open int. 4,022
Total put vol. 30	Put open int. 2,047

5-YEAR U.S. TREASURY NOTE—$100,000 principal value

Total call vol. 0	Call open int. 187
Total put vol. 0	Put open int. 1

3 p.m. prices of underlying issues supplied by The Chicago Corporation: T-Bonds 12% 124.20; 8¾% 96.01; 8⅞% 97.21; 9⅛% 100.20. T-Notes 7⅝% 96.13; 8¼% 99.02; 8¾% 100.01.

Options indexes were introduced in the 1980s and quickly became extremely popular, particularly before the October 1987 decline in securities prices. Table 20-3 shows the most active options traded on the Chicago Board and the American and New York exchanges as of June 10, 1988. These include both stock and nonstock options. It will be noted that in terms of volume, most options trading is in index options, and that the S & P 100 index option traded on the Chicago Board has the widest following of any single option. The Major Market Index traded on the AMEX and the NYSE Index traded on the New York are both index options. Indeed the only true stock option that made the list of most popular options trading on the Chicago Board on June 10 was the IBM June 115 call option.

The possibility of using puts and calls on individual stocks to hedge against price movements has previously been noted. Is there any social benefit to the trading of index options described in this section? Or are they pure gambling on price movements in abstract numbers? These questions have evoked some controversy. Basically, options package the risk components of investments in units that can be traded separately from the underlying stocks. Index options permit investors with large and diversified portfolios to hedge against broad price movements. On the other hand, index options appear to many to be legalized gambling on price movements in stock prices generally.

§20.4 Commodities Trading in General

Commodities trading, primarily based in Chicago, and to a lesser extent in New York, has existed for more than a century. Until relatively recently, it did not involve trading in securities, but that has changed significantly in recent years. The options trading described in the previous sections illustrates the gradual broadening of the products traded on these traditional commodities exchanges, particularly the Chicago Board of Trade. This section deals with traditional commodities trading; the following section briefly discusses financial futures.

§20.4.1 The Spot Market

The traditional commodities market consists of two separate markets. The market for commodities available today — commodities located in warehouses or storage silos — is the *cash market* or *spot market*. Table 20-4 shows cash market prices for June 10, 1988. These products may be sold by sample or quality designation or description. They are actual goods available for delivery. This market is used by suppliers, producers, and users of the various commodities that are traded. The prices of many commodities are quite volatile and may change quickly. Most of the trading and speculative interest in commodities is not in the cash market, however, but in the futures market described in the following paragraphs.

Table 20-3

MOST ACTIVE OPTIONS

CHICAGO BOARD

		Sales	Last	Chg.	N.Y. Close
CALLS					
SP100	Jun260	32260	1¾	— ⅝	257.95
SP100	Jun255	24809	4½	— ½	257.95
SP100	Jun265	20627	9-16	— 5-16	257.95
SP100	Jun250	8037	8⅜	— ⅜	257.95
I B M	Jun115	7841	2	+ ¼	116⅛
PUTS					
SP100	Jun255	25221	2¼	— 7-16	257.95
SP100	Jun250	17709	15-16	— 5-16	257.95
SP100	Jun260	12096	4½	— ⅜	257.95
SP100	Jun245	7955	½	— 3-16	257.95
SP100	Jul250	7451	4½	+ ⅛	257.95

AMERICAN

		Sales	Last	Chg.	N.Y. Close
CALLS					
Apple	Jul40	5552	5	+ 1	44½
MMIdx	Jun410	3501	3⅜	— ⅞	407.61
MMIdx	Jun415	3485	1 11-16	— 13-16	407.61
Apple	Jul45	3290	1 11-16	+ 9-16	44½
MMIdx	Jun420	3185	13-16	— 7-16	407.61
PUTS					
MMIdx	Jun405	3269	4	— ¼	407.61
MMIdx	Jun400	2317	2¼	— ⅛	407.61
MacMil	Jun70	1817	⅛	— 11-16	75⅞
MMIdx	Jun395	1308	1½	— 1-16	407.61
MMIdx	Jun390	1298	1	....	407.61

NEW YORK

		Sales	Last	Chg.	N.Y. Close
CALLS					
NY Idx	Jun155	580	11-16	— 3-16	152.89
IrvBk	Jun65	558	1¼	+ ¼	65
Maytag	Jul25	441	¾	— 3-16	23½
IrvBk	Jul65	371	2¾	+ ½	65
CSoup	Aug25	216	2	+ ⅛	25⅞
PUTS					
NY Idx	Jun150	365	½	— 5-16	152.89
NY Idx	Jun155	243	2⅞	+ ⅜	152.89
NY Idx	Jun152½	102	1 7-16	+ 1-16	152.89
AmStd	Jul75	100	⅛	+ 1-16	77¼
NY Idx	Jun145	80	⅛	— ⅛	152.89

§20.4.2 *The Commodities Futures Market*

Table 20-5 shows the quotations for the *futures* markets for two staple agricultural commodities — corn and oats — for June 10, 1988. Unlike the spot market, the futures market reflects trading in hypothetical units of corn or oats for delivery at specific times in the future. The futures market for corn is a good example. Table 20-5 reflects trading on June 10, 1988 in hypothetical 5,000 bushel units of corn for future delivery: July, September and December,

484

Table 20-4

CASH PRICES

Friday June 10, 1988.
(Quotations as of 4 p.m. Eastern time)

GRAINS AND FEEDS

	Fri	Thurs	Yr.Ago
Barley, top-quality Mpls., bu	3.30-.40	3.10-.25	1.90
Bran, wheat middlings, KC ton	82.00	75.00	36.00
Corn, No. 2 yel. Cent-III. bu	bp2.41	2.36½	1.75
Corn Gluten Feed, Midwest, ton ..	95.-125.	95.-125.	91.00
Cottnsd Meal, Clksdle, Miss. ton	197½-210	197½-212½	151.25
Hominy Feed, Cent-III. ton	76.00	75.00	57.00
Meat-Bonemeal, 50% pro. III. ton .	335.00	335.00	230.00
Oats, No. 2 milling, Mpls., bu	3.05	3.00-.05	1.56
Sorghum, (Milo) No. 2 Gulf cwt ...	4.52	4.39	3.57
Soybean Meal,			
Decatur, Illinois ton.................	284.-287.	281.-284.	197.50
Soybeans, No. 1 yel Cent.-III. bu ...	bp8.47½	8.49½	5.59
Sunflwr Sd No. 1 Duluth/Supr cwt	11.00	10.95	8.50
Wheat, Spring 14%-pro Mpls. bu ..	4.42	4.37	3.00¼
Wheat, No. 2 sft red, St.Lou. bu ..	3.53	3.52½	2.53½
Wheat, No. 2 hard KC, bu	3.77½	3.68½	2.69

FOODS

	Fri	Thurs	Yr.Ago
Beef, 700-900 lbs. Mid-U.S.,lb.fob .	n.a.	1.09	n.a.
Broilers, Dressed "A" NY lb	x.6626	.6571	.5018
Butter, AA, Chgo., lb.	1.32	1.32	1.44
Cocoa, Ivory Coast, $metric ton ..	g1,873	1,870	2,091
Coffee, Brazilian, NY lb.	n1.23	1.23	1.10
Eggs, Lge white, Chgo doz.	.48-.54	.48-.54	.57
Flour, hard winter KC cwt	9.65	9.65	7.90
Hams, 17-20 lbs, Mid-US lb fob	n.a.	67.00	n.a.
Hogs, Iowa-S.Minn. avg. cwt	49.50	50.00	61.75
Hogs, Omaha avg cwt	47.50	48.25	61.50
Pork Bellies, 12-14 lbs Mid-US lb ..	n.a.	.50	n.a.
Pork Loins, 14-17 lbs. Mid-US lb ...	n.a.	1.12	n.a.
Steers, Tex.-Okla. ch avg cwt ...	74.75	74.75	70.50
Steers, Feeder, Okl Cty, av cwt ...	87.15	87.15	77.00
Sugar, cane, raw, world, lb. fob ...	.0992	.0977	.0633

FATS AND OILS

	Fri	Thurs	Yr.Ago
Coconut Oil, crd, N. Orleans lb. ...	xxn.26	.26	.21½
Corn Oil, crd wet mill, Chgo. lb. ..	n.25	.25	.23½
Corn Oil, crd dry mill, Chgo. lb. ..	n.25	.25	.22½
Cottonseed Oil, crd Miss Vly lb. ..	n.26	.26	.19½
Grease, choice white, Chgo lb.	b.14¾	.14¾	.13½
Lard, Chgo lb.	.17½	.17½	.14½
Linseed Oil, raw Mpls lb.	n.a.	n.a.	.25
Palm Oil, ref. bl. deod. N.Orl. lb. .	n.22¾	.22¾	.17
Peanut Oil, crd, Southeast lb.	n.32	.32	.25½
Soybean Oil, crd, Decatur, lb.	.2502	.2524	.1586
Tallow, bleachable, Chgo lb.	.17	.17	.13¼
Tallow, edible, Chgo lb.	.18½	.18½	.16

FIBERS AND TEXTILES

	Fri	Thur	Yr. Ago
Burlap, 10 oz. 40-in. NY yd	n.2845	.2845	.2400
Cotton 1 1/16 in str lw-md Mphs lb	.6372	.6340	.7163
Print Cloth, poly/cot. 48-in. NY yd	s.51	.51	.65
Wool, 64s, Staple, Terr. del. lb.	4.50	4.50	2.70

METALS

	Fri	Thur	Yr. Ago
Aluminum ingot lb. del. Midwest .	q1.26-.32	1.26-.32	.73¼
Copper cathodes lb	p1.17-.20	1.15-.18	.74¾
Copper Scrap, No 2 wire NY lb	k.84	.82	.54¾
Lead, lb.	p.36	.36	.36
Mercury 76 lb. flask NY	q355-365	345.-355.	315.00
Steel Scrap 1 hvy mlt Chgo ton	105.-113.	105.-113.	82.50
Tin composite lb.	q4.4132	4.4200	4.1770
Zinc High grade lb	p.60-.63	.60-.63	.46½

MISCELLANEOUS

	Fri	Thur	Yr. Ago
Rubber, smoked sheets, NY lb.	n.72½	.72	.50¾

PRECIOUS METALS

	Fri	Thur	Yr. Ago
Gold, troy oz			
Engelhard indust bullion	459.03	456.87	457.10
Engelhard fabric prods	481.98	479.71	479.96
Handy & Harman base price	457.60	455.45	455.45
London fixing AM 4571.0 PM ...	457.60	455.45	455.45
Krugerrand, whol	a450.00	457.75	456.75
Maple Leaf, troy oz.	a464.00	472.25	469.00
American Eagle, troy oz.	a464.00	472.25	469.00
Platinum, (Free Mkt.)	569.50	579.00	587.00
Platinum, indust (Engelhard)	580.00	577.00	585.00
Platinum, fabric prd (Engelhard)	680.00	677.00	635.00
Palladium, indust (Engelhard) ...	129.75	129.50	139.00
Palladium, fabrc prd (Englhard)	144.75	144.50	154.00
Silver, troy ounce			
Engelhard indust bullion	7.070	7.155	7.720
Engelhard fabric prods	7.565	7.656	8.260
Handy & Harman base price	7.080	7.105	7.700
London Fixing (in pounds)			
Spot (U.S. equiv. $7.1300) ...	3.9185	3.8450	4.7535
3 months	4.0015	3.9260	4.8550
6 months	4.0880	4.0120	4.9500
1 year	4.2715	4.1905	5.1500
Coins, whol $1,000 face val	a5,295	5,425	5,980

a-Asked. b-Bid. bp-Country elevator bids to producers. c-Corrected. d-Dealer market. e-Estimated. g-Main crop, ex-dock, warehouses, Eastern Seaboard, north of Hatteras. j.-f.o.b. warehouse. k-Dealer selling prices in lots of 40,000 pounds or more, f.o.b. buyer's works. n-Nominal. p-Producer price. q-Metals Week. r-Rail bids. s-Thread count 78x54. x-Less than truckloads. z-Not quoted. xx-f.o.b. tank-cars.

1988, and March, May, July, September, and December of 1989. On June 10, 1988, one could buy or sell corn in 5,000-bushel units for future delivery in December, 1988 for $2.83 per bushel, or corn for delivery in December, 1989 for $2.54 a bushel. These transactions must be in the standard 5,000-bushel units. Let us assume that you decide on June 10, 1988 to purchase 5,000 bushels of corn for December, 1988 delivery. For simplicity, let us further assume that the price of December 1987 corn when you actually entered into this transaction is $2.85 per bushel. As a result of this transaction you have made a commitment to buy 5,000 bushels of corn next December; if the purchase were actually carried out, the transaction would involve $14,250 ($2.85 × 5,000). On the other hand, it is essential to realize that you have not actually bought any corn in the physical sense: You have simply committed yourself to buy corn next December at $2.85 per bushel.

The price of December 1987 corn varies from day to day, hour to hour, and minute to minute during each trading day for reasons to be discussed

Table 20-5

FUTURES PRICES

Friday, June 10, 1988

Open Interest Reflects Previous Trading Day.

	Open	High	Low	Settle	Change	Lifetime High	Low	Open Interest
—GRAINS AND OILSEEDS—								
CORN (CBT) 5,000 bu.; cents per bu.								
July	260	262	255	257¾	+ 4	262	174	54,703
Sept	269	270½	263½	265½	+ 3¼	270½	180¾	30,072
Dec	283	283	275	278¼	+ 3½	283	184	93,272
Mr89	287	290	281½	284½	+ 2¾	290	193½	12,866
May	292	292½	286	288½	+ 3	292½	207½	4,329
July	292½	294	288	289	+ 2½	294	233	2,244
Sept	267	269	267	267¼	+ 3¼	275	245	227
Dec	254	258½	253	253	+ 1	270	235	1,347
Est vol 65,000; vol Thur 77,540; open int 199,060, +3,150.								
OATS (CBT) 5,000 bu.; cents per bu.								
July	260	260	260	260	+10	260	144	2,957
Sept	263½	263½	263½	263½	+10	263½	143	3,469
Dec	266	266	263	265	+ 9	266	162	2,742
Mr89	259	260	254	255	+ 5	260	171	596
Est vol 1,000; vol Thur 3,768; open int 9,805, +181.								

shortly. Both the Chicago Board of Trade (where your purchase was executed) and the securities broker that placed your order are responsible for the performance of your obligation to buy the corn. Therefore, when you "buy the future," that is, when you enter into the contract to buy 5,000 bushels of corn at $2.85 per bushel next December, you must post some money to assure that you will carry out your commitment. When you buy the future you will be required to put up perhaps 10 percent of the total purchase price of $14,250, or $1,425 in cash. This up-front payment is called *margin*, but it differs in a fundamental way from a margin purchase of stock discussed in §18.16. In a purchase of stock on margin, the broker is actually lending the investor funds to purchase shares, and the margin required is actually a down payment on the purchase price. In a margin transaction for stock, interest is charged on the unpaid balance. In the case of margin in a commodities future transaction no credit is extended to buy anything; the margin in this context is somewhat analogous to a performance bond. Further, no interest is charged on a commodities future transaction since no funds have been advanced by the broker.

The futures market does not differentiate between buyers and sellers with respect to margin: If you believed on June 10 that corn prices were going down, you could sell the future, that is, enter into a contract to sell 5,000 bushels of corn in December, for $2.85 per bushel through your broker. The terms would be precisely the same as though you had purchased corn: You would have to post about $1,425 margin with your broker.

§20.4.3 The Purchase or Sale of Commodities Futures or of the Commodities Themselves

A speculator who expects the price of a commodity to go up purchases a futures contract for that commodity; a person who expects the price to go down sells a futures contract. One interesting aspect of futures trading is that a person can buy or sell commodities for future delivery in the futures market, speculating on the prices of commodities for years without ever acquiring, owning, or selling the commodities themselves. A speculator in corn, for example, never needs to own a single grain of real corn despite a lifetime of trading in corn futures.

Virtually none of the delivery obligations created by futures contracts actually leads to delivery of the commodity. In order to see how this works, let us follow through on the preceding hypotheticals to show a speculation in corn futures. Let us assume first that you buy a corn futures contract on June 10, 1988 for $2.85 per bushel. Over the summer, the drought continues to worsen, the potential corn harvest continues to decline, and the price of corn continues to spiral upwards. By November 10, the price of December 1988 corn has risen to $3.15 per bushel. Clearly, you have made a profit, but how do you realize upon it? In the world of commodities futures you do not "assign" or "turn in" or "sell" your contract to buy. Nor do you await delivery and then sell the corn itself on the spot market. Rather, you simply enter into another futures contract to sell December 1988 corn at $3.15 per bushel on November 10. When this transaction is executed, you have *netted out* or *closed out your position*. Since you now have commitments both to buy and to sell the standard trading unit of December 1988 corn, you do not owe the market any corn and the market does not owe you any corn. At that point your account with your broker reflects only the purchase of December corn for $14,250 and the sale of December corn for $15,750 ($3.15 × 5,000) for a profit of $1,500. You are neither long nor short in corn. Your cash account with the broker, available for future commodities speculation now contains $2,925, the profit on the transaction in December corn plus the $1,425 cash originally put up as the performance bond.

This process of netting out, of course, works equally well if you originally sold a corn future. You simply buy a corn future with the same maturity, and your position is netted out. This process is so well established, so universal, that it is reflected in the commission structure for commodities futures. Only a single commission is charged for the dual step of buying a future and then closing it out. Thus, in the normal and routine futures transaction, if a position has not been closed out and the date of delivery is drawing near, one avoids the nuisance of accepting or tendering delivery by entering into an offsetting contract. This is not to say that deliveries under futures contracts never occur. If a user of corn, a producer of corn oil, say, decides it needs the corn in December, it simply does not net out its position; then delivery of 5,000 bushels of real corn is required under the standardized futures contract. A speculator who fails to net out similarly would have to make or accept delivery. This transaction, however, would be in the form of a warehouse receipt: A speculator who is long in corn runs no risk of awakening one morning to see a truck pulling up with 5,000 bushels of corn to be dumped in his front yard.

For every futures transaction, there must be both a buyer and a seller. The process, however, is as totally anonymous as on a securities exchange: The buyer has no idea of the identity of the seller and vice versa. Indeed, since the Chicago Board of Trade guarantees each trade, it in effect becomes the buyer for each seller and the seller for each buyer, once the transaction has been verified. Because of the settlement process that is followed, there is also no limit on the number of futures contracts that can be written. Theoretically, there may be more open contracts to deliver grain in the future than all the grain that actually exists in the world. Usually, however, the numbers are more modest. Table 20-5 provides information as to the number of futures contracts opened on June 10, 1988: approximately 65,000 futures contracts in corn. Further, the third item in the bottom line, "open int 199,060" indicates that there exist 199,060 contracts for future delivery of corn that have not yet been closed out by an offsetting purchase at the close of trading on that date.

As the date of delivery draws nearer, the open interest declines as more and more speculators net out. On the delivery date, the open interest is down virtually to zero.

§20.4.4 Commodities Futures Trading Is Speculative

Futures trading may lead to huge speculative gains or losses on rather small investments. In the above example there was a return of $1,500 on a $1,425 investment in 5 months: That is an annualized return of over 250 percent per year. Of course, the buyer assumed a considerable risk by purchasing that December 1987 corn. If the price of corn had declined, the loss could easily have exceeded the initial $1,425 investment. If the price of December corn had declined to $2.50, for example, the buyer would have incurred a loss of $1,750 (5,000 × 2.50 = 12,500 − 14,250 = −1,750). If it had dropped to $2.30, the loss would have been $2,750 (5,000 × 2.30 = 11,500 − 14,250 = −2,750). Before losses of these magnitudes would occur, the broker would have had to be assured that the buyer had sufficient assets to cover the loss — either free capital or freshly posted additional margin made after a margin call — or the broker would close out the transaction on its own. See §20.4.2.

There is so much speculation possible in commodities futures because (1) commodities often exhibit substantial price movements, and (2) a purchaser's or seller's net gain or loss on a futures transaction is measured by the price movement of a large amount of the commodity, but the actual capital invested is approximately 10 percent of the total value of the commodity. Again, it is a species of leverage, though in this case there is no actual use of borrowed capital.

§20.4.5 Marking to Market

Margin calls are common in the commodities futures business since only a small payment is required to carry a much more substantial position. In the foregoing example, a $1,425 payment enables one to have the advantages or risks of price movements on 5,000 bushels of corn worth ten times the amount of the payment. In this market, each person's account is *marked to market* on a daily basis. Marked to market simply means that the margin position of the account is recalculated each day. The price used is the price set forth in the

"Settle" column of Table 20-5. If the price moves in a favorable direction, the account, when marked to market, will show a surplus over the minimum needed to carry the position: That surplus may be withdrawn or used to buy additional futures contracts. In other words, one can "pyramid" a successful futures speculation very easily. If the price moves in an unfavorable direction, the margin in the account is marked down. The Chicago Board of Trade limits the maximum price movements that can occur in a single day in the futures market. Trading is suspended when the maximum change in a single day occurs. This enables all accounts to be marked to market before trading is resumed the next day.

$20.4.6 The Trading Floor for Commodities Futures

Trading in commodities futures is quite unlike trading on the New York Stock Exchange and other securities exchanges. The Chicago Board of Trade is a place, where traders come to trade. The trading for each commodity takes place in separate *pits*, which are large depressions in the floor: Persons trading contracts for a specified month stand on the same step or level within the pit. Trading is by outcry and hand signal, with purchasers and sellers of the futures often trading on small price movements. You may have seen photographs of this hectic process — traders screaming and shouting in the pits. Repeated outcries of price are necessary because prices remain valid only during the outcry. Because of price volatility and the small margins required to acquire futures positions, this trading is hectic and fortunes may be made or wiped out in very short periods of time. Traders (unlike speculators) rarely carry overnight a net short or net long position.

$20.4.7 Hedging Transactions

Commodities futures are widely used by producers and users of commodities to hedge against future price changes. A farmer growing corn, for example, may know that his corn will be harvested and ready to market in July 1989. The futures price for July corn is about $2.92. If that price is acceptable to the farmer for his crop, he can lock in an approximate $2.92 price by selling one or more July corn futures in the approximate amount of his expected harvest. If the price of corn declines, he can sell his corn at a loss but recoup that loss on the profit on the futures contract (since he can close out the account by buying July corn for substantially less than $2.92). If the price goes up, the farmer has a loss on the futures contract, but is able to sell his harvested corn above $2.92: Again the two transactions should largely offset each other. A manufacturer that uses corn in its manufacturing process may similarly ensure itself of reliable raw material prices for an extended period in the future by buying futures contracts. Farmers or users of commodities may also hedge by buying or selling commodities "for forward delivery" at fixed prices without using the standardized futures market.

§20.4.8 Futures Trading Differs from Trading in Options

Futures trading resembles option trading, but there are important differences. An option does not commit the purchaser of the option to do anything; if the price moves in the wrong direction the purchaser of the option simply lets it expire. A futures contract, on the other hand, commits the purchaser to close out the position: If the price moves in the wrong direction, the purchaser of the futures contract has to take a loss that grows steadily as the price moves further in the wrong direction. In the financial futures market discussed in the next section, we will see that that is a very significant difference indeed.

The margin required in a futures transaction is also superficially analogous to the purchase price of an option. Again, however, there is a difference. The price paid for an option is the cost of obtaining a power to enter into a transaction: The premium becomes the property of the writer of the option. On the other hand, the margin required in a futures contract is a guarantee of performance and remains the ultimate property of the person entering into the contract.

It was noted earlier that the *writer* of an option is at the risk of market forces. In a futures contract, both sides of every contract are subject to the risk of market forces.

§20.5 Financial Futures and Options to Buy Futures

Today, most of the excitement in the futures business is in financial and index futures, not commodities futures. Standardized contracts to buy or sell foreign currencies at stated times in the future — British pounds in 25,000 pound units, Canadian dollars in $100,000 units, Japanese yen in 12.5 million yen units — are actively traded. Interest rate futures in treasury bonds, and 5-year treasury notes are traded in $100,000 units; treasury bills are traded in $1 million dollar units. All of these financial futures can be bought or sold for approximately 10 percent down, and constitute speculation on interest rates or foreign exchange rates.

From a dollar standpoint, the most active trading in all futures contracts today occurs in stock and bond indexes. Table 20-6 reflects the June 10, 1988 trading in these indexes. A major difference between commodities futures and these financial futures is that it is usually impractical to deliver the financial futures on the delivery date: One must always settle in cash for the difference between the contract price and the present level of the index.

Because futures carry with them the risk of loss from adverse price movements in excess of the amount initially invested, a logical development is the creation of put and call options on financial or commodities futures. Indeed, some instruments of these types have been created but they have not been as popular as the straight financial futures trading on the S & P 500 index. Table 20-7 is an example of price quotations for options on futures contracts. This lack of popularity has probably been a result of the complexity of the security thereby created and the difficulty of relating its value to the value of the underlying commodities or indexes.

Table 20-6

FUTURES PRICES

Friday, June 10, 1988

Open Interest Reflects Previous Trading Day.

—INDEXES—

MUNI BOND INDEX(CBT)$1,000; times Bond Buyer MBI

	Open	High	Low	Settle	Chg	High	Low	Open Interest
June	87-29	88-16	87-29	88-11	+ 17	89-26	70-03	5,857
Sept	85-17	86-09	85-17	86-03	+ 20	88-08	81-02	8,230
Dec	83-25	84-06	83-24	84-03	+ 18	86-29	80-16	518
Mr89	....	....	....	82-09	+ 18	85-05	78-25	412
June	80-24	80-24	80-18	80-18	+ 18	80-24	77-06	424

Est vol 4,000; vol Thur 4,029; open int 15,441, −172.
The index: Close 88-23; Yield 8.25.

S&P 500 INDEX (CME) 500 times index

	Open	High	Low	Settle	Chg	High	Low	Open Interest
June	272.20	274.25	269.80	271.10	− .35	347.90	190.00	52,547
Sept	274.00	276.45	271.95	273.10	− .20	343.50	193.00	73,202
Dec	276.00	278.40	274.00	275.05	− .15	278.40	252.20	1,217
Mr89	279.00	279.90	275.50	276.45	− .15	279.90	253.90	100

Est vol 69,322; vol Thur 79,565; open int 127,066, −1,854.
Indx prelim High 273.21; Low 270.20; Close 271.24 +1.04

NYSE COMPOSITE INDEX (NYFE) 500 times index

	Open	High	Low	Settle	Chg	High	Low	Open Interest
June	153.60	155.00	152.50	153.05	− .15	194.60	113.00	3,892
Sept	154.65	156.25	153.50	154.30	....	156.25	128.50	3,175
Dec	155.70	156.70	155.70	155.30	....	156.70	137.95	797
Mr89	....	....	....	156.30	+ .05	156.20	144.25	230

Est vol 9,076; vol Thurs 10,921; open int 8,094, −801.
The index: High 153.82; Low 152.35; Close 152.89 +.53

KC VALUE LINE INDEX (KC) 500 times index

	Open	High	Low	Settle	Chg	High	Low	Open Interest
June	237.55	239.30	235.80	239.00	− 1.80	287.00	177.20	1,857
xSept	245.60	247.60	244.30	245.85	+ .65	247.60	225.00	1,106
xDec	....	....	....	248.35	+ .65	240.00	237.25	10

Est vol 700; vol Thur 908; open int 2,973, −197.
X- New index: High 241.81; Low 240.26 ; Close 241.23 +1.00

MAJOR MKT INDEX (CBT) $250 times index

	Open	High	Low	Settle	Chg	High	Low	Open Interest
June	408.80	412.80	406.70	407.00	− 1.20	478.00	373.00	5,730
July	410.00	414.10	408.00	408.20	− 1.10	414.10	376.70	325
Sept	411.80	414.50	409.00	409.20	− 1.10	543.30	249.00	116

Est vol 5,000; vol Thur 6,215; open int 6,187, −240.
The index: High 411.72; Low 406.56; Close 407.61 +.96

§20.6 Arbitrage: Program Trading in Index Futures and Stock

The development of index options and index futures described in this chapter open up a variety of new computerized trading strategies involving arbitrage. Arbitrage is the process of taking advantage of small price differences in equivalent securities. Such differences may arise from different maturity dates on equivalent securities, trading in different geographical markets, or trading in securities with different forms but equivalent or interrelated values. At the present time, index options, index futures, and the underlying securities that comprise the indexes all trade simultaneously in different markets. It is almost impossible for an individual to determine whether the prices of the 500 stocks that make up the S & P 500 stock index are selling at a price below what their value should be in the futures market for the S & P index. Computers, however, now permit arbitrage transactions across markets of this type. Computerized trading programs (using the DOT LIST computer facility) may involve simultaneous purchases of long positions in a package of several hundred securities (in round lots) that mimic the S & P 500 index with the simultaneous sales of S & P 500 index futures on the Chicago Board of Trade futures market. This

Table 20-7

FUTURES OPTIONS

Friday, June 10, 1988.

—AGRICULTURAL—

CORN (CBT) 5,000 bu.; cents per bu.

Strike	Calls—Settle			Puts—Settle		
Price	Jly-c	Sep-c	Dec-c	Jly-p	Sep-p	Dec-p
240	19½	35	49	1½	10	11½
250	12	34	43	4½	15	15
260	8¾	30	38	10	24	20
270	4¾	26	34½	16	....	25
280	....	22½	30½	....	....	28
290	....	20	26½	....	....	36

Est. vol. 20,000, Thur vol. 10,557 calls, 2,396 puts
Open interest Thur 60,055 calls, 46,462 puts

—INDEXES—

MUNICIPAL BOND INDEX (CBT) $100,000; pts. & 64ths of 100%

Strike	Calls—Settle			Puts—Settle		
Price	Jun-c	Sep-c	Dec-c	Jun-p	Sep-p	Dec-p
84	4-22	3-10	2-41	0-02	1-08	2-35
86	2-24	2-01	1-51	0-03	1-61	3-40
88	0-43	1-13	....	0-14	....	....
90	0-07	....	....	1-47	....	....
92	0-01	....	....	....	....	....
94	....	....	....	....	....	....

Est. vol. 150, Thur vol. 18 calls, 181 puts
Open interest Thur; 24,391 calls, 25,101 puts

NYSE COMPOSITE INDEX (NYFE) $500 times premium

Strike	Calls—Settle			Puts—Settle		
Price	Jun-c	Jly-c	Sep-c	Jun-p	Jly-p	Sep-p
150	3.75	6.60	8.80	0.50	2.65	4.90
152	2.25	5.35	7.60	1.15	3.45	5.60
154	1.20	4.25	6.65	2.10	4.25	6.45
156	0.45	3.30	5.45	3.35	5.25	7.45
158	0.30	2.40	4.50	4.95	6.35	8.45
160	0.10	1.65	3.65	6.95	7.60	9.60

Est. vol. 26, Thurs vol. 37 calls, 50 puts
Open interest Thurs 678 calls, 837 puts

S&P 500 STOCK INDEX (CME) $500 times premium

Strike	Calls—Settle			Puts—Settle		
Price	Jun-c	Jly-c	Sp-c	Jun-p	Jly-p	Sep-p
260	11.70	16.30	19.75	0.60	3.30	6.90
265	1.35	12.50	16.35	1.25	4.45	8.40
270	3.80	9.50	13.40	2.70	6.10	10.35
275	1.55	6.50	10.70	5.45	8.40	12.55
280	0.50	4.35	8.30	9.40	11.20	15.55
285	0.15	2.75	6.20	14.05	14.60	....

Est. vol. 6,323; Thurs vol. 4,098 calls; 2,535 puts
Open interest Thurs ; 25,070 calls; 24,421 puts

kind of trading is known as *program trading*. Because there are many arbitrageurs involved in program trading, and because all programs may dictate the simultaneous purchase or liquidation of long positions on the New York Stock Exchange in very large amounts, program trading undoubtedly contributed to the October 1987 market collapse, to the increase in volume of trading on the NYSE, and to the wild trading swings that have occurred with increasing frequency in that market. Indeed, concern has sometimes been expressed about the possibility of manipulation of the underlying prices of securities on the NYSE in order to profit in the index futures or options markets.

§20.7 Hedging and Portfolio Insurance

A second major source of index futures trading prior to the October 1987 break in securities prices is a bundle of strategies usually known as *portfolio insurance.* It is widely believed that these strategies also contributed significantly to the October 1987 market break and were largely unsuccessful in preventing substantial losses.

An institutional investor that holds a portfolio of securities similar to that reflected in the Standard & Poor 500 index may hedge that position by selling S & P 500 index futures in much the same way that a farmer with a long position in the form of a crop in the ground can hedge against a price decline. See §20.4.7. Portfolio insurance (sometimes called *dynamic hedging*) does not strive to produce a riskless portfolio. Rather, it attempts to offset the potential decline while not eliminating the possibility of gain (as a true hedge does) in the case of a market rise. This is accomplished by buying or selling with the movement of the market: selling index futures when prices are declining and buying futures when prices are rising. During the October 1987 market collapse, these strategies became impossible to execute because they dictated the sales of index futures in a volume that the market was unable or unwilling to absorb.

§20.8 Other Trading Strategies Involving Options or Futures

The creation of a variety of new derivative securities has revolutionized the traditional securities markets for large investors. It is usually cheaper in terms of commissions and brokerage fees to effect major changes in portfolio strategies by transactions in the futures markets than by the sale and repurchase of an entire portfolio of securities. For example, a predominantly debt portfolio can be converted rapidly to equity by simultaneously selling bond futures and buying stock index futures. Of course, commission costs will be incurred if the underlying debt portfolio is ultimately liquidated and equity investment substituted. However, these transactions may be delayed indefinitely through the use of index futures.

Tactical Asset Allocation (TAA) is the name sometimes given to an investment strategy for large institutional investors that concentrates on classes of investments — e.g., equities, debt securities, and money market funds or cash equivalents — rather than on specific securities. These programs are computer-driven and rely on the purchase and sale of financial futures rather than on transactions in the underlying securities themselves. This strategy is attracting many institutional investors that utilized portfolio insurance or dynamic hedging before October 19, 1987.

A closing illustration as to the complexity of modern financial transactions may be appropriate. The following is the description (taken from *The Wall Street Journal*, May 2, 1984, p. 2, col. 3) of the strategy of *reverse conversions*, a rather arcane strategy that involves attempting to make profits from interest income on short stock positions:

> The crux of the strategy is the short sale of stock. The seller sells borrowed shares, and proceeds are deposited in his account at the brokerage firm that lent him those shares. The lender pays the short seller interest on the deposit, a current

annual rate of about 9½ percent. The lending broker also is free to relend the proceeds elsewhere at a higher rate. Eventually, the short seller must buy back the shares for return to the lender. . . .

Before the seller buys back the stock and thus closes out his position, he needs to hedge himself against loss. He does that by buying call options in the S & P [100] index, because the value of these options rises more or less in tandem with the price of the stocks.

If the index rises, the options grow in value, offsetting any loss on the short sales of the stock. If the index declines, the option loses value and ultimately could expire worthless, but the investor realizes offsetting gains from the short sales.

To offset the cost of the call options, the investor uses the third leg of the strategy — selling put options on the index. The put options rise in value as the index declines. Thus, if the index does decline, the investor will lose money on his sale of the puts but will make money on the short sales. And if the index stays the same or rises, the put options expire worthless and he pockets the money he got for selling them.

Publicity about this arcane strategy arose because of concern that it might involve forward trading in the options market based on knowledge that large volumes of trading in the underlying stocks on the NYSE would occur by the same or mutually cooperating individuals. Clearly, markets in which these types of strategies are executed are not for beginners and neophytes.

VII

◇

A SURVEY OF CORPORATE PRACTICE

CHAPTER 21

WHAT IS CORPORATE PRACTICE?

§21.1 Introduction

The practice of business or corporation law, particularly with large firms in big cities, is often viewed by law students today as the ultimate in success in the practice of law. This view is not universally held today by law students and law professors: It certainly was not the general view held by many law students during the turbulent years of the late 1960s and early 1970s, and it may not be again some time in the future. But a recent study shows that today corporate practice is widely viewed as interesting and challenging as well as being more remunerative than many other types of practice.

A corporate lawyer is simply one whose practice involves representing business clients. Most substantial businesses are incorporated, so that most business clients are corporations and hence "corporate" and "business" are to some extent interchangeable when describing this type of practice. Many businesses, however, are conducted in other forms, usually partnerships and limited partnerships, and corporate practice traditionally encompasses these types of business forms also.

Corporate practice involves challenging and diverse problems. Problems may range from the mundane — simple review of business transactions such as contracts, leases, security agreements, and the like — to the wildly esoteric such as the management of contested takeovers of corporate businesses. Staples of corporate practice include organizing and financing of new business entities, advising a large publicly held corporation in a variety of internal and business matters, "doing deals" involving mergers or the acquisition or disposition of corporate assets, and solving the problems of succession from one generation to the next of a valuable closely held business. Obviously, not all corporation lawyers handle problems throughout the range of business activities (though many do); as in other areas of law practice, individual lawyers and firms tend to specialize in certain areas or subareas.

A basic distinction among lawyers in corporate practice is between those who practice in the traditional manner with law firms or as solo practitioners and those who are employees of corporations — inside legal counsel. The balance of this chapter is devoted to a description of traditional corporate legal practice, while Chapter 22 discusses the lawyer who is an employee of the corporation for which he or she renders legal services.

§21.2 Traditional Corporate Legal Practice

Most traditional corporate practice is centered in large and medium-sized firms in the large cities. These firms employ new associates each year, promote associates to the rank of partner usually only after five or more years with the firm, and provide a great deal of on-the-job training for would-be corporate lawyers during the period they are associates. In many of these firms, only a small fraction of all associates ultimately become partners.

Some traditional corporate practice is also performed by small firms or even individual practitioners in large cities. There are also lawyers involved in corporate practice in smaller cities and towns, though typically they are there because one or more important clients are located there. Small firms or solo practice are the norms of practice in small cities and towns. Probably most corporate lawyers with small firms or in solo practice worked at one time as an associate for a large or medium-sized firm in a large city, though some may have received training from individual practitioners, governmental agencies, or in corporate legal departments. A very few may have successfully opened their own practices fresh out of law school.

Many lawyers handle some corporate practice matters but do not specialize exclusively or primarily in corporation or business law. Rather they may be engaged primarily in other types of practice, such as trial or negligence or labor law work, but also handle some business matters. In a sense, these lawyers are involved in corporate practice also. In bad economic times, a fair amount of corporate practice may be bankruptcy practice, or at least representing debtors or creditors in working out their problems. Real estate lawyers may also engage in some business practice, particularly in connection with the syndication of large real estate ventures. As with most broad descriptions of complex and varied legal practices, there are many exceptions and the lines between corporate and other types of practice in individual cases may be indistinct, and may change over a period of time.

§21.3 What Does a Corporate Lawyer Do?

There is no single or simple answer to the question of what a corporation lawyer does. Such a lawyer may be a counselor, a planner, a drafter, a scrivener, a negotiator, an investigator, a litigator, a lobbyist, a friend, or a person to be blamed when things go wrong. Indeed, every experienced corporate lawyer probably has at one time or another found himself or herself in each of these roles.

Most corporate practice is office practice and does not involve extensive litigation. When litigation involving publicly held corporations erupts, it tends to be complex, massive litigation, involving large sums of money and large numbers of lawyers. Often this litigation arises in connection with large and fast-moving business transactions and must be resolved in a very short period of time; success is measured not by entry of a judgment but by whether a judge can be persuaded to grant (or deny) a temporary restraining order. Many large firms maintain litigation departments that specialize in this type of litigation; some smaller firms also specialize in this type of litigation. In corporate litigation, there are often multiple defendants, and different firms represent different defendants, so that the list of record counsel often reads like the "Who's Who" of corporate practice in that city or state, or sometimes in many different states. While most lawyers in corporate practice have some contact with litigation, it is usually not a central portion of their practices.

It may be helpful to describe the most typical types of corporate lawyers while recognizing that many corporate lawyers do not specialize in only one of these categories.

§21.3.1 A Legal Adviser to Corporations

Perhaps the most typical function of a corporate lawyer is that of principal legal adviser to one or more corporations with respect to the central operations of those corporations. Such a lawyer may be the general counsel of the client while still engaged in the independent practice of law; he or she may devote most of his or her time to the affairs of that client; or, depending on the legal problems faced by that client, may devote most of his or her time to the affairs of other clients but remain on call to the corporation. Such a lawyer is referred to as an *outside general counsel*. At one time, it was customary for outside lawyers to serve as general counsel of corporations, and it is still common in smaller corporations today; the general counsels of most large publicly held corporations today are full-time corporate officers who are compensated by the corporation in the same manner as other corporate officers and who do nothing but represent the corporation. Such a general counsel is referred to as an *inside general counsel*. Inside general counsel are usually supported by a full-time legal staff who are salaried employees of the corporation and who also do nothing but work for and represent the corporation. A lawyer in outside practice who is acting as a legal adviser to such a corporation quickly becomes accustomed to dealing with inside general counsel and recognizes that he or she will be called upon only to discuss difficult problems that inside counsel does not wish to handle in house. The relationship between inside and outside counsel is a complex one that is described briefly in the following chapter.

A lawyer with general responsibility for the corporation's legal business — whether as general counsel or as an outside adviser to a general counsel — may be expected to address legal issues in any area relevant to the activities of the client, though the client may also have specialized legal counsel (either inside or outside) in areas such as patent law, federal and state taxation, environmental regulation, antitrust, Employees Retirement Income Security Act (ERISA), and others.

§21.3.2 The Securities Law Specialist

A second type of corporation lawyer is a specialist in securities law. Every general counsel of a publicly held corporate client must be familiar with the broad outlines of securities law, including the disclosure obligations of publicly held corporations, the rules against insider trading, exemptions from registration of issues under the Securities Act of 1933, the registration process, and the controls mandated over securities sold pursuant to an exemption. However, many specialists in securities law are not general counsel of a corporation. Modern securities law involves so many significant and broad-ranging questions that the securities law specialist for a major publicly held corporation is also in a central position with respect to the corporation's activities and regularly advises one or more corporate clients in many sensitive areas: for example, disclosure obligations to the Securities and Exchange Commission, shareholder relations, the manner of raising capital, the creation and maintenance of adequate internal controls against inadvertent violations of law, the handling of questionable payments, and the management of shareholder litigation.

Lawyers in securities practice may have narrow subspecialties. For example, lawyers or firms may specialize in municipal bond law, in mutual fund regulation, or in the registration of certain classes or types of companies.

§21.3.3 The Takeover Specialist

A relatively new and glamorous facet of securities law is the takeover specialist and the law firms actively engaged in takeovers. Major firms have developed around the nucleus of legal business generated from the modern wave of acquisitions and takeovers. These firms may be on either side of a transaction: In one case they may counsel clients about initial defenses against takeovers and in the next they may be involved in managing the aggressor's attempt to take over a different target. Litigation is a well-accepted tactic in takeover attempts, usually involving suits being filed simultaneously in several different jurisdictions and courts.

Legal fees paid in connection with takeover attempts, while substantial, are dwarfed by the fees paid to brokerage and investment banking firms that provide capital and render economic advice and assistance to the protagonists. In the 1980s several successful lawyers in takeover practices have left the practice of law to join brokerage and investment banking firms in order to "do deals" and (presumably) to share in the larger fees paid to the economic (as contrasted with the legal) participants in such transactions.

§21.3.4 The Securities Law Plaintiff's Bar

A relatively small group of litigation-oriented lawyers are involved in shareholder litigation against corporations and their directors and officers. Practically all of this litigation is on a contingent fee basis and is pejoratively described as *strike suits* by lawyers who represent the corporation and its management in such litigation.

§21.3.5 Miscellaneous

Many corporate lawyers are involved in a wide variety of traditional corporation law problems without falling specifically into any of the categories described above. Some specialize in specific problem areas while many others handle a large variety of business matters. Many of the problems involve small closely held businesses where the major problems of shareholder relationships are entirely different from those in the large publicly held corporation. Problems of closely held businesses involve formation, financing, planning, and negotiation. The lawyer may be involved in the formation of new corporations or small enterprises; he or she may form numerous limited partnerships to allow a client involved in real estate activities to finance its operations. Financing may involve the negotiation of loan agreements or agreements for the sale of stock: Precise knowledge of the scope of the exemptions from registration under the Securities Act of 1933 and the applicable state securities statute (the blue sky law) is essential in this type of activity. The lawyer may also be called upon to advise owners whether to go public by registering shares under the Securities Act of 1933 for sale to members of the general public. Planning involves anticipation of problems that arise when adjusting or terminating the interests of the owners of small businesses. A not uncommon problem in the modern era is the treatment of interests in closely held corporations in connection with divorces or property agreements in contemplation of marriage. Planning often involves negotiation. For example, financial planning for individual participants may involve working out agreements among participants in corporations to allow the older participants to liquidate their interests and the younger participants to obtain control, or to allow the principal owners of the corporation to retire and transfer control down to younger generations with the minimum cost in transfer taxes. Or the transaction to be negotiated may involve a simple sale of the assets of the corporation or of some or all of the stock of the corporation to outside interests. Lawyers that handle closely held corporations also may handle issues relating to larger corporations. In a sense, this is the most general type of corporate law practice.

The categories of corporate practice described in this section are not always sharply defined or mutually exclusive. There is also a considerable degree of specialization. Indeed, some lawyers draw a distinction between a business practice and a corporate practice, reserving the latter term for the representation of large corporate clients, the practice of securities law, "doing deals" involving mergers and the acquisition or disposition of corporate assets, and engaging in takeover wars. There are many corporate lawyers, almost all of whom practice with large firms in the major cities, whose practices fall into these categories. However, many lawyers who practice extensively in these areas also handle other problems described in this section and view their practice as a corporate practice.

§21.4 What Skills Are Needed by a Corporate Lawyer?

Perhaps the simplest and most naive conception is that the skills of a corporate lawyer are learned almost automatically through experience. In this view, one joins a large and affluent law firm with a thriving practice as an associate; after several years of drudgery and hard work, one hopefully "arrives," makes partner, and then relaxes into the comfort of a successful practice, where the hours are short, most of the hard or dirty work is delegated to associates or more junior partners, and the financial rewards are substantial. In this scenario, one lives happily ever after when one is promoted to partner.

This vision is hopelessly overglamorous and simplistic. If one were to follow an average, successful senior partner in a corporate law practice through his or her daily schedule for a week or so, it would quickly become apparent that his or her success is based on skills, knowledge, and sophistication acquired from years of experience and study, and is dependent on continued hard work and long hours. These skills can be broken down into several broad categories:

1. The average corporate lawyer must have intimate familiarity with a number of discrete areas of law that are currently covered in part in law school: federal income taxation, corporation law, agency and partnership, securities law, antitrust, contracts, the modern law of products liability, the Uniform Commercial Code, and probably several other commercial subjects as well.

2. In addition, the successful corporate lawyer must have a good working knowledge of basically non-legal concepts: corporate finance, financial accounting, practical management techniques in large enterprises, how the securities markets work, and the unique perspectives of bankers, brokers, insurers, and other persons or organizations whose cooperation or assistance may be essential for the continued successful operation of any corporation. This kind of knowledge is rarely taught in law school; some of it may be taught in business courses in or out of law school, but most of it is still learned the hard way: through on-the-job experiences. Hopefully, some of it has been learned by a careful reading of the earlier chapters of this book.

3. Depending on the particular client and the type of practice the lawyer is in, the successful lawyer may also have to be conversant with a variety of unique business practices or specialized or exotic areas of law of interest to the immediate client and probably not taught anywhere in law school: perhaps commercial practices in international trade in wild animals, the highway testing procedures followed by the Division of Engineering of the Department of Transportation of the state of South Dakota, the intricacies of those statutory abominations known as the Employees Retirement Income Security Act or the Tax Reform Act of 1986, the commercial law of Nigeria, or current policies of the United States Government with respect to trade with the Union of South Africa, to take a few examples. All of this knowledge, information, and background, furthermore, must be kept fully current so that the client has the benefit of today's perspective, not yesterday's.

4. A final attribute of the typical successful corporate lawyer is that he or she combines good business and common sense with substantial interpersonal skills. While most corporate lawyers rarely see the inside of a court room, they

spend a good part of their time on the telephone, talking daily with clients, other lawyers, accountants, and other business people. They are giving advice, structuring transactions, negotiating, "doing deals," overseeing corporate formalities, drafting agreements, memoranda, or letters, giving formal legal opinions, and dealing with various federal and state agencies. They may deploy and be responsible for the activities of junior partners and associates within the law firm. The skills needed to handle these and other multiple functions probably are to some extent innate but they are also interpersonal skills that can be significantly improved through experience and practice.

Obviously, one does not become a skilled corporate lawyer overnight. On the other hand, one also does not need a strong business background before law school in order to be a corporate lawyer. Many lawyers with successful corporate practices have prelaw backgrounds in areas other than finance, accounting, or business. One such lawyer (who provided invaluable commentary on an earlier version of this chapter) described himself as "someone who majored in 'Culture and Behavior,' a combined major in psychology, sociology, biology, anthropology, and linguistics." And that is not unusual. A business background basically helps only in the second skills category described above. Virtually all successful corporate lawyers began their careers, either in law school or shortly out of law school, without a great deal of knowledge, sophistication, or experience. After all, everyone has to begin someplace.

§21.5 The Growth of Specialization in Corporate Practice

The practice of corporate law has not remained static but has gradually changed over time. It is probable that equally great changes will occur in the future. Perhaps the most important recent trend is the increase in specialization. As the law business has become more complex, specialization has steadily increased: Either an entire firm specializes in a specific area or one or more partners in a firm specialize in one area while other lawyers in the firm specialize in other areas. Most large corporations retain a number of different lawyers in order to take advantage of this specialization: tax lawyers, securities lawyers, pension specialists, labor lawyers, antitrust specialists, patent lawyers, customs lawyers, immigration lawyers, government contracts specialists, and specialists in Commerce Department export regulations, to name only a few. Of particular note is the growth of "boutique" law firms that may specialize in large case litigation or in specific areas such as bankruptcy or labor law, and offer to provide expert, specialized service at lower costs than the traditional large, multiple-specialist law firm.

§21.6 A Corporate Law Practice Is Not Always a Bed of Roses

While the psychological and financial rewards of a successful corporate practice are great, it should be recognized that there is considerable personal stress associated with a high-level corporate practice. Modern corporate law practice is typically highly competitive with law firms competing on a genteel (or not so genteel) basis for business. While many law firms have long-standing historical relationships with specific clients, these bonds have usually weakened in recent years or have ended abruptly with the disappearance of a client through merger, buyout, or liquidation. Increasingly, a client who is not entirely satisfied feels free to go elsewhere, and the original lawyer is usually not told of the dissatisfaction: He or she may learn of it or sense it only when the amount of work he or she is being asked to do for a client declines. The lawyer may learn these unpleasant facts by hearing that another lawyer or law firm has been asked to handle a matter he or she would normally have expected to handle. Part of the insecurity of large client corporate practice arises from the fact that clients often expect prompt answers or prompt actions and success is usually judged not by how good or how bad the legal services have been but on how well the client comes out in the matter. There is, furthermore, the uncomfortable fact that large and important clients sometimes are abruptly taken over by other companies with the likely consequence that even if one's legal work is impeccable, that client's legal business may be gradually or abruptly shifted to different law firms in whom the new owners have more confidence.

Finally, there is the attestable fact that partners in law firms are generally expected to bring in new business as well as keep existing clients happy. Business-getting by many lawyers is even more chancy than handling clients. It is true that there are a few lawyers who have clients forming lines at their door with no apparent effort on their part. These are the "rain makers" who produce business that helps to sustain other lawyers in the firm. There are also some firms that have so much business that work must be turned away, so that a relatively small premium is placed on bringing in new clients. These lawyers and firms are exceptional, however. For most people who become partners in law firms with substantial corporate practice, individual success is partially measured by their success in bringing in business as part of an overall contribution to the firm. In general, success is by no means guaranteed for partners or for associates.

Lawyers in firm practice have been classified as "finders," "minders," and "grinders." One can classify lawyers in corporate practice on this basis.

§21.7 The Economist Looks at What a Corporate Lawyer Does

In recent years there has been a wealth of studies by economists or lawyers with economics training analyzing business transactions and corporation law concepts from the standpoint of economics. The roles of corporation lawyers have been partially subjected to this analysis. (The discussion below is largely based on a provocative analysis of this subject by Professor Gilson which appears at 94 Yale Law Journal 239.)

The economist begins by distinguishing actions that *create value* from actions that merely affect the *distribution of value*. For example, if a lawyer is engaged in negotiating a contract on behalf of his or her client with another lawyer who is also representing a client, the lawyer who is more skillful in negotiation techniques may be able to cut a better deal for his or her client at the expense of the client with the less skillful lawyer. Certainly, many lawyers engage in contract negotiation and similar activity of this type all the time. However, this function is not highly regarded by the economist who argues that in such a negotiation, what one client gains, the other client loses. In other words, it is a zero sum game and the lawyers are not creating value but merely rearranging its distribution between the two clients. When viewed from the perspective of both clients combined, the lawyers have contributed nothing to the profitability of the transaction, and indeed the clients in the aggregate are worse off because each must pay a fee to a lawyer. The economist further suggests that when viewed from an *ex ante* perspective (i.e., before the negotiation begins), the clients will be aware that the lawyers are providing no net benefit to the transaction. Further, in commercial or corporate transactions, both parties usually have the assets to hire sophisticated lawyers. Each side should therefore realize that if one side hires a skillful lawyer to effect the distribution of benefits, the other side will in all probability do the same thing with the result that the lawyers cancel each other out and neither client gains significantly in the distributional sense. Thus, the long-range consequence, in the world hypothesized by economists, should be that both clients will decide that it is in their combined best interest not to hire lawyers at all.

To most lawyers, this final conclusion flies in the face of experience. It assumes a degree of rational cooperation between clients which is certainly unrealistic in most competitive negotiations between persons who have no reason to trust each other. Further, in first-time transactions someone must usually produce the necessary documentation — whether it be a contract, a letter agreement, a bill of sale, or a deed — and thus there will usually be a lawyer representing at least one of the parties, so that the other side will also employ a lawyer. On the other hand, every lawyer recognizes that in situations where clients deal with each other repeatedly in similar transactions (or where virtually identical transactions such as bank loans occur with different parties), there is a tendency to minimize or eliminate entirely the role of lawyers and negotiate directly. The documentation then is often based on the documentation of the earlier deals. In this situation, the clients may refer expressly to the benefit of avoiding the lawyers' fees.

Not all functions of lawyers, however, merely affect the distribution of gains. Professor Gilson starts his analysis of these "socially useful" functions of lawyers by suggesting that most corporate transactions involve the sale of capital assets that have value solely because of the prospect of future cash flows. Further, the pricing of such capital assets in a perfect economic world is established by the *capital assets pricing model (CAPM)*, which under idealized circumstances results in market forces establishing the value of capital assets without the intervention of lawyers. (See §2.9 for a discussion of how the CAPM actually prices such assets.) However, the real world does not approximate these idealized circumstances on which CAPM is based, which include assumptions (1) that all investors have common time horizons (i.e., they all measure returns over the same time period), (2) that all investors have the same expectations about future risks and returns associated with the asset in question, (3) that there are no transaction costs, and (4) that all information is costlessly available to all investors. The "socially useful" roles of lawyers, according to Professor Gilson, are activities that reduce the disparity between the real world and the idealized world underlying the CAPM. Gilson identifies four such activities:

1. The lawyer may facilitate transfer of information between buyer and seller by negotiating the representations and warranties made by the parties in the contract of sale;

2. The lawyer may supply information to the buyer by way of legal opinions;

3. The lawyer may assist in the creation of mechanisms by which the buyer may verify the accuracy of information, typically through due diligence reviews, holdbacks of portions of the purchase price for a limited period, workout agreements, or similar arrangements; and

4. The lawyer may serve as a reputational intermediary, ensuring the buyer of the seller's honesty and reliability (or vice versa).

Gilson also identifies other important functions of lawyers: they may (1) suggest techniques to bridge differences in expectations of future returns and (2) serve as architects of complex acquisition transactions by recognizing and taking advantage of the fact that different acquisition techniques lead to economically indistinguishable results and yet have widely varying legal and tax consequences and procedural requirements.

What is one to make of this innovative analysis? It deals, of course, only with one facet of the role of corporation lawyers — the acquisition transaction — albeit an important facet and one that involves very large amounts of money and lawyers' fees for many firms. Corporate lawyers engaged in such transactions recognize that their activities usually "create value" rather than merely redistribute it — a common expression of this idea is that if the deal is not advantageous from both parties' standpoint it is not a good deal. Lawyers also recognize that they propose mutually advantageous ways to structure novel transactions and that they verify that the often elaborate documentation that surrounds complex transactions in fact carries out the parties' intentions. On the other hand, from the day-to-day standpoint of a practicing corporate lawyer it probably makes little difference whether he or she is creating value or affecting distribution of gains; in either event the goals and needs of the client — the service to be rendered — determine the lawyer's actions, not the benefit of society as a whole.

Gilson's analysis is also useful in that it emphasizes the importance and seriousness with which lawyers should take their role in giving legal opinions (discussed in Chapter 23).

INSIDE COUNSEL: LAWYERS WHO WORK FOR A CORPORATION

§22.1 Introduction

This chapter describes briefly the role of lawyers who are officers or employees of a corporation. The top legal officer of a corporation is called the *chief legal officer* or *CLO*; he or she may have the formal title of *general counsel*. Historically, the top legal officer of a corporation was a partner in a law firm (or the law firm itself); today, virtually all general counsels of large, publicly held corporations, are full-time salaried officers or employees of the corporations.

A major development in the practice of corporate law has been the growth of inside legal staffs of corporations. The importance of inside lawyers should not be underestimated: Today much of all corporate legal work is done in house. Estimates indicate that 20 percent of all licensed lawyers are currently employed by corporations. Many corporations have legal staffs that rival law firms in size and diversity (as many as 200 or 300 attorneys in the case of a major corporation such as Exxon or General Electric, with many smaller corporations having legal staffs of 70 or more), with compensation levels comparable to those paid by independent law firms. Lawyers employed by corporations have their own independent organization, the American Corporate Counsel Association; committees of the American Bar Association and state bar associations also deal specifically with the roles of such lawyers. The functions performed by these inside staffs, and the relationships between inside and outside lawyers while handling the legal business of the corporation are major topics considered in this chapter.

§22.2 The Large Corporation and Its Need for Legal Services

Large corporations today have a continuing need for legal services that requires the availability of full-time legal assistance in the form of an internal legal staff. For one thing, the sheer magnitude of operations of a large corporation means that at any one time it is constantly involved in legal disputes of one kind or another. A large corporation may have dozens of plants and hundreds of offices scattered throughout the world: Any one of them may give rise to local litigation of various kinds. It may have subsidiaries incorporated in many different states and foreign countries. Also any large business has constant and continuing problems in regulatory areas: environmental, safety of employees, safety of products, governmental licensing, and so forth. State and local tax problems are also constant and continuing. The federal income tax problems of a large corporation by themselves are often sufficiently complicated to involve the full-time activities of several lawyers as well as auditors and accountants. Thus, a large corporation is almost constantly involved with legal problems and litigation of varying degrees of importance, and may have literally hundreds of lawyers with various kinds of skills performing legal services of various kinds for it. It seems only common sense for corporations to have some kind of chief legal officer with an internal legal staff simply to keep track of things.

In addition, most publicly held corporations have large and active programs that can best be described as preventive law. Corporations conduct their business through delegation of authority to thousands of employees, overseen by more senior employees. The compensation of many of these employees may be fixed wholly or partially in terms of output, productivity, or success; in the giant bureaucratic structure thereby created, programs to monitor employee conduct to ensure fidelity to governmental policies and general legal principles are necessary if the corporation is to stay out of trouble.

Large corporations are almost continuously involved in monitoring legislation or administrative action at the federal and state level. Many corporations retain special counsel in Washington, D.C., and in selected state capitals to handle specific lobbying matters or to look after the general interests of the corporation. Some of this work may be handled by trade associations of which the corporation is a member (again usually overseen by the corporation's general counsel, particularly for possible antitrust problems), but most corporations supplement the trade association work with activities of retained counsel in Washington.

Many corporations engage in significant international trade; not only is international business transactions a specialized area of law in its own right but problems regularly arise in such arcane areas as classification disputes with United States Customs, or the applicability of export license restrictions on high technology products by the United States Department of Commerce or Department of Defense. Many corporations have foreign subsidiaries, foreign plants, and foreign offices. These foreign operations also give rise to a large amount of legal business; most publicly held corporations have retainer arrangements with lawyers in foreign countries; large law firms have often opened offices in foreign countries in order to better serve their clients there. These arrangements may benefit both the law firm (since otherwise the legal business of the client in those countries would go by default to independent counsel in these areas) and the client (whose affairs will be handled by persons more familiar with their operations).

Large corporations also obtain legal advice on a large variety of non-litigation matters more regularly than individuals. Indeed, corporations probably rely on attorneys to a greater extent than individuals engaged in similar activities, and they tend to look at legal services somewhat differently than individuals or small businesses. There are several reasons for this. Many corporations have inside legal staffs that are salaried; they are available at no additional cost for advice on a variety of matters. All corporations also regularly budget for legal services, treat such costs as a regular, recurring cost, and are accustomed to seek legal advice regularly. Smaller businesses and individuals, of course, also make regular provision for legal services, but they usually do not use such services regularly and to the same degree. In addition, a large publicly held corporation is usually managed by professional managers who do not own a substantial portion of the shares of the corporation; since they are managers and not owners their actions are subject to monitoring and review by more senior executives, the board of directors and ultimately the shareholders, governmental agencies, and the securities markets. In this milieu, consultation with lawyers about potential legal problems that might arise from proposed actions may be viewed as a sensible precaution from a personal standpoint, particularly since the cost is borne by the corporation and not by the person seeking the consultation.

§22.3 The General Counsel

As indicated above, it is customary for large corporations to denominate a lawyer as general counsel or chief legal officer. In the larger corporations this person is usually an officer and a salaried employee; in smaller corporations and even in some of the larger ones he or she may be a member of an outside firm who devotes most or all of his or her time to the affairs of the corporation.

As the chief legal officer, the general counsel has ultimate responsibility for all legal matters affecting the corporation. If litigation turns out disastrously from the corporation's standpoint, or the corporation is found to have violated securities law or environmental regulation requirements, the general counsel has the ultimate responsibility, or at least will have to explain how things could have gone so wrong. Similarly, the general counsel usually has responsibility for the government-related efforts of the corporation in the form of lobbying and dealing with regulatory agencies. Obviously, the general counsel must be a skilled and sophisticated lawyer, familiar with all major facets of the corporation's business and comfortable dealing with governmental authorities.

In most corporations, however, the general counsel is much more. He or she is also the head of the corporate legal department discussed in §22.4, and as such, has the responsibility of managing and deploying a legal staff that may rival a large law firm in size and have a budget running into the millions of dollars per year. A great deal of time must be spent managing the department, controlling costs, implementing departmental procedures and policies, and developing a cadre of trained lawyers. Obviously, substantial managerial talents are required that probably exceed those required of managing partners of a large law firm.

Another important facet of the role of general counsel is that the position is traditionally one of influence and importance on nonlegal issues within the corporation. General counsel are also assigned nonlegal management responsibilities. They may serve on high-level task forces or committees within the corporation that deal with major business concerns. In periods of stress within the corporate structure, the general counsel may be assigned to head sensitive nonlegal departments such as safety, transportation, or real estate. The general counsel is usually familiar with corporate operations and his or her advice may be sought on numerous business questions as they arise.

The general counsel is also influential within the corporation because he or she is usually close to the center of power. The general counsel is personally selected by the chief executive officer (CEO), reports directly to that officer, and enjoys friendly and close relationships with him or her. In most corporations, the general counsel is viewed as the CEO's lawyer. Many CEOs select the general counsel in part as an adviser and in part as a lawyer. Further, the general counsel may serve as a member of the board of directors and the executive committee of the corporation. Even where the general counsel is not on the board of directors, he or she usually attends board meetings and is an adviser to the board as well as to the CEO. As a result, the general counsel is known to individual members of the board of directors who may come to rely on his or her judgment. Because of the close relationships that often develop, it is not uncommon for the general counsel to move into the executive suite and ultimately become the chief executive officer of the corporation. Indeed one study reveals that today more than 15 percent of all top managers of publicly held corporations began their careers as lawyers.

The close relationship between the general counsel, the CEO, and the board of directors is sometimes sensitive. In a sense, the general counsel advises both the board of directors and the CEO, even though he or she is usually selected by the CEO; while the interests of the CEO are usually parallel with the board of directors, they are not always. Further, the applicable ethical standard complicates matters because it states that the corporation is the general counsel's client, thereby suggesting that the general counsel owes duties to other constituencies in the corporation, particularly the shareholders. In the rare circumstances where the interests of the CEO, the board of directors, and the shareholders diverge, say, in takeover situations or the negotiation of an employment contract for the CEO, the general counsel may feel so inherently conflicted that he or she recommends that independent counsel be hired at least for the members of the board of directors who are not directly employed by the corporation.

The perspective of the general counsel employed by the corporation usually is not identical with the perspective of an attorney in private practice with the corporation for a client. The general counsel is a high-level member of the management team who works toward the corporate goals. He or she concentrates on a single business and is closely aligned with the success of that business. Some independence of approach is thereby inevitably lost if for no other reason than the general counsel is so close to the corporation, its affairs, and the persons running it. Of course, the lawyer in private practice also seeks to further the client's interests and is aligned to some degree with the success of the client.

But the outside lawyer usually has a number of clients and is not so closely tied to a single client. He or she may readily advise a client that a transaction is probably unlawful and should not be pursued even though well aware that the advice will not be happily received. General counsel should of course also advise the corporation not to pursue a transaction upon reaching the conclusion that the transaction in question is probably unlawful. The general counsel, however, may be more reluctant to reach this conclusion knowing the importance of the transaction to corporate management. Indeed this is why outside counsel may be retained to make an independent review of a contemplated transaction. The suggestion that independent counsel be retained may come from the board of directors or the CEO; it may also come from the general counsel who recognizes the need for an independent perspective (or possibly prefers that the bad news comes from another source). For the same reason, both third parties and governmental agencies are sometimes unwilling or reluctant to accept legal opinions prepared by inside counsel and insist that a legal opinion be given by independent outside counsel.

§22.4 The Growth of Corporate Legal Departments

In talking about the relative roles of inside or house counsel (attorneys employed by the corporation) and outside counsel (law firms or individual attorneys retained by the corporation), it is helpful to talk about history and recent trends.

The role of general counsel evolved along with the modern corporation. Most large corporations also created skeletal legal staffs to assist the general counsel at a relatively early time. However, until quite recently these staffs were almost always small and handled only the most routine legal matters: For example, they might be involved in the preparation of minutes of meetings of the board of directors, the preparation of simple patent applications and routine contracts, the closing of real estate transactions, and the searching of titles of potential oil and gas leases. More substantial legal matters were almost universally handled by outside lawyers. As late as the 1950s and 1960s it was common for a large corporation to have historical connections with a specific law firm that did (or oversaw) virtually all the significant legal activities of the corporation. All of the important legal work of the corporation was in fact handled by or under the direction of the favored law firm or a favored specific partner in the firm. These relationships continued over long periods; one or more partners of the law firm also were often members of the board of directors of the corporation and the general counsel may have had prior association with this firm if he or she was not currently a partner in the firm. Sometimes the firm maintained office space within the corporate offices, or vice versa.

In this setting, virtually all of the interesting, challenging, and significant legal work (and a great deal of the routine work as well) was handled by the outside law firm. That firm also was regularly involved in selecting specialized or local counsel, when that was felt to be necessary, and overseeing the performance of those attorneys. The internal legal staff had virtually no challenging work and became the backwater of the legal profession. This view of the position of the inside legal staff was certainly shared by the partners and associates of the dominant law firm. The law firm might successfully place associates who did not make partner on the client's inside legal staff in order to cement the continuing relationship and at the same time provide a suitable spot for the junior attorney where he or she could do little harm. Even with the upgrading of the internal legal staffs that has occurred in recent years, a tinge of this old attitude may continue to exist in some lawyers today.

The systematic upgrading of internal legal staffs in terms of quality, size, and prestige has largely been fueled by economic considerations. During the 1960s and 1970s, large corporations faced an explosion of regulatory activity and products liability litigation. During this period, the corporate general counsel and the favored law firm were not only forced to become familiar with new regulatory requirements but also increasingly to practice preventive rather than reactive law. The lawyers found themselves increasingly involved in the establishment and monitoring of legal compliance systems or participating in corporate planning discussions about future economic activities so that legal problems could be anticipated and prepared for. Virtually none of this important work could be trusted to the inside legal staffs as they were then constituted. As the quantity of legal work increased with the burst of regulatory and litigation activity in the 1960s and 1970s, the legal bills submitted to corporations by favored law firms grew dramatically. While this was of course ideal from the standpoint of the law firm, cost-conscious corporate executives realized that legal costs were getting out of hand. The most obvious way to reduce these costs was to improve the capability of the inside legal staff to handle more matters.

Upgrading the capability of inside legal staff is not very different from upgrading the capability of an independent law firm. Imaginative general counsel must be hired with the direction to increase the legal staff in size and improve its quality; salaries must be improved; systematic attempts must be made to attract more competent lawyers, train them in much the way associates in law firms are trained, and give them more challenging work. As legal costs continued to rise, more and more corporations adopted this approach.

Many outside law firms initially welcomed the trend toward the upgrading of internal legal staffs, since at the time legal business was booming and the improved internal staff freed the firm's partners, associates, and paralegals from many routine matters. Eventually, however, the development of substantial in-house legal staffs put strain on traditional relationships with outside law firms, as well as compelling the forging of new cooperative techniques between the inside and outside attorneys. To consider the most extreme scenario, picture a senior partner of a law firm in the 1950s with a historic relationship with a corporation that had only a tiny internal legal department. That partner was in a most enviable position: he or she presumably had the complete confidence of the CEO and the individual members of the board of directors. For many years, the firm had handled virtually all the legal work of the corporation; while much of the work had been routine and in fact delegated to junior partners or senior associates, the work was partially attributable to the senior partner and was reflected in his or her remuneration from the firm. As the volume of legal services continued to increase, the remuneration of our hypothetical senior partner also increased.

Now, new inside general counsel is appointed specifically to reduce overall legal costs by moving work to an increasingly sophisticated internal law department and by moving isolated pieces of work to other law firms. Assume that one major source of legal work involves the regular and routine acquisitions of smaller firms by the corporation in order to obtain desired locations or desired products or inventory. Such an acquisition program is traditionally a major source of remunerative and recurring legal business. The first step by the new general counsel is the assignment of a newly hired inside lawyer to assist the outside firm in one or more acquisitions: After a few transactions, the outside firm is told that the inside lawyer is now in overall charge of the acquisition and will report directly to the general counsel and indirectly to the corporate officer charged with overall responsibility for acquisitions; and the law firm will be consulted if any unusual problems arise. Gradually, more and more acquisitions work is taken over entirely by inside counsel so that eventually most deals are handled entirely without the assistance of outside counsel and the amount of work performed by the firm and the senior partner for the client noticeably declines.

If one puts oneself in the position of the senior partner of the outside firm in this scenario, it is easy to see why there might be some bitterness and friction. The outside firm in effect trained the inside lawyer to take over a portion of the firm's business and the senior partner views the decline in business as threatening his personal future. When this pattern recurs in other areas of specialized work, such as managing litigation, tax, and securities regulation, relationships often become increasingly strained. Perhaps the senior partner or the firm with historic connections with the client might seek to return to the good old days by getting the general counsel fired or at least his or her responsibilities cut back. Generally, such efforts would not succeed, since the inside general counsel has effectively reduced the cost of legal services without any noticeable diminution in quality. Indeed, efforts to undermine the position of the general counsel might make matters worse, since the basis for the unhappiness of the senior partner and the outside firm would be fully understood by top management which could not be expected to be sympathetic.

Once the historic ties between law firm and client are broken and the independence of inside counsel firmly established, it is common for the corporation, through its general counsel, gradually to place legal work with other firms in an effort to obtain the best legal services at the best price. As a result the historic ties have declined further and most large corporations now routinely place outside legal work with several different law firms. Many corporations, of course, still have close historical connections with specific law firms that provide a substantial amount of continuing legal work for the corporation, with legal fees running into the hundreds of thousands or millions of dollars per year. It is clear, however, that this pattern is not what it was 25 years ago. Inside staff has responsibility for many substantive matters, often including the handling of litigation, that only a few years ago would routinely be delegated to outside counsel. If legal fees have increased, it is because the corporation's need for legal services of the type now provided by outside counsel has increased.

§22.5 The Diverse Work of Corporate Legal Departments

A modern corporate law department resembles a large or medium-sized independent law firm in many respects. It has a number of secretaries, a law library, word processing equipment, branch offices, and most of the amenities found in a law firm. It is usually divided into divisions or sections reflecting specializations — litigation, claims, law compliance, patents, etc. It has junior and senior lawyers with varying degrees of managerial responsibility: Senior lawyers oversee the work and development of the junior ones. There are "minders" and "grinders"; "finders," however, are unnecessary. It has an active recruitment program for new lawyers; it may have a summer intern program for law students. There are differences, however. Since it only represents one client, the maintenance of complex time records for billing purposes is usually dispensed with (though some legal departments maintain hourly records for cost allocation purposes). In a law firm, a junior associate may advance by putting in a lot of billable hours; this approach is usually not possible in a legal department, though hard work is usually noticed and appreciated much the way it is in any important job. Also, the legal department is headed by a single person rather than a pluralistic bevy of partners. The chief legal officer or general counsel of the corporation is also the head of the internal legal staff. Since that staff itself may be the size of a law firm, it is obvious that in many corporations, general counsel is as much a manager of the legal department as a lawyer.

Furthermore the law department is structured with the needs of a single client in mind. There may be a fair amount of decentralization, with the department maintaining small staffs at each of the major plants and offices of the corporation. These satellite departments may be headed by a single person who reports to the general counsel, or each staff member may be assigned to a section or division of the central office. Rotation between the central and field offices may occur routinely or even randomly in order to retain the discipline of the central office and a spirit of cohesiveness.

There are other, more subtle differences also. Much of the legal work of a law department involves preventive law rather than reacting to problems that come into the office. Inside lawyers are regularly involved in antitrust review, environmental review, and compliance programs of various types. They are called upon to develop policy statements for employee relations, to review audit questionnaires to be sent to factory managers, to establish policies for the retention or destruction of documents, and so forth. They may be asked to sit in on planning or other committees within the corporation. They may review all publications and press releases of the corporation to avoid claims of defamation or inadvertant violations of disclosure obligations. They may review reports dealing with overseas payments, political contributions, and the like.

Inside legal staff are usually involved in formal legal matters of the employing corporation and its subsidiary and affiliated corporations. The general counsel or members of the legal staff may fill the position of secretary of such corporations; even if not, the staff is almost always involved in the process of meetings, agendas, certification of records, and assuring that the various legal requirements applicable to corporations have been met. The legal staff may also be involved in shareholder relations, transfer problems relating to share certificates, and similar matters.

The inside legal staff may also be expected to provide legal services to officers and employees. This usually involves matters of interest to the employer, such as conflict of interest problems, the availability of employee benefit plans, and so forth. But a limited amount of personal assistance on estate, financial, or tax planning, and similar matters may also be provided for senior management.

Like the general counsel described previously, inside lawyers quickly become familiar with their employer's business and problems. They may become involved in business decisions as well as legal ones. Their attitudes, also like the general counsel's, may be somewhat different than the attitude of outside lawyers: They tend to feel that their basic goal is to further the policies of the corporation. They view themselves as facilitators and expeditors of their employer's goals to a greater extent than many outside lawyers would.

§22.6 The Control of Litigation and Law Work Performed by Outside Lawyers

Even in corporations with legal staffs of a hundred lawyers or more, much of the corporation's legal business is still handled by outside counsel. It is simply not cost-efficient for even the largest legal staff to maintain lawyers with experience in all local or specialized areas. It is also not cost-efficient to maintain a legal staff large enough to handle the peak loads of legal business: Such a staff would be significantly underutilized in other periods.

Matters on which the assistance of outside counsel is likely to be requested obviously varies widely from corporation to corporation, depending on the strengths and weaknesses of the internal corporate legal department. There are some areas, however, in which probably all corporations enlist the assistance of outside counsel. These include:

1. Problems entailing special expertise not found in the legal staff, such as immigration law;

2. Problems that dictate the presence of counsel on a continuing basis but that are geographically distant from the offices of the corporation;

3. Major litigation that involves the use of skilled litigation counsel and extensive supporting legal services;

4. Proxy fights and attempted unwanted takeovers by cash tender offer of control of the corporation;

5. Issues involving sensitive internal matters such as conflict of interest, indemnification of officers and directors or questionable payments where inside counsel may not create the appearance (or reality) of objectivity and unbiased advice;

6. Issues relating to the effectiveness of the inside legal department in handling the law business of the corporation; and

7. Antitrust litigation.

On the other hand, the inside legal department is most likely to develop expertise in areas where recurring problems arise: product liabilities claims not involving death or serious injury, workmen's compensation, labor relations, employment benefit claims, and general business matters such as breaches of routine contracts and leases. Many legal departments maintain extensive in-house litigation departments primarily to handle most of the litigation arising in these areas. It is generally cheaper to litigate with salaried attorneys than it is to pay high hourly rates charged by outside attorneys that contain a profit factor. Savings may arise from taking advantage of the knowledge and expertise of inside counsel thereby avoiding the expense of educating outside lawyers about the details of the client's business. Repetitive or recurring litigation is particularly likely to be handled entirely in house, assuming that the volume does not exceed the capacity of the litigation section of the inside legal department. Where the inside lawyers must try a case in a rural or remote location, local counsel will usually be retained in essentially the same way as local counsel is retained by large firms when called upon to handle local matters.

It is generally accepted today that the inside legal department is in charge of the legal business of the corporation and speaks on behalf of the corporation on legal matters. After the cutting of the umbilical cord between a corporation and its historic law firm, inside counsel decides not only which issues outside counsel should be consulted upon, but also the identity of the outside counsel selected and the fee arrangement with that counsel. Where outside counsel is retained in connection with important matters, however, the relationship between inside and outside counsel is often a delicate one. Inside counsel is the point of contact for the outside lawyer with the corporation. Often inside counsel will vigorously participate in the development of strategy with respect to how that litigation should be handled: Indeed inside counsel may insist that his or her views as to strategy should be followed. On the other hand, many private lawyers are accustomed to receiving assignments from corporate clients and then receiving complete deference to their professional judgment. These two perspectives are clearly on a collision course. Obviously, many potential problems may be avoided by a clear understanding as to who is ultimately responsible for the case and who will make the final strategic decisions.

In another sense, outside counsel controls the substantive and policy aspects of the matter for which he or she has responsibility. That lawyer has ethical responsibilities to the client, not to the inside lawyer who states that he or she represents the client. If the lawyer feels that strategies being insisted upon are unwise or inappropriate, the lawyer should raise the question within the inside legal department, going up to the general counsel, if necessary. Many corporate legal departments have guidelines for handling such disagreements between inside and outside lawyers. In the most extreme cases, the lawyer may be compelled to resign if he or she is unable to persuade the client as to the appropriate strategy.

CHAPTER 23

THE FINE ART OF GIVING LEGAL ADVICE AND OPINIONS

§23.1 Introduction

Most business lawyers spend a good part of their time giving advice to their clients (or considering what advice to give them). The issue may involve a proposed contract, a proposed business strategy, or almost anything that a corporate client becomes involved in. The mark of a successful corporation lawyer in giving advice can be simply stated: He or she must consistently give advice that the client believes it can rely on, and that, when followed, usually leads to the desired result (which may simply be that nothing bad happens when the advice is followed). If this is the ultimate test of success, obviously a fair degree of luck helps the average lawyer along with the skills, knowledge, expertise, and experience described above.

In addition to advice, corporate lawyers are often asked to give written legal opinions on a variety of matters, ranging from the reasonableness of a settlement offer to the legal consequences of proposed important commercial transactions. The process of giving formal legal opinions turns out to be surprisingly complex, and is the second major topic of this chapter.

§23.2 Informal Legal Advice

Clients often ask for advice about a proposed business transaction. They may want an informal opinion as to whether the transaction is lawful, whether it is consistent with loan or other commitments that the corporation has previously undertaken, whether it will lead to a desired tax treatment, or many other questions. Such advice is in effect an informal legal opinion. Most of these requests are made informally, usually by telephone, and only an informal response is expected. A telephone call asking "John, is there any reason we can't do X?" is typical. There is little problem if the lawyer is familiar with what X is and what the relevant legal rules are: The lawyer can then give his or her views immediately and with confidence. Certainly, the more experience a lawyer has had with the affairs of the client, the more opportunities he or she will have had to investigate X in the past and the more confident the lawyer can be that the advice being given off the cuff is basically accurate.

Quite possibly the facts surrounding X are complicated and the full implications of the proposed decision are difficult to appreciate. It is sometimes not easy to follow the complex twists and turns of a description of a novel factual situation while trying to figure out what the precise issue is and formulating a response. One of the most important intuitive skills that a lawyer can possess is the ability to sort out the relevant from the irrelevant and sense what questions should be asked of the client in order to get an accurate picture of the situation. In this type of situation, it may be useful for the lawyer to summarize or restate his or her understanding of the facts before the conversation is terminated.

Unfortunately in some situations the lawyer will *not* be certain that he or she knows the answer to a question that is basically legal in nature. The question may be phrased abstractly, divorced from any factual situation, or it may be phrased in terms of a simple factual situation that starkly raises a direct legal question. If the relevant statutes or regulations are on the lawyer's desk, they can be consulted during the course of the telephone call, though first readings of complex text while carrying on a telephone conversation are obviously very unreliable. More likely, the lawyer will feel it necessary to break off the conversation to do research (or ask other lawyers), promising to call the client back shortly. While it sometimes may be a bit embarrassing to do this on a question the lawyer feels he or she should know the answer to, bad advice is worse than no advice. If a person is not confident of the correctness of his or her advice, the only safe thing to do is to delay an answer — "Let me check and I will call you back later today," or "Let me think about that," or "Let me run that by somebody else before telling you what to do." (This last response has the potentially negative implication that the lawyer lacks confidence in his or her own judgment.)

In all of these situations in which the lawyer is not certain of the answer, it is very dangerous to refer to some general legal principle as possibly providing the answer to the question since there may well be a more specific legal principle that is directly applicable to the question that is presented: The only way to find this out is to check.

All of these problems must be approached with the realization that a lawyer who gives the wrong offhand advice may cause the client to lose confidence in the lawyer and in his or her law firm, the cardinal sin of a junior lawyer.

§23.3 How Conservative Should the Lawyer Be in Appraising Risks?

What attitude should a lawyer adopt in giving advice about business transactions? Should he or she be negative or positive? Should all possible legal risks be pointed out? Or only the most serious ones? Before a client requests advice from a lawyer, that client will often have thought about the proposed transaction a great deal, and will have decided that it badly wants or needs to enter into it. In this situation, when it asks the lawyer for advice, it is seeking to combine two discrete and potentially conflicting kinds of advice from the lawyer. First, it wants objective and reliable informal legal advice that accurately predicts the likely consequences of various courses of conduct. Second, it almost always wants advice that will permit it to follow the course of conduct (or one of several possible alternative courses of conduct) that it has preliminarily determined to be most profitable or most desirable for it to follow.

Given this reality, it hardly pays in client relations to always conclude that there are legal risks that make the transaction unattractive. A lawyer's natural inclination is to "nitpick" a proposal and raise all sorts of major or minor concerns of varying degrees of likelihood about a proposed course of conduct. On the other hand, almost nothing in this life is certain, and if a transaction is important to the corporation but unlikely to get it into serious trouble, a lawyer is not giving good service to the client if he or she overstates the risks. The client wants the lawyer to make an assessment of the probability of a risk as well as of the fact of its existence. A lawyer who is too cautious will find that his or her clients are not happy with the advice, and will soon be seeking advice from other lawyers who are not so squeamish. On the other hand, most business actions that a lawyer sees entail some measurable or immeasurable degree of legal risk. (If the client believed there was no legal risk it probably would not incur the cost of getting an opinion in the first place.) Thus, a lawyer who always tells his or her corporation what it wants to hear about a course of conduct is probably not giving the client good service. Certainly that is true when the conduct actually entails serious and potentially unacceptable risks. When the client gets into serious trouble while following the advice, as will probably occur sooner or later, the lawyer may well lose the client.

In every case the lawyer must resolve the apparent dilemma created by these two polar extremes. There is no way to resolve it in the abstract; everything depends on the concrete problem and the concrete circumstances. However, a few observations may help. In the first place, it obviously is a tremendous help if the lawyer has a good working knowledge of the client's attitude about the assumption of risk. The lawyer should understand the public environment in which the client operates, and whether its management can "stand the heat" if a course of conduct gives rise to litigation against the corporation or creates problems, for example, through adverse publicity or inquiries from governmental authorities. A legal adviser to a corporation in a sense must be more than a lawyer. The advice he or she gives must take into account the circumstances of the corporation as well as the legal issues that are raised. Along the same line, it is also helpful if the lawyer knows quite a bit about his or her client and its business so that he or she can estimate how important the proposed transaction really is to the client. When I first entered practice, I was surprised to find out that the senior lawyer I was working for subscribed to all the trade papers in the areas in which our clients operated, regularly obtained copies of all public filings by them, and generally tried to keep as familiar with the clients' activities as he could. At the time, it seemed to me to be a lot of work with no apparent payoff. Over the next few years, however, it became apparent to me that his knowledge about the details of his clients' activities were often invaluable when he assayed risks and pitfalls.

Secondly, it is sometimes possible to reduce the risks of a desired course of action significantly by changes in the structure of the proposed transaction that do not significantly affect the economics of the transaction from the standpoint of the client. This last qualification is a highly important one, that is elaborated upon further in the following section. Normally, a lawyer should not suggest changes that affect the basic nature of the deal: He or she is being asked for his opinion on the deal as presented, and not a different (and less profitable) one.

Third, as described in some detail in §23.5, it may help to respond to difficult questions in writing rather than giving purely oral advice. However, when all is said and done, the lawyer may have to give difficult advice in close circumstances with the real possibility that the relationship with the client is riding on the outcome.

§23.4 The Distinction Between Legal Advice and Business Advice

When giving advice to clients, it is important to keep in mind the fact that the client is usually asking for legal advice rather than business advice. Usually a client does not want to know that the lawyer believes that the proposed transaction is hare-brained and unlikely to be profitable under the best of circumstances. If the client wanted business advice he or she would ask someone with expertise in business. Assume, for example, that a client in the donut business, who is not naive or unfamiliar with business generally, comes to you with a proposal that would place 50 of his donut shops within a ten-block radius in a city. An observation that this plan is unlikely to succeed because the shops are not sufficiently dispersed geographically and will compete with each other is clearly business advice, and probably would be viewed, at best, as gratuitous. Presumably, the client knows something about donut shops, has considered that possibility and has concluded that the plan does not suffer from such an obvious defect. Of course, as with all broad statements, there are exceptions. The business advice of some lawyers may be sought by clients because of the lawyer's unusual skill and experience. Where lawyers develop this skill it is not uncommon for them to move gradually away from the legal profession and into business. In other situations, the friendship between the lawyer and the client's representative may be so close that the lawyer may feel comfortable in raising business concerns, usually by asking the client to describe how it is expected that the arrangement will be profitable. And a different rule is unquestionably applicable when a lawyer is representing an unsophisticated client who may be unaware of risks and is about to take a potentially disastrous step. But those are not the normal situations; usually a lawyer's legal advice is all that is sought, and one should be cautious about volunteering personal views about business considerations.

Unfortunately, the line between legal and business advice is not at all clear-cut in many situations. A suggestion that financing may be obtainable from X is obviously business advice, but in some circumstances may be sympathetically received since many sophisticated clients may not have investigated all possible financing sources, and there is really no harm in asking. Advice that the plan may be unlawful, that it would require obtaining a license, or what-have-you, clearly involves legal advice. Advice that a plan of recapitalization should be first submitted to important lenders or trustees may be either. A recommendation that a physical count of inventory should be made before the purchase price for a business is paid, may be a sensible precaution no matter whether the advice is classed as business or legal in nature, though any sophisticated purchaser of small retail businesses is aware of the importance of such a count.

As indicated above, if a lawyer is representing an unsophisticated client, the lawyer often gradually assumes the roles of both legal and business adviser. Where an unsophisticated client is involved, business risks should be pointed out clearly, forcefully, and without hesitation. To take an extreme example, a lawyer who is handling the estate of a corporate executive may learn that a securities broker has suggested to the widow that she attempt to augment the size of the estate by engaging in options trading (a highly speculative and sophisticated market described in Chapter 20; a market in which it is easy to lose one's entire capital investment in a very brief period). Probably every lawyer in this situation would feel compelled to speak up and warn the widow of the dangers of following the advice of the securities broker. This general type of situation is probably more common than many people realize: Most sophisticated business lawyers at one time or another represent relatively unsophisticated clients. In these situations, the client may end up relying on the lawyer for both financial and legal advice. Usually the lawyer should try to persuade the client that he or she should seek appropriate business advice, and that reliance on a lawyer for advice on such matters is not desirable. Often, however, the client is happy with the lawyer's advice or is unwilling to incur the cost of direct business advice or does not know who to ask.

When a lawyer is asked to give advice about a transaction that poses some significant legal risks, he or she may recognize that the risks will be lessened by changing the deal in some respect. In recommending changes, however, the distinction between business-related changes and formal changes that do not affect the basic economics of the transaction should be kept in mind. A suggestion that a significant change be made in the business terms of the proposed transaction — for example, that a lease should be changed into an outright conveyance, that the price should be increased, or that a covenant against post-employment competition should be taken out of a proposed employment contract — normally should not be proposed by a lawyer when giving advice on the transaction if he or she believes the term is important to the deal. On the other hand, on legal matters or on mixed legal and business matters where the effect on the business aspect of the deal does not appear to be substantial, the lawyer should stick to his or her guns if he or she believes that the position of the client is improved by the proposed change. For example, it is rarely essential to tie up either side with a covenant not to compete for a long period, such as ten years. A shorter period may provide the essential protection needed and increase the likelihood that the transaction will go through.

§23.5 Informal Letters of Advice

If the facts are complex or the downside risks of one course of conduct or another are substantial, it is usually desirable to respond in writing to a request for advice rather than orally. In part this is defensive, since the lawyer can set forth in a letter his or her understanding of the facts, and can make express qualifications that may not be fully appreciated when given orally. In effect, the letter formalizes the advice and makes clear on what assumptions it is based, and the chance of misunderstanding is significantly reduced as a result. In part it avoids the dangers inherent when giving an off-the-cuff response without an opportunity to do adequate investigation or research since one can do research in connection with the preparation of the letter. On the other hand, there is always some risk that the letter may fall into unfriendly hands or be held to be discoverable because it falls outside of the lawyers' work product or lawyer/client privileges. Obviously, one should also be aware of the canons of ethics and not recommend (either orally or in writing) that the client engage in unlawful action, though the dangers of putting such advice in writing are so obvious that a lawyer who does so is probably asking for whatever happens.

A letter to a client discussing alternative courses of action is similar to an informal written opinion, though it may not be cast as an opinion letter. An informal opinion letter usually deals with the lawyer's conclusions as to rights and obligations arising from completed transactions while a letter of advice deals with contemplated transactions. The line, however, is not at all clear. For example, letters reviewing an offer of settlement of pending litigation and making a recommendation to the client whether or not to accept the offer, expressing an opinion as to whether a contemplated transaction would violate certain covenants in a loan agreement, or considering whether the corporation may indemnify a corporate director for expenses incurred in defending against litigation, all have some of the characteristics of a letter of advice and of an informal opinion.

An informal written opinion is sometimes referred to as a *speaking opinion* if it discusses alternatives, considers applicable legal precedents, and weighs various policy and strategic considerations. A speaking opinion often is a qualified opinion, and should be distinguished from the more formalized written opinions described in the following section.

When writing letters of advice or informal opinions to clients there are rules of thumb which are little more than common sense. First, every opinion or letter of advice should be freestanding, that is, understandable on its own face without any need to refer to other documents for factual descriptions, other people's opinions, or other considerations. As a result, such letters should state what the legal question is, and where appropriate, include a brief statement of the relevant facts. Where necessary, other documents may be attached to the letter as exhibits, though there are problems with the excessive use of this device.

Second, every opinion or letter of advice should expressly set forth the assumptions on which the writer is proceeding.

Third, a client wants an answer, not an inconclusive discussion of legal principles that gives little or no practical guidance as to what to do. In other words, you do have to come to a conclusion and let the client know what it is, clearly and unambiguously. If the outcome is genuinely uncertain (because, for example, it depends on the categorization of conduct or on factual inferences drawn from the facts), you must say so.

Fourth, where the proposed transaction does involve some appreciable uncertainty or risk, the lawyer should give the client some estimate of its magnitude, if that is possible. It is probably a mistake, however, to give probabilistic estimates in actual numbers if—as is usually the case—the numbers are made up out of thin air or are based on purely impressionistic judgments. There is a danger of giving an appearance of precision when actual numbers are used that usually is not justified. Phrases that often appear in opinions include "a strong case," "the better of the argument," and "not free from doubt." On the other hand, when assessing worst-case probabilities it is important to remember that in the real world most worst-case scenarios do not actually occur. When evaluating risks and benefits there is a natural tendency by all lawyers to concentrate on the risks to the exclusion of the benefits, or at least to overstate the risks.

Fifth, it is usually unnecessary to cite or discuss cases (though that may be necessary if one case is squarely in point or otherwise appears to be determinative). It is also usually unnecessary and undesirable to have footnotes referring to legal principles or authorities; an opinion or letter of advice should not look like a brief or a legal memorandum submitted to another lawyer in the firm. The client is usually not a lawyer, and a lawyer's analysis is not likely to be very helpful. On the other hand, footnote discussion of tangential but relevant issues is sometimes helpful in that it permits the inclusion of qualifications without distracting the client from the main point.

Finally, the letter should be limited to the problem and should not opine on a variety of matters that are not really involved and have not been carefully considered. The danger of broad statements, obviously, is that a client may rely on them in other or different contexts even though the facts are materially different and even though the opinion states expressly that it is limited to the facts stated.

§23.6 Formal Legal Opinions in Connection with Commercial Transactions

Formal legal opinions are usually required of counsel in virtually all important business transactions. The purpose of these opinions, unlike the informal opinions or letters of advice described in the previous section, is to confirm and ensure that certain desired legal relationships have been or will be created upon the closing of a specified transaction. A bank receiving corporate promissory notes or debt instruments in exchange for the payment of millions of dollars is giving up a lot of money for several pieces of paper: The lender's only real assurance that the pieces of paper create rights against the borrower and its assets is the opinion of an attorney. Such a lender is obviously not willing to accept an opinion that the loan might be repaid under some circumstances: A qualified or speaking opinion is simply not acceptable unless the qualifications are very narrow and fully acceptable to the person relying on the opinion.

Formal opinions on certain types of legal relationships are so common that law firms usually create forms for the guidance of its partners and associates when preparing opinions. The most common types of opinions are the following:

1. Opinions that a corporation is "duly incorporated, validly existing and in good standing" in a specific state;

2. Opinions that a corporation is "duly qualified and is in good standing under the laws of X state" (or, more dangerously, "of every jurisdiction where the business done by it or the property leased or owned by it requires such qualification");

3. Opinions that the corporation has power "to own its properties and conduct its business as now being conducted and to perform its obligations" under the agreement in question;

4. Opinions that the corporation has "corporate power to execute, deliver, and perform" a contract or other commitment;

5. Opinions that an agreement or other document was "duly authorized, executed, and delivered" by a corporation;

6. Opinions that certain shares of stock "have been duly authorized, validly issued and are fully paid and nonassessable;"

7. Opinions that, upon closing a transaction, a purchaser "will have acquired valid title [to designated property] free and clear of security interests, liens, claims, and encumbrances;"

8. Opinions that to the knowledge of the lawyer the transaction in question "does not conflict with or constitute a breach or violation of any of the terms of" other specified documents, such as the articles of incorporation, bylaws, outstanding indentures, or all outstanding judgments or decrees;

9. Opinions that registration of a securities issue is unnecessary; and

10. Opinions that the lawyer knows of nothing that would render inaccurate any material statements made by the client in any of the relevant documents.

This list of opinions is not complete. Opinions are often requested relating to specific regulatory problems, the priority of liens, the absence of defaults, and other matters. Lawyers may be called upon to give opinions that depend in part on the law of other states. A firm requested to give such an opinion may hire local counsel and rely (either expressly or implicitly) on their opinion. This is not essential, however. Many national law firms routinely express opinions on Delaware corporation law, for example, since it is so widely applicable that many lawyers in other states are comfortable expressing opinions as to that law. A national law firm, however, would probably retain local counsel if, for example, it were asked to express an opinion with respect to the application of the corporation law of West Virginia.

The opinions described above are usually addressed to a single person, sometimes the client but more commonly a participant in a transaction with the client. Principles of privity probably restrict the circle of potential plaintiffs in suits against the attorney. However, some legal opinions are informally distributed widely throughout the investing public even though they may be addressed to a limited number of persons. Formal opinions are required in connection with certain registrations with the Securities and Exchange Commission; those opinions may appear in registration statements or even on the face of the securities themselves. It is not clear that the scope of liability in such cases is as restricted as the lawyer giving the opinion undoubtedly hopes.

The precise words used in a formal written opinion are often items of serious dispute among lawyers. Many firms have standard opinions that they want to be used in specific transactions while the other side may have a differently worded opinion form that it wishes to use. Whether or not issues of substance are involved or whether the disagreement is legal hair-splitting is often doubtful. In any event, extensive negotiation over the precise wording of opinions is quite common. Also controversial is the so-called "golden rule" of opinions negotiation: Never ask for an opinion that you would be unwilling to give if you were on the other side. While many lawyers profess to follow this golden rule, it is not uncommon for firms to have two sets of opinion forms, one that they proffer when asked to give an opinion, the other they ask the other side to give when representing the client relying on the opinion. Another rule followed by many lawyers is never tell a client that a closing is being delayed because the lawyers are still negotiating over the language of legal opinions.

Many firms have instituted quality-control procedures to ensure that formal opinions binding the firm are given only in appropriate circumstances. Some firms have created independent opinion committees to review a proposed opinion before it is released; others require that a partner not connected with the matter review the opinion before it is released. Many firms supplement these requirements with a loose-leaf guide setting forth the policies of the firm with respect to opinions and listing factual or legal issues that must be investigated before giving specific opinions. These quality-control procedures were widely adopted following a consent decree accepted by a major New York law firm publicly agreeing to the institution of such procedures.

At first blush it is a little scary to give an essentially unqualified opinion, for example, that a $100,000,000 loan contract constitutes a "legal, valid, and binding obligation" of the debtor. What if the attorney is wrong? Does that mean the lawyer, the firm, and the firm's insurer are all liable for $100,000,000? It is important to recognize that an opinion is not itself an insurance policy; the opining lawyer is liable for negligence or malpractice but is not liable for being in error in the absence of negligence or malpractice. On the other hand, negligence or malpractice may well be found if a lawyer fails to check some obvious possibility. Certainly few lawyers are willing to give an opinion unless they are as sure as they reasonably can be that they will be found to be correct, even when being subjected to the risk of judicial hindsight. It is damaging, expensive, and embarrassing to have an opinion called into question in a subsequent proceeding.

The fine art of giving formal legal opinions can best be appreciated by an example. If a lawyer is called upon to give an opinion that a contract is "legal, valid, and binding," he or she must make an investigation in order to satisfy himself or herself that the essentials of a contract exist and that the agreement has been properly authorized, executed, and delivered by the corporation. The lawyer should also examine the agreement in order to make sure that the agreement does not contain unenforceable provisions such as usurious interest rates or liquidated damages clauses that might be construed as unenforceable penalties. (If the contract does contain such clauses, it is customary to state expressly that the opinion does not address the enforceability of those clauses.) Presumably it would be negligence not to verify, for example, that the officers executing the contract were duly authorized to do so. This in turn will probably compel reliance on a certificate of the corporation's secretary that certain actions were duly taken by the corporation's board of directors, and in order to make sure that there is no misunderstanding, the opinion may recite that the opining lawyer relied on the certificates of corporate officers in this regard. Even if the lawyer verifies that all the procedural steps have been taken, and that the contract does not contain inherently unenforceable clauses, other qualifications to the opinion are necessary. An unqualified opinion that the agreement is "valid, binding, and enforceable" takes no account of the bankruptcy laws that enable debtors to defer making payments and to obtain discharges of obligations in some situations, and most opinions therefore contain an express qualification for bankruptcy and insolvency. Would a lawyer be negligent if he or she failed to insert the routine bankruptcy exception? Probably not, but why take a chance when a $100,000,000 transaction is involved?

Some lawyers request that the opinion given by the other side state that the agreement "is enforceable in accordance with its terms." Does that add anything to the opinion that the contract is "legal, valid, and binding"? A fair amount of billable time has been spent on issues such as this. A careful lawyer that is requested to give a "valid in accordance with its terms" opinion may first resist on the ground that it does not add anything, but if the other side insists, he or she may shift ground slightly and treat the additional phrase as an opinion that the agreement is *specifically* enforceable in accordance with its terms. Since specific performance is a discretionary, equitable remedy, no one can opine that it will be available in all circumstances; hence, the opining lawyer may argue, if you want a "valid in accordance with its terms" opinion, that opinion must be further qualified by the addition of language such as "except as enforcement may be affected by the availability of equitable remedies or the applicability of principles of equity." And so goes the fine art of writing formal opinions.

There is a substantial and growing literature on formal legal opinions, and the new lawyer should obviously consult this literature as well as the form file that the firm maintains, before embarking on this sea of esoterica. The problem, however, cannot be readily solved by library work. The precise language of individual opinions may vary to some extent, and it is important to recognize that apparently innocuous language may create treacherous problems not unlike those associated with the "legal, valid, and binding" opinion used as an example above. Furthermore, even language that seems clear, for example, that a corporation is "duly organized" and "validly existing in good standing" in its state of incorporation, may not be so clear. An article on this type of opinion suggests that the "litany of time-honed phrases" is "replete with fuzzy nouns and slippery adverbs [and] is susceptible to a broad range of interpretations." (Fitzgibbon and Glazer, Legal Opinions on Incorporation, Good Standing, and Qualification to Do Business, 41 Bus. Law. 461 (1986).)

A new lawyer should not enter blindly into any negotiation with other lawyers about a legal opinion without first acquainting himself or herself with the potential pitfalls associated with a specific opinion. Indeed, an inexperienced lawyer who does so may be viewed as violating the canons of ethics for undertaking a matter for which he or she lacks the background and experience.

◆ GLOSSARY

Abstract Company. *See* Title Company.

Abstracting a Judgment means filing a copy or summary of the judgment in the public records. Pursuant to state statute, such a judgment then becomes a lien on all the nonexempt real property owned by the judgment debtor in the state or locality. Abstracting a judgment is a simple and relatively inexpensive way to collect upon a judgment since the judgment debtor may not convey clear title to any of his or her real estate affected by the lien without obtaining a discharge of the lien.

Accelerated Cost Recovery System (ACRS) is an accelerated depreciation system that was permitted under the Internal Revenue Code before 1986.

Accelerated Depreciation permits the allocation of relatively larger amounts of depreciation deductions to the early years of an asset's life. Accelerated depreciation produces increased tax deductions in the early years of the life of the asset.

Accounting involves the collection, summarization, and reporting of financial data by a business. It also involves the computation of profit and other measures of the financial health of the business.

Accounts Payable on a balance sheet are amounts owed to suppliers based on deliveries of supplies and raw materials on credit.

Accounts Receivable on a balance sheet are amounts due from customers not represented by promissory notes. Accounts receivable typically arise from the sale of goods on credit and may be due upon billing or upon payment terms of up to 90 days.

Accredited Investors in securities law parlance are investors who possess sufficient sophistication to "take care of themselves" and do not need the protection of the registration provisions of the Securities Act of 1933 to determine whether to purchase securities. Under Regulation D promulgated under that Act, offers of securities may be freely made to accredited investors.

Regulation D contains a precise definition of accredited investor. *See* Private Offering; Regulation D.

Accrual Basis Accounting is a method of accounting for transactions that recognizes and takes into the accounting system transactions when they have their primary economic impact rather than when cash is received or disbursed. On the revenue side, that time is usually the rendering of service or the sale of goods even though they may not have been billed and even though there may be no right to immediate payment. On the expense side, costs are taken into the accounts when the benefit occurs, which is typically when the revenues to which they relate are earned. The ultimate goal of the accrual system is the matching of expenses with corresponding revenues to the maximum extent possible.

Accrual of Costs or expense items occur for accounting purposes (that is, they must be taken into the business's accounts) when the benefit they provide occurs, which is typically when the revenues to which they relate are earned. *See* Accrual Basis Accounting.

Accrual of Revenue Items occurs for accounting purposes (that is, they must be taken into the business's accounts) when they have their primary economic impact, not necessarily when cash is received or disbursed. Thus revenue items may accrue even though they have not been billed and even though there is no right to immediate payment. *See* Accrual Basis Accounting.

Accrued Expenses Payable on a balance sheet is a catchall category for amounts owed to other business creditors that fall within neither the Accounts Payable nor the Notes Payable category. Accrued expenses payable may include amounts owed to employees for wages and salaries on the date of the balance sheet, interest on open accounts not reflected as promissory notes, amounts owed to federal, state, or local governments for taxes, fees to attorneys, insurance premiums, required pension plan contributions, and a variety of other similar items.

Accumulate/Bail-Out Strategy in income tax parlance means the common strategy used before the 1986 tax amendments to reduce overall corporation/shareholder taxes. Since tax rates were generally lower for corporations than for individuals at practically all levels of income, profitable C corporations ended up paying less tax than if the same income were allocated directly to individuals. The accumulate/bail-out strategy involved a long-term accumulation of excess undistributed earnings within the corporation followed by a liquidation or sale of the corporation's stock or its assets in a transaction that qualified for long-term capital gain treatment and permitted the accumulation to be distributed to shareholders at favorable tax rates. The corporation also had the use of funds saved by taking advantage of the lower corporate tax rate during the period of accumulation. This strategy is no longer attractive following changes in tax rates in the 1986 amendments and the elimination of favorable tax treatment for long-term capital gains.

Accumulated Depreciation on a balance sheet is a negative item subtracted from "fixed assets" equal to the total of all prior deductions for depreciation in earlier years for assets still being depreciated by the corporation. Accumulated depreciation is sometimes referred to as the "Less: Accumulated Depreciation" item, or the "Depreciation Account" or "Depreciation Reserve." Accumulated depreciation is, however, purely a balance sheet item and does not represent an actual account or reserve.

Accumulated Retained Earnings Statement is a financial statement that describes the relationship between the statement of income and the balance sheet of a business. The accumulated retained earnings statement may also cover additional capital contributions by, or capital distributions to, shareholders; such capital transactions may also be presented in a separate statement usually called Statement of Changes in Equity Accounts. *See* Retained Earnings.

Acid Test. *See* Quick Assets Ratio.

ACRS. *See* Accelerated Cost Recovery System.

Actuaries determine rates, returns, and the like for life insurance policies or annuities for the life or lives of persons on the basis of average life expectancies. Life expectancies are determined from recorded data, particularly records of mortality that show numbers of persons of various ages and occupations who die each year.

Add-On Interest is the method used for computing interest on most small consumer loans (either cash loans or loans to finance the purchase of major consumer items). Add-on interest is calculated on the original loan amount for the entire period of the loan even though periodic payments reduce the unpaid principal.

Additional Capital Paid In Respect of Common Stock is a balance sheet item that reflects the amounts paid by investors in excess of par value when the stock was originally issued.

Adjustable Life Insurance Policy is a life insurance policy that allows an individual to switch protection from term insurance to whole life insurance or back, subject to specified restrictions. *See* Term Life Insurance; Whole Life Insurance.

Adjustable Rate Mortgage (ARM) in real estate parlance is a mortgage that provides for periodic adjustments to the effective interest rate on the mortgage based on changes in a market interest rate or index of interest rates. Usually, these adjustments are reflected by changes in the amount of the monthly payment on an annual or semiannual basis. An Adjustable Rate Mortgage is also known as a Variable Rate Mortgage or a VRM. *See* Conventional Mortgage; Alternative Mortgage.

Adjusted Basis in tax parlance is the basis of property with adjustments: (1) *plus* capital improvements made by the seller, purchase commissions originally paid by the seller, legal costs for defending or perfecting title, and so forth, and

(2) *minus* returns of capital, depreciation claimed as tax deductions, depletion, deducted casualty losses, insurance reimbursements, and the like. *See* Basis.

Adjusted Gross Income for federal income tax purposes equals Total Income minus adjustments to income (employee business and moving expenses, pension plan deductions, and alimony). *See* Total Income.

After-Tax Dollars is a shorthand phrase for the concept that dollars paid by employees into retirement plans may have been subject to federal income tax when originally earned. The phrase is used most commonly when comparisons are being made with an alternative method of payment involving before-tax dollars. Before-tax dollars are involved if the employee may deduct the payments from taxable income or if the employer may make the payments directly, taking a deduction for them, without the payments being included in the employee's income for federal income tax purposes. After-tax dollars are also involved whenever the employee sets aside personal funds or makes voluntary contributions to the plan from his or her own personal funds. Similarly, a contributor to an annuity uses after-tax dollars if he or she must pay income taxes on all dollars earned, and then must make contributions to fund the annuity out of the dollars that remain.

Aggressor in corporation law parlance is the corporation (or individual or group of individuals) that is seeking to take over a target corporation.

AICPA. *See* American Institute of Certified Public Accountants.

All Holders Rule is a rule adopted by the Securities and Exchange Commission (following the *Unocal* opinion by the Delaware Supreme Court) that prohibits a public offer by the issuer of shares to all shareholders except one or more specifically designated shareholders.

Allowance for Bad Debts (or allowance for doubtful accounts) is a balance sheet item that reduces accounts receivable to reflect uncollectible accounts. The amount of this item is usually estimated based on the prior collection history of the business.

Alternative Minimum Tax in federal income tax parlance is a separate method of calculating a taxpayer's liability if the taxpayer has taken advantage of specified tax preference items. *See* Tax Preference Items.

Alternative Mortgage in real estate parlance refers to a mortgage that contains interest and/or payment terms that differ from the traditional conventional mortgage. *See* Fixed Rate Conventional Mortgage.

American Institute of Certified Public Accountants (AICPA) is the professional association of certified public accountants.

American Stock Exchange (AMEX) is a securities exchange located in New York City that lists for trading securities issued by somewhat smaller companies than those traded on the New York Stock Exchange.

AMEX. *See* American Stock Exchange.

Amortize or **Amortization** means periodic payments are to be made to gradually reduce and ultimately eliminate a larger amount. In the classic level-payment real estate mortgage, for example, the loan is amortized over the period of the loan by monthly payments that are fixed in advance and remain constant throughout the life of the mortgage. A portion of each payment represents interest and the remainder reduces (amortizes) the loan. Amortize may also be used in other contexts. For example, the amortization of assets for accounting purposes means the process of accounting for intangible assets (e.g., copyrights or patents) and deferred charges (e.g., organizational expenses, research and development costs, or "dry holes" in oil and gas exploration) by taking periodic charges against income to reduce and ultimately eliminate these assets from the financial statements.

Amount Realized in tax parlance is part of the calculation of gain or loss on a sale or exchange of property. Amount realized includes the cash received for the property on a sale or the fair market value of the property received in exchange for the property. Selling expenses, including brokerage commissions paid by the seller reduce the amount realized. In the case of property subject to a mortgage, the amount realized also includes the amount of mortgage debt which the seller is relieved from paying as a result of the sale. *See* Gain or Loss.

Anchor Tenants in real estate parlance are major tenants for commercial real estate projects, such as shopping centers or office buildings. Depending on the type of project, anchor tenants may include department stores, grocery stores, and the like. The design of the commercial project may be developed in cooperation and conjunction with the anchor tenants, who typically pay significantly lower rental on a square-foot basis than smaller tenants.

Announced Dividend Policy. *See* Regular Dividend.

Announcement Date for a dividend is the date of the press release that a cash or stock dividend is to be paid or a distribution is to be made.

Annualized Interest is the basis on which many interest rates on discounted debt with maturities of less than one year are quoted. Annualized interest rates facilitate comparisons between different issues with different periods before maturity.

Annuitant is the person receiving an annuity. The annuitant may but need not be the same person as the creator of the annuity.

Annuity is a stream of payments to be made at fixed intervals in the future.

Antidilution Provisions in convertible debentures or convertible preferred shares are provisions that adjust the conversion ratio for share dividends, share splits, the issuance of additional common shares, and similar transactions affecting the underlying common shares into which the convertible securities may be converted.

Any or All Offer in corporation law parlance is an offer to purchase all shares tendered to an aggressor by shareholders of the target without regard to the number.

Appraisal. *See* Valuation.

Appraisal Right means the statutory right of a shareholder in certain limited circumstances to have the value of his or her shares judicially determined and to be paid that amount in cash. This right is also known as Dissenters' Rights or the Right of Dissent and Appraisal.

Arbitrage is a market strategy for profiting on small differences in market prices of two different but equivalent securities in the same or different markets, or in the market prices of the same security in two different markets, or the same securities available now for delivery at two different times in the future.

ARM. *See* Adjustable Rate Mortgages.

Article 8 of the Uniform Commercial Code deals primarily with transfer of investment securities: shares of stock and long-term debt instruments. It also includes a variety of other provisions, such as a special statute of frauds for sales of investment securities.

Article 9 of the Uniform Commercial Code deals with security interests in personal property.

Articles of Incorporation is the basic corporate document filed with the appropriate state agency to form a corporation. It is the basic constitution of that particular corporation. In some states this basic document is known as the charter or the certificate of incorporation of a corporation.

Asset Acquisition Transaction in corporation law parlance is the acquisition of a business by purchasing all its assets, usually including even liquid assets such as cash and cash equivalents. In an asset acquisition transaction, the purchase price is paid to the selling corporation, not to its shareholders: There are no immediate tax consequences to the shareholders unless the proceeds are distributed to them. Businesses are often acquired through asset acquisitions for tax reasons and to limit the exposure of the purchaser to contingent or undisclosed liabilities. *See* Share Acquisition Transaction; Personal Holding Company.

Asset Coverage of Debt is a measure of how secure a holder of debt is about receiving repayment of that debt. It is obtained by subtracting current liabilities from total assets and dividing by the amount of the debt, all computed at book values. *See also* Cushion.

Assignee is a person who takes personal or intangible property by a transfer from an owner. The transfer is an Assignment; the transferor is the assignor. An Assignment is usually a voluntary transfer but the word may also sometimes be used to refer to an involuntary transfer.

Assignment for Benefit of Creditors is a state law substitute for a bankruptcy proceeding. It proceeds on the theory that the debtor has recognized the hopelessness of his or her financial situation and has voluntarily decided to turn his or her available property over to a trustee or receiver for the benefit of creditors to be administered and divided up on an equitable basis.

Assume a Mortgage in real estate parlance refers to an agreement by a purchaser of real estate to purchase a property subject to an existing mortgage and to promise to make the required payments on that mortgage.

Assumed Name is a name under which a proprietorship, partnership or corporation conducts business. *See* DBA.

Assumption of a Mortgage. *See* Assume a Mortgage.

Audit Manuals are manuals created by accounting firms to guide partners and associates when conducting an independent audit of the financial records of a business.

Auditors are independent certified public accountants who prepare and certify the financial statements of a business.

Authorized but Unissued Shares in corporation law parlance are shares that the corporation is authorized to issue under its articles of incorporation but has not yet issued.

Authorized Capital of a corporation is a term that today has no single meaning. It originally meant the number of shares the corporation was authorized to issue multiplied by the par value of those shares. Today, given the widespread practice of nominal par value shares and shares without par value (shares to be issued at a consideration set by the board of directors) the term has no real meaning. Authorized Capital may be used as a synonym for Authorized Shares.

Authorized Shares of a corporation is the number of shares that the corporation is authorized to issue under its articles of incorporation.

Automatic Stay in bankruptcy law parlance refers to the stay on collection procedures by creditors that automatically follows the filing of a voluntary or involuntary bankruptcy petition.

Back-End Load. *See* Load.

Back-End Transaction in corporation law parlance is the transaction that follows the successful acquisition by an aggressor of a majority of the target's shares. In the back-end transaction, the minority shareholders in the target are eliminated through a cash-out merger. A back-end transaction is also sometimes called a Mop-Up Merger. *See* Cash-Out Merger.

Badges of Fraud are transactions presumed to be in fraud of creditors under the Uniform Fraudulent Conveyance Act.

Balance Sheet Insolvency. *See* Insolvency.

Balance Sheet is the most fundamental financial statement, which restates the fundamental accounting equation, Assets = Liabilities + Equity.

Balance Sheet Test in corporation law parlance is a test of the validity of a corporate distribution that prohibits distributions to shareholders from specified capital accounts on the balance sheet. *See* Distribution; Dividend.

Balloon Note is a note that requires periodic amortization payments but the unpaid balance comes due before the payments amortize the full borrowed amount. The final, large payment is the "balloon," which may have to be refinanced. In some contexts, an interest-only note or even a note without periodic payments may be referred to as a balloon note.

Bankers Acceptances are short-term debt instruments the payment of which are guaranteed by a commercial bank. Bankers acceptances originate in commercial transactions and payment may also be guaranteed by the participants and by a lien on the goods involved.

Bankrupt has several varied and loose meanings. In the most technical sense, bankrupt means a person who is the subject of a federal bankruptcy proceeding. At one time it also meant a person who had committed one or more acts of bankruptcy (a concept that was eliminated from the Federal Bankruptcy Code in 1978 but continues to be referred to in the literature). It may also mean a commercial trader who is insolvent (either in the equity or balance sheet sense). It also may be used most generally as a synonym for insolvent.

Bankruptcy Judge is a federal official who presides at bankruptcy proceedings. A bankruptcy judge is not an Article III judge and has limited powers. Orders by a bankruptcy judge may be appealed to the presiding federal District Judge.

Basis in tax parlance is the investment the seller of the property has in property. Basis is the cost or purchase price of the property paid or incurred by the seller in acquiring the property. *See also* Adjusted Basis; Substituted Basis; Stepped-Up Basis.

Basis Book is a set of tables used to calculate yield-to-maturity for marketable debt securities at various prices, coupon rates, and dates of maturity.

Basis Point in debt securities trading parlance is a change in yield-to-maturity of $1/100$ of 1 percent. Thus a change of price of 50 basis points equals a change in price sufficient to change the yield-to-maturity of a debt security by $1/2$ of 1 percent, a major movement in price for most debt securities.

Bearer Paper refers to a negotiable instrument that may be negotiated merely by delivery of the paper itself. The alternative to bearer paper is a negotiable instrument payable to the order of a specific person.

Bearhug in corporation law parlance is an approach by an aggressor to a target proposing a friendly acquisition. In this approach, a veiled or explicit threat may be made that if the target chooses not to negotiate, an unfriendly takeover attempt addressed directly to the target's shareholders may be undertaken.

Bearish Sign is a sign that market prices should move downward.

Bear Raid is a campaign of short selling that is designed to drive down the price of a marketable security. Bear raids were very common before and during the early years of the 1930s but have become rarer in part because of restrictions imposed by the SEC on short selling.

Before-Tax Dollars is a shorthand phrase for the concept that certain amounts may be set aside for the benefit of employees or others without the beneficiaries being required to include in their income tax returns the amounts so set aside. Usually the benefits received by the beneficiaries will be taxable income when received, so the before-tax dollars do not escape taxation permanently. *See* After-Tax Dollars.

Beneficiary of a Life Insurance Policy is the person to whom the face value of the life insurance policy is paid upon the death of the insured. *See also* Owner of a Life Insurance Policy.

Bid and Asked Quotations are price quotations in securities markets set by market-makers in the over-the-counter market or specialists in the securities exchanges.

Big Eight refers to the eight major firms of certified public accountants in the United States that act as auditors for most publicly held corporations.

Binder in insurance parlance is a temporary policy of insurance covering the period while the insurance company assesses the risk of writing a regular policy. It is a preliminary commitment to insure against a risk. Insurance agents usually have authority to issue binders even though they may not have independent authority to bind the insurance company to a regular policy. In real estate parlance a binder issued by a title company is a preliminary report of the status of title to a property.

Blank Shares. *See* Series of Preferred Shares.

Blended Price in corporation law parlance is the combined price of a front-end loaded tender offer on a per share basis. Such an offer consists of a high initial price for the front end and a lower price for the back end. The blended price is the average of the two. An analysis concluding that shareholders will receive the blended price assumes that all shareholders will behave rationally and tender their shares to the aggressor.

Block Positioners in securities parlance are upstairs brokerage firms that participate in block trades with their own capital if the entire trade cannot be entirely placed with institutional investors. *See* Block Trade; Upstairs Brokers; Institutional Investors.

Block Trades are trades in securities involving blocks of 10,000 or more shares.

Blockage in securities trading parlance is the phenomenon that a large block of publicly traded shares may be difficult to dispose of on the market if the market is thin or the shares inactively traded. A discount for blockage when valuing a large block of inactively traded shares may be appropriate.

Blue Chip Stocks are securities issued by the very largest and most secure domestic corporations, typically the leading firms within their industry. The Dow Jones Industrial Average of 30 stocks is usually viewed as the most accurate reflection of price movements in blue chip shares. Blue chip may also refer only to the 30 companies that make up the Dow Jones Industrial Average.

Blue Sky Laws in securities law parlance are the state statutes that require public offerings of securities to be registered.

Board of Directors of a corporation has the statutory responsibility of managing, or overseeing the management of, the corporation's business.

Bond is a long-term debt instrument that is secured by a lien or mortgage on specific corporate property. Many bonds are publicly traded. The word bond is also used more broadly to refer to all long-term marketable debt securities, whether secured or unsecured. *See* Debt Instrument; Debenture.

Book Value (of a Business) means the value of the residual interest in the business (i.e., what remains after subtracting liabilities from assets) according to the financial records of the business. Book value is an accounting concept rather than a true measure of value, though it may be a rough surrogate of value and its ease of calculation may justify its use in a variety of situations.

Book Value (of an Asset) is the value of the asset as shown on the books of the business. It is equal to historical cost minus depreciation deductions taken in prior accounting periods and may bear little or no relationship to the amount that may be obtained upon the sale of the asset.

Book Value (of Shares) means the value of those shares calculated on the basis of the values shown in the books of the company. Book value is calculated on a per share basis; in a simple capital structure consisting only of common shares, book value equals shareholders' equity divided by the number of shares outstanding. In more complex capital structures, values must be assigned to shares with preferential rights before the book value of the common shares may be calculated.

Bookkeeping is the systematic recordation of every transaction entered into by a business.

Bootstrap Transaction (in Commercial Real Estate) is a transaction in which the purchaser or developer is able to borrow 100 percent of the construction and development cost and use the later cash flows to repay the loans and thereby pay for the land and improvements with no further personal investment.

Bootstrap Transactions (in Corporation Law) are transactions in which the assets of a target corporation are used to pay for its own purchase. They are highly leveraged since virtually the entire purchase price is borrowed on the strength of the acquired company's earnings or cash flow. Excess cash owned by the target or the proceeds of sales of lines of business not essential to the target may also be used to satisfy this acquisition-created debt.

Bottom Line (of a Balance Sheet) is not a meaningful figure and should be distinguished from the bottom line of an income statement.

Bottom Line (of an Income Statement) shows the results of operations over the period covered by the statement. The bottom line is usually called Net Income. Many income statements may have one or more intermediate bottom lines: *See* Gross Margin, Operating Profit, Total Income, Income Before Provision for Federal Income Taxes, Net Income for Year Before Extraordinary Items. It is important when using the phrase bottom line to have a clear understanding as to which measure is being referred to. Net Income is sometimes called the bottom bottom line.

Brackets. *See* Tax Brackets.

Bridge Loans (in Real Estate) are loans that bridge the gap between the available first lien financing and the equity funds that a developer has available to finance the project. Bridge loans are usually for intermediate periods and may be secured or unsecured. It is often contemplated that bridge loans will be rolled over as they mature into longer-term debt. Mezzanine Financing is one species of bridge loans.

Bridge Loans (in Corporation Law) are loans by investment bankers to aggressors to enable the aggressor to acquire shares of the target.

Broad Tape in securities trading parlance is the news service tape operated by Dow Jones.

Broker in securities trading parlance is a securities firm that is executing an order for a customer with a third person. A securities firm that buys or sells securities is a dealer. Large securities firms commonly act both as broker and as dealer in OTC securities, and may act as both a broker and a dealer in the same transaction if suitable notice is given to the customer.

Buildup in the parlance of annuities is the amount by which the value of a deferred annuity increases from the return on funds invested in the annuity before the annuity payments begin.

Bullish Sign is a sign that market prices should move upward.

Bunching of Income in tax parlance is including in one taxable year income or gain from activities or efforts over several years. Bunching has adverse tax consequences in any progressive rate structure, but the effect has been lessened significantly by the 1986 amendments to the Internal Revenue Code.

Business in the broadest sense means any asset or group of assets that promise to produce a flow of cash or income in the future. It generally includes all gainful activity other than employment.

Bust-Up Acquisition in corporation law parlance is an acquisition of a publicly held corporation with a view toward selling off some or all of the components of the acquired business. Usually the proceeds are used to pay down the indebtedness incurred to acquire the corporation.

Buy a Future in securities law parlance means to enter into a contract to buy a standard amount of a commodity or financial contract at a specified date in the future.

Buy Down Option. *See* Pledged Account Mortgage.

Buy-Sell Agreement in corporation law parlance is a type of share transfer restriction that commits the shareholder to sell, and the corporation or other shareholders to purchase, the shares owned by the shareholder at a fixed or determinable price upon the occurrence of a specified event. *See* Option Agreement.

Buying Term and Investing The Difference is insurance law parlance for attempting to replicate the rights created by a whole life insurance policy by buying term insurance and investing the differential in premiums in an income-producing savings account.

Bylaws are an internal set of rules for the governance of a corporation. Bylaws deal with such matters as elections, notices, size of board of directors, restrictions on the transfer of shares, and similar matters. A single section or subsection of the bylaws is usually referred to as a bylaw. The bylaws may usually be amended either by the board of directors acting alone or by the shareholders.

Calendar Year means a reporting period chosen by a business for accounting purposes that ends on the last day of the calendar year.

Call is an option to purchase a designated security at a fixed price for a limited period. *See* Strike Price; Option Writer. In a different context, call means a demand to post additional capital. *See* Margin Call.

Callable Shares. *See* Redeemable Shares.

Cap is a maximum amount for a commitment, payment, liability, or transaction. For example, in commercial real estate financing, lenders often decline to provide more than 95 percent of the contemplated construction cost; the 95 percent figure is a cap.

Capital Account of a partner reflects amounts invested by each partner in the business. In some instances, income may be credited directly to this account. *See* Income Account.

Capital Asset in tax parlance means any property held by a taxpayer other than inventory, property held primarily for sale to customers, depreciable and real property used in a trade or business, and several other less important items of property.

Capital Gain in tax parlance means the gain from the sale or exchange of a capital asset. For many years, long-term capital gains were taxed at a significantly lower rate than other forms of income, but this special tax rate was eliminated by the 1986 amendments. *See* Gain; Sale or Exchange; Capital Asset.

Capital Loss in tax parlance means the loss from the sale or exchange of a capital asset.

Capital of a Corporation is its assets minus its liabilities. It includes capital paid in for shares actually issued and retained earnings.

Capital Stock. *See* Stated Capital.

Capital Structure of a corporation refers to the mix of debt and equity in the permanent or near-permanent capitalization of the corporation. Depending on the context, capital structure may also refer to the mix between preferred and common shares in the equity capitalization of the company.

Capital Surplus in corporation law parlance is contributed capital of a corporation that is in excess of the aggregate par values of the issued shares of a corporation. Capital surplus is defined by statute in some states. Depending on the context, capital surplus may also refer to the excess of a corporation's assets over its liabilities, i.e., the capital of the corporation. *See* Par Value; Stated Capital; Paid in Surplus.

Capitalization Factor in valuation parlance is a number used to multiply estimated earnings or cash flow in determining the value of a business. The capitalization factor is the reciprocal of the discount rate when determining the present value of a perpetual stream of payments in the future with the same degree of risk and uncertainty. The capitalization factor is also called the multiplier.

Capitalization of Expenses in accounting parlance means that funds expended are treated as an investment in an intangible asset rather than as current expenses for the production of income. Capitalized expenses are usually written off in a later accounting period when revenues to which they relate are generated.

Capitalization of Income (or Earnings) is a well-recognized method of estimating the value of a business by discounting future income or earnings estimates. An estimate is made of future income or earnings and a capitalization factor is applied to that estimate. *See* Capitalization Factor.

Capitalized Organizational Cost is an asset item that reflects an accounting decision to treat the cost of organizing the company as an asset rather than as an expense. Companies usually amortize or write off such assets through periodic charges to income.

Capitalized Research and Development Cost is an asset item that reflects an accounting decision to treat research and development costs as an asset rather than as a current expense in order to match later revenues arising from that research and development with the expenses incurred to develop those revenues.

Cash as a balance sheet item includes not only funds on deposit in checking accounts, but also cash equivalents, such as United States treasury bills or notes, certificates of deposit, commercial paper, bankers' acceptances, and money market accounts.

Cash Basis Accounting is a method of accounting for transactions based on the time that payments are received or made. Salaries and other income items are entered when they are received; payments are entered when they are made.

Cash Dividend is a dividend by a corporation that is paid in the form of money.

Cash Flow Analysis consists of estimates of the future intake and outgo of cash by a business. Such analysis may be described as a statement or a projection.

Cash Flow is a measure of inflows and outflows of cash from a project or business. In commercial real estate the cash flow may be computed on a gross

541

basis (without taking into account necessary payments such as monthly mort-gage payments or management costs) or on a net basis (subtracting such expenses from the gross cash flow). Income tax savings from losses are treated as part of the cash flow from the project or business.

Cash Market. *See* Spot Market.

Cash-Out Merger in corporation law parlance is a transaction authorized by modern state corporation statutes that permit some shareholders to be com-pelled to accept cash or property for their shares while other shareholders receive (or retain) equity interests in the continuing business. Shareholders eliminated from a business through a cash-out merger may have a statutory right of dissent and appraisal if they are dissatisfied with the terms of the cash-out transaction.

Cash Sale/Credit Sale Distinction is a doctrine that permits retailers to avoid usury problems. It allows the seller to establish a higher price for credit sales than for cash sales of the identical goods without the difference being consid-ered interest under the usury statute. This distinction is also known as the Time-Price Differential.

Cash Surrender Value of a whole life insurance policy is the dollar value of the policy. It is the amount that may be obtained from the insurance company if the policy is surrendered or the amount that may be borrowed by the owner from the insurance company. The cash surrender value is also referred to as the cash value of the policy.

Cash Tender Offer in corporation law parlance is an offer made by an aggressor directly to the shareholders of the target corporation to purchase all or a specified number of shares at a designated price. The tender offer price is usually set significantly above the current market price for the target shares in order to encourage shareholders to tender their shares.

Cash Value of a whole life policy is its cash surrender value. *See* Cash Surrender Value.

CATS. *See* STRIPS.

C Corporation in tax parlance is a corporation that has not made the S Corporation election. *See* S Corporation.

CDs. *See* Certificate of Deposit.

Centralized Management refers to the attribute most clearly evident in cor-porations in which management of the business may be vested in persons with little or no ownership interest in the business. If there is centralized manage-ment, changes in ownership of the business do not directly affect who is entitled to manage the business.

CEO. *See* Chief Executive Officer.

Certificate of Deposit is a document that evidences the deposit of funds with a bank or financial institution for a fixed term at a specified interest rate.

Premature withdrawals usually involve forfeiture of some or all of the earned interest. Certificates of deposits are better known by their acronym CDs.

Certificate of Incorporation. *See* Articles of Incorporation.

Certified Public Accountants (CPAs) are individuals who have qualified as professional accountants.

Chapter 11 Reorganization permits corporations and individuals who are not hopelessly insolvent to obtain protection from creditors in federal bankruptcy court in order to devise a plan to pay off some or all of their outstanding liabilities; the plan must be approved by certain categories or percentages of creditors as well as by the bankruptcy court. During the period of reorganization, the debtor usually continues to manage its business and assets. In the plan of reorganization, some creditors may be compelled to accept partial or deferred payments or equity interests in the debtor in lieu of previous current obligations. Many businesses that file for reorganization ultimately emerge as successful and profitable businesses.

Chapter 13 Reorganization is somewhat similar to reorganization under Chapter 11. Major differences are that Chapter 13 reorganization is available only for individuals, approval of the plan of reorganization requires court but not creditor approval, and all debts must be paid in full.

Charging Order in partnership law is the procedure that must be followed by an individual creditor of a partner in order to obtain satisfaction of his or her claim from the partner's interest in the partnership.

Charter of Corporation. *See* Articles of Incorporation.

Checkbook Accounting. *See* Cash Basis Accounting.

Chicago Board of Trade is the principal commodities futures exchange. It provides trading markets for financial futures, options on shares, options on commodities futures, and options on financial futures.

Chicago School refers to theories espoused by a group of conservative law professors and economists to explain legal phenomena in economic terms. The Chicago School has been particularly influential in its analysis of takeovers and related phenomena.

Chief Executive Officer (CEO) is the person with ultimate responsibility for the management of a publicly held corporation. The CEO may have been the entrepreneur that built up the business at an earlier stage, but more likely he or she is a professional manager who never was the principal owner of the business.

Chief Legal Officer of a corporation is the inside general counsel. The position is sometimes referred to by its acronym CLO or by the term general counsel.

Claims Made Insurance is liability insurance that provides protection only for claims made during the period the policy is in force. Most liability insurance is of this nature.

Class A Stock is a designation commonly given to a class of common shares when there is more than one class of common shares outstanding. It also may be given to a class of participating preferred shares. *See* Participating Preferred Shares.

Clean Opinion in accounting parlance is an opinion by certified public accountants that financial statements have been prepared on the basis of generally accepted accounting principles and consistently with prior years, and that they fairly present the results of the business's operations.

Cleaning up the Balance Sheet is a slang phrase for transactions that reduce debt and otherwise appear to improve the financial strength of a corporation. For example, a corporation may call convertible debentures at a time when the conversion is forced so that most debenture holders will elect to convert their debentures into common shares rather than permitting them to be redeemed.

Clearly Reflect Income in tax parlance is the test applicable to determine whether specific accounting principles may be adopted for income tax purposes.

Clear the Market in securities trading parlance is a price in a market that causes the supply of the stock at that price to equal the demand for the stock at that price.

Close Corporation. *See* Closely Held Corporation.

Closed-End Investment Company is an investment company that has outstanding a fixed number of shares that are traded either on a securities exchange or over-the-counter. *See also* Open-End Investment Company.

Closely Held Corporation is a corporation with relatively few shareholders. Typically a closely held corporation is one in which (1) the number of shareholders is small, (2) there is no outside market for its shares, (3) all or most of the major shareholders participate in its management, and (4) the free transferability of shares is restricted by agreement. A closely held corporation is sometimes called a Close Corporation.

Closing Costs in real estate parlance are a variety of fees, charges, and points that a purchaser or seller must pay in connection with the sale of the real estate. *See* Points.

Closing Inventory in accounting parlance is usually determined by physical count with a value being assigned in accordance with standardized conventions. *See* Cost of Goods Sold.

Closing is the second step in important commercial transactions, where the parties meet to formally complete the transaction: to make payments and deliver deeds, bills of sale, mortgages, or other documents. Ownership usually changes hands at the closing, though possession of the property may have been delivered at another time. A closing may or may not entail an escrow arrangement. If it does not, cash payments are in the form of certified or bank checks and documents are executed and delivered at the closing pursuant to a script prepared by the person in charge of the closing.

Closing Officer is the person who is responsible for a real estate closing. Typically he or she makes sure that all necessary documents have been properly executed and received, receives and deposits checks, and so forth. Most real estate closings involve an escrow arrangement with the closing officer being responsible that the terms of the escrow are followed, ensuring that all documents are recorded in the proper order and that payments are made to the persons entitled to them.

Closing out a Position in commodities futures trading means purchasing or selling an offsetting contract so that the speculator neither owes nor is owed any of the commodity. Closing out a position is also called Netting out the Position.

Commercial Annuities are annuities sold by life insurance companies or other financial institutions. Most commercial annuities are for the life of one or more persons and involve calculations based on mortality tables.

Commercial Credit Reporting Agency is an agency that compiles financial information and credit files about individuals and businesses and provides credit reports upon payment of a fee. Individuals and businesses are entitled under federal law to have access to the information in the Agency's files.

Commercial Paper is a generic term for short-term promissory notes, checks, and other negotiable instruments issued by businesses or individuals. Commercial paper is also used more narrowly to refer to short-term debt instruments issued by leading finance companies and industrial concerns that are widely viewed as riskless short-term investments for excess capital. Commercial paper in the latter sense is publicly rated by rating agencies as to the risk of default.

Commodities Markets consist of two interrelated markets: the spot market and the futures market. *See* Spot Market; Futures Market.

Common Shares are the basic proprietary units of ownership of a corporation. They represent the residual ownership interest in the corporation. Common shares may be referred to by a variety of similar names: common shares, common stock, capital stock, or, possibly, simply shares or stock (in corporations with only a single class of shares). The two fundamental characteristics of common shares are that their holders are (1) entitled to vote for the election of directors and on other matters coming before the shareholders and (2) entitled to the net assets of the corporation (after making allowance for debts and senior securities) when distributions are to be made, either during the course of the life of the corporation or upon its dissolution.

Comparables in real estate parlance are prices at which similar nearby properties sold in the recent past.

Composition is an agreement between a debtor and two or more creditors by which the creditors agree to accept a payment in partial satisfaction of their claims and forgive the balance.

Compound Interest is computed on the assumption that the interest earned in the previous periods is left with the borrower and treated as principal thereafter, itself to earn interest in the following period. In most real-life situations, the assumptions underlying the compound interest calculation are more realistic than those underlying the simple interest calculation. *See also* Simple Interest.

Compound Interest Tables are tables that calculate the present or future value of payments, annuities, etc. for one dollar of investment over various periods and at various interest rates.

Compounded Quarterly means that interest is calculated at the end of every three months and the resulting interest is treated as principal in the following quarter.

Conduit Tax Treatment in tax parlance means the method of tax treatment applicable to partnerships by which the partnership files an information return and each partner includes in his or her personal income tax return the allocable portion of income or loss without regard to whether actual distributions have been made. The nature or quality of each item, i.e., long-term capital gain or loss, is also usually preserved in the tax returns of each partner. This method of taxation is also sometimes called the pass-through method of taxation. A similar method of taxation is also applicable to S corporations and to many investment companies.

Construction Lender for a commercial real estate construction project advances funds as construction proceeds to enable the contractor to complete the construction. In advancing these funds, the construction lender relies on architects' or engineers' certificates as required by the construction loan agreement to ensure that work to date has been performed properly and that a designated stage or percentage of completion has been attained. The construction lender is also known as the interim lender. *See also* Permanent Lender.

Construction Loan is an interim loan made by a Construction Lender to provide funds for the construction of a real estate project. It is usually assumed that upon the completion of construction a long-term loan (called a Permanent Loan) will be obtained to pay off the construction loan. Construction loans are usually made in reliance on a commitment by a responsible lender that a permanent loan will be made upon completion of construction.

Constructive Receipt in tax parlance is the principle that a cash-basis taxpayer must take into income amounts that are unqualifiedly available to him or her even though not actually reduced to the taxpayer's control.

Contingent Liabilities in the accounting sense are claims that do not qualify as liabilities in the accounting sense and therefore do not appear on the balance sheet as such. Material contingent liabilities should be referred to in the accompanying notes to the financial statements. Contingent liabilities in the more generic sense are liabilities whose validity or amount are actively disputed.

Continuity of Life refers to an attribute of a business form (most clearly evident in corporations) by which changes in the identity of owners of the business do not affect the continuity of the business form itself. A corporation possesses continuity of life while a partnership generally does not to the extent it is dissolved upon the death or withdrawal of a partner.

Contra Account on a balance sheet is an account on the asset side that reduces another asset account. An example of a contra account is Less: Accumulated Depreciation. A contra account is also called a Negative Asset Account.

Contract for Deed is a type of real estate transaction in which the purchaser enters into a contract agreeing to make specified payments over a period of years in return for entitlement to immediate possession and use of the property. Title, however, is conveyed to the purchaser only after the last required payment is made. Contract for deed is sometimes referred to as an installment sales contract for real estate.

Contract in securities trading parlance is the standard trading unit for options or futures. In the case of options on securities it is an option to purchase or sell 100 shares of the specified security.

Contributed Capital. *See* Invested Capital.

Contributor to an Annuity. *See* Creator of an Annuity.

Contributory Plan is a qualified retirement plan in which employees are required to make contributions as well as the employer. The employees' contribution is with after-tax dollars; the employer's with before-tax dollars. *See* Qualified Retirement Plan; Before-Tax Dollars; After-Tax Dollars.

Control of a Corporation is usually viewed as residing in the shareholder or shareholders who have the power to vote more than 50 percent of the voting shares of the corporation. However, where share ownership is diffuse, a significantly smaller percentage may carry with it effective working control. In another sense, control of a publicly held corporation is vested in its incumbent management, who may in fact select members of the board of directors and determine the business policies of the corporation. Control may also be defined in other ways in specialized contexts. For example, for the purpose of determining control in tax provisions relating to nonrecognition of gain or loss from transfers of property to a newly organized corporation, control means ownership of at least 80 percent of the voting stock of the corporation and at least 80 percent of all other classes of stock.

Control Share Acquisition in corporation law parlance is the name of the Indiana statute upheld by the United States Supreme Court in CTS Corporation v. General Dynamics Corp. of America, 107 S.Ct. 1637 (1987). This statute defines a control share acquisition as any acquisition that causes the shareholder's percentage of ownership to exceed 20 percent, 33⅓ percent, or 50 percent. A person making a control share acquisition of an Indiana corporation does not obtain the right to vote the newly acquired shares unless a majority of disinterested shareholders (excluding both the shares owned by the acquirer of the control shares and the shares owned by incumbent management) vote to grant voting rights to the acquirer.

Control Shares in a closely held corporation are the shares owned by a majority shareholder or group of shareholders. In rare instances there may not be an identifiable block of control shares in a closely held corporation.

Conventional Loan in real estate parlance is a long-term loan at a fixed interest rate that is secured by a first mortgage on the real estate and is amortized by level payments over the duration of the loan. Depending on the context, conventional loan may also mean a loan made by a savings and loan institution that is not insured by a governmental organization such as the Federal Housing Authority or the Veterans' Administration.

Conversion Ratio in convertible securities is the ratio between one share of the convertible security and the number of shares into which it may be converted. For example, a convertible preferred share that may be converted into two shares of common has a conversion ratio of 2:1.

Convertible Preferred Shares are preferred shares that are convertible at the option of the preferred shareholder into common shares at a specified price or at a specified ratio. Upon conversion, the preferred shares disappear.

Cooking the Books is a slang phrase for fraud or chicanery in accounting.

Corner in securities trading parlance is a market strategy in which a person or group of persons buys up most of the floating supply of shares in order to compel short sellers to cover at very high prices.

Corporation is most usefully viewed as a fictitious legal entity that possesses the same business powers as an individual. A corporation protects shareholders from personal liability on corporate obligations because the fiction is that the corporation, not the shareholders, is liable on the debt. The fictitious entity is created by a public filing with the secretary of state (or other designated public official in the state of incorporation) and the payment of a filing fee.

Cost of Goods Sold in accounting parlance is usually calculated by taking the value of Opening Inventory, adding additions to inventory during the period and subtracting the value of Closing Inventory. Opening and closing inventory are determined by physical count and value is assigned in accordance with standardized conventions. *See* LIFO; FIFO.

Coupon Bonds are long-term debt instruments that are transferred by delivery and have attached coupons representing future interest payments. *See* Coupons.

Coupons on long-term debt instruments represent future interest obligations of the issuer. Each coupon reflects a single interest payment due at some time in the future.

Coupon Clippers is a slang term for the owners of bearer bonds who clip coupons representing their periodic payments of interest.

Coupon Rate of a bond or debenture is the relationship between the face amount of the bond and the amount that is paid as interest each year on the bond or debenture. The name comes from the fact that many bonds or debentures bear interest coupons to reflect the interest payment obligation.

CPAs. *See* Certified Public Accountants.

Creative Accounting is a slang phrase for adopting accounting practices that are novel and skirt close to a line of impropriety or unacceptability.

Creative Financing is a generic term for a wide variety of innovative financing techniques, usually involving a higher degree of speculation and risk than standard financing.

Creator of an Annuity is the person who makes the payments required to create an annuity. The creator of an annuity may also be described as the contributor to the annuity.

Credit means a right-hand bookkeeping entry.

Credit Check is a report provided by a commercial credit reporting agency on the assets and bill-paying history of an individual or business. Some agencies provide a considerable amount of additional information that may be relevant in assessing the credit risk or a contemplated transaction (e.g., information about bill-paying history). A credit check is sometimes called a credit report or a credit history.

Credit Life Insurance is declining-balance term insurance sold in connection with the making of a loan that provides that if the debtor dies the loan will be paid off by the insurance proceeds.

Credits in federal tax parlance are amounts that may be subtracted from the tax due on a return in partial satisfaction of the liability shown on the return. *See also* Deductions.

Crown Jewels in corporation law parlance are valuable assets or lines of business owned by a potential target corporation. Such assets may be sold to third parties or placed under option at bargain prices as a device to defeat an unwanted takeover attempt.

Cumulative Dividends on preferred shares are preferential rights that do not disappear if dividends are not paid in some years, but are carried forward so that both all arrearages and the current year's dividends must be paid in full before any dividends on common shares may be declared.

Current Assets on a balance sheet consist of cash plus other assets that normally may be expected to be turned into cash within a year (or in a few cases in a longer period constituting the business's normal operating cycle).

Current Liabilities on a balance sheet consist of obligations to be satisfied out of current assets, usually including all liabilities that become due within a year.

Current Ratio is a measure of short-term stability of the business. It is the ratio between current assets and current liabilities.

Current Replacement Cost is an experimental accounting system required by the Securities and Exchange Commission for reporting companies. This system involves an alternative income statement created by calculating depreciation deductions on the basis of current replacement cost rather than historical cost.

Current Yield in securities parlance is the relationship between the current market price of a bond or debenture and the annual interest payments on that security. It differs from the true yield or yield-to-maturity in that no account is taken of whether the security is purchased at a premium or a discount over its value at maturity. *See* Yield-to-Maturity.

Cushion in corporation law parlance is the excess of a corporation's assets over its liabilities. From the standpoint of potential creditors, the cushion ensures that the corporation will be able to repay debt out of assets on liquidation.

Danger Signals are indications that a business is not in as strong financial condition as the financial statements might indicate. Traditional danger signals include a declining rate of growth or a rate of growth smaller than the industry as a whole, unusual turnover of key personnel, changes in auditors, and a gradual slowdown in the rate of payment of liabilities. Many danger signals cannot be detected by examining the financial statements.

Day Order in NYSE trading parlance is a limit order that provides that if the order is not filled during the trading day, it is to be filled at the closing market price at the end of the day.

DBA means "doing business as" and is used to identify the trade or business name under which a firm is conducting business.

Dealer in securities trading parlance is a securities firm trading for its own account. Large securities firms commonly act both as broker and as dealer in OTC securities and new issues, and may act as both a broker and a dealer in the same transaction if suitable notice is given to the customer. *See also* Broker; Underwriter.

Dealt In Flat in bond trading parlance means that no apportionment of interest is made between buyer and seller of the security. Bonds that are dealt in flat are either in default or of such speculative character that any interest payment is uncertain or unlikely.

Debenture is a negotiable long-term debt instrument that is unsecured. Debentures may be publicly traded. The word bonds is often used to refer to debentures as well as bonds in the narrower sense. *See* Debt Instrument; Bonds.

Debit means a left-hand bookkeeping entry.

Debit Cards are plastic cards issued primarily by banks that are similar to credit cards but all charges are automatically subtracted from the customer's bank account as soon as the merchant reports it.

Debt Instrument is an instrument that reflects unconditional obligations to pay specific sums at a date in the future and usually to pay interest in specified amounts at specified times in the interim. Promissory notes, bonds, and debentures are all debt interests.

Debt Securities are traditionally viewed as bonds or debentures. Treasury bills and notes are also sometimes referred to as debt securities. Debt securities in theory must ultimately be repaid, though maturing debt may often be rolled over.

Debt/Equity Ratio is the ratio long-term debt bears to the total shareholders' equity in the corporation. The debt/equity ratio is a measure of the amount of debt in the permanent capitalization of the business. It is stated as a ratio: Thus, a 3:1 debt/equity ratio means that long-term debt is three times shareholders' equity.

Declining Balance Insurance is term insurance with a face amount that gradually declines while the premium remains constant. Credit Life Insurance or mortgage life insurance are common examples of declining balance insurance. *See also* Face Amount Insurance.

Declining Balance Method is an accelerated depreciation system.

Deductions in tax parlance are amounts that may lawfully be deducted from adjusted gross income in calculating taxable income. *See also* Credits.

Deep Discount Bonds in securities trading parlance pay current interest rates well below effective market interest rates and therefore trade at deep discounts. *See* Zero Coupon Bonds.

Deferral of Gain or Loss. *See* Recognition of Gain or Loss.

Deferred Charges. *See* Prepaid Expenses.

Deferred Interest Rate Mortgage is a graduated payment mortgage with a fixed payment and a fixed date of maturity. However, initial payments for the first several years are fixed at such a low level that they do not cover the interest cost of the loan. Such a mortgage involves Negative Amortization.

Deficiency in debit collection parlance arises when the proceeds of the sale of foreclosed property are not sufficient to discharge the loan (as is usually the case). The creditor continues to have an unsecured claim against the debtor for the amount of the deficiency and may reduce it to a judgment, a so-called deficiency judgment, and collect on it in the same manner as any other judgment.

Defined Benefit Plan is a qualified retirement plan in which the size of the employer's contribution is determined on an actuarial basis to provide employees with designated benefits upon retirement (e.g. a retirement benefit equal to 2 percent of the employee's average salary over the last three years of his or her employment multiplied by the number of years of employment). *See also* Defined Contribution Plan.

Defined Contribution Plan is a qualified retirement plan in which the size of the employer's contribution is determined each period on a basis unrelated to the size of promised retirement payments. For example, contributions may be established as a percentage of the employer's profits during the period in question or of the actual salary paid to the employee during that period. *See also* Defined Benefit Plan.

Delaware Block Approach is a judicial method of estimating the value of shares for purposes of the statutory right of dissent and appraisal. The Delaware

Block approach combines value estimates based on earning power, market value of shares, and underlying asset values in determining the ultimate value of shares. In Weinberger v. UOP, Inc., 457 A.2d 701 (Del. 1983), the Delaware Supreme Court abandoned the Delaware Block Approach as the sole method of valuation in judicial appraisal proceedings, but other state courts may continue to follow this method of valuation.

Depletion of Assets for accounting purposes means the process of accounting for the gradual exhaustion of natural resources through the process of development and use.

Depreciation Account. *See* Accumulated Depreciation.

Depreciation of Assets for accounting purposes means the process of accounting for and writing off plant and equipment to reflect its gradual wearing out. Depreciation in an income statement reflects the portion of the original purchase price of each depreciable asset that is allocated to the current accounting period as the cost of gradually using up that asset. It should be distinguished from the Less: Accumulated Depreciation item in the balance sheet, which represents all prior deductions for depreciation of all depreciable property in the asset account.

Depreciation Reserve. *See* Accumulated Depreciation.

Derivative Securities are securities the value of which are based on or derived from price movements in individual shares (usually NYSE-traded), on changes in stock index levels that reflect a hypothetical portfolio of publicly traded securities, or price movements in commodities futures or other securities.

Designated Order Turnaround is the computerized trading system operated by the New York Stock Exchange. It is usually referred to by its acronym DOT.

Dilution in the case of shares of publicly held corporations arises when new equity securities are issued at a price or for a value that is less than the value of the interests of the current shareholders. Dilution may involve either the market value or the book value of already outstanding securities, or both.

DIM in real estate parlance is an acronym for deferred interest mortgage. A DIM involves Negative Amortization.

Discharge in Bankruptcy is the order entered by the bankruptcy court discharging a bankrupt from pre-filing debts. A discharge in bankruptcy does not cover all debts and may be withheld entirely in the event of specified types of misconduct by the bankrupt.

Discount means generally a reduction or subtraction from a designated amount.

Discount Factor is the number used to reduce the value of a dollar payable at a specified time in the future at a specified interest rate to its present value. A discount factor is the reciprocal of the future value of one dollar over the same time period and interest rate.

Discount for Lack of Alienability is a discount applied when valuing publicly traded shares that are subject to a restraint that permits transferability only to certain classes of persons or prohibits transferability to designated classes of persons.

Discount for Lack of Marketability is a discount applied when valuing publicly traded shares that are subject to significant legal restraints on transferability. *See also* Discount for Minority Interest.

Discount for Loss of Key Person is a discount applied when valuing either publicly traded or closely held shares when the fortunes of the company appear to be closely tied to a single individual.

Discount for Minority Interest is a discount applied when valuing noncontrolling interests in closely held corporations.

Discount for Restrictive Agreements is a discount applied when valuing publicly traded shares that contain a restriction that they must be first offered to the corporation or other designated person before being sold on the open market.

Discount Point. *See* Points.

Discount Rate is the interest rate used to determine the present value of a right to receive a specified payment at a specified time in the future. Discount rate is also the name of the rate set by the Federal Reserve System on loans to commercial banks. This is the wholesale cost of money from the perspective of banks; the retail rate is the prime rate. The discount rate is set by the Federal Reserve System partially on political and partially on economic considerations. Changes in this rate receive considerable publicity.

Discounting Future Payments to Net Present Value refers to the process by which amounts payable at different times are made comparable by reducing all payments to their present value. *See* Discounting; Time Value of Money; Net Present Value.

Discounting generally means reducing or subtracting from a designated amount.

Disguised Dividend. *See* Informal Dividend.

Dissenters' Rights. *See* Appraisal Right.

Distribution in corporation law parlance is a general term referring to any kind of payment (in cash, property, or obligations of indebtedness) by the corporation to one or more shareholders on account of the ownership of shares. A distribution need not be made proportionately to all shareholders. An important type of distributive transaction is the repurchase by the corporation of its own shares from a shareholder.

Diversification is the principal strategy suggested by modern portfolio theory. It involves investing in a variety of different investments rather than placing one's entire resources at the individualized risk of a single business or single type of investment.

Diversified Investment Company is an investment company that limits its investments in any one corporation to a small fraction of its total assets. Diversified investment companies may also limit the percentage of assets that may be invested in any one industry.

Dividend in corporation law parlance means a distribution by a corporation to its shareholders out of its current or retained earnings.

Dividend Preference in connection with preferred shares means that the preferred shares are entitled to receive a specified dividend each year before any dividend may be paid on the common shares.

Dividend Received Deduction in tax parlance is a deduction available to corporations for a major portion of dividends received from other corporations. The amount that may be deducted depends in part on the percentage ownership of the receiving corporation in the dividend paying corporation.

Do-It-Yourself Annuity is a plan by which a person desiring an annuity decides to replicate the desired payments from investments without actually purchasing an annuity from a writer of commercial annuities.

DOT. *See* Designated Order Turnaround.

Double Declining Balance Method is an accelerated depreciation system.

Double Entry Bookkeeping is the almost universal method of bookkeeping in use today for all but the smallest and simplest businesses. It is based on the principle that every transaction entered into by a business affects at least two accounts in the balance sheet and each effect must be recorded separately on the balance sheet. Double entry bookkeeping is the cornerstone on which modern accounting is built.

Double Exempt Municipal Bonds are bonds that are exempt from state income taxes as well as federal income taxes.

Double Tax Problem in tax parlance refers to the fact that income earned by a C corporation is first taxed at the corporate level and then taxed a second time at the shareholder level if the income is thereafter distributed to shareholders in the form of dividends.

Dow Jones Average is an average of the stock prices of 65 major Blue Chip Stocks. It is subdivided into industrial, transportation, and utility subcomponents, and averages for each of the subcomponents are also maintained.

Downstairs Brokers in NYSE trading parlance are brokerage firms who only deal with other brokers on the floor of the New York Stock Exchange. *See also* Upstairs Brokers.

Downtick in securities trading parlance means that the current price quotation is below the price at which the last transaction occurred. *See also* Uptick.

Drawing Account is a partnership account created to permit partners to draw periodic amounts without regard to the actual fluctuations of income or loss within those periods. A drawing account usually closes out into the partner's income or capital account at the end of each year.

Due on Sale Clause in mortgages provides that the face amount of the mortgage comes due upon the sale of the property. Due on sale clauses are used to prevent trafficking in below-market interest rate mortgages and to require the buyer to refinance upon a purchase.

Earnest Money is a nominal payment that usually accompanies a proposed contract of sale presented by the hopeful buyer to the seller of real estate.

Earnings per Share is a basic measure of the profitability of a corporate business. Earnings per share equal net earnings divided by the number of shares outstanding. *See also* Fully Diluted Earnings per Share.

Effective Rate of Interest is the mathematical relationship between the amount of interest paid and the amount and term of the loan. The effective rate of interest is sometimes called the Yield.

Effective Tax Rate in a progressive income tax rate structure is the ratio between the amount payable as tax on the return and the amount of income shown on the return. Income in this calculation is usually measured as taxable income as shown on the return but may also be calculated on adjusted gross income or total income. *See* Adjusted Gross Income; Total Income; Taxable Income.

Efficient Capital Market Hypothesis states that securities prices currently reflect all public information about the prospect of individual companies and the economy as a whole at any time. As a result, the next movement of any securities price is random (based on additional information as it becomes available) and not a function of prior price movements. Another corollary of this hypothesis is that it is not possible consistently to do better than the market as a whole on the basis of analysis of available information.

Employee Business Expenses for tax purposes are ordinary and necessary expenses incurred by an employee in connection with his or her employment. Such expenses are deductible subject to a floor of 2 percent of total income.

Employee Retirement Plans are retirement annuity plans created by employers for the benefit of their employees.

Endowment Life Insurance is an insurance policy that provides for premiums greater than those required for a whole life policy so that the policy becomes fully paid up at an earlier time. An endowment policy may be created so that it is fully paid up after a specified period (e.g., 20 years) or when the insured reaches a specified age (e.g., 65). *See* Fully Paid Up Policy; Whole Life Policy.

Entrenchment in corporation law parlance is a pejorative term used by courts when concluding that defensive tactics adopted by a target corporation to defeat an aggressor were excessive under the circumstances and deprived the target shareholders unreasonably of an opportunity to sell their interest in the target.

Equity in an accounting sense means ownership or net worth. It has nothing to do with equitable principles or the historical division of the English judicial system into courts of law and equity.

Equity Insolvency. *See* Insolvency.

Equity Insolvency Test. *See* Insolvency Test.

Equity Kicker in real estate parlance relates to provisions in a junior mortgage that give the mortgagee the right to acquire an equity interest in the project at a bargain price as an inducement to persuade the mortgagee to make a subordinated junior loan.

Equity Participation Loan is an innovative financing technique in which the lender receives some percentage of the developer's equity in the project in exchange for a reduction in the terms of the payback of the mortgage. An equity participation loan is sometimes referred to simply as a participation loan.

Equity Securities are securities that represent ownership interests in the corporation. Typical equity securities are common shares and preferred shares.

ERISA stands for Employee Retirement Income Security Act. ERISA is the basic federal statute that defines and regulates Qualified Retirement Plans.

Escrow means that payments and documents relating to a transaction have been placed in the custody of an independent third person with instructions to take steps to complete the transaction when specific actions have been taken and specific conditions have been met. Payments and executed but undelivered documents held by the third person are said to be held in escrow.

Established Business is a business that has been in existence for a significant period and has had substantial growth. If the business, when it started up, had sales of, say, $150,000 per year, the same business, when established, will have sales perhaps 10 or 20 times as large. Established businesses are usually incorporated but their shares may be owned by a relatively few persons, often including the original entrepreneur and other persons.

Estimated Tax is tax parlance for that portion of the Pay as You Go tax collection system that requires taxpayers with significant amounts of income not subject to withholding to file quarterly declarations of estimated tax and to make a payment with respect to estimated taxes with the declaration.

Ex Dividend Date refers to a policy established by securities exchanges to determine whether the buyer or the seller of shares traded close to the dividend date is entitled to a dividend. Ex dividend means without the dividend: A purchaser on or after the ex dividend date does not acquire the right to receive the dividend.

Exact Interest is calculated by treating the year as consisting of 365 or 366 days, as the case may be, and ignoring months. With the development of modern calculating devices, the computation of exact interest, like the calculation of compound interest, has been greatly simplified. *See also* Ordinary Interest.

Excess Liability Insurance. *See* Umbrella Insurance Policies.

Exchange Offer in corporation parlance is an offer by an aggressor to exchange its own debt or equity securities for the equity securities of the target. It is an alternative device to a cash tender offer to seek to obtain control of a target. Today most exchange offers involve aggressor debt securities being offered for target equity securities.

Exclusion Ratio for deferred annuities is the ratio applied to each annuity payment to determine what portion is a tax-free return of capital to the annuitant and what portion is taxable income. *See* Tax Deferral.

Exclusive Listing in real estate parlance means that a real estate broker has been given the sole right to sell the property for a specified period and is entitled to a commission if the property sells during that period whether from its efforts or from the efforts of the owner or others.

Execution Sale is a public sale of part or all of a judgment debtor's nonexempt assets by a public official in order to satisfy the judgment.

Exempt from Execution refers to property of a debtor which by state or federal law cannot be levied upon to satisfy a judgment.

Expenses for the Production of Income for tax purposes are ordinary and necessary expenses incurred by a taxpayer in connection with his or her income-producing activities.

Extension Agreement is an agreement between creditors and a debtor that gives the debtor additional time to pay the debts but does not forgive them. Extension agreement may also refer to a variety of other contracts, such as agreements extending a relationship beyond a stated termination date or agreements extending the period of an applicable statute of limitations. *See also* Composition.

Extra Dividend. *See* Special Dividend.

Extra Risk Life Insurance Policies are policies written for persons with known medical problems, such as apparently controlled cardiovascular disease or a history of successful treatment for cancer.

Extraordinary Items in accounting parlance are nonrecurring items that materially affect the operating results of a business. On income statements, such items are usually separated out and shown at the very bottom of the statement after the calculation of operating profit that represents the earnings capacity typical of the firm, and an estimate of the taxes due on that operating profit. Extraordinary items themselves may or may not give rise to additional income tax adjustments, which are usually shown separately as part of the effect of the extraordinary item.

Face Amount Insurance is term insurance for a fixed amount payable upon the death of the insured during the period the policy is in effect: Premiums for face amount insurance increase gradually as the insured gets older. *See also* Declining Balance Insurance.

Fair Market Value of a business is the price that would be established by a buyer and a seller in an arms-length negotiation for the purchase and sale of the business, both being ready, willing, and able to enter into the transaction, under no compulsion to enter into the transaction, and having essentially complete information about the relevant factors.

Fair Price Amendments in corporation law parlance are amendments to Articles of Incorporation adopted by publicly held corporations that preclude subsequent mergers or related transactions with major shareholders except at prices that meet specified standards. Such amendments are designed to prevent unfair Back-End Transactions, and ultimately serve as a defense against unwanted takeovers.

Fair Price Statutes in corporation law parlance are state statutes enacted by several states that specify minimum prices for Back-End Transactions for a period of time following the purchase of shares.

FASB stands for Federal Accounting Standards Board, the organization primarily involved in developing Generally Accepted Accounting Principles.

Fed in securities trading and banking parlance is a short-hand reference to the Federal Reserve Board.

Federal Estate Tax is a tax due on the estate of a decedent upon his or her death. It is not an income tax but is levied upon the value of the assets includable in the taxable estate of the decedent.

FHA Mortgages are residential real estate mortgages the payment of which are insured by the Federal Government. FHA insurance is not available for very large transactions.

FIFO. *See* First In First Out.

Financial Accounting involves the preparation of financial statements primarily for the benefit of investors, creditors, regulatory agencies, employees, and others. Financial accounting is usually contrasted with Management Accounting.

Financial Futures are futures contracts in a variety of financial instruments, e.g., foreign currencies, United States Treasury debt securities, and stock and bond indexes.

Financials is a shorthand term for financial statements.

First In First Out (FIFO) is an inventory valuation method that assumes that the earliest item in inventory is the first used.

First Mortgage. *See* Senior Mortgage.

Fiscal Year means the reporting period for accounting purposes chosen by a business that ends on a date other than December 31. A fiscal year may vary slightly in length from a period of precisely 12 months.

Fixed Assets in accounting parlance are property, plant, and equipment. Such items are usually recorded on the balance sheet at historical cost. Plant and equipment is depreciated over its expected life while land is a fixed asset that is not depreciable. *See* Accumulated Depreciation.

Fixed Rate Conventional Mortgage (FRCM) in real estate parlance is a long-term mortgage that provides for a fixed interest rate and level periodic payments that totally amortize the loan upon the final payment.

Flim Flam means the use of fraud, fictitious entries, or unusual accounting principles in order to mislead, usually by overstating income or assets or understating liabilities. Flim flam in accounting is often called Cooking the Books.

Flip-In Poison Pills in corporation law parlance grant shareholders additional financial rights in the target (e.g., the right to acquire additional shares or indebtedness issued by the target corporation at a bargain price) when the poison pill is triggered by a cash tender offer or a large acquisition of target shares by an aggressor.

Flip-Over Poison Pills in corporation law parlance grant shareholders additional financial rights in the aggressor when the poison pill is triggered by a cash tender offer or a large acquisition of target shares by an aggressor. The usual flip-over provision grants shareholders in the target the right to purchase shares in the aggressor at bargain prices (e.g., the right to purchase $200 worth of the common shares of the tender offeror for $100 in the merger) in the event of a Back-End Merger between the target and the aggressor within a designated period after the pill is triggered.

Float when referring to travelers checks is the pool of funds representing amounts paid by individuals who have bought travelers checks but not yet used them.

Floating Supply of Shares. *See* Street Name Shares.

Floor in tax parlance means a minimum amount below which no deduction for expenses is allowed. If expenses exceed the minimum amount, the excess amount is deductible.

Floor (of the Exchange) means the trading area in the building of the New York Stock Exchange, the Chicago Board of Trade, or similar exchanges, where securities or futures are traded.

Floor Traders on the New York Stock Exchange are individual members of the Exchange who may trade for their own account as well as acting as broker for others.

Flyspeck in real estate parlance is a trivial defect in the title that is unlikely to have any practical significance or effect and does not make the title unmarketable. *See* Marketable Title.

For Sale by Owner when used in connection with residential real estate implies that no brokerage commission is involved.

Forced Conversion of a convertible security in securities trading parlance occurs when the convertible is called for redemption at a time when the price of the underlying conversion security, the conversion ratio, and the redemption price are such that it is profitable for all security holders to convert their convertible securities rather than permitting them to be called for redemption.

Foreclosure in real estate parlance is the process by which a lender on a defaulted loan sells the property at public sale in order to obtain full or partial satisfaction of the debt. Foreclosure may also refer to the process to enforce a security interest in personal property, though in the case of consumer goods it may involve repossession. Typically, personal property is also sold and the proceeds applied to the payment of the debt, though the sale may not be a public sale.

Form 1040 is the long tax return form used by individual taxpayers with substantial taxable income not subject to withholding or with substantial deductions. More simplified forms may be used by many taxpayers who have smaller incomes or who do not itemize deductions.

Fortune 500 in corporation law parlance is the list of the 500 largest corporations as determined by *Fortune* Magazine.

14D Statement is a statement that must be filed with the SEC by a person who has made or is about to make a public cash tender offer for shares of a target corporation.

Fraud on Creditors. *See* Fraudulent Conveyance.

Fraudulent Conveyance (also called Fraud on Creditors) is a state law doctrine designed to protect creditors from transactions entered into by debtors that have the purpose or effect of hindering or defeating the creditor's ability to collect on his or her indebtedness.

Free Transferability of Interest refers to the attribute of business forms by which owners of a business may sell or transfer their interests in the business without legal restriction. Free transferability of interest theoretically exists in all corporations unless there are restrictions on transfer, but as a practical matter the power to transfer is likely to be theoretical in closely held corporations since there is no market for shares. Free transferability of interest may also exist in limited partnerships for interests of limited partners.

Fresh Start is the slang term often used to describe the discharge that is available under the federal bankruptcy laws for most individual debtors that enables one to be relieved of the obligations owed to unpaid creditors.

Front-End Load. *See* Load.

Front-End Loaded Tender Offer is a cash tender offer in which it is announced that the Back-End Transaction will be effected at a lower price than the initial offer for the controlling interest of the target made in the tender offer itself.

Full Cost Oil Companies are oil companies that capitalize the cost of the dry holes: The reported costs of their reserves include the cost of drilling unsuccessful as well as successful wells. *See* Successful Efforts Oil Companies.

Fully Diluted Earnings per Share are earnings per share computed on the assumption that all outstanding options to purchase shares, conversion rights to convert into common shares, and warrants or rights to acquire common shares, have been exercised. Fully diluted earnings per share represent what the earnings per share would have been at the worst, assuming all options have been exercised and all conversions have been made.

Fully Paid Up at 65 Policy. *See* Endowment Policy.

Fully Paid Up Policy is a whole life or endowment insurance policy in which the cash surrender value equals the face value of the policy, and there is no remaining component of life insurance to be paid from premiums.

Future Value of a Present Sum is the amount by which a present sum will grow at a specified compound interest rate during a specified period.

Futures Market for commodities is the market in which contracts for future delivery of standardized amounts of the commodity are traded. *See also* Spot Market.

GAAP. *See* Generally Accepted Accounting Principles.

GAAP Statements are financial statements prepared in accordance with Generally Accepted Accounting Principles.

GAAS. *See* Generally Accepted Auditing Standards.

Gain or Loss on a transaction in tax parlance equals the Amount Realized minus the Adjusted Basis of the property.

Garbage is a slang term for the useless computational results obtained when inadequate, incomplete, or inaccurate data is manipulated by precise statistical or mathematical methods. The phrase "garbage in — garbage out" (GIGO) is often used in this context.

Garnishment is a procedure by which a judgment creditor may execute upon ("garnish") amounts owed to the judgment debtor. A writ of garnishment is served on a person who owes the judgment debtor money and commands that person to pay the amount owed to the garnishing creditor rather than to the judgment debtor. Bank accounts are the most common garnished property: Some states wholly or partially exempt certain types of payments from garnishment, such as wages or salaries.

General Partnership is a partnership without limited partners. The word "general" may be omitted unless the context requires that a distinction be made between a limited partnership and a general partnership. Thus, partnership alone means a general partnership. *See* Partnership.

General Utilities Doctrine in tax parlance is the principle that permitted corporations, upon liquidation, to avoid the realization of gain from appreciation in the value of its assets. The General Utilities Doctrine was repealed in the 1986 tax amendments.

General Warranty Deed includes a general warranty by the seller that his or her title is valid as against the world. General warranty deeds may be known by different names in some localities. *See also* Special Warranty Deed; Quit Claim Deed.

Generally Accepted Accounting Principles (GAAP) are the accounting principles that form the standard for financial reporting for publicly held corporations in the United States.

Generally Accepted Auditing Standards (GAAS) are auditing standards prepared by the American Institute of Certified Public Accountants that deal with the manner in which CPAs carry out independent examinations of the financial statements of companies.

Going Naked. *See* Naked Options.

Going Private in corporation law parlance is a transaction in which a publicly held corporation eliminates all public shareholders and returns to the status of a closely held, unregistered corporation. Many going private transactions are effectuated by Leveraged Buyouts, but there are other transactions that may also be used for the same purpose.

Going Public means the process by which a business, almost always a corporation, raises capital by selling securities to members of the general public. Going public usually requires registration of the securities to be sold with the Securities and Exchange Commission under the Securities Act of 1933 and with state security commissions in the states where the securities will be offered. This registration process for an initial public offering may be difficult and expensive.

Golden Parachutes in corporation law parlance are lucrative severance contracts for top management whose employment with the corporation may be terminated upon a successful takeover by an aggressor.

Good to Cancelled in NYSE trading is a Limit Order that is not a Day Order.

Goodwill in a broad sense refers to intangible assets such as business reputation and name recognition that are not assets appearing on a balance sheet. To the extent goodwill does appear as an asset on a balance sheet it is a questionable entry that may reflect only a balancing entry for prior transactions; for example, if a company buys a bundle of assets for more than the sum of their individual fair market values, the excess may be entered as "goodwill." It is rare for such an asset to have any tangible or realizable value. Many companies write off such assets through periodic charges to income.

GPARM (or GP/ARM). *See* Graduated Payment Adjustable Rate Mortgage.

GPM. *See* Graduated Payment Mortgage.

Grace Periods in promissory notes or mortgages are provisions that allow the debtor to correct defaults or make up missed payments for specified periods after the default.

Graduated Payment Adjustable Rate Mortgage (GPARM) is a mortgage that combines a graduated payment feature with an adjustable interest rate. This type of mortgage may also be referred to as a graduated payment/adjustable rate mortgage (GP/ARM). *See* Adjustable Rate Mortgage; Graduated Payment Mortgage.

Graduated Payment Mortgage (GPM) has a fixed interest rate and a fixed time for repayment like a fixed rate conventional mortgage (FRCM). However, the monthly payments under a GPM start out at a lower level than those called for by the equivalent FRCM, but thereafter rise periodically, usually in three or four steps. *See* Fixed Rate Conventional Mortgage.

Greenmail in corporation law parlance is an agreement by an aggressor and a target corporation, following the acquisition by the aggressor of a substantial holding in target shares, by which the target corporation agrees to buy the target shares owned by the aggressor at a price that is usually above market and certainly above the aggressor's cost. In return the aggressor agrees to make no further purchases of target shares for an extended period.

Gross Cash Flow. *See* Cash Flow.

Gross Margin in accounting parlance equals net sales minus cost of goods sold. Gross margin is an income statement entry.

Gross Profit in accounting parlance equals net sales minus value of opening inventory minus additions to inventory plus value of closing inventory. Gross profit is an income statement entry.

Group Life Insurance is term insurance that is made available, usually at special premium rates, to members of a group such as all employees of a specific employer, members of a social or professional organization, and so forth.

Guaranteed Payment in partnership law is a salary payable to a partner that is independent of the amount of partnership earnings allocable to the partner.

Handshake Partnership is a partnership created without a formal written partnership agreement, often entered into without legal assistance.

Head of Household in tax parlance is an unmarried person who is not a surviving spouse and who maintains a home for a dependent child or relative.

Heavily Leveraged, when referring to a corporation, means a corporation with a high Debt/Equity ratio.

Hedge in securities trading parlance is a general term that describes a transaction designed to protect an existing holding or position from adverse price movements. For example, a speculator who has sold a stock short may hedge the risk by purchasing a call option on the same stock. In commodities futures trading hedgers are persons, such as farmers or users of agricultural commodities, who assure future prices by entering into commodities futures transactions. For example, a farmer with a corn crop in the ground may hedge his or her projected harvest against price decline by selling a corn futures contract. Similarly, a manufacturer using raw corn in its manufacturing processes may ensure future supplies at an assured price by buying corn futures contracts roughly matching its needs for raw corn. The effect of hedging by the farmer and/or manufacturer usually is to transfer the risk of price movement to a market speculator willing to take that risk.

Historical Cost of an asset means its original cost or purchase price. Historical cost also includes subsequent investments in or the cost of improvements to the asset.

Holder in Due Course is a person who acquires a negotiable instrument by endorsement for value and without knowledge of possible defenses. A holder in due course may enforce the promise of payment set forth in the negotiable instrument free of most defenses that the debtor might have had if suit had been brought directly by the creditor on the underlying transaction.

Holding Company is a corporation that invests exclusively in controlling interests in several operating companies and itself has no other business.

Home Equity Loan is a loan or line of credit secured by a mortgage on a person's residence that may be drawn upon for a variety of personal needs. Interest on home equity loans is tax deductible even if the proceeds are used for personal purposes.

Homestead means a person's personal residence. A homestead is exempt from execution in whole or in part in many states.

House Counsel are lawyers who are employed by the inside legal department.

H. R. 10 Plans. *See* Keogh Plans.

Hybrid Securities are securities that have some of the characteristics of debt and some of the characteristics of equity.

IOU is a simple acknowledgement that a debt exists.

In House means that legal work is to be done by lawyers employed by a corporation rather than by lawyers or a law firm in the traditional lawyer/client relationship.

Income (in the accounting sense) means revenues minus expenses.

Income Account of a partner reflects the undistributed income allocable to the partner in prior and current accounting periods. In some partnerships, the income account is periodically closed out into the capital account. In smaller partnerships, income may be allocated directly to the capital account. *See* Capital Account; Drawing Account.

Income Before Provision for Federal Income Taxes in accounting parlance equals total income less interest on long-term debentures. Income before provision for federal income taxes is an income statement item.

Income Bonds are bonds on which the obligation to pay interest is limited to the amount of corporate earnings in each accounting period.

Income Depletion was a method of tax accounting formerly used for the depletion of oil and gas reserves. Income depletion permitted the deduction from taxable income of a specified amount of income arising from development of the reserves each year rather than a specified amount of the cost of acquiring the reserve.

Income in Respect of a Decedent in tax parlance is income received by the estate of a decedent attributable to services of the decedent, such as fees for services provided by the decedent before his or her death. Income in respect of a decedent is includable in the federal income tax return of the estate.

Income Splitting in tax parlance is the division of a single income among two or more persons for tax purposes. If the persons involved do not have additional outside income, income splitting always results in a lower aggregate tax bill on the income, though the advantages of income splitting were reduced by the 1986 tax amendments.

Income Statement is a basic accounting statement that shows the results of operations over a designated period, usually monthly, quarterly, or annually.

Incontestability Clause in life insurance policies prohibits a life insurance company from cancelling a policy for fraud or nondisclosure after the lapse of a specified period, called the contestability period. Following the expiration of this period the policy is said to be incontestable.

Increased Dividend in corporation law parlance is a decision by a publicly traded corporation to increase the amount of its regular or announced dividend. *See* Regular Dividend.

Index Fund is a mutual fund that attempts to replicate the performance of the market as a whole, usually by investing in a pattern that is comparable to the mix of securities in a major market index such as Standard & Poor's 500 stock index.

Index Futures are futures contracts in a variety of widely followed securities indices, particularly the Standard & Poor's 500 share index. *See also* Portfolio Insurance.

Individual Retirement Accounts (IRAs) permit certain employees whose employers do not have a qualified retirement plan to make retirement contributions to a special account.

Inflation Accounting generally describes a number of experimental accounting systems that are designed to reflect the impact of inflation on accounting statements.

Informal Dividend in corporation law parlance is a payment of salary, rent, interest, reimbursement of expenses, or similar transaction by a corporation to one or more of its shareholders that is a substitute for a dividend. Such a payment is also sometimes referred to as a Disguised Dividend. *See* Distribution.

Inside General Counsel to a corporation is a full-time corporate legal officer compensated by the corporation in the same manner as other corporate officers.

Insolvency (or Insolvent) has two quite different meanings. The most common meaning is that the debtor is unable to meet its obligations as they come due. This is usually referred to as "Equity Insolvency" or "insolvency in the equity sense." The second meaning is that a debtor's total liabilities are greater than the value of his or her nonexempt property taken at a fair valuation. Insolvency in the latter sense is referred to as "Balance Sheet Insolvency" or "insolvency in the bankruptcy sense." Balance sheet insolvency requires reference to accounting principles in its application.

Insolvency Test in corporation law parlance is a test of the validity of a corporate distribution that prohibits distributions to shareholders if the effect is to make the corporation unable to pay its debts when they fall due. This test is also known as the Equity Insolvency Test. *See* Distribution; Dividend.

Instinet is a computerized trading system for institutional and non-NYSE member brokerage firms to trade among themselves.

Institutional Investors are large investors who primarily invest other people's money. They include life insurance companies, pension funds, investment companies (divided into Closed-End and Open-End Funds), bank trust departments, charitable foundations, educational institutions, and similar organizations.

Institutional Trading Departments are divisions of upstairs brokers that specialize in trading with and on behalf of institutional investors.

Insurable in life insurance parlance refers to a person who can demonstrate that he or she is in reasonably good health and engages in activities of average risk.

Insured in a life insurance policy is the person whose demise triggers the obligation of the insurance company to pay the face value of the policy.

Intangible Assets in accounting parlance include patents, trademarks, franchises, goodwill, capitalized organizational cost, or capitalized research and development costs. Intangible assets is a balance sheet item. *See* Goodwill.

Interest Cushion is the difference between the interest owed by a business and the total income of the business. The interest cushion is a measure of the ability of a business to carry debt and the risk of a default on that debt. In some contexts, the interest cushion may be referred to simply as the cushion. *See* Cushion; Net Interest Coverage.

Interest is the amount paid by a borrower for the use of the lender's money. Interest may also be viewed as the cost of a loan to a borrower and the return from owning capital to the lender.

Interest-Only Mortgage is an alternative mortgage that contains loan provisions that provide that, for the first years of the loan, payments need only equal the interest payable on the loan. Principal is amortized beginning at the end of the interest-only period. *See* Alternative Mortgage.

Interim Financing in real estate parlance is short-term financing obtained during periods when permanent loans are expensive or difficult to obtain. The purchaser hopes that financing conditions will ease and a permanent loan may later be obtained to pay off the interim financing. It may also sometimes refer to a construction loan. *See* Permanent Loan.

Interim Lender. *See* Construction Lender.

Intermarket Trading System (ITS) is a computerized trading system that links trading in specific securities on the regional and New York securities markets.

Internal Rate of Return (IRR) is a method of capital budgeting by businesses. The IRR is the discount rate that equates the present value of the expected cash outflows with the expected cash inflows of a contemplated investment. When alternative investments are under consideration, the business should select the one with the highest internal rate of return.

Internal Revenue Code of 1986 is the official name of the statute that made major changes in the federal income tax laws in 1986.

Intrinsic Fairness is the standard adopted by the Delaware Supreme Court in evaluating self-dealing transactions between a parent and subsidiary corporation. The intrinsic fairness standard is applied to transactions that have not been appropriately approved by disinterested directors of the subsidiary.

Intrinsic Value of a warrant, right, or option is the difference between the call, strike, or exercise price and the current market value of the security to which the warrant, right, or option relates. *See* Time Value.

Inventories in accounting parlance on a balance sheet include goods needed by the business in production of its end product: raw materials, partially finished goods in process of manufacture, all goods on hand that are ultimately consumed in the production of goods, and finished goods ready for shipment. The inventory of a retail operation may consist almost solely of finished goods.

Inventory Turnover Ratio in a manufacturing or retail business is a measure of whether the company's inventory is too large for its level of operations and whether inventory turns over quickly or not.

Invested Capital (or Contributed Capital) of a corporation is the capital received by a corporation in exchange for its shares.

Investment Company is a corporation that invests only in marketable securities of other corporations. *See* Closed-End Investment Company; Open-End Investment Company.

Investment Interest in tax parlance is interest on obligations incurred to buy or carry investment property. Under the 1986 amendments such interest is deductible only to the extent the taxpayer has income from the investments.

IRAs. *See* Individual Retirement Accounts.

Joint Venture is a type of business form that can best be described as a limited-purpose partnership. Most partnership rules are applicable to joint ventures.

Journal in bookkeeping is the first set of entries made when a transaction occurs.

Judgment Debtor means a person against whom a final money judgment has been entered.

Junior Mortgages are subordinated mortgages, e.g., second or third mortgages. They carry higher interest rates than first mortgages because of the significantly higher risk.

Junk Bonds are below-investment grade bonds, as determined by one or more bond rating services, often issued in connection with takeover attempts.

Keogh Plans are self-employed retirement plans that in effect permit the self-employed to make retirement contributions with before-tax dollars. A self-employed individual may make contributions to a Keogh Plan (up to a specified maximum) and deduct the payment from his or her federal income tax return. Keogh Plans are also known as H.R. 10 Plans.

Last In First Out (LIFO) is an inventory valuation method which assumes that the last item added to inventory is the first used.

LBO. *See* Leveraged Buyout.

Ledger in accounting practice means a separate sheet or sheets created in order to consolidate and record all entries relating to a single balance sheet or income item. Ledger accounts are often called "T accounts" because they traditionally are kept on sheets that look like a balance sheet to facilitate the entry of right hand and left hand entries. Depending on the context, ledger may be used more generally to mean any page in a set of financial records, or even the entire set of financial records themselves.

Left Hand Side (of a balance sheet) is the asset side even though it is printed above rather than to the left.

Legal Opinions in connection with transactions confirm and give assurance that certain desired legal relationships have been or will be created upon the closing of the specified transaction.

Less: Accumulated Depreciation. *See* Accumulated Depreciation.

Letter Ruling in tax parlance is a ruling by the Internal Revenue Service on the tax consequences of a proposed transaction.

Letter Stock in securities law parlance refers to publicly traded shares of stock that are subject to restraints on transferability usually imposed to ensure the continued availability of an exemption from registration under the Securities Acts.

Letters of Intent in real estate parlance are written indications from possible commercial tenants of their interest in renting space in a commercial development not yet built. Letters of intent are often submitted to potential lenders as part of an application for a permanent loan. Letters of intent may or may not be legally binding.

Leverage is the advantage obtained from the use of borrowed money when acquiring income or cash flow-producing property.

Leveraged Buyout in corporation law parlance is a transaction by which incumbent management of a corporation, usually with the assistance of outside financing sources, purchases all publicly owned shares of the corporation and takes the corporation private. Most of the purchase price for the shares is borrowed and is assumed by the corporation taken private in the leveraged buyout. A leveraged buyout is often referred to as an LBO or MBO (for management buyout).

Leveraged Capital Structure is a capital structure that has large amounts of debt capital in relation to equity capital.

Leveraged Recapitalization in corporation law parlance is a series of transactions in which a corporation borrows additional amounts in order to distribute those amounts to its shareholders directly or indirectly. A leveraged recapitalization substitutes debt capital for equity capital and makes a potential target in a takeover attempt less attractive. A transaction in which a potential target borrows large amounts of money in order to increase its debt/equity ratio and distributes the cash to shareholders in the form of a share repurchase program or extraordinary distribution is also known as Leveraging Up.

Leveraging Up. *See* Leveraged Recapitalization.

Levy means to sell certain property at an execution sale.

Liabilities in the accounting sense are recognized debts or obligations to someone else, payable either in money or in something reducible to money, in an amount that can reasonably be estimated at the time the balance sheet is prepared. Not all liabilities in the legal or lay sense are liabilities in the accounting sense.

Lien is an intangible interest in property that secures the payment of a debt. A lien allows the creditor, if the loan is not repaid, to seize the property subject to the lien to satisfy the unpaid loan. Usually the property is sold and the proceeds applied against the unpaid loan. *See also* Security Interest.

Life Expectancy of a person is the actuarial determination of the period he or she is expected to live. The life expectancy of a person is an essential aspect of many insurance or annuity calculations.

LIFO. *See* Last In First Out.

Limit Order is an order to buy or to sell securities on an exchange at other than the market price when the order reaches the securities floor.

Limit Order Book is the book in which a record of limit orders is maintained by the specialist in a stock. It may either be a physical book or an electronic book.

Limited Partner is a partner in a limited partnership who is not liable for the partnership debts. A limited partner may lose the shield of limited liability if he or she takes part in control of the business.

Limited Partnership is a partnership that consists of at least one limited partner and one general partner. Limited partnerships differ from general partnerships in that there are one or more partners, called "limited partners," who are not personally liable for the debts of the partnership and who are not expected to participate in the day-to-day affairs of the partnership.

Line of Credit is a common kind of open arrangement between a bank and a customer by which the customer may borrow money as needed up to a stated maximum. Interest is usually charged only on amounts actually borrowed, though fees may be charged when creating or renewing the arrangement.

Liquidation Preference in connection with preferred shares means that the holders of preferred shares are entitled to receive a specified distribution from corporate assets in liquidation (after provision has been made for corporate debts) before the holders of common shares are entitled to receive anything.

LIST is the name of the part of the DOT computerized trading system operated by the New York Stock Exchange that allows arbitrageurs and others to trade lists of securities instantaneously.

Listed Shares on the New York Stock Exchange are the shares that are traded on the floor of the Exchange. To be listed, companies must meet certain size and securities holdings requirements and enter into a listing agreement with the Exchange.

Listings in real estate parlance are properties that have been listed for sale with a real estate broker. *See* Exclusive Listing.

Load in mutual fund parlance is an additional charge imposed on an investor when he or she invests in an open-end investment company (a Front-End Load) or when he or she redeems his or her shares in that investment company (a Back-End Load). Front-end loads are more common than back-end loads. A front-end load is usually called a Sales Load.

Lock-Up Options in corporation law parlance are options on Crown Jewels or on shares of the target that are granted to friendly third parties as a device to defeat an aggressor's takeover attempt.

Long Lead Time means that costs must be incurred for the production of an item for an extended period before revenues are received.

Long Position in securities trading parlance means that the trader owns more of a security than he or she owes to the market.

Long Term in tax parlance, when used in the context of capital gains or losses, means the statutory holding period for capital assets. This period is six months but sometimes in the past has been one year.

Long-Term Liabilities on a balance sheet are liabilities due more than one year from the date of the balance sheet.

Loss on a transaction in tax parlance equals the amount by which the Adjusted Basis of the property exceeds the Amount Realized.

Lower of Cost or Market is an accounting principle that requires inventory or marketable securities to be promptly marked down to market value if that value is less than its cost.

Maintenance in securities trading parlance refers to the level of asset coverage in a margin account that triggers a call for additional capital to be added to the account. *See* Margin Call.

Majority Consent Procedure in corporation law parlance refers to the provisions in the Delaware General Corporation Law and a few other state statutes that allow the shareholders of a corporation to act by written consent of the holders of a majority of the shares without a meeting.

Management is a general term that describes the officers and high-ranking employees of a business, usually a corporation.

Management Accounting involves the preparation of internal reports and analyses for the benefit of management. These reports are usually not prepared in accordance with GAAP and may involve analyses of highly confidential information such as controls and costs. The preparation of these internal reports is usually contrasted with Financial Accounting.

Management Consultant Firms offer a variety of services to business managers: decision-making, planning, valuation, accounting, and taxation. These firms employ persons with experience in accounting and auditing as well as management decision-making.

Margin is the amount of capital a customer must deposit with a broker to engage in Margin Transactions in securities under regulations established by the Federal Reserve Board. For several years the requirement has been 50 percent. Margin when used in connection with commodities futures trading is a deposit — a performance bond — that provides assurance that a speculator in commodities futures has available assets to cover short-term losses if the market moves adversely to his or her interest. *See also* Maintenance.

Margin Account is an account with a broker in which purchases on margin or short sales are authorized.

Margin Call is the request by a broker for additional capital when the value of a portfolio containing margin transactions or short sales has dropped to the point that an additional contribution of capital is necessary under applicable maintenance requirements.

Margin Transactions in securities involves borrowing money from a broker to buy more shares of marketable securities. *See* Margin.

Marginal Tax Rate in a progressive income tax rate structure is the rate of tax applicable to the last dollar earned by the taxpayer. *See also* Effective Tax Rate.

Marked to Market refers to the process by which the value of each commodities futures account is recalculated each day on the basis of the Settle Price. If the value of the account is below a specified level, the speculator must deposit additional capital in the account or the futures positions will be closed out by the broker.

Market for Control in corporation law parlance is the theory adopted by some members of the Chicago School of law and economics that there is a market for control of publicly held corporations, and that the effect of that market ultimately is to eliminate inefficient managers. It was also argued that this market is interstate in character and not subject to regulation by the states. Market for control may also be used to describe the phenomenon that the value of a publicly held corporation (established by an outside cash tender offer or internal leveraged buyout for all the shares of the corporation) is apparently greater than the total market value of all the outstanding shares established by the securities markets immediately before the transaction in question is proposed.

Market Maker in the over-the-counter securities market is a dealer who announces its continued willingness to both buy and sell a specific stock. The price at which a market maker is willing to sell (the asked price) is somewhat higher than the price at which it is willing to buy (the bid price).

Market Order is an order to buy or to sell securities at the market price.

Marketable Securities are securities for which a regularly established trading market exists. Securities may be marketable even though the market is "thin" and trades occur relatively infrequently.

Master Limited Partnership is an organization that issues depository receipts for limited partnership interests so that they may be publicly traded. Publicly traded limited partnerships exist primarily for tax reasons: Recent legislation has reduced the attractiveness of this form of business organization.

MBO stands for Management Buyout. *See* Leveraged Buyout.

Members of the New York Stock Exchange are persons or firms that have acquired seats on the Exchange and are entitled to trade securities on the floor of the Exchange. *See* Seats.

Mezzanine Financing. *See* Bridge Loans.

Miller-Modigliani Theorem states that the aggregate value of a corporation's securities is independent of the amount of debt in the corporation's capital structure. This theorem is valid only with certain simplifying assumptions, including elimination of the tax advantage of debt.

Money Market Account is an interest-bearing bank account. Usually the depositor is permitted to write checks on the account, sometimes with restrictions as to size and number each month.

Money Market Fund is a mutual fund that invests only in short-term, virtually riskless investments. Money Market Funds bear names such as cash management accounts, liquid asset funds, and the like. Money market funds usually attempt to keep their net asset value at one dollar per share so that the fund appears to be similar to an interest-bearing bank account. Many money market funds permit checks to be written against the account.

Mop-Up Merger. *See* Back-End Transaction.

Mortgage Life Insurance is declining-balance term insurance sold in connection with a mortgage that provides that if the borrower dies the mortgage will be paid off by the insurance proceeds. Mortgage life insurance is also called mortgagor life insurance.

Mortgagee Policy in real estate parlance is a title insurance policy that protects only the interest of a mortgagee. A mortgagee policy may leave the owner dangerously exposed if an unexpected title defect surfaces. *See also* Owner's Policy.

Multiple Payment Annuity is a deferred annuity for which the contributor makes periodic payments. Many employer-created pension plans in effect involve multiple payment annuities.

Multiple Listing Service in real estate parlance is a centralized listing system for residential real estate properties that have been listed with brokers for sale. A multiple listing service gives all participating brokers in the community access to all properties.

Multiplier. *See* Capitalization Factor.

Municipal Bonds are bonds or debentures issued by states, municipalities, and state-created taxing authorities. They carry lower interest rates than other debt instruments because the interest is exempt from federal (and sometimes state) income taxes.

Mutual Fund is the common name for an Open-End Investment Company.

Mutual Life Insurance Company is an insurance company that does not have shareholders: Its board of directors is elected by its policyholders, and excess earnings of the company are paid to policyholders in the form of annual dividends. In a mutual company, policyholders are somewhat analogous to owners of the company. *See also* Stock Life Insurance Company.

Naked Options are standard put or call options written by a person who does not own the underlying securities (in the case of call options), or does not have the financial resources to purchase the shares if the options are exercised (in the case of put options). Such options are also called Uncovered Options. Writing naked options is also sometimes referred to as Going Naked.

Narrow Tape is the Dow Jones tape that sets forth securities transactions. *See* Broad Tape.

NASD. *See* National Association of Securities Dealers.

NASDAQ. *See* National Association of Securities Dealers Automated Quotations.

National Association of Securities Dealers (NASD) is a semi-public association of securities dealers active in the Over-the-Counter Market.

National Association of Securities Dealers Automated Quotations (NASDAQ) is a computerized price quotation system for the more heavily traded securities in the Over-the-Counter Market. *See* Bid and Asked Quotations.

National List refers to the portion of the Over-the-Counter Market that consists of widely traded, active securities issues that fall somewhat below the standards for listing in the National Market System. Price quotations for National List securities are reported in bid-and-asked form but volume figures are supplied by principal market makers.

National Market System is the portion of the over-the-counter market in which the most active and widely held securities in that market are traded. The principal market makers for these securities report actual trades and prices so that the reporting of such transactions is indistinguishable from those of the formally organized exchanges. There are several market makers for each National Market System security. *See* Over-the-Counter Market; National List.

Negative Amortization in real estate parlance occurs when the payment terms of a mortgage provide for payments in early years of the mortgage that do not cover the interest charges. The difference is called negative amortization: It is added to principal to be amortized in later years when payments have increased. Negative amortization may also occur in transactions involving property other than real estate.

Negative Amortization Mortgage is a mortgage that provides for negative amortization during the time the loan is outstanding. *See also* Fixed Rate Conventional Mortgage; Alternative Mortgage.

Negative Asset Account. *See* Contra Account.

Negative Cash Flow means that the disbursements of a project exceed its receipts. A negative cash flow means that the cash being generated by the project is not sufficient to cover its cash needs and that additional infusions of capital may be required if the negative cash flow continues.

Negative Income Items are expenses that reduce the owner's equity account.

Negotiable Instrument means an instrument that is in negotiable form. An instrument is in negotiable form if it (1) is signed by the maker, (2) contains only an unconditional promise to pay a sum certain in money, (3) is payable on demand or at a definite time, and (4) is payable to order or bearer.

Negotiation of a negotiable instrument means that it is transferred to a Holder in Due Course. *See* Negotiable Instrument; Holder in Due Course.

Net Asset Value of investment company shares equals the value of the investment company's portfolio divided by the number of outstanding shares of the investment company. *See* Investment Company.

Net Cash Flow. *See* Cash Flow.

Net Change in securities trading parlance is the change between the closing price of the security on the day in question and the closing price on the previous trading day.

Net Income in accounting parlance is the traditional bottom line of an income statement that shows the results of business operations for the period in question. Net income may be broadly defined as revenues minus expenses. If the business has material extraordinary and nonrecurring transactions during the period, the comparable bottom line may be called net income for year before extraordinary items. The extraordinary items, and the tax consequences of those items, are then shown as special entries below the net income for year before extraordinary items figure. Where extraordinary items appear, the appropriate net income item to use for comparative purposes (either historical comparisons with earlier years of operations or comparisons with other businesses) is net income for year before extraordinary items. *See* Extraordinary Items. *See also* Gross Margin; Operating Profit; Total Income; Income Before Provision for Federal Income Taxes.

Net Interest Coverage is a financial measure of the ability of a business to carry debt. It is the ratio between income before interest and taxes and the annual interest payable on the business's long term. Net interest coverage is usually expressed as a multiple of the amount of interest due; for example, a business with income of $100 and annual interest charges of $20 has a net interest coverage of 5. *See also* Interest Cushion.

Net Present Value is a method of capital budgeting by businesses. A minimum rate of return is established on projects that the business has determined is necessary for its financial health. All estimated outflows and inflows of a project are reduced to present values using this discount rate, and the present value of outflows are subtracted from the present value of inflows to obtain the net present value of the project. The contemplated investment is attractive if the net present value is positive; if it is zero or negative, the investment is unattractive. In a broader context, net present value may also may mean current value.

Net Profit Ratio is a financial measure of the profitability of a business as a function of sales. It is the ratio between Net Income and gross sales.

Net Quick Assets is a financial measure of the ability of a business to meet immediate obligations. It is Quick Assets minus Current Liabilities.

Net Sales in accounting parlance means Gross Sales minus returns.

Net Working Capital is a financial measure of the short-term stability of the business. It is the difference between Current Assets and Current Liabilities.

Netting out a Position. *See* Closing out a Position.

New Money generally refers to additional capital contributions or payments that are being discussed.

New York Stock Exchange is the principal secondary market for trading in corporate securities.

New York Stock Exchange Composite Index is an index of price movements of more than 1,600 securities listed on the New York Stock Exchange.

Nine Bond Rule in NYSE parlance is the rule that permits members of the exchange to deal with bonds in the over-the-counter market when the number of bonds involved exceeds nine units of $1,000 each.

No Load Fund is a mutual fund that does not charge a sales load. *See* Load.

Nominal Par Value Shares are shares that have a small par value if they are issued for a consideration that is significantly greater than par value.

Nominal Rate of Interest means the quoted rate of interest, which may diverge from the effective rate of interest because of the manner of calculation, the length of periods used, and so forth.

Nonasset Assets are balance sheet asset items that have zero realizable value. The most common items of this type appear in the intangible assets account: goodwill, organizational expense, capitalized promotional expense, or capitalized development costs.

Noncontributory Plan is a qualified retirement plan in which only the employer makes contributions. *See* Qualified Retirement Plan; After-Tax Dollars.

Noncurrent Assets on a balance sheet consist of all assets that are not classified as current assets.

Noncurrent Loans. *See* Problem Loans.

Non-GAAP Statements are financial statements prepared in accordance with a set of accounting principles that depart from generally accepted accounting principles in one or more respects.

Nonparticipating Life Insurance Policy is a policy that is not entitled to receive dividends. Such policies are usually written by stock companies. *See also* Participating Life Insurance Policies.

Nonrecourse Loan is a loan secured by property in which it is agreed that in the event of default the holder may foreclose on the property but may not hold the maker personally liable for any deficiency.

Nonrecurring Dividend. *See* Special Dividend.

No Par Shares. *See* Without Par Value.

Notes Payable in accounting parlance is a balance sheet item that reflects amounts due to banks and other lenders in connection with loans that mature during the following 12 months. The portion of a long-term loan payable in installments that is due to be paid within 12 months is also included in notes payable.

Notes to Financial Statements are the textual material and comments that accompany the auditor's opinion and financial statements.

Novation is the substitution of one debtor for another on an obligation with the consent of the creditor.

NYSE. *See* New York Stock Exchange.

October 19 Collapse refers to the dramatic decline in securities prices and securities indices that occurred on October 19, 1987.

Odd Lot in securities trading parlance is a trading order that involves less than a round lot of securities. *See* Round Lot.

Off-Book Liabilities in accounting parlance are commitments that need not be reflected as liabilities on financial statements. Typical off-book liabilities include obligations under pension plans in future years and long-term leases. Contingent liabilities, such as litigation, the probability of future product liability claims, tax claims, and the like may also be referred to as off-book liabilities. Material contingent and off-book liabilities should be referred to in the notes to the financial statements.

Officers of a corporation are appointed or elected by the board of directors; their functions are to conduct the business on a day-to-day basis and to carry out the policies established by the board of directors. In large publicly held corporations, the officers of the corporation are referred to as Management.

150 Percent Declining Balance Method is an accelerated depreciation system.

Open-End Investment Company is usually called a Mutual Fund. It is an investment company that does not have a fixed number of shares outstanding. Rather, it stands ready at any time to issue new shares to persons desiring to invest in the fund and repurchase or redeem its own shares at net asset value (or in some cases at a small discount below net asset value) from investors who wish to liquidate their positions. An open-end company has no fixed capitalization; as it grows or declines in size, the number of its outstanding shares also grows or declines.

Open Interest in commodities futures trading parlance means the number of futures contracts that are outstanding and have not been netted out.

Opening Inventory in accounting parlance is usually determined by the physical count at the close of the preceding accounting period with value assigned in accordance with standardized conventions. *See* Inventory; Cost of Goods Sold.

Operating Expenses in an income statement are expenses that are not allocable directly to the cost of goods sold.

Operating Margin is a financial measure of the profitability of a business. It is the ratio of pretax income to gross sales. The operating margin is also known as the Profit Margin. Generally, increases in sales cause dramatic improvements in the operating margin since some costs (e.g., rent and main office expenses) are fixed and do not rise or fall in proportion to volume. Correspondingly, a decrease in sales volume may cause a disproportionately large decline in the operating margin.

Operating Profit in accounting parlance is an income statement item that equals gross margin minus operating expenses.

Operating Revenues means the revenues of a business not involved primarily in selling goods. Operating Revenues is analogous to cost of goods sold in a business primarily involved in selling goods.

Opinion Shopping is a tactic engaged in by some publicly held corporations to obtain favorable accounting rulings on material items. The corporation may threaten to change independent auditors if a more favorable opinion is not reached or inquire about the position of a prospective auditing firm on the items in question before retaining that firm.

Option Agreement in corporation law parlance is a share transfer restriction that commits the shareholder to sell, but does not commit the corporation or other shareholders to purchase, the shares owned by the shareholder at a fixed or determinable price upon the occurrence of a specified event. *See also* Buy-Sell Agreement.

Ordinary Interest is calculated on the assumption that a year consists of 360 days divided into 12 months of 30 days each. Ordinary interest is still used by many banks, and in the computation of interest on corporate, agency and municipal bonds. *See also* Exact Interest.

Ordinary Life Insurance. *See* Whole Life Insurance.

OTC (or O-T-C) stands for over-the-counter. *See* Over-the-Counter Market.

Other Assets in accounting parlance is a balance sheet item that includes miscellaneous assets such as debts owed to the company that mature in more than one year, minority interests in independent businesses that the company plans to retain indefinitely, and the like.

Other Income in accounting parlance is an income statement item that reflects earnings from dividends, interest, or rent not connected with the entity's principal business.

Out of the Money Option is an option that has no intrinsic value. *See* Intrinsic Value.

Out Years are years in the relatively far distant future in which payments are to be received or made. In estimating present values of a stream of payments, payments in out years make a relatively small contribution to the present value of that stream.

Outside General Counsel to a corporation is a lawyer who is acting as general counsel of the client while still engaged in the independent practice of law. An outside general counsel may devote most of his or her time to the affairs of the corporation, or, depending on the legal problems faced by the corporation, may devote most of his or her time to the affairs of other clients but remain on call to the corporation.

Over-the-Counter Market for securities consists of a large number of brokers and dealers who deal with each other via computer or telephone, buying and selling shares for customers or for their own accounts. Most brokers and dealers active in trading in the over-the-counter market are members of the National Association of Securities Dealers. The over-the-counter market is a vast and informal network of securities brokers and dealers that has become increasingly competitive with the traditional securities exchanges in handling securities trading.

Overcapitalization means that the corporation has available liquid assets in excess of business needs. A publicly held corporation that is overcapitalized may be subject to takeover bids from aggressors or leveraged buyout proposals since the excess assets may be used to pay off a portion of the debt incurred to finance a takeover of the corporation.

Owner of a Life Insurance Policy is the person who has the power to exercise a number of important options with respect to the policy: to name or change the designation of the beneficiary, to borrow against the policy or pledge it as security for a loan (if it has a cash surrender value), and to surrender the policy or decide to let it lapse for nonpayment. Usually the owner of the policy is the person who pays the premiums; the owner and the insured may be the same person but they need not be, and indeed it is often advantageous from an estate tax standpoint for them to be different persons.

Owner's Policy in real estate parlance is a title insurance policy that protects the title of the owner as well as the title of a mortgagee.

Owner's Equity in accounting parlance is the phrase customarily used on partnership or proprietorship balance sheets to describe the permanent capitalization of the business contributed by the owners as well as undistributed earnings from prior periods. It may also be called capital or capital contributed by partners.

Pac Man Defense in corporation law parlance is a defensive tactic that involves a cash tender offer by the target for a majority of the aggressor's shares.

Paid in Surplus. *See* Capital Surplus.

PAM. *See* Pledged Account Mortgage.

Par Value is an arbitrary amount assigned by the articles of incorporation to common and preferred shares in many states. Par value was originally a representation of the price at which shares were to be issued. Thus common shares with a par value of $100 were to be sold at $100 per share. Modern practice today has departed from this practice: In par value states the virtually universal practice is to issue par value shares for a price higher than par value. As a result, the par value assigned to shares is not a valid guide either to present value or to original issue price. Its sole relevance today is that it determines the amount of permanent capital and capital surplus in the original capitalization of the corporation. The Revised Model Business Corporation Act and the statutes of an increasing number of states eliminate the concept of par value except for internal planning purposes. In debt securities parlance par value of a bond or debenture is the face amount of the bond: usually $1,000 or a multiple thereof.

Partially Cumulative Dividends on preferred shares are usually of the "cumulative to the extent of earnings" type, that is, the dividend is cumulative in any year only to the extent of actual earnings during that year. *Compare* Income Bond; Cumulative Dividends.

Participating Bonds are bonds or debentures on which the amount of interest payable increases with corporate earnings.

Participating Life Insurance Policy is a policy that is entitled to share in dividends declared by the life insurance company. Such policies are usually written by mutual companies. *See also* Nonparticipating Life Insurance Policy.

Participating Preferred Shares are shares that are entitled to the original preferential dividend, and after the common receives a specified amount, they share with the common in any additional distributions in some predetermined ratio.

Participation Loan. *See* Equity Participation Loan.

Partnership at Will is a partnership that may be dissolved at any time by the express will of any partner without liability to any other partner.

Partnership for a Term is a partnership that is to continue for a specified term or until the occurrence of a specified event. A partner in such a partnership has the inherent power to dissolve the partnership, but that act may constitute a breach of contract by the dissolving partner.

Partnership is a business owned by two or more persons as co-owners. In most states partnerships are governed by the Uniform Partnership Act. *See also* General Partnership; Limited Partnership.

Passive Activities in tax parlance are all rental activities and trade or business activities in which the taxpayer does not materially participate. Investment activity is not passive activity. The ownership and rental of commercial or residential property is a passive activity even if the owner participates in decisions on matters such as who should be tenants. Otherwise, material participation means that the taxpayer is involved in the operations of the activity on a regular, continuous, and substantial basis. Losses from passive activities are deductible only to the extent the taxpayer has income from passive activities.

Pay as You Go in tax parlance refers to the tax withholding and estimated tax provisions of the Internal Revenue Code that are designed to ensure that all or most of the tax due is withheld by employers or paid by taxpayers as estimated tax payments during the taxable year as income is earned.

Payment Date for a corporate distribution is the date the checks or certificates are actually mailed. In a corporation with large numbers of shareholders, the payment date is set between two to four weeks after the record date in order to permit the corporation to go through the mechanical processes of making the distribution in the proper amounts to the thousands or millions of record holders. *See* Record Date.

Payment Options for deferred annuities are the elections available to an annuitant prior to the time of the first payment as to the duration of the annuity. Common options are for the life of the annuitant, or the life of the annuitant with a specified number of payments guaranteed, or for the combined lives of the annuitant and his or her spouse.

Penalty Against Unreasonable Accumulation of Surplus is a penalty tax designed to prevent corporations from being used as repositories of undistributed earnings as a tax avoidance device. This tax was of considerable importance before the 1986 amendments when individual tax rates were higher than corporate rates; today it is rarely advantageous to accumulate surplus in a C corporation. When applicable, this penalty tax provides a strong incentive to pay dividends to shareholders. *See* C Corporation; Accumulate/Bail Out Strategy.

Pension Plan provides retirement benefits to employees. A pension plan is usually a qualified defined benefit plan but the term pension plan is often used more broadly to refer to a defined contribution plan or even to any type of qualified or nonqualified retirement plan.

Perfection of a security interest in property makes the security interest valid against subsequent creditors of the debtor, the bankruptcy trustee, and possible good faith purchasers of the property. Perfection usually requires a public filing with a public office, though security interests in many types of property may be perfected automatically or by taking other steps, such as taking possession of the collateral.

Permanent Lender in real estate parlance is a lender that makes the permanent loan on a commercial real estate project. *See* Permanent Loan.

Permanent Life Insurance. *See* Whole Life Insurance.

Permanent Loan in real estate parlance is a loan made upon the completion of a commercial real estate project that is for a long term (perhaps 20, 25, or 30 years) and provides for amortization of the loan over that term. The proceeds of a permanent loan are used to pay off the interim or construction lender. The permanent lender's decision to make the loan is based on an evaluation of the projected economics and cash flow of the completed project.

Perpetual Annuity is an annuity that continues forever. The present value of a perpetual annuity equals the reciprocal of the applicable discount rate.

Personal Exemptions in tax parlance means the flat amount that a taxpayer may deduct from adjusted gross income for him or herself, his or her spouse, and for dependent relatives in the taxpayer's family.

Personal Holding Company is an investment company that is closely held by a few shareholders. A personal holding company is created when a closely held corporation sells all its business assets and then remains in existence.

Personal Identification Number (PIN) is a security device designed to prevent the possessor of a stolen or lost credit card from using it to withdraw cash or cash-equivalents from automated teller machines. This number must be entered manually by the user to effectuate the transaction.

PI stands for principal and insurance. The PI payment on a real estate mortgage is the amount necessary each month to pay interest and amortize principal.

PIN. *See* Personal Identification Number.

Pink Sheets. *See* Sheets.

PITI stands for principal, interest, taxes, insurance. The PITI payment on a real estate mortgage is the PI payment plus the required payments to be held in escrow by the lender in order to pay real estate taxes and casualty insurance premiums each year.

Pits are the trading areas for commodities and financial futures contracts. They are large depressions in the floor of the trading area with steps — persons trading contracts for a specified month stand on the same step or level within the pit.

Plain Vanilla Securities is securities trading slang for traditional investments such as shares of stock or debt instruments.

PLAM. *See* Price Level Adjusted Mortgage.

Pledged Account Mortgage (PAM) is a deferred interest or graduated payment mortgage in which a fund is created at the closing to finance the lower initial payments. In creative financing, the seller may make a payment to this fund. If the seller makes a contribution, the arrangement is sometimes known as a Buy Down Option.

Points in real estate parlance are charges made at closing by a mortgagee. A point is a charge equal to 1 percent of the loan amount; a lender who charges 3 points on a $100,000 loan in effect imposes an additional $3,000 fee at closing. A point is also sometimes called a discount point. In securities trading parlance a point means one dollar when discussing price movements of equity securities.

Poison Pills in corporation law parlance are special issues of preferred shares or debt securities with rights that are designed specifically to make unwanted attempts to take over the issuing corporation difficult, impractical, or impossible. A poison pill grants additional rights to shareholders upon the occurrence of a triggering event such as an acquisition of a substantial block of shares or a tender offer by outside interests. *See* Voting Poison Pills, Flip-In Poison Pills, and Flip-Over Poison Pills.

Porcupine Provisions. *See* Shark Repellants.

Portfolio in securities trading parlance is the different investments held by a single investor at any one time.

Portfolio Insurance is a trading program that attempts to offset market declines in the value of investment portfolios by selling index futures when prices are declining and buying futures when prices are rising. Portfolio insurance does not strive to produce a riskless portfolio (as a true hedge does) but rather to offset potential declines while not eliminating the possibility of gain in the case of a market rise. Portfolio insurance did not successfully prevent huge portfolio losses in the October 1987 price collapse, and is viewed by many persons as having contributed to the magnitude of that decline. *See also* Program Trading.

Positive Cash Flow means that the project produces more cash than the out-of-pocket disbursements necessary to operate the project. Projects with positive cash flows are self-supporting and do not need periodic infusions of capital.

Positive Income Items in accounting parlance are revenue items.

Posts on the New York Stock Exchange Floor are the locations at which trading in specific securities occur.

Preferences are transactions by debtors that favor one creditor over another and are voidable to a limited extent if the debtor thereafter becomes the subject of a federal bankruptcy proceeding.

Preferred Dividend Coverage is a measure of the financial security underlying a preferred dividend. It is the ratio between the net income of the corporation (after payment of interest and taxes) and the amount payable to the preferred shareholders as preferential dividends. The difference between the preferential dividend and the net income of the business is sometimes referred to as the Preferred Dividend Cushion.

Preferred Dividend Cushion. *See* Preferred Dividend Coverage.

Preferred Shareholders' Contract in corporation parlance means the provisions in the basic corporate documents that describe and define the terms and rights of preferred shareholders.

Preferred Shares are shares that have a preference over the rights of common shares either in dividends or in liquidation, or in both. Preferred shares usually (but not always) have limited financial rights and are non-voting shares.

Prepaid Expenses in accounting parlance is a balance sheet account that is used in connection with the concept of accrual to allow expenses paid in one period to be reflected in the income statement in another accounting period. In effect prepaid expenses are "parked" in this asset account on the balance sheet until they are taken into account in the income statement under principles of accrual. Prepaid expenses are also sometimes called Prepaid Charges, Prepayments, or Deferred Charges.

Prepaid Income in accounting parlance is a balance sheet account that is used in connection with the concept of accrual to allow receipts in one period to be reflected in the income statement in another accounting period. In effect prepaid income items are "parked" in this liability account on the balance sheet until they are taken into account in the income statement under principles of accrual.

Prepaid Rent is an example of a Prepaid Expense or Prepaid Income item.

Prepayment Penalty in real estate parlance is a charge for prepaying the principal of a mortgage before it is due. A prepayment penalty is nominally justified as a charge to help defray the cost of accepting a prepayment and redeploying the funds into another mortgage. In fact, prepayment penalties are usually viewed by mortgagees simply as another way of modestly increasing the profitability of the lending business during periods of stable interest rates, since most mortgages are refinanced when properties are sold and prepayment penalties may be imposed.

Price Level Adjusted Mortgage (PLAM) is a mortgage in which the interest rate and the term of the mortgage are fixed, but the outstanding balance is adjusted periodically in accordance with changes in some agreed-upon price index.

Primary Markets in securities parlance are markets in which corporations who wish to raise capital sell their new securities. *See also* Secondary Market.

Prime Rate is the interest rate that is usually (and not always accurately) defined as the rate large commercial banks charge large borrowers that run essentially no risk of default. It is the "weather vane" rate for loans by banks and other institutions to individuals and businesses.

Private Annuity is created by the transfer of property by one person to another in exchange for a promise by the recipient to make fixed periodic payments for the life of the transferor. A private annuity is an annuity based on the credit of the recipient who is not in the business of writing annuities. A private annuity may be advantageous because it permits deferral of income taxation on gain realized upon the transfer of the property.

Private Offering in securities parlance is the sale of securities by an issuer without registration under the Securities Act of 1933 to a limited number of investors pursuant to exemptions for transactions not involving a public offering. *See* Regulation D; Accredited Investor.

Private Placement in securities parlance is the sale of securities by well-established or large publicly held businesses in large amounts to a limited number of institutional investors. Private placements usually involve debt securities secured by liens on real estate or machinery or equipment, or on all of the assets of the corporation. They are known as private placements since they are effected without registration of the securities for public sale under the Securities Act of 1933 or state blue sky laws.

Problem Loans in real estate parlance are loans that are in default, but the owner has not given up and the mortgages have not been foreclosed. Problem loans are also sometimes referred to as Noncurrent Loans.

Pro Forma Cash Flow Projections are projections or assumptions of cash flow made on the assumption that certain transactions have been entered into. Pro forma cash flow projections may be in the form of computer-generated spread sheets or documents with titles such as "projected cash flow."

Pro Forma Financial Statements are statements that are recast to reflect the results of prior operations on the assumption that a transaction that involves the amalgamation, divestment, or adjustment of a business had been in effect during the period of the financial statements.

Professional Corporation is a specially designed business form that enables professionals, such as lawyers, doctors, and dentists, to obtain the benefits of incorporation consistently with ethical requirements of the profession that require a personal relationship between professional and client or patient. The tax advantages of incorporation have been largely but not entirely eliminated; today the limited liability that may be available to shareholders in a professional corporation appears to be the principal incentive for professional incorporation.

Profit and Loss is a synonym for Income.

Profit Margin. *See* Operating Margin.

Profit Sharing Plan is a type of qualified defined contribution plan in which the amount of the annual contribution is based on the profits of the employer. *See* Qualified Retirement Plan.

Program Trading in securities parlance consists of Arbitrage transactions, often involving the simultaneous purchase or sale of index futures contracts and the offsetting sale or purchase of bundles of common shares in the traditional securities markets.

Progress Payments in real estate parlance are payments made to the general contractor by the interim lender as construction progresses.

Progressive Income Tax Rates are tax rates on income that themselves increase as income increases. For example a rate structure that taxes income under $10,000 at 14 percent and all income in excess of $10,000 at 28 percent is progressive.

Projections are estimates of future income or cash flow prepared by a business. The SEC permits projections to appear in public financial statements to a limited extent.

Promissory Note is paper that states that the debtor "promises to pay to the order of" the creditor the amount of the debt, together with interest; unlike an IOU, a promissory note contains a promise to pay as well as an acknowledgment of a debt.

Property Dividend in corporation parlance is a dividend by a corporation that is paid in the form of property, not money.

Proposed Regulations in tax parlance are contemplated regulations that the Internal Revenue Service has published for comment but has not yet promulgated. Proposed regulations may be pending for many years and may be relied upon by taxpayers to a limited extent.

Proprietor is the owner of a proprietorship.

Proprietorship is a business individually owned by a single person.

Proxy Fight in corporation law parlance is a proxy solicitation by a nonmanagement group in opposition to the solicitation of management. The purpose of the opposition solicitation is usually to persuade shareholders to vote for an alternative slate of directors. Proxy fights, however, may have more limited goals, such as opposing a proposal by management to adopt antitakeover defenses. A proxy fight has sometimes been used in connection with takeover battles in an effort either to take over control of the target in the face of substantial defenses or generally to put pressure on incumbent management.

Proxy Solicitation Machinery in corporation law parlance is the complex of factors that leads most shareholders in publicly held corporations to support management proposals.

Public Land Records in real estate parlance are the documents recorded in the office of the appropriate public official and the indexes maintained by that official. These records are not widely used in most jurisdictions since they are not normally organized on a tract basis. *See* Title Company.

Public Offering in securities law parlance is an offer by an issuer to sell securities to the public. A public offering is not defined in the Securities Act of 1933 but has been construed by case law to mean an offering, without regard to size, in which one or more offerees need the protection of the Securities Act of 1933. State blue sky laws usually contain a numerical definition of public offering that may be coupled with a prohibition against the use of public solicitation or advertisement. *See* Registered Offering.

Public Sale means a sale at public auction.

Publicly Held Corporation is a corporation that has outstanding shares held by a large number of people. While there is no minimum number of shareholders that defines when a corporation becomes publicly held, corporations with shares traded on the securities exchanges, or shares for which there are published price quotations, are publicly held corporations. Corporations that have made a registered public offering of shares are also usually viewed as publicly held corporations even though the number of shareholders may be relatively small and transfers of shares relatively infrequent. The most important distinguishing features of publicly held corporations are: (1) the existence of a public market for their shares so that investors can come and go relatively easily, and (2) the wide availability of relatively current information about their activities.

Publicly Traded Fund is another name for a Closed-End Investment Company.

Purchase Money Security Interest is the phrase used by the Uniform Commercial Code to describe the security interest obtained by a seller of goods for a loan of all or part of the purchase of the goods.

Purchase on Margin. *See* Margin Transaction.

Pure Preferred Shares. *See* Straight Preferred Shares.

Put into Play in corporation law parlance means that a corporation has been made the target of a takeover attempt.

Put is a standardized option to purchase a designated security at a fixed price for a limited period. *See* Strike Price; Option Writer.

Qualified Opinion with respect to financial statements is an opinion by the auditor that contains one or more qualifications, exceptions, or reservations.

Qualified Retirement Plan is a pension or profit-sharing plan that meets the requirements of the Employee Retirement Income Security Act (ERISA) and the Internal Revenue Code. Contributions may be made to a qualified plan by the employer for the employee's retirement program without the contributions being included in the employee's tax return and without affecting the deductibility of the contributions from the standpoint of the employer.

Quarterly Declarations of Estimated Tax must be filed by taxpayers who have substantial amounts of self-employment income, income from personal investments, or other sources not subject to withholding, such as gambling or stock market trading. A payment of estimated tax may have to accompany a quarterly declaration if it reveals an estimated underpayment of tax.

Quick Assets in accounting parlance are assets that can be used to cover an immediate emergency. Quick assets consist of cash, marketable securities, and current receivables. Quick assets differ from current assets in that inventories are excluded. Bankers and others considering short-term loans to a business often rely on a quick asset analysis.

Quick Assets Ratio is a financial measure of the ability of a corporation to meet current liabilities. It equals quick assets divided by current liabilities. This ratio is also called the Acid Test.

Quit Claim Deed in real estate parlance is a deed that conveys whatever title the seller possesses without any warranty of any kind. Quit claim deeds may be known by different names in some localities. *See also* General Warranty Deed; Special Warranty Deed.

Rainmakers are lawyers in law firms who bring in legal business in excess of what they can handle personally.

Random Walk means that the next movement of any statistic is as likely to be down as it is up.

Ratio of Accounts Receivable to Average Daily Sales is a financial measure of the turnover rate of accounts receivable. It is calculated as gross annual sales divided by the number of selling days in the year.

Ratio of Inventory to Current Assets is a financial measure that evaluates whether the business is investing too heavily in inventory. It is the percentage that closing inventory bears to current assets. *See also* Inventory Turnover Ratio; Ratio of Sales to Inventory.

Ratio of Sales to Fixed Assets is a financial measure of whether the capital invested in productive facilities by a business is being used efficiently in that business. It is the ratio between sales and fixed assets. The ratio of sales to fixed assets is particularly useful in "before and after" examination of a proposed substantial enlargement of productive facilities.

Ratio of Sales to Inventory is a financial measure that evaluates whether the business is investing too heavily in inventory. It is the ratio that gross sales bears to closing inventory. *See also* Inventory Turnover Ratio; Ratio of Inventory to Current Assets.

Real Defenses may be asserted by the maker of a negotiable instrument, even against a holder in due course. In other words, the claim of a holder in due course may be defeated by real defenses such as infancy, incapacity, or illegality of the transaction.

Realization of Gain or Loss in tax parlance means that a transaction involving a sale or exchange is closed for the purpose of determining the gain or loss from the transaction. However, a realized gain or loss is includable in the taxpayer's return for the year in question only if the gain or loss is recognized. *See* Recognition of Gain or Loss.

Realization of Revenue in accounting parlance means the time when revenues should be taken into the accounting records as income. The usual rule is that revenues are realized when the business becomes unconditionally entitled to their receipt, not when payment is received. Thus, in the case of a contract for the sale of goods revenue may be realized when the goods are shipped rather than when the contract is entered into or when payment is made.

Recognition of Gain or Loss in tax parlance means that a realized gain or loss is to be taken into account as a taxable transaction. If a realized gain or loss is not recognized it is said to be deferred to a later year. *See* Realization of Gain or Loss.

Record Date for a dividend determines in whose name specific checks or share certificates are to be issued: The check is made out to the order of (or the certificate is made out in the name of) the person or persons who are the holders of record on the books of the corporation at the close of business on the record date. Entitlement to the dividend is determined for publicly traded shares by the Ex Dividend Date.

Redeemable Shares are shares that may be retired at the option of the corporation upon the payment of a fixed amount for each share. Such shares are often called Callable Shares. Preferred shares are usually redeemable while common shares almost always are not.

Refinancing of a Mortgage involves obtaining a new loan to pay off the old loan secured by the mortgage. A mortgage is usually refinanced when the property is sold.

Regional Exchanges are securities exchanges located outside of New York. The principal regional exchanges are Philadelphia, Cincinnati, Boston, Midwest, and Pacific.

Registered Bonds are debt securities that have been issued in the name of the owner, called the registered owner. Registered bonds do not have interest coupons; periodic interest payments are made to registered owners by check much the same way as cash dividends on shares of stock. Registered bonds are transferred by endorsement rather than merely by delivery as is the case with Coupon Bonds.

Registered Corporations in securities law parlance are corporations with securities registered under the Securities Exchange Act of 1934.

Registered Offering or Registered Public Offering means a public offering of securities that has been registered with the SEC under the Securities Act of 1933 and the appropriate state securities commissions.

Regressive Tax Structure is a structure of tax rates that result in lower income taxpayers being taxed at a higher effective tax rate than taxpayers with higher incomes.

Regular Dividend in corporation law parlance means the announced dividend in a specified amount that may be expected to be declared periodically. A regular dividend policy is also referred to as the corporation's Announced Dividend Policy.

Regulation D is the principal private offering exemption under the Securities Act of 1933. Under Regulation D substantial amounts of capital may be raised by private sales of equity securities to accredited investors so long as offers to other persons are limited and controlled. *See* Accredited Investor.

Regulations in tax parlance refers to the voluminous regulations issued by the Internal Revenue Service to implement the Internal Revenue Code. Regulations often involve substantive tax issues and usually have the force of law. *See also* Proposed Regulations.

Reinsurance is the process by which an insurance company transfers some of the risk of loss it incurs to other insurance companies. Reinsurance permits diversification of risk by insurance companies.

Reorganization. *See* Chapter 11 Reorganization; Chapter 13 Reorganization.

Replacement Cost or Replacement Value is an experimental accounting system in which more current or realistic asset values are substituted for historical cost. *See* Current Replacement Cost.

REPOs are short-term loan transactions that take the form of a sale of marketable securities by the borrower to the lender coupled with a commitment by the borrower to repurchase the securities at a higher price on a specified date in the future. Assuming that the securities are appropriately segregated, the risk of loss is slight because the lender may sell the underlying securities if the borrower fails to honor its commitment to repurchase the securities.

Retained Earnings in accounting parlance are earnings from prior accounting periods that have not been distributed to shareholders as dividends but have been retained by the business. Retained earnings at the end of an accounting period equals retained earnings at the beginning of the period plus net income for the period minus dividends declared during the period.

Return on Equity is a financial measure of how much a business is earning on each dollar of owners' investment. It is the ratio of net income to net worth. When applied to GAAP statements it is broadly comparable from company to company and from industry to industry even though it is affected to some extent by the accounting conventions that have been adopted.

Return on Invested Capital is a financial measure of the effectiveness of the deployment of invested capital by the business. It is the ratio that net income plus interest on long-term debt bears to net worth plus long-term debt.

Reverse Annuity Mortgage in real estate parlance is a mortgage that provides monthly payments to the owner of the mortgaged property. These payments are secured by the mortgage in increasing amounts based on the accumulated equity in the residence.

Reverse REPOs are short-term loan transactions identical to REPOs except the transaction is initiated by a dealer who wishes to borrow securities in order to sell them in anticipation of a price decline. *See* REPOs.

Reverse Stock Split in corporation parlance involves an amendment to the corporation's articles of incorporation that (1) reduces the number of shares outstanding and (2) provides a method of converting the outstanding shares into the smaller number of new shares. Though called a split, the transaction actually involves an amendment to the articles of incorporation.

Right Hand Side (of a balance sheet) is the liability and equity side even though it may be printed below rather than to the right.

Right of Dissent and Appraisal. *See* Appraisal Right.

Rights in securities trading parlance are short-term options to purchase securities from the issuer at a fixed price, expiring within one year. Rights may be publicly traded. *See also* Warrants.

Risk Arbitrageurs in corporation law parlance are speculators who actively accumulate shares that are offered in the market following the announcement of a cash tender offer. Risk arbitrageurs tender shares so acquired to the aggressor (or to the highest competing bidder).

Roll Over Mortgage (ROM) in real estate parlance is a long-term mortgage in which the interest rate and monthly payments are renegotiated periodically. Caps are provided on the maximum adjustment permitted in any single adjustment.

Rolling over Debt means obtaining a new loan shortly before the maturation of older debt and using the proceeds of the new loan to pay off the maturing debt.

ROM. *See* Roll Over Mortgage.

Round Lot in securities trading is a standard unit of trading. On the New York Stock Exchange it is usually a unit of 100 shares though in some lightly traded shares the unit may be 10 shares.

Sale and Leaseback in real estate parlance is a transaction that is economically equivalent to a mortgage in that the financier buys a commercial property from the developer and then immediately leases it back for fixed or determinable rentals over a long period that usually exceeds the estimated life of the improvements.

Sales for Forward Delivery in commodities trading are contracts to provide specific commodities for future delivery. Such sales differ from traditional commodities futures contracts principally in that they are not necessarily the standardized commodity in standardized contract form used in futures trading.

Sales Load. *See* Load.

Schedule C in tax parlance is the form used by proprietors to reflect the income or loss of their business in their personal income tax returns.

S Corporation in tax parlance is a tax election that may be made by corporations with relatively few shareholders and a simple capital structure. If this election is adopted, corporate income is passed through to shareholders individually and the double tax problem of C corporations is largely avoided. *See* Double Tax Problem; C Corporation.

Seats on the New York Stock Exchange authorize holders to go onto the trading floor of the Exchange and deal in securities. Most owners of seats today are brokerage firms.

Secondary Markets are markets in which persons who already own outstanding shares and wish to sell them deal with persons who wish to buy shares. *See also* Primary Market.

Section 203 of the Delaware General Corporation Law is an antitakeover statute that regulates back-end transactions. It generally prohibits a wide variety of transactions between the corporation and a shareholder owning more than

15 percent of the corporation's shares within a period of three years after the transaction in which the shareholder acquired the shares.

Security Interest is the phrase used by the Uniform Commercial Code to describe the intangible interest that a creditor may obtain in personal property or intangibles to secure payment of a debt.

Sell a Future in commodities trading parlance means to enter into a contract to sell a standard amount of a commodity, such as corn, at a specified date in the future.

Seller of an Annuity is the entity that agrees to make the annuity payments. Sellers are usually life insurance companies in the business of selling annuities and life insurance. The seller of an annuity may also be described as the writer of the annuity.

Senior Mortgage is a mortgage to which other mortgages are junior or have been subordinated. A senior mortgage is also called a First Mortgage.

Series of Preferred Shares in corporation parlance are preferred shares in one or more series that may be created by the board of directors without shareholder approval upon terms determined at the discretion of the board of directors. Under many state statutes, the articles of incorporation must authorize a class of preferred shares and further authorize the board of directors to create one or more series from within that class and to vary any of the substantive terms of each series. The class of preferred shares out of which series may be created is often called blank shares. Some statutes permit the articles of incorporation to create new classes of shares as well as series out of a specific class of blank shares.

Settle Price in commodities futures trading is the price that is used to mark all open positions in commodities futures trading accounts to market each day.

Settlement Sheet in real estate parlance is the document that shows all the receipts and disbursements of money by the closing officer in connection with the sale of real estate.

Sham Transactions in tax parlance are transactions that appear to have no business purpose other than to reduce tax liabilities. The Internal Revenue Service may ignore such transactions in the computation of income tax liabilities.

Share Acquisition Transaction is corporation law parlance for the acquisition of a business by a purchase of all or most of the outstanding voting shares of a corporation. In a share (or stock) acquisition transaction, the purchase price is paid directly to the selling shareholders and not to the corporation. The purchaser of a business through a share acquisition transaction takes the business subject to all contingent or undisclosed liabilities. *See also* Asset Acquisition Transaction.

Share Dividend (or Stock Dividend) is a distribution of shares of common stock by a corporation to its shareholders in proportion to their shareholdings. Thus, a 10 percent share dividend means that the corporation issues one new share to each shareholder for every ten shares held; a holder of 100 shares will receive 10 new shares when the distribution is made, owning 110 shares in all. *See also* Share Split.

Share Split is a distribution of shares of common stock by a corporation to its shareholders in proportion to their shareholdings. Thus a "2-for-1 split" involves the corporation's issuing an additional share for each share already owned, so that a shareholder who owned 100 shares before the split owns 200 shares after the split. A share dividend and share split are usually treated differently for accounting purposes on the books of the corporation. However, a share split differs from a share dividend in degree more than in kind. A share split usually involves a substantial increase in the number of outstanding shares whereas a share dividend involves a smaller increase. Further, a regular dividend policy is not likely to be adjusted for a share dividend, but usually will be adjusted in the case of a share split. *See* Share Dividend.

Share Transfer Restriction limits the power of a shareholder to dispose of his or her shares. Such restrictions are widely used in closely held corporations for purposes such as permitting other shareholders to determine with whom they are associated in the business and ensuring a minority shareholder of a market for his or her shares in specified circumstances. Share transfer restrictions are also widely used in publicly held corporations to assure that transfers do not occur that may jeopardize the availability of securities law exemptions or the S corporation election. *See* Option Agreement, Buy-Sell Agreement.

Shared Appreciation Mortgage in real estate parlance is a mortgage under which the lender shares in any increase in value of the project upon its sale or refinancing.

Shareholders are persons who own shares of a corporation.

Shareholders' Equity on a balance sheet consists of two parts: (1) the permanent capitalization of the business contributed by the shareholders, and (2) retained earnings.

Shares of Stock are the fundamental units into which the proprietary interest of a corporation is divided. The word shares alone is often used to describe shares of stock.

Shark Repellants in corporation law parlance are changes made in a corporation's articles of incorporation or bylaws designed to make it difficult for a new majority shareholder to replace the incumbent board of directors or to impose additional costs on the corporation in the event of a successful takeover. These provisions are also sometimes called Porcupine Provisions.

Sheets (or Pink Sheets) is a daily overnight publication containing representative price quotations for less heavily traded stocks in the over-the-counter market.

Short Position in securities trading parlance means that the trader owes more shares to the market than he owns. A similar description is that short position refers to short sales that have been entered into but have not been covered by purchases.

Short Sale in securities trading parlance is a transaction that enables an investor to speculate on a price decline to the same extent as a purchase of shares constitutes speculation on a price increase. A short seller borrows shares from his or her broker and sells them immediately, planning to repurchase them and replace the borrowed shares after the price drops. A short sale is treated as a margin transaction. A short sale "against the box" is a short sale at a time when the seller owns shares to cover the transaction but elects to borrow shares and sell them. The "box" referred to is a hypothetical safe deposit box in which the share certificates are stored. *See* Margin Transaction.

Show Stopper in corporation law parlance is an event of such seriousness that it causes the abrupt termination of a takeover attempt.

Shrinkage of inventory means unaccountable losses of inventory, whether due to pilferage, failure to maintain adequate records, spoilage, or other cause.

Signature Loan is an unsecured loan made solely on the borrower's signature.

Simple Interest is computed on the assumption that the earned interest is withdrawn every period so that each period's interest is computed on a stable principal. Simple interest is calculated by multiplying the rate by the number of periods and multiplying the result by the amount of the loan. *See also* Compound Interest.

Single Premium Deferred Annuity is an annuity purchased for a single payment today with annuity payments to begin at some future time.

Single-Premium Variable Life Insurance Policy is a life insurance policy created by a single payment or series of payments. The portion of the payment not needed immediately for insurance premiums is placed in an accumulation account. The owner of the policy usually may direct the manner in which the funds in the accumulation account are invested and may borrow from the account much as though it were the cash surrender value of a traditional whole life policy. The amount of the insurance provided under the variable life insurance policy is adjusted periodically to ensure that the earnings from the capital invested in the policy are not immediately taxable to the owner of the policy. Variable life insurance policies have significant tax deferral benefits and are sold more for the tax and investment benefits than for the insurance benefits.

Sinking Fund Provisions in corporation law parlance require the issuer of preferred shares or debentures to set aside a specified amount each year to retire a portion of the shares or debentures that are outstanding. More broadly, a sinking fund provision may refer to any similar type of arrangement for the gradual reduction of a debt or obligation.

Small Order Execution System (SOES) is an automated execution system maintained by the NASD for securities traded in the National Market System. This system permits automatic execution at the best available price quotation of orders for national market securities of up to 1,000 shares. *See* National

Market System; Over-the-Counter Market; National Association of Securities Dealers.

SOES. *See* Small Order Execution System.

Speaking Opinion is an informal written legal opinion that discusses alternatives, considers applicable legal precedents, and weighs various policy and strategic considerations.

Spec Houses in real estate parlance are houses or apartment complexes built by a speculator who has no buyer for the property but who plans to find a buyer and resell the property after it is improved.

Special Dividend in corporation law parlance is a one-time dividend by a corporation with an announced dividend policy: It does not create an expectation that a similar payment will be forthcoming in future years. A special dividend is sometimes called a Nonrecurring Dividend or an Extra Dividend.

Special Warranty Deed in real estate parlance is a deed with a warranty by the seller that his or her title is valid as against any act of the seller but does not warrant good title against the world. Special warranty deeds may be known by different names in some localities. *See also* General Warranty Deed; Quit Claim Deed.

Specialist is the Market Maker of securities on the New York Stock Exchange. He or she maintains the record of limit orders and is obligated to trade as a dealer in an effort to maintain an orderly market.

Spot Market in commodities trading is the market for commodities for current delivery. The spot market is also called the Cash Market, and prices in this market may be called Cash Prices.

Staggered Board of Directors in corporation law parlance is a board that has been divided into two or three groups with one group to be elected each year. A staggered board is sometimes used as a defensive measure against unwanted takeover attempts.

Standard & Poor's 500 Index is an index that reflects the price movements in listed securities issued by 500 leading corporations.

Standard Deduction in tax parlance means a deduction that a taxpayer may take instead of itemizing personal expenses.

Standstill Agreement in corporation law parlance is an agreement between a target and an aggressor under which the aggressor agrees not to increase its holding in the target beyond a specified size for a specified period of time.

Start-Up Business is a new business just getting under way, usually in the form of a proprietorship or a small partnership.

Stated Capital in corporation law parlance is the aggregate par values of all issued shares of a corporation. It may also be described simply as Capital Stock or Capital. Capital contributed in excess of stated capital is defined in some state corporation statutes as capital surplus. States that have eliminated the concept of par value generally also eliminate the distinction between stated capital and capital surplus. *See* Capital Surplus.

Statement of Changes in Financial Position is a financial statement that reclassifies accounts appearing in the balance sheet and income statement in order to focus on the flow of funds or working capital during the accounting period. It describes how a company acquired working capital during the accounting period and what it did with it.

Statement of Changes in Owners' Equity Accounts is a financial statement that presents changes in invested capital during the accounting period in addition to changes reflected in the Accumulated Retained Earnings Statement.

Statement of Changes in Retained Earnings is another name for the Accumulated Retained Earnings Statement.

Statement of Source and Application of Funds is another name for the financial statement called Statement of Changes in Financial Position.

Step Transactions in tax parlance are transactions that are linked together but are apparently independent. The Internal Revenue Service may treat step transactions as a single transaction for tax purposes.

Stepped-Up Basis in tax parlance arises upon the death of a person owing appreciated property. The basis of that property is automatically increased or "stepped up" to the fair market value of the assets on the death of decedent. The appreciation of property owned by a person at his or her death is never taxed because of the step-up in basis on death.

Stock Acquisition Transaction. *See* Share Acquisition Transaction.

Stock Bonus Plan is a qualified profit-sharing plan in which contributions are made in the form of shares of the employer rather than in cash.

Stock Life Insurance Company is in form a traditional corporation with shareholders who purchase stock in the company and who are entitled to elect the company's board of directors. Dividends in a stock company are paid to the shareholders, not to the policyholders as in a mutual company. In a stock company, policyholders are more analogous to customers of the company than to owners. *See also* Mutual Life Insurance Company.

Stock. *See* Shares.

Stop Order in NYSE trading is a limit order to sell when the price has declined to a particular point or to buy when the price has increased to a particular point.

Straddle in options trading parlance is the simultaneous purchase of a put option and a call option on the same security. In a straddle, the speculator profits if the price moves significantly in either direction.

Straight Bankruptcy is the traditional Chapter 7 bankruptcy proceeding that leads to the liquidation of assets owned by the bankrupt and possibly to his or her discharge from unpaid debts. *See* Discharge in Bankruptcy.

Straight-Line Depreciation allocates the expense of using up an asset by taking the difference between its original cost and its estimated scrap value, dividing by the number of years of the asset's estimated useful life, and taking that amount each year as depreciation of the asset.

Straight Preferred Shares are preferred shares with cumulative dividend rights but without conversion rights or participating dividend rights. Most preferred shares traded on the major securities exchanges are straight preferred shares. Straight preferred shares may also be known as Pure Preferred Shares.

Straw Party in real estate parlance is a person (or corporation) without substantial assets who executes a promissory note on behalf of the developer of real estate in order to avoid imposing personal liability on the developer. Some straw parties provide this service for a fee. A straw party may also be used in transactions not involving real estate.

Street Name Shares in securities trading parlance refers to shares that are registered in the names of New York brokerage firms and are traded among brokers simply by delivery. At any one time the number of shares registered in street name is very large. The supply of street name shares is sometimes referred to as the Floating Supply of Shares.

Street Sweep in corporation law parlance is the purchase of shares directly from arbitrageurs and speculators immediately after an unsuccessful tender offer. The "street" is Wall Street.

Strike Price of an option is the fixed price at which the specific option in question is exercisable. *See* Put; Call.

STRIPS (Separate Trading of Registered Interest and Principal of Securities) are zero coupon bonds issued by the United States Treasury. Brokerage firms may create equivalent securities by removing the coupons from treasury bonds and depositing the stripped bonds with an appropriate depository. These securities are known by feline acronyms such as CATS or TIGRS.

Stub End of a transaction in securities trading parlance is the portion of a large transaction that is not disposed of or covered before the transaction is effected.

Subordination of a Claim means that other creditors are entitled to collect the amounts due them before the holder of the subordinated claim. Subordination may be voluntary, as when a creditor agrees to accept a second mortgage with knowledge that the holder of the first mortgage has priority; or it may be involuntary, as when a bankruptcy court orders a loan subordinated because of inequitable conduct by the holder. A lien securing a subordinate loan may be described as a subordinate lien.

Subrogation means stepping into the shoes of another. For example, following the payment of a claim by an insurance company, the company is subrogated to the rights that the claimant may have against third parties, and may pursue those rights.

Substantial Underpayment of Estimated Tax is tax parlance for the failure to make sufficient payments under the Pay as You Go tax collection procedure to avoid statutory penalties imposed after the filing of the final return for the year in question.

Substituted Basis in tax parlance is the principle that in the case of property acquired by gift, the basis in the hands of the donee is the same as the basis in the hands of the donor. *See* Basis; *See also* Stepped-Up Basis.

Successful Efforts Oil Companies are oil companies that expense dry holes immediately; these companies are known as "successful efforts" companies since the reported costs of reserves include only the cost of drilling successful wells. *See* Full Cost Oil Companies.

Sum of the Digits Method is a method of calculating depreciation deductions on an accelerated basis. *See* Accelerated Depreciation.

Supermajority Provisions in corporation law parlance are provisions in Articles of Incorporation or Bylaws that require certain actions to be approved by more than a simple majority of the affirmative votes of shares. Supermajority provisions are widely used as takeover defenses by requiring merger transactions proposed by substantial shareholders to receive supermajority approval.

Supplemental List in securities trading parlance refers to a portion of the over-the-counter market that involves securities that are not as widely traded as National List or National Market System securities but are nevertheless sufficiently widely held that financial newspapers carry bid and asked quotations for them. *See* National Market System; National List; Over-the-Counter Market.

Surcharge of Directors in corporation law parlance means that a judgment has been entered against directors requiring them to restore to the corporation distributions to shareholders or other payments to third parties that were found to be improper or illegal. A director authorizing a payment may be surcharged even though he or she received no direct benefit from the payment.

Surviving Spouse in tax parlance is a person whose spouse has died within the previous two years; a surviving spouse is entitled to use the special tax rates applicable to married couples.

Sweep is an arrangement by a bank by which a customer's noninterest bearing checking account is periodically examined (swept) and any excess funds are moved to an interest-bearing money market account. Similarly, a sweep of option accounts by brokerage firms occurs shortly before expiration to ensure that all options with value are exercised prior to expiration.

Sweetener is securities law parlance for a valuable right, option, or warrant given to an investment banker or broker as an incentive to ensure effective distribution of an issue of securities.

Swing Shares in a closely held corporation are shares that hold the balance of power between two factions.

Syndicate in securities law parlance is a group of brokers and/or dealers who participate in the public distribution of an issue of securities.

T Account. *See* Ledger.

Tactical Asset Allocation in securities trading parlance is a complex of computer-driven trading strategies in which large investors move quickly among debt portfolios, equity portfolios, and cash equivalents. Tactical asset allocation usually involves the extensive use of financial futures and financial options.

Takeover Movement is a general term describing the wave of forced takeovers that began in the late 1960s and was continuing at the time this book was written.

Take Subject To in real estate parlance is an agreement by a purchaser of real estate to purchase subject to an existing mortgage; the purchaser must make the required payments under threat of losing the property, but has no personal liability with respect to the mortgage.

Taking a Bath in accounting parlance is a tactic in which a business, having a single bad year, lumps as many write-offs in that year as possible so that a return to predictable increases in profits becomes possible in later years.

Tape in securities trading parlance refers to the tape operated by Dow Jones which reports securities transactions. It is sometimes called the Narrow Tape. *See also* Broad Tape.

Target Corporation in corporation law parlance is the object of a takeover attempt by another corporation (or by an individual or group of individuals).

Tax Accounting is the phrase customarily used to describe the accounting principles that must be followed by businesses in determining income for federal income tax purposes. Tax accounting departs from GAAP principles in important respects.

Tax Avoidance is the reduction of one's taxes by structuring or timing transactions in a legal way.

Tax Brackets are the different levels of income subject to different tax rates under federal or state income tax statutes.

Tax Deferral means delaying the reporting of income or gain on a transaction to a later period. For example, deferred annuities provide tax deferral because the buildup is not subject to tax as it is earned. The tax is deferred until payments begin on the annuity itself. *See* Exclusion Ratio.

Tax Evasion is the improper or unlawful reduction of one's taxes by omission, misstatement, fraud, or misrepresentation.

Tax Preference Items in tax parlance are the items that must be taken into account by a taxpayer in connection with the calculation of the Alternative Minimum Tax. Tax preference items include accelerated depreciation on property, capital gains deductions, portions of incentive stock options excluded from income, and percentage depletion.

Tax Shelters in tax parlance are investments whose primary purpose is to provide tax deductions for high-income persons to allow them to protect or shelter other income from tax. Most tax shelters were sharply limited or eliminated entirely by the 1986 tax amendments.

Taxable Income in tax parlance equals adjusted gross income minus allowable itemized personal deductions (or the standard deduction if one does not itemize) minus the allowance for personal exemptions.

Teaser Rates are low initial monthly payments for graduated payment mortgages (GPM) that are sometimes heavily advertised. The ads usually do not warn that payments increase materially over the life of every GPM.

Term Insurance is a type of life insurance that provides only basic life insurance protection. It provides for payment of the face amount of the policy upon the death of the insured during the term of the policy. Term insurance is pure insurance, based on actuarial data as to the probability of death occurring within the fixed period of the policy with no savings account feature. As a person gets older the cost of term insurance increases. *See also* Whole Life Insurance.

Thin Corporation is a heavily leveraged corporation with most of its debt held by the corporation's shareholders. A thin corporation may also be referred to as a thinly capitalized corporation.

Thin Market is a market in which there are relatively few traders and securities offered for trade. The market for many over-the-counter securities and for debt securities are often thin markets.

Thinly Traded Shares are shares issued by smaller companies that are publicly traded on the over-the-counter market, but by reason of their size or the number of shareholders, the volume of trading is small.

13D Statement is a statement that must be filed with the SEC by a person who has acquired 5 percent or more of the voting shares of a publicly held company. The statement must be filed within 10 days after the purchase that causes the holding to exceed 5 percent.

TIGRS. *See* STRIPS.

Time Value of a warrant, right or option is the difference between the Intrinsic Value of the warrant, right or option, and its current market value. *See* Intrinsic Value.

Time Value of Money is the basic concept that dollars payable in the future are always worth less than dollars payable immediately.

Time-Price Differential. *See* Cash Sale/Credit Sale Distinction.

Tin Parachutes are severance contracts for middle-level management of a corporation faced with the threat of a takeover. *See also* Golden Parachutes.

Title Assurance in real estate parlance is the process by which the buyer is assured that he or she receives good and marketable title free and clear of liens or title defects, including easements and intangible interests in property.

Title Company is a private company that has created an index for real estate records by tracts rather than by the names of grantors and grantees in order to facilitate searches of title. The records maintained by a title company are called a title plant. A title company is also called an Abstract Company.

Title Insurance is a method of title assurance that provides indemnification against defects in title not specifically excepted from coverage by a title insurance company.

Title Plant. *See* Title Company.

Title Report is a statement of the results of a title search conducted by an attorney or a title company.

Toehold in corporation law parlance is the purchase by a aggressor of an initial holding of shares in a target.

Torrens System is a method of land registration provided by local governments in some areas of the United States.

Total Income in tax parlance equals gross receipts minus trade and business expenses and expenses directly connected with other gainful, nonemployment activity. Total income in accounting parlance is an income statement item that equals operating profit plus other income.

Trade Name is an assumed name used by a business.

Trade or Business Expenses in tax parlance are ordinary and necessary expenses incurred by a business in connection with the generation of revenues.

Trading Floor of an Exchange is the area where trading in listed securities takes place. The trading floor is often referred to simply as the floor of the Exchange or the floor.

Treasury Shares in corporation law parlance are shares that were formerly issued but have been reacquired by the corporation and are held in the corporation's treasury until they are cancelled or resold. The Revised Model Business Corporation Act and some state statutes have eliminated the concept of treasury shares, treating all reacquired shares as authorized but unissued shares.

Trial Balance is a device used by accountants to make sure that they have not inadvertently transposed or omitted figures. It takes advantage of the mathematical equality of the two sides of all balance sheet to provide a check on the accuracy of the accountant's work.

Triggering Events in corporation law parlance are the events that trigger a poison pill. *See* Poison Pill.

Triple Exempt Municipal Bonds are municipal bonds that are exempt from state and city income taxes as well as federal income taxes.

True Yield in securities parlance means yield-to-maturity. More broadly, true yield means the mathematical calculation of the relationship between the total return from owning the security and the market price. *See* Yield-to-Maturity. *See also* Current Yield.

Trust Fund in corporation law parlance is a common law doctrine dating back at least to the nineteenth century that to some extent views the assets of a corporation as a trust fund for the benefit of creditors. The application of a trust fund concept may lead to directors being held personally liable to creditors or shareholders being required to restore a distribution to the corporation upon the suit of creditors.

Trustee in Bankruptcy is a person with responsibility for ensuring that all assets subject to the bankruptcy proceeding are recovered and properly administered for the benefit of creditors.

2 Percent in 10 days, Net in 30 Days means that the creditor is offering a cash discount: On a $1,000 purchase on credit, payment of the debt within ten days earns a $20 discount. The debt becomes overdue after the expiration of 30 days.

UFCA (Uniform Fraudulent Conveyance Act) is a uniform statute relating to fraudulent conveyances. It has been superseded by the Uniform Fraudulent Transfers Act.

UFTA (Uniform Fraudulent Transfers Act) is a uniform statute relating to fraudulent conveyances.

Umbrella Insurance Policies provide excess liability coverage over and above the amount provided by a basic liability insurance policy. Such policies are sometimes called Excess Liability Insurance policies. A person with $300,000 of liability insurance, for example, may be able to purchase an umbrella insurance policy providing protection between $300,000 and $10,000,000 at a relatively modest premium.

Uncovered Options. *See* Naked Options.

Underwriter is a person or organization who purchases securities from the issuer for resale or who sells securities as an agent for the issuer.

Unearned Income in accounting parlance is a balance sheet liability account created to "park" receipts on account of income allocable to future periods until they can be taken into account in the income statement under principles of accrual.

Uninsurable in life insurance parlance is a person who cannot demonstrate that he or she is in reasonably good health or who engages in activities of extraordinary risk. Many uninsurable persons may obtain some insurance by paying a higher premium.

Unlisted Properties in real estate parlance usually refers to residential or other real estate that is for sale but has not been listed with a broker. In another context, it may also refer to properties that have been listed with a broker but have not yet appeared in the multiple listing service. *See* Multiple Listing Service.

Unrealized Appreciation is the increase in value of an asset that has not been realized by sale or disposition. Unrealized appreciation may not be taken into the asset accounts under GAAP, but accounting principles under state dividend statutes may permit the practice.

Unreasonable Accumulation of Surplus. *See* Penalty Against Unreasonable Accumulation of Surplus.

Upstairs Brokers in NYSE trading parlance are brokerage firms that deal with the public. They transmit orders to the floor of the Exchange. Upstairs and Downstairs, when referring to brokers, describe the physical location of brokerage offices in the New York Stock Exchange building.

Uptick in securities trading parlance means that the current price quotation is above the price at which the last transaction occurred. Under SEC regulations a short sale may be effectuated only on an uptick or zero uptick. *See* Zero Uptick; Short Sale.

Usury Statutes purport to limit the maximum interest rate that may be charged on loans to individuals to a specified level.

VA (Veteran's Administration) Mortgages are residential real estate mortgages the payment of which is guaranteed by the federal government. VA insurance is available only for veterans and for modest transactions.

Valuation means establishing the value of a business or an asset.

Value usually means the price established for an item by transactions in the item between willing buyers and sellers in a market. Value also may be used in the senses of the value of the asset to the user, or the cost of reproducing or replacing the asset. In accounting parlance value usually means historical cost.

Value Line Composite Index is an index of price movements based on 1,650 stocks traded on the New York and American Stock Exchanges and over-the-counter.

Variable Annuity is a deferred annuity in which the amount of the annuity ultimately paid depends on the investment success of a fund managed by the writer of the annuity.

Variable Interest Rate Bonds are bonds on which the amount of interest payable is adjusted for changes in interest rates. The result is that changes in market interest rates are represented by increases or decreases in the annual yield rather than by changes in the price of the security, as in the case of fixed-income securities.

Variable Premium Life Insurance Policy is a life insurance policy that provides that premiums are decreased if the company's investment income increases to a specified amount as a result of rising interest rates and inflation.

Variable Rate Mortgage. *See* Adjustable Rate Mortgage.

Venture Capital Funds pool equity or risk capital from a variety of sources in order to provide capital to promising start-up and established businesses.

Voting Poison Pills in corporation law parlance grant increased voting rights for shareholders other than the aggressor when the poison pill is triggered. For example, when a voting poison pill is triggered by a cash tender offer from an aggressor, all shares owned by persons other than the aggressor may become entitled to ten votes per share while the voting rights of the aggressor are unchanged.

VRM (Variable Rate Mortgage) is another name for Adjustable Rate Mortgage.

Walk Away in real estate parlance is the ability of a developer to abandon an unprofitable project, leaving the mortgagee to deal with it. The ability of a solvent developer to walk away from a project may depend on whether he or she is personally liable on the mortgage. A developer who abandons a project is sometimes described as having "walked."

Wall Street Option refers to the power of shareholders in publicly held corporations to sell their holdings if they are dissatisfied with their investment in the corporation.

Warrants are transferable long-term options to acquire shares from the issuing corporation at a specified price. Warrants are usually outstanding for periods in excess of one year. Warrants may be publicly traded and listed on securities exchanges. *See* Rights.

W-4 is the form employers provide to employees to determine or adjust the amount of withholding of federal income taxes the employer must make from each periodic payment of wages or salary.

White Knight in corporation law parlance is a friendly alternative suitor for a target corporation.

Whole Life Insurance provides a fixed benefit on the death of the insured with premiums that remain level from the date of the inception of the policy until the maturation of the policy upon the death of the insured. Whole life policies have a cash surrender value. Whole life policies are also called Permanent Life Insurance or Ordinary Life Insurance policies.

Williams Act refers to the 1970 amendments to the Securities Exchange Act of 1934 relating to cash tender offers.

Wilshire 5,000 index is an index of price movements covering 5,000 stocks traded on all the major securities markets.

Window Dressing in accounting parlance is a technique in which year-end transactions are entered into solely in order to improve the appearance of the year-end figures.

Without Par Value refers to shares that are issued without par value. The phrase developed in states with par value statutes that also included the option to issue shares without par value. The financial provisions of such shares are integrated into the statutory par value structure. In addition, the Revised Model Business Corporation Act and statutes of several states have eliminated the par value concept entirely; shares issued under such statutes are not usually described as being without par value, though they differ only in minor respects from shares issued without par value under par value statutes. Shares without par value are sometimes referred to as No Par Shares.

Workout is generally a process by which a leading or principal creditor of a debtor in serious financial difficulty takes over the operation of the debtor's business, or requires the debtor itself to modify business operations in cooperation with lenders, so as to develop the cash flow necessary to repay the outstanding indebtedness. The business may be a real estate project in financial difficulty.

Workout Agreements are agreements for the sale of a business in which a portion of the purchase price is determined (or "earned" or "worked out") by the performance of the business during a period following the sale. *See* Workout Period.

Workout Period is the period during which business operations are measured in order to establish the purchase price of a business under a Workout Agreement.

Wrap-Around Mortgage is an assumption-related device that was originally designed for use in connection with the financing of commercial real estate but is also used for the quiet assumptions of mortgages on residential real estate. A wrap-around mortgage is a second mortgage the payments from which are used in part to continue the payments on the first mortgage.

Write-Off of an asset occurs when its book value is reduced to zero either by depreciation or depletion deductions or by a direct adjustment to the asset account.

Writer of an Annuity. *See* Seller of an Annuity.

Writer of an Option is the investor who commits to sell the optioned securities at the strike price in the case of a call or to buy the optioned securities at the strike price in the case of a put.

W-2 is the form employers provide to each employee to show the wages paid to the employee and the amount that has been withheld from the employee's wages for the year. One copy of this form must be attached to the employee's federal income tax return.

Yield. *See* Effective Rate of Interest.

Yield-to-Maturity is the discount or interest rate that makes all future payments to be received on account of a debt security equal to the market value of that security. *See also* Current Yield.

Zero Coupon Bonds in securities trading parlance are bonds or debentures that pay no interest and are sold at significant discounts from face value. A zero coupon bond is often referred to as a Zero.

Zero Uptick in securities trading parlance means that the current price quotation is above the price at which the last transaction that involved a change in price occurred. Under SEC regulations a short sale may be effectuated only on an uptick or zero uptick. *See* Uptick.

Zero. *See* Zero Coupon Bonds.

Zeroing out in tax parlance means adjusting the affairs of a C corporation so that the double tax on earnings can be minimized or eliminated. The usual technique involves the distribution of earnings in the form of salary or other tax deductible payments by the corporation to the shareholders. However, zeroing out is not always practical, since only "reasonable" salaries or other business expenses are deductible by the corporation. *See* Double Tax on Earnings.

INDEX

Index

Index

Index

Index

Index

Index

Index

Index

Index

Step transactions, federal income taxation, 12.4

Stepped-up basis, federal income taxation, 12.17

Stock bonus plan, 5.8

Stock life insurance company, 6.3

Stock. *See* Share or Shares

Stockholders' equity, balance sheet item, 8.2.2

Stop orders, NYSE trading, 18.5

Straddle, options trading strategy, 20.2.3

Straight bankruptcy, 10.8

Straight line, depreciation accounting system, 8.6.1

Straight preferred shares, pricing of, 15.5

Straw party, use to avoid personal liability on note, 3.7

Street name shares, 18.17

Street sweep, after unsuccessful tender offer, 17.8

Strike price, put or call option, 20.2

STRIPS (Separate Trading of Registered Interest and Principal of Securities), zero coupon treasury bonds, 18.21

Stub end, securities transactions, 18.7

Subrogation, 4.10

Substantial underpayment of estimated tax, penalty for, 12.13

Substituted basis, federal income taxation, 12.17

Successful efforts oil companies, 8.6.4

Sum of digits method, depreciation accounting system, 8.6.2

Supermajority provisions, as defensive tactic, 17.12.1

Supplemental list, over-the-counter securities, 18.13

Surcharge of directors, 16.3.1

Survey, in connection with purchase of real estate, 4.11

Surviving spouse, federal income taxation, 12.10

Sweeps
  option accounts prior to expiration, 20.2.1
  bank account transfers to interest-bearing accounts, 19.6

Sweeteners, distribution of securities, 15.8

Swing shares, in close corporation, 11.8.3

Syndicates, distribution of securities, 13.16.3

T account, 7.5

Tactical asset allocation (TAA), investment strategy, 20.8

Takeover specialist, as corporate lawyer, 21.3.3

Takeovers
  aggressors' profits from unsuccessful attempts, 17.18
  back-end transactions following, 17.5
  by open market purchases, 17.6
  cash out mergers, 17.5
  consensual, 17.19
  defenses
    generally, 17.9.3

  state statutes, 17.14, 17.14.1, 17.14.2
  tactics, 17.12
  economists' analysis, 17.2.4
    effect on economic concentration, 17.2.3
    economic or social desirability, 17.20
  front-end loaded offers, 17.9.3
  generally, Chapter 17
  insider trading in, 17.7
  institutional investors' role, 14.5
  junk bonds in, 17.9.3
  leverage as key, 17.17.2
  mop-up mergers, 17.5
  prototype example, 17.3
  put into play defined, 17.7
  risk arbitrageurs' role, 17.7
  sources of cash for aggressors, 17.17
  state and local political attitudes toward, 17.2.5
  street sweeps following unsuccessful attempt, 17.8

Taking a bath, accounting technique, 9.14

Taking subject to, outstanding mortgage, agreeing to pay distinguished, 4.18

Tape, reporting of securities prices, 18.14

Target, of takeover attempt, 17.1

Tax. *See* Federal income taxation
  accounting
    accrual basis compared to GAAP, 12.16
    generally, 12.14
  audits
    described in notes to financial statements, 9.7
    probability of, 12.4
  avoidance
    generally, 12.4
    variable life insurance, 6.10
  claims not discharged in bankruptcy, 10.9
  deferral
    on annuity buildup, 5.5
    variable annuity, 5.6
  evasion, 12.4
  generally, Chapter 11
  planning, importance of marginal rate, 12.5
  preference items
    alternative minimum tax, 12.12
    corporate, 12.20.1
  savings, in cash flow analysis, 3.3
  shelters
    C corporation income, 13.9.1
    effect on of 1986 Tax Act, 12.11
    generally, 12.6
    limited partnership as, 13.5.1
  tables 12.10
  valuation issues in, 11.8.1

Taxable income, federal income taxation definition, 12.9

Tax Reform Act of 1986, 12.1, 12.3

Teaser rates, graduated payment mortgage, 4.16

Tenants, subject to lien of mortgage, 3.6

Term life insurance
  benefits of compared with whole life insurance, 6.11
  generally, 6.7

627

Index